STATE BY STATE

This feature examines standards, laws, and other pertinent issues as they differ across the United States, displaying the range of policies and regulations teachers and school districts address each year.

State by State

Family and Community in the State of Massachusetts

The Massachusetts Department of Education's website has several areas of interest to parents. In Massachusetts, parents are allowed to send their children to schools in communities other than the city or town in which they reside with tuition being paid

WORKING WITH PARENTS

Working with Parents

Teachers are able to show parents how their children are using technology in school by hosting a Computer Family Night. After deciding on a date and time, the children can type and print personal invitations to their families. As families arrive in the computer lab, a digital camera or video camera is used to take their picture and this picture is put onto a disk. After the disk is loaded into the computer, the parents can add a 30-second message in their native language, scan photos brought from home,

This feature emphasizes the importance of teachers working effectively with the parents and families of students at every grade level.

NAEYC MARGINAL ICONS

Icons appear throughout the book to highlight appropriate practices as outlined by the National Association for the Education of Young Children.

TECHNOLOGY MARGINAL ICONS

Appearing throughout the book, these icons indicate opportunities or suggestions for effective use of technology in the early childhood classroom.

Educating Young Children

from Preschool through Primary Grades

LAVERNE WARNER

Coordinator and Professor of Early Childhood Education
Sam Houston State University

JUDITH SOWER

Master Teacher in Residence
Sam Houston State University

PEARSON

A and *B*

Boston   New York   San Francisco
Mexico City   Montreal   Toronto   London   Madrid   Munich   Paris
Hong Kong   Singapore   Tokyo   Cape Town   Sydney

Series Editor: *Traci Mueller*
Development Editor: *Alicia Reilly*
Editorial Assistant: *Janice Hackenberg*
Marketing Manager: *Elizabeth Fogarty*
Composition and Prepress Buyer: *Linda Cox*
Manufacturing Buyer: *Andrew Turso*
Cover Administrator: *Joel Gendron*
Editorial–Production Service: *Matrix Productions Inc.*
Interior Designer: *Ellen Pettengell*
Photo Researcher: *Kathy Smith*
Illustrations: *Omegatype Typography, Inc.*
Electronic Composition: *Omegatype Typography, Inc.*

For related titles and support materials, visit our online catalog at www.ablongman.com

Between the time website information is gathered and then published, it is not unusual
for some sites to have closed. Also, the transcription of URLs can result in unintended
typographical errors. The publisher would appreciate notification where these errors
occur so that they may be corrected in subsequent editions.

Photo credits appear on page 542, which is an extension of the copyright page.

Library of Congress Cataloging-in-Publication Data

Warner, Laverne, [date]
    Educating young children from preschool through primary grades / Laverne Warner,
Judith Sower.
        p. cm.
    Includes bibliographical references and index.
    ISBN 0-205-36659-7
    1. Early childhood education—United States. 2. Effective teaching—United States. 3.
Curriculum planning—United States. I. Sower, Judith. II. Title.

LB1139.25.W37 2004
372.21—dc22

2004041099

Printed in the United States of America

10 9 8 7 6 5 4 3 2 1   RRD-IN   09   08   07   06   05   04

☆ Contents

Chapter Four Teaching Children with Special Needs 118

Chapter Five Teaching in a Prekindergarten Classroom 162

Chapter Six Teaching in a Kindergarten Classroom 198

Chapter Seven Teaching in a First-Grade Classroom 244

Chapter Ten Using Technology in the Early Childhood Classroom 360

Appendix A Developmental Red Flags for Children Ages 3 to 5 461

Appendix B Checklist for Diversity in Early Childhood Education and Care 464

Bonus Chapter Teaching in a Fourth-Grade Classroom 468

⭐ Preface

Take a journey through the classrooms of Mrs. Flores, Mrs. Riehl, Ms. Thomas, Mrs. Strabinski, Ms. Chang, and Mr. Gedelian, all teachers with a passion for teaching and the commitment to meet the needs of their children every day they arrive at school. These prekindergarten through fourth-grade teachers hold certifications in their respective states, and theirs are positions of dignity and responsibility in their communities. State funding and legislative mandates control the school districts they teach in, but each teacher organizes his or her classroom and plans curriculum with the freedom that all professionals hold who make daily decisions for their clients' welfare. Judging instructional appropriateness requires their diligence in knowing their children and reaching out to children's families to ensure educating the whole child. For these six teachers, their children come first!

Principles and tenets of early education are global in nature. How they apply to various age levels depends on the teacher's understanding of her children's needs, how children learn, and the definition of expected learning outcomes. When *Educating Young Children from Preschool through Primary Grades* was conceptualized, my co-author and I recognized that curriculum books, for the most part, describe theoretical aspects of curriculum development without much thought to classroom application. The unique characteristic of our book is its description of six classrooms from prekindergarten through grade 4, demonstrating six teachers' decision-making skills, teaching styles, and insights into their children's developmental needs.

Questions about differences between kindergarten and second-grade classrooms or how teachers of 4-year-olds vary their teaching strategies differently from third-grade teachers are obvious. But there are other questions, too. How can principles that guide the first-grade teacher in her planning and implementation of lessons also guide teachers of young children in other grade levels? How can strategies appropriate for prekindergarten children be appropriate for 8-year-olds?

We have written a book to answer the questions that preservice teachers, graduate students, administrators, parents, and other curious parties might have about early education. Chapters One and Two of the text delve into the history of early education and the major theories associated with teaching children of any age. Chapter Three presents information about the importance of teacher planning and classroom organization. We discuss children with special needs in Chapter Four, but we emphasize diversity in all chapters. Information about Head Start is included in Chapters One and Five, and information about bilingual education and English as a Second Language programs appears in Chapters Four and Five. The sections in each chapter labeled Dimensions of Diversity highlight diverse populations and how schools plan and implement instruction for all groups of children. Issues and Trends provides insight into current concerns facing teachers and schools in the twenty-first century, with special emphasis on the No Child Left Behind legislation.

Then we take visits to six different teachers' classrooms. The heart of this book is the description of each classroom and the activities that go on in them. Mrs. Flores emphasizes social-emotional development and self-expression in her 4-year-olds. Mrs. Riehl's kindergarten class is learning about writing and how to conduct oneself when in school. The major emphasis in Ms. Thomas's classroom is reading instruction. In second and third grade, Mrs. Strabinski and Mrs. Chang continue helping children become independent readers and begin focusing on mathematics, science, and social studies standards. Mr. Gedelian helps us view fourth-grade ventures and the opportunities that 9-year-olds have in elementary schools.

How to address state standards and guidelines with appropriate instruction is a major dilemma early childhood teachers face, no matter the age they teach. The last three chapters of the book deal with classroom technology, parental involvement, and issues surrounding professionalism. Our book recognizes that school districts must answer to state and national standards, and accountability is necessary to demonstrate that tax dollars are spent equitably.

Though we were unable to include data from every state (this book would have become far too long), we have included sections entitled State by State that focus on standards, laws, or other pertinent information displaying the range of policies and regulations that teachers and local school districts address each year. State agency websites for any of the 50 states and Washington, D.C., provide comprehensive information about individual state education regulations concerning children and the teachers who serve them.

Another unique feature of this book is the What Teachers Are Saying sections of each chapter. In spring 2001, we distributed surveys to teachers in a number of school districts across the United States. Their survey responses gave us teachers' perspectives on a variety of topics—technology, use of classroom centers, philosophical orientations, children with special needs, approaches to literacy and reading development, and play as a teaching tool. Teachers have strong opinions about their teaching, which we share throughout the book.

Judy Sower and I hope you enjoy reading our book because we have become increasingly committed to early education as we have written and rewritten. As with any labor of love, numerous people helped us with the product, and we want to recognize them for their support of

our efforts. Sharon Lynch, Phil Swicegood, and Diana Nabors are colleagues in the Department of Language, Literacy, and Special Populations at Sam Houston State University who gave us special assistance. Lauren Grein, student clerical assistant, was a lifesaver on occasion. Vic Sower, Judy's husband, provided technical assistance and moral support from the very beginning of the project, and his experience as an author proved invaluable to us. Laverne's sister, Doris Phelps, also critiqued the manuscript and provided insight from an elementary principal's viewpoint.

Thanks, too, to our students who participated in a pilot study with the manuscript during the 2002–2003 school year. They gave us important feedback as we conducted final editing and revising duties. Special thanks go to Mary Sue Zoch, Tatum Stone, Amanda Marek, April Blackmon, Kim Williams, Amy Crisler, and Shelley Jones for spotting errors that required last-minute editing. What an inspiring letter Peggy Hutson, a first-year teacher and former student, wrote us as we were in the final stages of revising the text. We were compelled to share her thoughts!

A number of the photographs included in the book are from schools and centers in the Texas area. Special thanks goes to Pam Payne, pre-kindergarten teacher at Huntsville Elementary, and to Principal Morris Johnson and teachers at Samuel Houston Elementary School (Huntsville Independent School District, Huntsville, Texas). Teachers at Ford Elementary (Conroe Independent School District, Conroe, Texas) provided writing samples for the text, and their willingness to help is appreciated. Thanks to Kaye Mills, Director of Tomorrow's Promise Montessori School (Huntsville, Texas) for allowing us to snap additional photographs of her children.

We also want to thank Traci Mueller, our Allyn & Bacon editor, who guided us throughout the process. Her immediate response to phone calls and e-mails was exemplary. Alicia Reilly, development editor, also gave us invaluable assistance toward the end of the process. Additional thanks go to the reviewers who provided helpful suggestions as we wrote: Melissa Roberts Becker, Northeastern State University; Holly Craddock Harrison, University of New Mexico; Julie Ruelas, Los Angeles Mission College; and Michael Searson, Keen University.

If you are becoming an early childhood educator, we want to wish you well in your chosen field. Working with young children is a rewarding experience. We hope the chapters in our text convince you that early childhood education can become a professional effort worthy of all you can give.

Educating Young Children

from Preschool through Primary Grades

Chapter One

Early Education's Roots and Heritage

CHAPTER OVERVIEW

★ Do you know the origin of the field of early education?

★ Are you familiar with famous contributors to early education philosophy?

★ Have there been legislative influences on early education in the last century? If so, what are they?

★ What current issues face the education of young children in public school settings?

★ How successful is early childhood education as an educational field?

READING THIS CHAPTER WILL PROVIDE THE ANSWERS TO THESE QUESTIONS AND MORE.

I am already chomping at the bit to get back into my classroom to begin preparation for the up-coming school year. My mind is in reflective overdrive as I begin to plan for new and better ways to teach my lessons. Although I feel that we, both the students and I, learned and accomplished many wonderful things this year, there is still so much more that I hope to share and improve upon for next year. One of my biggest challenges is to add more opportunities for self-discovery in the same amount of time without the children feeling any additional pressure to learn and perform.

The expectations are incredibly high for all kindergarten students—ongoing district benchmarks, formative testing, assorted six-week math and language arts progress assessments, and end-of-year readiness tests. Pretty heavy stuff for little 5- and 6-year-old shoulders to carry—with many students being closer to the 4-year-old marker than to the 6-year-old marker! All this, plus the challenge of keeping the fun and excitement of being in kinder-garten passionately alive for my children.

Peggy Hutson
Kindergarten Teacher, Klein ISD
Klein, Texas

P.S. Yes, teaching kindergarten and spending my days with children is truly heaven on earth!

"**A**s the twig is bent," "The acorn doesn't fall far from the tree," and "Like mother, like daughter" are wise sayings that pass from generation to generation in the American culture, indicating the important foundation the early years have on children's development. Most of the research conducted during the 1950s (Hunt, 1961; Bloom, 1964) leading to the passage of the Economic Opportunity Act of 1964 relates directly to the impact of poverty on children's lives and the necessity of the federal government to provide equal access to the public school system. The government's attempt to provide early educational experiences in the form of Head Start summer programs and subsequently to year-round Head Start programs led state legislatures to understand the need for early education in public schools. Even Start, Home-Start, Jumpstart, and AmeriCorps programs are innovative federal programs unique to the 1990s that public schools are implementing across the nation.

HISTORICAL PERSPECTIVES

Insight into principles guiding child development is evident from the earliest time periods. When the words *early education* are mentioned, most people think about child care settings and home environments. Historically, philosophers thought about children within the contexts of their homes and families because public settings were unavailable to families for educational purposes. Plato maintained that the "right education" would develop "men of silver and gold"; Aristotle believed that the young should be taught and that a "sound and beautiful body was the outward expression of the sound and beautiful mind." Neither man thought of early education as anything more than the way children were educated in their homes (Braun & Edwards, 1971). Plato's philosophy included the tenet that both males and females should be educated.

Jean Jacques Rousseau (1712–1778)

Often credited with the beginning of early education (Seefeldt & Barbour, 1998), Jean Jacques Rousseau's work defines *naturalism,* a philosophy based on the belief that children should be educated from birth in natural settings. The influences of adult society and strict schooling were repulsive to Rousseau, and he touted education based on children's natural curiosities and providing environments to grow up freely without restrictive discipline (Rousseau, 1762/1947). Rousseau's philosophy was delineated in a work titled *Emile,* a story of a young boy who was removed from society to avoid the negative influences of civilization. The book served as a beginning point for the field of early education and the philosophical viewpoint known as naturalism.

Johann Pestalozzi (1746–1827)

Applying Rousseau's naturalistic philosophy in real-world situations, Johann Pestalozzi developed schools designed to educate children through play and sensory activities. His orphanage, a large farm for young boys, focused on children's growth through "object lessons" organized around hands-on experiences that provided a trade for the learners. Object lessons were a three-pronged approach to introducing knowledge and skills to youngsters, which included the use of concrete objects to practice what was being learned. Pestalozzi is often referred to as the father of industrial education because of his emphasis on teaching his young men to work with their hands (Bennett, 1926; Roberts, 1965; Braun & Edwards, 1971).

Pestalozzi was also a strong proponent of parent education. In 1801, he published a book titled *How Gertrude Teaches Her Children* designed to define his educational principles, which he posited were in line with the laws of nature. He emphasized a balance among three elements—the hands, heart, and head—and predicted a time when mothers would be able to educate the child entirely within the home. Spontaneity, self-activity, and the freedom to arrive at answers independently were key components of what became known as the *Pestalozzi method* (Silber, 1965).

Frederick Wilhelm Froebel (1782–1852)

Frederick Froebel, commonly known as the father of the kindergarten, introduced the concept that groups of young children can be educated in group settings. He prepared special materials and activities for the educational development of children, referring to them as "gifts" (wax pellets, small beads, lentils, and wooden sticks) and "occupations" (gardening, weaving, paper folding, singing, and drawing). Froebel's first kindergarten (the German word translates as "garden of children") focused on play as a cornerstone of learning for youngsters. Children were housed in a building that included a beautifully landscaped garden, and they had opportunities to spend time outdoors engaged in gardening activities (Froebel, 1912).

Froebel's esoteric discussion of children's learning and how the "gifts" related to knowledge of God and the spirituality they acquired was based on observation of children's needs, yet his description of these qualities was vague and often misunderstood. He established a teacher training school for young women that introduced his philosophy and methodology to students interested in becoming teachers. Froebel's programmatic components were important to the development of early learning in the United States.

Patty Smith Hill, professor at Teacher's College, Columbia University, noted of Froebel's work that "it is also agreed that the kindergarten can greatly contribute to reading facility in the grades by: (1) broadening the kindergarten child's first-hand experience; (2) by helping the child to gain from these experiences clear images and ideas which may be easily recalled through the printed page; (3) by helping the child to deepen and clarify the ideas gained through varied modes of expression and by better organization of these ideas in his work and play, including oral language; (4) by encouraging the child to utilize these ideas in his play purposes and plans, improving these in both content and form through the application and use of ideas gained in contact with people and things" (Hill, 1942, p. 1950).

John Dewey (1859–1952)

John Dewey was a proponent of a theory of experience as integral to learning. In *Experience and Education* (1938/1998), Dewey questioned traditional schooling, which focused on drill, practice, and memorization of facts. At the turn of the twentieth century, his work at the University of Chicago demonstrated challenging educational experiences based on the scientific processes to encourage child choice, self-discovery, and active exploration. Dewey's overall educational goals were the formation of positive habits and attitudes toward learning and hands-on learning, both of which arouse curiosity and strengthen initiative within individuals. Adults promote learning by allowing children to discover knowledge through individual activity and by responding to children's questions about their environment. The implications for modern classrooms are that children learn about democratic living through the give-and-take relationship between teachers and children in daily interactions (Dewey, 1938/1998).

Forerunners of Special Education

Jean Marc Gaspard Itard (1775–1838) was a French physician who specialized in diseases of the ear and educating the deaf. Most historians recognize Itard as the person who began the field of special education. His work with Victor, a young boy (perhaps age 12) found roaming naked in the forests, is described in *The Wild Boy of Averyon* (Itard, 1932). Though Victor's speech and behavior improved only slightly, Itard's experiment showed that "idiot children" could be rehabilitated with systematic educational methods (Hallahan & Kauffman, 1994).

Itard's student, Edouard Seguin (1812–1880), did most of his work in the United States and convinced many educators that children heretofore labeled as uneducable could indeed be taught. The significant ideas both men established as a foundation for contemporary special educators are:

- Planning for individualized instruction
- Sequencing educational tasks in an achievable series
- Emphasizing sensory stimulation in children
- Carefully arranging the child's learning environment
- Rewarding correct performance
- Tutoring in functional skills
- Believing that every child should be educated to the greatest extent possible (Hallahan & Kauffman, 1994)

Both Itard and Seguin influenced Maria Montessori's formulation of an educational philosophy that addresses the needs of all children, including those with special needs. Peggy Hutson, the first-grade teacher we met at the beginning of this chapter, was happy she had had exposure to children with special needs. Her first year of teaching she had a kindergartner with autism; and later she had a child who used a wheelchair.

☆ THE KINDERGARTEN MOVEMENT IN AMERICA

Throughout the latter half of the nineteenth century into the first decades of the twentieth century, the Froebelian method influenced teachers of America's young children. Froebel believed that women were apt teachers of young children, and one of his pupils, Margarethe Schurz, having studied in his teacher-training program for young women, began the first private kindergarten in America for six children (her own daughter Agathe, four cousins, and one neighbor boy). Her facility in Watertown, Wisconsin, is a small one-room building that has been preserved by the Watertown Historial Society. Her kindergarten opened in 1856.

Schurz's attendance with her daughter at a social function in Boston led to a chance encounter with Elizabeth Peabody. Peabody noted how precocious Agathe seemed to be and became curious about the implementation of the kindergarten concept in her city, especially in slum areas. She traveled to Germany to learn more about the kindergarten movement, though she did not study with Froebel. Her philanthropic work began in 1860, and soon kindergartens spread across the country (Snyder, 1972).

Susan Blow began a private kindergarten in her community of Carondolet, near St. Louis, Missouri, and her school was popular with area families. After operating the school independently for several years, she collaborated with William T. Harris,

Margarethe Schurz opened the first American kindergarten in Watertown, Wisconsin, in 1856.

the St. Louis School District superintendent, to open the first public school kindergarten in 1873 as a pilot program in the Des Peres School. Her success with 42 children caused the program to grow to nearly 7,000 students by 1889. Using Froebelian methodology and materials, which she had learned at the New York Institute for Kindergartners, Blow emphasized a child-centered approach to children's learning. She became recognized as a teacher trainer, organizing classes for young women in the afternoons and on Saturday mornings, sometimes with as many as 200 people in attendance (Carondolet Historic Center, 1982). Blow served as an Advisory Board member of the International Kindergarten Union (IKU), organized in 1892, and became one of its most popular speakers (Snyder, 1972).

Other influential persons who left their marks on early education in the United States include John Dewey (1859–1952) and Patty Smith Hill (1864–1946). Dewey's work at the University of Chicago during the latter part of the nineteenth century and the beginning of the twentieth century provided credibility to the systematic study of young children as learners. Dewey's ideals supported discovery learning and a child-centered curriculum, prompted by the child study movement at Clark University founded by G. Stanley Hall. Dewey influenced Patty Smith Hill, who incorporated his ideas into her kindergarten and primary-grade programs at Teacher's College, Columbia University, during the early twentieth century (Hill, 1942).

Hill's work blended with the development of the progressive kindergarten movement, which contrasted sharply with the conservative kindergarten movement led by Susan Blow (Hill, 1942; Evans, 1971). Hill's program emphasized creative play, and she developed and included unit blocks for children's play. Eventually the International Kindergarten Union (IKU) split in 1926 to form the National Association of Nursery Educators (NANE), the forerunner of the National Association for the Education of Young Children (NAEYC) (Hill, 1942). Alice Temple continued to lead the International Kindergarten Union, which eventually became the Association for Childhood Education International, another professional organization that addresses the needs of children in the early years (Hewes, 1976).

naeyc

☆ THE FEDERAL GOVERNMENT AND EARLY EDUCATION

Historically, the next significant impact on early learning came about during the Great Depression in the 1930s, when the Works Progress Administration (WPA) gave teaching jobs to out-of-work teachers. Many jobless professionals were retrained in this program to teach preschool and primary-age children. During World War II, demands were placed on citizens to provide care for children when mothers joined the workforce to manufacture munitions and other needed war equipment at factories and shipbuilding industries open for business 24 hours a day. Jimmy Hymes, one of early childhood's most illustrious leaders during the twentieth century, became manager of the Child Service Department for Kaiser Shipbuilding Corporation, developing a program that became a nationwide model for others to emulate (Braun & Edwards, 1971; Hill, P., 1942/1992). Hymes's legacy includes two publications that are classics in early childhood literature: *Behavior and Misbehavior* (1955) and *Teaching the Child under Six* (1968). He also edited yearly reports on the status of early education until his death in 1998.

The Economic Opportunity Act of 1964

President Lyndon Johnson's War on Poverty program in the mid-1960s and the passage of the Economic Opportunity Act of 1964 provided another impetus for the development of early childhood programs in public schools as well as in the private sector. At first, Head Start programs, which began in the summer of 1965, were half-day summer programs, usually eight to twelve weeks in length; eligible children from low-income families would be entering school for the first time in the fall of the year. Educational experiences were the main goal of Head Start programs, but they also provided medical, psychological, and health information services to the families served. After three years of study, the Westinghouse Corporation recommended that Head Start programs become full-year, full-day programs serving wider age ranges. Of all of the social services programs begun in the 1960s, Head Start is the only one to survive.

Documentation from several sources indicates that Head Start programs work for children (National Head Start Association, 2000; Epstein, Schweinhart, & McAdoo, 1996). Results reported by the National Head Start Association include the following: (1) Head Start improves delivery of health services; (2) poor children participating in Head Start go on to greater success in school and life; (3) Head Start provides positive long-term effects on parent or teacher ratings of antisocial behavior; and (4) programs positively affect school achievement, grade retention, and social adjustment in the long term. The Administration on Children, Youth and Families (ACYF) currently oversees Head Start programs, which have served close to 18 million youngsters since Head Start's conception in 1965. This figure represents about 20 percent of the population Head Start could serve if it had additional funding and staffing (National Head Start Association, 2000).

The Head Start movement became the impetus for emphasis in public schools on kindergarten and prekindergarten classrooms in succeeding decades. Legislative bodies recognized that early education is critical to the development of children's ability to learn. By 1982, most states required implementation of kindergarten programs. The practice of including prekindergarten programs in public schools has been sought by state mandate during the decade of the 1990s, and all but nine states currently have public school prekindergarten programs (Children's Defense Fund, 2000).

FEDERAL LEGISLATION AFFECTING PUBLIC SCHOOL EDUCATION

From the 1930s the government has taken an active role in developing laws that influence public school operations.

The Elementary Secondary Education Act of 1965

A second federal initiative, the Elementary Secondary Education Act of 1965 (ESEA), is another important legislative action that assists public schools in their endeavors to educate all children. Initially, ESEA provided the implementation and enhancement of school libraries and audiovisual equipment for every classroom (such as record players and overhead projectors). Through the years various Title programs have been added to this legislation, including curriculum development in the areas of reading and mathematics and the addition of teacher aides to classrooms. Telecommunications and technology applications are direct outgrowths of ESEA. Migrant education, family literacy programs, gifted and talented programs, prevention of and intervention with school dropouts, bilingual education and language acquisition programs, school facilities improvements, drug prevention programs, and the charter schools movement are funded through ESEA grants.

Title VII of the Elementary Secondary Education Act, known as the Bilingual Education Act, was a 1978 statute that encouraged the establishment of bilingual education programs for second-language learners or English-language learners (ELL) children. The implementation of bilingual and English as a second language (ESL) programs will continue to rise through the next decade. Numerous states rely on the federal government to appropriate funding for the growing numbers of Hispanic children in the U.S. population. *Children of 2010* (Washington & Andrews, 1999) reports that the fastest-growing populations in America are Hispanics and Asians, the result mostly of immigration and increasing birthrates. According to one estimate, by 2010 the Hispanic population in the United States will reach 42 million people.

In a 2001 rewrite of ESEA, states are required to bring all students to the proficient level on mandated tests no later than the 2013–14 school year. Schools in each state school district will make yearly reports of progress. If schools are identified as "needing improvement," they are required to develop plans for improvement. They must also receive technical assistance from their school districts (No Child Left Behind Fact Sheet, 2002).

Public Law 94-142

Another landmark legislative act is Public Law 94-142, the Education for the Handicapped Act (EHA), often referred to as the *mainstreaming law*. The law's intent was to place preschool children with disabilities in the "least restrictive environment" to provide an appropriate public education. With parental support and push, public school doors were open to children who had previously been denied access. The law, passed in 1975, gave states a three-year grace period to develop statewide plans for approval by the federal government, thus removing all but the most severely handicapped and disabled children from their homes and institutional care and placing them into public classrooms.

PL 94-142 required procedures for identifying children's physical and emotional problems and needs, testing and diagnosing children, and developing an individualized education program (IEP) to meet the needs of each child. The specific categories of disability that qualify a student to receive special education services are mental retardation (MR); emotional disturbance (ED); learning disabilities (LD); impairments in vision, hearing, speech, or language; deafness, blindness, orthopedic and other health impairments; and multiple disabilities. Children with special needs are eligible for free, appropriate, and individualized public education in the least restrictive environment. A nondiscriminatory evaluation is required and due process is established when parents have concerns about diagnoses. Schools are expected to take action to locate children who will qualify, and no student is to be excluded.

The process for reviewing a child is based on professional judgments and recommendations made by physicians and teachers. The family, in conjunction with school representatives including the child's classroom teacher and special educators, admit children to programs designed for their individual educational needs with periodic reviews of their progress. These individualized educational planning meetings require all individuals involved with children to provide input about their continued need for special services. More information about PL 94-142 is provided in Chapter 4.

ADA and the Individuals with Disabilities Education Act (IDEA)

In 1990, two federal laws impacting schools and communities were passed: the Americans with Disabilities Act (ADA) and Public Law 101-476, the Individuals with Disabilities Education Act (IDEA). The Americans with Disabilities Act (PL 101-336) established civil rights for the disabled, including equal access to job opportunities and education. ADA legislated access to public buildings, including schools. Communities were required to renovate streets and sidewalks to accommodate people with disabilities. Public restrooms had to be accessible for all people, and informational signs in buildings needed to be provided in Braille for the blind. Despite the strides made to help people with disabilities in the last decade, *CBS Evening News* reported in July 2000 that Americans with disabilities are more likely to live in poverty than their more able counterparts.

IDEA added autism and traumatic brain injuries to the list of categories considered as disabilities that public schools should accept. IDEA also provided funding to improve services to infants and young children, promoted programs that would include students with severe disabilities in the general education classroom, reduced placement in residential treatment facilities for students with severe emotional disturbances, and improved services for these children. IDEA also provided for the description of transition services for students at age 16 or older (age 14, if appropriate). This provision helps ensure that students receive the assistance they need to prepare for life after high school graduation.

In 1997, IDEA Amendments (Public Law 105-17) shifted its focus away from the implementation of a general curriculum to the IEP as the main tool for educating children with disabilities. In this law provisions for alternative educational placements are mandated as well, if it appears that children are likely to harm their peers within their classrooms. Transition services must be addressed at age 14. The law clarifies that children are not eligible for special education because of poor instruction or language differences and that when parents sign the consent form for the evaluation of their child, they are not consenting to a special education placement (Friend & Bursuck, 1999).

In the passage of the 1997 IDEA Amendments as defined by Early Childhood Intervention statute 300.7, the term *child with a disability* is defined as a child "having mental retardation, a hearing impairment including deafness, a speech or language impairment, a visual impairment including blindness, serious emotional disturbance, an orthopedic impairment, autism, traumatic brain injury, an other health impairment, a specific learning disability, deaf-blindness, or multiple disabilities, and who, by reason thereof, needs special education and related services" (Early Childhood Intervention 300.7).

In addition, the IEP must justify placement that is not in the general education classroom. A general education teacher must be a member of the team that writes the IEP. As of July 1, 2000, states were required to measure the progress of children in special education classrooms, either with the same assessment tools as the general student population or an alternative assessment procedure. If necessary, a behavior plan and strategies to accompany the plan must be included in the IEP.

⭐ EARLY INTERVENTION SERVICES

IDEA 1997 (Public Law 101-476) requires that local school districts participate in a transition planning conference for parents of toddlers with disabilities who are soon to enter preschool. The law calls for delivery of early intervention services in natural environments and clarifies the source of funding for early intervention services. Some local school districts plan infant and toddler programs that assist families in early education strategies for their young children. Others provide Preschool Programs for Children with Disabilities (PPCD).

These laws, plus others that have been enacted, imply that school districts across the nation have a high need for teachers trained as special educators. Usually, the demand for special education teachers is among the highest in all states each year, along with other high-demand areas in bilingual education, mathematics, and science.

⭐ NATIONAL EDUCATION GOALS PANEL

In September 1989, President George H. Bush convened governors from all 50 states for an Education Summit in Charlottesville, Virginia. An original six goals for the year 2000 were set and adopted, and two were added at a later date. In 1990, a National Education Goals Panel (NEGP) was established to publish annual reports about the nation's progress toward the achievement of the goals. The Goals 2000:

Schools have a high demand for teachers trained in special education.

Educate America Act was passed in 1994, under President Bill Clinton's administration, which established a National Education Standards and Improvement Council (NESIC) and added legislators to the NEGP. The goals were the following:

Goal 1: By the year 2000, all children will start school ready to learn.

Goal 2: By the year 2000, the high school graduation rate will increase to at least 90 percent.

Goal 3: By the year 2000, all students will leave grades 4, 8, and 12 having demonstrated competency over challenging subject matter including English, mathematics, science, foreign languages, civics and government, economics, arts, history, and geography, and every school in America will ensure that all students learn to use their minds well, so they may be prepared for responsible citizenship, further learning, and productive employment in our Nation's modern economy.

Goal 4: By the year 2000, the Nation's teaching force will have access to programs for the continued improvement of their professional skills and the opportunity to acquire the knowledge and skills needed to instruct and prepare all American students for the next century.

Goal 5: By the year 2000, U.S. students will be the first in the world in mathematics and science achievement.

Goal 6: By the year 2000, every adult American will be literate and will possess the knowledge and skills necessary to compete in a global economy and exercise the rights and responsibilities of citizenship.

Goal 7: By the year 2000, every school in the United States will be free of drugs, violence and the unauthorized presence of firearms and alcohol and will offer a disciplined environment conducive to learning.

Goal 8: By the year 2000, every school will promote partnerships that will increase parental involvement and participation in promoting the social, emotional, and academic growth of children (www.ed.gov/legislation/GOALS2000/TheAct/index.html).

All of the education goals affect public school early education, but Goal 1 (often called the "Readiness Goal") has attracted the most attention from early educators. The Southern Regional Education Board (1992) commented: "Any effort to address readiness effectively must reflect one basic truth: Learning does not begin with a child's entry into school; it begins at birth and is continuous throughout life. Learning is not limited to formal schooling. Success in school, and in life, is directly affected by many factors that may have little apparent relation to education" (p. 1).

Objectives for Goal 1 *were:*

- Children will receive the nutrition, physical activity experiences, and health care needed to arrive at school with healthy minds and bodies, and to maintain the mental alertness necessary to be prepared to learn, and the number of low-birthweight babies will be significantly reduced through enhanced prenatal health systems.
- Every parent in the United States will be a child's first teacher and devote time each day to helping such parent's preschool child learn, and parents will have access to the training and support parents need.
- All children will have access to high-quality and developmentally appropriate preschool programs that help prepare children for school. (NEGP, 2001)

America's Report Card

The Goals Panel is continuing its work into the twenty-first century, and annual report cards are released about the progress each state is making toward the eight defined goals. For example, the nation's scorecard for Goal 1 showed these Key Findings for 1999:

Goal 1: Ready to Learn

Areas of Improvement

- Thirty-seven states reduced the percentage of infants born with one or more of four health risks.
- Fifty states increased the percentage of mothers receiving early prenatal care.

- Forty-nine states increased the proportion of children with disabilities participating in preschool.

Areas of Decline

- In 36 states, the percentage of infants born at low birthweight has increased (NAEP, 1999).

Other Initiatives

In the 1990s legislators continued to tinker with early education programs, introducing Even Start and Jumpstart. Even Start allows individuals, usually mothers, of preschool children to work toward their high school equivalency diplomas and provides instruction as well to children. The goal of the program is to overcome illiteracy in America. Jumpstart and AmeriCorps programs are also federal initiatives designed to assist preschool children with one-to-one tutoring in school readiness skills. A private initiative, Home-Start, is an international program begun in the United Kingdom designed to promote the enjoyment of family life through interactions with paid volunteers.

No Child Left Behind Legislation

In January 2002, President George W. Bush signed into law Public Law 107-110, otherwise known as the No Child Left Behind Act. The three cornerstones of the No Child Left Behind (NCBL) law are (1) student and school accountability, (2) school choice for families, and (3) local flexibility in consolidating federal funds for any preauthorized purpose.

Issues and Trends

No State Left Behind

One of the components of the No Child Left Behind legislation is the accountability and assessment requirements placed on states. All states must develop academic standards and student achievement standards. After the annual student testing each year, a progress report is required by the state to determine "adequate yearly progress" for each school and district. States were required to begin corrective actions for low-performing schools after the 2000–2001 year and have 12 years to achieve the state-defined "proficient level." Adequate yearly progress is defined as (1) achievement based on academic indicators; (2) programs that are technically rigorous; and (3) standards that apply to individual schools, districts, and state levels of progress (ECS Special Report, 2002).

⭐ SCHOOL ORGANIZATIONAL STRUCTURES

During President Jimmy Carter's administration, legislation established the Department of Education (DOE), which opened with Shirley M. Hufstedler as its first Secretary of Education on May 4, 1980. The DOE is headquartered in Washington, DC, and ten regional offices are located across the states to assist with the department's mission and scope. The DOE's main purpose is to develop policy and administer federal funds that affect local and state school districts in the United States. An organizational chart is shown in Figure 1.1.

 Each state has its own department of education, often called an *education agency* or a *department of public instruction*. The chief education administrative officer in each state is called a *state superintendent* or *commissioner of education*. This person is

FIGURE 1.1 Organizational Chart for the Department of Education

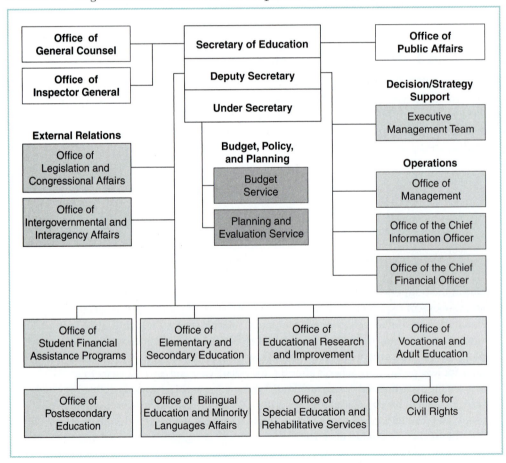

TABLE 1.1 Website Addresses for Education Agencies in the United States and the District of Columbia

Alabama	www.alsde.edu	Missouri	www.dese.state.mo.us
Alaska	www.eed.state.ak.us	Montana	www.metnet.state.mt.us
Arizona	www.ade.state.az.us	Nebraska	www.nde.state.ne.us
Arkansas	http://arkedu.state.ar.us	Nevada	www.nde.state.nv.us
California	www.cde.ca.gov	New Hampshire	www.ed.state.nh.us
Colorado	www.cde.state.co.us	New Jersey	www.state.nj.us/education
Connecticut	www.state.ct.us/sde	New Mexico	http://sde.state.nm.us
Delaware	www.doe.state.de.us	New York	www.nysed.gov
District of	www.k12.dc.us	North Carolina	www.dpi.state.nc.us
Columbia		North Dakota	www.dpi.state.nd.us
Florida	www.fldoe.org	Ohio	www.ode.state.oh.us
Georgia	www.doe.k12.ga.us	Oklahoma	http://sde.state.ok.us
Hawaii	http://doe.k12.hi.us	Oregon	www.ode.state.or.us
Idaho	www.sde.state.id.us/Dept	Pennsylvania	www.pde.psu.edu
Illinois	www.isbe.state.il.us	Rhode Island	www.ridoe.net
Indiana	www.doe.state.in.us	South Carolina	www.sde.state.sc.us
Iowa	www.state.ia.us/educate	South Dakota	www.state.sd.us/deca
Kansas	www.ksbe.state.ks.us	Tennessee	www.state.tn.us/education
Kentucky	www.education.ky.gov	Texas	www.tea.state.tx.us
Louisiana	www.doe.state.la.us	Utah	www.usoe.k12.ut.us
Maine	www.state.me.us/education	Vermont	www.state.vt.us./educ
Maryland	www.msde.state.md.us	Virginia	www.pen.k12.va.us
Massachusetts	www.doe.mass.edu	Washington	www.k12.wa.us
Michigan	www.michigan.gov/mde	West Virginia	http://wvde.state.wv.us
Minnesota	education.state.mn.us	Wisconsin	www.dpi.state.wi.us
Mississippi	www.mde.k12.ms.us	Wyoming	www.k12.wy.us

Source: National Education Goals Panel (2001).

often a political appointment or, on occasion, an elected official. For website addresses for the agencies in the United States and in the District of Columbia, see Table 1.1.

Teachers discover as they enter the teaching field that education agencies, both at the state and federal levels, are responsive to the political administrations governing them. Congress and state legislatures respond to public sentiment by enacting legislation that reflects voters' current thinking about public education. Public funding of schools, state curriculum mandates, specific curriculum areas studied in classrooms, teachers' salaries, the length of the school year, the daily schedule, assessment procedures, appointments to the state board of education (or elected board members), and other relevant influences on local school districts are decided by politicians who may or may not have knowledge about school operations. Recent political trends include legislating achievement at higher levels of academic excellence and ensuring that children can read by the completion of third grade.

Each local school district has its own superintendent, and individual campuses have their own principals, professionals who are certified by the state in which they reside. Local school boards are also composed of elected individuals representing their communities whose efforts are voluntary. Board members have minimal training about school board service, yet they are called upon to oversee the implementation of budget and policy concerns in school districts, whether they serve in large metropolitan districts or small rural ones. A typical school board agenda (from the Denver Public Schools in Denver, Colorado) is shown in Figure 1.2.

Citizens who serve on local school boards have a range of reasons for choosing to run for office, not always altruistic or noble. Balancing the educational needs of children and the political whims of any given community is a process that has often amused and irritated educators throughout the decades. At the far extreme, burning textbooks and banning library books result from public and parental interest in their children's education. In a few situations, taxpaying citizens may become heatedly involved in a variety of issues affecting their children's education, from the appointment of a new football coach to whether or not drug testing should be implemented in their schools.

A number of states and communities have their own associations or unions that are called upon to serve as advocates for educators. When decisions are made by the superintendent and/or school board that affect teachers and their abilities to do their jobs, these groups can assist in reversing policies or reinstating teachers to their positions if necessary. Watchdog groups are essential in maintaining the integrity of school board actions and superintendents who may not be performing adequately. The National Education Association (NEA) and the American Federation of Teachers (AFT) are two such groups that have state and local affiliates among their ranks.

⭐ STATE MANDATES

After the establishment of the Department of Education in 1980, one of the first assignments for Secretary Hufstedler was organizing a task force to study the status of education in the United States. In 1983, *A Nation at Risk* was released, a report suggesting that public education was not well organized from state to state, not adequately funded, and not representative of quality indicators. In the decade that followed, states began to develop statewide curriculum initiatives, scrutinize teacher education programs and implement professional assessments of teachers and their performance in classrooms.

One compelling reason for developing state curriculum guides is that inequalities in the breadth and scope of curriculum content existed among school districts within and among states. Children who relocated during the course of a school year would be placed in grade levels that might or might not match their educa-

FIGURE 1.2   A Sample School Board Agenda

Press Release

November 30, 1999
For Immediate Release

TENTATIVE AGENDAS FOR BOARD OF EDUCATION MEETINGS DECEMBER 2

The Denver Board of Education has three meetings set for Thursday, December 2. The meetings will be held at 900 Grant St.

At 4:00 p.m. in the first floor board room, staff will report on:

- The district's Y2K preparations
- School counselor program
- A program evaluation and presentation from P.S. 1

Following staff reports, the Board will adjourn to room 706 for a work session. The following items are scheduled for discussion:

- Hiring policy
- Historical designation of facilities
- Charter school recommendations
- School report cards
- Northwest school design

The Board's monthly public hearing is scheduled for 7:00 p.m. in the first floor board room. As of Tuesday, 11 speakers had signed up to discuss such items as district procurement procedures and the following charter school applications: Apollo Charter School; Denver Arts & Technology Academy Charter School; Richard Milburn High School; and Challenges, Choices and Images Charter School.

tional progress. Even within any given school district, discrepancies in educational expectations and curriculum organization would exist among various school campuses. Having a minimum state-mandated curriculum ensured some sense of quality and academic standards among school districts within a state.

State education agencies are continuing to work to develop curriculum standards that assist teachers and school districts in their preparation for classroom teaching. States organize in a variety of configurations to achieve the standards of excellence they hope to achieve. In Texas, as an example, the Texas Education Agency formed committees composed of classroom teachers, campus administrators, university faculty, and state agency representatives to develop the state's Texas Essential Knowledge and Skills (TEKS). Input from other educators in the state and from professional organizations representing various curriculum areas and grade-level constituencies was solicited to finalize the TEKS prior to sending them to the state legislature for legislative action. For information about state curriculum standards, go to the websites of individual states.

⭐ STANDARDS AND ASSESSMENT

Curriculum content and assessment go hand in hand. States recognize that educational progress will not be accomplished unless mechanisms are in place to demonstrate that learning is being achieved in their classrooms. Public understanding of assessment creates a dilemma in early education because taxpayers often view assessment as paper-and-pencil tests. Parents also believe that their children are not learning anything unless there is some kind of concrete demonstration that knowledge is being acquired. Often, documentation of learning is in the form of worksheets or other rote activities (memorizing the well-known "Alphabet Song" sung to the tune of "Twinkle, Twinkle, Little Star," for example, or repeating addition facts). Children might impress their families with rote learning, but memorized facts have little meaning to the children who recite them.

Early educators understand that assessment can and should take a variety of forms, acknowledging young children's specific needs. The National Association for the Education of Young Children (NAEYC) and the Association for Childhood Education International (ACEI) have papers showing the negative results of standardized testing of young children (NAEYC, 1987; Perrone, 1991). The professional thinking of these organizations influenced politicians when one task force sponsored by the National Association of State Boards of Education (NASBE) discussed Goal 1 of the National Education Goals Panel. In its report titled *Caring Communities: Supporting Young Children and Families* (1991) the National Task Force on School Readiness chaired by Bill Clinton recommends the use of performance-based assessment, referred to as *authentic assessment*.

Performance-based assessment requires teachers to use observational techniques to record information about their children. Checklists describing skills to be observed and portfolios including samples of children's work are the backbone of authentic assessment. Teachers circulate among children as they participate in classroom activities, assist them with challenges they face, and determine their level of performance based on knowledge of child development and their understanding of individual children's interactions with objects and people in the classroom. *Caring Communities* (1991) recognizes that "teachers need better ways to capture children's work and behavior. Assessment helps teachers understand children's progress, how their minds work, and how to extend and enrich their learn-

naeyc

State by State

Assessment

North Carolina utilizes performance-based assessments in kindergarten through second grade, but more standardized measures are utilized by third grade. The Public Schools of North Carolina report the following information on their web page:

GRADES K–2

Teachers in kindergarten, first, and second grades use a portfolio approach based on a checklist of goals and objectives to keep track of children's progress during the year. The state is considering a new "Ready for School" measurement to determine if students are ready for school and to alert the school to a child's needs.

GRADE 3

During the first three weeks of school, all third graders take the North Carolina Pretest–Grade 3. Students in this grade also take reading comprehension and mathematics tests at the end of the third grade, end-of-grade (EOG) tests.

Basic Facts

- Multiple-choice tests
- Pretests: measure knowledge and skills from grade 2 in reading and mathematics as specified in the North Carolina Standard Course of Study.
- EOG tests: measure reading comprehension and mathematics.

Source: Public Schools of North Carolina (2001).

ing. Credible assessment is also crucial to assure families and policymakers that teachers will retain strong responsibility for student progress" (p. 36).

ACCOUNTABILITY IN SCHOOL DISTRICTS

The development of state competencies and assessment procedures requires school districts to demonstrate how they are meeting the competencies. Accountability presents a two-pronged dilemma to local school districts because (1) standardized measurements do not always consider all the variables that occur in measurement, and (2) teachers begin to construct their curriculum and lesson choices around the standardized measurement. This second phenomenon is often referred to as "teaching to the test." Educators and many public citizens recognize the diminished opportunities for learning in classrooms where this "teaching to the test" phenomenon takes precedence in teachers' decisions about classroom instruction.

States report the scores for local districts, develop statewide recognition systems for those that have been performing well and, in some instances, provide funding for districts that meet state competencies and deny or reduce funding for low-performing schools. "Teaching to the test" often means that teachers focus on discrete facts and lower-level thinking skills that are easily tested. Higher-order thinking and the ability to synthesize information and make connections with what is already known becomes secondary to classroom instruction, and children are shortchanged in the process. In rare instances, school administrators and teachers may even resort to changing children's test scores so that the state indicators appear to have been met.

Overall, state bureaucracies are aware of their ranking among other states. An example of this awareness is shown in a 2001 report from the Superintendent of Utah's Department of Education, who writes: "The 2000 results indicated that the majority of kindergartners can grasp the basic concepts of print (they recognize the front of a book and know when its right side is up, and recognize signs and other words in their environment), and can comprehend the simple story in the assessment" (Laing, 2001, p. 12).

⭐ EARLY CHILDHOOD EDUCATION DEFINED

naeyc

The National Association for the Education of Young Children (NAEYC) defines early childhood education as programs that serve children from birth through age 8 (Bredekamp & Copple, 1996). Public schools and state education agencies define early childhood education more narrowly because states have few children younger than age 4 enrolled. Most states recognize early childhood education as public classrooms that serve children in the preschool years (ages 3 to 5). *Educating Young Children from Preschool through Primary Grade(s)* describes early education as classrooms that serve children from prekindergarten through grade 4. Younger children may be enrolled if they are classified as children with disabilities and if schools offer programs for youngsters with special needs.

Child Development Principles

Continuous study through the latter half of the twentieth century indicates that critical child development principles must guide the formation of curriculum content that is child centered and in tune with children's needs (Darling-Hammond, 1997). The major principles guiding appropriate practice for young children ages birth through 8 are identified by Sue Bredekamp and Carol Copple, editors of *Developmentally Appropriate Practice in Early Childhood Programs* (1997), published by

naeyc

the National Association for the Education of Young Children (NAEYC). The 12 principles are as follows:

1. Domains of children's development—physical, social, emotional, and cognitive—are closely related. Development in one domain influences and is influenced by development in other domains.

2. Development occurs in a relatively orderly sequence, with later abilities, skills, and knowledge building on those already acquired.
3. Development proceeds at varying rates from child to child as well as unevenly within different areas of each child's functioning.
4. Early experiences have both cumulative and delayed effects on individual children's development; optimal periods exist for certain types of development and learning.
5. Development proceeds in predictable directions toward greater complexity, organization, and internalization.
6. Development and learning occur in and are influenced by multiple social and cultural contexts.
7. Children are active learners, drawing on direct physical and social experience as well as culturally transmitted knowledge to construct their own understandings of the world around them.
8. Development and learning result from interaction of biological maturation and the environment, which includes both the physical and social worlds that children live in.
9. Play is an important vehicle for children's social, emotional, and cognitive development, as well as a reflection of their development.
10. Development advances when children have opportunities to practice newly acquired skills as well as when they experience a challenge just beyond the level of their present mastery.
11. Children demonstrate different modes of knowing and learning and different ways of representing what they know.
12. Children develop and learn best in the context of a community where they are safe and valued, their physical needs are met, and they feel psychologically secure. (pp. 10–15)

Peggy Hutson, the first-year teacher we have quoted earlier, calls to mind these 12 principles every day she teaches. She writes: "I am most grateful for my early childhood specialization. I find that my studies of the *young child* and *developmentally appropriate practices* have been most useful in preparing me to successfully self-manage my own classroom and to anticipate the needs of my students. With the help of my husband, both financially and creatively, my classroom is awesome—a true investment to benefit the cognitive-social-emotional growth of my children."

⭐ PROFESSIONAL ISSUES IN EARLY EDUCATION

Recognition of early education as a field implies that it faces professional issues impacting practices in and out of classrooms. As American cultures and school environments change, the charge to early childhood educators is to define the field more clearly and address problems and challenges as they arise. Professional organizations, national policy makers, state legislatures, local school districts, and parents or interested parties make daily decisions that influence children's lives. Following are some of the critical issues facing early educators in America.

Developmentally Appropriate Practice

naeyc

In the 1980s, the National Association for the Education of Young Children made a decision to define developmentally appropriate practice in the field of early education. The first edition of *Developmentally Appropriate Practice in Early Childhood Programs* was published in 1986, with a second edition following in 1987 and subsequent editions through 1997. Early childhood special educators were one of several groups who felt that the original description of appropriate practice did not recognize children with special needs (Bredekamp & Copple, 1997). Early childhood professionals continued a decade-long dialogue about what is "appropriate practice."

The 1997 revised edition acknowledges more clearly that developmentally appropriate practice is based on a collection of information from a number of sources about what is appropriate for any given child. Parents, teachers, administrators, and medical personnel are all involved in describing an individual child's behavior and needs, allowing collective decisions to be made in the best interests of the child. Developmentally appropriate practice is summarized simply by saying that it is:

1. What is known about child development and learning
2. What is known about the strengths, interests, and needs of each individual child in the group
3. Knowledge of the social and cultural contexts in which children live (Bredekamp & Copple, 1997, p. 9).

Bredekamp and Copple (1997) recommend that the definition of *developmentally appropriate practice* should continue to evolve. When programs and curriculum become rigid, then the emphasis has shifted from what children need to what adults think they should learn. Bredekamp and Rosegrant (1995) cite the difficulty in reconciling national goals with professionals' interactions with children within classrooms: "Potential negative effects of national standards include the threat to both integrated curriculum and emergent curriculum, the risk of expectations becoming standardized without regard for individual and cultural differences, and the danger of establishing inappropriate performance standards" (p. 11).

Elementary Error versus the Early Childhood Error

naeyc

Bredekamp and Rosegrant (1992) also recognize another problem associated with defining early education. Most people think about child care when the words *early education* are mentioned, and *child care* usually brings images of happy children playing in classrooms and on playgrounds. In some situations, child care professionals have limited educational training, and their interaction in young children's educational experiences is poor. The *early childhood error* is the belief that adults and environments minimally affect children's growth and development. Consequently, individuals working in child care centers may not even assert an active role in educating children.

The *elementary education error* exists when professionals believe children can be educated with methods and instructional practices that are more appropriate for older groups of students. The downward escalation of curriculum (often referred to as the *push-down curriculum*) results from the elementary education error. What this means is that material appropriate for second graders is "pushed down" to first-grade classrooms and teachers attempt to teach children information that would be more appropriate for older children.

Early educators maintain that appropriate practices for young children need to be utilized even with older groups of children. Integrative classroom instruction, center-based environments, and emergent curriculum should occur as children move from preschool settings into the primary grades. This position, described by Barbour and Seefeldt (1993), defines children's development as "continuous, sequential and hierarchical" and recommend a developmental continuity by:

- Eliminating artificial barriers, such as grade or group placement according to achievement tests, that negate continuity of achievement and progress as children move from the preschool to the kindergarten and through the primary grades
- Planning curriculum that provides a spiral of knowledge, skills and experiences from preschool through the primary grades
- Ensuring smooth transitions for children as they move from the preschool to kindergarten and primary grades (p. 11)

Brain Research

Recent brain research findings about the first three years of children's lives and how their brains are formed is influencing the field of early education. The *nature versus nurture* debate continued during most of the twentieth century, but now neurobiologists and data from neuroscience laboratories are suggesting that much of the early formation of the brain correlates with early experiences that infants have. Before infants are born, millions of brain cells develop that "map" connections in the brain after birth, allowing babies to see, hear, and begin language development. Positive environmental experiences stimulate brain synapses, and impoverished and detrimental environments negatively influence brain development (Kotulak, 1997).

For educators, the implications of current brain research are yet to be explored fully. Certainly, brain research will influence how teachers work with children, and policy makers are attempting to develop and fund resources to support parents of the youngest children in our society. Schiller's *Start Smart* (1999) recommends strategies for educators to follow to enhance brain development and functioning. Some of her techniques include (1) making sure children get enough water to drink,

(2) using music and aromas in the classroom, (3) providing enough physical activity for children (including cross-lateral movements), (4) sharing a hearty laugh periodically, (5) learning a second language, and (6) ensuring nutritious foods for children.

Sylwester (1995) suggests that brain-based curricula may emerge that enhance children's native abilities instead of imposing skills that are unnatural for their understanding. Children are born with potential based on the nature their parents give them, and what happens to them after birth is as significantly critical to their development as their native abilities. Early education provides teachers with opportunities to capitalize on the nature *and* nurture children bring with them to schools. With training and experience, committed teachers can indeed make a difference in children's lives.

☆ ISSUES FACING STATE EARLY EDUCATION PROGRAMS

Every U.S. state has its own set of problems when implementing educational programs.

Teacher Preparation and Training

Goal 4 of the National Education Goals Panel (NEGP) posited that by the year 2000, the teaching force in the United States would have access to programs for the continued improvement of their professional skills and the opportunity to acquire the knowledge and skills needed to instruct and prepare all American students for the twenty-first century (NEGP, 1993). The impact on teacher preparation institutions across the nation related to state legislative action that restructured schools and colleges of education, and an emphasis on earlier field experiences in public schools as a requirement. States implemented approaches for improving the quality of their beginning teachers by (1) requiring state performance exams, (2) strengthening the content knowledge expected of entering teachers, (3) developing alternative certification programs, (4) establishing initial certifications and professional certifications requiring additional training and experience, (5) requiring schools and universities to have induction-year programs, and (6) mentoring teachers who need assistance with their performance.

Professional organizations continue to investigate the strength of teacher preparation programs. The National Council for the Accreditation of Teacher Education (NCATE) prescribes a set of standards that were developed in conjunction with the National Association for the Education of Young Children (NAEYC) to determine the quality of baccalaureate and postbaccalaureate programs in early education. A 2001 standards revision outlines rubrics for Key Elements to show what teacher education candidates in early education know and can do in their classrooms. The emphasis on performance-based standards will guide teacher education programs in more successfully evaluating their teacher candidates. Additionally, the Association for Childhood Education International (ACEI) developed similar standards revisions with NCATE to accredit K–6 teacher education programs.

Other professional groups studying teacher preparation programs are the National Professional Teaching Standards Board (NPTSB) and the Interstate New Teacher Assessment and Support Consortium (INTASC), both of which are developing initiatives that focus on professional performance as much more than a "technicist" approach to classroom teaching. All three groups—NCATE, NPTSB, and INTASC—are recognizing that subject matter standards for teacher candidates will also include an expectation that teachers will know how to collaborate with others in order to improve their practice (Darling-Hammond, 1997).

Mentoring New Teachers

The estimate is that approximately 50 percent of the teaching force drops out of teaching within the first five years. Consequently, states and schools districts are developing programs to mentor new teachers as they come into their systems. All new teachers are assigned a veteran teacher in their grade level who is willing to guide individual novices as they tackle the challenges of the first year in the classroom. New teacher induction programs are often available from universities where teachers received their original training.

Many teachers credit their longevity at public schools to mentor teachers. One of your authors, Laverne Warner, would have left classroom teaching after her first year had it not been for Ruth Matthews (deceased), whose title as Reading Supervisor allowed her to visit and critique first-year teachers in her school district. Peggy Hutson claims that her mentor teacher and her principal were lifesavers time and again throughout her first year. "Oh, how many questions I asked and how much advice they shared with me!" she declares.

Charter Schools

The charter school movement is an outgrowth of the National Education Goals Panel work that recommends to communities that they exercise more involvement in the organization of the local school district and how it addresses needs of children and their families. Federal dollars became available in the 1990s for states to distribute if worthy proposals were submitted to establish schools that work under the auspices of the local school district yet separately from its usual operations and functioning. According to the Children's Defense Fund, 1,605 charter schools existed across the United States in 1999 (Children's Defense Fund, 2000).

Usually, parents, teachers, and community leaders set up charter schools and secure funding through local school districts. Though charter schools are public schools, they are not required to follow most laws governing school districts. However, they may not charge tuition for their services, nor may they discriminate against any student for reasons of ethnicity, national origin, gender, or disability. Charter schools must demonstrate accountability for the instruction that is given to students.

School Retention

The National Household Education Surveys (Zill & West, 1997) indicate that one child in seven in the United States is required to repeat kindergarten or enters kindergarten late. When children repeat kindergarten, their performance as first and second graders was worse than other first graders. The profile of children who had delayed kindergarten entry or were retained in kindergarten is that they are males whose birthdays were late in the year prior to their kindergarten entry (July through December). If children are retained in kindergarten, they are more likely to receive negative feedback from their teachers and more likely to be retained again as they move through the elementary grades.

Zill, Collins, West, and Hausken (1995) identify five other risk factors affecting children's achievement as they enter schools:

- Mother has less than a high school education
- Family is below the official poverty line
- Mother speaks a language other than English as her primary language
- Mother was unmarried at the time of the child's birth
- Only one parent is present in the home (DSO-PS-95-15)

The major issue associated with retaining children in prekindergarten or kindergarten relates to their developmental growth. Four- and 5-year-olds often have growth spurts that give them an opportunity to move ahead quickly even if it initially appeared that they were not performing well. The issue of retention requires that parents and schools work together to determine what is the best recourse for specific children. These surveys conducted by Zill and West indicate that children who have delayed kindergarten entry perform better than children who had entered kindergarten at the prescribed age.

Facilities

The U.S. Department of Education's "Condition of America's Public School Facilities: 1999" reported that most public school buildings are at least adequate, but 75 percent need some work. Factors such as heating, plumbing, roofs, fire alarms, ventilation, security, and air quality were rated by 903 public schools surveyed by the National Center for Education Statistics. The majority of schools reported that one feature of their building was either unsatisfactory or adequate, and only a few of the schools had plans for major repair, renovation, or replacement. President Clinton called for $2.5 billion in school modernization funds that would be interest free for school districts to modernize buildings with another $6.5 billion for urgent repairs. Time will tell whether these funds make a difference or not in the improvement of school plants.

Technology

The age of technology has arrived, and educators recognize the importance of learning and applying technology in their classrooms. Children are arriving at

Many school districts across America need new facilities, and many buildings require renovation.

school with a sophisticated knowledge of computers and what computers are capable of doing. Goal 6 of the National Education Goals Panel acknowledges that Americans need to be able to compete in a global economy. Being able to successfully compete means computer knowledge is essential.

Federal and state grant money has become available within the last five years to facilitate technology applications in schools and classrooms. The use of technology

 What Teachers Are Saying

Technology Applications

"My first-grade class uses the computer lab in our school once a week for 40 minutes."

"We have a computer lab in our school, but it is so outdated it is almost useless!"

"We use the computers we have in our room, but we are allowed to sign up to use the lab if we want to."

Response from a veteran teacher:

"When I first entered the field, I had the belief that computers did not belong in early childhood classrooms. But I've changed my mind in recent years. The children we're teaching right now are in the age of technology, and their computer skills will need to be far superior to ours. Starting preschool/primary children on computers gives them an opportunity to become skilled early with less fear of what computers can do for them."

in classrooms presents a number of problems to educators. Technology is difficult to integrate into the curriculum because an emphasis seems to be on drill, not discovery learning, and higher-order learning is limited. For more information about computer use in classrooms for young children, see Chapter 10 of this text.

EARLY CHILDHOOD ISSUES FACING SCHOOL DISTRICTS

School districts routinely evaluate their resources to determine how to best serve their clientele. Consequently, decisions about a variety of issues confront policy makers.

Half-Day/Full-Day Kindergarten Programs

The last 20 years of public funding for kindergarten programs has seen a change in scheduling of kindergarten programs. Most kindergarten programs in public schools during the 1960s and 1970s were half-day programs. This situation prevailed because fewer mothers were working out of their homes, and many schools had adequate transportation funds to take children home or pick them up during the middle of the day. The increased number of single-parent families and the necessity for school boards to adequately allocate school tax funds are leading many districts to rethink their attitudes about the length of kindergarten programs.

naeyc   In NAEYC's *Kindergarten Policies* (Peck, McCaig, & Sapp, 1988), the authors contended that giving parents choices about half-day or full-day programs is the best practice. In the twenty-first century, however, this option seems less attractive because many parents need after-school care to accommodate their working hours and family schedules.

The critical issue surrounding half-day versus full-day scheduling relates to what is happening in the programs. A half-day program may be adequate for children's academic and social needs, but research indicates that full-day kindergarten programs benefit young children, especially when they enter the primary grades (Rothenberg, 1995). No matter the length of the school day, the quality of the kindergarten program is the noteworthy feature in children's success. Rothenberg, as well as Peck, McCaig, and Sapp, recommend developmentally appropriate settings that engage children intellectually. Full-day programs assure that instruction and assessment will not be rushed to the point that children are stressed by their experiences.

After-School Care

The relationship between the length of the kindergarten day and the need for after-school care is obvious, and many school districts are exploring approaches for caring for children who need supervision beyond the school day. Currently, children who need extended day care are placed in programs that are funded by family-supported tuition rates. The Children's Defense Fund (CDF) estimates that only one child in ten is receiving child care assistance, and children of all ages need safe places to go when the school day is over. CDF (2000) reports that "the lack of good school-age options places children at risk; juveniles are more likely to be the victims of violent crime in the hour after the end of the school day than at any other time" (p. 50).

A joint report from the U.S. Departments of Education and Justice titled *Working for Children and Families: Safe and Smart After-School Programs* (2000), lists nine elements common to high-quality after-school programs: (1) goal setting and strong management; (2) quality after-school staffing; (3) low staff/student ratios; (4) attention to safety, health, and nutrition issues; (5) effective partnerships with community-based youth, juvenile justice, and law enforcement organizations; (6) strong family involvement; (7) coordination of learning with regular school learning; (8) linkages between school-day teachers and after-school personnel; and (9) program evaluation. For the full text of the publication, go to the DOE website (www.ed.gov) and search for the report by its title.

Parent Involvement

An old proverb states, "The child's first teacher is his parents." The Readiness Goal discussed earlier in this chapter focuses on children within the contexts of their families. *Caring Communities* (1991) recommends family-focused policies and services to achieve Goal 1 and the child's readiness for school.

Specific forms of service to parents should include:

- Parent involvement in developmental programs for children
- Family support programs
- Assistance in locating and selecting early childhood and family support programs
- Support for parents from employers
- Voluntary initiatives to strengthen families (pp. 30–31)

New teachers will notice as they go into classrooms for the first time the numbers of parent programs that are available at all levels of schooling. Parent-Teacher Associations (PTAs) and Parent-Teacher Organizations (PTOs) still exist, but now schools offer parent training programs and training for Grade Equivalent Diplomas (GED certificates). Opportunities are available for parent volunteerism, and schools encourage families to become connected. Children's achievement depends on parents' efforts.

Diversity

The changing face of America shows a widening range of cultural and ethnic groups. Teachers will be challenged to meet the needs of children who represent an increasing demographic diversity in and out of classrooms. Helping children realize that living in America means living in an inclusive community requires educators to be comfortable with their own culture, yet they should recognize that other cultures are welcome in a democratic society. Citizens who read newspapers or watch daily television news programs understand that biases still exist in America and around the world. Racism, sexism, homophobia, discrimination against those

---

Dimensions of Diversity

Demographics

The changing demographics of America within the next decade will be profound. As Washington and Andrews predict in *Children of 2010* (1999), the fastest-growing group in the United States are Hispanics who are emigrating here from Mexico, Central America, Puerto Rico and the Caribbean, and South America. They poignantly ask these six questions: "To make full participation in democracy accessible to all children of 2010, what changes must *you and I* make in our (1) lives, (2) professions and workplaces, (3) communities, (4) values, (5) socioeconomic system, and (6) commitment to activism?" (p. 164) One critical issue is whether educators will be ready for the demographic changes that are coming.

---

who are different in some way—all these problems are the foundation of violence and criminal actions in our society. Even childhood bullies act on a bias of some kind when they attack others in and out of their classrooms.

Poverty

The gap between the "haves" and the "have nots" in America has risen within the last two decades. According to the Children's Defense Fund's *Yearbook 2000*, economic growth made by Americans in the latter part of the twentieth century benefited the wealthiest one-fifth of all families. CDF also reports that 18.9 percent of American children live in poverty, and the number of families living below the poverty line fell for the fifth year in a row in 1998. When families of children younger than age 6 are considered, then the estimated number of families living in poverty rises to 25 percent (Seefeldt & Barbour, 1998). The poor are getting poorer, the rich are getting richer, and the middle-income family has to work harder to maintain an acceptable standard of living.

When children of poverty enter school, meeting their educational needs is difficult to manage. Taking care of youngsters' physical needs for food, clothing, and shelter will become a first and ongoing priority. Caring teachers who are able to utilize school district and community resources to assist families of children in poverty discover that their efforts will enhance the children's abilities to learn. Title I of the Elementary Secondary Education Act (ESEA) provides for low-income neighborhoods to receive extra funding to ensure that reading, writing, and mathematics are taught.

Child Abuse

Child abuse is a concern of federal and state agencies and has been for a number of years. The federal government passed the Child Abuse Prevention and Treatment Act in 1974, providing funds to state agencies to strengthen child abuse and neglect systems. Research on the occurrence of child abuse and neglect shows that in 1997 an estimated 3 million children were reported to state child protective agencies. Between 40 and 80 percent of abuse occurs in families who also have problems with alcohol and drugs. Child abuse is more likely to occur when some other form of domestic violence is present (Children's Defense Fund, 2000).

Abused children often grow up to be abusers themselves because they have learned unhealthy relational patterns that are difficult to break. The Children's Defense Fund indicates that the issue affecting children most negatively is domestic violence. Teachers are called upon each year to recognize signs and symptoms of abuse or domestic violence, and they should report suspected cases to authorities. During orientation sessions to school districts for new teachers, an administrator often describes policies and procedures for reporting suspected child abuse. If teachers are still unclear about what they should do, contacting the school nurse or the state's child abuse hotline should solve the problem.

Abuse comes in a variety of forms, but teachers can detect child abuse and neglect by observing children's demeanor and behavior in their everyday interactions with them. Inappropriate clothing for the season, unexplained bruises or bleeding, difficulty in walking or sitting, developmental lags, being fearful of going home, frequent absences from school, being overly withdrawn or aggressive, and having unusual sexual knowledge are a few of the physical signs that indicate that abuse and neglect are occurring (Seefeldt & Barbour, 1998). For more information on child abuse, see Chapter 12 of this text.

School and Community Violence

Overall school violence rates are declining, according to the Children's Defense Fund (2000), but the public's reaction to school shootings and community crime has prompted federal and state governments to develop initiatives to prevent and reduce violence in schools. The Departments of Education and Justice collaborated to develop the Safe Schools/Healthy Students Initiative, which provides funds to communities that address the following six elements:

- Providing a safe school environment
- Establishing prevention and early intervention programs that address violence, alcohol, and other drugs
- Ensuring student access to school and community mental health preventive, treatment, and intervention services
- Creating early childhood psychosocial and emotional development programs
- Working for educational reform
- Implementing safe school policies (p. 117)

The efforts teachers make to enhance children's understanding of one another, to teach negotiating skills, and to help children solve their own social problems are the foundation for eliminating school and community violence. An excellent resource for learning these techniques is *Early Violence Prevention, Tools for Teachers of*

Young Children (Slaby, Roedell, Arezzo & Hendrix, 1995), published by the National Association for the Education of Young Children.

Program Quality

From its inception, NAEYC has emphasized the need for quality care and education. Training and credentialing high-quality teachers, appropriate staff–child ratios, understanding child development, recognizing children's needs, and setting standards for the profession are goals the organization has addressed throughout the years (NAEYC Archives, 1976; Bredekamp & Copple, 1997). Ongoing research of the field supports the need for quality. The Organization for Economic Co-operation and Development (OECD) analyzed policies and services in 12 countries (including the United States). *Starting Strong: Early Childhood Education and Care* (Neuman & Bennett, 2001) cites the issue of raising the quality of services as prime concern. Recommendations from the report suggest that the United States needs to create a comprehensive early care and education system that collaborates with public education to address the issues of child poverty and diversity and support research to inform policy making.

⭐ EARLY EDUCATION WORKS

The news is positive: Early Education works! A 1999 report on the Abecedarian Study (Campbell & Ramey, 1999) reinforces the concept that early intervention influences children's lives. The longitudinal project studied children from infancy to age 21, yielding data that suggest that intervention provides higher scores on reading, cognitive, and math tests as compared to the scores of children who did not receive intervention. Additionally, children enrolled in high-quality child care programs were more likely to hold skilled jobs and attend college.

The New York State Education Department's *The BALANCED VIEW: Early Childhood Education, Part 1: What Research Tells Us* (2000) reports that preschool programs for disadvantaged children yield achievement gains as well as social-emotional outcomes such as self-esteem, motivation, and social behavior. Effects on school performance, as well as on long-term socially accepted values and behavior, are evident. Quality indicators characteristic of good early education programs include: "curriculum content, teachers and teaching practices, class size, onset and duration of services, intensity of services, and parent involvement" (pp. 1–2).

Teachers who use developmentally appropriate practices are most effective, and they are more likely to take advantage of "teachable moments" throughout the school day. Best practices include:

- Engaging children as active learners
- Individualizing work
- Allowing children to move at their own pace
- Encouraging individual choice

- Encouraging children to use language to express ideas
- Praising children for their accomplishments and viewing errors as normal development
- Using flexible time schedules dictated by children's needs
- Recognizing the value of play and modeling how to play imaginatively
- Establishing integrated and meaningful learning centers
- Varying activities from active to quiet, planned to spontaneous, small group to large group, and brief to sustained
- Providing opportunities for outdoor exploration (p. 2)

During 2000, the National Research Council released two documents exploring further the influence of early education on young children: *Eager to Learn: Educating Our Preschoolers* and *From Neurons to Neighborhoods: The Science of Early Childhood Development.* Both publications underscore the need for better understanding of child development and the assurance that children will be placed in quality care and educational settings.

Eager to Learn (Bowman, Donovan & Burns, Eds., 2000), published by National Academy Press and compiled by the National Research Council, reports a review of research by a number of professionals in early education and related fields. Among its findings are these:

- Cognitive, social-emotional, and motor development are complementary, mutually supportive areas of growth all requiring active attention in the preschool years.
- Responsive interpersonal relationships with teachers nurture young children's dispositions to learn and their emerging abilities.
- Both class size and adult–child ratios are correlated with greater program efforts.
- While no single curriculum or pedagogical approach can be identified as best, children who attend well-planned, high-quality early childhood programs in which curriculum aims are specified and integrated across domains tend to learn more and are better prepared to master the complex demands of formal schooling. (p. 6)

The National Research Council teamed with the Institute of Medicine for a two-and-a-half-year project to evaluate and integrate early childhood development science. Recommendations about the care and education of young children evolved in *Neurons to Neighborhoods* (Shonkoff & Phillips, 2000) based on four overarching themes:

- All children are born wired for feelings and ready to learn.
- Early environments matter, and nurturing relationships are essential.
- Society is changing, and the needs of young children are not being addressed.
- Interactions among early childhood science, policy, and practice are problematic and demand dramatic rethinking (p. 4).

Shonkoff and Phillips (2000) draw these conclusions from their study:

> In summary, the well-being and "well-becoming" of young children are dependent on two essential conditions. First is the need for stable and loving relationships with a limited number of adults who provide responsive and reciprocal interaction, protection from harm, encouragement for exploration and learning, and transmission of cultural values. Second is the need for a safe and predictable environment that provides a range of growth-promoting experiences to promote cognitive, linguistic, social, emotional, and moral development. The majority of children in the United States today enjoy the benefits of both. A significant number do not (p. 413).

Classroom teachers can provide both conditions for children who need them.

More from Mrs. Hutson

"Whew!" she writes. "Here are a few of this year's special kindergarten events from our busy calendar: Johnny Appleseed's Birthday, Grandparents' Day, 9/11 Day of Remembrance, Red Ribbon Drug Prevention Week, Bike Rodeo, Four Seasons Fashion Show, Career Day, Halloween/Fall Festival, Columbus Day, Rhyme Time, Turkey Strut Walkathon, Thanksgiving Feast and Parade, Three-Dimensional Shapes Day, Gingerbread Baby's Cookie Decorating Bash, Hanukkah/Christmas/Kwanzaa celebrations, Happy New Year, Martin Luther King Day, 100th Day of School, Chinese/Vietnamese New Year, Groundhog Day, Mardi Gras, Valentine's Day/Friendship Day, Presidents' Day, Rodeo/Texas, Our Texas Day, St. Patrick's Day, April's Fool/Joke Day, Passover/Easter Egg Hunt/Spring Party, Wedding for the Letters Q and U, Kindergarten Round-Up, 'Kid-Fest' Olympic Sports Field Day, Nursery Rhyme/Mother Goose Day and Parade, Popcorn/Popsicle Day, *Cinco de Mayo*, Mother's Day Craft and Card, and our last week of school activities: Father's Day Craft and Card, Game Day, Sand Day, Pajama/Read-In Day, Autograph Day and our Teddy Bears' Picnic finale. Not to mention ongoing mini-classroom celebrations—'Zero the Hero' every 10th day of school, 'Star Student of the Week,' 'Lost Tooth' Club, 'Happy Birthdays, Cha-Cha-Cha,' and weekly Show and Share.

"All this without even listing the district and state's specific kindergarten curriculum requirements that I'm mandated to teach: phonics/phonemic awareness, concepts of print, emergent writing/spelling, sequencing, patterns, opposites, numbers through 31, sorting by attributes, three-dimensional shapes, fractions, money, time, simple addition and subtraction and units on social studies (including character education, manners, rules, etc.), science and health/safety."

SUMMARY

Educators and policy makers have been interested in early education for a long time, and school positions that allow work with young children are becoming attractive to teachers who understand the importance of the early years. The emphasis the government is placing on high-quality settings for preschool/primary children and the knowledge that is being shared with young families are hallmarks of the last decade and the result of the National Education Goals Panel work. Problems still exist in the field of early education, but communities collaborating with schools and policy makers can attempt solutions that involve the participation of all American citizens.

DISCUSSION QUESTIONS

1. Use question 1 under Chapter Activities to develop small group discussions about each issue. Be prepared to report to your class about the topic your group discussed.
2. Survey your class to determine which historical character the class was most familiar with. Why do you suppose the person in question was selected?
3. Did any members of your group attend Head Start when they were preschoolers? Ask these persons to tell about the experiences they remember.
4. Are any members of your group working with Head Start, Home-Start, Jump-start, or Even Start? Give these persons an opportunity to tell what they know about their programs.

SUGGESTED CHAPTER ACTIVITIES

1. Go to any one of several state websites to find how each state addresses the following issues:
   state standards
   state assessment
   teacher preparation and training
   charter school opportunities
   demographic reports
2. If you do not know, find out the name of the state superintendent or commissioner of education for your state. Find the names of the members of the state board of education.
3. Interview one or more experienced teachers to learn what issues they faced as new teachers. Compare their answers with what you know about contemporary public school issues.
4. Talk to an administrator in your local district to learn which federal programs are available in the schools in your community.
5. Ask a teacher to tell how she determines appropriate practice for the children in her classroom.

Chapter Two

Influences on Contemporary Early Education

CHAPTER OVERVIEW

★ Have you noticed distinct differences in practices among classrooms you have visited? Have you wondered why these exist?

★ What does it mean to say that teaching practices are intentional?

★ Who are the major contributors to educators' thinking about best practices?

★ Are you aware of the major philosophical orientations individuals hold toward the education of children?

★ How is philosophy translated into program implementation?

THIS CHAPTER PROVIDES INFORMATION TO HELP YOU FORMULATE ANSWERS TO THESE QUESTIONS.

On the very last day of school, my husband went with me early to install my projector. My goal was to run a slide show for the children and their parents of all the photos I had taken of our classroom activities and students throughout the year. I was out of the room when the opening bell rang. Gary said that all was quiet until the bell rang and then, "All hell broke loose—a stampede of little children came storming into the room." (My boys are always fastwalking at the speed of light— semiracing to see who is first to get to the classroom each morning!) They quickly swarmed around Gary, who was sitting in one of the tiny kindergarten chairs working madly to get my new projector up and running.

The group of boys began to pepper him with questions, not waiting long enough between their questions for him even to answer. He says that the one-sided interrogation went something like this:

"Who are you?"

"Where is Mrs. Hutson?"

"Is Mrs. Hutson sick today?"

"Doesn't she know that it is the last day of school?"

"Are you our substitute?"

"What are we going to do today?"

"What are you doing to Mrs. Hutson's computer?"

"You're not allowed to touch Mrs. Hutson's computer without her permission."

"How old are you?"

"I bet that you are really, really old."

"No, he's not old."

"Yes, he is, too, old—look at his hair."

"But he doesn't have that much hair."

"See, his hair is gray."

"Hey, I know who you are!"

"Are you Mrs. Hutson's Dad?"

Peggy Hutson

Contemporary practices in any professional field do not exist in a vacuum. The history of understanding about any topic influences how problems and solutions are addressed. In the medical field, for example, patient treatment is based on the cumulative knowledge doctors have acquired about the body and how it responds to medicine and scientific practice. Treatments considered cutting edge a year or so ago become outmoded because of the availability of new technologies and medicines. Ongoing medical research also affects physicians' day-to-day work, and severe medical conditions often require experimental programs to assist in healing the sick.

Classroom practices and beliefs about how children learn change as well, just as the medical profession changes its practices. How classrooms are managed is influenced by years of work in classrooms by a vast number of teachers and ongoing research about what constitutes *best practices* with children. Educators learn early in their professional careers that change is the only constant, and methods and classroom strategies that were acceptable ten years ago are now passé.

In education, a stronghold in formulating policies affecting educational settings and classroom teaching is public opinion. Voters elect public officials from the community, state, and national levels who pass legislation about public school funding, which children are served, who can be certified, and other issues relating to school functioning. From an historical perspective, teachers observe pendulum swings in public thinking that vary from an emphasis on skill acquisition to an emphasis on integrated learning and holistic approaches to instruction. Cycles tend to rotate on a 20-year pendulum swing, and the recent wave of standard setting has placed emphasis on skill acquisition (sometimes known as the *back-to-basics movement*).

Who actually judges what classroom practices are best for children? Educators expect their professional organizations to define *best practices* because these entities are able to receive input from a broad constituency to clarify a body of knowledge on which all can agree. In early childhood education, a phrase that is heard over and over is whether a program's philosophy is "developmentally appropriate" or whether practices are designed to fit the age and culture of specific individuals in

Dimensions of Diversity

Developmentally Appropriate Practice

One of the cornerstones of developmentally appropriate practices is *"knowledge of the social and cultural contexts in which children live* to ensure that learning experiences are meaningful, relevant, and respectful for the participating children and their families" (Bredekamp & Copple, 1997, p. 9). To locate NAEYC's position statement titled "Responding to Linguistic and Cultural Diversity: Recommendations for Effective Early Childhood Education," go to www.naeyc.org (in the section labeled Position Statements). Guidelines are provided for working with children, working with families, professional preparation, and programs and practices.

the school. Bredekamp and Copple (1997) and the National Association for the Education of Young Children rightfully contend that practices should not be "either/or," but rather "both/and" in intent. Children do need skills, and children do need opportunities to integrate learning. Smart teachers recognize the need for both explicit and holistic instructional methodologies.

naeyc

Teachers in quality programs perceive that an "either–or" approach to instruction will not meet every child's needs. Utilizing their understanding of children's needs and their repertoire of teaching strategies to work with children individually, teachers work with small and large groups of children to maximize the potential that each child has for acquiring knowledge. Observing and assessing children becomes an ongoing process to allow for teachers' effective instructional planning.

This chapter will define major philosophical orientations that currently influence public school teachers. Though each philosophy will appear to be a pure approach to instruction, observers will not always recognize one true approach in a classroom when they visit. What observers see during the course of each day's instruction is a continuum of practices that represent each of the philosophies. Teachers rely on their knowledge of theoretical perspectives in order to produce a schedule and routine that meets the needs of their children within the constraints of the school district they serve. More information about the continuum of teaching practices will be described in Chapter 3.

 ## MAJOR PHILOSOPHICAL ORIENTATIONS

The broad categories of philosophical orientations are (1) **nativist theory,** (2) **maturationist theory,** (3) **psychosocial theory,** (4) **sociocultural theory,** (5) **cognitive-developmental theory, and (6) behaviorist theory.** Each orientation views child growth and development in distinctively different ways, a range of thought portraying children, at one extreme, as individuals who control their own destiny to ones, at the other, who are controlled completely by their environment and the adults who guide them.

Nativist Theory

Nativist theory holds that children are prewired for learning and development, that children grow and develop in natural and predictable patterns. Pure nativist thinking maintains that children develop their own individual growth and downplays the impact of adult guidance and the environment in which children live. Jean Jacques Rousseau (1712–1778), an early nativist, believed that environments have negative influences on children; placing them in natural or pastoral settings, he held, would protect children from the influences of evil societies. More recently, linguists such as Noam Chomsky posit that the brain is wired for language acquisition, another example of nativist thinking.

Maturationist Theory

Closely aligned to nativist thinking, **maturationist theory** attempts to describe children's characteristics at various ages without regard to their culture or experiential background (Jalongo & Isenberg, 2000). Specifically, maturationists draw a normative and descriptive portrait of children based on physical, social-emotional, and cognitive development milestones in children's lives. Much of the research on children and their development was conducted early in the twentieth century as a result of the Child Study Movement that began in Europe during the late 1800s.

Maturationist theory often refers to children's growth as "ages and stages," suggesting that children are more alike because they are the same age than they are unlike. Any chart or profile of children showing their development in specific areas (physical, language, social-emotional, and intellectual) at specific ages is an example of maturationist theory.

Psychosocial Theory

Psychosocial theory takes a maturational view of development as well. Erik Erikson, discussed later in the chapter, is a major proponent of psychosocial theory. He views individual progress within the context of humans' social and emotional crises at predetermined stages in their lives. Strongly influenced by Anna Freud, his mentor and teacher, Erikson describes "eight stages of man," defining challenges throughout the lifespan. The successful completion of each challenge provides ego strength for individuals, thus allowing them to become more successful as they approach yet another ego task.

Sociocultural Theory

In **sociocultural theory** the importance of the people in children's learning environments takes precedence. Lev Vygotsky, a Russian linguist and educator, clearly defined the role that parents and teachers play in the development of thinking processes and language in young children. He emphasized play as an important variable in children's growth, especially as it relates to their understanding of representation and symbolic thought. He believed that children are able to accept roles during play and maintain these roles as a representation of the thought processes they are acquiring. Vygotsky's discussion of children's ability to learn independently influences modern classrooms when teachers observe children and guide them to higher levels of conceptual development.

Cognitive-Developmental Theory

Cognitive-developmental theory is the framework used by researchers who study children within the context of their environments. They recognize that all children are born with the potential to learn, but they acknowledge that environmental factors contribute to children's development. Critical factors in the environment are the home and community, health and nutrition, educational opportunities, and interactions with adults and other children. Cognitive-developmentalists view children as learners who, through time and experience, learn from their environment.

Cognitive-developmental theorists are often referred to as *constructivists* because they believe that children construct whatever knowledge they acquire through experiences and human interactions. Children who live in a rural area will have concepts about farms, farm animals, and daily chores and know the names of farm buildings such as *barn, silo, dairy,* and *smokehouse.* Children who grow up in a city will know concepts and words that relate to their own metropolitan area, words such as *high-rise apartment, condominium, skyscraper,* and *traffic jam.* Piaget's constructivist theory, an example of cognitive-developmental theory, is delineated more fully later in the chapter.

Behaviorist Theory

Behaviorist theory is not a new development. Studies of behaviorism began with E. L. Thorndike's law of effect, Pavlov's salivating dogs, Watson's white rabbit, and, in the United States, B. F. Skinner's Skinner box. Behaviorists believe that external factors, such as a mother's reprimand or a teacher's praise, motivate children to behave in certain predictable ways. A classroom approach that utilizes stars, stickers, overt praise, or other external prizes capitalizes on behaviorism as one strategy for managing children's classroom behaviors. The use of behaviorism techniques is widespread in American culture, but early educators recognize that behaviorism has its limitations, a concern that will be addressed later in the chapter.

 **WHY KNOW ABOUT THEORETICAL ORIENTATIONS?**

Being aware of these philosophical orientations will help teachers more clearly define and defend the practices they exhibit in their classrooms. Instructional practices are intentional. Relationships with children develop when teachers strive to meet the needs of individuals assigned to them. Some children need more challenges than others; some children need more nurture than others; still others need an opportunity to become independent. Broad understanding of the learning philosophies discussed here allows teachers to make professional judgments about the relationships they establish with their children and choose practices matching the children they serve.

⭐ MAJOR THEORISTS

Each philosophical orientation has a strong proponent to support it.

Arnold Gesell (1880–1961)

Gesell provides an example of pure nativist thinking. His work emphasizes inherited traits and age-related personality components in individual development, and his collection of normative data is extensive, spanning decades of study on the characteristics of children. Gesell and his associates (Louise Bates Ames and Francis Ilg) listed extensive hierarchies of attributes describing typical behaviors of children from infancy through adolescence. The Gesell Institute of Human Development, opened in 1950 to honor Dr. Gesell, continues his research today.

Trained examiners plan predefined criteria of maturity using the Gesell Developmental Assessments, which describe normal behavior patterns in children. Results of assessments are compared to average child development norms in four areas: personal-social behavior, neurological-motor growth, language development, and overall adaptive behavior (Gesell Institute of Human Development). Other professional resources for parents and professionals plus schedules of workshops for teachers are available by contacting the institute online (www.gesell institute.org).

Erik Erikson (1902—1994)

A strong prototype of maturationist thinking, Erik Erikson refined psychosocial theory, describing social-emotional and sexual development in humans. Erikson's work emphasizes the need to understand human social-emotional development from birth to old age. Often referred to as the "eight stages of man," Erikson's theoretical perspective was influenced by Freudian psychology. Erikson's eight stages appear to be more pertinent to classroom application, whereas Freud's theory is recognized as psychoanalytic and clinical in its approach to severe psychological and emotional problems.

Erikson (1963) describes eight challenges or tasks that individuals face as they grow and mature. The tasks are framed as opposites, showing positive and negative growth areas. How people manage the polar nature of the tasks or obstacles is critical to the overall development of emotionally healthy beings, and their successful achievement at each stage lays a foundation for future mental health as they mature. This principle is easily understood in the context of a specific case. If a child has difficulty with autonomy versus shame or doubt and the ego task is not completed with positive results, then the child will continue to have difficulty with the remaining stages as he or she grows into adulthood.

Early educators need to have an awareness of Erikson's theory because the quality of the relationships they establish with young children correlates with their understanding of youngsters' emotional development. An adage of unknown origin has it that "children care to learn when they learn that teachers care." When teachers acknowledge the emotional issues children face at each age, their classroom curricula will allow learning experiences that facilitate children's self-awareness and stable passage from one stage to another. Daniel Goleman's (1995) recent suggestion that emotional intelligence is as important as cognitive development further supports the credibility of Erikson's theory. Erikson's first four stages (those that affect the early years more profoundly) and a brief description of each are given here.

Trust versus Mistrust. This first stage helps infants and 1-year-olds learn that the environment and the people in it can be trusted. Beginning at birth and continuing until age 2, children tackle the issue of learning trust or mistrust. Caregivers and other adults should be responsive to children and the needs they have during this stage. If they are hungry, children need food. If they are frightened or feeling isolated, children need affection. If they are hurt, children need attention and reassurance that the pain will go away soon.

If conditions are ideal, children pass through this stage with a basic sense of trust. Most recognize, though, that ideal conditions do not exist in children's lives, so a sense of mistrust is instilled in children as well. Balancing these opposite emotions is the essence of Erikson's theory. If children manage conceptions of their world more positively (with trust) than negatively (with mistrust), they are more capable of tackling the next hurdle they encounter as they age.

Autonomy versus Shame or Doubt. The ego task that faces 2- and 3-year-olds is that of becoming aware of themselves as autonomous people. The opportunity to express autonomy is directly associated with toilet training and learning self-control with urination and defecation events. Toilet training occasionally becomes a battleground for parents and children because adults do not recognize the need for children to develop their own elimination schedule. Occasionally, parents are unaware of their role in toilet training, leaving the responsibility for child care center personnel and allowing children far too much freedom in deciding when they will learn toilet etiquette.

During this stage, the polar emotion is that of shame or doubt. These feelings surface when too much external pressure is placed on children during toilet training or when adults are insensitive to accidents or mistakes children make about their ability to manage their own behavior. Children, generally, want to become socialized, and they have as much concern as their parents and caregivers when an error in judgment occurs because they have been so busy playing or engaged in some relevant activity that they forget to tell someone they need to "go potty."

Initiative versus Guilt. This third stage will be the one that most affects the prekindergarten and kindergarten teacher. Four- and 5-year-olds tackle the ego task of taking charge of their participation and engagement in play activities and having to become responsible for their actions. Because of the physical maturity of their bodies, children now have the capability of being more active in their activities. They engage thoroughly in their play, are easily distractible, and often do not comprehend the consequences of their behaviors. The impulsiveness of this age means that children will rush into a street after a wayward ball without thinking about vehicles, which have the right-of-way on the road. They make decisions to take toys they want for play, and they seem oblivious to the crying child they have hurt, though often unintentionally.

Teachers of children at this age become socializing agents influencing children's behaviors. Their instruction of problem-solving skills, negotiation, and understanding others' points of view pave the way for greater self-regulation in children's behavior. A teacher who says to a child, "Hey, Ted, you're being too rough," has not taught him anything about self-control, and Ted may only respond with, "Yeah, I know."

The teacher has an opportunity to say, "Ted, let's talk about your behavior. Do you know how you're affecting your friends?" Then the teacher can continue to help the child see that Fran is now crying because he knocked over her block tower, and the teacher can ask him how he might feel if he were in the same situation. The gentleness with which the teacher approaches this situation will influence Ted's understanding of his own impulsiveness and, through time and experiences, will guide Ted in becoming more sociable in his activity with others. Katz and

State by State

California

State standards address competencies that children will learn during their years in preschool and elementary schools. Among these are three social-emotional tasks as defined by the **California** Department of Education's (2000) Prekindergarten Guidelines:

1. The preschool child must learn self-regulation of emotions and behavior. This self-regulation means learning not to act on impulse, especially on aggressive impulse. Perspective taking and language skills are essential to this task.
2. The child must learn to express feelings in socially appropriate ways.
3. The child must develop satisfying social relationships with other children and adults. During the preschool years children gradually learn how to negotiate social relationships, enter into play with others and take the perspective of others. By the age of 5, many children are capable of a high degree of true cooperation and sharing. (p. 12)

McClelland (1997) reiterate this thinking about the importance of social interactions during the preschool years, and an in-depth discussion of this socialization process is described in Chapter 5.

Erikson was influenced considerably by Sigmund Freud's concept of children's interest in opposite-sexed parents or caretakers (the Oedipus and Electra phase) because he indicates that children begin to have infatuation-like fantasies about their opposite-sex parent or caretaker. A 4-year-old girl, for example, may have a secret desire to steal away her father's affection for her mother. She may indeed say, "When I grow up, I'm going to marry my Daddy." Young children also perceive their teachers as sexual beings. This explains why preschool males seem to fall in love with their teacher, and mother perhaps becomes somewhat jealous of this "new woman" in her child's life. Other examples demonstrating behaviors typical of Erikson's theory in public school classrooms are shown in Figure 2.1.

The significant impact of this stage of development on children correlates with adults' dealing with specific problems as they arise. If teachers and parents punish or scold children too harshly, children develop polar feelings of guilt. Addressing issues of masturbation and sex play as they occur requires that teachers recognize that these events are normal behavior in children's lives. Their attitude in talking to children about how to handle their urges is critical to the children's later development. This initiative-versus-guilt stage is also important in the development of a child's conscience.

Industry versus Inferiority. The ego task of early and middle childhood is necessary to understanding primary-age through preadolescent children's desire to learn. Another interpretation of this stage is *competence versus incompetence,* which means that 6- to 12-year-old children develop a sense of themselves as learners during this phase, and they are beginning to comprehend an "I can do it" attitude about themselves and their abilities (Hendrick, 2003).

Children's view of themselves as readers, mathematicians, scientists, musicians, athletes, dancers, and so on becomes the focus of the early grades in school. Children develop positive self-esteem if the classroom experiences they have are appropriate for them. Teachers need to continue caring and nurturing children in their classrooms because positive emotional relationships yield greater achievement rewards for students (Darling-Hammond, 1997).

Children tend to remember polar learning experiences, those that were quite positive or those that were extremely negative, long into adulthood. Recalling having to sit in the corner for talking in first grade or being sent to the principal's office in third grade are school memories that last a lifetime. Remembering being able to read a story for the first time or performing a solo during a second-grade parent program helps children think positive thoughts about their academic excellence. Doing classwork, being called on by the teacher for academic responses, playing childhood games on the playground, taking home schoolwork, participating in special celebrations in schools—all these memories of tasks accomplished accumulate, assisting the child in becoming competent (or industrious). Failing consistently at any one of these activities ensures that the child will feel incompetent (or inferior). The

FIGURE 2.1 Typical Behaviors Demonstrating Erikson's Theory in Public School Classrooms

4- and 5-Year-Olds

- Children cry easily at this age, especially if they do not get what they want immediately.
- Children interpret accidental and hurtful behavior by others as intentional, and they often respond with anger and aggression.
- Children do not interpret their feelings in the same that way that adults understand them. Teachers will need to spend time helping children identify and manage their feelings when they occur.
- Children respond to others in the same manner that adults have responded to them through the years. If children are abused or belittled in their homes, they will exhibit shy or timid behaviors or they will be continually aggressive toward others.
- Social skills, such as taking turns and remembering to say "please" and "thank you" do not come naturally to children at this age. The teacher's best strategy is modeling the appropriate behavior to the youngsters in her care.
- Children's play behaviors and interactions with others are critical to their development as social beings.

6- through 8-Year-Olds

- Children continue to have difficulty understanding their emotions, but they are usually more capable of managing impulsive behaviors.
- Emotional outbursts will still occur among some children, but they are more infrequent and rational discussion when they occur will help children continue to develop less impulsive behaviors.
- Children begin to understand the need for classroom rules and routines, especially if teachers allow for their input in developing reasonable standards of conduct for all to follow.
- Children prefer consistent management from adults (getting to bed at the same time every night, having lunch at the same time, developing a predictable classroom routine, etc.), because these procedures assist in developing their own self-management skills.
- Children still need parental support as they become attuned to themselves as learners.
- The teacher's attitude toward children's emotional development and social inclusion is a critical element in developing class community and children's care and concern for others' problems and behaviors.
- Class projects that assist children in developing a sense of social problems in the world (world hunger or environmental issues) help the students in understanding in an elementary sense the responsibilities they have to others in their community.

long-term consequences of feeling competent or feeling incompetent are critical issues in predicting children's success as they move through school.

Erikson's four remaining stages, though not truly pertinent to the early childhood teacher, are mentioned here, because teachers are dealing with specific emotional tasks themselves as they develop as professionals. The *identity versus role confusion* stage lasts from about age 12 to age 20. Adolescents are beginning to take on an adult identity and the life choices they make during this time will affect their development in early adult years and perhaps into old age.

Most students in teacher preparation studies are in the *intimacy versus isolation* stage. Spanning ages 20 to 30, young adults are preparing for the lifestyles they want to pursue, and they are making decisions about the individual they will spend their adult years with. The seventh stage is *generativity versus stagnation*. Individuals are pursuing career opportunities and developing family relationships with their offspring during this stage. Most adults achieve advancements in their career pursuits toward the end of this stage (from ages 30 to 50), and they realize how important their children (and the lives of others' children) are.

The last stage is labeled *ego integrity versus despair*. At about age 50, people begin personal reflection on their lives and what they have accomplished as adults. From an outsider's viewpoint, self-evaluation during this period appears to be a "midlife crisis," as some individuals change their lives drastically because they did not like what they had become as adults. Though most people continue to be as productive in their career pursuits and as caring as ever with their personal relationships, they

 What Teachers Are Saying

Philosophical Orientations

"Learning about Vygotsky has helped me be more aware of the point at which a child 'stalls' in a particular learning area. Teacher help at this point can boost the child to a new level of learning." —*a second-grade teacher*

"I believe Gardner's theory of multiple intelligences embraces the diverse population we encounter as teachers. Being open to each and every intelligence will promote success in our classrooms." —*a kindergarten teacher*

"Piaget has most influenced my thinking as a teacher. I learn more about and from my children when I watch them. That is why cooperative learning is such a match for me. The children become the teachers and I only facilitate." —*a third-grade teacher*

"I keep my professors' photos on my classroom shelf. They speak silently to my heart each day. Sometimes I even find myself muttering to their photos, asking for wisdom or for an extra burst of patience and energy—especially during times of unexpected, perplexing, semi-humorous challenges." —*Peggy Hutson, a first-year kindergarten teacher*

view life and tackle life's opportunities with more zest and enthusiasm than previously. They often choose activities that they want for themselves instead of doing what others ask of them. They are more likely to take better care of their health and to seek personally meaningful activities and lifestyles than previously. Often, the parenting responsibilities that were essential for the previous *generativity versus stagnation* stage are behind them, allowing for more personal freedom.

Lev Vygotsky (1896–1934)

Vygotsky's research interests, though cut short by his premature death, focused on the development of language in children. His recognition that social models, most often adults, are essential for children to refine their cultural and language knowledge is the hallmark of his theory. According to Bodrova and Leong (1996), the basic principles of Vygotskian theory are: (1) children construct knowledge, (2) development cannot be separated from its social context, (3) learning can lead development, and (4) language plays a central role in mental development (p. 8).

Vygotsky believed that very young children develop *pseudoconcepts* showing they have preliminary knowledge about objects in the environment. A 2-year-old might erroneously refer to a *horse* as a *cow* because of the similarities in their body frames and her own previous experience with cows. To obtain a more accurate conceptual understanding, an adult (or older child) might say, "That's a horse, not a cow. Cows have udders and give us milk, but horses don't. We ride horses." The child's false understanding is corrected because of adult modeling.

Vygotsky also proposed that children's play is critical to their mental development. Symbolic thought, representation, and reasoning are fostered through children's play behaviors. Vygotsky defined play as a "tool of the mind" that allows children to explore roles and acquire information about the rules governing the roles. If a child chooses to be a puppy dog in a play scenario, then his behaviors throughout the play experience must adhere to puppy dog behaviors. The puppy would not talk or pretend to eat lunch at the kitchen table. Instead, he would bark or whine and pretend to eat from a doggie bowl (Bodrova & Leong, 1996).

Vygotsky introduced two terms that have become important to educators. The **zone of proximal development** defines how children use language models to enhance their own learning experiences. Children can and do acquire certain levels of learning on their own, and Vygotsky urges adults to take a hands-off approach to their knowledge acquisition (Frost, Wortham, & Reifel, 2001). Many situations arise, both in and out of classrooms, when children need assistance to move to another level of understanding. The connections adults help children make, moving them to a higher level of conceptual development, occur in the zone of proximal development. For example, children will assimilate knowledge about print on their own, but teachers can assist children in understanding another level of print recognition by naming the letters or pointing out that words have consistent patterns.

Vygotsky referred to the learning environments adults prepare for children as **scaffolding.** Placing an abundance of books, puzzles, and other learning materials in the classroom is evidence of scaffolding. A teacher who has planned a unit on dinosaurs might bury chicken bones in the sandbox to assist children in learning the terms *paleontology* and *paleontologist*. Field trips to community businesses or government buildings or bringing special speakers into the classroom are a form of scaffolding. Scaffolding occurs in the home as well, when parents purchase educational materials for their children or take them to a children's museum in an effort to enhance their curiosity.

Scaffolding relates to the social and cultural environments children live in, thus accounting for Vygotsky's sociocultural orientation. Children who live in New England learn that a cold drink is called *pop,* whereas children in other areas of the country will call it *soda.* In the southern United States, a cold drink is often referred to as a *coke,* though the preferred drink might be a Dr. Pepper or a Pepsi. Scaffolding has strong implications for teachers of second language learners. Children who learn a language other than English as they mature might encounter learning difficulties because of their backgrounds, not because of their inability to learn. Teachers must consider social and cultural differences when they work with all children, no matter their heritage.

Piaget (1896–1980)

Piaget was not an educator, but his background as an epistemologist led him to study the behaviors his children exhibited as infants and, eventually, to study thousands of children (now known as the Geneva Studies). Epistemologists examine behaviors of organisms (in this case, children), and formulate theories about why organisms behave as they do. The result of Piaget's decades-long study led to a theory of cognitive development, which influenced educators' perceptions of children's thinking processes (Piaget, 1977).

Piaget believed that children's thinking and conceptual development preceded language production and that experiences in the environment and social interactions with others assisted in clarifying the knowledge (or schemata) they acquired. Twin processes—assimilation and accommodation—maintain a state of **equilibrium** within children. Children *assimilate* stimuli (or data) from their environment and use the information as they formulate thoughts and language. When new information from the environment causes children to think in a new or different way, they are said to *accommodate* the data. **Disequilibrium** occurs when the environment or an interaction challenges children. In order to return to equilibrium, children must accommodate the new data into their internal schema.

Rachelle, age 2, saw a billy goat walk across her front lawn one day, and she turned to her caregiver and said, "Look! Doggie." The adult responded by explaining that the animal was actually a goat and that the differences between this creature and Smoky, the large neighborhood dog, were that it had horns on its head and hooves on its feet. The puzzled child repeated the words, "Billy goat?" "Yes, it's a billy goat, not a dog," and the child repeated, "Billy goat," showing a satisfied expression indicating that her disequilibrium had stabilized. Equilibrium returned with the explanation she had heard. Conceptual development and acquisition of knowledge occur in similar ways every day that children learn.

Two young boys explore scientific phenomena in a preschool classroom.

Piaget's years of study also indicated that children do not think in the same way that adults think. He labeled their individualistic thinking as *egocentric.* As children mature, have social and educational experiences, and interact with the environment and other people, their thought processes change. Infants rely on innate reflexive abilities to make sense of their environment, and thought processes do not appear until toward the end of their first year. In this first stage, defined by Piaget as the **sensorimotor stage,** children use reflexes, motor activity, and sensory data to begin making sense of the information they receive.

The second stage, which begins around 18 months to 2 years, is characterized by children's interest in symbolic representation. Piaget called this the **preoperational stage,** indicating that children's thought processes are becoming consolidated based on the experiential evidence they receive from their environment. Children appear to be developing memory, and they begin to recognize familiar objects and repetitive events in their daily activity. A 3-year-old might begin talking about a circus he attended as if the circus trip happened quite recently when in fact it happened six months earlier.

The latter part of the preoperational period is marked by children's growing awareness of social and cultural knowledge, but children still rely on egocentric understanding in defining what they know. One 4-year-old named a squirrel living in her yard "Homer"; every time she saw another squirrel, she called it "Homer." Her label continued for several months before she realized that the squirrel that lived in her back yard was not the same squirrel she saw when she played in the neighborhood park.

Preoperational children are demonstrating Piaget's description of *logico-mathematical* knowledge. They understand events from one perspective, and they learn differing viewpoints from people and objects that they encounter. One child may comprehend the word *hot* in relation to heat or warm temperature. But she has an opportunity to learn another meaning when she witnesses her grandmother dip a chip into Mexican salsa and say, "Wow, that's hot." When she dips her own chip into the salsa and repeats her grandmother's utterance, she has a new comprehension of the word *hot.*

Other terms that define preoperational reasoning are centration and concreteness. *Centration* is the child's attending to one element in a situation and ignoring all other components of the situation. A child's belief (described previously) that every squirrel she sees in the community is the same squirrel living in her back yard demonstrates centration. Another example is when children group all red objects together without noticing that some are triangles and some are squares.

Concreteness is the child's understanding of objects in concrete terms. Abstract vocabulary escapes their logic. If someone reports that she "lost mother this year," a child will respond by saying, "Let's go find her." Or if a parent asks a child if she can sing a song *high,* the child will stand on his tiptoes to sing the song. See Figure 2.2 for more examples of preoperational thinking by young children.

The **concrete operations stage** emerges when children begin to understand knowledge in a more adult manner, especially if concepts are concrete in nature. Comprehension of mathematical and scientific phenomena is similar to adult interpretations of data and environmental stimuli. Beginning at about age 8, children are able to see opposite viewpoints of events, have flexibility in thinking, and are capable of defining terms with concrete examples. Piaget's analysis of these new processes is that children are now capable of reversible thought, they are able to *conserve,* and they can do operations that require dealing with mass, weight, and time.

Eight-year-olds can explain that 9 plus 7 is the same as 7 plus 9. They recognize that the numeral 10 can be subdivided into five 2s, two 5s, one 8 and one 2, one 7 and one 3, and so on. Asked to define the word *love* or another abstract term, they will use concrete expressions that show what the word means to them. They might say that love is hugs and kisses or describe it as the feeling parents have for their children or that they have for their parents.

The concrete operations stage implies that teachers need to work carefully with children in their classrooms to ensure students' understanding of mathematical and scientific processes that are occasionally taught in rote fashion. Third graders may not truly understand what a multiplication problem like 4 times 5 actually means. If children understand the concept first at a concrete level, learning the multiplication tables as techniques needed to save oneself time will become more meaningful to children.

The final stage, which Piaget described as the **formal operations stage,** begins at about age 11 and continues through age 16. In this stage children become capable of doing abstract thinking and suggest alternative solutions to problems. The foundation for the formal operations stage begins in the early years, and what children learn in the early years is critical to the development of this fourth stage. Transition periods exist among the stages, and children will vacillate from time to time from one type of thinking to another. Rich learning experiences in and out of classrooms facilitate children's movement toward higher levels of thinking.

Maria Montessori (1870–1952)

One European who had tremendous impact on early education in America was Dr. Maria Montessori, the first Italian woman ever to graduate with a medical degree. Her work can be classified as maturationist in nature because she defined stages in

Figure 2.2 Examples of Preoperational Children's Thought Processes

Example 1: Egocentrism

Bill, age 6, asks his first-grade teacher after lunch, "Teacher, can I keep my dessert until later in the day?"

His teacher smiles and answers, "Yes."

At dismissal time, the teacher learns at the same time as Bill that his ice cream dessert has melted into his lunch box and all over his cubby. Unfortunately, this teacher did not understand preoperational thinking, and she chided Bill for having been so foolish.

Example 2: Centration

Shelly, age 4, is talking to her aunt on the phone. "Oh, I see a bluebird in my yard," her aunt said.

"That must be the bluebird that lives in my yard," replies Shelley, who lives about 60 miles from her aunt.

Example 3: Faulty Preoperational Reasoning

A mother accidentally bumps her 4-year-old daughter with the grocery sack as she is removing groceries from the back seat of the family car. "Oh, honey, I'm so sorry to have bumped you. I know that hurt. It was an accident, and I didn't mean to hurt you."

"Yes, you did!" wails the child loudly enough for the neighbors to hear.

Example 4: Egocentrism, Incomplete Conceptual Development

"Austin, how do you spell your name?" asked his preschool teacher on the first day he came to class after he turned 4.

"I'm 4," said Austin.

"That's your age, Austin—I need to know how to spell your name." replied his teacher.

Austin held up his fingers and said, "One, two, three, four."

"Thank you, Austin," said his teacher, making a mental note to help this child become aware of the print in his environment. Then she wrote Austin as she thought it was probably spelled, checking later with the office to determine that she had spelled his name correctly.

Example 5: Centration

A prekindergarten child went into the cafeteria with her class and teacher, where the children were required to tell the cafeteria servers if they were on free or reduced lunch. Emily had just learned this procedure, and when Mrs. Baker asked if she had free or reduced lunch, the child said, "I'm 4, not free."

continued

Figure 2.2 *continued*

Example 6: Egocentrism

A noted dentist named Dr. Cole had died in the local community where Marcus lived, and Marcus had heard the news during the morning prior to going to his pre-kindergarten class in the afternoon. When he arrived at school, he announced to his teacher and classmates with much chagrin in his voice, "Old King Cole is dead."

Example 7: Faulty Concept Development

The music teacher came to the school's annual "Hag Day," dressed as only a hag could look. One of the kindergarten children who came to her classroom only once a week asked, "Who are you?" When the music teacher told him who she was, he looked puzzled. She certainly did not look like the music teacher he knew!

Example 8: Egocentrism

Raymond, age 4, had been standing in a line far too long, and when the principal stopped to talk to his teacher in the hall, he had had enough. His piercing scream to express his displeasure for having to wait so long lasted only a few seconds, but the principal gave him a scowl to express his displeasure for Raymond's misbehavior.

The teacher, though, understood the problem and Raymond's inability to express in words what he was feeling. She reached down, put her arm around him and told him gently, "We'll be back in the classroom in just a few minutes." As they made their way back to the classroom, she held Raymond's hand for support.

Example 9: Preoperational Reasoning (leading to an illogical conclusion)

Jenetta, age 3, playing near her grandmother's chair, accidentally knocked off one of Granny's house shoes from her crossed legs. The child picked up the slide-type shoe and tried to replace it on Granny's foot. Turning the slide upside down, backward, and sideways, never managing to get the shoe back onto Granny's foot, Jenetta finally dropped it on the floor and said, "It doesn't fit."

children's development that she labeled as "sensitive periods" and planned definite learning experiences for each specific stage.

Montessori believed that a prepared environment was crucial to children's education. Her philosophy stemmed from an interest in "idiot children" housed in the psychiatric clinic when she served as an intern at the University of Rome. She worked with the French educators Jean Itard and Edouard Seguin and read their works. Both had extensive experience with mentally retarded children and were strong proponents of sensory training. Montessori's ideology and methodology blossomed when she had an opportunity to open the Casa dei Bambini ("Children's House") in inner-city Rome in 1907, communally owned by the parents, mostly young women whose husbands had died or abandoned their families, now living in the tenement building where the school was housed.

The Roman Association of Good Building established the Casa dei Bambini "to offer, free of charge" a program that addressed "the education, the health, the physical and moral development of the children . . . in a way suited to the age of the children" (Braun & Edwards, 1971, p. 116). Montessori's experience with mentally retarded children supported her belief that children learn through their senses. Consequently, she developed over 1,400 materials designed to heighten the awareness children had for their environment and the concepts they learned about their world. More information about Montessori practices is provided later in the chapter.

Howard Gardner (1943–)

Gardner's work in **multiple intelligences theory** is an example of the work of a recent theorist impacting classroom practice. A Harvard psychologist, Gardner developed profiles of intelligence areas, proposing that individuals have the potential to enhance the intelligence areas based on their genetic structure and the constraints of the environments in which they live. He analyzed the lives of numerous people whose strengths in music, athletics, language, and mathematics made them famous, determining how they achieved greatness in their respective fields. His nine intelligence areas and classroom practices are defined later in the chapter, though Gardner acknowledges that more intelligence areas may exist than the ones he has targeted. More research in this area is needed.

⭐ RECOGNIZED PROGRAM MODELS

Educators use theoretical perspectives to develop programs based on the major tenets of the theorists described here. Piaget and Montessori hold the most influential positions in current practice, though Vygotsky's theory has taken precedence within the past ten years. Other influences include the Italian Reggio Emilia centers and Gardner's multiple intelligences theory.

High/Scope

Both High/Scope and Project Construct programs are based on the assumption that teachers know Piagetian theory. The Perry Preschool Program, as it was known in the 1960s, paved the way for the High/Scope Program Model. A researcher, David Weikart, became interested in determining how program development impacts children's lives. He divided a group of children from low-income families into two. One group attended a high-quality preschool program, and the other attended a regular program in the Perry Elementary School in Ypsilanti, Michigan. Weikart defined high-quality preschools as those that have well-trained teachers who work and plan together as a team with a well-defined curriculum and utilize parent involvement in the implementation of the program (Weikart, 1989).

The basic components of the High/Scope Program Model are an environment that allows for child choice, a daily schedule that provides for planning, doing, and then reviewing what has been accomplished (called Plan-Do-Review) and observant adults who facilitate children's activity and help them synthesize knowledge acquired throughout the day. High/Scope identifies Key Experiences that are critical ingredients in developing cognitive abilities in children. Key Experiences include Creative Representation, Language and Literacy, Initiative and Social Relations, Movement, Music, Classification, Seriation, Number, Space, and Time (Hohmann, 1995).

High/Scope-trained teachers carefully orchestrate children's introduction to symbolic representation by introducing them to the concrete object (the index understanding), then to a picture of the object (referred to as the symbol level) and finally to the sign level of representation (the actual word). Designing activities that allow children to progress through these levels of representation (index, symbol, sign) provide meaningful experiences for children to draw upon when it is necessary to reflect on their own learning. Looking at, smelling, cutting, and tasting a cantaloupe (index) leads to recognition of the object by looking at a picture of it (symbol), and finally the word *cantaloupe* (sign) is introduced.

Levels of operation are incorporated into the curriculum framework as well. Two levels of operation—motor and verbal—are inherent in any classroom experience children may have had throughout the course of the day. They are engaged with materials and learning opportunities (motor level), they talk about what they have done (verbal level) and, eventually, through experience they begin to write about what they are learning. Children learn by working with learning materials and interacting with peers, and teachers help them consolidate the knowledge they are acquiring by talking with the children about their activities (Hohmann, Banet, & Weikart, 1979).

After years of study, Weikart and his associates have determined that quality programming affects children's behavior in several ways: (1) they are more likely to graduate from high school, (2) they are less likely to become delinquents during adolescence, (3) they are more likely to attempt postsecondary education, and (4) they are more likely to obtain and retain jobs. The cost to taxpayers because of programs like High/Scope yields benefits because of reduced need for costly special education programs and fewer needs for criminal justice services as children become adolescents (Weikart, 1971).

Project Construct

Another program model based on Piagetian theory is Project Construct, emerging from work completed by the Missouri Department of Elementary and Secondary Education. In *Understanding the Possibilities: A Curriculum Guide for Project Construct* (Murphy & Goffin, 1992), a framework is laid out for teachers who want to plan for more constructivist curriculum development. Teachers who use Project Construct recognize that children acquire knowledge or "make meaning" through their own activity, following the old adage, "When I do, I learn." Environmental design, daily practice, and opportunities for learning have a child-centered perspective, and curriculum emerges within the context of the classroom and children's needs and interests.

Transforming oneself into a constructivist teacher takes time because teachers tend to rely on methodologies that they remember from their own childhood. They often observe classroom teachers who use traditional instructional strategies when they progress through teacher preparation programs and the opportunity to observe in constructivist classrooms is rare. The ability to analyze children's conceptual development and adjust instruction accordingly requires a strong foundation in Piagetian theory, keen observation skills, and flexibility with a wide range of instructional strategies.

Murphy and Goffin's text and workshops conducted each year focus on what individual children learn as a consequence of the interactions they have with the environment and the people in it. A traditional classroom requires third graders to know how many feet are in a mile, as an example. Instead of memorizing that 5,280 feet are in a mile, the constructivist teacher takes her class on a walking field trip to experience how far it is to walk a mile. The learning is in the conceptualization of a mile, not in remembering a fact that may or may not have meaning for 8-year-olds. Helping children achieve intellectual autonomy becomes one goal for teachers, eliminating the need for children to memorize irrelevant facts and figures, spend countless hours on meaningless worksheets, and practice skills in isolation from events that could have practical application for learners.

Curriculum in Project Construct is based on play and integration of classroom experiences to assist children in acquiring knowledge. The teacher poses social problems for children to solve through a variety of tactics emphasizing flexibility in thinking and attacking concerns with proactive strategies that they learn from their teacher (or other adults) and from peers. The problems children solve should be based on children's interests and need to be authentic. The teacher's role is to facilitate meaningful study based on her observation and assessment of emerging interests.

Building a bird feeder for winter birds is a "real" problem that requires children to do some planning and organizing for actual construction, achieving the ultimate goal of placing a bird feeder on the playground near the classroom. The study can continue with the addition of books and videos about birds, searching the Internet for information about specific observed birds, and recording the amount of food that various birds eat each day. Children move to higher levels of achievement in literacy by dictating or writing stories about the knowledge they are acquiring and discovering various ways to keep records of learning. The teacher keeps records, too. The information he or she collects is gleaned through observations, prepared checklists, photographs of children's work, and stories children write. Assisting with synthesis of learning as the study winds down provides additional information for the teacher to collect. Information about the learning that is going on in the classroom is easy to share because teachers have documented records for reporting purposes. Children synthesize knowledge by preparing displays showing what they have accomplished and learned.

Montessori Programs

Montessori had four major pedagogical beliefs about young children's learning. She believed that adults needed to have *respect for the child;* she was interested in allowing children *freedom* to learn and self-paced education; she proposed that children would learn if they were placed in a *prepared environment;* and she thought that teaching materials needed to be *autotelic* (instructional in nature and self-correcting). Her concept of *normalization* suggests that children grow and develop in predictable fashion, leading to her description of *sensitive periods.*

Montessori's Casa dei Bambini was a beautiful center, which included plants and a feeling of airiness created by large windows, allowing light to shine in for much of the day. Materials were placed at the child's level in spaces that were designed for the specific material, and children learned that the materials would be returned to that space when they were finished working with them. Even in modern-day Montessori settings, the materials are placed in spaces in the center that remain ever fixed for that particular material. The Pink Tower, for example, will always be found in the same spot in the classroom in the same configuration. Following this recommendation allows children to develop a sense of order about their surroundings.

Montessori also believed that the *directress* (or teacher) had a unique role in the classroom. In the role of observer, the Montessori teacher has the responsibility to determine the level of achievement children have and to challenge them to another level of understanding. Instruction was accomplished in one-on-one interactions with individual children who were left to their own devices to choose materials and the time and place they wanted to use them. Once it appeared that the child's interest in a specific activity was waning, the directress then took the responsibility for introducing another concept with the same material or showing the child how to use another material. Montessori believed that children learn by doing, and teachers need to observe children's learning and adjust instruction accordingly to be effective.

Montessori described *sensitive periods* in children's learning. These periods are clearly defined in Montessori's writings as specific phases of development when children are most receptive to certain stimuli:

Birth–3 years	absorbent mind
	sensory experiences
1½–3 years	language development
1½–4 years	coordination and muscle development
	interest in small objects
2–4 years	refinement of movement
	concern with truth and reality
	awareness of order sequence in time and space
2¼–6 years	sensory refinement
3–6 years	susceptibility to adult influence
3½–4½ years	writing
4–4½ years	tactile sense
4½–5½ years	reading (Orem, 1974, pp. 128–129)

Motor education, sometimes referred to as "Practical Life" activities, was designed to give children freedom of movement in the classroom. The ultimate goal was the development of self-management skills in children, which included experiences such as washing tables, pouring water into pitchers, folding linen napkins, cutting carrots or celery, scissors work, buttoning, lacing, and opening and shutting drawers. The button and lacing frames are popular Montessori materials in most early classrooms even today. Other motor education activities might include sweeping, washing napkins, brushing and caring for animals, and watering plants.

Montessori methodology is carefully designed to maximize instruction children are receiving from the materials they are using. An observer in a Montessori classroom might notice a 3-year-old carefully using a large soapy sponge to clean a table from top to bottom and then from left to right, following that activity with another wet sponge to rinse the soap from the table (again in top-to-bottom and left-to-right motions), and later to dry the table with a cloth in the same top-to-bottom and left-to-right motions. Or a 5-year-old who has spent time cutting cheese into cubes with a dull knife has an opportunity to serve another child in the classroom by placing cheese cubes on a cheese server, and the recipient has the right to accept or refuse the offer.

Sensory education includes numerous materials that develop children's tactile, visual, and auditory senses to a fine degree. Color tablets, for example, require children to differentiate tints of a certain color from darkest to lightest. Steel cylinders help children discriminate among various weights, sizes, and even temperatures. Blocks are graded by length and width to challenge children to order them by placing them in a specific sequence to resemble stairs. Cylinder insets cause children to make decisions between the circumference and height of each piece that fits into a wooden puzzlelike base. If the child makes a mistake, one of the pieces will not fit, obliging the child to rethink his work. Tracing geometric designs is thought to help children move from concrete thinking to more representational thought (Evans, 1971).

One of the most well-known materials Montessori developed were her "sound jars." Since then, early educators have used these materials to help children with aural discrimination. Children are not only expected to listen to differences in intensity of the materials inside the jar but also to sequence the materials from softest to loudest sounds. The tone bells assist children in hearing the fine quality of musical sound they make. Another important concept Montessori emphasized was the lesson of silence.

Montessori believed in teaching young children to read. The Italian language has but one sound per letter, and the method of decoding print Montessori used capitalized on this aspect of the language. The vowels in Italian are short, and this simplifies the process of reading the language. Instead of introducing the letter of the alphabet to children by their names ("this is an *a*" or "this is an *l*"), Montessori introduced the *sound* of the letter to children. Once children knew all of the *sound* names, they had an easy process of "sounding" out the letter names to make a word. "*Mm—a—tuh*" became *mat,* and children could "read" the word whether it was one they comprehended or not.

Montessori classrooms promote independent learning through self-paced activities.

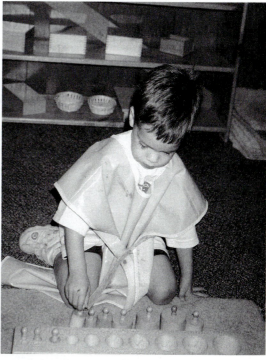

This young boy is participating in sensory training in an orderly prepared environment as defined by Montessori methodology.

Writing became simple, too, because children were asked to listen for the sound of the letters in a word. Montessori originally used sandpaper letters to facilitate the process through sensory training. The vowels are usually shown in a different color from the consonants. The directress begins writing instruction with three-letter words that usually had a personal reference to the child. Once a word was learned, such as the word *cat*, it was easy to introduce *hat, sat, fat,* or *rat*. The procedure from recognizing words to reading words is gradual, and children participate in numerous concrete experiences before being asked to read a word aloud.

Concrete activities are also essential to the development of number concepts. The Golden Beads are materials that are grouped together in units, tens, hundreds, and thousands. Long before their understanding of the figure *1562,* children are taught to recognize the spot each number holds. If they recognize which numeral is in which place, then they are able to count out *one thousand, five hundreds, six tens,* and *two ones* with the Golden Beads. Again, concept formation is gradual, but children begin to comprehend that volume increases because of the placement of the specific numeral in a number. Montessori believed, too, that the concept of *zero* should be introduced to young children (Montessori, 1914).

Issues and Trends

Alternative Certification

Teacher shortages across the United States caused many states to develop opportunities for individuals with bachelor's degrees to achieve elementary- or secondary-level teaching certifications. Alternative certification programs are available through local districts, some universities, and regional and state education agencies. The National Association for Alternative Certification (NAAC) has as its main goal the improvement of preparation programs for noncertified individuals. The No Child Left Behind legislation (ECS Special Report, 2002) classifies teachers who participate in alternative certification programs as highly qualified.

Montessori training is also offered to noncertified individuals. Anyone who seeks to become a directoress must hold a bachelor's degree and receive training in Montessori education in an approved facility (www.montessori.edu).

Two professional groups represent the Montessori methodology, Association Montessori Internationale (AMI) and the American Montessori Society (AMS). Numerous institutes within the United States deliver her methodology to students in training to become directresses. The differences between the AMI and AMS relate to the degree to which the Montessori Method is applied in classrooms. The AMI group upholds a stricter approach to the Montessori methodology; children are encouraged to be independent in their work, and interactions with others in the classroom are curtailed. The AMS organization espouses more creative approaches to instruction and recognizes the need for children to express themselves through artistic and musical endeavors and to socialize with one another in dramatic play and organized outdoor games (Orem, 1974).

Montessori's philosophy has generally been criticized for its lack of creativity and the lack of interaction among children in the program (Evans, 1971). However, the quality of the 1,400-plus materials she developed for classrooms indicates how important her circle of influence is in educational settings. Many educators believe Montessori was a woman "ahead of her time." Gordon and Browne (2003) report that over 100 public schools have programs based on her philosophy in early childhood settings.

Multiple Intelligences Theory

As discussed earlier in this chapter, Harvard-based researcher Howard Gardner introduced the multiple intelligences theory (MI theory) to the nation with a book titled *Frames of Mind: The Theory of Multiple Intelligences* (1983). His novel interpretation of the intellectual development of humans has evolved from an original seven intelligence areas to nine. Gardner readily acknowledges that more intelli-

gence areas are possible and encourages more research to identify and define each area. Goleman's
treatise on *Emotional Intelligence* (1995) is only one
study that proposes yet another intelligence area
and the need to understand and nurture it.

The nine areas currently defined by Gardner
are (1) verbal/linguistic intelligence, (2) logical/
mathematical intelligence, (3) visual/spatial intelligence, (4) bodily/kinesthetic intelligence, (5) musical intelligence, (6) interpersonal intelligence,
(7) intrapersonal intelligence, (8) naturalistic intelligence, and (9) existentialist intelligence. See Figure
2.3 for descriptions of each of the intelligence areas.
Persons usually possess strengths in more than one
identified intelligence area.

Often described as different ways of learning
and teaching, MI theory implies that each individual has areas of strength and weakness that educators can capitalize on in classroom teaching.
From a historical perspective, the verbal/linguistic
and logical/mathematical intelligence areas have
formed the basis for most classroom instruction.
The three Rs (reading, 'riting, and 'rithematic) approach to organizing classroom instruction becomes outdated when teachers begin thinking
about the talents and abilities children bring to
their classrooms each and every day.

*MI theory supports children's acquisition of visual-spatial
knowledge, easily developed through easel painting.*

Gardner's theory emphasizes that each intelligence area is a potential area for
development. Governing factors determining the intelligence areas that surface in
individuals are (1) genetic inheritance, and (2) environmental influences. Musicians
like Bach and Beethoven had native genetic structures, which provided the impetus to highest achievement when they were born into families of musicians. An
athlete may be "born" an athlete, but being born an athlete is only true to the degree that environmental influences allow him or her to excel.

When teachers understand intelligence areas, they are attuned to the strengths
and weaknesses of their children and can provide learning experiences promoting
each of the intelligence areas. The implication of teaching to multiple intelligences
is that the environment and daily activities are planned so that each intelligence
area is touched upon during the day. Providing reading, writing, and math experiences is a foundation in any public school classroom, but teachers with knowledge of MI theory provide music, physical education, theater and movement
experiences, social activity, self-reflection, and nature study, areas that do not often
appear in daily routines.

Multiple intelligences theory has made a critical impact in the early education
arena because children are not "schooled" in literacy and mathematics concepts as

FIGURE 2.3 Descriptive Characteristics of Nine Multiple Intelligences Areas

Verbal-Linguistic Intelligence

- Adept at verbalizations
- Enjoyment of public speaking
- Enjoyment of books and reading, puns, jokes
- Find pleasure in writing prose and poetry
- Discover word patterns, rhyme, and alliteration
- Often early reading and writing

Logical-Mathematical Intelligence

- Skill at solving number problems
- Enjoyment of puzzles and challenging conundrums
- Enjoyment of games that require logical thinking to play
- Facility with numbers and money
- Using number patterns and novel approaches when working with numbers
- Able to solve number and logic problems at a very young age

Visual-Spatial Intelligence

- Able to observe fine discriminations in colors, designs, and patterns
- Able to develop elaborate block structures and construct intricate designs with Lego blocks
- Enjoyment of art exhibits and demonstrations of artistic techniques
- Able to imagine placement of furniture and pictures in an empty space
- Skill in design and architecture
- Observing details in artwork

Bodily-Kinesthetic Intelligence

- Able to maximize the potential their bodies have for athletic endeavor
- Well coordinated and poised in demeanor and activity
- Enjoyment of dancing and movement
- Responsive to music with tapping or clapping
- Making time for physical activity
- Not able to sit still for long periods of time

Musical Intelligence

- Enjoyment of musical activity (listening and performance)
- Singing or humming while doing daily activity
- Responsive to music and rhythm when they occur
- Discovering pleasure in writing music and rehearsing with musical instruments
- Hearing the music and sound in nature before seeing its beauty
- Entranced with music and sounds at an early age

continued

Figure 2.3 *continued*

Interpersonal Intelligence

- Enjoyment of meeting new people and connecting with previous acquaintances
- Appearance of talking only to the person they are visiting
- Able to become a super salesperson
- Wanting to be with people, even when they are quite young
- People oriented, never shy away from a crowd
- Considered to be friendly and easy to talk with

Intrapersonal Intelligence

- Enjoyment in being self-reflective
- Seeming to possess wisdom beyond their years
- Happy to work alone
- Often exhibiting solitary play behaviors, even as youngsters
- Not relying on others for personal happiness

Naturalistic Intelligence

- Attuned to natural events and phenomena
- Cultivating beautiful yards and gardens (possess "green thumbs")
- As children, always bringing home stray animals
- Knowledge of natural science and animal behavior
- Able to name almost any plant and tell what each needs to survive
- Enjoyment of camping and hiking trips in natural settings

Existentialist Intelligence

- An uncanny sense of spiritual concepts
- Asking questions that appear to be "beyond their years"
- Expressing concern for others
- Possessing an understanding of global issues
- Not minding being alone for long periods of time
- Able to amuse themselves when they are alone

---

yet. They rely on physical and sensory experiences to learn what they can learn from an environment, and good early educators use these two areas to capitalize on instruction. Using musical experiences to teach rote information (the "Alphabet Song," for example) assists children in learning drill and practice material with a pleasurable activity. Chants, fingerplays, literature, and games are avenues to teaching a child who might otherwise not respond to traditional methods of instruction, which become the norm for elementary grade instruction.

Some curriculum areas are already addressing multiple intelligences theory with specific recognizable instructional movements that attend to areas of potential learning. The whole-language movement that gained popularity in the 1970s and 1980s directly relates to Gardner's verbal/linguistic intelligence and how children acquire knowledge in this area. Davis (2001) recommends that classroom centers in early education meet the individual intelligence needs of children by adding teaching materials and props. See Figure 2.4 for her suggestions.

Behavior Modification

The use of behavior modification presents a sticky issue to teachers in classrooms of young children, because early education experts argue at length that behaviorism is not good for young children. Observers, though, will note that use of behaviorism abounds in public schools and, in fact, in the American culture. Grades are a type of reward system that have existed in public school education for a hundred years. Receiving a salary is another type of reward system that the American workforce thrives upon. Many people would choose not to work if they were not paid adequately, and, most assuredly, people stop working in some positions because they feel that the pay received does not compensate them for the work they produce.

Behavior modification was born in clinical settings—witness salivating dogs and Skinner boxes. Awarding good behavior and ignoring bad behavior is the essence of behaviorism. Classrooms that utilize behavior modification strategies are ones that are teacher dominated and teacher directed. Children have limited choices in what they will learn, their misbehavior is not tolerated, and the classroom behavior they exhibit receives immediate positive rewards or negative responses. Children begin to feel that they are not in control of their own actions. These responses are referred to as *reinforcing consequences* (Skinner, 1968), and teachers are taught specific steps to follow in order to reinforce or eliminate behaviors they want. Skinner is not in favor of punishment per se, but he does admit that its use will only be effective if administered immediately after a classroom infraction.

The steps teachers follow when making decisions about behavior modification strategies to use when they want to change a child's behavior are the following: (1) observe the child's current behavior, carefully recording when it occurs and what prompts the misbehavior; (2) determine the reward system that the child will respond to; (3) write a description of the desired behavior; (4) develop a plan of action to eliminate the behavior; and (5) implement the plan with periodic reviews to analyze the effects of the reward system and what plan might need to be next followed (Hendrick, 2003). These steps are well documented and are shown to work if applied consistently.

When it is practiced with groups of children, behavior modification means that teachers define classroom rules and then reinforce good behavior or ignore bad behavior. Lavish praise, stickers, stars, or some other extrinsic reward are used to achieve the end goal of "good" classroom behavior. Some teachers even use special privileges, such as a popcorn party on Friday, if everyone in the class adheres to the preset classroom standard during the entire week.

FIGURE 2.4 Modifying Classroom Centers to Enhance Intelligence Areas

Center	Modification	Intelligence Enhanced
House Center	Add recipes and cookbooks, phonebooks, clocks, and calendars	mathematical-logical
	Add writing and drawing tools and paper	linguistic, bodily-kinesthetic, spatial
	Add artwork to decorate walls (both prints of masterpieces and children's works)	spatial
	Add tools for "repairs"	bodily-kinesthetic
	Add books, magazines, and newspapers	linguistic, naturalist, existentialist
	Add tape player and music tapes, radio	musical
	Add table games	spatial, interpersonal
	Add role-playing materials, dress-ups, and mirrors	interpersonal and intrapersonal, bodily-kinesthetic
Book Center	Add books that highlight the domains of each intelligence by their content or format	linguistic, logical-mathematical, musical, spatial, bodily-kinesthetic, interpersonal, intrapersonal, naturalist, existentialist
	Add a listening center and books on tape	linguistic, musical
	Add class, small group, and individually created books	linguistic, spatial, interpersonal, intrapersonal
	Add puppets (store bought, teacher made, and child created)	spatial, bodily-kinesthetic, linguistic, interpersonal, intrapersonal
	Add flannel boards and flannel board stories	bodily-kinesthetic, spatial, linguistic
	Add graphic representations of concepts and of comparisons of books read	mathematical-logical
	Add books in other languages, including sign language, and especially those represented by student backgrounds and family histories	linguistic, bodily-kinesthetic, intrapersonal
	Add dress-ups or costumes that tie to highlighted books	spatial, linguistic, interpersonal
	Add a computer with appropriate software that highlights symbol systems	bodily-kinesthetic, linguistic, existentialist, naturalist, musical, spatial
Puppet Center	Add puppets that represent people who use the various intelligences in their work	intrapersonal
	Add child- and teacher-made puppets	spatial, bodily-kinesthetic
	Add tape player with instrumental music (purchased and classroom created)	musical
	Add opportunities for problem-solving role play	mathematical-logical, interpersonal, linguistic, intrapersonal
	Add individual, small group, or class-created scenery	spatial

continued

FIGURE 2.4 *continued*

Center	Modification	Intelligence Enhanced
Puppet Center (continued)	Add opportunities for child-created plays that present material learned in the content areas (math, science, social studies)	mathematical-logical, naturalist, interpersonal, existentialist, linguistic
	Add opportunities for child-created plays based on books and poetry	linguistic, musical
	Add different types of puppets and puppetry, especially those represented by children's cultural and family heritage backgrounds	bodily-kinesthetic, intrapersonal, spatial
Woodworking Center	Add measuring tools	mathematical-logical
	Add a variety of tools and materials	spatial, naturalist, bodily-kinesthetic
	Add opportunities for collaborative projects	interpersonal
	Add books and writing materials	linguistic, mathematical-logical
	Add tape player with sounds of tools (large and small) at work	musical
Art Center	Add measuring tools	mathematical-logical
	Add a variety of materials from the natural world	naturalist
	Add prints of artworks and self-portraits by masters	spatial, intrapersonal
	Add opportunities for collaborative projects	interpersonal
	Add opportunities to create stories about artist- and child-produced projects	linguistic
	Add a variety of tools and media	spatial, bodily-kinesthetic
	Add opportunities to ponder and discuss masterpieces	existentialist, linguistic
	Add opportunities to create art while listening to music	musical, bodily-kinesthetic, spatial
Science (or Nature) Center	Add opportunities to gather materials outside and to categorize and identify them	naturalist, bodily kinesthetic
	Add opportunities to experiment	existentialist, interpersonal, mathematical-logical
	Add opportunities to describe, create stories, and label materials	linguistic, spatial
	Add tape player and tapes of nature sounds	naturalist, musical
	Add puzzles and games	spatial, interpersonal
	Add books (purchased and student made)	linguistic, spatial
	Add classroom pets	intrapersonal, naturalist, interpersonal

Behavior modification is widespread because it works. Novice teachers in public school classrooms discover quickly that children do not always respond easily and quickly to the problem-solving approach to behavior management that they may have been taught in their university studies. They observe experienced teachers across the hall who "get their children under control" in a matter of days because they resort to behaviorism as a strategy for encouraging class conformity.

The question becomes, then, why early education experts oppose behaviorism so adamantly. Basically, the answer is based on the goal the teacher has in mind when she uses any management strategy. Is the goal to have a quiet class and impress the principal with "good children"? Or is the goal to help children develop autonomous, independent behavior that will promote healthy self-identity and self-management skills that last a lifetime? The latter goal is preferable, of course, but the time involved in building emotionally healthy personalities and self-controlled children is important to their development.

All parents and educators use behaviorism at some point in their relationships with children. But parents and teachers who demonstrate a sense of caring to children in their care and those who communicate adequately about the need for rules and routines are also building a relationship that is not based on reward alone. Positive relationships are based on mutual trust and respect, elements children need as they develop. The long-term result is children who behave because they like themselves and want to show care for others they meet in day-to-day interactions. Most successful teachers use behaviorism initially to organize an environment that is conducive to learning, but they move quickly to encouraging self-development within their children.

☆ OTHER CONTEMPORARY INFLUENCES

Early childhood educators are aware of other modern influences that affect their profession.

Reggio Emilia

An Italian program that has gained popularity in recent years is Reggio Emilia, which is an excellent prototype for nativist theory. Named for a specific northern region of Italy, the innovative educational approach to working with preschool children began shortly after World War II. The city government began funding the program in 1963 for all children, and governmental funding and support of the schools started in 1967. Reggio's uniqueness is that 3- to 6-year-old children stay in the same classroom with the same teacher (*pedagogista*) the entire time they are enrolled in the program.

The features that define Reggio Emilia classrooms relate to intrinsic qualities that are best described by the learning style of each child as well as the interests of specific groups of children. Emphasis is placed on children, teachers, and parents working together as a team to determine what is studied. This team approach requires children to enter their community, do in-depth study of their environment, and then express themselves in all the visual and verbal modes they possess.

The phrase "the hundred languages of children" suggests that children are using every ability they have to express what they know—through numerous art media, elements of design, movement, music, architecture, discussion, debate, pantomime, puppetry, writing, and activity they can discover. Once children have expressed themselves in a product, reconstructed the product, evaluated their productions, and added fine detail to the quality of the production, they display their work for all to observe. What is achieved are wondrous works of art and scientific endeavor that amaze most onlookers because the children's work resembles the results that much older students might achieve (Edwards, Gandini, & Forman, 1998).

Reggio classrooms have about 25 children in them with two teachers. Other members of the staff include a cook and part-time and full-time auxiliary adults. The schedule of the day is from 8 a.m. until 4 p.m. Monday through Friday from September 1 until June 30 of each year. Early arrival time and extended day care are also provided as needed. A Community Advisory Council consisting of elected parent representatives, teacher and staff representatives, and citizens from the community govern schools.

One teacher, called an *atelierista* (art teacher), works with other teachers and children in each preprimary school in Reggio Emilia. All centers have an *atelier* (art room) that is used for activities and projects during the year. Curriculum for Reggio Emilia is difficult to quantify, because it varies from program to program and from teacher to teacher. Teachers use similar techniques in planning for classroom experiences, but they allow children to become full partners in the decision-making process that leads to classroom activity.

Once a decision is made about a topic of study, the teacher's role is that of documentation collector. She transcribes children's comments, takes photographs of their work, and provides for materials and classroom activities to facilitate children's learning. Many field trips are taken into the community to collect information and observe phenomena that will develop a project that becomes the backbone of the classroom experience (Hendrick, 1997).

One major difference between what happens in Reggio Emilia schools and what happens in America's public school classrooms is the image of the child that Italians hold. They view children as people with intense curiosity in the world about them, and they stimulate the intellectual spirit within children to explore their surroundings to learn what they have not known before. They attempt to give children a variety of perspectives of events and objects in the community (Gestwicki, 1999).

If children show an interest in buildings and how they are constructed, for example, then trips to building sites are planned so that children can observe what is happening. The study results are that children may differentiate between historical and modern buildings. Or they may observe one-story structures and compare them to multiple-story structures. They investigate door frames, window casings, floor tiles, wall patterns, paint textures, room design, and lighting fixtures. They return to the classroom to design and build their own structures. They revisit buildings for further scrutiny and use the new information as they continue to develop their project. Learning is firsthand, meaningful, and ongoing, and children are involved in the entire process. They are equal partners with their teachers in learning.

Educators often ask if the Reggio Emilia concept could be translated into American practice, and attempts to bring the concept to the United States are occurring (Hendrick, 1997). The differences between Reggio Emilia schools and U.S. schools are directly connected to the differences in the Italian and American cultures. Italians do not usually pursue the "American dream," and their culture is generally more leisurely, more family oriented, and less concerned about wealth and fame. Their culture is rich in artistic and historical context that is not evident in America. Using an emergent curriculum concept in American classrooms is a noble goal, but teachers would spend a great deal of time "educating" parents about the reasons the Reggio way is good for their children.

The Project Approach

An opportunity to "engage children's minds" is how Katz and Chard (2000) define the project approach. The use of projects is not a new educational practice because projects originally became popular in the United States as a result of study conducted by John Dewey (University of Chicago) at the beginning of the twentieth century. Project study continued during World War II when teachers in England searched for every imaginable instructional resource they could find to facilitate learning in underground basements of the safest buildings, which served as makeshift classrooms and also as potential bomb shelters, if needed. The collection of "stuff" that became teaching tools turned into creative products that children developed as a result of studies they initiated about objects and events relevant to their lives. This movement, often referred to as the Open Education movement, consequently influenced practices in the United States during the 1960s and 1970s.

Features that characterize project study are that (1) topics are of interest to children, (2) the study is relevant and meaningful to the children who choose it, (3) resources in the community are readily available to conduct the study, (4) the study will meet district and state-mandated curriculum goals, (5) parents can become involved in the activities of the project, and (6) a variety of skills and knowledge is inherent in the study so that children's acquisition of knowledge will be met at their level of comprehension (Katz and Chard, 2000). As a rule, projects are less structured in format than systematic instruction, and in some instances their use in classrooms begins to look more playful and less academic than other types of learning. Katz and Chard (2000) indicate that three types of projects may develop: (1) investigative, (2) construction, and (3) dramatic play.

Projects are easily adaptable to several grade levels. A prekindergarten project study might focus on the grocery store or the hospital. Using knowledge that children have from prior experiences with each of these units or planning field trips to the grocery store or to the hospital facilitates discussions within the classroom, in reading books that relate to the study, and developing questions that would guide children to further study of the topic. Recording information (or drawing pictures)

Integrated learning is a major focus of the Project Approach.

obtained while on the field trip and eventually setting up a class grocery store or hospital for dramatic play extends the children's learning. Third graders might be more interested in a study of pond life or of making comparisons among several city parks in the area. The determination of classroom project study is made conjointly with children and their teachers and should always be based on the children's interests.

Project studies are also flexible in length of study. A dog study emerged with 3- and 4-year-olds in a lab school setting one spring that lasted for about six weeks. The study had originally been set to last about three weeks, but after a trip to a local veterinarian office the children transformed their home living center into a vet's office; their dramatic play continued for several more weeks before it began to wane.

Getting parents involved is another key ingredient in successful project studies. Having parents and children working together to find information to share with other members of the classroom, inviting parents in as resource people, or having special end-of-project celebrations are important elements in the development of projects. Children expend effort and time to record the information they are collecting during the phases of project study. Whatever data results they acquire and documentation may be shared with parents, other classrooms in the school, or administrators in the building.

Project studies are different when compared to the traditional unit or thematic study that is traditionally used in preschool and primary classrooms, though they appear to have common traits. Themes are planned and directed by teachers, and the intent of instruction is purposeful with preplanned objectives in mind. Themes are an example of systematic instruction. Project instruction, on the other hand, may be as purposeful, but it is definitely planned with children's input and direction as it progresses. What each child learns will depend to some degree on which tasks each person has selected and the level of involvement that has been given within the child's range of abilities and skills.

Teachers facilitate learning, and their participation is clearly defined through three specific phases of project work (Chard, 1994a, 1994b). The three phases are further organized into six work stages that include (a) *design and planning* (initial idea and planning), (b) *implementation and development* (doing and recording and discussion), and (c) *concluding the work* (final product and sharing).

Assessment procedures are part of the development of projects, too. Again, the difference between units or themes (systematic instruction) and projects is clear.

Systematic instruction shows:

- How the child is acquiring skills
- The pace of learning
- The response to instruction
- Areas of learning difficulties
- The effectiveness of practice tasks (Chard, 1994a, p. 48)

Project work shows:

- How the child is applying skills
- Whether the child understands when to use skills
- The child's approach to work
- The depth of the child's understanding
- How resourceful the child is in the solution of problems
- How well the child is able to collaborate with others in the pursuit of common goals (Chard, 1994a, p. 48)

Project studies and the Reggio Emilia approach have a number of similarities for the reason that all curriculum ideas that grow out of emergent interests of children will have similarities in common. Katz and Chard (2000) admit that systematic instruction is necessary in America's public schools because of the emphasis on goals and objectives from district and state mandates. They advocate the use of project studies, which provide excellent opportunities for children to practice skills in meaningful ways. Projects are a foundation for the intellectual life of the child that systematic instruction cannot effectively support.

Multiage Classrooms

Housing children of multiple ages together in one room is as old as the one-room schoolhouse concept of America during the 1800s. What is distinct about the modern multiage concept is the reason for its existence. In the 1800s teachers and resources were scarce, and children often were required to work in the fields with their parents or go on a hunting trip with their fathers in order to survive hard winters and arid summers. Bringing in a specially trained teacher often took years of recruitment efforts, and communities could not afford to pay more than one teacher to work in the school, nor could they provide adequate housing for more than one classroom.

Multiage classrooms in modern practice are developed for educational purposes, not out of necessity. Putting two or three grade levels together in one room with the same teacher has educational merit. Katz, Evangelou, and Hartman (1990) take a proactive stance for the use of mixed-age groupings, because their study indicates children of several ages working together yields educational benefits. Their Executive Summary in *The Case for Mixed-Age Grouping in Early Education* (1990, p. v) summarizes the positive research conducted on multigrade classrooms. Among the findings they observed were that (1) multigrade classrooms resemble family and neighborhood groupings, (2) social development is enhanced by experiences in multigrade classrooms, (3) older children stimulate intellectual development within younger children in the classrooms, (4) peer tutoring and cooperative learning are beneficial to the tutor and the learner, (5) grade-level barriers are broken down to provide more conducive learning settings for children, and (6) multiage classrooms have been successful around the world.

Another benefit to children is that older children are in the position of becoming leaders in their classrooms, and they tend to take on more responsibility in their groups. They model prosocial behaviors that younger children emulate, and self-control begins to improve in younger children. Evidence exists that older children provide more complex play situations for younger children to learn. The social effects also benefit isolated older children who need opportunities to practice social behaviors. The development of a "caring community" as defined by Bredekamp and Copple (1997) is enhanced with the use of multigrade classroom experiences.

Cognitive development is increased in multigrade classrooms as well. Older children are in the same classroom with a teacher they had in previous years, and this situation allows the teacher to plan more specifically for individual needs of the children in his or her group. Because children are familiar with the environment and the expectations of the teacher, they feel comfortable taking risks that they may not have taken when they were the younger members of the group. Their learning challenges the younger members of the class group because they observe "experts" in action while they are the "novices" (Katz, Evangelou, & Hartman, 1990, p. 26).

One variation of the multigrade classroom is called *looping.* In looping experiences, children stay with the same teacher for two years (first and second, as an example). Then the teacher "loops" back to a new group of children after the second year of instruction is complete. This recent innovation eliminates the need teachers have at the beginning of each year to get to know their children, thus saving valuable instructional time that might be lost during the first few weeks of school. The teacher also gains a more beneficial relationship with the parents of her children, and this bond creates a strong home–school connection that strengthens what children can learn in their school setting.

SUMMARY

In early childhood theory, six orientations toward teaching and learning exist: (1) nativist theory, (2) maturationist theory, (3) psychosocial theory, (4) sociocultural theory, (5) cognitive-developmental theory, and (6) behaviorist theory. In any early childhood classroom, the teacher's work will demonstrate principles from each of these theories. Prototype programs include Piagetian-based programs such as High/Scope and Project Construct, Montessori programs, and Reggio Emilia.

Research conducted on multigrade classrooms and multiple intelligences theory by Howard Gardner and others support other teaching strategies available to teachers in public school early childhood classrooms. Teachers who choose programs that build autonomy, independence, and self-control in children are building emotionally healthy adults.

DISCUSSION QUESTIONS

1. Discuss each of the theories described in this chapter. Which one of them most closely represents your thinking about teaching young children?
2. With a group of peers, develop an interview to use with a Montessori directoress. After each group member has conducted an interview, compare notes with one another.
3. Discuss anecdotes you have observed that document the four stages of cognitive growth as defined by Piaget.

SUGGESTED CHAPTER ACTIVITIES

1. Visit at least two schools or centers that are prototype programs described in this chapter. Write a compare-and-contrast paper about your observations.
2. Recall a classroom experience from your own childhood that made an impact on you. Determine from your knowledge of the early childhood orientations described in this chapter which orientation your teacher possessed. Defend your answer.
3. Visit in an early childhood classroom, and make a list of materials you see in the classroom that could be classified as self-teaching and self-corrective.
4. Ask your parents if they can recall any incident from your preschool years that defined your preoperational thinking. Or ask a parent of a young child a similar question.

Chapter Three

Planning and Implementing Appropriate Curriculum for Young Children

CHAPTER OVERVIEW

★ What kinds of information do teachers need to know about teaching and learning prior to entering their classrooms to teach?

★ What is the Cycle of Learning and Teaching?

★ Are some teaching strategies more effective in early childhood classrooms than others?

★ What is the Teaching Continuum?

★ Why do young children spend time playing while they are in school? Is this not time wasted?

★ What are basic principles of planning lessons and thematic units?

READING THIS CHAPTER SHOULD PROVIDE ANSWERS TO THESE QUESTIONS.

I moved my desk out into our hall to make room for a housekeeping/dramatic play area in my class-room. I now keep the desk covered with a "seasonal/themed" tablecloth and use it as a discovery/ science/display table. Of course, many of the other veteran teachers think that I'm bonkers for giving up my classroom desk. Oh, well, I never was one for "thinking inside the box" anyway!

Peggy Hutson

Classrooms of young children are vibrant, active places designed to encourage children to think, interact with others, discover the joy in living, make errors, and learn from their errors. The learning process continues daily with routine experiences coupled with challenges arising with novel activities and exposure to the environment. When someone enters an early childhood classroom, their observations might lead them to believe that children's explorations are spontaneous, and their learning is somewhat haphazard. After all, young children are "just children."

Closer observation, though, yields an understanding that the environment is carefully organized, and the teacher has methodically planned for children's acquisition of knowledge and skills. Planning and implementing appropriate curriculum and day-to-day activities are the backbone of educating young children in all early childhood classrooms, and teachers who become adept in planning and implementation produce more able learners. One phrase that describes the work teachers perform is *developmentally appropriate practice*, defined previously in Chapter 1.

naeyc

⭐ DEVELOPMENTALLY APPROPRIATE PRACTICE (DAP)

naeyc

Explaining developmentally appropriate practice (DAP) is simple. DAP is teaching children what they need to know using practices that match their developmental needs. Therein lies the dilemma, because teachers of young children all around the nation ask time and again, "What is it that my children need to know? Do I prepare them for the next grade level? I know that play is important for their learning. Do I just let them play? Where is the balance between instruction and child-initiated learning?"

Planning for children correlates with teachers' abilities to make decisions about appropriate practice for the age and cultural backgrounds of the children in their classrooms as well as the specific needs of individual children. Some teachers exclaim, "I don't believe in teaching reading to kindergarten children," whereas others begin reading instruction on the first day children appear in the kindergarten classroom. A teacher in Florida would not even consider preparing an art activity about snow or winter (because of its lack of relevancy to her children), whereas a teacher in Minnesota searches for as many snow-related books and activities as she can find. One preschool child might express an interest in learning about dinosaurs, beginning to name all of the types of dinosaurs he knows, whereas another child has no interest whatsoever in prehistoric creatures.

naeyc

A concept defined by Bredekamp and Copple (1997) is the *early childhood teacher as decision maker*, which allows for variations in practices that are appropriate for children. When early educators inform their practice by knowing all they can know about their children as groups and individuals, their culture and their families, then decision-making processes are easier to manage. Facilitating learning and development implies that teachers know children's "learning styles, interests and preferences, personality and temperament, skills and talents, challenges and difficulties" (p. 40).

Consequently, one professional's decision about a specific practice may be responsive to her children and their families, whereas another professional might define the practice as inappropriate. A kindergarten teacher who does not believe in "teaching reading" to her 5-year-olds might actually plan such a literacy-rich environment saturated with numerous and relevant literacy experiences that her kindergartners learn to read naturally and spontaneously.

Meeting Children's Developmental Needs

Early educators value the importance of meeting children's needs. Knowing how children think, learn, interact, and react is essential to ensuring that their needs are met. Theorists, like those discussed in Chapter 2 (Piaget, Vygotsky, Dewey, Gardner, and Montessori, for example) have formulated approaches for analyzing children's development. Knowing that children do not think as adults think helps teachers determine the types of experiences children need to become better thinkers. Understanding that children need "hands-on" sensory activities correlating with their interests provides another view of children as learners.

Adults in classrooms of young children are attuned to children, and opportunities for their learning are different from classrooms of older children. Early childhood teachers recognize children's need for activity, stimulation, and challenge within an environment that provides safety, security, and an understanding that they are respected and valued. Preschool/primary age children should not be expected to sit for long periods of time, nor should they all be expected to learn the same things within the same time frame. Young children are individuals first, and treating them alike demeans their individuality and learning potential.

Knowledge, Skills, Feelings, and Dispositions Historically, early educators recognize children's complex make-up and development. Rousseau recommended that children should be placed in a natural environment so that they would not be affected by society's ills (Braun & Edwards, 1971). Dewey (1938/1998) recognized the role of experiences in education and suggested that positive habit formation related to children's interest and attitude toward learning. He advocated the use of environments that promote democracy and social opportunities for children, because their use supported a better quality of human experience.

Katz and Chard (2000) categorized and defined four types of learning that accompany educational experiences for young children. **Knowledge, skills, feelings, and dispositions** describe what and how children learn. *Knowledge* is the information children acquire intellectually. When the 18-month-old learns that some pickles are *sour* or that the family pet is a *cat*, these facts compose knowledge. *Skills* correlate with knowledge, and they demonstrate what children can do. A 6-year-old may be able to count to 20 by rote (knowledge), but the skill of counting 20 objects shows that the child can count rationally. Other skills include being able to

Young children are keen observers of their world, and planning classroom centers to promote observational experience assists learners to reach their full potential.

pick up a pencil and write (cognitive and physical skills), spell assigned words (cognitive skill), cut with scissors (physical skill), ride a bicycle or tricycle (physical skill) and negotiate and enter a selected play setting (social skill).

Usually schools focus on the development of knowledge and skills, and the degree of achievement in these areas is reported regularly to parents. Katz and Chard maintain that *feelings* and *dispositions* are critical components of the learning process. Feelings are significant to young children's ability to acquire knowledge. If children are tired, hungry, upset, or distracted, they are unable to focus on information that the teacher might deem important. Even adults who experience stress or disturbing news find that focusing on one's job or even normal conversation becomes difficult and sometimes impossible.

Feelings, of course, are the emotional reactions one has toward any given situation, but *dispositions* are an outgrowth of feelings. Katz and Helm (2001) refer to dispositions as "habits of mind." Children rely on their affective states (their feelings) to assist them in interpreting the experiences they have. When these feelings are positive, they develop healthy attitudes toward experiences and situations. When feelings are negative, they form unhealthy attitudes. If children have negative experiences in the educational setting, they form a dislike of school and their "habit of mind" is to avoid learning or rebel against events that occur in school.

Feelings and dispositions are more difficult to assess in the classroom, because their evidence is nebulous and solid data about their existence are not easily available. The need to obtain information about children's feelings and dispositions is essential in early education, for children form attitudes about school and their own abilities to learn at an early age. The development of *competence* in a number of arenas—intellectual competence, social competence, language and communicative competence—begins in early childhood, and children need positive cognitive and social experiences as a foundation for later educational experiences (Katz & Chard, 2000; Hendrick, 2003).

The Five Selves. Another way of viewing children is to analyze their development from multiple perspectives. Joanne Hendrick (2003) likens individual children to five specific selves—physical, social, emotional, creative, and intellectual. Each of these selves is a subcomponent of the whole child. Isolating one area (such as intellectual development) for instruction overlooks the overall vitality and mental health of children. When teachers plan for each of the five selves, they are meeting the needs of children's **developmental domains.** What this implies is that teachers think about the following characteristics of children as they plan.

Physical Development
- Place health and safety issues as a top priority in the environment
- Limit amounts of time children are required to sit for large-group activity (allow children opportunities to remove themselves from the group)
- Recognize when children are tired or ill and adjust accordingly
- Provide for indoor and outdoor play
- Allow children opportunities for naptime
- Plan for timely restroom breaks (if restrooms are not available in the classroom)
- Plan classroom spaces that provide for privacy
- Feed children and provide healthy snacks at appropriate intervals during the school day
- Recognize when children need water and provide access to water fountains
- Plan for movement and music experiences that allow for physical relief

Social Development
- Talk to children about acceptable social behaviors
- Hold group discussions about how children can get along together
- Model acceptable social behaviors
- Intervene when children are fighting with one another and help them work out their differences
- Help children understand others' viewpoints
- Establish class rules that respect children and teach them to respect others
- As children become more experienced in classroom activity, give them an opportunity to solve their own problems before intervening
- Join children's play on occasion
- Enjoy children and what happens in the classroom

Emotional Development
- Accept children's emotional outbursts as part of their development
- Verbalize labels for feelings children are demonstrating
- Talk to children about emotions people feel every day and help them understand that their feelings are normal
- Recognize that some children behave in certain situations because they do not know other, more acceptable behaviors
- Give children alternatives for dealing with their emotions by providing other acceptable activities
- Talk with children to assist them in understanding the realities of living (what they can change and what they need to accept)
- Tell children how you feel on occasion to demonstrate that all people have feelings
- Recognize signs of abuse or neglect and seek help for the child

Creative Development
- Provide many activities that allow children to express themselves (refer to Chapter 5 for information about self-expression activities)
- Encourage children to express themselves with a variety of media
- Prominently display children's artwork
- Provide time for children to sing and dance in the classroom
- Acknowledge children who suggest extraordinary solutions to problems or make comments that are different from those of other children
- Recognize that children's experiential backgrounds will give them perceptions of life that are unusual or unlike other children's perceptions
- Encourage children who seem to shy away from self-expressive activities
- Enjoy children's varying personalities

Intellectual Development
- Recognize that children are eager to learn
- Share children's enthusiasm for learning
- Plan activities that give children more knowledge about their world
- Provide choices for children about what they want to learn
- Use projects that utilize individual children's strengths as they work
- Plan learning that strengthens children's skills of observation, experience with solving problems and acquiring knowledge
- Assess children's knowledge for curriculum planning and reporting to parents

Meeting children's needs is a principle in early education that focuses on children's overall development first, and curriculum planning is placed in a secondary position. Yes, teachers want children to learn and schools emphasize knowledge and skill acquisition, but children also need to develop as individuals who understand democratic living and feel confident in themselves as learners and doers capable of addressing and solving problems that confront them daily. Meeting children's needs goes hand in hand with teachers' planning developmentally appropriate practice.

NAEYC approved a position statement in 2003 that defines Early Childhood Curriculum Assessment and Program Evaluation. The position statement is sponsored jointly by the National Association of Early Childhood Specialists in State Departments of Education (NAECS/SDE [www.naeyc.org/resources/position_statements/pscape.asp]).

☆ THE VALUE OF PLAY

Observers in early childhood classrooms often remark about the time children spend playing during the daily schedule. Historically, forerunners to modern-day practice recognized play as an integral part of early education. Froebel referred to play as "tiny seeds" that were the foundation for later learning. Montessori referred to children's activity as their work, their opportunity for self-expression and self-

Brain-Based Learning

Dr. Pam Schiller defines "Windows of Opportunity" for children's learning in her book *Start Smart* (1999). Using centers and allowing children to play supports all of the windows.

WINDOWS OF OPPORTUNITY

WINDOW FOR	OPTIMAL WINDOW	NEXT BEST OPPORTUNITY	FURTHER REWIRING POSSIBLE
Emotional intelligence	0–24 mos.	2–5 years	any age
Motor development	0–24 mos.	2–5 years	decreases with age
Vision	0–2 years	2–5 years	
Early sounds	4–8 mos.	8 mos.–5 years	any age
Music	0–36 mos.	3–10 years	any age
Thinking skills	0-48 mos.	4–10 years	any age
Second language acquisition	5–10 years	any age	

development of the whole personality (Orem, 1974). Patty Smith Hill (1942/1992) viewed play as an opportunity for a child to "experiment and discover his own ways and means for arriving at goals" (p. 1967). Simplistically, each of these individuals perceived play as an educational endeavor. (For more information about Froebel's concepts about play, go to www.geocities.com/froebelweb/webindex.html.)

Play supports children's physical, social, emotional, creative, and intellectual development. As a definition, play can be described as pleasurable, self-selected, and freely chosen, permitting children to suspend reality and imagine all they can become (Seefeldt & Barbour, 1998). The spontaneity of play behaviors is essential to healthy mental development.

Play correlates well with developmentally appropriate practice guidelines. Classroom play allows children to become members of a caring community of learners as they interact with others to establish democratic rules to guide their own behaviors. Play encourages children to pursue their interests and abilities

Not only is play a relaxing experience, but it also teaches children invaluable social skills.

through inquiry processes that cut across content disciplines (such as art, music, mathematics, science, language arts, and social studies). The intellectual integrity of curriculum content, which occurs as children participate in learning (or play), is the strength of developmentally appropriate practice.

⭐ PLAY THEORIES

Analyzing play and determining how and why children play is fascinating to theorists. Watching children engage in play led Vygotsky, a sociocultural theorist, and Piaget and Parten, both labeled as cognitive-developmental theorists, to formulate highly recognized theories about play. Their definitions of play vary as they considered children's ages and social-emotional development. Each theorist's perspective is organized in relationship to the component of development they were studying.

Vygotsky's View of Play. Vygotsky believed strongly in the language model of the adult, and his work with children was designed to show the essential roles that adults play in children's cognitive and language development. Infants rely on their caregivers for establishing emotional attachment, an ingredient in intellectual development. Adults respond with language to babies' coos, babbles, and first words, teaching them traditional games and rhymes like "Pat-a-Cake" and "This Little Pig Went to Market."

As infants become toddlers, they begin to manipulate objects in pretend ways, picking up a stick or ruler as an example and saying, "It's a horse. Giddy up, horsy!" Later, as they take on specific dramatic roles, they respond in their roles to the play setting, demonstrating knowledge they have about the role. A child who is playing the role of a bunny rabbit would not suddenly become a circus clown and exhibit behaviors uncharacteristic of rabbits.

During the preschool years, play becomes the leading activity, defined by Vygotsky as an optimal activity for development (Bodrova & Leong, 1996). Play sparks imagination, supports the development of symbolic function and concepts (through the use of children's words), and integrates feelings and thought. As children grow into the primary years and later childhood, play loses its importance because of societal emphasis on more formal learning settings. However, play continues to be valuable to children and adults as well to reduce stress and to provide comic relief when serious situations become too intense.

Piaget's View of Play. Piaget compiled data about children's play, composing his theoretical position on play in relationship to intellectual development. His *practice* or *functional* play observed during the sensorimotor stage is play that gives children opportunities to use their developing motor skill repeatedly (Piaget, 1962; Seefeldt & Barbour, 1998). When infants discover, perhaps by accident, that toys dropped onto the floor from the crib will be returned by adults, they delight in dropping the toy onto the floor again and again. Adults tire of practice play far sooner than babies do!

Symbolic play becomes evident during the preoperational stage of development, when youngsters begin substituting one object for another. Children declare that they are firefighters, police officers, superheroes, individual family members, animals, monsters, or TV and film characters and play their chosen roles with zest and a sense of reality. Four-year-old Max became Superman in his neighborhood learning center, donning a Superman cape each morning for approximately six months. When children add language and gestures, interact with others during the play period, and carry on the role for a long period of time, researchers label this activity as *sociodramatic play.* Sociodramatic play is essentially an extension of symbolic play as described by Piaget (Smilansky & Shefatya, 1990).

Constructive play also begins during the preoperational stage of development. Constructive play is descriptive, because it efficiently defines what children do when they build or construct with blocks and construction toys, model or sculpt using clay or playdough, paint, use writing implements—any activity that yields a product through children's efforts. Constructive play, according to Piaget, appears to be an outgrowth of practice play, and its repetition serves as a foundation for play with rules when children move to the concrete operations stage of development.

When children begin *play with rules,* they comprehend games and play experiences with more sophistication. They learn that rules are necessary to achieve the

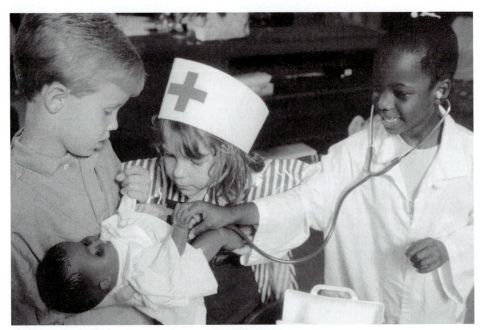

Symbolic play occurs as children substitute props for other objects, an intellectual marker as defined by Piaget.

goals of games and that violating rules brings penalties. Teams or groups of children band together for a similar purpose, and abiding by specified rules keeps harmony among children as they play. Whether the activity is a playground softball game or a classroom skit, the rules override the individual needs of those who are participants.

Parten's View of Play. Mildred Parten's (1932) classic study identified six stages of play based on the social interactions she observed among children as they played. Parten's stages include

- *Unoccupied play:* Children are not playing.
- *Onlooker play:* One child is watching another child or children play.
- *Solitary play:* Children are playing alone (solitary play may occur for a number of reasons).
- *Parallel play:* Children are playing in the same area of the classroom, perhaps playing with the same materials, but they are not interacting with others.
- *Associative play:* Children exhibit this play behavior when they join one play group, quickly moving to another group without any commitment to the original play (commonly observed among 4-year-old children).
- *Cooperative play:* Children play together working to satisfactorily plan and play with one another.

In summarizing the play theories discussed here, the main points are that (1) play activity requires physical skills and social-emotional expertise of children as they participate in play; (2) children learn from their play experiences; (3) play provides developmental growth in developmental domains; and (4) theorists view play as a valuable educational experience for children. Teachers can foster quality play by ensuring that sufficient time is allocated for classroom play and assisting children in planning play activities. Stocking classrooms with enticing play props, encouraging children to act out familiar stories, and demonstrating how their block constructions and projects can be useful when playing are other strategies teachers use to foster play (Bodrova & Leong, 1996).

Classrooms are not always harmonious, and disputes will arise when children play together. Teachers can alleviate classroom tensions by redirecting violent play and modeling negotiation and problem-solving skills to resolve disagreements. Occasionally older children can become mentors in play situations to model for younger children how to enter and maintain play with others (Bodrova & Leong, 1996).

Play Therapy

Some schools and communities have access to play therapy services, a therapeutic counseling approach to working with children who have emotional problems. Play therapy is an approach based on client-centered counseling theory introduced by Carl Rogers in the twentieth century. Virginia Axline (1947) developed a non-directed play therapy structure that gives children opportunities to play in a specially prepared playroom filled with toys and materials. As therapists work with individual children on a one-on-one basis, they establish rapport, accepting

Dimensions of Diversity

Developmentally Appropriate Practice

Understanding people of different races and ethnic groups, religions, sexual preferences, and cultural beliefs is a democratic principle that teachers need to instill in young children. The developmentally appropriate practice guideline to "create a caring community of learners" is the foundation of children's comprehension of human compassion. Freeing humans of biases and prejudices liberates the human spirit, according to McCracken (1993), who advocates four commitments in valuing diversity: (1) study society's perpetuation of racism and oppression, (2) reflect on personal participation in oppressing ourselves and others, (3) examine ways cultures may retain their integrity as they learn to interact in the larger community, and (4) effect change of oppressive systems (pp. 7–12).

the children as they are. Through careful observations of children at play and discussions of feelings that appear during the play activity, therapists facilitate children's crises by assisting their ability to sort out problems and arrive at personal solutions. Classroom teachers are not professionally trained to use play therapy, but knowing the therapeutic value of play should support teachers' defense of play activity as valuable to children.

★ PROMOTING PLAY IN CLASSROOM CENTERS

Applying play activity in classrooms appears through special areas designated as *centers*. Classroom centers form the basis for child-initiated learning, which leads to their acquisition and consolidation of knowledge (Bredekamp & Copple, 1997). Centers are appropriate instructional tools for young children because they (1) give children choices of activity, (2) provide opportunities for integration of knowledge, (3) allow children to learn while finding pleasure in their tasks, (4) promote conceptual development across various subject areas; and (5) recognize children's developmental needs.

Centers are introduced to children at the beginning of the school year, and teachers usually open only a few at a time to facilitate management issues. Using centers might become boring to children during the year if the materials and equipment in them remain stagnant. Teachers are observant of children's behaviors during center time, and they add new materials and even new centers to avoid lackadaisical interest and play in these centers. The most commonly used centers in preschool/primary classrooms are briefly described here.

Home Living Center

The Home Living Center often has other names—Housekeeping Center, Family Center or House Center. Generally, the Housekeeping Center allows children to take on roles from their families (mother, father, children, babies, pets, etc.) and "play-act" scenarios they observe in daily living. Social reenactments and language development are strengths of the Home Living Center, because children simulate interactions they have observed in their own homes. The give and take of the specific roles players imitate strengthens symbolic thought as learners internalize knowledge about the rules governing the selected characters being enacted (Leong & Bodrova, 1996). To be exact, a child who is imitating a pet cat would not begin to talk in a play setting because rules governing cats are that they purr, meow, or hiss—they do not talk.

Block Center

Popular with both genders, the blocks and the Block Center were introduced by Froebel (1912) as part of his "gifts" package and were restructured by Patty Smith

Hill (1942/1992), who made them larger, with heavier wood, to encourage physical exercise and social cooperation. Early educators plan Block Centers in their classrooms to encourage construction work as children build houses, buildings, bridges, stairs, and other configurations for play behavior. As children exercise and socialize, they are developing mathematics concepts (geometry, specifically) and learning scientific principles governing force and motion. Having a variety of block shapes and sizes available provides more creative thought when children put together their structures.

Manipulatives Center

Puzzles, pegboards, geometric boards, Legos, Lincoln logs, beads to string, Cuisenaire rods, attribute blocks, dominoes, checkers, commercial board games, and teacher-made folder games are staple items in the Manipulatives Center. Sometimes called the Puzzle and Games Corner, materials in this center require children to use fine-muscle skills to manipulate objects to achieve a predetermined goal. The following skills are strengthened by using manipulative-type toys.

- Seeing part–whole relationships (puzzles)
- Copying patterns (pegboards, geometric boards, attribute blocks)
- Building replicas of larger structures (Lego blocks, Tinkertoys, Lincoln logs)
- Developing number and numeral concepts (Cuisenaire rods, pegboards, geometric boards, attribute blocks)
- Following rules of board games (commercial games)
- Identified skills inherent in specific folder games

Early materials organized by Froebel (his "gifts") and Montessori (her academic materials) are forerunners of modern manipulative items, which are easily available through teacher supply stores and catalog warehouses. Preparation of teacher-made folder games is discussed more fully in Chapter 7.

Book Center

The Book Center, Reading Center, Literacy Center, or Book Corner is prominently placed in classrooms of young children. Designed to attract children's interest in books, the Book Center houses books, tapes of recorded stories, compact discs, and stuffed toys as well as flannel board story sets. Most early educators place a moderate number of books in the center, rotating them on occasion to maintain interest in the area. Special-interest books relating to unit or project studies going on in the classroom are often placed in the center. Books placed in the center are ones that teachers have read to the children prior to their placement there. A variety of choices are available in order to meet a wide range of children's interests.

Writing Center

Writing Centers include paper, pencils, washable markers, crayons, stencils, printing stamps and stamp pads, stickers, decals, chalk and chalkboards (sometimes, child-sized), discarded greeting cards, envelopes, and other supplies to encourage writing and designing printed materials. The purposes of the Writing Center in preschool are threefold: (1) assisting children in understanding writing concepts, (2) supporting children's initial attempts to write, and (3) providing opportunities for children to do invented writing. As children progress into the primary grades, the center's purposes extend to include: (4) writing words children are learning to read and spell, (5) developing journals, logs, or summaries of subject matter content (often correlated with specified themes or classroom learning), and (6) writing expository and creative stories. Purposes also coordinate with school district curriculum guides that underscore the need for children to learn letters and words and acquire phonemic awareness. For further information about Writing Centers, refer to Chapter 6.

Outdoor Center

Developmentally Appropriate Practice in Early Childhood Programs, revised edition (Bredekamp & Copple, 1997) recommends daily gross-motor activities for preschool children and physical education experiences for primary-age children. Schools usually plan playground space for children, though budget expenditures

FIGURE 3.1 The National Program for Playground Safety Report Card

_____	Is there trash on the ground?
_____	How many adult supervisors are on the playground at recess?
_____	Is the surfacing underneath the equipment hard (concrete, asphalt, dirt, or grass) or soft (wood chips, sand, rubber, or pea gravel)?
_____	Do the swings and slides have enough soft surfacing underneath them, or is it displaced?
_____	Do the swings have twisted or broken seats?
_____	Is there anything sticking out of the ground that would trip you when you are running?
_____	Does the equipment have any chipped or peeling paint?
_____	Does the metal equipment have any rust?
_____	Are there any holes or cracks in plastic equipment?
_____	Does the wooden equipment have any rough wood or splinters?
_____	Are there any nails or bolts sticking out of the play equipment?
_____	Is there any place that your fingers might get stuck or pinched when you are playing?

for high-quality playgrounds are limited. In many communities, child care centers develop and manage playgrounds with age-appropriate equipment, which are often superior to public school facilities.

Play equipment found in Outdoor Centers are swings, climbing apparatuses, and transportation toys. A major design element in planning playgrounds is space encircled with a fence and locked gate for safety's sake. Play areas should be near bathroom facilities and a drinking fountain (Marotz, Cross, & Rush, 2001). Sometimes water and sand tables (discussed later in this chapter) are positioned on playgrounds.

The National Program for Playground Safety (NPPS) advocates four considerations in planning and assessing playgrounds: (1) supervision, (2) age-appropriate equipment, (3) safe fall zones, and (4) equipment maintenance. Teachers and children alike can use the NPPS Report Card (Figure 3.1) to determine the safety of their playground areas (NPPS, 2001).

Art Center

The Art Center is a place in the classroom where self-expression reigns. Young children do not always have the language they need to communicate what they know or feel, and self-expressive outlets become important to their emerging thinking and skill development. Art Centers should promote all types of media

Children's art is an excellent form of self-expression.

and materials for artistic expression: crayons, markers, scissors, sponges, paint, finger paint, manila paper, newsprint, poster board, scrap paper, brushes, rollers, printing materials, and other supplies. Easels and drying racks should be available, and the Art Center is best placed near a classroom water source.

Odds and ends of fabric, sequins, buttons, pipe cleaners, glitter, rickrack, stickers, natural phenomena (such as leaves and twigs), empty boxes, discarded socks, and Styrofoam balls are items that can encourage self-expression. Paint smocks (or discarded shirts) are essential to keeping children clean during art activity, and large plastic tarps on the floor eliminate paint spills on the floor and facilitate cleanup. The Art Center provides the foundation for children's views of themselves as competent learners and doers, and its use in the classroom directly supports the creative self. You may recall that self-expression is the foundation of Reggio Emilia curriculum (refer to Chapter 2).

Music Center

Another center that facilitates self-expression is the Music Center. The Music Center introduces children to singing, movement, music making (usually with rhythm band or handmade percussion instruments), and sometimes to music composition. Equipment in the Music Center includes a record player and records, a CD player and CDs, rhythm band instruments, children's musical picture books, and posters or pictures of musical instruments and music ensembles. If musical materials are limited, the teacher may not open the center as a choice on a daily basis, choosing to plan large group singing or movement activities instead. In planning group experiences, the teacher may choose to accompany children's voices with a recorder, ukulele, or guitar, because young children do not need piano accompaniment, which tends to drown out their singing. Singing without accompaniment is always the best option.

The Music Center promotes firsthand investigation of music and musical instruments representative of native and world cultures. The arts are a critical precept in defining cultures and their values. Both music and art curricula are discussed more thoroughly in the chapter on prekindergarten education (Chapter 5).

Centers allow children to play, of course, but they also teach children numerous skills that serve as a foundation for knowledge acquisition throughout their lives. See Table 3.1 for skills children learn in various centers.

☆ OPTIONAL CLASSROOM CENTERS

Other classroom centers appear in early childhood settings, but their use is less common than the centers described previously. Occasionally, some of the centers described are set up for a short time or for a specified purpose. In other situations, teachers establish optional classroom centers, either because of their personal

TABLE 3.1 Skills Taught in Various Centers

HOME LIVING CENTER	MANIPULATIVES CENTER	WRITING CENTER	ART CENTER
Social skills	Attributes of objects	Experimentation with	Fine-motor
Social roles	Math skills, including	pencil and paper	development
Practical living skills	patterning shapes,	Concepts of print	Art elements (line,
Self-management skills	seriation, classifi-	Fine-motor skills	color, space, com-
Parenting skills	cation, matching,	Cutting with scissors	position)
Language development	cardinal and ordinal	Composition (with	Concept of artists
Potential for nutritional	numbers, sequencing	print and art	Use of art media
knowledge	Problem-solving skills	materials)	Pride in
Collaboration with others	Fine-motor skills	Emergent writing	accomplishment
Responsibilities of	Foundations for writing	Writing one's name	Sculpture
assumed roles		Using writing tools	Self-expression

BLOCK CENTER	BOOK CENTER	OUTDOORS CENTER	MUSIC CENTER
Math skills (balance,	Concepts of print	Science knowledge	Appreciation of music
height, length,	Care of books	Physical knowledge	Aural discrimination
proportion, organi-	Vocabulary	Enjoyment of nature	Singing
zation, patterning,	development	Physical endurance	Vocabulary
shapes)	Story sequence	Taking risks	development
Social skills	Plot and	Perfecting physical	Phonemic awareness
Construction skills	characterization	abilities	Musical concepts
Self-management skills	Storytelling	Group games	(pitch, tempo,
Collaboration with	Emergent reading	Physical development	melody, dynamics)
others	Foundations for		Singing games
Problem-solving skills	reading		

preferences for certain types of play or because they have available space in the classroom.

Discovery Centers

Discovery Centers are essentially ever changing because they connect with ongoing classroom discussions, seasonal events, and thematic topics. The Discovery Center might be a repository for fall leaves and nuts in October, a water and ice experiment in December, a classroom post office in February, and table space for classroom plants and flowers when spring arrives. Discovery Centers support children's participation in bringing items from home to put in the center. Discovery Centers entice children to observe and experiment with materials placed on them by the teacher or classroom peers. Their development is often spontaneous as children observe scientific phenomena in nature.

Dress-Up Center

The Dress-Up Center is usually developed in association with the Home Living Center, or it may also be called the Dramatic Play Center. Teachers should recognize that having a Dress-Up Center depends on space availability and how much time can be allocated to dramatic play activities. Basically, the Dress-Up Center is an area of the classroom housing costumes or clothing that will encourage certain types of play (becoming a story character, being an astronaut, pretending to be firefighters, police officers, or mail carriers, for example). When classroom space is limited, teachers of young children often organize prop boxes containing theme-related paraphernalia, which may be placed in the classroom when a topic is discussed (Barbour & Desjean-Perrotta, 2002).

Science Center

Froebel's emphasis on gardening in his kindergarten and Dewey's promotion of scientific processes in classrooms of young children are forerunners to the Science Center. Like Discovery Centers, Science Centers add a distinctive difference to classrooms in that they focus specifically on scientific phenomena and the scientific method. This area of the classroom most often houses classroom pets (gerbils, hamsters, hooded rats, birds, or rabbits), aquariums filled with fish, terrariums, and plants. Certainly, teachers and children will add seasonal artifacts from nature as they occur each year.

When teachers introduce the scientific method, they ask children to observe phenomena, formulate hypotheses, about items, brainstorm strategies for learning additional information, testing hypotheses, and summarizing their findings. This sample activity appropriate for second grade applies the discovery method.

1. Place several commercially prepared pinwheels on the Science Table along with a few hand fans and an electric fan.
2. If children appear interested, show them how pinwheels move when the hand fans and the electric fan are applied.
3. Ask children questions about why the pinwheels move faster with the electric fan and whether other natural forces could move the fan.
4. Test some of the suggestions children offer about making the pinwheels move (blowing water or pouring water on the pinwheels).
5. Ask children to record their findings on a large poster or in their individual science logs.
6. Include books showing windmills or turbines that perform as a consequence of nature's energy.

Sand Table

Often found in preschool classrooms, Sand Tables are excellent pieces of equipment for teaching children about quantity, mass, measurement, and comparisons

Water tables are a favorite center choice of preschool children.

of weight. Measuring cups, small shovels, pails, sieves, sifters, and other plastic toys add to the table's appeal. One teacher of 4-year-olds transformed the Sand Table into an archeological excavation and encouraged her group to dig for bones she had hidden in the sand. Sand Tables also provide creative outlets for children's imaginations, being more attractive to children if teachers change the play pieces available in the center.

Water Table

Another center placed in preschool classrooms is the Water Table. Children acquire some of the same scientific and mathematical knowledge in the Water Table that they acquire in the Sand Table. Many of the same play items found in the Sand Table are placed in the Water Table. Adding food coloring to the water periodically or using soap bubble solution instead of water are variations in water play that will teach children new information about their environment. When children play in the Water Table, they need smocks to protect their clothing, and protection for the floor eliminates messy cleanups.

Puppet Center and Puppet Stage

The Puppet Center promotes language development and language arts concepts in classrooms of young children. Puppets and puppetry are closely aligned with literature, and some teachers include puppets in their Book Corners. Commercial

State By State

Planning

The development of state standards affects teacher planning in every classroom. Often no standards are set for prekindergarten or kindergarten classrooms. Nevertheless, teachers in the preschool grades must be aware of the standards that are set for children in the primary-grade classrooms so that their planning will serve effectively as a foundation for later learning. **South Dakota** has established specific science standards for kindergarten children in several areas of science.

KINDERGARTEN NATURE OF SCIENCE STANDARDS
Students Will:

1. Actively participate in science activities.
2. Observe and ask questions about the world around them (example: Where does rain come from?).
3. Show an interest in and willingness to investigate unfamiliar objects and events.
4. Use their senses and simple instruments to make observations (example: magnifying glasses, balance scales).
5. Safely conduct simple experiments to answer questions.
6. Use nonstandard units of measurement to compare objects.
7. Use scientific thinking skills (example: observing, communicating, and comparing).

KINDERGARTEN PHYSICAL SCIENCE STANDARDS
Students Will:

1. Use sensory descriptors to describe objects (example: sweet, sour, rough, smooth).
2. Explore objects in terms of physical attributes.
3. Find similarities and differences between various objects.
4. Study water in solid and liquid form.
5. Observe physical changes in matter (example: melting, freezing, bending, tearing).
6. Explore magnetism, describe its effect on various materials, observe that magnetic force can pass through various materials and that some magnets have useful applications.
7. Describe the motion of various objects found in their world (example: cars, swings).
8. Explore vibration and sound.
9. Determine which of two objects is hotter or colder.
10. Explain how thermal energy can be produced from many other forms of energy (example: burning, rubbing objects together).

KINDERGARTEN LIFE SCIENCE STANDARDS

Students Will:

1. Sort living from nonliving things.
2. Describe the basic needs of living organisms.
3. Recognize similarities and differences in diverse species.
4. Compare size, shape, and structure of living things (example: grasses to trees, birds to mammals).
5. Describe changes that are part of common life cycles (example: seed to flower to fruit to seed).
6. Recognize that offspring of plants and animals are similar, but not identical to their parents or one another (example: pets and plants).
7. Explore ways in which organisms react to changing conditions (example: animals' coats change in the winter; people sweat in hot weather and shiver in cold weather).
8. Describe the flow of energy in a simple food chain.
9. Describe ways that plants and animals depend on each other.
10. Explore the habitat.
11. Explain the importance of conserving water or other resources at home and school.

KINDERGARTEN EARTH/SPACE SCIENCE STANDARDS

Students Will:

1. Explore how shadows are made.
2. Describe major features of the Earth's surface (example: rivers, deserts, mountains, valleys, oceans).
3. Compare rocks, soil, and sand.
4. Describe simple Earth patterns in daily life (example: weather observations).
5. Describe what causes day and night.
6. Identify observable objects in the day and night skies.

KINDERGARTEN SCIENCE, TECHNOLOGY, ENVIRONMENT, AND SOCIETY STANDARDS

Students Will:

1. Recognize technology in school, home, and community (example: computer, pencil, refrigerator, Velcro, fire truck).
2. Describe ways technology makes life easier for people.
3. Care for the environment around the school (example: pick up litter, paper).
4. Recognize ways to reuse various materials.
5. Explore how science helps bring water and energy to the home and school.
6. Identify how science is used to make everyday products (example: paper, pencils, desks).

varieties are available for teachers and schools to purchase, and school libraries stock puppets for teachers to check out during the year.

Handmade puppets are easy for children to handle as an art project, and their own creations emerge behind the puppet stage in story retellings and creative productions by individual children as well as groups. Asking parents to contribute paper plates, Styrofoam and paper cups, Styrofoam balls, tongue depressors, paper sacks, discarded socks, pipe cleaners, and decorative sewing materials leads to self-expressive, fun-loving creations for puppetry activities. Coupling the Puppet Center with the Art Center facilitates the puppet-making process.

Construction Center

MacDonald (1996) describes children's potential learning in the Construction Center (often known as a Woodworking Center) as (1) developing fine-motor skills, (2) developing perceptual awareness and pincher control, (3) expressing themselves and their thoughts and feelings through construction materials, (4) repeating simple patterns, and (5) experimenting with a variety of materials. Construction Center equipment and toys are hammers, nails, pieces of wood, a saw, a vise, measuring tools, and safety goggles (several pairs so they will be available to all children playing in the center). Many teachers introduce the Construction

Competence with computer applications is essential for children growing up in the twenty-first century.

Center to their classes by first placing Styrofoam packing pieces or thick cardboard in the center so that children can experiment with construction-type activities with a minimum of difficulty. As children become proficient with construction tools, small pieces of soft wood are the next logical addition.

Computer Center

Many public schools own computers, but sometimes children are only able to receive computer instruction in computer labs. The recent trend toward teaching children of all ages technology applications implies that teachers of young children will have one or more computers in their classrooms. The Bonus Chapter near the end of the book provides comprehensive information about classroom technology and the decisions teachers need to make about appropriate computer use with young children and managing computer use in classrooms.

Special-Interest Centers

A prekindergarten teacher assists her children in their decision to change the Home Living Center into a Veterinarian's Office. A first-grade teacher brings in produce boxes from a nearby supermarket so children can set up a grocery store as part of their study of their community. A third-grade teacher puts up a bulletin board and display center to show her souvenirs and photographs from her recent trip to the Galapagos Islands. These three teachers are demonstrating their need to develop Special-Interest Centers, which are an outgrowth of classroom study. Special-Interest Centers complement and accessorize thematic units, and their inclusion provides a more realistic study for children than other centers. These centers depend on resources available, and they remain in the classroom for short periods of time. They also complement project studies (see Chapter 2 for more information about project development).

Special Skills Centers

Teachers who perceive children's need to develop specific skills plan Special Skills Centers. Two examples are a Cutting Table in kindergarten for children who need practice cutting paper in a straight line or a second-grade teacher who sets up a Dictionary Study Center for youngsters who need additional help with alphabetizing words. Special Skills Centers are unique to each classroom, established for small groups of children for only a few

Occasionally, teachers plan individual instruction time with children while other children participate independently.

TABLE 3.2 Examples of Special Skills Centers per Grade Level

	SPECIAL SKILLS CENTER	MATERIALS	SKILLS
KINDERGARTEN	Folder Games Center	Shapes and shape forms	Matching
		Buttons and numeral cards	Rational counting
	Ordering Table	Color tablets	Ordering lightest to darkest
		Cuisenaire rods	Ordering shortest to longest
		Various-sized patterns	Ordering smallest to largest
	Number Table	Abacus	Counting
		Pegs and numeral cards	Matching
FIRST GRADE	Matching Table	Word cards and pictures	Matching
		Letter cards (lower and capital case)	Matching
		Numeral cards and set cards	Matching
	Ordering Table	Numeral cards	Ordering by quantity
		55 buttons	Ordering rows showing next number as one more
SECOND GRADE	Poetry Table	Samples of poetry	Creating poetry
		Poetry anthologies	Copying favorite poems
	Puzzles Table	Rubik's Cube, tangrams	Problem solving
		Art supplies	Creating personal puzzles
THIRD GRADE	Games Table	Chess set, dominoes, and checkers	Problem solving Thinking skills
	Architecture Center	Slide rules and compasses	Design and map skills
	Author Corner	Vocabulary word cards	Vocabulary development
		Calligraphy pen and ink	Handwriting development

days. Teachers often use these centers as opportunities for giving children direct instruction about skills that they need to acquire. Other Special Skills Centers are listed in Table 3.2.

☆ THE CYCLE OF LEARNING AND TEACHING

naeyc

The process of leading children to new information is called the *Cycle of Learning and Teaching* (Bredekamp & Rosegrant, 1992). This cycle indicates that learners bring prior knowledge to the learning setting (awareness), and they follow a process (exploration and inquiry) to a climax when they are able utilize their new knowledge (utilization). The cycle acknowledges that children need others to assist them in achieving a higher level of conceptualization (much like Vygotsky's zone of proxi-

FIGURE 3.2 The Cycle of Learning and Teaching

	What Children Do	What Teachers Do
Awareness	Experience Acquire an interest Recognize broad parameters Attend Perceive	Create the environment Provide opportunities by introducing new objects, events, people Invite interest by posing problem or question Respond to child's interest or shared experience Show interest, enthusiasm
Exploration	Observe Explore materials Collect information Discover Create Figure out components Construct own understanding Apply own rules Create personal meaning Represent own meaning	Facilitate Support and enhance exploration Provide opportunities for active exploration Extend play Describe child's activity Ask open-ended questions—"What else could you do?" Respect a child's thinking and rule systems Allow for constructive error
Inquiry	Examine Investigate Propose explanations Focus Compare own thinking with that of others Generalize Relate to prior learning Adjust to conventional rule systems	Help children refine understanding Guide children, focus attention Ask more focused questions—"What else works like this?" "What happens if . . . ?" Provide information when requested—"How do you spell . . . ?" Help children make connections
Utilization	Use the learning in many ways; learning becomes functional Represent learning in various ways Apply learning to new situations Formulate new hypotheses and repeat cycle	Create vehicles for application in real world Help children apply learning to new situations Provide meaningful situations in which to use learning

Source: Bredekamp & Rosegrant, 1992. Reprinted by permission.

mal development implies). Learners learn, but teachers facilitate their learning, especially when they recognize the existence of the learning and teaching cycle. See Figure 3.2 for a graphic representation of the Cycle of Learning and Teaching.

What Teachers Are Saying

Planning for Children's Learning

"The zone of proximal development is crucial for scaffolding learning, and miscues are a better mindset for learning than 'mistakes.'"—*a first-grade teacher*

"I've found that the developmentally delayed students I work with make incredible gains when learning within their zone of proximal development—when instructed in a way that enhances their strengths. All too often these students have checked out mentally because of the lack of challenge."—*a special education teacher*

"Piaget's descriptions of children's cognitive development serve as my (now unconscious) guide to planning developmentally appropriate activities, topics, and materials for my children."—*a kindergarten teacher*

The Cycle of Learning and Teaching emphasizes the sociocultural elements of educational environments. Children are capable of learning within the range of social and cultural experiences they bring to the classroom. Islamic or Jewish children who have had no experience with Christianity could be confused by the sight of a classroom Christmas tree. Their personal interpretation of this Christian practice will require adult clarification before children understand why the Christian culture celebrates the birth of their religious leader in this peculiar way. The second-language learner feels unacceptable and incompetent in classrooms where English only is spoken and acknowledged, and addressing their language needs becomes the responsibility of the school and its teachers.

The Cycle of Learning and Teaching has four components: awareness, exploration, inquiry, and utilization. *Awareness* is the step learners take when they enter a new learning setting. As awareness applies to classrooms, the teacher plays an important role in organizing the environment for optimal learning to occur. Exposure and experience are critical elements during the awareness phase. Early educators should allow children time and opportunity to become familiar and comfortable with their classroom to maximize learning potential.

Exploration is comprehension of the elements available in a learning setting. Children's senses are attuned to potential learning, and their curiosity is heightened as they observe and explore the environment to develop conceptual understandings. Like children's exposure to a new classroom, any person who has traveled away from home or abroad recognizes immediately the differences between other communities and their own. How individuals interpret new learning elements is distinctly personal, whether correctly or incorrectly analyzed, and is continually updated through exploration and activity.

Exploration allows children to create personal meanings, and they develop general understandings and concepts, which lead to the *inquiry* phase of the cycle. During this phase, teachers help children in refining knowledge and correcting misunderstandings children have about what they know. The following anecdotes describe how the inquiry process works.

Refining Knowledge

1. A third-grade child uses word attack skills she knows to try to pronounce the abbreviation *etc.* When her classmates laugh, the teacher explains to them that *etc.* is actually an abbreviation, which is correctly pronounced *et cetera.*
2. Children in prekindergarten often believe that letters appearing in their names are theirs alone. Teachers assist them in recognizing that individual letters appear in many words, a generalization that is important to emergent reading and writing.

Correcting Misunderstandings

1. When a 4-year-old child incorrectly identifies a cow's udder as penises, the teacher might respond by saying, "They look like penises, but cows have udders. Udders let calves drink milk from their mothers."
2. If a 6-year-old observes a classroom plant and declares, "That looks like poison ivy. I'm allergic to poison ivy," then his teacher will need to find a picture of poison ivy and show the youngster the differences between poison ivy and the plant in the classroom. Reassuring the child that "not all plants are poisonous" helps him feel secure in the classroom environment.

The last component in the Cycle of Learning and Teaching is *utilization*. Children's abilities to apply the information they are learning through group discussions, in pretend play, and through verbal, pictorial, and written representations allow them to achieve the utilization phase. If children know about environmental safety signs, for example, their ability to name them, draw pictures of them, pick out the signs as they are named by the teacher, and obey them during play when they appear in the Block Center demonstrate utilization of knowledge.

Much like the scientific method, learning does not end at the utilization phase. What happens instead is that the Cycle of Learning and Teaching begins anew. The learning process is ongoing as long as the environment provides stimulation and motivation to children for acquiring more knowledge. The teacher's role continues as she plans environmental changes to challenge children to acquire new knowledge.

⭐ THE TEACHING CONTINUUM

naeyc

The Cycle of Learning and Teaching implies that learners and teachers have responsibilities during daily classroom activity. The *Teaching Continuum* demonstrates that teachers use a compendium of strategies to facilitate learning processes. The interaction between teachers and children is active and complex and depends heavily on teachers' abilities to analyze learning situations and respond to children with appropriate comments and instruction. This interaction corresponds well with developmentally appropriate practice principles that suggest that learning should be (1) age appropriate, (2) individualized, and (3) culturally sensitive.

The Teaching Continuum also implies that a balance exists between teacher-directed and child-initiated learning. Bredekamp and Rosegrant (1992) developed the continuum as a reaction to criticism in the profession that developmentally appropriate practice, as originally defined, did not meet the needs of some subgroups of children. Recognizing that individual children and various groups, no matter their age, will need different learning experiences suggests that teachers must know a variety of techniques for facilitating learning in their classrooms. The continuum acknowledges that children with special needs or children from other cultures do not respond to learning environments in the same way that children in another classroom will react. Figure 3.3 shows the Teaching Continuum as organized by Bredekamp and Rosegrant with a compendium of strategies from nondirective to directive techniques. The chart defines each strategy and gives an example of classroom application for each. In their discussion of the continuum, Bredekamp and Rosegrant (1992) maintain: "Every one of these behaviors occurs in adult-child interactions. The percentage of time each behavior is used will vary depending on the activity and the child. All of these behaviors are appropriate at certain times and under certain conditions. Disproportionate use of any one behavior renders it ineffective" (p. 39).

⭐ EMERGENT CURRICULUM

naeyc

Early educators who are true to the principle that curriculum should follow children's needs and interests are fully aware of a concept known as *emergent curriculum.* In their book of the same title, Jones and Nimmo (1994) describe why emergent curriculum is preferable to state or district curriculum. They state: "In early childhood education, curriculum isn't the focus, children are. It's easy for teachers to get hooked on curriculum because it's so much more manageable than children are. But curriculum is *what happens* in an educational environment—not what is rationally planned to happen, but what actually takes place" (p. 12).

A teacher who decides to develop a thematic study about dogs because she observes children pretending they are dogs during center play is acknowledging emergent curriculum. Extending a preplanned unit study because children show more than usual interest in the topic is another example of emergent curriculum. A news event in the community or nation (such as a natural disaster or a terrorist attack) might prompt an appropriate study about their occurrence for children in the primary grades. Some teachers prepare prop boxes filled with objects pertinent to a variety of studies, just to be prepared when they observe a theme emerging. Prop boxes stimulate dramatic play, too (Barbour & Desjean-Perrotta, 2002).

The elements supporting emergent curriculum are (1) adults as playful learners collaborating with children, (2) acknowledging that curriculum is process oriented, not product driven, (3) recognizing that knowledge is not static, (4) assisting chil-

FIGURE 3.3 The Teaching Continuum

NONDIRECTIVE	MEDIATING	DIRECTIVE

Acknowledge / Model / Facilitate / Support / Scaffold / Coconstruct / Demonstrate / Direct

Classroom Examples of the Teaching Continuum

Teaching Strategy	Application
Acknowledge: Attending to children's activity and giving encouragement	"Mia, I notice that you have been sharing your crayons with Trey today."
Model: Showing children appropriate classroom behaviors (sometimes implicitly and sometimes explicitly)	"Geoffrey, let's talk about the problem you're having with Chi Li in the Block Center." (implicit) "While we are in Circle Time, can we all sit like this?" (explicit)
Facilitate: Temporarily assisting children during a specific learning setting	"Andy, let me hold the door for you while you take the blocks to the playground."
Support: Facilitating learning with greater involvement from the adult	"Anna Marie, tell me if you need help while writing your story for your Mom."
Scaffold: Setting up classroom challenges to encourage children to move to another level of development (based on Vygotskian theory)	"You may have already noticed that I've added some floor puzzles to the Manipulatives Center. I believe you'll be able to use them on your own, but if you need help, I'll be available when you want to try one of them."
Coconstruct: Teachers and children work together simultaneously as learners	"I don't know much about spiders, Vic, and your question is a good one. Let's look at this book to see if we can find an answer to your question."
Demonstrate: Commonly used in classrooms, demonstrating information to children that might be unsafe for them if they were to use discovery learning	"Let me show you this demonstration, which shows what fires need to grow and spread, and let's talk about ways we can put out a fire."
Direct: Intrusively intervening into children's learning environments (used in limited situations)	"You know, when you climb on that counter and jump off, you risk falling and hurting yourself or one of your classmates. Wait until you go out on the playground where you can climb."

dren in understanding they are responsible for their own learning, and (5) knowing that children do not arrive at school with the same knowledge and experiences (Jones & Nimmo, 1994).

Realistically, teachers approach curriculum and lesson planning with predetermined goals and objectives in mind. On the first day of school, teachers must know how they will proceed through the day with their group, and they should have a long-term view of what they hope to accomplish during the school year. Their willingness to reorganize and refine their thinking about educating young children, however, demonstrates their understanding that interactions with children are more important than preset curriculum mandates. Emergent curriculum is best practiced in its purest form.

☆ LESSON PLANNING

Lesson plans, sometimes called *learning* or *activity plans,* are road maps to ensure that teachers achieve predetermined goals and objectives in their classroom. Without them, classrooms appear to be chaotic, and teachers become inefficient in their roles as instructional leaders. Good teachers write and implement lesson plans because they are at the heart of learning and teaching. Many school districts recommend a specific lesson plan format, and some require teachers to turn their lesson plan book in to be checked by the principal or assistant principal on a weekly basis. Lesson plans are a must for a substitute teacher if the teacher is ill or takes a personal day from the classroom.

Basically, the lesson plan cycle includes the following elements:

- A lesson title
- Objectives, usually written in behavioral form (the rationale for the lesson)
- Introduction to the lesson (called a Focus or Anticipatory Set)
- Brief description of the activities that will be used during the body of the lesson (showing premarked textbook pages, if children are using texts)
- If necessary, a description of practice activities children will use to demonstrate they are learning what is planned
- Lesson closure (a review of the information that has been presented during the lesson)
- A description of follow-up activities
- A description of evaluation procedures
- A listing of classroom resources needed to teach the lesson

An example of a first-grade lesson plan is shown in Figure 3.4.

What Are Goals and Objectives?

Goals and objectives define the rationale for the lesson. They answer the question onlookers might ask: "Why is the teacher doing this activity?" In the planning process, educators distinguish between goals and objectives because of the specialized nature of the planning they are doing. *Goals* are more general in scope, describing what children will learn during the school year. Examples of goals include:

1. Children learn to write their names in kindergarten.
2. Children will learn to read in first grade.
3. Children are introduced to cursive handwriting toward the end of second grade.
4. Children learn their multiplication facts in third grade.

FIGURE 3.4 A Sample First-Grade Lesson Plan

(*Note:* This lesson is the beginning phase of an ongoing mural children will develop as the Transportation Unit is initiated. It is developed for the first-grade level. The rationale for the lesson is to focus on the concept of transportation, define what the word *transportation* means, and consolidate the knowledge children have about transportation and why it is important to the community).

Lesson Title: Transportation Mural

Objectives: After this lesson, children will be able to:

- Simply define the word *transportation.*
- Name types of transportation their families have.
- Identify three types of transportation they have observed in the community.
- Tell one reason why transportation is important to the community.
- Name the type of transportation they used to come to school.

Focus:

Ask children to tell how they arrive at school each morning. Have pictures available of cars, buses, bicycles, or children walking to hold up as each are mentioned.

Body of the Lesson:

1. Read *This Is the Way We Go to School,* by Edith Baer.
2. Develop a group discussion about transportation and ensure that children can define the word *transportation.*
3. Tell the children that a classroom study of transportation is beginning. Ask them to brainstorm the types of transportation they would like to study, and record their responses on a chart or overhead transparency. Have transportation models available to assist children in their brainstorming. Remind children that transportation types appear in the air and on water. Talk about the reasons people rely on transportation in the community.
4. Describe the classroom mural that they will contribute to each day as another transportation type is studied. Ask for volunteers to paint butcher paper to resemble a highway. As the study progresses, children will draw and cut out examples of transportation vehicles to place on the large mural that is situated in the hallway for other children to view.

Closure:

Review what the word *transportation* means. Ask children to name one type of transportation as they leave the lesson setting for center activities (or list the type of transportation they use to come to school).

continued

FIGURE 3.4 *continued*

Follow-Up Activities:

Ask children to look for transportation vehicles as they leave school for the day. Encourage them to write the names of observed vehicles in a content log and bring their listing to school the next day. Have sentence strips available in the Writing Center so they can write the words to display in the classroom.

Evaluation: In small groups or individually, ask children to name two types of transportation and tell one reason why transportation is important to the community.

Resources:

Book, 10-foot length of butcher paper, gray paint and brushes, plastic vehicle toys, pictures of transportation types, chart paper.

Objectives, on the other hand, are specific descriptions of learning during an individual lesson. Education experts recommend that objectives include the behaviors teachers want to observe in children during or after lesson presentations and that the degree of achievement children exhibit be included to ensure account-ability. Often called *behavioral objectives,* they are composed of three subparts: (1) *what* children will learn, (2) *how* they will demonstrate their learning, and (3) the *proficiency level* they will exhibit. Translating this definition into written form for a second-grade mathematics lesson on adding two-digit numbers is shown here.

The What (Behavior Expected)

Children will be able to:

Identify two-digit numbers.
Demonstrate their answers to simple addition problems with Cuisenaire rods.
Explain how simple two-digit addition problems are solved.
Formulate an hypothesis about solving addition problems when the units column projects an answer more than nine.

The How (Condition)

By solving several simple two-digit problems with Cuisenaire rods and on paper.
By verbally explaining the process they used to solve their problems.
By using a problem that will cause the units column to move beyond the numeral 9.

Proficiency Level

With 80 percent accuracy   *or*   Four out of five times.

When the subparts are put together, the objectives read as follows.

Children will be able to:

1. Identify two-digit numbers from a list shown on the chalkboard with 100 percent accuracy.
2. Demonstrate answers to simple addition problems with Cuisenaire rods and on paper with 80 percent accuracy.
3. Explain to peers how simple two-digit addition problems are solved while using Cuisenaire rods and paper and pencil.
4. Formulate an hypothesis about solving complex addition problems when the unit's column projects an answer more than 9 using Cuisenaire rods four out of five times.

Each of these objectives are *observable* and *measurable*, both characteristics of teaching and learning essential to classroom accountability.

The age and development of the child determine whether objectives are planned with individuals or groups of children in mind. The younger the child (or if the child has special needs), the more critical individualization is in developing objectives. Table 3.3 shows other examples of behavioral objectives for individuals and groups.

TABLE 3.3 Examples of Individual and Group Objectives

INDIVIDUAL OBJECTIVES	GROUP OBJECTIVES
After individualized instruction, Alex will name three colors from a group of crayons with 100% accuracy.	After group instruction, children will be able to record three characteristics of crocodiles in their content logs with 100% accuracy.
Judy will demonstrate self-control during Circle Time three days this week after personal discussion with her.	Children will be able to name at least one onomatopoeic word after the lesson.
Adilia will follow three simple directions with 100% accuracy after individualized instruction about following directions.	During the week, children will exhibit increasingly cooperative behaviors after a group discussion of the word *cooperation*.
After pairing Maria with another child in the classroom, she will show that she is able to enter a play setting without aggressive behavior throughout the entire week.	After group discussion with the boys in the class, they will demonstrate that they can keep their bathroom area clean.
Jordan will demonstrate his knowledge of numerals one through ten by writing them while I sit with him and give him encouragement with 100% accuracy.	After class review of colors, children will be able to name the three primary colors and the three secondary colors.

What Is the Lesson Focus?

Like a well-planned speech, the lesson *focus* is the technique teachers use to focus children's attention on the plan of the lesson. The focus does not need to be dramatic, but it does need to attract children's interest and motivate them to attend to the content of the lesson. Teachers will use books and pictures, artifacts and props, media productions (teacher-prepared *PowerPoint* presentations, overhead transparencies or commercial productions), and other strategies for obtaining and maintaining children's interest in lesson content.

Classroom guests can serve as a lesson focus, or the teacher might put an object into a mystery box for children to guess what is inside. Mystery boxes, often created by the teacher, are attractively decorated and used frequently to develop curiosity among children about their contents. Teachers who dress up in special clothing appeal to young children, too. Figure 3.5 describes costumes teachers might wear for preselected themes to introduce lessons and unit studies to children.

What Is the Body of the Lesson?

The lesson itself is essentially the *content* teachers want children to learn. If teachers could say to children, "This is what I want you to learn," and children could respond accordingly, teaching would be easy. But adults even have difficulty learning

FIGURE 3.5 Costumes to Use in Lesson Focuses

Topic	Costume Suggestion
Apple or Farm Theme	Johnny Appleseed clothing; overalls or jeans and a straw hat
Alphabet	Purchase fabric and clothing that have alphabet letters on them
Animal Unit	Put on animal masks or ears to represent various animals
Color Theme	Dress according to the color studied each day
Occupations Unit	Collect hats worn by people in various occupations to wear when their jobs are introduced
Seasonal Studies	Appropriate clothing representing each season: Fall: sweaters and warm hats Winter: coats, wool scarves and hats Spring: gardening clothing Summer: sun hats and sunglasses
Popular Literary Characters	Simple costumes and props representing storybook characters—magic wands, wizard hats, cloaks and capes, baskets, or burlap bags

in this fashion, so lessons should be carefully planned to ensure children's learning. Lesson cycles include the introduction of content geared to children's ages and development, practice with remembering the information, application of skills, and a review of the information that has been presented.

The key to good lessons is planning interesting and varied activities that will cause children to be actively engaged while discovering pleasure in learning. Preschool children need gross-motor activity and concrete applications of information, whereas primary-grade children are capable of increasing intellectual stimulation, moving ever closer to abstract thought. Songs, fingerplays or poems, stories, books, discussions that allow all children to participate, graphic representations (such as charts and photographs), games, and movement activities are among the lesson activities that will engage youngsters. If children appear bored or distracted, they are not learning.

Teachers should remember, too, that children's experiential foundation is limited because they are young. No matter the age, then, if teachers want children to learn about seeds, then bringing several (from peas to sunflower seeds to magnolia seedpods) into the classroom represents the best practice. Hands-on data are essential to young children's learning. Field trips to actual sites are preferable to pictures of a nearby ice cream factory or the local newspaper business. Integration and consolidation of knowledge are implicit in playing with, talking about, collecting sensory data on, and eventually reading about content. Good lessons recognize *who* children are and *how* they learn.

What Is the Lesson Closure?

The lesson *closure* is a simple review of the content of the lesson. Finding out what children have learned is easy: Ask them! What teachers discover when they provide children with opportunities to tell what they know is twofold: (1) what children's personal interpretations of the lesson content are, and (2) how much of the lesson content has been absorbed. Presenting the content in another lesson setting is necessary, on occasion, because learners do not comprehend totally and wholly any concept with one presentation. Teachers should make plans to work with individual children if drill and practice sessions will assist in concept development. Teaching is an ongoing process, and daily interactions with the teacher and classroom materials and supplies are imperative for children to learn what is expected of them.

Asking Better Classroom Questions

During lessons, and throughout the day, teachers need to ask children questions that challenge their thinking. Teachers use memory-level or rote-level questions easily. Questions such as "What are the colors in the flag?" "What is the name of our school?" "What is your address?" "Recite the alphabet" are all designed to find out what knowledge children have. Higher-level questions, on the other hand, require children to think about their answers and move them to higher levels of thought. A question like "Who are the characters in this story?" can be easily changed to "Why did the Little Billy Goat Gruff go across the bridge first?" Or "Why do you think the troll was protecting the bridge?" are much more interesting questions, and they motivate children to envision some creative answers.

⭐ PRINCIPLES THAT GUIDE EFFECTIVE LESSON PLANNING

The outcomes of lesson planning and classroom activity are proof to teachers that they are doing their jobs proficiently and effectively. Keeping in mind the following principles of planning gives teachers a sense of "mission accomplished" as they deliver the lesson plan presentations.

- The younger the child, the shorter lessons should be.
- Having clear objectives in mind streamlines the lesson plan procedures and implementation.
- Capitalize on children's expressed interests and questions during the lesson to ensure that attention is maintained (known in education circles as *teachable moments*).
- Make connections to prior learning that children already have acquired. These connections form a bridge to new learning.
- Review previous lessons and decide when additional instruction is necessary.
- Vary activities during lessons to maintain interest and increase learning (songs, fingerplays, games, and movement experiences are appropriate choices).
- Provide one or more activities for the physical self while the lesson is presented (if nothing more than standing or stretching).
- Use questions to challenge children to do higher-level thinking. Too many rote-level questions become humdrum and seem interrogative.
- Not all lessons are successful; be aware of when to stop the lesson cycle and move to another activity.
- Enjoy the lessons as they are presented. Feelings and dispositions are strengthened when teachers demonstrate that they delight in learning.

Final Comments about Lesson Planning

Novice teachers benefit from fully writing out lesson plans. In doing so, they begin to think like more experienced educators. As teachers become more accomplished with writing lesson plans, they organize an outline format as a reminder of the questions they want to ask or the activities they want to use in their instruction. Through the years, teachers accumulate resources and materials that aid them in their planning and implementation of lessons; therefore, pulling together a lesson for children is easily and quickly accomplished. No matter the ease of organization, teachers *always* have objectives in mind for their instruction. Without objectives, teaching is ineffective and learning is haphazard.

THEMATIC UNITS

Typically, when observers amble through school buildings, they will see evidence that children are learning about various topics of study. Books, bulletin boards, pictures, artwork, teaching materials, and instructional aids point to a particular study for the classroom (or the entire school) during a specified time period. Teachers usually plan these thematic studies in response to school district curriculum guides or other educational mandates. Occasionally, teachers will plan as a grade-level team to organize yearly units of study they want for their children. *Thematic unit development* is traditional practice, whether correctly applied or not, and future teachers require knowledge of planning units and their implementation.

What are the steps in developing thematic units? First, teachers need to decide what topic is to be studied and when it will be introduced. Brainstorming a set of goals for the theme helps them determine the specific knowledge areas and skills children should learn. Once goals are set, the process of developing daily lesson plans complete with precise objectives is easier to manage. The second step is to collect resources in the classroom, from the school library, and from the community. To novices, this step appears to be a last plan of action, but teachers need instructional materials, books, authentic props, audiovisual aids, equipment, and supplies on hand to effectively implement unit development. The availability of these resources strengthens content organization.

The third step in unit construction is to decide upon age-appropriate activities that will best introduce the knowledge and skills children should learn. As plans spring forth, teachers should evaluate each in light of their children's needs and interests, reviewing the Principles That Guide Effective Lesson Planning, described earlier in this chapter. Figure 3.6 shows questions teachers must ask themselves in their deliberations about specific thematic topics.

The decision about which lesson will introduce the topic to children is the fourth step in unit development. The enthusiasm children generate for the study as a consequence of the introductory lesson likely affects the success of future lessons about the topic (see Figure 3.4 for a sample lesson introducing the transportation theme).

The fifth step in developing themes is preparing the classroom for instruction. This preparation includes putting up bulletin boards, bringing in display items, placing topical books in the Book Center, contacting and visiting possible field trip sites, scheduling classroom guests, and collecting materials and supplies children will need for their lesson activities. Now the teacher is ready to start teaching the unit!

 PROJECT STUDIES

Project studies, discussed thoroughly in Chapter 2 under the sections on Project Construct and Project Approach, are similar to thematic unit studies because they

FIGURE 3.6 Teacher Deliberations about Proposed Thematic Topics

Proposed Topic	Grade Level	Questions Teachers Ask Themselves
Pets	Prekindergarten	"Are my children mature enough to handle a classroom pet?"
		"How will children respond if the pet dies during the year?"
Sounds and Music	Prekindergarten	"Will this unit become so noisy that others in the building will complain?"
		"How much supervision will be necessary to protect classroom musical instruments from destruction?"
Fire Station	Kindergarten	"Is a fire station nearby that we can walk to? Transportation funds for field trips are limited this year."
		"Have any of the children experienced a fire in their home that might cause fear or trauma to them during classroom discussions?"
Zoo Animals	Kindergarten	"How do I reconcile my feelings about exploitation of animals when I introduce this topic to children?"
		"There's not a zoo nearby that we can visit. Is this topic as relevant and meaningful as it should be or is there another topic we can study?"
Weather	First grade	"Will children become frightened when we talk about tornadoes?"
		"Will a classroom demonstration of evaporation adequately help first graders learn the concept? Is it a concept first graders need to learn?"
Space and Sky	First grade	"What is the best approach for introducing an understanding of planets to first-grade children? Is this essential knowledge for them to learn?"
		"Would it possible to plan an evening sky-watching event?"
Money	First grade	"My children don't have good concepts of money, especially coins. How will I help them learn about change and making change?"
		"Will Juan need instruction about Mexican money? He's going back to Mexico in June."
Cheese Industry	Third grade	"How can I make this topic relevant to my children here in Louisiana?"
		"If I tried making cheese in the classroom, how long would it take and how smelly would it become?"
Water Treatment Plant	Third grade	"Could there be information on the Internet that we can explore about water purification and sanitation?"
		"I feel sure Merida's wheelchair will prevent her taking our field trip to the city water plant. I wonder what I can plan for her instead?"

are topical in design. Their development and implementation are child initiated, with teacher guidance to guarantee that maximum learning opportunities are available to all children in the classroom. Recall from Chapter 2 that three phases undergird project studies, and three project types evolve: dramatic, investigative, and constructive. Projects allow children essentially to take control of the classroom environment.

Project studies are a prototype of emergent curriculum because they grow out of children's interests and observations of their school and community. When notices appear in the community about an upcoming county fair, children's motivation to participate in fair events or finalize art products for display heightens the introduction of a theme about fairs and bazaars or carnivals. Projects also represent the best teachable moment for sharing information about a perceived topic.

As with thematic units, once teachers decide that time is appropriate for further study about a topic, they collect resources to capitalize on children's interest and they formulate the goals and objectives about learning that are to be achieved. From this point, projects become divergent in six ways.

1. Children compile their collective knowledge with teacher assistance (through webs, charts, or graphs).
2. They brainstorm questions to be answered.
3. They generate activities about how to find the answers to their questions.
4. They investigate as much information as they can (with teacher assistance and facilitation).
5. They use their knowledge in dramatic play or by building structures that represent their knowledge.
6. They display their knowledge and share information with classroom guests. (Katz & Chard, 2000)

The teacher has roles as facilitator, mentor, monitor, and support system for children as they work. She *facilitates* by noticing the potential for study that emanates from children, by asking questions, by recording information (if children are not old enough to record their own) or encouraging them to record what they know, and by providing resources that are not readily available in the classroom. She *mentors* children when she models strategies for finding information, works with individuals who need more assistance than others, and describes various techniques to record data. As a *monitor,* the teacher surveys the ongoing project to keep children focused on their study, asking pertinent questions or making suggestions to deepen the project study, and bringing in additional resources if children's interest continues.

The teacher's role as a *support system* is obvious by her continued encouragement of children as they work, the individual assistance she provides for children who are less skilled or knowledgeable than their classmates, and her contacts with parents or guardians about children's work. In one sense, she is a public relations agent as she invites in other schoolchildren, administrators, and parents or guardians to enjoy the work children are producing.

Sample project studies are categorized here under the three project types.

DRAMATIC PLAY	INVESTIGATION	CONSTRUCTION
PREKINDERGARTEN OR KINDERGARTEN Using props obtained on the fire station trip to pretend to be firefighters	Asking the fire station to bring a pumper truck onto the school playground	Building a fire station with blocks or boxes; using playground equipment as a pretend fire station
PRIMARY GRADES Reenacting favorite classroom books or stories (teachers secure representational clothing)	Analyzing books on the same topic, recording their similarities and differences; comparing stories from various countries	Writing and compiling books based on popular classroom stories in the Writing Center
KINDERGARTEN OR PRIMARY GRADES Learning songs, fingerplays, and poems about fish or other pond animals	Taking a field trip to a nearby park, pond, or fish hatchery	Constructing a terrarium for hatching tadpoles; developing a wall mural
PRIMARY GRADES Bringing large plastic containers into the classroom for children's experimentation	Using a Venn diagram to differentiate between submarines and other ocean transports	Building a classroom submarine with a large refrigerator box and other scrap materials
SECOND OR THIRD GRADE Organizing a skit about early pioneers to present to another class in the school	Viewing a video or film about pioneer life	Preparing a time line depicting the Westward Movement
SECOND OR THIRD GRADE Planning a 1970s dress-up day	Interviewing parents and guardians and neighbors about life in the 1970s	Graphing results of neighborhood surveys about life in the 1970s

DIVERSITY AND CURRICULUM PLANNING

If early educators become aware of cultural, ethnic, and gender differences among children, their classrooms will play a role in liberating the human spirit. King, Chipman, and Cruz-Janzen (1994) indicate that ethnicity, gender, and social class affect children's development. Trawick-Smith (1997) explains that developmental variation in children's behavior, language, and learning style can be defined by life's experiences and children's adaptation to their home and community environments. One recommendation by Nilson (2001) is that educators recognize and acknowledge that families from other countries do not have the same values as Americans. Becoming more aware of diversity issues within the classroom aids in planning curriculum, which incorporates democratic principles of living.

☆ SUMMARY

Teacher planning assures children's learning. Preparing the classroom and organizing for instruction are critical elements in successful teaching. Teacher understanding of the Cycle of Learning and Teaching, the Teaching Continuum, the organization and management of classroom learning centers, and lesson planning aid them in becoming proficient as early educators. Recognizing differences among children supports the evolution of a caring classroom community.

Balancing children's developmental needs with state and school district expectations obliges teachers to know their children well for effective delivery of instruction with age-appropriate strategies. Whether systematic unit instruction is utilized or emergent curriculum evolves, teachers must capitalize on teachable moments to maximize children's education.

☆ DISCUSSION QUESTIONS

1. Talk to a preschool or primary grade teacher to find out about a recent unit of study he or she used in the classroom, asking some of the following questions:
   - What resources in the school and community did the teacher use to accomplish the unit instruction?
   - Was the study an example of emergent curriculum, or was it part of the school district's curriculum?
   - Did the study produce a class project?
   - What goals and objectives did the teacher plan to achieve during the unit?
   - How did children react to the study?
   - What changes in planning will the teacher make if he or she uses the theme again?
   - Would the teacher use the same unit in the classroom a second time? Why or why not?

   Be prepared to discuss the answers to these questions with your classmates. What differences are there among teachers?
2. Collaborate with a group of your classmates to brainstorm materials and supplies that could be placed in a Weather Station Center for a second-grade classroom.
3. In a small group, select a favorite childhood story ("Little Red Riding Hood," "The Three Little Pigs," or "The Gingerbread Man," for example). Brainstorm questions to use with children that will challenge them to "think outside the box."

☆ SUGGESTED CHAPTER ACTIVITIES

1. Recall a play experience you had as a child. Can you categorize the play as an example of play as defined by Piaget, Vygotsky, or Parten?
2. Using what you have learned about lesson planning in this chapter, write a lesson plan that you could use with a small group of children in the Music Center.
3. Write a brief paper about what the Cycle of Learning and Teaching means to you. Can you describe how the Cycle of Learning and Teaching applied as you learned to drive a car?

Chapter Four

Teaching Children with Special Needs

CHAPTER OVERVIEW

★ How do disability laws impact the general education teacher?

★ Do you understand the differences in the educational placements for children with disabilities?

★ Can you describe some accommodations that might be made in the general education classroom for children with special needs?

★ What is the difference between bilingual education and ESL?

THESE ARE A FEW OF THE QUESTIONS THAT
WILL BE ANSWERED WHEN YOU READ THIS CHAPTER.

Teaching children with special needs can be very rewarding for teachers. It is through working with these children that teachers can have a profound impact on their lives and development. A teacher who has high expectations and devotes the time needed can determine the entire course of a child's education and emotional well-being. A teacher's greatest reward comes from making a difference in a child's life. Often children with special needs need the extra encouragement that comes from the teacher's telling them that they can learn to do this. Years of struggle, lack of success, and taunts from others take their toll on these children. Building them up psychologically is an important step in beginning to help them.

"I will never forget the night that my phone rang and a man asked if I was the person who had taught in a certain public school 15–20 years ago. I said that I was indeed that person, and this man said, 'You might not remember me, but you were my teacher back in third grade. I am now 22, and I found you by looking you up on the Internet. I want to let you know how much you have influenced my life and that I am the man I am today because of you.' We spent over an hour on the phone. I did indeed remember him. He was one of those children who tug at a teacher's heart. Although he had an IQ in the gifted range, his learning disability made it very hard for him to learn to read. I had thought of him often in the years after he left elementary school. You see, I had him in my resource classroom for 3 years. I remember what a hard time I had trying to convince him that he was intelligent. He had been so beaten down by his shcool experience that by the third grade he felt like he was dumb and a failure. He is doing very well now, he told me. What a priceless gift he gave me that night!"

I t is important for teachers to have an understanding of legal issues, various types of disabilities, and possible placements for children with disabilities. Included in this understanding is knowledge of the many acronyms used in education, such as IEP, LRE, and ARD. With more and more children being included into the general education classroom, teachers need to be aware of some common accommodations and modifications and know how to plan for the successful inclusion of these children.

★ MAJOR LAWS AFFECTING STUDENTS WITH DISABILITIES

There have been several major pieces of legislation affecting the education of students with disabilities since 1973. These laws carry significance for general education teachers and special education teachers alike, who must equally comply with the law in working with children with disabilities. With the exception of Section 504 of the Rehabilitation Act of 1973, these laws were discussed in Chapter 1.

Rehabilitation Act of 1973, Section 504

Before the year 1973, legislation involving students with disabilities consisted of support to aid children who were blind, deaf, and in state hospitals or institutions.

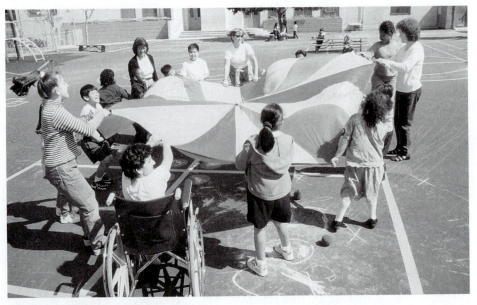

All children like to be included.

In 1973, Congress passed the Rehabilitation Act, Public Law 93-112, Section 504, which defined who was considered a "handicapped person," defined "appropriate education," and prohibited discrimination against students with disabilities by anyone receiving federal funds. Section 504 states that schools are prohibited from assigning students with disabilities to segregated classes and that students may only be assigned to segregated classes or separate facilities when this placement is necessary for students to obtain an equal educational opportunity. Students may not be assigned to segregated classes based on intelligence tests alone, and assessments must also include achievement tests, aptitude tests, adaptive behavior evaluation, teacher recommendations, evaluation of the student's physical condition, and information about the student's cultural and social background. Section 504's definition of a disability includes any mental or physical impairment that limits a major life activity such as learning, breathing, working, caring for oneself, manual tasks, walking, seeing, hearing, and speaking. There is no listing of what specifically qualifies as a disabling condition under 504, but cultural, environmental, and economic disadvantages as well as low-average intelligence are excluded from the definition of disability (Richards, 1997).

Some of the more common disabilities and medical conditions that qualify children to receive Section 504 accommodations are attention deficit disorder (ADD), attention deficit/hyperactivity disorder (ADHD), and problems such as asthma or depression. Some medical conditions that involve medications taken by the children may affect their alertness and ability to sustain attention. Obviously, this will have an impact on the education of these students and will qualify a child under Section 504 for modifications in the general education classroom. Sometimes children who have ADHD will be eligible for special education under the IDEA umbrella if this is also accompanied by a learning disability, emotional disturbance, or one of the other federal categories of disabilities.

Children with disabilities recognized under IDEA are required by law to be educated to the maximum extent appropriate with general education or nondisabled students. These students also may not be excluded from participation in extracurricular activities on the basis of their disability. A main concern of parents is the suspension or removal of their child. Under existing law, if a student is suspended or removed for more than ten consecutive days, this would constitute a change in placement. Before a change in placement can be made, the school would be required to provide notice to the parents and conduct an evaluation. Once this has been done, the placement is to be determined by a team of people who know the student and can understand the evaluation information (U.S. Department of Education, 1998a).

The law also requires districts to make a concerted effort to search for eligible children and not simply wait for these children to come forward and identify themselves. This effort must extend throughout the range of the school ages, not just be directed toward young children (Richards, 1997). Once children who might possibly qualify are identified, parents must then be notified of the rights of the child, told how the district will meet the needs of their child, provide parents with information about procedural safeguards, and clearly state the district's duty to provide a free, appropriate public education (Richards, 1997). Notice should be provided to parents before any committee meetings and actions.

Children who do not fit into one of the categories of disability but who do qualify under Section 504 become eligible for accommodations and modifications *in the general education classroom,* not the special education classroom. Once a child is considered for the accommodations under Section 504, that child's teachers may be asked to participate in a 504 conference. This conference is held with a team of people that may include teachers, administrators, counselor, and school nurse. It is held to discuss modifications for a child in the general education classroom. An accommodation under Section 504 made for a child with ADHD might be as simple as seating the child close to the teacher and giving the child an assignment notebook. Teachers need to be aware of children who receive accommodations in their classrooms and make sure that they follow the specified accommodations.

History of Education of Children with Disabilities

In 1975, Congress enacted the Education for All Handicapped Children Act. Before the enactment of this law, many individuals with disabilities lived in state institutions in restrictive environments that provided only minimal clothing, food, and shelter. With the passage of PL 94-142, individuals with disabilities were guaranteed a free, appropriate public education (FAPE) in every locality in the United States, regardless of the disability or the severity of the disability. This law was a response to concern over the blanket exclusion of children with disabilities from public education. This law provided financial assistance to the states to help with compliance. The law also provided due process necessary to ensure that the rights of these children were protected (IDEA, 2001).

Efforts were also made to improve the evaluation and assessment of these children. The law required that evaluations be conducted in the child's native language and be free from racial and/or cultural bias. In addition, the child must be assessed in all the areas related to the disability. For example, if the child demonstrated symptoms of a speech or language problem, the language pathologist would assess the child. If the child demonstrated problems with walking or postural control, then the physical therapist would assess the child in this area. Children with disabilities were eligible for special education and related services beginning at age 3 and continuing through age 21. Related services would include transportation, audiological services, speech therapy, occupational therapy, physical therapy, psychological diagnosis and evaluation, assistive devices such as Braillewriters or special computers, and medical or counseling services. Basically, any service that is needed by the child for *educational purposes* can be considered a related service (PL 94-142, 1992).

Placement for the child under this law must be in the **least restrictive environment (LRE)**. The least restrictive environment clause means that students with disabilities will receive their education in the schools and in the classrooms they would attend if they had no disability. For most children with disabilities, this will be in the general education classroom. These children would receive daily support through the special education teacher or instructional aide in the general education classrooms. Or the children might leave the general education classroom at specific times to go to the instructional support center or the resource room. If the disability is such that the child needs more assistance than is possible in these situations, then the child will be placed in a particular educational program, usually in a self-contained classroom, but will still be "mainstreamed" with the general education students to the greatest extent possible (U.S. Office for Civil Rights, 1999). This might occur at times such as lunchtime, recess, and possibly physical education, art, and music. The most restrictive placement for a child with a disability would be in a residential setting where there would be no interaction possible with children without disabilities.

Determination of the least restrictive environment can be a complicated process and is based on the answers to several questions.

Will the child be able to progress and learn in the general education classroom?
If not, will support with supplementary aids and services allow the child to be successful in the general education classroom?
What interventions can be attempted to help the child succeed?
If the child is still not successful, what other interventions can be tried?
What benefits will the child receive by staying in the general education classroom?
Will the child benefit academically and nonacademically from being in the general education classroom?
Is the education of the other students impacted adversely by the inclusion of the child with special needs?
Does the child require an inordinate amount of the teacher's attention?

These questions are related to the potential success of the child in the general education classroom. All of these bits of information are taken into consideration in determining the LRE for each child (Yell, 1995). Decisions about placement must be reviewed annually and changes made accordingly (PL 94-142, 1992).

Under PL 94-142, the teacher's responsibilities consist of attending the annual Admission-Review-Dismissal (ARD) meeting, participating in the development of the Individualized Education Plan (IEP), implementing and assessing the specific IEP objectives that are to be taught in the general education classroom, and reporting to the parents and others at the ARD meetings. The IEP is tailored to each child's needs. It contains the specific goals and objectives that the child should achieve in the coming year, steps toward each goal, and related services that are needed. The teacher's report must include not only the status of mastery of the IEP objectives, but also how the child is functioning and has adapted to the placement and successes and concerns in all areas of the school experience.

In 1990 the act was renamed the Individuals with Disabilities Education Act (IDEA) or Public Law 101-476. IDEA was enacted to promote programs that include students with severe disabilities. More funding for projects was extended to infants and toddlers, the term *handicapped* was replaced by the term *disability,* and "people-first" language was instituted. No longer would children with disabilities be referred to in such terms as *the autistic* or *the blind;* the focus now would be

Improving Education Results for Children with Disabilities Act of 2003 (H.R. 1350)

In April 2003, another reauthorization version of IDEA was introduced and passed by the U.S. House of Representatives. Advocates for children with special needs believe that this bill will significantly weaken support and services for children. H.R. 1350, the Improving Education Results for Children with Disabilities Act of 2003, contains several areas of concern for parents and teachers of children with special needs. In an effort to reduce paperwork for teachers, this legislation establishes a voluntary three-year IEP option and eliminates the use of short-term objectives. Parents may feel pressured to accept a three-year IEP instead of the annual IEP. Lawmakers used the No Child Left Behind Act (NCLB) as justification for the elimination of the short-term objectives, but the NCLB act only focuses on reading and math academic achievements, with science to be added in 2007–2008. For a child with special needs, the related skills of mobility, independent living, and assistive technology are also very important skills that demonstrate a child's progress.

The act further weakens the educational prospects for children with special needs by changing the expectations that teachers will meet the highest requirements to wording that states that teachers will be "appropriately and adequately prepared." Parents also must now wait one month before their complaints can proceed to due process, regardless of the problem. The act will require parents to present their case in a mandatory resolution session, and they are not reimbursed for attorneys' fees. If the case continues to a due process hearing, only issues that were originally in the complaint or resolution session can be raised. When the case has proceeded to due process, the governor of each state will determine the amount of attorneys' fees that will be reimbursed to the parents but will set no limits on fees paid by the school districts to their attorneys. This act further impacts children with special needs by requiring 15 percent of IDEA funds to be used for prereferral support and services that would pay for remedial assistance for all children with academic problems. In the area of discipline, the schools can remove a child from his or her placement based on the violation of any school rule, whether or not the behavior is related to the child's disability.

The bill changes the definition of a free, appropriate public education by adding that an appropriate education is one that is reasonably calculated to provide educational benefit that enables a child with special needs to access the general education curriculum. When districts are determining whether a child has a specific learning disability, they will not be required to take into consideration any severe discrepancy between the child's achievement and intellectual ability. Students who have not been diagnosed by a physician or other person certified by the state as having a disability should not receive services. This applies to learning disabilities and behavioral problems, both of which are perceived as being overidentified because of vague and ambiguous definitions. The general education teacher is not required to attend the IEP meeting if there are no issues to be discussed that pertain to the child's participation in general education. Practically the only positive change in the bill, in the view of special education advocates, is the provision that children with vision problems must be provided with textbooks that are appropriate for them in a timely manner (H.R. 1350: Summary of Major Changes, 2003: An Analysis of H.R. 1350, 2003).

placed on the humanity of all individuals, who would be referred to as people or children first, with the disability placed afterward. This would change the language from *the disabled* to *people with disabilities,* from *the autistic* to *children with autism,* or from *the blind* to *children who are blind.*

In 1997, when IDEA was reauthorized, it became mandatory when the child reaches age 14 for a statement about the transition of the child into adulthood to be included in the IEP. When the child reaches age 16, an individual transition plan must be developed. The transition plan identifies the vocational, educational, and independent living needs that are expected when the student completes the public school program. This requirement was added in an attempt to ensure that the child receives the kind of education that would prepare that child for independent adulthood. For instance, the transition plan for some special education students may be to attend college. If students do not take college preparatory courses in high school, it will be extremely difficult for them to gain admission to a college or university. If nothing else, students would be severely delayed in being able to pursue a college degree. For those students not attending college, the transition plan must address issues and skills related to them that will lead to the most independent and productive lives possible.

Also under this reauthorization, the behavior of each student in school is to be specifically addressed in the **admission-review-dismissal** (**ARD**) meeting (IDEA, 1997). It will be determined at this meeting if the child is able to follow the same discipline plan that the general education child follows. If so, then this decision will be noted. If not, a specific behavior management plan will be developed for the child as part of his or her IEP (IDEA, 1997). This behavior plan must specify the exact steps that are to be taken when an infraction of the school rules occurs. It is the teacher's responsibility to follow the discipline plan that is set out in the IEP in dealing with behavior problems that arise.

☆ THE REFERRAL PROCESS

The general education teacher is often the first person to suspect that a child might have a learning disability, mental retardation, or some other type of disability. When this is the case, or when the parents suspect a problem and want their child tested, a certain procedure must be followed. Before an official referral is made, there is a prereferral process. This process is in place to assure that sufficient time and effort have been put forth and that children are not merely arbitrarily tested for special education. First, the child's name will be submitted to the intervention or screening team. This team consists of teachers trained in the process, in addition to other school personnel such as the school nurse, an administrator, and possibly the school counselor. The teacher who is concerned about one of his or her students will complete a form stating the reasons for the concern, strategies and interventions that he or she has implemented to assist the student, the results of these interventions, and any other pertinent information.

Once this initial paperwork is submitted, the screening team will review the information provided by the teacher and will begin the process of assembling information on the child. The screening team will proceed to gather information from other people in the school who have contact with the child. The team will review the child's attendance, talk to the nurse to see if there are health problems, talk to the counselor to see if there are any known extenuating circumstances, check test scores and previous report cards for problems in previous years, and check to see if the child has been seen in the office for excessive discipline problems. The team will then make recommendations and suggestions to the teacher for dealing with the problems, and they will follow up to see if these interventions have helped. If there continues to be a problem, the team may recommend that the child be referred for a full individual evaluation by a multidisciplinary team to determine if there is a disability requiring special education services.

A number of procedural safeguards must be followed in the referral process. Before a child can be evaluated, the parents must be notified and must give informed consent for the individualized evaluation. When parents give their consent for this testing, they are only giving permission for the testing, not for special education placement. The educational team will administer the appropriate tests. Usually these consist of an IQ test to determine the child's IQ and achievement tests to determine the level of functioning in academic and developmental skills. Information will also be gathered from the parents and teachers about how the child is functioning in the classroom and in the home environment. Testing by the educational team may reveal the presence of a learning disability or mental retardation.

The criteria for a diagnosis of learning disabilities vary from state to state. In some states, learning disabilities are identified by a discrepancy between IQ and achievement. Other states require varying delays and examine other sensory processing deficits and adaptive behavior.

Once the testing is complete, the parents are notified of the IEP meeting. The parents must receive written notification at least five days before the scheduled IEP meeting. This notification must also itemize all the issues to be discussed by the school. Parents may request rescheduling of the IEP meeting if the time is inconvenient, and every attempt will be made to accommodate the parents so that they can attend. Besides the special education teacher, the general education teacher must also attend this meeting.

Specific Diagnostic Tests

Of all the intelligence tests given to children today, the Wechsler Scales of Intelligence is the one most widely used (Pierangelo & Giuliani, 1998). There are two different scales of this test that may be administered to young children. They are the Wechsler Preschool and Primary Scale of Intelligence (WPPSI-III) and the Wechsler Intelligence Scale for Children (WISC-IV). These tests are administered by a psychologist or educational diagnostician to an individual child and take between 60 to 75 minutes to administer. They are standardized, norm-referenced tests, and scores are reported as Verbal, Performance, and Full Scale IQ. The verbal tests measure general information knowledge, abstract and concrete reasoning, computation, vocabulary, common sense reasoning, attention and concentration, immediate auditory memory, and working memory. The performance tests measure visual memory, attention to detail, visual perception, ability to reproduce designs, object assembly, visual motor dexterity (pencil manipulation), visual discrimination, visual motor speed and accuracy in learning new tasks, and planning capability. One reason that this test is so widely used is that there is strong evidence of its **validity** and **reliability,** it is easy to use, it is well organized, and it correlates highly with academic achievement. The Wechsler does have several weaknesses, however, including possibly some culturally biased questions and lack of distinction of IQ scores below 40, making it less able to distinguish lower levels of retardation (Pierangelo & Giuliani, 1998).

Other intelligence tests that might be used are the Stanford-Binet Intelligence Scale, the Kaufman Assessment Battery for Children, the Leiter International Performance Scale–Revised, the Columbia Mental Maturity Scale, the McCarthy Scales of Children's Abilities, the Slosson Intelligence Test–Revised, and the Comprehensive Test of Nonverbal Intelligence. These tests must also be administered individually by a psychologist or educational diagnostician.

Once an IQ is obtained, the child may have his or her academic skills evaluated through achievement tests. Achievement tests measure a child's performance at all ages and grade levels in basic skills such as reading, language, writing, spelling, and math. Tests may include components that assess oral reading, silent reading, and comprehension and can be used to determine specific strengths and weaknesses in the subject areas (Pierangelo et al., 1998). Classroom teachers or special education teachers may administer many of these tests. Scores are often reported in terms of age equivalence, grade equivalence, or percentile rank. Commonly used tests include the Woodcock-Johnson Tests of Achievement–Third Edition, the Wechsler Individual Achievement Test–Revised, the Test of Early Reading Ability, and the Test of Early Mathematics Ability.

Test-Related Vocabulary

It is important for the teacher to understand some basic terms that the diagnostician may use during the assessment reporting phase of the IEP meeting. Teachers may be called upon to explain these terms to parents later and also when parents receive results from other types of testing that the district may require. (See Figure 4.1.)

THE IEP MEETING

The IEP committee consists of an administrator, the child's current teacher, an assessment person (if evaluations were conducted), the child's parents, and the child, if appropriate. These are the official members of the IEP committee. The parent may invite other individuals to the meeting, but these people are not part of the official committee. Parents who anticipate having problems with the school may bring an advocate to advise them. Organizations exist that provide advocates and advice to parents who want to ensure that their child's rights are not violated. If the parents bring a tape recorder into the meeting, the school will probably tape the

Figure 4.1 Basic Test Vocabulary

Achievement test	Test that measures knowledge or skills about specific subjects such as reading, math, or science.
Age equivalent	Score reported in the estimated age level that corresponds to a given score. Scores are reported in years and months. A score of 7–4 would mean that a child's performance was the same as the average score of children who were 7 years, 4 months old in the reference group used when the test was developed.
Criterion-referenced test	Performance is measured by mastery of specific skills or criteria, not against others who took the same test.
Grade equivalent	Score reported as an estimated grade level that corresponds to a given score. Scores are reported in grades and tenths of a grade. A score of 3.4 would mean that the child's score is the same as the average score of children in the fourth month of third grade in the reference group used when the test was developed.
Norm-referenced test	A test that compares one individual's performance to the performance of his or her peers.
Percentile rank	The percentage of children who scored at or below a given score. A 58th percentile rank means the child scored as well as or better than 58% of the children in his/her norm group who took the test.
Reliability	The extent to which the test is stable and consistent when given to the same individual on different occasions.
Standard error of measurement	The extent to which chance errors may cause the score to vary. The smaller this is, the more desirable the test is.
Standardized test	A test that has been normed with a specific group or population and then has the mean, standard deviation, standardized score, and percentile calculated.
Validity	The extent to which the test measures what it is intended to measure.

Adapted from Pierangelo & Giuliani (1998).

meeting as well. Minutes will be kept of the meeting, and the parents will receive copies of these minutes and all other forms completed during the meeting.

Some districts have developed forms preprinted with district and school information that basically contain a checklist or "fill-in-the-blank" form that reduces the amount of writing done in the actual meeting. These forms may be extensive, sometimes up to 12 or more pages covering specified issues such as accommodations, goals and objectives, behavior plan, and transition plan. During the IEP meeting, the results of the evaluation are presented and eligibility for special education is determined. Then appropriate placement of the student is discussed and determined. If the child qualifies for special education, the committee determines the least restrictive environment for the child and which related services will be provided. Often these meetings are scheduled during the teacher's conference period.

If this time is not convenient for the parents, the meeting can be scheduled at another time during the day, and the general education teacher's class may be covered by an aide during the meeting. The IEP meeting may also be scheduled before or after school hours to accommodate the parents.

Sometimes IEP meetings may extend for much longer than anticipated. If, after a reasonable time, the IEP committee is not able to reach agreement on placement, services, or any other issues, then the meeting may be adjourned and reconvened at another time. At the completion of the IEP meeting, the required members of the IEP committee sign the IEP report and check whether they agree or disagree with the decisions made. All efforts must be made for the committee to come to a consensus about the decisions that have been made. Once the placement decision has been made, the IEP will be developed.

 ## Working with Parents

Parents are one of the most constant presences in the child's life and should be considered part of the overall collaboration team as an education plan is developed for a child with special needs. Although parents are not expected to meet on a daily basis to discuss educational problems that have developed, no one knows the child as well as the parents, and parents can offer insight into their child's development. They can save the teacher time by reporting effective practices used at home and in previous classroom settings. Parents can be involved in the educational process by being taught ways to work with their child at home and by coordinating home and school efforts to work with the child in consistent ways. If teachers are trying to teach a child to tie his or her shoes in a specific manner, parents can be taught that same method and can work with the child on this task at home. If the school is teaching one way and the parents are teaching another, it may delay the child's learning. Parents should be treated as a valuable resource and should be involved in the educational process of their children.

 # THE IEP

The **Individualized Education Plan (IEP)** is a legal document that describes, among other things, the services, goals, and objectives for a specific child for the school year. The IEP committee develops appropriate educational goals for the child. Parents and teachers are involved in the process, and the IEP is reviewed annually and revised as necessary. Parents are equal partners, under the law, and school personnel must work with them in developing the IEP. In addition to the parents and the child's current teacher, someone from the school who is qualified in special education must be on the IEP team. If appropriate, the child may also be involved in the IEP meeting and the development of the IEP. Parents who are not satisfied with the IEP may refuse to sign the document and pursue due process options (IDEA, 1997).

The child's current level of educational performance, yearly goals, and the instructional objectives that must be met in order to achieve those goals are a part of the IEP. How the child will be evaluated and the objectives measured will also be included in the IEP. The committee determines the extent to which the child will participate in the general educational program, what special and related services will be needed, when these services will begin, and the amount of time per day or week that the child will receive these services. All of these points will be stated in this document (PL 94-142, 1992). For example, if the child is to receive speech therapy, the IEP states the amount of time and how often each week that the child will receive speech therapy. Speech therapy might be listed on the IEP as occurring twice a week for 30 minutes each session. If the child is 14 years old or older, the IEP must address transition services. At the annual review one year later, the team will go over the IEP and note whether objectives and goals were met from the previous year. Occasionally, a child's IEP will prove to be either too hard or too easy. In either case, the teacher can and should request an IEP meeting to make the necessary adjustments. Any changes to the IEP must be done in a formal meeting and not simply arbitrarily changed by the teacher.

An example of an annual goal on a student's IEP might read that the "child will improve in reading by six months by the end of the year." This means that the child, who may have been reading on a beginning second-grade level at the beginning of the year, will be reading on a grade level of 2.6 (second grade, sixth month) at the end of the year. This does not mean that the child is on grade level or even close to grade level; this child might be in the fourth grade and reading on a beginning second-grade level. It does mean that the child is expected to progress by six months in his or her reading ability. The IEP also states how this gain will be measured—for example, by standardized test or criterion-referenced tests. Short-term objectives to help this child achieve this goal might deal with phonics, sight words, context clues, or other reading strategies.

IEP objectives are written as behavioral objectives. This means that they contain three parts: the condition under which the desired behavior will occur, the behavior description that will occur, and the criterion that will be used for mastery of the objective. An example of a behavioral objective for sight words might be written as follows: "Given a random list of 20 second-grade sight words, George will read the words with 80 percent accuracy." The "random list of 20 second-grade sight words" is the *condition*. The *behavior description* is "will read," and the *criterion* is "with 80 percent accuracy." The behavior description must be an observable behavior.

Objectives written using the words *know* and *learn* are vague and not measurable. Objectives written with words such as *read, say, write, add, subtract, state, spell,* and *point* contain observable descriptions. The criterion may be stated as a percentage or as the number correct out of the total number of attempts, such as three out of four times. There is no set percentage for the objectives. It is common, however, to see objectives written that will allow a child with a disability to receive a passing grade if he or she attains 60 percent accuracy. This percentage may be adjusted up or down depending upon the skills, the subject matter, and the child's ability. A child who is not very verbal may have an IEP objective that states that he or she will participate in singing songs with the class 50 percent of the time. Though this percentage might seem low, for a child who is doing very little talking and participating it may be a very reasonable goal. (See Figure 4.2.)

NAEYC cautions teachers that care must be taken to guard against inappropriate practices in assessing children with special needs. Assessment needs to be more comprehensive and precise than "is usual with typically developing children. The assessment activities must describe (a) children's development in detail, (b) their needs in various environments, (c) the influences of the social and physical environment, (d) their preferences, (e) their usual styles of responding and patterns of engagement, and (f) factors than motivate their learning" (Bredekamp & Rosegrant, 1992, p. 107).

If assistive technology services are needed, they are to be specified in the IEP. These would include such items as specialized computers, magnifiers, special chairs, or any devices that are necessary for that child's education. Devices may be low tech, such as a paper clip used to allow a child to turn the page of a book, or high tech, such as a sound system that requires the teacher to wear a microphone connected to the child's hearing aid system. These devices help the child to overcome problems that occur in the everyday school environment.

In determining the accommodations that the child will need, the IEP team discusses discipline management as well as accommodations and adaptations for instruction. The IEP committee determines if the child can follow the discipline plan in place for the general education students. If not, then a behavior management plan will be developed specifically for the child. This plan might include in class time outs, frequent breaks, positive reinforcement of some type, a **behavior contract,** or other types of accommodations and consequences, either positive or negative. It may also include steps that need to be followed in dealing with escalating behavior.

Accommodations or adaptations that deal with instruction are numerous and include many different types, from materials to actions on the part of the teacher or child. Some examples of accommodations involving materials include the use of calculators, taped materials, large-print materials, computers, and manipulatives. Examples of accommodations that involve teacher actions include reading the test aloud to the child, reducing the reading level, reducing the length of assignments, allowing oral tests, or verbalizing steps in a task. Some accommodations involve actions on the part of the child. These include assigning a buddy and allowing the child to ask the buddy for help at specific times, allowing the child to move to another desk if he or she is distracted, or allowing the child to decide when to take a break and practice stress-reducing techniques if the child starts to lose self-control.

Beginning teachers sometimes make the mistake of listing many accommodations, thinking that they are providing extra help for the child. If the child needs an accommodation, then the accommodation needs to be used. If the child doesn't really need all the accommodations that the teacher has listed, however, then the teacher is doing that child a disservice by providing unnecessary accommodations that might lead the child to become dependent instead of independent. It is important for the teacher to realize that the parents or the child have the right to insist that any accommodations listed on the IEP be provided. The goal should be to have the child

FIGURE 4.2 Sample Page of an IEP

Texas ISD
*INDIVIDUAL EDUCATIONAL PROGRAM (IEP)[1,2]

[X] *INSTRUCTIONAL SERVICES   IEP DATE: 10/17/2001
[ ] *RELATED SERVICES   [ ] DRAFT _____
   SPECIFY: [ ] ACCEPTED BY ARD COMMITTEE

Future Accountant	3423232323	From: / / To: / /
NAME OF STUDENT	ID NUMBER	DURATION OF SERVICES

Wonder Elementary	05	English	ESL [ ] Bilingual [ ]
SCHOOL	GRADE	LANGUAGE OF DELIVERY	

PARENTAL NOTIFICATION STATEMENT
Written IEP Progress Reports will be provided to the student's parent(s) at least every ___ weeks to regularly inform parent(s) of their children's progress toward meeting annual IEP goals. These Progress Reports are provided on the same timely basis as are provided to parent(s) of non-disabled children, and are in addition to regular reporting for all children.

INSTRUCTIONAL AREA	LOCATION	IMPLEMENTORS
SMR/ECH	[ ] Special Education	[ ] Special Education
	[ ] General Education	[ ] General Education
	[ ] Other:	[ ] Parent(s)
		[ ] Student
		[ ] Other:

LEVELS OF PERFORMANCE

*GOAL   THE STUDENT WILL MASTER SPECIFIC 24 MONTH LEVEL COGNITIVE SKILLS ADDRESSING THESE IDENTIFIED EDUCATIONAL NEEDS: naming, picture recognition

*SHORT TERM OBJECTIVES Future will be able to	*LEVEL OF MASTERY CRITERIA	*METHOD OF EVALUATION	EVALUATION CODES						
			DATE	DATE	DATE	DATE	DATE	DATE	DATE
			CODE	CODE	CODE	CODE	CODE	CODE	REGRESSION
CS51-carry out one-step directions	daily for 2 weeks	2							
									YES / NO
CS53-repeat two digits	2 of 3 times x 3 weeks	2,7							
									YES / NO
CS55-match objects to picture	7 of 8 trials	2,7							
									YES / NO
CS60-use names of familiar objects	twice daily for 2 weeks	2							
									YES / NO

METHOD OF EVALUATION		EVALUATION CODES	
1 = Teacher Made Tests	5 = Conferences	* = Not Yet Addressed	N = Not Mastered
2 = Observations	6 = Work Samples	C = Continue	W = Work In Progress
3 = Weekly Tests	7 = Portfolios	D = Discontinued	Y = Mastered
4 = Unit Tests	8 = Other:	M = Mastered	

[1] Goals and objectives for English as a second language and/or primary language development shall be included for limited English proficient students as appropriate.

[2] Criteria and schedule must allow for determining student's eligibility for participating in extracurricular activities.

* Denotes required items

FIGURE 4.3 A Sample Modifications Checklist

Name of Student _____   Date of IEP meeting _____

The IEP committee has determined that the following modifications will be necessary.

__ Modifications not needed or not applicable   Regular Discipline Plan   __ YES   __ NO

__ Modifications needed are checked   __ YES __ NO   Behavior Management Plan   __ YES   __ NO

A. Assignments
- 1. __ Extra time for completing assign.
- 2. __ Reduce assignments
- 3. __ Opportunity to respond orally
- 4. __ Taped assignments
- 5. __ Other: _____

B. Instruction and Materials
- 1. __ Short instructions (½ steps)
- 2. __ Immediate feedback
- 3. __ Use of study carrel
- 4. __ Extra time for written assign.
- 5. __ Highlighted materials
- 6. __ Taped materials
- 7. __ Assignment notebooks
- 8. __ Extra time for oral response
- 9. __ Large print materials
- 10. __ Peer to read
- 11. __ Repeat directions
- 12. __ Verbalize steps
- 13. __ Study aids
- 14. __ Manipulatives
- 15. __ Other: _____

C. Testing Situations
- 1. __ Extra time
- 2. __ Testing by sp. ed. personnel
- 3. __ Reduce reading level
- 4. __ Reduce number of items
- 5. __ Adapt test format
- 6. __ Provide word bank
- 7. __ Use calculator
- 8. __ Manipulatives
- 9. __ Other: _____

D. Support Services
- 1. __ Peer Tutor
- 2. __ Resource
- 3. __ Co-Teacher
- 4. __ Support Center
- 5. __ Other: _____

E. Grading Criteria

F. Behavior Management
- 1. __ Proximity control
- 2. __ Clearly defined limits
- 3. __ Frequent breaks
- 4. __ Positive reinforcement
- 5. __ Frequent reminders of rules
- 6. __ In-class time out
- 7. __ Behavior contract
- 8. __ Call home
- 9. __ Other: _____
- 10. __ None needed

G. Health/Safety

H. Assistive Technology/ Equipment
- 1. __ Communication Device
- 2. __ Computer Access
- 3. __ Word Processor
- 4. __ Calculator
- 5. __ Decoder
- 6. __ Other: _____
- 7. __ None needed

function in the classroom as close as possible to the general education student and to have as few accommodations as necessary for achieving success. (See Figure 4.3.)

Grading for children with disabilities may also be modified in several ways. The child who goes to the resource room may have his or her grade from this class averaged in with the grade from the general education teacher. Or the child may be graded only on mastery of the objectives on the IEP. Because children with special needs generally need more time on assignments and tests, they can be graded on their work for accuracy. The teacher would take the number of correct answers, divide by the number of problems attempted, and use the result as the grade on the assignment. On a writing assignment, the grade might be divided into sections with one grade assigned for creativity and content and another grade assigned for mechanics such as spelling and punctuation.

⭐ PLACEMENT OPTIONS FOR CHILDREN WITH DISABILITIES

Placement options for children with disabilities range from least restrictive, the inclusion classroom, to most restrictive, a separate facility or even homebound. Placement of children with disabilities is decided on an individual basis.

The Inclusion Classroom

The position of the Division for Early Childhood of the Council for Exceptional Children (and adopted by the National Association for the Education of Young Children) on inclusion is that "inclusion, as a value, supports the right of all children, regardless of their diverse abilities, to participate actively in natural settings within their communities. A natural setting is one in which the child would spend time had he or she not had a disability. Such settings include, but are not limited to, home and family, play groups, child care, nursery schools, Head Start programs, kindergartens, and neighborhood school classrooms" (1993).

The terms *inclusion* and *mainstreaming* have been used interchangeably, but they do not mean the same thing. The inclusion philosophy sees the child as receiving the accommodations and support needed to learn in the general education classroom. The mainstreaming philosophy, on the other hand, sees children with disabilities as being educated in a separate classroom, with integration to the maximum extent possible with general education students (Smith, Polloway, Patton, & Dowdy, 2001). Inclusion in the general education classroom allows the child, as a member of the community, to be taught by the same talented teachers as the child without a disability and to develop social relationships with these children (Schattman & Benay, 1992). The child with the disability and the general education teacher receive support in the form of special education personnel, assistive technology, and modifications and accommodations made in the curriculum and the physical environment. By law, the majority of children with special needs will be educated in the general education classroom.

No Child Left Behind and the IEP

Many questions have been raised with regard to the impact of the No Child Left Behind Act and special education. Members of professional organizations are contacting their respective organizations in an attempt to obtain clarification of various issues. One area of concern expressed by state directors of special education is the parent's right to remove a child from a failing school and place that child in another school. If the child has an IEP that was developed at the first school, does the IEP team have to meet and sanction the change in placement and does the new school have to provide all the services that the IEP states? Some schools may not have the same placement options, for example, and if the school is required to provide the placement option listed in the IEP, this could require a school to expend significant amounts of money and may exacerbate the shortage of special education teachers, if schools are required to set up duplicating programs (National Association of State Directors of Special Education, 2002).

How Their Schools Handle Inclusion

"This is the most difficult year I have had in 29 years. I have three very disruptive behavior problems, three ADD children, two other children who probably fall into that category, two very low LD children, two ED children, and two at-risk children. I have 23 total children in my classroom." —*a second-grade teacher*

(Fortunately, most principals do not overburden a teacher with children with special needs and will remove some children from the class should this happen. The wise principal knows that this situation is not good for the teacher or the children.)

"Our special education teachers prepare teachers and work with them when special needs children are in our classroom." —*a third-grade teacher*

"Sometimes I do not feel I modify the assignments enough for students with special needs." —*a second-grade teacher*

(A new teacher should feel free to ask more experienced teachers or the special education teacher for assistance.)

Instructional Support Center/Content Mastery Room/Achievement Center/Tutorial Classroom

Districts may call these classrooms by several different names, but their purpose is to offer an alternative to the resource classroom that is less restrictive while still meeting the needs of the children. These classrooms receive children who need help with an individual lesson or assignment or who need accommodation or modification for an assignment or a test, such as additional time or having parts read aloud to them. With this type of program, the child is often the one who decides when to go to the **Content Mastery** room for help.

All general education teachers give the Content Mastery (CM) teacher a copy of their lesson plans each week. This allows the CM teacher to know what the students are working on in each classroom and thus to provide more efficient help when the child arrives. Some schools are using local money to help support the Content Mastery program, thereby opening up these classrooms and special assistance for any child in the school, whether the child is in special education or general education. Schools that use only federal IDEA funds for this program are required to restrict it to the special education children.

The Resource Classroom

Students with disabilities may receive instruction in certain subjects in the resource classroom. For instance, a child with a learning disability who is experiencing difficulty in math may go to the resource room for math instruction during the time that the general education students are having math in their classroom. Time spent in the resource room may vary, depending on the amount specified by the IEP. A special education teacher staffs the resource room, and students come in and out during the day for different subjects. This model of delivery of special education services is commonly found in schools.

The Self-Contained Classroom

The self-contained special education classroom serves children with disabilities in isolation from the general education children. These children receive their instruction in all the core subjects in this classroom. Sometimes but not always, these students will be mainstreamed with the general education children for lunch, physical education, art, and music, and there may be little chance for these students to interact with general education students during the school day.

Other Placements

Other placement decisions for children with disabilities may be such that a child is placed in a separate school or facility that contains other special education classrooms. Sometimes children will be bused to another campus so that they can attend school in a cluster program designed just for children with a certain disability.

These classrooms often contain children with moderate to severe problems such as mental retardation, emotional and/or behavioral disorders, autism, or multiple disabilities.

For some children, even placement at another campus may not be appropriate. If a placement in a cluster program or special school is not deemed appropriate, then the child may be placed in a residential facility or in a hospital or may receive homebound instruction. Obviously, these are the most restrictive and least desirable environments, and they should be used only as a last resort.

☆ FEDERAL CATEGORIES OF DISABILITIES AND SOME COMMON CLASSROOM ACCOMMODATIONS AND MODIFICATIONS

In the following sections, several accommodations will be discussed for each type of disability identified by IDEA. Accommodations suggested for one type of disability might be used successfully with several other types of disabilities, and there will be much overlapping. The key to successful modification is to try any and all accommodations that seem appropriate, use the ones that work for each child, and discard the rest.

Modifying the amount and/or difficulty of a child's work is a common adjustment. Teachers, parents, even other children may say that it is not "fair" to the other children when a teacher modifies the amount or the difficulty of a child's work. An appropriate response would be to ask if it is fair that some children get to wear glasses in class when others do not, or is it fair that some children get to use hearing aids while others do not? Coursework accommodations fall into the same category. They are necessary for the children who need them to be successful in school, but the average general education child does not need them. Without accommodations in classwork, assignments, or the environment, the child with special needs will be unable to remain in the general education classroom and receive an appropriate, individualized education.

Whether a child has a disability or not, a good teacher will carefully consider all aspects of the classroom environment and will plan and teach to maximize the learning of all the children. The teacher knows which children have problems with attention and places their desks in an area as free from distractions as possible. The teacher knows that all children learn best when they receive frequent feedback and strives to provide this feedback for all the children. The teacher also knows that children will be more successful when they feel that they are a true and valued part of the classroom.

When the teacher considers the placement of individual children's seats, there is no one set rule that says that children with attention deficit hyperactivity disorder must be placed close to the teacher's desk or to the front of the room. Placement of the child's seat will vary greatly depending upon the child's disability and attentional needs. Many different places may need to be tried before the best placement for a child is found.

Frequent feedback is extremely important, not only for children with disabilities, but for all children. The teacher should be on his or her feet constantly, monitoring and checking for understanding of skills and concepts and reteaching as needed. How sad that teachers have been known to assign 30 math problems and then sit at their desks and do something else while the students work the problems. Two days later, when the teacher finally grades the papers, she discovers that Cindy worked most of the problems incorrectly. Not only did Cindy practice solving problems incorrectly, but it has been several days before the teacher realized this fact and tried to reteach the skill to her. Cindy may have also compounded the problem by practicing the assigned homework incorrectly, too. How much better for Cindy if the teacher had seen on that first day that Cindy did not understand and retaught her that first day!

Beginning teachers, especially, need to keep in mind that not all assignments have to be done independently by the children and graded. The class could work the first three problems. Then the answers could be self-checked as volunteers put the problems on the board. The teacher, of course, is moving around the classroom during this time and noting which children need extra assistance. The teacher can then pull these children into a flexible group and reteach the skill as the others complete the assignment.

A very simple way not only to provide additional assistance to children but also to give them a feeling of belonging is to assign buddies. Assigning a buddy to children with special needs is a simple, easy accommodation that can be most helpful. The teacher might want to assign a buddy to all the children or just let children ask for help from a child sitting beside them. If a buddy is assigned to a child with special needs, this buddy should be asked if he or she wants to help. There always seem to be several children in every classroom who enjoy being helpers. Children should never be forced or made to feel guilty because they do not want to be a helping buddy. Some children prefer not to be a buddy, not because they dislike children with special needs, but because they prefer to work more independently and alone. They would respond in the same manner if they were asked to buddy with a child without a disability. Buddies should be changed periodically or be given the opportunity to change. Even children who have special needs themselves can participate in the buddy program by helping another child, either in the same class or in a lower grade level.

The teacher wants to make all the children feel important and a valued part of the classroom family. One way to do this is through classroom jobs. Some typical classroom jobs are Line Leader and Messenger; other types of jobs suitable for the classroom are Computer Lab Attendant (shut down the computer and printer each day); Attendance Clerk (remind the teacher to mark the attendance at the appropriate time and take the attendance to the office); Door Closer/Opener; floor monitor (inspects floor for trash); Pet Attendant (feeds and cleans the cage of the classroom pet), Monitors for each center (inspect and make sure that the centers are straight at the end of the day); Classroom Librarian (check out books to individual children); and Teacher's Helper (assist the teacher in passing out materials). A teacher can privately brainstorm all the possible jobs in the classroom and develop a list before the start of school. Jobs may be assigned to children, or children may fill out an "application" and "apply" for a specific job. Jobs should be rotated periodically because not every child, unless the class is small, will have a job. A simple job or two should be kept aside for any new children assigned to the classroom. By giving a new child a job, the teacher can help that child adjust and feel a part of the class.

Children with disabilities should be included in classroom jobs, too. Some accommodations may be needed for specific jobs and, obviously, some jobs will be difficult for a child with certain disabilities to do independently. A child who is unable to use his or her hands will not be able to feed and clean the cage of the classroom pet without another child as a partner. A simple modification made for a child who uses a wheelchair will allow that child to be in charge of the classroom lights. If the light switch is out of reach for the child, the teacher can use a low-tech device such as a yardstick, ruler, or cardboard and tape it to the switch, thereby allowing the child to have this job. For an example of a classroom jobs chart, see Chapter 7.

Learning Disabilities

Of students with disabilities, children with learning disabilities (LD) account for 51.2 percent of the population between the ages of 6 and 21, with four boys identified to every girl (U.S. Department of Education, 1998b). This means that most general education teachers can expect to have children with learning disabilities in their classrooms. Children with learning disabilities have normal or above-average intelligence but may be behind in one or more academic areas. These children might have a cooperating special education teacher visit the classroom to assist the teacher and the students; they might go to the Content Mastery classroom as help is needed; or they might go to the resource classroom for certain academic subjects at specific times during the day.

Two of the most common accommodations made for children with learning disabilities are also the easiest to implement. It may take a child with a learning disability two to three times longer to do the same amount of work as a child without a disability. Knowing this, the teacher can provide this extra time. The other accommodation is related to work amount. Teachers may assign fewer problems or questions but allow the same amount of time as the general education child has. In math, for example, instead of assigning 20 problems, the teacher can assign 10 problems that have been carefully selected to include all problem types. If a grade must be given, it is figured as a percentage of the number correct out of the 10 problems. A child who has problems with math might be assigned the easier problems in the section first. Then the teacher will closely monitor the child's work before he or she attempts the harder problems. Again, the teacher must take the time to decide which problems should be done and provide constant feedback to the child.

The teacher also needs to make these accommodations in a way that does not embarrass the child. The problems the child is to do could be circled or listed on a card and placed discreetly on the child's desk. It would be highly inappropriate for the teacher to yell across the classroom, "Oh, Johnny, you just do problems 1 to 10. Those are the easiest."

The general education teacher needs to be aware that, in addition to extra time, these children may need extra assistance. A child who has trouble reading will probably also experience problems in math word problems, science, social studies, and any other subject in which a significant amount of reading is required. A simple accommodation that is useful for the entire class is to allow all the children who come across a word or words not known, not just the child with special needs, to ask a neighbor. This practice also helps keep the special education child from being singled out. Obviously, if the reading disability is severe, it would not be appropriate or desirable to have children ask each other to read every other word. In this case, the teacher might need to tape-record the lesson for the child.

Listening and following directions seem to be constant problems for children with learning disabilities. The teacher should give instructions in brief, clear, short sequences and check frequently for understanding. It also helps to provide a written copy of the instructions, either on the board for all the students to reference, or placed on a child's desk for that child to reference. Asking a child with a learning disability to repeat the instructions lets the teacher know if the instructions were understood. The teacher may even need to present this child with directions a few steps at a time. "Johnny, get your science book out." "Now, turn to page 30." Once this is accomplished the teacher can then tell Johnny what the assignment is.

Modifications that are less easy for the teacher to implement include highlighting or tape-recording the textbooks and retyping tests to allow more space between items, less on a page and fewer choices if it is multiple choice or matching. Even among modifications that are more difficult for the teacher, some will be easier than others. Tape-recording the textbook will be much easier and faster than highlighting the book because of the need to make a careful choice about what to highlight: Once highlighted, the book cannot be unhighlighted.

The use of cooperative grouping, interest grouping, and flexible grouping based on a specific need or skill can be very beneficial for all children. Cooperative groups are formed around a shared goal. The students are organized so that everyone in the group has a job. Jobs vary in difficulty. Two jobs in cooperative groups that could be done by almost any child in the class are the job of assembling or collecting materials and the job of encouraging the group. Obviously, the student who must record the progress of the group or the information gathered has a much harder task and will need to have the skills necessary to accomplish this job. The cooperative grouping method works well in situations where classroom experiments are to be done by small groups. Interest grouping occurs when the child places himself or herself in a group based on interest in a topic that will be studied by the group. Even if the material seems too advanced for a given child, interest in the topic will be a powerful motivator. Flexible groups will be assembled as the teacher recognizes children's needs. Only those children who are having problems with a specific skill, such as capitalization, will be assembled together for the reteaching of the skill.

Mental Retardation

Placement of children with mental retardation will vary from district to district. Again, the least restrictive environment will be the general education classroom, and districts with an inclusion philosophy will place most of these students there, with the proper support. However, some districts tend to place only children with mild mental retardation in the general education classroom, and children with moderate and severe mental retardation are placed in self-contained classrooms, sometimes segregated to one campus within the school district. Children with mild mental retardation usually have an IQ range of 55–70. Children with moderate mental retardation usually have an IQ range of 40–55, and children with severe mental retardation usually have IQs below 40 (Smith et al., 2001).

Adaptive behavior is taken into account in placing children with mental retardation. The term *adaptive behavior* refers to how well children fit into society, how well they are able to function independently and function in a social world. A deficit in adaptive behavior might be explained better by the following example. You are sitting in a movie theater, eating popcorn and watching the movie, when suddenly the stranger sitting next to you reaches over and grabs a handful of popcorn from your container. This is socially unacceptable behavior. Teachers who have children with mental retardation in their classrooms also need to work on adaptive behavior skills that help these children fit into society in a less conspicuous manner.

Accommodations for children with mental retardation really begin with a series of questions. The answers to these questions determine the direction and changes necessary for the accommodations. The first question should be: Can this student do the same work as the general education student? If the answer is "yes," then accommodations may take the form of extended time or fewer items required. In the art classroom, the child with mild to moderate mental retardation could be expected to participate in most of what is done in class. For academic areas, a second question should be asked: Can this child do the same work, but with modifications and/or support? Participation in a social studies or science lesson might involve the assistance of a peer tutor or instructional aide for the child to be successful.

If the answer to this question is "No, the child is not able to do the same work" (because the child does not have the cognitive ability to do the task), then the next question is asked: Can this child do the same type of skill, but at a lower or easier level? A child with mental retardation in the mild to moderate range is in the regular third-grade classroom for math. The third graders are practicing regrouping in addition. Although the child is unable to add numbers at this level, he or she is able to practice adding sums to 10. This is the same type of skill—addition—but at an easier level. A child with moderate to severe mental retardation is in the second grade, and it is time for reading. Obviously, the child will not be able to read on a second-grade level, but this same child can still practice skills that have meaning on a level appropriate to him or her. The child can learn to recognize words that are personally important in everyday life, such as *boys, girls,* and *exit.* For this child, reading means being able to read these words.

If the child is unable to do any activity related to what is being studied in the inclusion classroom, then the question must be asked: What skills does this child need that will help him or her to lead a more independent life? These skills, known as *life skills,* include such tasks as being able to dress oneself, button and zip clothing, or fix a sandwich. Alternatively, are there some skills on the IEP that the child can work on during the instructional period? For example, when the other children are answering questions about a reading assignment, the child with mental retardation can be answering questions as part of the language goals from the IEP. When the general education teacher views the education of the child with mental retardation in this manner, it becomes easy to see how to make the necessary modifications.

Of course, hands-on learning, the use of manipulatives, and the assistance of other children in the class will go a long way in helping these children function successfully in the classroom. The teacher should always keep in mind that what is taught should be relevant to the child's life, both now and for the future. Too often in the past, these children have practiced the same skills, such as putting pegs into a pegboard, year after year after year. Rather than rote repetition of such skills, their school time should be spent on learning skills that will allow them to be as independent and self-sufficient as possible. These might include learning to make a sandwich, button a shirt, or use the washing machine.

Autism

Autism is a pervasive developmental disability that significantly affects verbal and nonverbal communications, social interactions, and educational performance (Spinelli, 2002). There are several characteristics of children with *autism* that make it hard for them to function in an inclusion classroom. These children have difficulty relating to others, often avoid eye contact, may display repetitive behaviors such as rocking or hand flapping, may have impaired language, and generally do not handle change in the environment or daily schedule well.

The most important accommodation for these children is to keep the environment as consistent as possible. This means the actual setup of the room remains constant and the daily schedule is followed as closely as possible. Routines are important and provide the child with a sense of security. Even with a constant schedule, children with autism may have a difficult time changing activities and this may bring on a tantrum. Schmit, Alper, Raschke, and Ryndak (2000) found that children with autism responded somewhat more successfully to changes in activities when they were cued using photographic images along with verbal cues that one activity is ending and another is about to begin. Other ways to allow the children to communicate involve Picture Exchange (Ryan, 1990), in which a child will exchange a picture of what he or she wants for the actual object. Communication boards showing pictures that express meaning can also be made. When the child points to the picture of a toilet, he or she is indicating a need to use the restroom. Likewise, a

This child is using a communication board to communicate his needs.

picture of a glass means that the child wants a drink. A weighted vest may help children who fidget to calm down (Grandin, 1999). Many children with autism are visual thinkers. Teachers can take advantage of this trait by using pictures of nouns and actions to teach whole words associated with those pictures. Incorporating tactile experiences is also beneficial (Grandin, 1999).

Communication Disorders

The U.S. Department of Education reports that approximately 2 percent of school-age children have a speech or language disorder (1999b). A *speech disorder* may involve problems with articulation, fluency, or voice. A *language disorder* may involve problems with comprehension and/or spoken or written language (Smith et al., 2001). Accommodations for these students involve an increase in teacher behavior. The teacher should allow students to finish their own sentences and not try to guess what they are saying. The teacher should work with the speech therapist and reinforce what the child is learning in speech therapy in the classroom. Centers in the classroom provide a natural setting for these children to practice language skills, learn new vocabulary, and interact with children who provide good models. Cooperative group work also allows them exposure to children without communication problems and is an authentic way to encourage children with a problem to talk and communicate. The use of music, songs, poems, and "big books" or repetitive books are also motivating ways for children to practice speaking the language.

Visual Impairments

A child with a *visual impairment* may have sight that ranges from complete blindness to low vision. Obviously, a child who is completely blind will need more modifications and accommodations than a child who has low vision. Children with low vision need to sit close to the board or overhead. They may require large-print books, a page magnifier, or materials prepared on the computer using a large-size font. Paper for writing may need to have wider, darker lines to aid the child. Computers make these types of modifications simple to do. Care should be taken to shield the chalkboard from any glare from the windows. Children who are blind may use a Braillewriter or specialized computer. Taped books and lessons may also be needed.

    Arrangement of the classroom is an important accommodation for children with a vision impairment. For the safety of this child, the other children need to be taught to keep the floor clear of obstacles. Materials should remain in the same place for the duration of the school year. This modification will allow the child to be as independent as possible. Be sure to have people identify themselves as they approach a child with a visual impairment as well as tell the child when they are leaving and walking away. It can be very embarrassing to not realize that a person has left and still be talking with no one there. The use of hands-on activities and instruction as well as cooperative grouping are both good strategies to employ with these children.

Hearing Impairment

Children may have *hearing impairments* that range from mild to severe. These children often have speech and language problems because of the hearing impairment. They may wear hearing aids. Sometimes the teacher will wear an FM device that transmits speech directly to the child's ear or hearing aid. Sign language may be taught to assist the child with communication. Accommodations might include a buddy to assist the child by helping him or her find the correct page in the book and follow other directions given by the teacher or an interpreter who stays with the child and signs what is going on in the classroom. The teacher needs to face the child at all times when talking, which allows the child to have an unobstructed path for the teacher's voice and also places the teacher's mouth in view if the child is also relying on lip reading. When the teacher writes on the blackboard, then, she must turn around before talking about what she has just written on the chalkboard. The teacher and other children should talk in a normal manner, not exaggerate their words. The teacher should wear neutral-colored clothing to minimize eye distraction in children who read lips; bright clothing tends to draw the eye and make it harder for the child to read the teacher's lips.

Deaf-Blindness

Deaf-blindness in a child is defined by IDEA (1997) as hearing and vision impairments that have so severely affected the child's communication skills and learning needs that he or she cannot be educated without supplementary assistance in a special education class for children who are hearing impaired, vision impaired, or possess multiple disabilities. These children must be taught at a very basic level using the sense of touch and enhancing any residual vision or hearing through the use of hearing aids or other assistive technology.

Orthopedic Disabilities

Orthopedic disabilities are physical disabilities that affect the child's educational performance (Smith et al., 2001). A wide range of diseases and disorders can put a child in this category. Some of these include cerebral palsy, spina bifida, amputations, and muscular dystrophy. If there is severe small-motor impairment, the child may be fitted with a head stick, a stick that is attached to a band and worn around the head. The child uses this stick to operate a computer or other technological devices or even to operate a motorized wheelchair. Mouth sticks serve the same purpose. Spoons and other implements may attach to the wrist or hand to allow a child who is unable to grip with the hand to manipulate the spoon through wrist or arm action.

New computer technology will allow a child who is unable to speak the ability to communicate through a voice synthesizer. Messages can be composed by using an eye scan. The child will gaze at an alphabet board and spell words that the computer will then speak. Teachers need to remember that the fact that a child cannot speak does not mean that the child will not be able to learn to read. As technology advances

This child is using a high-tech laser communication board.

along these lines, it becomes imperative that teachers teach children who are unable to speak to read and to spell so that they will be able to use the new technology.

Other modifications will have to be made in the classroom. If the child uses a wheelchair, the room must be arranged with wide aisles and a desk or table that allows the wheelchair to slide underneath so that the student may have an appropriate writing and working surface. Even with the wide aisles, it will still be necessary for the other children to keep items picked up and out of the way of the walker or wheelchair. Materials should be placed at a reachable level when there is a child using a wheelchair in the classroom. During writing, a child might use the computer and a head stick to write his or her story. A buddy may get the child's books out of the desk and open them to the correct page. Tests may be done orally, if the child is able to speak. The child may use an alphabet board to spell out his or her needs, or a communication board, as discussed in the autism section, may be necessary.

Other Health Impairments

To be classified as *other health impaired* (OHI), students must have chronic or acute health problems that limit their strength, vitality, or alertness (Smith & Smith, 2000). Some conditions that might cause these types of problems are AIDS, asthma, diabetes, and cancer. Medications taken for these illnesses can cause problems with attention and alertness. Close contact needs to be maintained among school officials, teachers, parents, and medical personnel. The child's schedule may need to be arranged around the periods when he or she is most alert, and frequent rest periods may be necessary.

In 1991, the Department of Education issued a clarification about children with attention deficit hyperactivity disorder. Part B of the regulations now list children with ADHD as eligible under the conditions of OHI. Not all children who are ADHD will be eligible to receive special education, but each child will be evaluated as to eligibility. The child must qualify under Section 300.7 and must need special services because of that disability. Section 300.7 defines an OHI impairment as one in which a child displays limited strength, vitality, or alertness (Office of Special Education Programs, 1999). ADHD remains an area of controversy while being the fastest-growing area of eligibility in this decade.

Emotional Disturbance

To be eligible under the diagnostic category of *emotional disturbance,* a child must manifest inappropriate behaviors to a marked degree over a long period of time, adversely affecting educational performance (Culatta & Tompkins, 1999). A child who suddenly begins displaying violent, aggressive aberrant behavior could not immediately be classified as having an emotional disturbance because the behavior has not existed over a long period of time. The child has obvious issues that need to be addressed, but the general education teacher should not seek to have this child tested for an emotional disturbance because the child will not qualify.

The behaviorist theory predominates in classrooms for children with emotional disturbances. Teachers in these classrooms often employ a *token economy* in which the children are rewarded with tokens or some objects that can be collected and used to "buy" or be exchanged for something. The tokens might be used to purchase extra computer game time or items from a classroom store. Teachers will often use positive reinforcement to increase the desirable behaviors. When a child stays seated and raises his or her hand, for example, the teacher reinforces this behavior with praise, a sticker, or possibly a piece of candy. Receiving this reward encourages the child to repeat the behavior. *Levels systems* are often used for children with emotional disturbances. A levels system associates school privileges with appropriate behavior, and the child earns the right to school privileges at specific levels in the token economy. These systems have been criticized for requiring the child to earn the right to be included in general education.

The child with an emotional disturbance may sign a contract with the teacher. (See Figure 4.4.) A contract states what the child is expected to do as well as both the positive consequences that will occur when the child follows the contract and the negative consequences that will occur when the child fails to live up to the terms of the contract. It is signed by both the child and the teacher and kept close at hand in order to be reviewed by the child and teacher as needed.

The academic accommodations that have been suggested for the child with a learning disability are also appropriate for some children with an emotional disturbance. In addition to the academic side of the situation, the behavioral side must

FIGURE 4.4 A Sample Contract Used in Public Schools

_____ will do the following when in Mr.
(Student's name)
Quinn's classroom.

1. Stay in my seat when working on class assignments.
2. Raise my hand and wait for Mr. Quinn to call on me.
3. Complete my work without complaining.

Mr. Quinn will let me select one of the following activities at the end of the day
when I have followed this contract.

1. Five extra minutes on the computer.
2. Good note home to parent.
3. Special sticker.

Consequences for not following this contract will be:

1. Loss of 5, 10, or 15 minutes of recess (1st, 2nd, 3rd offenses).
2. I will call my parents (4th offense).
3. I will spend the next day in the Time Out Room (5th offense).

_____   _____
Student's signature   Teacher's signature

Date _____

also be addressed. The child is likely to have a behavior plan that has been developed by the IEP committee. This plan probably includes positive rewards for exhibiting the correct school behavior and consequences for inappropriate behaviors. It may require the teacher to mark a folder every 15 to 30 minutes to indicate if the child is attending and working as he or she should or to indicate if there is a problem. Collecting information such as this allows the teacher to determine problem times of the day and to track how well a tried intervention is working.

If the child is in an inclusive classroom, the special education teacher may help the general education teacher pinpoint possible factors that are contributing to the inappropriate behavior and make suggestions of ways to change the environment to keep these conditions from occurring. For instance, the special education teacher might observe that Ricky begins displaying signs of frustration before he erupts in a tantrum. Helping the general education teacher to "read" the signs of this beginning frustration and intervening with assistance may help Ricky to control the aggression he displays when frustrated. Close collaboration between the special education teacher and the general education teacher is needed when the child with an emotional disturbance is being initiated in the general education classroom.

When the child is successful in the general education classroom, then his or her time in the classroom is gradually increased. Close tabs are kept on the child, who may be returned to the special education classroom for the remainder of the day if a problem develops. The child will come back to the general education class the next day. The general education classroom can be very rewarding for a child who has been in a self-contained special education environment. Children in these special classrooms often sit in a study carrel, a desk with three high sides, and work independently or one-on-one with the teacher the entire day. The environment is carefully controlled and behaviors are carefully monitored and recorded.

An effort should be made to identify areas and topics of interest to the child who has an emotional disturbance. Then the teacher can use these interests in planning lessons in the classroom. A child who is interested and involved shows fewer behavior problems.

Traumatic Brain Injury

Traumatic brain injury is acquired brain damage that has occurred because of an external physical force. The injury results in total or partial functional disability and thereby affects the educational performance of the student (Culatta & Tompkins, 1999). How the disability manifests itself depends upon the nature of the injury and the area of the brain that received the damage. There may be problems with speech, memory, behavior, academics, motor skills, vision or hearing, or some other problem or combination of problems.

Because this type of injury shows no set, predictable impairment, the accommodations that the teacher uses will be related to how the impairment is manifested. If the child has vision problems, then the accommodations should be similar to those used with vision impairments. With brain damage several areas of the brain may be affected, and this might mean trying accommodations and modifications specific to several disabilities. The child may have problems with emotional control, attention, and speech. Because of the varied manifestations of traumatic brain injury, all modifications used with children should be evaluated for effectiveness and all types of modifications should be tried.

Multiple Disabilities

Multiple disabilities are defined as the combination of impairments that cause such severe educational problems that the child cannot be accommodated in a special education setting for only one of the impairments. These disabilities include mental retardation and blindness or mental retardation and physical disabilities, but not deaf-blindness (IDEA, 1997).

Because of the cumulative effects of several disabilities, these children need highly individualized supports in several major life areas. Goals are generally directed toward maximizing the child's independence in daily living. Regardless of the severity of the disabilities, these children have been successfully included in general education environments when families and schools are committed to inclusive education.

State by State

Assessment

Many states, such as **New York,** "permit the following testing accommodations on the State's elementary assessments in English language arts and mathematics":

1. Oral reading or signing of reading passages (not listening selections), multiple choice questions, and/or extended response items.
2. Use of a calculator or abacus on mathematics tests measuring calculation skills such as addition, subtraction, multiplication, or division.
3. Use of a spell/grammar checking device on tests measuring spelling and/or grammar.
4. Deletion of spelling, paragraphing and/or punctuation requirements on tests assessing spelling and/or grammar. (New York State Department of Education, 2002)

☆ CHILDREN WITH OTHER SPECIAL NEEDS

Not all children who need extra assistance fall into one of the categories recognized by the federal government. These children also need to be recognized by the teacher as needing special assistance.

Attention Deficit Hyperactivity Disorder

The cause of *Attention Deficit Hyperactivity Disorder* (ADHD) has been the subject of much debate and experimental treatment over the years. Causes have been attributed to everything from fathers who do not pay enough attention to their children and teachers who do not pay enough attention to their students to an invented disease that doesn't exist (Breggin & Breggin, 1995). Teachers will hear comments from parents that teachers are just trying to dope up kids so that they will behave in class and that large numbers of children are being placed on medication unnecessarily. The argument may soon be settled as science uses technology to investigate this condition. More children labeled as ADHD are being studied using new brain-scanning technology. Previously, brain scans required the use of radioactive isotopes, and subjecting the brains of children to this type of evaluation was not suggested. Scanning techniques no longer require the use of radioactive isotopes and are considered very safe. These scans are showing differences between the brains of children with ADHD and those without (Rogers, 1998).

Attention deficit hyperactivity disorder is not listed as a separate category of disability under the law that would allow a child to receive special education. However, the U.S. Department of Education (1999) indicates that these students can be served under the existing categories. It is not uncommon for this disorder to be found in conjunction with learning disabilities or emotional disturbance.

ADHD may also fall in the category of other health impairment (OHI) since the educational performance of children with this disorder can be negatively affected.

The diagnosis for ADD or ADHD is made using the criteria from the *Diagnostic and Statistical Manual of Mental Disorders–Fourth Edition* (1993). Six or more symptoms must be present to a significant degree (inattention or hyperactivity impulsivity), persist for at least six months, with some symptoms occurring before age 7. The child experiences these problems in two or more settings, and the problems cause significant impairment in social, academic, or occupational functioning. Criteria under the inattention category include descriptors such as carelessness in work, problems with sustained attention, difficulty in listening, failure to complete assignments, distractibility, poor task completion, and disorganization. Criteria under the hyperactivity-impulsivity category include descriptors such as fidgets and squirms, gets up out of seat, runs about, difficulty playing quietly, always on the go, talks excessively, blurts out answers, has difficulty waiting, and often interrupts (DSM–IV, 1993).

Teachers may be asked to rate a child's behavior in the classroom using a rating scale. The rating scale will list a behavior, such as fidgets, and the teacher will mark whether this behavior occurs on a scale from very often to not at all. Behaviors may include such characteristics as hums constantly, shy, excitable, fearful, and fearless. Some scales will include opposites. Obviously, a child who scores a "very often" on fearful will not score very often on fearless. Some items such as these are used to check the accuracy of the person doing the scoring, so the teacher should carefully read and reflect on each item asked. This scale may be used in making the initial diagnosis of ADHD. If medication is tried, the teacher may be asked to complete the rating scale again. This will help to show the effect, if any, of the medication.

Medications for ADHD that are prescribed most often are stimulants, of which Ritalin is the best known. Sometimes antidepressant medications are used instead of a stimulant. Research has shown that medication is effective in 70–80 percent of the children (Spencer, Biederman, Wilens, Harding, O'Donnell, & Griffin, 1996). If medication is prescribed, the teacher should be sensitive to the child's feelings and refrain from making statements such as, "Did you take your medicine this morning? It sure doesn't seem like it!" and "Did you remember to stop by the nurse and get your medicine? You know you can't do your work without it."

Current brain studies using MRI scans are showing a physiological difference in the functioning of the brains of people diagnosed as ADHD. Brain scans are allowing scientists to view the brains of children with ADHD and without ADHD. Sixteen boys aged 8 to 13 years received MRIs (magnetic resonance imaging) scans before and after receiving Ritalin medication. Ten of these boys had ADHD. The scans showed, interestingly enough, increased blood flow to the areas of the brain that help regulate attention in the boys who had ADHD and less blood flow to the brains of boys without ADHD after taking Ritalin (Rogers, 1998). The increase of blood flow confirmed the reason for the increased attention in the boys with ADHD. Interestingly, Ritalin had the opposite effect on the boys who did not have ADHD. It is possible that MRI scans may be one day used in the diagnosis of ADHD.

Despite headlines in newspapers reporting that huge numbers of children are being "drugged" in an attempt to control their behavior in school, research shows that in 1998 only 12.5 percent of children who met the criteria for ADHD were being treated with stimulants. The children were more likely to receive school-based interventions and counseling than medication (Jensen, Kettle, Roper, Sloan, Dulcan, Hoven, Bird, Bauermeister, & Payne, 1999). Research has also shown that the use of medication does not translate into an increased risk that children will become drug abusers and does not significantly impact growth (Pancheri & Prater, 1999). A study by Greene, Biederman, Faraone, Wilens, Mick, & Blier (1999) found that the sole predictor of drug and alcohol abuse was social impairment of children, not whether they were on medication for ADHD. Headlines stating that larger numbers of children than ever are taking medication for ADHD are true because our school population has increased in numbers over the years, but the percentage of children now taking medication has decreased (Jensen et al., 1999).

Because some schools have required that children with ADHD take medication before they are allowed to attend school or return to school after a suspension, state legislatures are passing legislation to bar schools from recommending or requiring parents to place their child on medication. Connecticut prohibits school personnel from even discussing drug treatments with parents (Zernike & Petersen, 2001).

Other available treatments for ADHD vary widely in quality. Parents need to realize, for example, that no one monitors the efficacy of Internet websites that promise help or a cure, where people with no credentials may be pushing nonconventional therapy that is, at best, untried and useless and, at worst, harmful to children. Some of these unproven treatments are dietary supplements that include blue-green algae, pycnogenol, vitamin B6, and caffeine pills. Little is known about the long-term effects on young bodies of taking these supplements, and they should be regarded with extreme caution. Treatments that are not based on medication or supplements range from restrictive diets to transcendental meditation to chiropractic intervention to neurotheraphy using biofeedback.

One older alternative treatment is the Feingold diet, which eliminates artificial colors, flavors, and preservatives from the child's food. Other dietary treatments attempt to identify foods that are causing unwanted behaviors. This is a very difficult and time-consuming process. Some success has been reported with eliminating certain foods; however, the numbers are very small (Brody, 1999). A parent who intends to implement this diet will have to send all the child's food to school each day in order to ensure that the child's diet remains free from additives.

In dealing with children with ADHD, the teacher must try to distinguish behavior that results from the ADHD and is something the child cannot do or control from behavior that results from the child's refusal to do something or noncompliance. Treatment for noncompliant behavior requires different strategies—namely, setting of specific rules, reinforcing compliance, and using techniques to reduce noncompliance. Behavior that results from the child's inability to remain still, however, should be handled by finding ways to allow the child to move and be active (Waddell, 1988). Research has shown that children with ADHD respond, or are more sensitive, to the use of rewards than children who do not have ADHD (Tripp & Alsop, 1999).

CHADD (Children and Adults with Attention-Deficit/Hyperactivity Disorder), the national organization for people with ADHD, believes that preventive intervention strategies should be used by school personnel in dealing with children with ADHD. A proactive discipline strategy must be used that will anticipate situations where the child may have problems and will take preventive measures. School personnel usually need specific training in these methods (CHADD, 1999). CHADD believes that positively reinforcing appropriate behavior is much more effective than using negative consequences and that schools should develop a continuum of consequences for inappropriate behaviors. These consequences should be shown to be effective in reducing inappropriate behaviors, and the least intensive interventions possible should be used. CHADD further advocates that schools train children in appropriate social skills behaviors and in self-control. Careful monitoring of interventions should be done, and the effectiveness of interventions should be noted on a child-by-child basis.

Training children to use appropriate social skills is becoming more common. One type of program that seems to be gaining in popularity is the Boys Town approach to social skill training developed in Nebraska at the Girls and Boys Town facility. This approach is based on the belief that children cannot be held accountable for their behavior until they have been taught the appropriate behavior. The approach has step-by-step directions for teaching children and covers the social skills that are necessary in the school setting. One social skill teaches children how to get the teacher's attention in the appropriate way. Positive skills are also addressed with lessons in such behaviors as giving compliments (girlsandboystown.org, 2001).

The types of behaviors that the child exhibits determines the accommodations necessary. If the child is constantly moving out of his or her seat, more space can be allotted around that child's desk or chair and masking tape can be placed on the floor about 1 foot out from the desk. The child can then be allowed this space to wiggle and squirm and stand up. As long as the child stays within the masking tape, there will be no negative consequences for "out-of-seat" behavior. It is essential that the child's feet touch the floor; care should be taken to avoid chairs that are too big for young children, particularly those with ADHD. The child's placement in the classroom is also important. There is no one correct placement, but it should be away from distractions such as windows, doors, and computers. Even if the computer screen is only displaying the various program icons, children with ADHD may find them more interesting than what the teacher is doing at the board. The teacher needs to experiment to find the best seat placement for each child. The room and the teaching plan alike need to be well organized and structured while the teacher maintains an atmosphere that allows for movement and frequent breaks. High-interest activities will keep all the children engaged to a greater degree. Good lesson plans will help achieve this.

Like the child with an emotional disturbance, the child with ADHD might have an individual contract with the teacher that specifies behaviors expected of him or her. The teacher needs to watch the child for special interests. A child who is motivated by computers might work for extra time on the computer. He or she might also be allowed 5 extra minutes of computer time each day as a positive consequence for following the terms of the contract. This child can also be considered for the job as computer assistant, or some other job in the classroom that appeals to him or her. The child who has fulfilled the terms of the contract has earned the privilege of holding that job.

Giving all children a few minutes of "wiggle breaks" not only helps the child with ADHD, it also helps all the children to be more attentive. The teacher can do simple things such as have the children stand, without talking, and model the different actions that the teacher makes. The teacher can also appoint a child each time to lead the wiggle break. If possible, a quick trip outside that allows the children to run to the fence and back (or a certain distance), take a walk around the block, or do some simple exercises can also refresh them. Certainly, the teacher who punishes the child with ADHD by withholding recess will be punishing himself or herself in addition to denying the child the opportunity to have needed physical activity. Instead of sitting out recess, the children can walk or run laps around the playground. This kind of break helps the children to have the physical activity that children with ADHD need.

Children can be taught to monitor their own behaviors. If a child is often out of the seat, the teacher can first make tally marks to determine exactly how frequently this behavior occurs. The teacher can then talk to the child and explain why it is important for him or her to stay in the seat. The teacher can tape a card or small piece of paper on the desk and teach the child to make tally marks each time the out-of-seat behavior occurs. This self-monitoring allows both the child and the teacher to notice exactly how often the behavior is occurring and to record improvements in the behavior.

Because children with attention problems will often need to have the steps in the assignments repeated in some fashion, the teacher needs to find unobtrusive ways to offer this assistance. As the child begins an assignment, the teacher can tell the child to put his or her name and date on the paper. The teacher can continue moving about the room and giving short, brief instructions for all the children. Then the teacher can return to the child with ADHD and make sure that he or she has heard and understood the next direction. The teacher continuously monitors and provides assistance to the child as needed. Tasks and assignments should be broken down into small steps with prompts and cues used as needed. This constant monitoring ensures that the child will be working on the correct assignment. Teachers who fail to monitor their children will find that everyone else is finished when the child with ADHD hasn't even found the page yet.

The amount of work will probably need to be shortened for the child with ADHD. Unfinished work should not be assigned as homework in addition to homework that is already required. If it is assigned as homework, each day the child will get further and further behind. At a certain point, he or she will quit making the effort to do any of the work because of the overwhelming amount accumulated. Do allow additional time for completion of assignments and provide immediate feedback on what is correct as well as what is wrong.

Because organizational skills are usually a problem, spending a few minutes at the beginning and end of each day helps the child get organized. Take-home folders with one side marked "Stays at home" and the other marked "Return to school" will help the child and the parent with homework and will also ensure that other important papers needed by the school will actually make it back to school.

Whenever possible, provide visual aids such as assignments written on the board and material displayed in graphs, charts, and pictures. Checklists are helpful with long or complicated assignments. These checklists are a step-by-step listing of the tasks involved; each item can be checked off by the child as each step is completed.

At-Risk Children

Children from situations of poverty, as well as those who are abused or neglected, often have difficulty keeping up academically with other students. They may exhibit unacceptable social behaviors and are often considered at risk. *At risk* usually refers to the fact that these children may have or may develop learning and/or behavioral problems in school. These children do not qualify for any type of special education, although they may have special needs.

Emphasis should be directed toward bringing these children up to grade level in all subject areas. Homeless children and/or children who are constantly moving between schools will have gaps in their learning and will need to be helped with instruction specifically directed toward these areas. This help may be offered during the school day in the form of one-on-one tutoring, or it may be offered before or after school. Cooperative grouping helps such children to feel successful. The use of mentors from the community may also help provide them with the positive role models that may be lacking in their lives. Individual teachers may exert an incredible influence over these children. Many rags-to-riches stories are attributed to a special teacher.

If the child comes to school without proper food or clothing, help with these basic needs is a priority. A hungry child will be less able to learn. Talking with the principal and the cafeteria manager may help the teacher develop a way to feed the child without paying for the food out of the teacher's own pocket. Appeals to the Parent-Teacher Association (PTA) usually will produce clothing appropriate for the weather, warm jackets and coats in the winter and shorts in the spring. The clothes may be hand-me-downs, but PTAs have also been known to buy new clothes for such children.

Bilingual Education and English as a Second Language

Children who speak English as a second language (ESL) or who have limited English proficiency (LEP) make up more than 6 percent of the children enrolled in public and private schools (Scarcella, 1990). Of these, 66 percent are in the elementary grades (National Center for Research on Cultural Diversity & Second Language Learning, 1995). Research has shown that it will take these children between six and eight years to achieve the same oral skill level as native speakers of English (Collier, 1987). Understanding this fact enables general education teachers to have realistic expectations for second-language learners.

There are three main instructional approaches for limited-English-speaking children (Miller, 2000). The *immersion* approach teaches all children in the general education classroom in English, with no added provisions for any type of assistance. Children are "immersed" in English and are expected to pick up the language and the content through this immersion. This approach has traditionally been the form of instruction used with limited English speakers in our country (Miller, 2000).

The *bilingual* approach teaches reading and writing in the child's native language concurrently with formal and informal instruction in oral English. Children enrolled in bilingual education classrooms may have their subjects taught in their primary language first. The goal of bilingual education is to produce children who are fluent readers and writers in two languages. As they master the English language, the subjects will be presented more and more in English, depending upon the level of English language development of the students.

The *English as a Second Language* (ESL) approach teaches oral English skills, usually in a pullout program, before any reading instruction begins. ESL programs focus on teaching subject matter in English and are less concerned about the child's retention of language ability in another language. Teachers in general education classrooms may have ESL children in their classroom for most of the day. The children may only go to the ESL classroom for an hour or two a day but spend the remainder of the day in the general education classroom.

In the United States, most bilingual education classes deal with Spanish-speaking children. It is hard to have bilingual education for children from countries that speak languages other than Spanish because it is difficult to find certified teachers who are fluent in those languages. For children who speak no English, the development of a communication board such as those mentioned for children with disabilities can help the child and the teacher communicate basic needs.

The teacher who understands Vygotsky's theory (see Chapter 2) is aware that children, especially limited-English-speaking children, will learn by constructing their own knowledge through the activities presented in the classroom, through their play experiences, and through the social context presented every day in the school environment. Indeed, this view is supported by NAEYC's position statement (2002) on linguistic and cultural diversity. "For young children, the language of the home is the language they have used since birth, the language they use to make and establish meaningful communicative relationships, and the language they use to begin to construct their knowledge and test their learning. . . . Language development is essential for learning, and the development of children's home language does not interfere with their ability to learn English. Because knowing more than one language is a cognitive asset, early education programs should encourage the development of children's home language while fostering the acquisition of English" (p. 1).

naeyc

Language acquisition can be greatly facilitated by the use of centers in the classroom. Language becomes important to the child as the child interacts with other children and participates in play. The home center will especially be beneficial because familiar roles and scenarios are acted out in the center.

Some accommodations that can be made for these children include a buddy to help them, allowing them extra time to process speech—both in listening and trying to respond, responding to what they are saying without constantly correcting their language, using simple language and speaking slowly, using cooperative learning groups and centers, using manipulatives and hands-on activities as much as possible, using gestures, and using routines in the classroom (Vaughn, Bos, & Schumm, 2000). Use of visuals during instruction will help the children to understand the vocabulary and to gain a better grasp on concepts presented. The visuals may be pictures, story maps, or graphic organizers such as Venn diagrams or webs (Gersten & Baker, 2000).

The National Center for Research on Cultural Diversity and Second Language Learning has identified 10 principles that should be kept in mind when teaching children with limited English proficiency, regardless of the approach that is used:

1. Being bilingual is an asset to be fostered.
2. It is rare for both languages to be equally developed in all children.

3. Cultural patterns in language use will vary among children.
4. It is normal for children to code switch, or interchange the two languages, within a single sentence.
5. Children learn a second language in many different ways. Prior experiences, opportunities the teacher makes available, and motivation all have an influence on the learning of a second language.
6. Language, whether Spanish or English, must communicate meaning.
7. A language-rich environment is needed for language to flourish.
8. Teachers should encourage children to experiment with language.
9. Being careful in wording questions, activating prior knowledge, and being aware of the pace of the lesson increases the children's achievement in learning Spanish and English.
10. Classroom activities should incorporate the real-world knowledge and experiences of the children. (1995)

Gifted and Talented Children

Although children who are identified as gifted and talented may not be thought of as having special needs, they do indeed have special needs that require accommodations in the general education classroom. The U.S. Department of Education (1993) recognizes that this group of children needs different educational experiences from their peers and their curriculum should be adjusted to meet their higher levels of ability. These children possess outstanding talent or perform at high levels when compared with their peers. This high performance may be in the intellectual, artistic, or creative area, and these children may show unusual leadership ability or strengths in specific academic areas (Walker, Hafenstein, & Crow-Enslow, 1999).

While an integrated-thematic approach can be used and adapted to meet the needs of these children, some children identified as gifted and talented (G/T) may be placed in pullout programs similar to the resource room that offer enrichment instead of remediation. Some schools may bus these children to a central location on certain days to special classes composed entirely of G/T children. Some schools may offer these children placement in a magnet school that offers acceleration in certain classes. A child who is gifted in math or science might attend a magnet school that contains, in addition to the regular classes, classes that are accelerated in math and science.

Dimensions of Diversity

Issues in Diversity

New terms and acronyms are constantly developing in the field of education. Currently, the term *English-language development* (ELD) is being used to describe all types of instruction that deal with English-language skills, whether written or oral (Gersten & Baker, 2000). This term is proposed as a replacement for *English as a second language* (ESL), *English for speakers of other languages* (ESOL), and *English-language learners* (ELL).

For the child who is gifted and talented and remains in the general education classroom most of the time, there are several options open to the general education teacher. The teacher can offer the child opportunities for enrichment within the classroom setting. This does not mean that the child does ten worksheets instead of the five that the other children will be doing; this means that the child might research a topic in much more depth than the other children do and produce a product that is considerably more complex than those of the other children. For instance, instead of drawing a picture and writing a summary about a book that has been read, a third-grade child who is gifted in language arts might produce a board game based on the book, and then make the board, pieces, and rules for the game. The child could then teach the game to the other students in the class.

Another choice open to the teacher is to *compact* the curriculum. This means omitting sections of the curriculum, for this child only, that are repetitive and unnecessary for a child who quickly grasps new ideas and materials (Clark, 1992). Sections that are quickly learned may have the amount of practice greatly reduced. The teacher, principal, and parent need to discuss what happens when the child has finished the entire subject and half the school year remains. Does the child begin the next grade level material? Or does the child then investigate in detail some area of interest?

Accommodations should be made that will allow the children to learn to use higher-level thinking skills. These are skills such as analyzing, synthesizing, classifying, inferring, and summarizing.

analyzing	separating into parts to determine the nature of the whole
synthesizing	reasoning from the general to the particular
classifying	to organize according to a category
inferring	to conclude from evidence
summarizing	presenting in a condensed form

Using Howard Gardner's multiple intelligences theory (see Chapter 2), the teacher can determine the child's interests and talents and use those areas to enrich the curriculum for the child. Knowledge of Gardner's theory can provide the teacher with a guide for accommodations and modifications. A child who has a strong logical mathematical intelligence will enjoy puzzles, games that require logical thinking, patterns, working with numbers, and money and logic problems. Modifications in the kindergarten classroom include providing more instruments for measuring in the sand and water play areas, harder puzzles, more cooking experiences, and adding measuring instruments in the woodworking area.

APPLYING ACCOMMODATIONS AND MODIFICATIONS IN A REAL-WORLD SCENARIO

Although teachers may be familiar with the laws, varying disabilities, special needs, and accommodations and modifications relating to their students, how does this knowledge translate into action for a teacher who receives a new child with special needs in the classroom?

Children can be very accepting of differences.

Joseph: A Case Study in Preparing for a Child with Special Needs

It is January 15 and Ms. Patrick has just been told by the counselor in her school that tomorrow she will be getting Joseph, a child with moderate mental retardation, who is transferring from another school district. Joseph is 6 years old, a year older than the other kindergarten children. Even so, he is functioning on a level of a 3-year-old and has speech problems that make him difficult to understand. Ms. Patrick has also been told that the IEP will not be available for a few weeks, and she is concerned about what to teach Joseph until the IEP arrives. How can Ms. Patrick prepare for Joseph?

When a teacher is notified that a new student with special needs is on the way, there is no cause for panic and dread. Clear thinking on the part of the teacher, however, can ease the transition for the child, the teacher, and the other children in the class. Ms. Patrick knows that Joseph will be immature in comparison to the other children in the classroom. Her first concern is one of communicating with Joseph. What will she do if she can't understand what he is saying? How will she know when he needs to use the restroom? Reviewing the section on children with mental retardation in her college textbook, she notices the information about a communication board and so she uses her computer to make a simple communication board that has a picture of a toilet, a glass, a happy face, a sad face, and a plate of food. Already she begins to feel better. The problem of communication can be handled that first day for the necessities.

Ms. Patrick decides to assign Raymond to be Joseph's buddy. Raymond has shown special kindness to the younger children out on the playground and she thinks he will be a good buddy for Joseph. She wants to ensure that Joseph will feel successful his first day. Ms. Patrick remembers her university professor saying to keep a job or two for new children coming into the classroom to help them feel successful and a part of the class immediately. She has reserved the classroom job of "door opener" in anticipation of the day that she would have a new student. The "door opener" opens the door when the class is ready to exit for lunch, physical education, or for any other reason. This child gets to stand directly behind the line leader. Ms. Patrick believes that Joseph can do this job, and she thinks having him directly behind the line leader will help him become familiar with the school more quickly.

Without an IEP, Ms. Patrick thinks about what she will plan for Joseph to do until the IEP comes. Using her college textbook as a guide, Ms. Patrick asks herself if Joseph will be able to do the same work as the other children with or without modifications or accommodations, and she decides that he will be able to participate in a great portion of the school day with very few modifications or accommodations. He will be able to go to centers with the other children. There might be problems in getting along with the others, but Joseph should be able to participate in center time. Lunch and outdoor time should hold minimal problems, as should music and movement time. Although there are no records from Joseph's previous school yet, Ms. Patrick will call Joseph's parents tonight and ask what skills he has been working on at his old school.

Now Ms. Patrick examines the other times of the school day. She thinks of her schedule and mentally notes all the other different activities that occur during the day. Her kindergarten children engage in writing, circle time, math, and shared reading. She ponders each time and activity and thinks of accommodations that may be needed. Most of her children are able to write, draw, and recognize their names. This may be a problem for Joseph, although he can certainly use the same materials as the other children during this time. She makes a mental note to evaluate his recognition of his name and his skill with pencils and crayons.

One area that may be a problem is circle time. If Joseph has never been included in a circle time before, he may not know the appropriate behaviors. Ms. Patrick has a little stuffed bear named Bailey that all the children love. She decides to place Joseph right beside her during circle time and let him hold Bailey. Another challenging time may be shared reading because he may never have been exposed to shared reading before. Ms. Patrick uses "big books" many times during shared reading. She decides that for tomorrow she will work using a big book that the children really enjoy. This big book also allows for movement and noise during the reading and will help ease Joseph into shared reading. She may even let him stand beside her and hold her pointer as she moves the pointer under the words.

In math the children have been making different representations of the number 6 using manipulatives and then writing the equations. Although this activity is probably too difficult for Joseph, he should be able to use the manipulatives in other ways. Ms. Patrick can even assess his counting ability by asking him to hand her different numbers of bears. She may also attempt to have him sort the bears by color into colored cups. He also may be able to string beads, place pegs in the pegboards, or do one of the very simple puzzles that she has on shapes.

Ms. Patrick feels a sense of excitement as she gets ready for bed that night. She knows that she has made good plans that will allow Joseph to be successful tomorrow, and she believes that she can include Joseph successfully in her classroom. How different this story would be that next day if Ms. Patrick simply walked in unprepared and tried to react to things as they happened. Ms. Patrick, Joseph, and the other children might have experienced a very long, frustrating, and stressful day. Because she planned well, Ms. Patrick's day will go relatively smoothly.

Planning will not end for Ms. Patrick after this first day; this is just the beginning. She will constantly be observing, not only Joseph, but all the children and evaluating what is working and what needs to be changed. This evaluation is continuous throughout the day, day after day. As Ms. Patrick observes the children, she will note strengths as well as weaknesses in them, and she will plan to meet any needs they have, whether those needs be in the area of academics, or physical, or social-emotional needs. As she observes, she will also be anticipating problem areas and planning for eventualities. With Joseph, each day will bring the need for possibly different materials or adaptations of materials in the classroom. What Ms. Patrick will find is that understanding how to meet Joseph's needs through specialized instruction and modification of materials will become easier and easier. Although Ms. Patrick did not think of seeking assistance from the special education teacher when she learned that Joseph was to be in her class, she now works closely with the special education teacher in making these plans, accommodations, and modifications for Joseph.

☆ COLLABORATING WITH THE SPECIAL EDUCATION TEACHER

The special education teacher visited Ms. Patrick the next day and provided Ms. Patrick with assistance in planning instruction, materials, and ideas for making modifications. Effective collaboration between special education and general education comes from a shared concern for the education of all the children. Collaboration is the voluntary working together of people for a shared goal. It requires effective communication as problems are addressed and solutions are brainstormed, implemented, and evaluated. Because of specialized training, the special education teacher may have simple ideas and suggestions that will assist the general education teacher in a variety of ways. Constant dialogue between and among the teachers will benefit the general education teacher as well as the child with special needs. Though a majority of the collaboration takes place within the school as teachers implement the IEP, parents should also be a part of this collaboration.

 SUMMARY

Understanding the laws dealing with children with special needs helps the teacher remain in compliance with those laws. Understanding the types of disabilities recognized by IDEA helps a teacher know which children can receive special education services and need to have an IEP. As more attention is focused on children with ADHD, the teacher needs to have a greater understanding of what this may mean for both the teacher and the child in all areas of school life, in addition to types of treatments that may be tried with the child. Understanding some common types of accommodations and modifications for all children with special needs helps the teacher be more successful in planning for these children, and the ability to apply this knowledge helps ensure the success of the teacher and the children in her care.

☆ Discussion Questions

1. Discuss the laws affecting students with disabilities. How have they changed over the years?
2. Describe the referral process.
3. What are the different placement options for children with special needs?
4. Describe some common modifications and accommodations that can be used with children with special needs. How easy or hard would these modifications and accommodations be to implement?

☆ Suggested Chapter Activities

1. Interview a general education teacher. Ask how many children with special needs are included in the classroom. What types of special needs do they have? What types of modifications and accommodations are made? Which ones work best?
2. Research more modifications and accommodations for one of the specific disabilities and present them to the class.
3. Contact your local school district and ask about their G/T program. How are the children served? Are they part of a pullout program, or do they attend a special school? Visit a G/T classroom and notice the types of activities the students are engaged in.
4. Using the following case study and the information provided, plan for this student to be included in your class.

Becky: A Case Study

You have been told by the counselor that tomorrow Becky, a child with very limited vision, will be a part of your first-grade class. Becky also has ADHD but is not currently on any type of medication. Because of her vision, she will be seeing a special teacher who assists children with visual problems. Unfortunately, your small district has limited resources and this teacher has to visit many children on different campuses throughout the district. She will only see Becky twice a week for 60 minutes each time. Becky will be your responsibility the remainder of the time. Becky is behind approximately one year in her language arts skills. Writing is also a problem, and Becky's combined problems of vision, ADHD, and lack of interest in writing make writing a very challenging time for her. Plan for Becky's first day in the class. How will you structure your writing time to meet Becky's needs and control for her behavior? Be very detailed in your answer.

5. Locate other parent organizations for specific disabilities. What kinds of help and information do they provide? Do they have a website? If so, visit the site and notice if there is assistance for parents and for teachers. How valuable are the suggestions and information?

Teaching in a Prekindergarten Classroom

C H A P T E R   O V E R V I E W

★ What specific educational needs do prekindergarten children have that older children do not?

★ How do Head Start and Bilingual Education programs affect prekindergarten education?

★ What does it mean that children are developing impulse control?

★ Why is fine arts curriculum an important area of learning for 4-year-olds?

★ Are states developing standards for 4-year-old classrooms?

★ What other issues are pertinent in the prekindergarten classroom?

R E A D   T H I S   C H A P T E R   T O   F I N D   T H E   A N S W E R S   T O   T H E S E   Q U E S T I O N S   A N D   O T H E R S   Y O U   M I G H T   H A V E .

Four-year-olds are intensely curious, active, and wide-eyed learners. Even the shyest 4-year-olds are interested in ongoing events, and their questions give evidence that they want and need answers. "Why?" is a typical response when a phenomenon catches their attention and causes bemusement. Their "why" questions are complex ones and not always easily answered. Teachers will find that replying to "why" questions with "Why do you think this is happening?" fosters a sense within children that they can think for themselves.

Physically, 4-year-olds are more capable of moving around the classroom and playground with ease than younger children. They are not as clumsy as they were at previous ages, and they find pleasure in physical activities (for example running, hopping, and jumping). When they play, they play with gusto and wholehearted energy. Occasionally, they enjoy simple group games, such as "Duck, Duck, Goose" or "Red Light, Green Light." A scheduled time for physical activity assists children in managing the demands of classroom experiences, which require them to be more sedate than their bodies allow them to be.

Prekindergarten children are egocentric. Their self-centered nature is exhibited in numerous ways each day as they blurt out answers during Circle Time or cry when even the slightest bump from another indicates they are being attacked. They want to be chosen first for the lunch line, and they pout when they are not chosen to participate in a specific desired center

choice. When 4-year-olds spy something they want, they take it without thinking about the repercussions. They express themselves in view of their immediate wants and needs and, in general, think about themselves before thinking about others.

Four is an age that is unsettling and emotionally uneasy. When the feelings of these children are hurt, they cry immediately or lash out with their fists. They readily cling to their mothers or teachers when their personal space is violated, but they also want to be bold and courageous, even in the face of new situations. Their actions demonstrate simultaneously the dual emotional states of independence and vulnerability.

Children at this age do not make easy transitions, and they do not make friends quickly. They enjoy being with others their age, but remembering the prosocial behaviors necessary for becoming an acceptable member of the group takes practice and reminders from the teacher about how to interact with others. The intellectual learning that 4-year-olds accomplish depends heavily on their understanding of themselves in relation to others.

Consistency and stability are cornerstones for the development of social-emotional well-being in 4-year-olds. The adults in their lives should be nurturing, responsive individuals who recognize children's needs. Assisting children in getting along with one another, alleviating the stresses they feel in group settings, helping them learn to assert themselves in social situations, and providing support during daily classroom routines are essential contributions teachers make to their 4-year-olds.

Mrs. Flores arrives at school every morning at 7:15 a.m., and a number of her children begin arriving shortly thereafter. The early childhood center where she works is unique in her urban district because 98 percent of the population of the school is Hispanic. As parents depart for their jobs each morning, having the school open at an early hour alleviates their concerns for leaving their children alone at home until school starts. Mrs. Flores is bilingual and can converse in Spanish; she and her colleagues are certified as bilingual-education or English-as-second-language teachers. The majority of her children speak Spanish, as do their parents. Mrs. Flores recognizes that her knowledge of Spanish is a comfort to parents who need to converse in Spanish.

The early childhood center is a novel concept for Mrs. Flores's large metropolitan school district, and the area of the city where it is located has many young families living in several apartment complexes near the school. Currently, the center houses only prekindergarten and kindergarten classrooms, but within the year a building will be completed that will house grades 1 through 3. As children move into upper elementary grades, a nearby middle school will accommodate their educational requirements.

Breakfast is served to all children who come to school each morning, and lunch is prepared for children who arrive at school at noon. Mrs. Flores would prefer to keep the same group of children all day, but state funding prohibits extending the length of the day beyond four hours. Her morning instructional time is 8 a.m. to 11 a.m., and the afternoon session begins at 12 noon and continues until 3 p.m. Breakfast is served at 7:30 a.m., and lunch is served at 11:30 a.m.

The school's parent center is popular with the families the school serves. Numerous mothers come to the center during the day to parenting classes or to read information the center keeps in stock for the school's clientele. Mrs. Flores has reserved the center on two consecutive Friday evenings in November for evening festivities for her two groups of children. The family gatherings in past years have been quite successful in building a sense of community within the school.

The school board and administration have discussed the need to lengthen the prekindergarten day to allow 4-year-olds to undergo the fullest educational experience, but local funds are not available to supplement state funding. A full-day program would solve some families' problems for child care when children are not in school. Fortunately, a nearby Head Start program provides transportation to school for afternoon prekindergarten children and transportation to its center for the morning children who are enrolled. Some parents make arrangements for neighbors and family members to care for their children when the 4-year-olds are not in school.

Mrs. Flores recognizes that prekindergarten programs in her state are established with one goal in mind—to prepare children for kindergarten. The legislation creating 4-year-old education indicates that children with language deficiencies or needs for second-language acquisition are eligible to attend prekindergarten. Generally, schools in her state have interpreted the law to mean that children who qualify for free or reduced lunch programs are the target population for prekindergarten education. This interpretation implies that mostly low-income families attend the prekindergarten program in her center.

In her own pedagogical philosophy, Mrs. Flores does not agree that children need to "get ready for kindergarten"; she asserts time and again that schools should enhance children's everyday lives with experiences that maximize their potential for learning. She believes that all children are learners, but she recognizes that her responsibility as teacher is that her 4-year-olds learn information that will ease their transition into kindergarten instruction. Her goal is to meet this task with appropriate practices that fulfill the needs of the children in her care.

WHAT PREKINDERGARTNERS ARE EXPECTED TO LEARN

Most state guidelines for prekindergarten programs focus on (1) oral language development, (2) initial literacy skills (understanding the role of print in the environment), (3) mathematical skills, and (4) social/emotional knowledge. The California Department of Education (2000) also defines motor-skill development as an area of learning. The skills children are expected to acquire in each of these areas are delineated here.

Oral Language Development

- Ability to speak well enough in their native language for others to comprehend them (though some speech errors may occur)
- Rudimentary understanding of the turn-taking cycle in conversational speech
- Ability to listen to others and make appropriate responses when requested
- Ability to retell familiar stories while adults prompt to prolong the storytelling activity
- For second-language learners, acquisition of basic information about the second language of the school culture

Initial Literacy Skills

- Ability to recognize one's name in print
- Initial understanding that print has meaning
- Recognition that pictures in a book convey meaning
- Ability to hold a book appropriately while looking at it
- Preliminary development of writing activity (scribbles and invented spelling)
- Ability to express themselves through pictures, movement activities, and music

Mathematical Skills

- Ability to count orally to 10 (or higher) by the end of the school year (ordinal principle)
- Ability to count rationally to 10 using concrete objects (cardinal principle)
- Understanding the importance and use of numerals in the environment
- Ability to name basic shapes
- Ability to work six- to eight-piece puzzles
- Ability to classify items based on one characteristic (all the red beads, blue beads, green beads, etc.)
- Rudimentary understanding of pattern construction
- Rudimentary understanding of comparison and descriptions of quantities
- Use of reasoning in attempting to solve mathematical problems (such as how many napkins are needed at snack time)

Social/Emotional Knowledge

- Ability to tell name, address, and phone number
- Ability to get dressed with adult assistance
- Ability to take care of bathroom needs with minimal adult assistance
- Ability to eat without assistance
- Initial understanding about regulating involvement in classroom activities (with some adult assistance and intervention)

- Ability to enter a play situation and sustain play activity with other children
- Ability to label one's own emotions and identify their source
- Understanding the need to control one's own emotions

Motor-Skill Development

- Beginning to coordinate motor activity (which is not complete until age 5)
- Increasing amount of time spent on any given movement (speed)
- Initial ability to balance one's body in space
- Increasing agility and ability to change directions rapidly and accurately
- Increasing strength and power for producing motor activities (Stork, 2000)

Prekindergarten guidelines and standards vary from state to state, though school districts often provide direction for teachers in prekindergarten classrooms. Interpreting standards is a critical issue because policy makers and administrators do not always understand 4-year-old children. If mandates are interpreted narrowly, instructional practices in prekindergarten classrooms can evolve into a skill-and-drill approach focusing on rote memorization with beginning reading and math goals, which are not appropriate for the young child.

Prekindergarten classrooms help young children become learners. The Cycle of Learning and Teaching and the Continuum of Teaching Strategies discussed in Chapter 3 are instructional frameworks that prekindergarten teachers should review before entering their classrooms. Using a model of emphasizing inquiry and utilization strategies without adequate awareness and exploration of the learning environment will overwhelm preschoolers and destroy their dispositions to learn (Katz & Chard, 2000).

⭐ PREKINDERGARTEN SCHEDULE AND CLASSROOM LAYOUT

Developmentally appropriate prekindergarten classrooms promote children's abilities (1) to make choices, (2) sustain self-directed activity, (3) carry on interactions with others, and (4) follow through on self-selected tasks. Four-year-olds are young children who are capable of determining their own interests, and classroom environments should allow them an opportunity to pursue their personal preferences to nurture their individual abilities.

Mrs. Flores understands that her children need experiential development, not academic instruction, and her classroom planning demonstrates her commitment to enhancing children's potential for learning. Consequently, she organizes classroom centers to allow for children's choice making among activities that are designed for their development. Her center choices include Home Living, Dramatic Play, Block, Art and Music, Library, Manipulatives, and Special Interests. (See Chapter 3 for further discussion of early childhood classroom center development and implementation.)

The School Day

Mrs. Flores begins each prekindergarten session with an instructional strategy labeled "Table Activities." When children arrive each day, materials are set out on the classroom tables for children to explore and experiment before their regular routine. Table Activities, designed to assist children's transition from their school meal, allow choices among experiences, which focus on fine-motor development. The manipulative choices include putting together puzzles; placing pegs in pegboards; tracing shapes or stencils; cutting with scissors; matching shapes; playing with magnetic alphabet letters; using the Etch-a-Sketch toy, Tinkertoys, or Lincoln logs; or writing and drawing in their class journals. Throughout the year, the focus on the manipulative items changes to match children's growth and challenge them to move to higher levels of information about literacy and numeracy. A typical prekindergarten school day is shown in Figure 5.1.

Center Time provides Mrs. Flores with an opportunity for working with children individually or in small groups. Early in the prekindergarten year, she uses an individualized assessment instrument to determine each child's physical development, how much knowledge each child has about print and numerals (cognition), and how well each gets along with others in the classroom (social-emotional development). By using a predetermined set of guidelines to determine problem areas children may exhibit, teachers are able to establish curriculum guidelines for individualizing instruction to meet the needs of learners. Often curriculum guides in each school district establish these guidelines, which observe developmental areas such as social-emotional development, motor development, speech and language development, hearing, and visual acuity. Mrs. Flores usually consults an instrument developed by the Preschool Enrichment Team, Incorporated, titled "Developmental Red Flags for Children Ages 3 to 5" (see Appendix A

FIGURE 5.1 Mrs. Flores's Schedule for Morning and Afternoon Prekindergarten Sessions

Time	Activity	Time	Activity
7:30	Breakfast	11:30	Lunch
8:00	Table activities	Noon	Table activities
8:30	Circle Time	12:30	Circle Time
8:50	Center Time	12:50	Center Time
9:50	Milk break	1:50	Milk break
10:05	Outdoor time	2:05	Outdoor time
10:25	Storytelling or book reading	2:25	Storytelling or book reading
10:35	Music and movement	2:35	Music and movement
10:50	Prepare for departure	2:50	Prepare for departure
11:00	Dismissal	3:00	Dismissal

Mrs. Flores's Lesson Plan

Lesson Title: Learning about Our Hands
Objectives: After this lesson, children will be able to:

- Identify their hands on their bodies.
- Tell three things they do with their hands.
- Match pairs of hands by size and color.
- Demonstrate their knowledge of position words.

Focus:

Hold up hands and ask children to tell what they are. Introduce the song "Here Are My Hands."

Body of the Lesson:

1. Ask children to brainstorm ways they use their hands. Write their responses on a chart tablet.
2. Show children the picture book by Bill Martin, Jr., *Here Are My Hands.*
3. Play a follow the leader game asking children to put their hands above their heads, behind their backs, on their knees, in front of their faces, and so on.
4. Play a matching game requiring children to match a pair of hands based on size and color.

Closure:

Review what was discussed in the lesson. Use the chart tablet responses to remember how people use their hands.

Follow-Up Activities:

- Place the pairs of hand materials in the Manipulatives Center
- Have a photograph of a hand skeleton on the Science Table.
- Put Bill Martin's book in the Book Corner.
- On the playground, teach children how to do the wheelbarrow so they can "walk" on their hands.

Resources:

Teacher-made pairs of hands in various sizes and colors (laminated, preferably, for additional use); flip chart and marker; book (Martin, B. (1987) *Here Are My Hands.* New York: Henry Holt & Company); song:

"Here Are My Hands" (Tune: "The Farmer in the Dell")
Here are my hands,
Here are my hands,
I wiggle my fingers and point my thumbs,
Here are my hands.

My hands help me out,
My hands help me out,
I wiggle my fingers and point my thumbs,
And put them in my lap.

From B. Martin, *Here Are My Hands* (New York: Henry Holt & Company, 1987). Quoted by permission.

for an adaptation of this instrument). Other commonly used assessments are the Denver Developmental Screening Test (Frankenburg & Dodds, 1992), the Bracken Basic Concept Scale, Revised (Bracken, 1998), and the Boehm Test of Basic Concepts (Boehm, 2001).

Once children's developmental levels are determined, teachers are more capable of determining what areas of instruction each child needs. An excellent classroom strategy is to plan for small groups of children to work together while the other children in class are involved in center activity. Cliff, Wes, Mia, and Francine may need information about shape recognition, while Consuela, Britni, and Margo require instruction about naming colors. A 10-minute session with a small group of children is easy to manage while the class is busy elsewhere. Groups (or even individuals) rotate turns with the teacher and the classroom aide throughout the week to accomplish weekly instructional goals and objectives. (See the Lesson Plan box on page 169 for a sample lesson plan from Mrs. Flores's classroom.)

Using individual or small-group instruction provides more input to the teacher about children's achievement and analysis of their specific content needs. Keeping a checklist or anecdotal record showing children's progress allows for more accurate information about children's growth when parents come for school conferences. Samples of children's work (such as attempts to write one's name or drawing self-portraits) are easier to secure when small groups are utilized. Records also assist teachers in planning curriculum and lessons for individual children during the school year. More thorough discussion of the observational techniques mentioned here is presented in Chapter 7.

What Teachers Are Saying

Play

"We plan 45 minutes for center activity. The centers I have in my classroom are art, blocks, computers, sand, Lego table, scissor station, housekeeping, games, science, library, and doll house." —*prekindergarten teacher*

"In my classroom, I have dramatic play, literacy, art, music, blocks, fine and gross motor centers. We plan for one hour of center play. This supports our emphasis on oral language development in language arts." —*prekindergarten teacher*

"I try to include a variety of activities and materials to encourage phonemic awareness within my children. We have the usual centers, but this year I included an animals center. Now we have fish, a guinea pig, and bugs to talk about."

—*prekindergarten teacher*

☆ Head Start Programs in Public Schools

The Ewing Marion Kauffman Foundation (Mitchell, Stoney & Dichter, 2001) verifies that 41 states and the District of Columbia offer public prekindergarten financing. A number of state prekindergarten initiatives are affiliated with the Head Start Bureau and supported by the Administration for Children and Families (ACF) under the auspices of the U.S. Department of Health and Human Services. ACF (2001) reports that approximately 1,400 Head Start programs are available from community-based nonprofit organizations and school systems across the country. As mentioned in Chapter 1, Head Start was born in the mid-1960s as an answer to the pervasive cycle-of-poverty social problems in the United States. In 2001, the Head Start Bureau reported it had served a total of 19,397,000 children since 1965 (ACF, 2001).

Major components of Head Start are (1) education (focusing on intellectual, social, and emotional growth); (2) health (including immunizations and medical, dental, mental, and nutritional services); (3) parent involvement; and (4) social services (consisting of community outreach and referrals as well as emergency assistance and crisis intervention) (ACF, 2001). Among the cultural entities served by ACF are the American Indian Head Start Program and the Migrant Head Start Program. In 1994, the new Head Start Program Performance Standards were introduced and published as a final rule in the Federal Register in November 1996. The purpose of the national standards was to revise guidelines for high-quality Head Start programs to include standards for infants and toddlers and their families.

The Children's Defense Fund (2001) reported successes in Head Start programming by summarizing research studies that indicate:

- Low-income children in Head Start programs are less likely to be retained in one grade and more likely to graduate from high school.
- Children in Head Start programs have the knowledge and skills in literacy and numeracy allowing them to enter school ready to learn.
- Head Start children perform better on cognitive tasks than do their low-income peers without Head Start experience.
- Head Start children acquire the social skills essential for kindergarten success.
- Head Start programs are more likely to meet national accreditation standards for quality.

Funding for Head Start continues to be problematic. Communities that support Head Start programs are required to provide 20 percent of development funding. Local agencies do not have available funding or are unwilling to provide Head Start support, however; the Children's Defense Fund reported that Head Start reaches only about half of the eligible preschool children and 50,000 children out of 2 million eligible infants and toddlers. Other issues addressed by the Head Start Bureau and professional organizations are the need for universal Head Start programs for all preschool children and the training and credentialing of qualified

Head Start teachers. Recent legislation (Head Start Act, 2003) authorizes improvement in Head Start programs in four areas: (1) academic outcomes, (2) teacher competency and professional development, (3) collaboration with other programs and public schools, and (4) accountability for services.

☆ BILINGUAL EDUCATION AND ESL PROGRAMS IN PUBLIC SCHOOLS

Prekindergarten programs often serve bilingual children, especially those who live in states such as California, Florida, and Texas where the Hispanic population has grown tremendously within the last decade. According to Washington and Andrews (1999), projected Hispanic population will continue to grow, rising approximately 31 percent by 2010. The result will be an increased need for bilingual teachers in schools across the United States. In 2000, the U.S. Bureau of the Census presented the following educational data about Hispanics:

- Approximately 52.4 percent of Hispanics leave school prior to graduation.
- Hispanics compose 15 percent of the student population.
- Nevada and Arizona have the highest dropout rates.
- 90 percent of Hispanic students are in urban districts.
- 5.9 percent of Hispanic students attend private schools.
- 24 percent of prekindergarten children are Hispanic.

These data support the need for bilingual-education and English-as-a-Second-Language programs in public schools. State mandates often support beginning bilingual education and ESL programs in prekindergarten. Bilingual education models include Dual Language Schools, Two-Way Bilingual Education and Immersion Models, and Maintenance Bilingual Education programs, which have as their goal fluency in the first language and development of fluency in the second language. These programs are often referred to as *developmental programs,* and instruction is delivered in both Spanish and English while children are in school (Brisk, 1998).

Transitional-Bilingual-Education (TBE) models and English-as-a-Second-Language (ESL) programs work to prepare students for academic achievement in monolingual classrooms (Brisk, 1998). Teachers in TBE programs use children's native language while the children are learning English. When children acquire fluency in English, they are transferred to general classrooms, where they continue their education. ESL classrooms, on the other hand, provide total immersion in English, and children are expected to learn information at the same time that they are learning English.

Theoretical perspectives in second-language acquisition fall into two major categories: (1) environmentalist theories (behaviorism), and (2) nativist theories (natural learning processes) (Freeman & Freeman, 1994). Stephen Krashen's nativist theory has had the greatest impact on public school classroom practice. His Monitor Model, based on Chomsky's linguistic theory, is subdivided into five interrelated hypotheses.

Bilingual education classrooms help young children learn English.

Chomsky posited a *language acquisition device* (LAD) paradigm suggesting that humans have innate abilities to learn their first language with little effort. Krashen's hypotheses acknowledge Chomsky's LAD in the following ways:

- The *acquisition-learning hypothesis* differentiates language acquisition from learning. Speakers acquire language subconsciously in real-life situations. Learning, on the other hand, is a conscious process associated with direct instruction.
- The *natural-order hypothesis* applies to acquired languages, not language that is learned. Children learn that plurals exist and add *s* or *es* subconsciously without formal instruction. When languages are presented in a textbook, the natural order of language acquisition is subverted, and grammar is presented in an order unlike natural language acquisition.
- The *monitor hypothesis* is Krashen's explanation that learned language rules can assist children as they speak and write the second language. The monitor (usually the teacher or more proficient classmate) assists the speaker and writer during the process of delivering language. This process can speed delivery and helps children learn rules while they are producing language.
- The *input hypothesis* implies that people comprehend oral and written messages they observe in their environment. Comprehensible input will

Issues and Trends

Bilingual Education

The National Association for Bilingual Education (NABE) represents bilingual educators across the United States. Their legislative priorities for the 108th Congress were:

1. To continue to advocate for increased federal funding, particularly Title III of the Elementary Education Secondary Act (ESEA)
2. To focus on the needs of English Language Learners (ELL) who are disabled and should be served by the Individuals with Disabilities Education Act (IDEA)
3. To highlight the needs of ELL students as Head Start is reauthorized
4. To improve teacher recruitment and retention efforts for ELL classrooms
5. To work for legislation that will permit immigrant students to go to college and obtain permanent legal residency in the United States
6. To defend the civil rights of language-minority Americans (NABE, 2002)

effectively assist children in acquiring the second language, particularly if the input is slightly beyond their current language abilities.

- The *affective filter hypothesis* suggests that social-emotional factors can affect children's abilities to learn the second language. Children who are anxious, fearful, bored, or distracted will have difficulty acquiring the second language (Freeman & Freeman, 1994).

Researchers have attempted to define effective bilingual teachers and bilingual classrooms. In a synthesis of several research studies, Baker (1996) defines effective teachers as those who have high expectations of their students, are confident in their abilities to teach, use students' native language for instruction, and integrate the students' home culture and values into classroom activity. Lucas, Henze, and Donato (1990) presented several features of successful bilingual education schools in California and Arizona that emphasized the value and status of the language and culture of minority students, the importance of parent involvement, and the desirability of offering choices among courses to second-language learners.

⭐ THE ISSUE OF DIVERSITY

Diversity issues arise in prekindergarten classrooms depending on the population enrolled. Teachers who have evaluated children's biases (gender bias, racial bias, ethnic or cultural bias, bias toward children with special needs) discover a community of learners who recognize strengths and weaknesses in others yet accept their peers for who they are (Neugebauer, 1992).

Occasionally, a teacher may need to say, "Olga doesn't know how to speak English yet, but she's learning. Let's be patient with her." Or "Kirmani doesn't celebrate the holidays in the same way we do. Kirmani, can you tell the group about some of your holiday celebrations?" Or "Marcella dictated her story about her family to Mrs. Gonzales, our aide. Mrs. Gonzales, will you tell us what Marcella wrote for us?"

Head Start programs recognize multicultural elements in classrooms of young children by defining the following "Principles Supporting the Framework for Multicultural Programming in Head Start" (Head Start Multicultural Task Force, 2001).

1. Every individual is rooted in culture.
2. The cultural groups represented in the communities and families of each Head Start program are the primary sources for culturally relevant programming.
3. Culturally relevant and diverse programming requires learning accurate information about the culture of different groups and discarding stereotypes.
4. Addressing cultural relevance in making curriculum choices is a necessary, developmentally appropriate practice.

Dimensions of Diversity

Guidelines Addressing Cultural Diversity

The California Department of Education has developed a set of guidelines to ensure that classrooms for young children, whether they are in public or private settings, build respect for diversity. Characteristics for appropriate programs and activities defining how to follow the guidelines are provided in the department's *Prekindergarten Learning & Development Guidelines* (2000). These are the five guidelines:

1. The program encourages and supports appreciation of and respect for individual and group similarities and differences, making the acceptance of diversity a theme that is central to the classroom climate.
2. Program materials reflect the characteristics, values, and practices of diverse cultural groups.
3. Whenever reasonable, teachers engage in practices that are consistent with those from children's homes.
4. Teachers attempt, as much as possible, to learn about the history, beliefs, and practices of the children and families they serve, and they receive support for their efforts from the early care and education center.
5. Children are encouraged to recognize and develop strategies to use when they encounter social injustice, bias, and prejudice. (pp. 42–46)

5. Every individual has the right to maintain his or her own identity while acquiring the skills required to function in our diverse society.
6. Effective programs for children with limited English speaking ability require continued development of the primary language while the acquisition of English is facilitated.
7. Culturally relevant programming requires staff who reflect the community and families served.
8. Multicultural programming for children enables children to develop an awareness of, respect for, and appreciation of individual cultural differences. It is beneficial to all children.
9. Culturally relevant and diverse programming examines and challenges institutional and personal biases.
10. Culturally relevant and diverse programming and practices are incorporated in all components and services.

For full discussions of each principle, consult the website for the Head Start Bureau.

⭐ CREATING A CARING COMMUNITY OF LEARNERS

naeyc

Creating a caring community of learners is a major guideline of developmentally appropriate practice as defined by the National Association for the Education of Young Children (Bredekamp & Copple, 1997). When teachers work with children over a long period of time (nine months to a year), they begin to see a microcosm of the culture in which they live and work. The future doctor, politician, teacher, lawyer, plumber, sales person, engineer, professor, or carpenter emerge as unique individuals who are easily recognizable, even at age 4. Adults can point out the classroom diplomat, the hypochondriac, the "boss," the artist, and other personalities that begin to surface in the preschool years. If the classroom is well organized and the teacher's influence is consistent, children have potential for becoming all they can be (Bredekamp & Copple, 1997).

Developing a community of learners is imperative in a world that is becoming more diverse and as people lose contact with their extended families because of work relocations. Young children are frequently in single-parent families, and the adult in their classroom may provide the most secure level of consistency in their lives.

Helping children learn to care for others, the essence of a "community of learners," is a major goal in the preschool years. Adults discover that a good majority of their time is spent modeling cooperative behaviors, teaching youngsters appropriate verbal communications essential for cooperative living, reminding children to share, and planning cooperative activities that will reinforce prosocial behavior (Gestwicki, 1999). Hendrick (2003) describes children's needs as "immediate, intense and personal" (p. 249). Prekindergarten teachers quickly learn that developing social competence is an ongoing classroom endeavor.

Showing Respect for Children

The best approach for developing a caring community is, first and foremost, to be aware that children need to accept themselves as individuals. Adults who respect children help children to accept themselves. Nurturing teachers can demonstrate respect for children by listening to them, responding to their needs, giving them choices, and helping them grasp why certain decisions are made in their behalf. A 4-year-old may cry because her teacher insists that she clean up the classroom before leaving to go home at the end of the day. The teacher's kind explanation that she wants all children to take care of the classroom sends the message, "I care about you as a person, but all children in this classroom have the same responsibilities. I cannot let you avoid helping with cleanup just because you're upset." The child may still cry, but a rational explanation about the denial of the request will help her understand why the decision is made.

Respect for the child, a concept introduced by Montessori (1914), implies respect for the child's privacy and development toward independence. Allowing children opportunities to make choices and then abide by the consequences of those choices while ensuring their safety is one component in the overall relationship between adult and child that shows respect. Using threats, taking away privileges, yelling, or belittling children as forms of punishment limit what children can do for themselves. Instead, caring adults need to give children instruction about their activities, explaining what is appropriate behavior and what is considered inappropriate and why. On occasion, modeling the expected behavior and working side by side with children are essential for children's understanding of their responsibilities.

Respect is also developed when teachers assist children in dealing with their own emotions. An immediate reaction to a child's tantrum is often one of criticism by the adult. Telling the child to "stop that crying" or "don't behave like a baby" does not help the child analyze and define his own emotions. Young children interpret criticism from an adult as being labeled bad. Saying to the child, "I know you're upset— I would be angry, too, if Zach took away my toy," is a step toward allowing the child to verbalize his own feelings and eventually learning to tell Zach to find another toy until he is finished playing with the one he currently possesses. See Figure 5.2 for a summary of classroom practices that promote respect for children.

Recognizing Individual Needs

Recognizing individual needs is another element in giving children positive understanding of self and the sense that they are respected. Institutions generally take away children's individual rights. In public schools, an ever-increasing emphasis is placed on conformity, and children learn quickly to do what their teacher tells them to do to avoid getting in trouble or being labeled a problem child.

Child-centered teachers, however, limit the emphasis they place on conforming behaviors. If Juan needs a little more time to enter Circle Time, then the adult will begin her plans and acknowledge Juan when he joins the group. Bailey takes more time to eat her snack than others, but the supervising adult will allow for her leisure

FIGURE 5.2 Classroom Practices That Promote Respect for Children

Listening to children when they talk
Conveying warmth and nurture to children
Comforting children when they are upset, frustrated, or angry
Noticing when children accomplish new tasks or produce interesting projects
Communicating regularly with families and getting to know them well
Using positive discipline techniques that tell children how to behave
Preparing a classroom environment that meets children's needs
Planning activities that are appropriate for children's ages
Remembering promises made to children

instead of rushing her to gulp her food or tossing it out in order to keep schedules in place. Occasionally, children need private time with the teacher or another adult.

The types of children's needs can be categorized into five areas: physical, social, emotional, creative, and cognitive (Hendrick, 2003). When teachers plan experiences for children, if they plan for each of these five areas, then children's needs are met. The group schedule will flow more smoothly and children will be happier in their surroundings. The California Department of Education (2000) acknowledges that play environments promote language competencies, problem-solving skills, and social interactions in children.

Teaching Social Skills

Teaching social skills is another responsibility of the teacher in the prekindergarten classroom. Children follow adult models when learning to share, to take turns, to remember to say "please" and "thank you," to use appropriate table manners, and to greet and interact with individuals in their environment. Children are not born with "social graces," and these skills need to be taught by their parents and teachers. Even teaching children to "use your words, not your fists" becomes a challenge for adults who work with them.

When teachers notice that problems are arising on a routine basis and their modeling is not working, sometimes a small-group or Circle Time discussion can help youngsters learn what they need to know to be more social. "I noticed today during center choice selection that some of you excluded Austine, who wanted to join the block building session," a teacher might say. "What are some ways that we can solve this problem?"

Occasionally, the adult discovers that she needs to give children instruction about how to join a new play setting. Austine may have been "barging in" and joining the group instead of saying, "I want to join you," or "You look like you could use some help." Equally important is the child's understanding of the word "no" from her peers. The teacher may need to help her deal with rejection and make a decision about another activity she would enjoy instead of block play. "You can join this area later when Kyle and Trey are through with their play."

Teaching Problem-Solving Skills

Helping children acquire *problem-solving skills* is another goal for the preschool teacher (Reynolds, 2001). Children often have one approach to solving a problem (hitting or giving up, as examples), but they need numerous strategies for problem solving to help them grow into competent adults who can solve their own problems. Talking with children as problems arise and sharing alternative strategies for solving difficulties is a major approach to teaching problem-solving skills.

Setting up situations that require problem-solving activity is another strategy teachers might use. "Let's move the house furniture to another place in the classroom. Where should we put it? Is one place better than another? Let's look at the reasons why we should do this or why we shouldn't. Will everyone need to be involved in making the move? Are there easier ways to move the furniture instead of just picking up the pieces?"

As simple as it seems, problem-solving skills are learned by allowing children the freedom to solve problems on their own. Sometimes the adult stands back for a while in order to give children an opportunity to make a decision (this is permissible as long as children are safe). Sometimes the teacher says, "Have you considered putting the block on its side instead of the end?" or "What's another way we could clean up the lunch table?" Allowing children to share a repertoire of ideas serves as a teaching strategy for other children who have not acquired an understanding that most problems can be solved in more than one way.

Sharing stories about how adults make decisions, such as buying a new car or whether to go to Jack in the Box for tonight's meal, gives children information about decision-making skills. Group decision-making experience occurs when the class decides whether to buy a pet for the room, what type of pet it will be, and the pros and cons of each purchase. Obtaining a kitten from the local animal shelter may be fine, but keeping it in a cage during the school day is unacceptable. A hamster could be a good choice, but some hamsters bite. Working within the constraints of the classroom budget gives children some insight about the variables that need to be considered when decisions are made.

Helping Children Learn to Negotiate

Negotiating skills fit hand in hand with problem solving and social skill acquisition. Adult modeling and intervention help children in becoming proficient in negotiating for what they want (Reynolds, 2001). From a child's viewpoint, the easiest way to get something he wants is to grab it from another, with no concern about the victim's feelings. The "use your words, not your fists" rule needs to apply to all classroom situations, and teaching children how to get objects they want is as much a part of the prekindergarten curriculum as is learning to count to 10.

The victim's needs should be addressed as well, and experts recognize how important the message is to the bully if the victim is given attention and concern before addressing the actions of the bully (Katz & McClelland, 1997). The teacher's use of words provides a strong model to children about how they should behave in touchy situations. For example, the teacher might say, "I know you're hurting.

Tell Bruce how you feel about his snatching your toy. Use your words to tell him how upset you are."

Teachers' expression of emotions is as important as their recommendations that problems can be solved. "Duncan, you can see how upset Derek is because you snatched his truck. Let's talk about a way you can share the toy when Derek is through with it. What are some suggestions for solving this problem?" This scenario will need to be repeated numerous times before children are able to internalize the skills they need to negotiate their own problems. The teacher's patience in orchestrating many repetitions of this problem-solving activity will yield dividends as children mature and have more experiences with having their needs met. Other sample teacher responses are shown in Figure 5.3.

Helping Children Develop Self-Control

The development of *self-control* in children is the long-term outcome of teachers being patient and kind when dealing with children (Hendrick, 2003). The type of classroom guidance that focuses on children's gaining control over their own behavior refers to *intrinsic* motivation. Intrinsic behavior occurs when children behave in a certain way because they know that their behavior is appropriate and kind to others. In other words, children share because sharing makes them feel good. Children walk in a line down the hall because they understand that this is a safer procedure than running down the hall. Children remember to use words to express their displeasure or anger about a specific situation because they know that in doing so, they are being conscious of another's feelings, yet they are being assertive about their own rights.

Even some adults should learn more about being sensitive to others' needs. Instead of lashing out at children when she is angry, another prekindergarten teacher sits in her classroom "power chair" when she feels she is out of control. Her model assists children in learning about gaining self-control.

Classroom teachers have often relied on *extrinsic* motivators to encourage the kind of behavior children need (or at least the kind of behavior the teacher thinks children need). They provide stickers, stars, parties, and other extrinsic rewards to promote children's conformity to a set of classroom rules. Instead of asking children to understand the reason for rules, they immediately stamp the child's hand with a smiley face, taking away the intrinsic value children might feel for having been appropriate in their actions toward others.

Extrinsic motivators also demean what the children can accomplish for themselves. An overreliance on extrinsic rewards causes children to doubt their own instincts about what is "right" and what is "wrong." The dichotomy is that adults are trying to encourage children by giving them rewards for something they have done well, yet children receive the rewards, believing that their own judgments are not sound (Kohn, 1993). Eventually, children begin to look for rewards for everything they do. A teacher whose son had been inducted into the "rewards game" as he entered school asked his mother when he was in the second grade what he would get if he cleaned his room as she had requested. The mother's thoughtful response was, "A clean room."

FIGURE 5.3 Sample Teacher Responses to Children's Comments

Example 1

Child: "Teacher, look at my picture."
Teacher: "Yes, Mark, I see that you like red quite well."
Child: "It's my favorite color."
Teacher: "What do you like best about your picture?"

Explanation: The goal in this situation is to assist the child in evaluating his own work. The teacher has not placed a value judgment on the quality of the art, and she has commented about what she can actually see (the color red). By approaching the child's work in this manner, she allows the child to recognize for himself the accomplishment he has achieved.

Example 2

Child: "Teacher, Jeremy hit me."
Teacher: "What did you tell him?"
Child: "I told him I didn't want him to hit me any more."
Teacher: "Did he stop hitting you?"
Child: "Yes."
Teacher: "Then you know what to do when someone hits you, don't you?"
Child: Nods her head "yes."
Teacher: "I think you've learned something today about how to handle your own problems."

Explanation: The teacher is helping the child understand that she has handled her own problem with a classmate. By recognizing this behavior and acknowledging the child's handling of the problem, she allows the child to perceive herself as a problem solver.

Example 3

Child: "Yipppppppeeeeeeeeeel!" (as he knocks over Marjetta's block structure)
Teacher: "Hey, John, remember our rule about knocking over block structures?"
Child: "Yeah." (looking sheepish)
Teacher: "How can we help Marjetta with this problem? Looks to me like she's pretty upset."
Child: "I'll help her build a new structure."
Teacher: "Is that acceptable to you, Marjetta?"
Marjetta: "Sure, Mrs. Barton."
Teacher: "Yes, it appears that John forgot our rule. But I think he'll remember in the future, won't you, John?"

Explanation: The teacher has demonstrated the skill of negotiation to John and Marjetta. She also gently reminded John of a classroom rule essential to normal classroom functioning.

A prekindergarten teacher explained the difference between intrinsic and extrinsic factors that control behavior to a parent when he came to complain that his son had been hit on the playground. "I've told him to hit back when someone hits him," confided the parent.

"Let's talk about that, Mr. Gentry. Suppose your son has grown up and is standing at the checkout counter at the grocery store. Would you want him to turn around and hit the person behind him if that individual has accidentally bumped him with his cart?"

"Why, no, of course, not," exclaimed Mr. Gentry.

"That's what you're teaching your child to do—you're telling him that it's okay to use his fists when someone has hurt him, either purposefully or accidentally. In our classroom, we teach children how to handle their problems with words. This is a difficult but critical lesson to learn even though your child is only 4 years old. Learning to talk about one's problems rationally is a concept all children need to learn as they grow to maturity."

Recall that Vygotsky suggests that children learn self-control through play. When a child takes on the role of a pet, then the child can use only behaviors that pets exhibit. If the child comes out of his role to talk or perform some other nonpet behavior, then he shows that he is not able to manage himself during the course of the play (Bodrova & Leong, 1996).

Self-control also relates to one's personal habits as well. Thumb-sucking behaviors and masturbation are problems early educators observe in their classrooms on occasion. Children often resort to these habits when they are tired or experiencing emotional conflict (Hendrick, 2003). Children do not think of these behaviors as "bad," but rather as comforting actions when they need emotional support.

Responding sensitively to children who masturbate in public is essential to helping parents and children alike understand the social implications of their emotional demonstrations. Finding alternative activities for children to participate in is one solution (holding a teddy bear or doll, playing with clay or playdough, or doing easel or finger painting might be helpful substitutes), but adults also need to explain why the exhibited behavior is unacceptable. Telling children that masturbation is something that should be done in private in one's bedroom should assist in eliminating this unwanted behavior. Thumbsuckers will need many gentle reminders before this behavior disappears.

Preventing Negative Cycles of Behavior

Teachers also need to intervene when they observe that children's negative behaviors are standing in the way of their healthy emotional development. Evidence exists that negative behaviors are more easily addressed when children are young (Katz & Chard, 2000). As children grow older, both positive and negative behaviors become more firmly entrenched and helping children learn more effective strategies for socialization and self-control becomes more difficult.

Can classroom teachers and administrators ensure that caring communities of learners are being developed? One important element in the development of community is the *attitude of the teacher.* Teachers need to assess their own behaviors occasionally to determine if they are treating all children fairly and justly. Teachers sometimes label a child as a "problem" and thereafter whatever behavior the child exhibits is considered "bad."

Educators should guard against seeing any child as one-dimensional in personality, as an individual who will always behave in the same manner. If an adult observes restless, squirmy behavior in a child and thinks that this is a behavior problem, then the child's behavior will always seem negative. If the adult thinks instead that the child needs an opportunity to go to the playground to work out some of his or her restlessness, then the child's behavior seems less problematic.

Another strategy for ensuring more positive behavior in children is to show care and concern for their activities (another aspect of demonstrating respect to children). Getting to know children's families shows respect. Giving children an opportunity to talk about what they like to do, how they spend time with their families, family pets, and special family outings improves their belief that the teacher cares. Home visits, if permitted by the school district, enhance the relationship between the educator and the child.

Asking children to take responsibility in the classroom can aid in their becoming an integral part of the community group. Maybe Audra can be messenger for the week or Vir can be in charge of holding the flag during the pledge. Chrissy can be given the chore of feeding the fish for a few days, and then responsibility for specific jobs can rotate to others. All children need responsibilities for cleanup in the classroom, and remembering to take home their belongings at the end of the day adds to their growing sense of responsible behavior.

Children's respect for themselves grows as well when adults recognize their accomplishments. Encouragement and praise are not the same. Children need encouragement and acknowledgment that what they are doing has adult approval. Praise is often misused in classrooms as a strategy for controlling children's behavior instead of guiding it. When children do something worthwhile, the teacher's appropriate comment about the activity will help them develop a sense of pride in what they are doing. Charles needs to be able to say, "I did this myself."

Charles did tell his teacher one morning, "I'm learning to write my name, but don't tell my mother." She knew that his parents were pressuring their 4-year-old to learn to write, but the teacher's wisdom in allowing writing to occur naturally was more conducive to Charles's attempts to write. Charles felt more comfortable tackling the task at school because he was aware that the teacher would acknowledge his early scribbles without judgment and criticism.

Children learn how to get along with one another more easily during the preschool years.

Helping children learn how to ask for help is another aspect of community spirit. Children who help one another and respond to others' needs develop into adults who care for others. One prekindergarten teacher had a rule that children could call on another child for an answer during Circle Time if they did not have an answer to a question. Children learn more cooperative behaviors when a rule of this type exists in the classroom.

Teachers who know children well will make comments like, "I hope Pete goes into Mrs. Sawyer's kindergarten next year. He needs someone who will accept and stimulate his creative mind." Or a teacher might say, "I discovered throughout the year that Colin needs more careful supervision than others in my class. He never seems to know what to do unless I make a suggestion to him. Then he gets turned on and runs with the idea."

Or a parent may even say to her child's teacher, "I know Beverly is sensitive—she's always been like that. Thanks for reminding me that this is a problem we should work on. She loves school, but I don't want her sensitivity to become such a problem for her that she's unwilling to learn. Your recommendation that she needs more explanation about what others mean when they talk about her is a good one. I'll try to follow up with this plan of action."

⭐ OTHER EMOTIONAL ISSUES PREKINDERGARTEN CHILDREN FACE

Young children exhibit a variety of emotions when they come to school for the first time. The source of their emotions is not always obvious to teachers, and sometimes parents are unable to explain why their children behave uncharacteristically in the classroom. Some of the more common emotions demonstrated are fear, shyness, antisocial behavior, and aggressiveness.

Fear

Many children are afraid of new situations, and they need a responsible adult to give them comfort as they make transitions into new environments. One child may walk into a fast-food restaurant with confidence, whereas another child will see a room full of strangers who are frightening to her. Any setting can be disruptive to children's emotional well-being if they are not prepared for it. The school classroom can be overwhelming, too, and parents and teachers may need to give solace to the child who is fearful. Marcus's story, shared later in this chapter, is an example of a child who was afraid of his classroom despite having been to the actual classroom before he went to school.

Shyness

Shyness is a form of low self-esteem, and shy children are usually not confident within groups of children. They feel inadequate or incompetent, and their experiential backgrounds may not have prepared them for classroom activity. Shyness may also be an imitated behavior learned from parents who feel inadequate about school routines and rituals. The teacher's job is to put shy children at ease as quickly as possible and provide confidence-building activities for them. Prekindergarten settings should provide activity choices that children can use to express themselves safely and securely. Competence breeds confidence. Through time, children will feel comfortable with their abilities.

Sharing and Turn Taking

One of the most important social skills children learn during the prekindergarten year is the ability to share and take turns in groups of children. As Piagetian theory suggests, 4-year-old children are egocentric (see Chapter 2 for further discussion). *Egocentrism* implies that youngsters see the world from their own viewpoints, and they often behave as if no other children exist. Sharing and turn taking are acquired skills, not innate ones. Teachers can assist children in learning to share and take turns by:

- Explaining to children what sharing and turn taking are
- Noticing the skills and commenting positively when they are observed
- Continuing to explain what sharing and turn taking are
- Communicating to parents about the issue and giving them advice about supporting the learning at home
- Complimenting children when they share and take turns

Separation

Separation issues begin during infancy for children (Driscoll & Nagel, 1999), continuing until the end of childhood. Children seek familiar adults, and they feel more secure in everyday surroundings that help them feel comfortable and safe. Acquainting children with the school setting before they enter the new classroom usually alleviates separation anxiety for youngsters, but some children need more reassurance in separating from their parents or guardians, even if only for a short period of time. Children who have parents who are separated or are divorcing will likely have significant separation issues requiring professional intervention from outside the classroom.

Aggressiveness

Periodically, a few children exhibit aggressiveness or other challenging antisocial behavior, such as stealing or chronic lying, in prekindergarten classrooms. Generally, this type of misbehavior is limited and relates to a problem in the home setting. The behavior will disappear when the problem at home goes away. When the antisocial behavior continues, teachers should rely on a clearly defined plan of action to assist the child in demonstrating more socially acceptable behavior.

Chandler and Dahlquist (2002) recommend (1) repeated instructions about appropriate behaviors, (2) providing physical prompts to remind the child of appropriate behaviors (such as touching or hugging the child), (3) ignoring aggressive behavior, and (4) praising the child when compliant behavior is exhibited. Karly's story, shared later in this chapter, is an example of a child whose teacher dealt with her aggressiveness.

Dealing with Death

Death comes in a number of forms for young children—finding a dead bird on the playground, the death of a pet, deaths of grandparents, and even the death of a parent or sibling. Nagy (1948) studied children's understanding of death and defined three distinct developmental stages.

> *Stage 1* (up to age 5): Children have little understanding of death. They may know and use the word, but they have no comprehension of the concept of death. One 3-year-old said she did not want to die because she did not want all that dirt up her nose.
> *Stage 2* (from ages 5 to 8): Children have rudimentary understanding of death, but they believe they can escape death because they are young or they can use magic rituals to avoid dying. Their view is that the dead are underground carrying on their usual activities.
> *Stage 3* (beginning at about age 9): Children begin to understand death in the same way that adults view death. They see death as a permanent condition, and their grief begins to parallel the demonstrations of grief adults show.

Nagy (1948) explains that young children are most fearful of the death of their mothers. Preschoolers who are experiencing deaths of loved ones require close observation, sympathetic concern, and even referral for professional counseling (Gordon & Klass, 1979).

⭐ EXAMPLES OF A FEW CLASSROOM PROBLEM CHILDREN

The following descriptions are examples of children who presented problem behaviors to the teachers who worked with them. The teachers involved (1) observed the problem behavior, (2) analyzed the behavior to determine a course of action to take, (3) implemented the plan of action, (4) enlisted parental support for the plan, and (5) worked to a successful conclusion (Warner & Lynch, 2001).

Marcus

Marcus's cries could be heard all around the classroom and the center when he arrived at school the first day of the fall semester. His mother was trying to be

Guidelines for Social and Emotional Development

Most educators recognize the importance of social and emotional development for young children, and academic guidelines reflect the concept that 4-year-olds are beginning to develop a strong sense of self and autonomy. The **Texas** Education Agency has developed the following guidelines for prekindergarten children.

Prekindergarten children develop personal and social skills that enable them to function well within the social setting of the classroom. Children develop a sense of who they are and their capabilities, and establish positive relationships with others, which enables them to effectively participate in class and community and accomplish meaningful tasks.

(1) PERSONAL DEVELOPMENT

Children develop a sense of self in prekindergarten. They begin to show initiative in learning and begin to take greater responsibility for their own behavior. They learn to channel their energies in ways that promote effective learning experiences.

The child:

develops a sense of personal space
expresses interests and self-direction in learning
begins to show self-control by following classroom rules
begins to be responsible for individual behavior and actions
begins to show greater ability to control intense feelings (e.g., anger).

(2) SOCIAL DEVELOPMENT

Children develop interpersonal and social skills for communicating with others. They learn alternatives for resolving conflicts and communicating their needs and feelings verbally, and they begin to develop and maintain productive relationships with other children.

The child:

begins to share and cooperate with others in group activities
respects other people's space and personal belongings
begins to develop friendships with others
begins to express thoughts, feelings, and ideas through language as well as
    through gestures and actions
responds to the suggestions of others

(Texas Education Agency, 1997).

supportive, encouraging Marcus by reminding him that he had been to this classroom previously when his older brother Ryan was a prekindergartner here and that he knew Mrs. Hebert, his teacher.

"Marcus, remember you even came here this summer when I registered you for school," said Mrs. Muns. "You enjoyed riding the big trike, and you played with the blocks for a while. Ryan used to show you how to build tall buildings when he came to this classroom."

Mrs. Hebert soon knelt to Marcus's eye level and used her most soothing voice to comfort her new charge. She remembered that Ryan had made an easy transition to school; Marcus exhibited a different personality, however, and he appeared to be more dependent on his mother, grasping her hand even more securely this early morning. "You know, Marcus, I know you'll enjoy meeting the other children in our classroom, and I think you even know Sandy Louise. Doesn't she live in your neighborhood?"

"That's right," responded Mrs. Muns, "Let's go say 'hi' to Sandy. She can show you around the classroom. You know I have to go to work soon."

"Mrs. Muns, you're welcome to stay as long as you can until Marcus feels comfortable here," Mrs. Hebert said as she continued to talk soothingly to Marcus and pointed out to him the features of the room that he would be sure to enjoy during the day.

The days that followed were never easy for Marcus. Each morning the crying, clinging ritual continued when his mother arrived to drop him off before going to work. In each daily encounter, the parent and the teacher joined in their efforts to nurture Marcus, encouraging him to understand that his mother had to work and that he needed to stay at school during the day. Mrs. Muns brought favorite toys to leave with Marcus each day and departed with a kiss for her child and a promise that she would return at 11:30 a.m. Mrs. Hebert assisted Marcus by helping him draw pictures for his mother or write dictation for notes that he wanted to give her when she returned.

The success in this story came after many months of patient work between teacher and family to achieve the same goal for Marcus: that he would enjoy being in school. When dismissal time came, Mrs. Hebert reported to Marcus's mother about his progress during the morning, and she always said, "See you tomorrow, Marcus."

After six months or so, Marcus began to appear more comfortable in his relationships with others in the classroom and even seemed to look forward to going to school. Periodically, his fretting, crying behavior would occur again, but the consistency of the adults in his environment, at home and at school, helped him feel more secure about being away from home.

Mrs. Hebert wisely began thinking about an upcoming transition to kindergarten that Marcus would need to make soon, and she began talking to all the children in her classroom about what experiences they would have when they went to another classroom. In April, she decided a trip to the school's kindergarten wing would help Marcus and his classmates make the transition that they would face the following August.

Karly

Ms. Vasquez was beginning to feel frustrated with Karly early in the prekindergarten year. School had started in late August, and by mid-September Karly was already exhibiting the biting behavior she used in relationships with other children in the classroom.

"I don't know what to do," Ms. Vasquez told her principal. "Karly has bitten three children just this week, and each time I explain to her what the consequences of her action are. I keep telling Karly that biting doesn't help her make friends, but this explanation doesn't seem to faze her at all."

"Have you talked to her parents?" asked her principal. Ms. Vasquez said, "I have an appointment with them this afternoon, so maybe we can arrive at a logical solution to this problem."

Ms. Vasquez knew that biting was behavior typical of younger children, especially toddlers, but she had never before had a biter in her 4-year-old class. When she met Karly's parents, the information they gave her did not seem to throw light on the situation, either. Karly was an adopted child, so any tendency toward aggressive behavior was not information the parents knew about. They did report that Karly played with older cousins in the evenings and on weekends, and their interactions were of the "rough-and-tumble" variety.

According to her parents, Karly ate an adequate breakfast before coming to the center, so she should not be excessively hungry—one primitive theory about why young children bite. Ms. Vasquez told Karly's parents that biting often occurs in preverbal children, ones who do not have words to adequately express their emotions. Neither of these theories seemed to fit Karly's case.

Ms. Vasquez decided that she needed to do some data collection to answer the following questions: When did the biting occur? Who were her targets? Were there prompts or activities in the classroom that led to the biting? Did she seem angry when she was biting or was she frustrated?

After several weeks of observation and ongoing discussions with Karly about the consequences of biting her classroom friends, Ms. Vasquez decided that Karly's behavior related to lack of appropriate social opportunities with other children her age. She continued to talk to Karly when it appeared that biting was about to occur, and she visited with Karly's parents about finding more suitable companions for Karly to play with at home.

Again, the teacher's success with this problem did not come quickly. A nearby university offered play therapy to children and their families, and Ms. Vasquez recommended that the family seek this resource for help. They attended several sessions before the December break, but the play therapist was unable to report any breakthrough in determining the source of the child's misbehavior.

In early January Ms. Vasquez tried another technique. "Karly," she said, "When you feel like you need to bite someone, stop and tell yourself, 'No biting, no biting.' Can you do that?" Special educators label this technique *self-prompting* (Warner & Lynch, 2001).

Karly agreed that she could say the words "no biting, no biting" to herself, and Ms. Vasquez would take Karly aside each morning when she arrived to remind her of the self-talk strategy. Several more weeks passed before Karly finally was able to curtail her temptation to bite her classmates, who were usually quieter, shy girls who tended to cry when bitten, instead of saying assertively, "Don't bite me!" The teacher was careful each time an infraction occurred to give sympathy to Karly's victims and instruct them about dealing with her aggression, asking them to stay out of Karly's way when it appeared she might be ready to bite and to assert themselves about not liking her biting behavior.

Ms. Vasquez also began a vigorous campaign to smile at the end of each day Karly demonstrated appropriate social behavior by telling her, "I noticed that you made it through today without biting anyone. Don't you feel good about yourself because you didn't bite your friends?" Within about two months, Karly stopped biting others.

Luke

Mr. Morrison knew Luke because he was returning to his multiage classroom for the second year of a prekindergarten/kindergarten combination. He had remembered Luke as a 4-year-old child who was friendly, congenial, and intelligent, and he was looking forward to having another comfortable year with Luke. Luke knew the classroom rules, he was a leader with his peers, and he loved coming to school to learn. Mr. Morrison could not remember one single incident from the previous year that caused any concern that Luke's development was out of the ordinary.

The first day of school, Luke arrived late, but Mr. Morrison greeted him cheerfully and visited with him briefly to ask about his summer experiences. During group time, though, he noticed that Luke was not attending well, and he appeared to be deliberately causing a distraction for his classmates by banging his hands on the floor. Later in the morning, he heard Luke exclaim to a younger child, "Kelvin, you're not doing that right! Here, I'll show you how to write your name."

As Mr. Morrison approached the two children, Luke looked up and spat out with exasperation, "Look, teacher, Kelvin says he wrote the words *green light*. That doesn't say *green light*. He's wrong."

At first, Mr. Morrison believed that Luke was just having a bad day. After all, he had arrived late that morning. He may not have been feeling well. But in the days and weeks after school started, he noticed continuing negative behaviors and almost an unkempt look in the child's dress and demeanor. Luke occasionally threw temper tantrums, and he was becoming increasingly more aggressive with his peers. He would not participate during group time, and he spent most of center time disrupting other children's play activities. Certainly, a behavior change was evident to Mr. Morrison, and other professionals in the building who had not been acquainted with Luke from the previous year noticed his aggressiveness.

Was something going on at home that Mr. Morrison needed to learn about? Children react to stressful situations by lashing out at others, especially when they believe that they are in a safe environment and that no repercussions will occur from kind and patient adults. Mr. Morrison had provided a safe environment for Luke during the previous year, and Luke was using every strategy he could think of to indicate to his teacher that he had some problems on his mind. He just did not know how to say, "I've got a problem here, will you help me?"

Luke's mother was responsive to Mr. Morrison's phone call to discuss the problems Luke was having at school, and the information she shared was quite helpful to the concerned teacher. "Thanks for calling, Mr. Morrison," she said. "I've been meaning to call you, but I've just not had the time. You see, Luke's father has a new job that requires him to travel a lot, and I'm burdened with my mother's problems. She's dying with cancer, and I know that I'm not as patient with Luke as I need to be. We keep her at home with us as much as we can, but since school started I've had to take her to the hospital twice. I leave Luke and his brother with the neighbors, but our routine is disrupted and I know he is unhappy."

Mr. Morrison was relieved that Luke's parents were not divorcing and wasn't Luke being abused. His resolve was to talk to Luke every day to find out about his grandmother and to give him the additional support he needed during his family's crisis. Luke's problems were not going to disappear overnight, but Mr. Morrison believed that he could make a difference in Luke's understanding of his situation.

"Maybe it's time to sit down with Luke and read *Alexander and the Terrible, Horrible, No Good, Very Bad Day* (Viorst, 1972) with him. That will give us a chance to start talking," thought Mr. Morrison as he made his lesson plans for the following day.

Regina

Four-year-old Regina seemed like a pleasant child when she came to prekindergarten, but Mrs. Linn learned quickly that Regina did not fit in well with her peers. She was not an aggressive child, but she seemed frantic to join in with others when they were playing. Her social skills were absent, and she would rush into play settings with puppylike abandon, disrupting the play already in progress. Fortunately, the other children did not perceive that she was pushy and rarely complained of her interruptions because she was small and rather fragile. Most of the time, with a few adaptations on the part of the players, Regina became a member of the group after a few minutes.

Regina rarely attended well during the time she was at school. She did not appear to listen during Circle Time, and she stared dreamily out of a window or looked around the room with a dazed look on her face. Sometimes Regina would listlessly attend to something else in the classroom while the rest of the class was lining up to go out to the playground. When Mrs. Linn administered her first pediculosis check for nits (lice eggs) in the class, she discovered that Regina needed to be sent home from school with a note to her parents to take care of the problem. Mrs. Linn was surprised by this turn of events, because Regina appeared to be clean and her hair was thin—it was almost impossible for nits to grow on her hair.

Mrs. Linn knew that the nurse would come toward the end of the month to check every child's hearing and vision, and she was hopeful that indicators would appear during this visit to indicate problems Regina might have that could be corrected. Other strategies she determined to use in the classroom were to:

- Seat Regina close to her during Circle Time activities.
- Call Regina by name when transitional activities were necessary.
- Use a visual cue (a picture or object) to attract Regina's attention when she was seated in group activities.
- Give Regina some instruction about how to enter play settings.
- Check Regina's head when she came to school every morning.
- Send her to the school nurse for assistance if nits appeared again.

Mrs. Linn also decided that the time had come to talk to Regina's parents, though scheduled conference times were planned for a later time in the year. She wondered if the family had some unusual problems that were preventing Regina from becoming socially acceptable in the classroom. Perhaps a community agency would be available to help the family with whatever crisis might be facing them. The first step was a note home to Regina's mother, but she was aware that a home visit might be necessary to make contact with the family.

☆ HELPING CHILDREN EXPRESS THEMSELVES

A major goal in prekindergarten classrooms is to help 4-year-olds to express themselves orally and in print. The foundations of expression come in the form of art, music, and movement experiences (Bredekamp & Copple, 1997). The ability to scribble and make representational art forms and the ability to sing and move to music are essential ingredients of self-expression. Teachers who provide materials and time for exploration and experimentation with art and musical innovations lay the foundations for literacy development and children's sense of pride in their own work. Research evidence suggests that the addition of fine arts to the school curriculum promotes academic achievement in schools (Winner & Hetland, 2001).

Art

The visual arts in elementary schools are generally downplayed in favor of language arts and math instruction. Prekindergarten teachers, on the other hand, recognize more clearly the importance of putting marks on paper that represent print and representation forms because they understand the cognitive value of art. For young children, art is a form of visual thinking, and theorists from Arnheim to Fein to Carini to Howard Gardner support this conceptualization of art as a mental endeavor (Engel, 1995). Children's art demonstrates their thinking processes and provides adults a glimpse into their minds.

One authority on children's art, Victor Lowenfeld (1947), describes the following stages of development in early childhood and beyond.

- *Scribbling* (ages 2–4): Children begin to experiment with marks on paper as a means to express themselves; the first marks are usually dots and circles.
- *Pre-Schematic* (ages 4–7): Children refine their scribbles and begin to identify and label their marks on paper with names.
- *Schematic* (ages 7–9): Children draw forms that are easily identifiable by others; often these forms follow a set design (or schema) that recurs among drawings.

The keys to positive art experiences in prekindergarten classrooms are (1) plenty of classroom materials, and (2) time to explore the materials. Mrs. Flores's classroom features an Art Center that has two easels, a large drying rack, accessible materials, and a sink nearby. Materials include crayons, markers, scissors, manila paper, construction paper, newspaper, numerous varieties of paint, scraps of fabric, chenille strips, glue, paste, and other craft items, such as Popsicle sticks, tongue depressors, sequins, Styrofoam balls and cups, paper plates, and ribbon. Her stock of painting smocks is sufficient for all children to participate in the Art Center if they choose to do so. Her favorite art experiences for her 4-year-olds are shown in Table 5.1.

TABLE 5.1 Art Experiences for 4-Year-Olds

Torn paper art	Tissue paper art
Premade stamps and paper	Stamps and stamp pads
Wet chalk drawing	Tracing stencil shapes
Tracing one's hand	Painting with cotton balls
Finger painting	Flower petal painting
Handprint or footprint designs	Splatter painting (with teacher assistance)
Painting over doilies	
Marble painting	Blowing ink through straws
Making figures from precut shapes	Crayon relief over paper on leaves (or other textures)
Paper plate or Styrofoam cup puppets	
Puppets from discarded socks	Small-group mural painting
Painting rocks	Box sculptures
Aluminum foil ornaments	Papier-mache
Commercial stickers	Gluing objects onto paper
Sponge shape art	Clay or playdough
Collages with leaves or natural materials	Thumbprint art

Music

Musical experiences are a natural outlet for young children. They have favorite tunes, and they find delight in a musical session as well as older children do. The song "Jingle Bells" is as popular in May as it is in December. Teachers of young children do not need to be proficient musicians—they need only to be able to promote an enjoyment of music. The Music Educators National Conference (MENC) defines these characteristics of effective musical experiences for young children. They include teachers':

- Support of the child's total development—physical, emotional, social, and cognitive
- Recognition of the wide range of normal development in prekindergartners and the need to differentiate their instruction
- Facilitation of learning through active interaction with adults and other children as well as with music materials
- Planning of learning activities and materials that are real, concrete, and relevant to the lives of young children
- Provision of opportunities for children to choose from among a variety of music activities, materials, and equipment of varying degrees of difficulty
- Allowance of time for children to explore music through active involvement

McDonald (1979) suggests that 4-year-olds are ready for a steady introduction of easy-to-sing melodies that help them learn some basic concepts about music. Prekindergarten children can become aware that melodies exist and that melodies have a steady beat, can go up and down, and are repeated in easily recognized phrases. She also recommends that "music for the young child starts with exploration, imitation, experimentation which can lead to discrimination, organization, creation which, in turn, can lead to reorganization, production, and conceptualization" (McDonald, 1979, p. 8).

Mrs. Flores insists on using easy-to-sing songs with her 4-year-olds. Some of her children have musical talent, but most need music that will match the physiological structure of their young voices. She relies on the following well-known favorites because they fit a five- or six-note range that is appropriate for young children. Occasionally, she makes up new words for these familiar tunes when she needs a song about an unusual topic:

"Twinkle, Twinkle, Little Star"	"Hot Cross Buns"
"Mary Had a Little Lamb"	"The Farmer in the Dell"
"London Bridge is Falling Down"	"Alphabet Song"
"Baa, Baa, Black Sheep"	"Ring around the Rosies"
"This Old Man"	"Miss Merry Mack"
"Have You Ever Seen a Lassie?"	"Skip to My Lou"
"B-I-N-G-O"	"Bow Wow Wow"

Music provides numerous benefits in classrooms of young children. Singing helps children with memory acquisition, listening skills, vocabulary development, and storytelling. Children who have many singing experiences become better at-tuned to musical concepts, and they discover pleasure inherent in musical activi-ties. Evidence exists that suggests that music helps children develop positive self-concepts (Warner, 1999). Mrs. Flores tries to incorporate singing into her class-room plans every day.

Movement

Separating musical and movement activities in classrooms of young children is dif-ficult because they go hand in hand. Learning that songs have steady beats implies that children are moving to the music. Many songs require that children move to the beat of the music by adding predetermined movements or their own creative reactions to perform the song. Many musical recordings are designed for move-ment participation by marching, clapping, sliding, swaying, swinging, tiptoeing, pretending to skate, nodding, reaching, and bending. Popular musical games in early childhood classrooms expect children to participate in some way. The "Hokey Pokey" and "Looby Loo" are common examples of movement experiences for prekindergarten children.

Fundamental movement experiences fall into three movement categories: sta-bility, locomotor, and manipulative. Stork (2000, p. 40) classifies movement skills into these three areas:

LOCOMOTOR SKILLS	MANIPULATIVE SKILLS	NONMANIPULATIVE SKILLS
walking	throwing	turning
running	catching and collecting	twisting
hopping	kicking	rolling
skipping	punting	balancing
galloping	dribbling	transferring weight
sliding	volleying	jumping and landing
chasing, fleeing and	striking with rackets	stretching
dodging	striking with long-	curling
	handled implements	

Basic playground equipment, such as balls, ropes, hoops, a parachute, balance beams, lightweight rackets, mallets, slides, climbing bars, and tire swings allow for the development of these mentioned skills in a low-pressure environment that allows children to make choices. Teaching children simple games such as "Jump the Brook," "Duck, Duck, Goose," or "Red Light, Green Light" requires children to utilize these skills within the range of their abilities.

Sanders (2002) reminds educators that movement programs and youth sports programs have different purposes. Sports programs emphasize competitive-ness and skill acquisition beyond the abilities of 4-year-olds. Prekindergarten children need movement opportunities that assist preschoolers in improving self,

naeyc

participation, and cooperation. A foundation of movement experiences allows for the development of skills, which serve as a foundation for later involvement in sports activities.

Reporting to Parents

Many school districts do not establish prekindergarten report cards to send home with children, but prekindergarten teachers recognize the value of keeping parents informed about their children's progress. In Mrs. Flores's school, three established conference times are advertised and supported by businesses and employers in the area. These conferences are set at 12 weeks (November), 24 weeks (February), and 36 weeks (end of the school year). Mrs. Flores collects data for each child throughout the school year to share with parents or guardians during conference periods. Though these work samples are not portfolios in the truest sense (children did not choose what work to put into the folders), they do represent the progress children are making in the prekindergarten setting. (See Chapter 6 to learn more about portfolio development.)

Mrs. Flores also uses cameras in her classroom frequently. The school purchased a digital camera and video camera for each grade level, and Mrs. Flores brings them in regularly to take pictures of children in action. Often she sends home a print from the computer with a written explanation attached describing what a specific child is doing (and learning). Duplicates are kept for a class book, which she prepares for the children to review, because she places it in the Book Corner. Later in the year, she will use the video camera clips to prepare a video to share with the parents when they come to an end-of-the-school-year program. Her school asks parents to sign media permission forms at the beginning of the school year.

SUMMARY

Prekindergarten teachers nurture and support the children they teach, planning more fully for social and emotional activities than do teachers of older children. However, they recognize the learning capacity of their children, and they provide numerous enjoyable and challenging opportunities for children to learn about letters, numbers, their environment, and getting along with others. They plan regular Circle Times, center activity, snacks, outdoor play, and ample self-expressive experiences.

Prekindergarten teachers also look for signs that children need intervention services before entering kindergarten. Teachers of 4-year-olds are eager to meet children's parents because they recognize their important role as "children's first teachers." From the beginning of the school year, they make zealous efforts to provide information to families to assist in children's learning development.

⭐ DISCUSSION QUESTIONS

1. Interview a prekindergarten teacher, asking her to share stories about her most challenging children and how she handled their problems. Share these anecdotes with your class.
2. With your class, brainstorm some of your favorite games and songs from your early childhood. Be prepared to teach one of them to your classmates, if requested.
3. Discuss the populations represented in your community. How would knowledge of various groups influence the way you teach?

⭐ SUGGESTED CHAPTER ACTIVITIES

1. Begin a card file of art, music, and movement activities appropriate for 4-year-olds. Be prepared to add to it as you student teach and begin your own teaching years.
2. Find out the requirements in your state for allowing children to enter prekindergarten programs. Develop a list of reasons for providing or not providing universal prekindergarten for all children. Share these with your classmates.
3. Use a familiar tune to make up a new song about a topic that prekindergarten children might talk about. Use the topic *dogs* and set words to the tune of "Skip to My Lou."

Chapter Six

Teaching in a Kindergarten Classroom

CHAPTER OVERVIEW

★ What are the responsibilities of kindergarten teachers in developing children's understanding of the routines and schooling skills associated with going to school?

★ What information is essential for children to learn in kindergarten for later school success?

★ How do teachers facilitate conceptual development?

★ How do teachers organize for Circle Times?

★ What is emergent literacy?

★ What observational skills do teachers need in order to become better facilitators of children's learning?

USE THE INFORMATION IN THIS CHAPTER
TO DISCOVER THE ANSWERS YOU NEED.

The term that most accurately describes 5-year-olds is curious. *The pleasure teachers discover in teaching kindergarten children is 5-year-olds' instinctive motivation to learn everything they can learn. This characteristic clearly matches Erikson's description of the* initiative versus guilt *stage. Kindergarten children have a need to belong to the group. Sensitive teachers who take time to talk about their infractions and give them information for improving their classroom behaviors are sharing social knowledge that they need for future success in kindergarten and the primary grades.*

Generally, kindergarten children are congenial and eager to get acquainted with their peers. Their spats with others in the classroom last only a few minutes. Teachers can easily discuss social disputes that arise, and children understand reasonable classroom rules (though they may need more than occasional reminders from the teacher that the rules exist). Teachers who believe that children's forgetfulness of rules indicates insubordination and stubbornness need to rethink their positions. Encouraging children to exhibit prosocial behaviors will yield positive results. Five-year-olds are capable of taking turns, sharing materials and supplies, and negotiating for what they want, but the adults in their lives must take the responsibility to teach these social competencies.

Children's stress levels at this age are volatile, and teachers who place unrealistic expectations on them will observe signs of

frustration, frequent crying, and fretful behaviors. If children have constant stress in their lives over a long period of time, they may become withdrawn and shy, demonstrating frightened and oppressed behaviors uncharacteristic of young children. Occasionally, the time spent at school represents security and safety lacking in children's home lives.

Kindergarten children enjoy group experiences, but teachers should plan only one or two short Circle Times during the daily schedule (refer to Chapter 5 for planning effective Circle Times). Five-year-olds participate in classroom and musical games with zest, and simple playground games are appealing. Once teachers have an accurate understanding of children's knowledge and skills, they will use several small-group activities to ensure children's learning during the year.

Fives begin the year at approximately 45 to 55 pounds and have a weight gain of approximately six or seven pounds during the year. They have 20 teeth, and if dental care is sufficient, they should still have all of their baby teeth. In some children, the six-year molars begin to appear in the spring of the year. Eyesight is still becoming more focused, and kindergarten children need teachers who limit the amount of close, tedious work they are required to perform. Their level of physical activity requires a rest period during the day.

Unless youngsters have attended child care programs, social interactions away from home are almost nonexistent for 5-year-olds. The transition to school enrollment is problematic for youngsters whose social competence is limited. Some families are involved in church and synagogue activities, and religion classes allow social experiences with other children and families. Families who can afford the costs enroll their youngsters in dance and gymnastic classes, and T-ball is a favorite for both genders. Soccer is another group activity that appeals to some children. Parents need to be cautioned that experiences of this type are not conducive to the development of cooperative behavior and that some children respond negatively to them.

Five-year-olds still need opportunities for choices to assist in their emotional development. Offering children choices of activities in and out of school will allow them to find their own interests and talents.

Mrs. Riehl's fifth year as a kindergarten teacher in an urban inner-city school was beginning soon, and her school visit was to finalize the personalization of her classroom for the group of children she would have this school year. As she prepared labels of children's names to mark their individual cubbies, she recognized a few family names she had had in previous years. Being acquainted with her children and their parents was important to Mrs. Riehl, because she understood the need to develop alliances with families as early as possible in the school year.

The school community Mrs. Riehl teaches in is comprised of low-income families, and her school was built during the early 1970s when urban renewal funds were available from the federal government. Many of the children's families receive state aid, and most of the parents have low-paying, menial jobs. A number of the fathers are hourly construction laborers, and the stability of their jobs depends on good weather and the economy of the city. Some of the families do not have running water in their homes, and, occasionally, when families are unable to pay their utility bills, heat and electricity are not always available. For many, financial survival is a weekly and occasionally daily challenge. Mrs. Riehl remembers that two of her children's fathers are in the state department of criminal justice, and this issue is one that adversely affects both families.

The school district refers to Mrs. Riehl's building as a neighborhood school, and most of the children walk to school. A few families provide transportation for their children, but bus transportation is not provided by the school district. Free and reduced-cost lunches are available to children because of a grant the school district received from the U.S. Department of Agriculture. Families document their annual incomes to receive this food supplement, and approximately 90 percent of the children who attend the school are eligible.

The school also offers an after-school program, and many families take advantage of after-hours care. Because the majority of parents or guardians work, the service is necessary to protect younger children from coming home to empty houses at the end of the school day. Older children find safe haven at school, and school officials believe that the after-hours program deters the appearance of gangs and gang-related crime in the neighborhood. Evidence exists that black children are more likely than other racial groups to receive before- and after-school care. Mothers with less education (high school diploma or less) also need before- and after-school care for their children (West, Denton, & Germino-Hausken, 2000).

WHAT KINDERGARTNERS ARE EXPECTED TO LEARN

Kindergarten children are a unique group because their experiences in child care settings before their entry into kindergarten and their family and cultural backgrounds will vary. Their potential for school success is related to a number of variables in their lives. Curriculum guides outline the knowledge children should acquire during the kindergarten year, and they relate to the knowledge and skills that children bring with them to school. In public school settings, curriculum expectations are defined by grade-level groups of teachers and district curriculum coordinators, but many states have established taxonomies of knowledge and skill acquisition that influence what local districts do. The main emphasis in kindergarten is that children will learn what it means to go to school, but content-specific information is introduced as well.

Three major areas of instruction are: (1) language and literacy skills, (2) mathematical skills, and (3) schooling skills. *Language skills* refers to children's oral (speaking) abilities, whereas *literacy skills* refers to children's print awareness. Each of these areas, as well as schooling skills, is defined here.

Language Skills

- Ability to speak well enough for others to comprehend their conversations (with few speech errors)
- An understanding of the give and take of conversational speech
- Ability to listen to others and make responses when asked to
- Ability to retell familiar stories with few prompts

Literacy Skills

- Recognition of letters by the end of the school year
- An understanding that printed material has meaning
- Conceptual understanding of what a *word* is
- Ability to read and write one's name
- Ability to write letters when they are named
- Recognition of a few basic words
- Recognition of beginning and ending letter sounds in words
- Ability to point out rhyming words
- Ability to point out specific words in a sentence
- Ability to develop their own written stories (first through pictures; eventually through invented or conventional print)
(Kindergarten Teacher Reading Academies, 1999)

For additional information about emergent language and literacy skills, see *Learning to Read and Write: Developmentally Appropriate Practices for Young Children* (1998), the joint position statement by the National Association for the Education of Young Children (NAEYC) and the International Reading Association (IRA). This statement is available online at www.naeyc.org.

Mathematical Skills

- Ability to count orally to 20 (or higher) by the end of the school year (ordinal principle)
- Recognition of written numerals to 20 (or higher) by the end of the school year
- Ability to count rationally using concrete objects (cardinality principle)
- Knowledge of the numeral that comes after the last number in a series

- Ability to name the next object in a pattern sequence
- Beginning ability with addition and subtraction principles using concrete objects
- Understanding the importance and use of numerals in the environment
- Ability to name basic shapes
- Ability to work 12-piece puzzles

For more information about mathematics for young children, see *Mathematics in the Early Years* (Copley, 1999), *The Young Child and Mathematics* (Copley, 2000), and the "Developmental Checklist" in Catron and Allen's *Early Childhood Curriculum, A Creative Play Model,* 2nd edition (1999). The National Council of Mathematics Teachers' standards for Pre-K through Grade 2 can be found online at www.nctm.org.

Schooling Skills

- Preliminary skill in listening to small- and large-group discussions
- Becoming a participant in small- and large-group discussions
- Following simple classroom rules with teacher reminders
- Following three-step directions
- Responding appropriately to questions asked by the teacher
- Participating in preliminary social experiences requiring children to share materials
- Beginning experiences with taking turns during classroom activities
- Exhibiting cooperative play during Center Time
- Beginning experiences with lining up at the door for transitions to other parts of the building
- Participating in classroom cleanup duties in a reasonably consistent fashion

Mrs. Riehl's prior teaching experience in kindergarten makes her cognizant of the patience she will need to demonstrate on a daily basis to ensure that all of the cognitive and academic skills are successfully achieved by her children. Her understanding of the cultural background of her group also assists her in recognizing that time will be her ally as she repeats the information children will acquire throughout the year. The Children's Mental Health Foundations and Agencies Network (FAN) identified causal risk factors for early school failure (Huffman, Mehlinger, & Kerivan, 2000) as: (1) cognitive deficits, (2) early behavior problems, (3) parents' psychological problems, (4) problematic parenting practices, and (5) difficulties with peers and teachers (p. viii).

Once children fall into patterns of failure, teachers have the responsibility and the opportunity to intervene and eliminate *negative recursive cycles* as labeled by Katz and Chard (2000). Established patterns of failure become cyclical in nature with failure breeding more failure. Lack of adult support to overcome the negative failure patterns causes children to repeat the behaviors they know, because they have no knowledge of how to behave with more appropriate social responses and strategies. Teachers of young children must make a commitment to assist children in changing their failure-oriented attitudes (Katz & Chard, 2000). Mrs. Riehl's developmental perspective of children's progress ensures that she will carefully observe her children and plan classroom activities that are tailor-made for their needs.

Educators also have expectations that kindergarten children will have self-help skills. Kindergarten teachers spend some of their time with children helping them with zippers and buttons, reminding them to cover their mouths when they cough and sneeze, noticing when clothing is in disarray (boys' pants have open flies or girls' dresses are tucked into their underwear), and nurturing them when they are hurt or anxious. Basic self-help skills are part of the personal awareness repertoire children possess when they come to school (Catron & Allen, 1999). These skills include being able to:

- Dress themselves
- Take care of bathroom needs
- Feed themselves
- Demonstrate an understanding of personal hygiene needs
- Tell their name, address, and phone number
- Regulate their own involvement in classroom activities (recognizing their own needs for personal or quiet time)
- Take responsibility for personal belongings

CONCEPTUAL DEVELOPMENT IN THE EARLY YEARS

Kindergartners arrive at school with heads full of knowledge. The research reported in the 1960s leading to the development of Head Start programs and other federal initiatives supporting young children and their families suggests that children's intellectual development is most rapid during the years under age 8 (Hunt, 1961; Bloom, 1964). *From Neurons to Neighborhoods* (Shonkoff & Phillips, 2000) supports the earlier findings by stating that the ages from birth to school entry are years of strong intellectual and linguistic development.

The Early Childhood Longitudinal Study, Kindergarten Class of 1998–99 (West, Denton, & Germino-Hausken, 2000) reports that 5-year-olds come to school with the following specific skills.

- 66 percent can recognize their letters
- 29 percent understand beginning sounds
- 17 percent understanding ending sounds
- 94 percent recognize numbers and shapes and can count to 10
- 58 percent are able to compare relative sizes
- 20 percent are able to identify ordinal position of an object (first, second, third, etc.)

One perspective of the knowledge kindergarten children have is based on Sternberg's Triarchic Theory of Intelligence (2003). Sternberg refers to three types of intelligence: componential, experiential, and contextual. *Componential intelligence* is the type of knowledge that is measured by IQ and achievement tests. Thinking, memory, and information-processing skills make up componential intelligence.

Experiential intelligence relates to individuals' abilities to see connections between and among situations and objects, based on the backgrounds of experience they bring to a problem or event. *Contextual intelligence* is how people learn to fit into a setting or environment. Children who make smooth transitions into the school setting understand the clues from the environment that allow them to respond easily to the expectations of teachers and other school personnel.

A **concept** is essentially information children have about any area of learning. Piaget (1977) emphasized the development of cognitive structures, but concept areas include social, emotional, and creative domains as well. All conceptual development requires time and experience. For instance, an 18-month-old called her Easter eggs "Easter balls" because she had insufficient conceptual development to differentiate egg shapes and ball shapes. A year later, with more experience, she was able to label her eggs appropriately (with no memory of the previous error). Remembering to say "please" and "thank you" in appropriate situations or knowing to cover one's mouth when sneezing are two examples of social concepts children develop through time and experience. Children's ability to acquire the use of words and resist the impulse to hit another child when attacked is an example of emotional knowledge (contextual intelligence).

Kindergarten teachers' responsibilities in fostering conceptual development are threefold. They (1) assess the knowledge children already have when they come to school (most often through observation strategies, discussed later in this chapter), (2) provide firsthand experiences that help children add to their knowledge base (otherwise known as best practices), and (3) clarify children's misunderstandings as they occur. Teachers must first be aware that children's componential, experiential, and contextual intelligences will affect their growth potential during the kindergarten year and adjust their approaches accordingly.

Teachers should remember, too, that a Continuum of Teaching and Learning exists within any classroom group (as discussed in Chapter 3). In kindergarten classrooms, some children will have limited knowledge of position words (*behind, above, in front of, beside, on top of*) whereas others will be proficient with these concepts. Providing activities (a Circle Time lesson or an independent activity in a classroom center) to secure the concept for children with limited understanding is a component of the decision-making process teachers make every day. If teachers recognize that children have achieved a certain level of understanding prior to school attendance and build on that achievement, then children will profit from the school activity. (This recognition demonstrates Vygotsky's *zone of proximal development* theory discussed in Chapter 2.)

Teachers use a variety of strategies (from the Teaching Continuum) to facilitate conceptual development: (1) acknowledging, (2) modeling, (3) facilitating, (4) supporting, (5) scaffolding, (6) coconstructing, (7) demonstrating, and (8) directing (Bredekamp & Rosegrant, 1992). The teacher selects strategies depending on her insight into children's need for knowledge, the opportunity to deliver the instruction, and the relevancy of the concept to the individual child.

In telling kindergarten children about school fire drills, for instance, teachers will find the directive strategy is most effective (and essential). Telling each child

naeyc

about fire drills is not effective use of the teacher's time, nor does it provide children with a concrete experience with which to relate. Giving group instructions about fire drills and then practicing the skill is the teacher's preferred strategy from the teaching continuum. On the other hand, sitting in the Restaurant Center and *modeling* how to order from a menu is the most efficient strategy for children who are playing in that center.

Specific teacher techniques for enhancing conceptual development are: (1) asking children to demonstrate and tell what they already know, (2) asking questions to facilitate children's mental processing, (3) encouraging children to ask and answer their own questions, (4) helping children propose alternative solutions to solving problems, and (5) recognizing the value in creative responses (Hendrick, 2003). More specific examples of these techniques are the following:

- *Asking children to demonstrate and tell what they already know*

  "Cassidy, what do you know about growing flowers?"
  "Dodie, you visited the Children's Museum last week. What can you tell me about your visit?"
  "Your mother tells me you have a new puppy, Brandon. Tell us about it."

- *Asking questions to facilitate children's mental processing*

  "Look at these pictures showing the caterpillar's metamorphosis. Can you put them in order?"
  "Will this object float or sink? Why do you think it will float?"
  "In this picture, why do you think the little boy is crying?"

- *Encouraging children to ask and answer their own questions*

  "When the veterinarian comes to visit today, what questions do you want to ask her?"
  "Our new playhouse is arriving this afternoon, and we need to make room for it. Where will be the best place to put it?"
  "If we move the Block Center to make room for the playhouse, what are the best ways for moving the blocks?"

- *Helping children propose alternative solutions to solving problems*

  "Demetrius, when you stomp your feet like that, other children become angry with you. Let's talk about other ways to express your unhappiness."
  "Our plans for building the fire station aren't working well. Let's talk about other ways to build it."
  "Telling me that you could apologize to Chi Li is a good plan of action, but isn't there something else you could do to prevent this problem from happening again?"

- *Recognizing the value in creative responses*

  "Cruz, that's a great idea. I wonder if it will work."
  "Kimmie suggested that we put the plant outside in the sunshine. What do the rest of you think?"
  "I notice that you hum when you do your work. Is humming something you like to do?"

IMPORTANCE OF OBSERVING CHILDREN'S LEARNING

Teachers' responsibility to assess children's conceptual knowledge begins the hour children come to any program. Ongoing observations, accompanied by records of the observations, assist teachers in planning activities that meet children's needs and determine what learning is occurring. Watching children in authentic settings is the foundation for determining whether children are acquiring knowledge and skills, understanding and dealing with their feelings, and establishing positive dispositions toward learning. Eventually, teachers report progress and behaviors to parents and administrators, so keen observation of children is necessary.

How Do Teachers Meet Children's Needs?

Teachers need to know about children and how they develop. Reading a book about child development will help with initial understanding of children's needs. But watching children while they play, listening carefully when they respond in group settings, spending time interviewing them individually or in groups, and talking with children's parents are avenues for learning about youngsters. Observing children essentially implies that teachers need to know about their social, emotional, physical, and intellectual needs.

Children possess multifaceted personalities. They are social beings who have physical and emotional needs, yet educators also harbor the expectation that they are intellectual beings as well. Observations help teachers become architects in children's growth as they design and implement classroom activities to promote learning and development in all domains. Meeting preschool children's needs means that teachers think about the following issues.

Physical Development

- Place health and safety issues as a top priority in the environment
- Limit amounts of time children are required to sit for large-group activity (allow children opportunities to remove themselves from the group)
- Recognize when children are tired or ill and adjust accordingly
- Provide for indoor and outdoor play
- Allow children opportunities for naptime
- Plan for timely restroom breaks (if restrooms are not available in the classroom)
- Plan classroom spaces that provide for privacy
- Recognize when children need water and provide access to water fountains
- Feed children and provide healthy snacks at appropriate intervals during the school day
- Plan for movement and music experiences that allow for physical relief

Social Development

- Talk to children about acceptable social behaviors
- Hold group discussions about how children can get along together

- Model acceptable social behaviors
- Intervene when children are fighting with one another and help them work through their differences
- Help children understand others' viewpoints
- Establish class rules that respect children and teach them to respect others
- As children become more experienced in classroom activity, give them an opportunity to solve their own problems before intervening
- Join children's play on occasion
- Enjoy children and what happens in the classroom

Emotional Development

- Accept children's emotional outbursts as part of their development
- Verbalize labels for the feelings children are demonstrating
- Talk to children about the emotions people feel every day and help them understand that their feelings are normal
- Recognize that some children behave in certain situations because they do not know other, more acceptable behaviors
- Give children alternatives for dealing with their emotions by providing other acceptable activities
- Talk with children to assist them in understanding the realities of living (what they can change and what they need to accept)
- Provide many activities that allow children to express themselves (refer to Chapter 5 for information about self-expression activities)
- Display materials in the classroom that promote self-expression
- Encourage children to express themselves with a variety of media
- Tell children how you feel on occasion to demonstrate that all people have feelings
- Recognize signs of abuse or neglect and seek help for such children

Intellectual Development

- Recognize that children are eager to learn
- Share children's enthusiasm for learning
- Plan activities that give children more knowledge about their world
- Provide choices for children about what they want to learn
- Use projects that utilize individual children's strengths as they work
- Assess children's knowledge for curriculum planning and reporting to parents
- Plan learning that strengthens children's skills of observation, experience with solving problems, and acquisition of knowledge
- Assess children's knowledge for curriculum planning and reporting to parents

Creative Development

- Acknowledge children's creative responses to questions
- Provide opportunities for children to utilize their creative abilities
- Encourage children to make up songs or poems to share with their classmates
- Display children's creative products
- Invite in musicians and storytellers as models for children's creativity

- Utilize artists-in-residence programs provided by the school and community
- Introduce art collections of famous artists
- Occasionally play classical music as background music for children during Center Time

⭐ ARE CHILDREN LEARNING?

Experts recognize the time-consuming nature of assessing children (Beaty, 2002; Wortham, 1995), but without active observations and data collection, teachers are not adequately qualified to define what knowledge children need. Beaty (2002) recommends that children's assessment battery include self-identity, emotional development, play, prosocial behavior, large and small motor development, language and literacy skills, cognitive development, and art skills and imagination. Helm, Beneke, and Steinheimer (1998) recommend using children's classroom products as proof that children are learning. Collecting art, recording verbal language, allowing for musical and dance representations of knowledge, and constructing projects are concrete evidence for parents and others who are curious about children's learning experiences. Using classroom products is an example of *authentic assessment* because they show what children are capable of doing. Later in this chapter more information is shared about how teachers collect the data they need in reporting to parents.

Assessing Children's Literacy Knowledge

With the heavy emphasis placed by contemporary society on children's acquiring reading and writing abilities, teachers of young children need to be aware of their development in the literacy area. Children begin noticing and understanding print at an early age. Two-year-olds recognize the Jack in the Box sign or other pertinent markers in the environment that have meaning for them. When children show their

---

Issues and Trends

English-Language Proficiency Assessments

The No Child Left Behind legislation mandated state assessment plans by 2003 to demonstrate that English-language learners are acquiring English proficiency. Students must have an annual assessment of oral language and reading and writing skills in English. The assessments must be aligned with state content and academic achievement standards. The data are to be disaggregated within states, districts, and schools by gender, race/ethnicity, English-language status, migrant status, disability status, and economically disadvantaged status. Tests should be of adequate technical quality and include measures of higher-order thinking skills (Education Commission of the States Special Report, 2002).

knowledge of print, they are demonstrating the concept Marie Clay (1966) labeled as *emergent literacy.* Parents and guardians assist in emergent literacy development by reading to and talking about favorite books with children. Helping children "write" letters or notes to family members, reading brand names while grocery shopping and names of businesses and traffic signs to children while traveling in the car, playing musical games and chants, and repeating nursery rhymes to them are other activities that promote emerging literacy development (Combs, 2002).

Specific strategies teachers use for encouraging emergent literacy are:

1. Providing print-rich environments
2. Continuing to read interesting literature to children on a daily basis
3. Sharing big books with children
4. Helping children make the oral/written language connection
5. Setting up a class writing center
6. Encouraging children to write and share their writing (Henniger, 2002)

The prepared classroom, with its numerous opportunities to read and write, provides perfect opportunities for teachers to observe what children know about reading and writing. See Figure 6.1 for an example of one school district's description of beginning readers and writers.

⭐ STAGES OF WRITING

Children's development of writing skills grows out of their early attempts at *drawing* (Morrow & Asbury, 2001). Often, when young children are asked to write, they will draw a picture to indicate the story they wish to tell. Then "writing" moves to scribblelike attempts to make letters (almost resembling cursive writing). *Scribbling* resembles writing in that it is often formed from left to right, with the random pencil marks making a sound like that produced by writing.

Eventually, children begin to make *letterlike forms* that look like letter shapes at first glance. Actually, they are children's own creations, following a left-to-right sequence, which lead to the *reproduction of letter sequences.* Letter sequences are often strings of letters that children write again and again. They choose letters that are easy to write or that appear in their own names.

Phonetic spelling occurs as children begin to understand the connection between letters and sounds. One letter can represent an entire word, and vowel sounds are omitted. This invented spelling, as it is sometimes called, is the forerunner of *conventional spelling.* Conventional spelling produces writing that adults and other children can read and comprehend. For examples of each of these types of writing, see Figure 6.2.

Writing Centers

Watching children in the classroom Writing Center strengthens teacher's observations of literacy growth. Development that teachers can assess and document in the Writing Center includes

- Visual discrimination skills
- Eye-hand coordination skills
- Recognition of alphabet letters and numerals
- Children's attempts at writing alphabet letter and numerals
- Children's interest in the printed word
- Language skills (Herr & Libby, 1994)

Collecting samples of children's writing (and dating the product) provides evidence to parents that children are making progress in the literacy area.

FIGURE 6.1 One School District's Definitions of Emergent Readers and Writers

The Bay St. Louis–Waveland School District (Waveland, Mississippi) defines the emergent reader and writer as follows.

Beginning Reader (K–1)

Reading Strategies: Uses readinglike behavior. Knows that reading moves from left to right and from front to back. Understands that written language uses symbols to form words. Uses pictures to find meaning in texts. Reads environmental print.

Reading Responses: Smiles, claps, and listens attentively to stories. Responds artistically to stories. Retells favorite stories, rhymes, poems. Enjoys print and is curious to know its meaning. Reads pattern books from memory. Expresses personal connections to text.

Reading Interest and Attitude: Exhibits preferences for particular books. Chooses to read during free time.

Preletter Symbol Writer (K)

What the Writer Does: Uses pictures, scribble, and letterlike marks to communicate. Copies environmental print. Reads/explains own writing.

What the Writer Shows: Understands difference between pictures and print. Uses familiar symbols of writing.

Use of Writing: Uses pictures and print to communicate an idea.

Early Emergent Writer (K–1)

What the Writer Does: Copies words from the environment. Labels drawings. Writes simple messages. Attempts sentence writing. Uses sound–symbol connections. Exhibits hand preference for writing. Uses letter symbols (letters for part of a word) and pictures to communicate ideas.

What the Writing Shows: Experiments with letters, words, punctuation. Uses letter groups as words. Uses spaces in "writing." Demonstrates left to right movement in lines from top to bottom of page.

Use of Writing: Knows that oral language can be written.

FIGURE 6.2 Samples of Writing Stages

Scribbling

Letter
Sequences

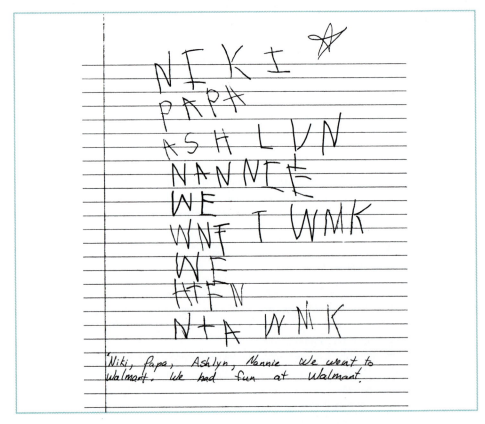

Phonetic
Spelling

Phonetic
Spelling

⭐ CLASSROOM LAYOUT

A carefully designed environment coupled with skilled adults who utilize class-room and community resources will produce tremendous intellectual and social growth in children throughout the kindergarten year. Classroom organization mo-tivates and challenges children if it is carefully planned with them in mind. Furni-ture purchases and design of the classroom are usually out of teachers' control, and many features are unchangeable (placement of electrical outlets, windows, doors, classroom restrooms, closets, cabinets, etc.) Arrangement of equipment, materials, and instructional aids, however, can benefit or hinder children's skills acquisition.

Experienced teachers seem to know how they want their classroom to look and what items will appeal to kindergarten children. New teachers should consider these recommendations for planning the classroom environment:

- Reserve an area for Circle Time experiences (see the discussion of Circle Time plans later in the chapter). The space can also be used for small-group instruction. A large circular rug will mark the area visually for children's use.
- Materials and instructional aids that children play with need to be readily accessible to them. Change or add new materials periodically to enhance children's interest in learning.
- Quiet centers need to be separated from centers that tend to be noisy. The Block Center should not be near the Book Corner because of the distractions of the more active center.
- Traffic flow is important as well. Children tend to run in large, open spaces. Organizing furniture to prevent running will assist children in participating in more intimate play activity.
- Use graphic organizers (signs on shelves, duct tape, or painted directions and lines on the floor) to assist children in knowing how the classroom space is used. A duct tape line at the classroom door helps children recog-nize what it means to "stand in line."
- One bulletin board in the classroom needs to be available for displaying children's work. Classroom bulletin boards are an integral part of the learn-ing environment, and teachers' effective use of bulletin board space en-hances thematic studies going on in the class. If possible, a smaller bulletin board near the door should be prepared for announcements to parents and guardians about upcoming school events.
- Place the Art Center and Water Table near a water source for cleanup ease. If a sink is unavailable in the classroom, opportunities to use these centers will be limited. Trekking down the hall to the restroom for paint cleanup on a daily basis is tiresome to teachers and out of the range of possibility for children's responsibility level.
- Have a preplanned system for allowing children to choose centers during Center Time. Careful explanation about the use of centers (how many can

be in each center and how children may change centers if they want) is part of the instruction teachers plan at the beginning of the school year.

- Classroom cleanliness is critical to children's health and safety, but ultra-organized classrooms do not appeal to children.
- Plan one space for privacy when children need to escape from the stress of classroom activity.
- Move the teacher's desk to the side of the classroom (almost out of sight) to help children understand that this is their classroom, not the teacher's.

Making the environment as inviting, comfortable, and attractive as possible is an invitation to children to come in and learn. Occasionally, classrooms become messy because of the work children are doing, especially in optimal periods of creative productivity. Generally, the classroom should be clean and orderly with an aesthetic, "homey" feeling that recognizes that children live and work in this setting. Hendrick (2003) refers to this quality as its *ambience*. Children's "home away from home" should help them feel nurtured and confident.

⭐ KINDERGARTEN CLASSROOM CENTERS

Kindergarten classrooms use centers of interest designed to pique children's curiosity. Five-year-olds are eager to learn (Bowman, Donovan, & Burns, 2000), and centers provide a variety of classroom activities children can use for knowledge acquisition. As defined in Chapter 3, classroom centers are valuable to children because of their capacity for offering children choices and providing conceptual development in a playful, nonthreatening atmosphere.

Space availability and school resources dictate the centers teachers will include in their classrooms. Mrs. Riehl's center choices coordinate with her overall objectives for the learning she hopes her kindergarten children will achieve by the end of the school year. Her interest in emergent literacy skills is the foundation for a Book Corner, and she has an abundant stock of books that she rotates in and out of the center throughout the year. Other centers include an Art Center, a Computer Center, a Block Center, a Puzzles and Manipulatives Center, a Puppet Center, a Writing Center, a Home Living Center (complete with dress-up clothing), and a Discovery Center. As the year progresses, she will add a Grocery Store Center, a Bakery Center and, in the spring, an Ice Cream Parlor Center, because these centers coordinate with themes she has planned.

Periodically, teachers will discover a need to rearrange or eliminate centers in the classroom. This action usually relates to children's changing interests or to development of projects, but teachers may also observe a need to challenge children with new center configurations and materials. In one classroom, children became so interested in the veterinarian clinic they had visited recently that they moved the furniture out of the Home Living Center to change it into a vet's office. The Puppet Center could become a Kindergarten Theater if children decide to plan a program for their families or for another class in the school. Even a Puzzles and

Manipulatives Center could become another area of interest if children have met all the challenges that were available to them in the original center.

Visitors (administrators and parents) should be able to envision the educational potential in a classroom setting. When a centers approach is used in any classroom, many adults believe that children are playing and not seriously pursuing educational objectives. Jones (1991) recommends that adding small posters describing what learning is going on in each center facilitates adult understanding of the playful learning that is occurring. A small poster in the Block Center might read

What children are learning in the Block Center is:

- Cooperation
- How to complete a project
- Spatial skills
- Mathematical skills

Planning for Multiple Intelligences with Centers

In an informal survey of early childhood teachers across the United States, Howard Gardner's Multiple Intelligences Theory was cited as a theoretical perspective that affected their classroom organization and instruction (Warner & Sower, 2001). In a nutshell, teachers of young children recognize that children have various strengths, and classroom centers meet the potential for providing learning for children in a package that both intrigues and challenges them. Children with strong logical-mathematical intelligence need the Puzzles and Manipulatives Center and the Block Center. Children with strong visual-spatial skills need the Art Center and the Puppet Center. Providing choices for center selection allows children to extend their strengths and explore areas of weakness in a safe environment.

In the process of learning, children eventually are able to concentrate on the linguistic and logical-mathematical intelligence areas. In the preschool and primary years, however, the broader the array of approaches to learning that teachers can provide, the more successful children become (West, Denton, & Germino-Hauskin, 2000).

Project Spectrum is a program founded in 1984 as a result of work by Howard Gardner leading to his formulation of a theory of multiple intelligences (MI theory) and David Feldman's theory of nonuniversal development. (Refer to Chapter 2 to review Gardner's MI theory postulated in his 1983 book *Frames of Mind: The Theory of Multiple Intelligences*). Feldman's book *Beyond Universals in Cognitive Development* (1994) questioned whether intellectual development is inevitable, suggesting instead that children learn gradually in various areas providing they have sustained exposure to cognitive domains in a conducive environment. With grant funds from several sources, Project Spectrum initially began with the goal of developing assessment strategies for the cognitive abilities of preschool children. After several years, the Project Spectrum research team began examining the use of a battery of cognitive assessments with kindergarten and first-grade children who were at risk for school failure. Eventually, researchers sought to discover if Project Spectrum could be used in public schools to promote academic achievement in eight discipline areas: language, math, movement, music, general science, mechanics and construction, social understanding, and visual arts (Chen, 1998).

The conceptual framework of Project Spectrum follows these steps:

- Introducing children to a range of learning areas
- Identifying children's strength areas using a Working Styles Checklist (see Figure 6.3)
- Nurturing children's areas of strength
- Using their strengths to lead children to other learning areas (Chen, 1998)

The Project Spectrum research team organized classroom activities for each of the eight discipline areas and encouraged teachers to use a combination of free-play and structured classroom plans to support children's intellectual development. Individual, small-group, and large-group activities allow teachers to diversify their approaches with children in order to maximize their learning. Parental support is solicited also to nurture each child's strength area. (For more information about Project Spectrum, refer to their website www.projectspectrum.com.)

Phipps (1997) discusses MI theory as it relates specifically to preschoolers in *Multiple Intelligences in the Early Childhood Classroom.* Phipps points out that labeling specific learning centers with names of the intelligence areas is not necessary. Any classroom learning center has potential for meeting the needs of several intelligence areas. Her discussion clearly shows how each center that early educators use can address and promote several intelligences within children (Phipps, 1997).

Meeting Children's Needs with Classroom Centers

Centers provide a natural approach for meeting individual children's needs in a variety of ways. Children who are initiating explorations with print and what print can do gravitate to the Writing Center, whereas those who are uninterested in print choose another center that matches their specific developmental needs. In any given classroom center, adults can observe children who exhibit expert levels of performance whereas others are only moderately engaged in the center activity. Still others may only be looking on, trying to decide whether they are ready to tackle the center's inherent challenges. These behaviors are reminiscent of Parten's play stages, defined in Chapter 3.

Many teachers are aware that children tend to return to the same center of interest day after day. Their concern is that other centers in the environment hold learning possibilities, and individual children are overlooking classroom opportunities to broaden their knowledge base. Early educators, however, recognize that children need repetitive experiences to deepen their conceptual understandings (Bredekamp & Copple, 1997); in most cases, children's continual return to their most enjoyed center builds on the skills and knowledge they are acquiring through its use.

Several strategies exist for assisting children in moving away from the familiar choices they make. The teacher's best choice is to talk about center choices both in group settings and in one-to-one conversations. It is helpful to remind children

FIGURE 6.3 Working Styles Checklist

Child _____   Observer _____

Activity _____   Date _____

Please mark which working styles are distinctive during your observation. Mark only when obvious; one from each pair need not be checked. Please include comments and anecdotes whenever possible and write a general, overall phrase that best describes how the child approaches the activity. Star (*) any outstanding working style.

Child is   Comments
   easily engaged in activity   _____
   reluctant to engage in activity   _____

   confident   _____
   tentative   _____

   playful   _____
   serious   _____

   focused   _____
   distractible   _____

   persistent   _____
   frustrated by activity   _____

   impulsive   _____
   reflective   _____

   apt to work slowly   _____
   apt to work quickly   _____

   conversational   _____
   quiet   _____

   responds to cues
     visual   _____
     auditory   _____
     kinesthetic   _____
   demonstrates planful approach   _____
   brings personal strength to activity   _____
   finds humor in content area   _____
   uses materials in unexpected ways   _____
   shows pride in accomplishment   _____
   attends to detail; is observant   _____
   is curious about materials   _____
   shows concern over "correct" answer   _____
   focuses on interaction with adult   _____

What Teachers Are Saying

Developing Classroom Centers

"I have always believed in play as being important for children's development. I taught kindergarten for several years, though, before I truly understood how play developed a sense of community among the children. Now that I am more aware, I spend more time developing centers that promote play."—*a kindergarten teacher*

"I use an abundance of hands-on experiences in my classroom. That way I can ensure that children are learning the concepts they need."—*a kindergarten teacher*

"Every summer I spend my time developing new folder games for my children. Most of them focus on phonemic awareness—how words rhyme and how letters sound. I want my kindergartners to have a strong foundation in literacy."—*a kinder-garten teacher*

during Circle Time that if the same people choose a specific center every day, then others do not have the chance to use the center. Often, in a group discussion children will make this statement or a similar one on their own. Group dynamics can provide an outlet for children to make a ruling that no one child can choose the same center for more than five days in a row. If not, the teacher needs to say, "Let's remember that our friends in our class need to play in all the areas of the classroom."

Individually, the teacher may pull one child aside and say, "Abby, you always choose the Home Living Center every day. Let me help you make another choice today. You can choose the Home Living Center later today or tomorrow."

Another strategy is to close specific centers on occasion. Children need a rational explanation for this choice. Centers can be closed for any number of reasons: materials or furniture are in need of repair; the area is required for project development; dramatic play from one area spills over into another space; or a place is needed for art projects to dry. Children can tolerate the closure of the Block Center for a few days if the grocery store project needs their space for project outgrowth. Closing centers on occasion is helpful for children in learning the realities of living.

Periodically using a centers rotation system can stimulate and motivate children to other learning areas in the classroom that are important to their cognitive development. First, teachers must recognize the importance of the social and emotional knowledge children acquire in center play, and arbitrarily adopting a rotation system might destroy the fun and enjoyment that centers bring to children. When centers are used only for cognitive development, the overall concept of educating the whole child is lost. A rotating centers approach needs to be used judiciously and with the best interests of children in mind.

Teachers can shape what is being learned in centers by adding more challenging activities. Eventually, the learning that children are doing in specific centers wanes unless challenges pique their further intellectual development. Hendrick (2003) recommends several ideas for moving children to another level of cognitive understanding:

- Increasing the number of items children work with at a time strengthens cognitive development
- Including memory applications as part of the process (remembering a missing item, as an example) as another approach to enhancing cognition
- Asking children to use another sensory modality (feeling objects instead of looking at them)
- Increasing the amount of information that has to be analyzed to figure out an answer
- Asking children to give verbal reasons for their decisions (p. 447)

Five-year-olds are challenged to record the information they are learning in journals or logs. At first, these records are pictorial, but by the end of the year some kindergarten children should be able to make marks on paper that resemble print and others can demonstrate conventional print. Challenge is inherent in activities that ask children to act out, talk about, or write about new knowledge.

☆ ISSUE OF RELEVANCY

No matter what planned experiences are implemented in the classroom, relevancy is the key to children's acquisition of knowledge. Having firsthand understanding of classroom topics makes a difference in children's conceptual understanding of the topic. Children are keen observers of their environment, and planning emerges within the context of their daily interactions with their home, school, and community. Sternberg (2003) refers to this phenomenon as *experiential intelligence.* Teachers' willingness to focus on children's experiences shows their understanding of appropriate curriculum development.

For example, children will be less interested in learning about Hawaii if they have no previous experience of Hawaii. Learning about spiders and their habits, on the other hand, appeals to children if someone happens to notice the spider web that appeared overnight in one corner of their playground. Teachers can take advantage of these spontaneous events to teach children about their surroundings. The advantage of *teachable moments,* as these situations are called, is that they capitalize on the naturally curious behavior of preschoolers and their need for immediate gratification.

Now might be an appropriate opportunity to review NAEYC position statement on Early Childhood Curriculum, Assessment, and Program Evaluation (www.naeyc.org).

☆ SCHEDULE OF THE DAY

Defining schedules for kindergarten classrooms depends on whether they are half-day or full-day programs. School districts in various states are mandated to offer certain types of kindergarten programs by their state legislatures. In the United

States, 33 states and the District of Columbia require either half-day or full-day programs. Only eight states and the District of Columbia have compulsory attendance statutes. Approximately 55 percent of America's children are enrolled in full-day programs, either in private or public school settings (West, Denton, & Germino-Hausken, 2000).

Mrs. Riehl's school uses a half-day three-hour schedule, which means that she has a total of 44 children daily. Her agenda, planned with other kindergarten teachers in the school, includes a morning Circle Time, an hour-long Center Time, snack, outdoor play, shared reading, and music and movement. She has collaborated with other teachers in her school to set the schedule.

Teachers who work in public schools need to follow daily schedules closely because their agendas interface with those of other teachers in the grade level and school. If they are tardy to lunch, for example, they find that they create problems for other teachers and grades, who are then unable to enter the cafeteria in a timely fashion. Generally, kindergarten teachers have more flexibility within the classroom to organize as they choose than do teachers in older grades, but when they leave their rooms they need to be in sync with the rest of the school.

⭐ HELPING CHILDREN LEARN CLASSROOM ROUTINES AND RESPONSIBILITIES

Routines provide security for children. Awareness of scheduled activities for the day and an understanding that the school environment is safe are foundations for children's ability to develop self-esteem. Children's familiarity with their surroundings and a patient, nurturing teacher are critical elements in youngsters' transition into the school environment. If parents and teachers develop a collaborative partnership early in the year, they will observe children's growth in all developmental domains as the year progresses.

The cornerstone of early childhood development is *self-regulation* (Shonkoff & Phillips, 2000). Self-regulation begins in infancy and includes the tasks of establishing day-night wake-sleep rhythms, regulating crying, regulating emotions, learning to attend, and regulating mental processes. These skills relate to the early relationships children have with parents or guardians and caregivers. Their development is also influenced by cultural variations in parenting as well as individual temperament. Children who arrive at school with problems in self-regulation present behavioral issues to their teachers and to others in the classroom.

Transitions

The times when children move from one activity to another or from one setting to another are labeled as *transitions.* Experienced early educators recognize the need to plan for transitions and execute procedures that facilitate changes smoothly and with minimum fuss (Gestwicki, 1999). The most significant transition for kindergartners is their entry into the classroom setting. Much of the planning teachers do for 5-year-olds during the first weeks of school entails introducing the classroom to their children and assisting them in learning routines and responsibilities that will help youngsters in being successful.

Other transitions occur in changing activities within the classroom day. When children are engaged in center play, teachers plan for moving children into another configuration such as Circle Time or lining up at the classroom door. Or if children are in a large group, teachers execute a plan of action to revert to center play. Other transition times include moving from room to room, walking down the hall to another school site, using the restroom, and leaving school at the end of the school day.

Merely lining up at the door is a challenge for young children, who are not usually familiar with directional terminology to "line up at the door" or "stand in a straight line." Often, "standing in a straight line" means kindergartners will stand at attention like some television soldier they have observed. When teachers tell children to line up, children will scramble to the door unless a transition procedure is in place. Teachers learn to say, "Children with lunch money may line up first," or "Children who brought their lunches from home may line up now." Other options are calling all children with clothes that are a certain color to line up first or telling children who are wearing shoes that lace, have Velcro, or are sandals or slip-ons that their time to line up has come. Figure 6.4 shares other transition ideas.

Classroom Signals

Teachers know that gaining children's attention is not always easy to do, so they decide upon signals with special meaning that they plan to use during the year and describe these signals to children. A common technique is *switching classroom lights off and on.* The signal, if carefully explained, is a nonverbal message that communicates the importance of the information that the teacher is planning to share. If a teacher has a small bell, *ringing the bell* serves the same purpose as the light-switching strategy.

Other preplanned signals are

1. *Raising one's hand* in the air and requesting that children do the same
2. *Singing a familiar song* until children are attending
3. *Repeating a well-known fingerplay* until children are attending
4. *Using a clapping pattern* and expecting children to imitate the pattern

Some teachers use a repetitive phrase that chants, "If you can hear my voice, clap once; if you can hear my voice, clap five times; if you can hear my voice, clap three times," until children are listening and responding. When children and teachers are familiar with one another, sometimes the teacher can stand quietly in place until children notice that she needs their attention.

The use of a *puppet* can draw children's attention to the teacher, too. One puppet is designated as a commentator on children's classroom activity and their behavior within a given event. The puppet might be reserved for an end-of-day discussion about the positive behaviors the teacher observed throughout the school

FIGURE 6.4 Transition Ideas

Ask children to move to another classroom activity or line up at the door in group formation by:

- Singing a familiar song
- Tiptoeing like a quiet elf
- Moving like a named animal (doing a crab walk; slithering like a snake; walking like a horse or cow)
- Pretending to fly like a bird
- Pretending to move like a giant, fairy, skater, or dancer
- Naming a specific category that allows small groups to move (type of transportation to come to school; or type of clothing children are wearing; color of hair or eyes)

Or use individual suggestions for transition:

- Moving when lightly tapped on the head
- Informally assessing children's knowledge of a specific concept (names or sounds of farm animals; colors on a traffic signal; identification of environmental print, such as community business names or familiar fast-food restaurants)
- Individually naming a picture flashcard
- Individually naming a specific selected shape
- Individually identifying a specific selected color
- Counting groups of objects
- Telling what number comes *before* or *after* a named numeral
- Naming favorite objects or activities (favorite color, food, game, book, television show, restaurant, etc.)
- Telling the names of their pets
- Naming their brothers and sisters
- Answering specific questions about their address and phone number
- Telling their birth date or naming the week day
- Describing what they enjoy about being in school

day. Asking the children to give the puppet an interesting name (Peppy Puppet, Michelangelo, or Puppet Monster) attracts children to pay attention to its comments.

The *magic wand* strategy works best when children are in group activities that teachers are leading. A commercial wand purchased from a local dollar store or through a teacher supply catalog serves in a cueing capacity to direct children's attention to the class calendar or a flip chart. The wand can also appoint specific children to take turns in a favorite game or to respond to questions the teacher has asked.

Taking Responsibility for One's Behavior

Preschoolers often view themselves as uninvolved in classroom infractions or want to blame others for their misdeeds. They may have puzzled or confused looks on their faces because they do not recognize a problem as a problem. Or they may stand aside helplessly as others take the responsibility that should be theirs. Knowing that cleaning spilled milk is the responsibility of the person who spilled it requires teacher patience and knowledge that this concept will need to be taught.

Children sometimes learn that saying, "I'm sorry," smoothes over an injustice they have committed, and teachers must be prepared to help children understand that apologizing does not always address the problem at hand. The teacher's description of a specific problem and facilitation of conflicts between and among children is part of the continued development of impulse control begun at earlier ages. Continuing to assist the aggressor in recognizing the pain and frustration the victim feels is another aspect of accepting responsibility for one's own behavior (Slaby, Roedell, Arezzo, & Hendrix, 1995). Refer to Chapter 5 for more information about problem-solving approaches to guidance.

Taking Responsibility for Specific Tasks

Assigning classroom tasks to specific children is a common practice in early childhood settings. Usually, these tasks are rotated among children on a daily or weekly basis. They include being Line Leader, Classroom Messenger, Plant and/or Pet Caretaker, Table Setter, and other roles as deemed essential by an individual classroom teacher. Introducing the Responsibility Chart and the work required in each of the classroom chores is completed within the first few weeks of school, but beginning this ritual on the first day is not necessary. Children have enough information to absorb on the first day, and their comprehension of basic classroom routines is more important than giving them additional responsibilities right away.

When teachers use a Responsibility Chart, they need to keep accurate records of the children who have taken classroom roles. Some children are capable of accepting responsibility, and they delight in an opportunity to provide classroom assistance. Other children with limited experience will require instruction or teacher modeling about carrying out their work. If a child is absent and misses an assigned turn, the teacher needs to remember the child's responsibility. Ensuring children a turn with their assigned tasks is important to children seeing themselves as an integral part of the group. (See Figure 7.3 in Chapter 7 for an example of a Responsibility Chart.)

Classroom Cleanup

One kindergarten teacher began receiving compliments from the school custodian about her abilities to teach though little evidence showed that he had ever observed her in action. After several weeks of compliments, she asked him why he thought she was such a great teacher. His response was, "Your children always clean up the room before they leave every day."

Giving children cleanup responsibilities is among the easiest ways to ensure children's growing abilities to exhibit classroom accountability. Cleanup is best scheduled at the end of the day, when children are preparing for school dismissal. Some school districts require all chairs to be placed on tables to facilitate the custodial crew when they come in to mop or clean the classroom floor. Picking up clutter from the floor and discarding litter and scrap paper can improve the appearance of the classroom. Providing a special box to allow for children to recycle scrap paper is another element in learning responsibility.

Children do not automatically participate in classroom cleanup, but their willingness to assist their classmates will improve if the teacher models the behavior herself. She can also compliment the children who are participating (or perhaps Peppy Puppet can praise). In extreme situations, using stickers or stamps to recognize the children who are doing their share of the work will serve to motivate the nonparticipants to engage in cleanup behavior. Eventually, the activity becomes a natural part of the schedule, and children will not need the extrinsic rewards to accomplish the cleanup task.

⭐ PLANNING FOR GROUP TIMES

One time during the day that presents special problems to teachers is known as Circle Time or Group Time. Circle Times are a traditional experience in preschools, and this group time is a forerunner of the more structured activities that are characteristic of primary-grade instruction.

Teachers who use their knowledge of children's interests in planning Circle Time experiences will have greater success than those who arbitrarily choose a concept or theme they believe is important for children to know. Remembering to include a variety of activities that appeal to children and to offer them intellectual stimulation enhances the overall impact that group times have on their learning. Choosing nonsexist and nonracist books and materials demonstrates teachers' sensitivity to the children they are teaching.

For kindergarten children, Circle Time activities should be approximately 20 minutes in length, preferably only 15 minutes at the beginning of the school year. If teachers are aware of their children's strengths and weaknesses, this time frame might extend as the year progresses. Sedentary activities cause children to be less responsive to the overall Circle Time plan. Provide for children's physical needs, and recognize when Circle Time experiences should come to a close.

Tips for Conducting Effective Circle Time Experiences

1. Be well planned, but be prepared to adapt to children's suggestions that emerge during the allotted time.
2. Develop a signal system (a bell, special song, or a recording) that indicates that it is time for Circle. Use this signal regularly.

Group time experiences are important to foster children's ability to participate in large-group learning activities.

3. Begin the Circle as soon as children begin joining the group. If teachers wait for everyone to join in, they may be asking some children to sit for a long time.
4. Plan the most significant experiences—new information or a lengthy book—for the beginning of Circle Time.
5. Allow time for children to interact with others during Circle Time. This practice helps make the time more meaningful to them.
6. Provide for physical activity during Circle Time (a song, fingerplay, or group game may allow enough relaxation for children to return to other planned activities).
7. Recognize that some plans will not work because of outside factors in the school or community (it is more difficult to plan during a holiday season, for example, or the week after daylight savings time changes).
8. Children can sit still for only so long, and wise teachers know that sometimes a better plan of action is to stop Circle instead of going on doggedly without much learning going on.
9. Decide whether it is necessary for all children to participate in Circle Time. A child who is easily distractible may ruin a positive group experience for the other children. Preferred practice is to allow the disruptive child to choose another activity while Circle Time is going on.
10. Model the enjoyment in learning for children during Circle Time. They need congenial teachers, and demonstrating pleasure in what you are doing will evoke positive responses from them.

A sample lesson plan framework is presented in Figure 6.5, a sample lesson plan from Mrs. Riehl's files in Figure 6.6.

Extending Circle Time Experiences

If the topic of discussion for Circle Times is indeed a good one to use with children, then it is appropriate to extend the cognitive activity beyond the time spent in the group. Planning and implementing follow-up activities that relate to the topic theme challenges and motivates children to pursue their interest in the information. If a planned springtime theme about meadows includes the reading of the book *Over in the Meadow* by Olive Wadsworth (1985), the teacher could include some of these activities as choices for children during Center Time:

- Have flannel board figures available in the Book Corner for story retelling.
- Include topic-related books in the Book Corner.
- Fill the Water Table with plastic animals represented in the book.
- Encourage children to record animal sounds on the classroom cassette recorder.
- Work with a small group of children to prepare a classroom terrarium.
- Add a turtle to the terrarium or Science Center.
- Put out a variety of art materials to encourage children to make one or more of the animals depicted in the book.
- If children's interest continues for several days, consider a walking field trip to a nearby meadow for observation purposes. The book could serve as a springboard for discussions about springtime animals, parks and ponds, or plants and flowers in the environment.

FIGURE 6.5 A Circle Time Plan Framework

- Signal that it's time to begin group activity.
- Sing a familiar tune as children gather to the circle area ("The Muffin Man" or "Yankee Doodle").
- Tell children the topic of discussion for the morning.
- Allow discussion to occur.
- Read a book about the topic, providing children an opportunity to respond as the pages are turned.
- Pretend to be a character in the book for movement activity or teaching a song that relates to the topic.
- Review quickly the major points made during the Circle Time discussion.
- Describe any follow-up activities that are planned for the classroom during the day.
- Transition to other scheduled classroom events.

FIGURE 6.6 A Sample Circle Time Plan

Theme: Farm Animals

- Flick the lights off and on and announce that it is time for Circle.
- Sing the usual Circle Time song. One teacher uses this song she composed to the tune of "London Bridge."

    Come to Circle for some fun, for some fun, for some fun.
    Come to Circle for some fun;
    What will we learn?

- Tell the children that the topic of discussion is farm animals. Ask who has been to a farm. Name the animals they have seen.
- Read *Barnyard Banter* (Fleming, 1994) and allow discussion of the events in the book.
- Play "Barnyard Frolic." Purchase two copies of a farm animals book and cut out the animals to glue on 9"x12" pieces of poster board (laminate to keep the material durable). Give individual children one picture each, using the matching set as prompts for the game. As each animal picture is held up, the child holding the identical picture must make the sound of the animal. When one round is completed, switch cards among the children to play the game again. One poster board piece needs to have the words *Barnyard Frolic* written on it. When this card is flashed, all children make their animal sounds at the same time.
- Depending on the length of the Circle Time and the interest of the children, a third activity could include singing and performing "The Farmer in the Dell."
- Describe to children an art activity they can choose during Center Time that would let them use inexpensive paper plates and a collection of art materials to make farm animal masks. Glue the masks on tongue depressors for children to use in dramatic play.
- Ask children to name their favorite farm animal as they transition to Center Time. (An optional transition could include allowing children to move to their selected center imitating an animal they talked about during Circle Time. Or the teacher could name an animal and ask individual children to make the sound for the animal.)

☆ LEARNING ABOUT THE COMMUNITY

Kindergarten children have a variety of experiences with the community in which they reside. Teachers of young children seek to broaden children's knowledge base, and a number of strategies are available for expanding children's concepts of community. Among the techniques teachers use are

1. *Photographs:* Snap pictures of familiar community businesses and restaurants children and their families visit regularly and organize the photos into a book about the community.

2. *Bulletin boards:* Use photographs of area community sites on a bulletin board about the community or clip pictures from magazines representing various establishments.

3. *Graphs:* Ask children to name places they visit in the community and prepare a graph of the most commonly visited sites.

4. *Webs:* Prepare a chart labeled *favorite store* or *favorite restaurant* and brainstorm community sites to place on the Web.

5. *Sharing children's writing:* Find time during the daily schedule to allow children to "read" from their journals or tell about community sites they visit regularly.

6. *Artifact collection:* Ask children to bring in objects they have discovered in visits to community entities (store fliers, sales slips, shopping and grocery bags, napkins, cups, and Styrofoam containers).

7. *Family contributions:* Ask parents and guardians to send photographs or other materials representing community business establishments.

Taking Field Trips with Kindergarten Children

The most effective strategy for exposing children to their community is to take field trips to various locations in the city. Field trips provide firsthand relevant information to children about their community surroundings. Mrs. Riehl is fortunate in being able to take walking trips in the neighborhood with her kindergartners. For several years, she has made trips to the post office, a nearby fire station, and the bakery housed across the street from the school. Her principal supports her decision to continue these class excursions, and she is planning to add a trip to an ice cream parlor in early May. Finding parent volunteers to accompany the children is a problem on occasion, but the principal assists in locating adults in the building who can serve as field trip monitors.

Inviting Guests into the Classroom

In some public school settings, field trips are banned or limited. These decisions by administrators and/or school boards are based on any number of local factors: (1) lack of finances for trips, (2) concerns about school liability (if an accident occurs), (3) unavailability of transportation (buses and drivers are scheduled with regular routes and duties), or (4) a misunderstanding of the educational value of class trips.

When field trips are not an option, teachers of young children invite guests into their classrooms for special one-time discussions or events. Guests may include police officers, firefighters, or specially trained drug prevention teams. Anyone willing to talk about his or her career, often parents of children enrolled in the class, is a potential visitor. Seefeldt and Barbour (1998) label these invited guest visits as *reverse field trips.* Before inviting someone to the classroom, teachers should evaluate (1) the relevance of the discussion to ongoing classroom study topics, (2) the guest's ability to relate to young children, and (3) the value of the contributions he or she will make.

One teacher discovered the value of having someone to assist children with their writing in the Writing Center and found a teacher education student who was willing to work for two or three hours a week when she was not attending school.

Some schools support Artists in the Classroom or Musicians in the Classroom projects. Storytellers and authors often have appointments in schools as well. These part-time employees receive reimbursements from community arts commissions or other grant funds, and their engagements in schools are limited. The goal of these programs is to provide educational experiences for children that might otherwise be prohibitive because of financial constraints.

⭐ CLASSROOM MANAGEMENT IN KINDERGARTEN

Working with children in classrooms implies that teachers are aware of the environmental impact on behavior and learning. Guidance of young children is founded on positive relationships between adults and their students, but environmental influences play a role as well in the overall development of positive behaviors. Teachers attempt to control the factors that diminish learning and create chaotic behavior, but all distracting elements cannot be removed from a classroom. For example, other school groups walking down the hall or even regularly scheduled lawn maintenance may disrupt classroom experiences. If the teacher's classroom is adjacent to the music room or library, children will need to adjust to the intrusiveness of the hallway traffic flow prior to becoming actively engaged in their own learning.

Classroom Rules

Keys to effective classroom rules are that they are (1) simple, (2) well defined, (3) worded positively, (4) easily communicated, and (5) displayed for all children to view. Some teachers use the first day of school to request children's input in developing classroom rules, for they believe that children will follow them more systematically if they have a hand in formulating the rules. Mrs. Riehl's class from the previous year had planned these rules:

1. Listen while others are talking.
2. Use indoor voices.
3. Walk in the classroom.
4. Share toys.
5. Talk about problems.

Kindergarten teachers often differentiate between "indoor voices" and "outdoor voices." Following this procedure helps children understand that different behaviors are expected in the classroom, whereas it is appropriate to run and make noise while on the playground. When children develop the rules and when they are prominently displayed, teachers can more easily say, "Let's review rule number three. Some of us are having difficulty remembering the rule."

Group Behaviors

Classroom rules are designed basically to guide group behaviors. Children with limited experiences with others are guided by their egocentric thinking. The implication for the classroom is that children do not always understand others' behaviors, often misinterpret what classmates and teachers are communicating, and they need continual reminders about why rules are important in getting along with one another. At the beginning of the school year, teachers find that reviewing the rules is a daily strategy that promotes an understanding of the expectations they have for their children.

Individual Behaviors

Most discussions of children's behaviors occur on an individual basis, though. Learning to control oneself is an individual process, and learning to "behave" requires instruction no different than planning for lessons and classroom activities. When kindergarten children misbehave, they have forgotten the rules, did not comprehend the rules initially, or misinterpret behaviors of others in reference to themselves. If Jeremy accidentally bumps

Posting classroom rules reminds children that rules exist and should be followed.

Briana in line, Briana may misinterpret the action as one that was deliberate, and the teacher's intervention to help each child understand the infraction is essential to children's social development.

The phrase "praise in public and reprimand in private" is one that facilitates children's learning of appropriate classroom behavior. When teachers take aside an offender, explain what the infraction has been, and describe alternate behaviors to exhibit, most "bad behavior" will disappear from the classroom. Children also respond when they know the consequences of their acts. Removing a privilege (such as being the classroom messenger for the day) or briefly isolating the child are techniques that teachers use to remind children of their responsibilities (Reynolds, 2001).

When children's behavior is severely reprimanded, negative consequences may result. Fields and Boesser (2002) suggest that anger and aggression, fear, and deceitfulness within children result from inappropriate adult punishments. Children also suffer damage to self-esteem and their ability to think critically and develop internal controls, and they miss learning opportunities. Adult stress and misperceptions of appropriate guidance techniques are precursors to classroom punishment (Fields & Boesser, 2002).

One problem arises in early childhood classrooms when some young children discover that they receive attention from their peers and teachers when they misbehave. A teacher who observes this negative social impulse needs to respond by limiting the opportunities for children to demonstrate "attention-getting" behavior, looking for positive comments she can give the child, and talking to parents about curtailing negative behaviors at home.

On occasion, children come to school as the only child in their family, and these children need instruction about how to get along with others. The only child is often a dominant personality in the classroom, and he or she demands attention from the teacher and peers. Talking to the child individually, defining the reactions of his or her classmates, and telling the child about more appropriate behavior will, over time, assist the child in developing prosocial behaviors essential for good school conduct.

Behaviors in Other Areas of the School

Scheduled trips to the library, cafeteria, or school gymnasium present opportunities for children to misbehave. Early in the school year, teachers need to tell children the specific routines to follow as they move from the classroom to another area of the building and carefully monitor the behavior until it is internalized. Schools usually provide graphic organizers in the building, such as painted lines or darker tiles on the hallway floor, which assist children in knowing how to "walk in a line." Reviewing expected behaviors before going to another part of the building will help children in their recollection of the rules. An example of cafeteria rules is shown in Figure 6.7.

Behaviors during Special Events

Planning for a field trip, attending a schoolwide program, or incorporating holiday ideas into the classroom can induce excitement that teachers will recognize as disruptive. Teachers' understanding that negative behavior emerges because of the situations involved is one step toward eliminating some of children's hyperactive behavior. Awareness of potential problems is an ally in heading off problems before they occur. Group discussions about how to behave and supervision of individual children who might be troublesome are two techniques teachers use to eliminate the emergence of negative behavior during out-of-the-ordinary school events.

FIGURE 6.7 Cafeteria Rules Chart

Use 6-inch voices.
Please walk in the cafeteria.
Eat your food politely.
Pick up all your trash around you.
Raise your hand for help.
Enter cafeteria quietly.
Stay seated until you are dismissed.

Promoting Cooperation and a Sense of Community

Teachers who are dedicated to achieving the goal of creating a caring community of learners will use what they know about child development, what they know about individual children, and information about the social-cultural context children live in to establish practices to meet their needs. Addressing and discussing social issues as they arise in the classroom helps develop this sense of community. *Starting Small,* a publication from the Teaching Tolerance Project (1997), defines social issues as understanding racial, ethnic, and gender awareness, building friendships, facing biases and discrimination, working toward inclusive classrooms, and helping children comprehend and deal with loss. The essence of community is the establishment of democratic principles in classrooms of young children.

Confronting biases and discrimination when teachers observe them is essential in developing a classroom democracy. On occasion, children exclude someone while they are playing because the person is of another race or gender. The teacher who steps in and makes an appropriate comment is a model for sensitivity to others. Saying, "Alby would like to join your block play; how can she help out?" communicates that all children can make contributions to classroom activity.

Introducing concepts of cultural diversity is another technique for helping children understand others. James Banks points out that introducing foods, art, holidays, celebrations, and other artifacts associated with another culture is a good approach to learning about others (Banks & Banks, 1993), and many teachers and schools routinely use these strategies to impart information about other cultures (examples are Black History or Hispanic Heritage months). Banks advocates, however, a more successful approach, what he calls "social action" (Banks & Banks, 1993). The social action strategy requires that children, with the assistance of their teachers, identify a problem within their school or community that affects special groups of people and then work to solve the problem.

Social action allows children to participate in making changes in practices that may be discriminatory. For example, first graders might notice that the door to the school cafeteria is too small for their classmate who has a wheelchair to enter on his own. Writing a class letter to the principal or the school board asking for the door to be widened would be social action at its best. Or pointing out to the music teacher that the all-school choir has no minority representation and requesting a solution or explanation would be another example of social action.

Communicating elements of cultural diversity to children's parents or guardians also promotes a sense of community. The changing demographics of America's children dictate that information should be disseminated to families about the make-up of the school and classroom. An easy strategy is to focus on the cultures represented within the classroom. Asking families to share an artifact representing their cultural background on a preset date or inviting individual parents in to talk to children will expand children's understanding of diversity. Planning a potluck supper with foods from a variety of cultures could become a schoolwide tradition if all teachers in the school work together. Newsletters, discussed more thoroughly in Chapter 11, offer opportunities to share information about diverse populations.

Dimensions of Diversity

Nondiscrimination Laws

All states have nondiscrimination laws that affect public school operations. The following is Wisconsin's Nondiscrimination Law.

Under Wisconsin law, section 118.13, Wis. Stats., no pupil may be excluded from a public school, or from any school activities or programs, or be denied any benefits or treated in a different manner because of:

sex	pregnancy	physical disability
race	parental status	mental disability
religion	marital status	emotional disability
ancestry	sexual orientation	learning disability
creed		

national origin (including a student whose primary language is not English)

The law requires each school district to submit an annual compliance report to the Department of Public Instruction and periodically conduct a self-evaluation of the status of pupil nondiscrimination and equality of educational opportunity.

Each school district is required to adopt written pupil nondiscrimination policies and complaint procedures and to designate an employee of the district to receive complaints of pupil discrimination. The complaint procedures must be included in pupil and staff handbooks.

A Checklist for Diversity in Early Childhood Education and Care (Peck & Shores, 1994) is shown in Appendix B.

Cooperative games also develop a sense of community. Egocentric behaviors are lessened when children are asked to play games that require them to work and plan together to solve a problem. One such game is called "Sticky Popcorn." In this game, kindergartners jump or hop about the play area and search for other sticky pieces of popcorn, sticking to them until the class becomes one big popcorn ball. A variation of the game is to include soccer balls in small circles of children who try to keep the balls inside as they jump up and down (Sobel, 1983).

Stunts requiring children to work together also promote cooperative behaviors. Big Snake and Little People's Big Sack are examples of cooperative activities to play in the gym or on a playground (Orlick, 1978). In playing Big Snake, children stretch out on their stomachs holding the ankles of the person in front of them. Two-person, four-person, or even eight-person snakes can slither and hiss across the gym floor, joining other snakes until one long snake emerges.

To play Little People's Big Sack, the teacher or parent volunteers need to prepare "big sacks" by sewing together light white sheets (ones children can see through easily) so that many children can get into one. The goal is for the children in the sack to shuffle, hop, crawl, or roll across the floor in one mass. The more children use the sacks, the easier it becomes to maneuver their bodies to work cohesively.

One well-known kindergarten game is Musical Chairs, which actually focuses on competitive behavior. Revising the game to eliminate the competition is the prerogative of teachers, and this one is easy to change. Instead of removing a chair each time the music stops, plan to have one less chair than children. The child who becomes "it" sings a song, recites a fingerplay, demonstrates a stunt, or is given the privilege of starting the music for the next round of play. Children like this variation, and the game can continue until they tire of playing it.

 ## Working with Parents

Children's entrance to an elementary school is a monumental step, and parents want to know about the progress their children are making. Most states label kindergarten as one of the primary grades in the K–12 scheme. Early educators, though, view kindergarten as a member of the preschool family, and they recognize the importance of establishing home–school relationships. Working with parents in kindergarten does not always require sending home report cards, but home–school communication is essential whatever its form.

Portfolio Development

A growing trend in education is to use portfolios to report information to parents. Classroom portfolios are samples of children's work collected together in a file or folio representing children's progress during the school year. Kindergarten teachers use them as a record for parents, administrators, and children, too. Their strength lies in the concrete evidence they present, and their use is appropriate at any grade. To show evidence of growth, portfolio entries must be dated each time something is added to the collection. In kindergarten, the teacher is the primary organizer of the collection, and she is attentive to including samples representing the broad range of children's learning from social and emotional learning to physical growth to cognitive learning. As children grow older, they have personal control over their work samples, and occasionally they have the opportunity to participate in a parent-teacher conference to describe their work and defend portfolio choices (Helm, Beneke, & Steinheimer, 1998).

What Is Included in Portfolios? The goal of portfolio development is to show children's growth, so anything that demonstrates classroom learning is appropriate. Photographs, videos, samples of invented writing, children's journals (if used), artwork, checklists and rating scales teachers have developed, and anecdotal records are appropriate artifacts for portfolios. Photographs can also be used in other situations—on bulletin boards or in class books showing a history of the kindergarten year. Videos are excellent for parent viewing, perhaps in a special end-of-year parent program.

Writing and drawing show definite progress over time, and their inclusion in a portfolio helps parents understand the developmental nature of learning while showing evidence that children are acquiring knowledge. Many teachers ask their kindergarten children to draw self-portraits at the beginning of the school year and then again in May. Giving children the drawings at the end of the school year to compare is an eye opener to them, and some will exclaim that they did not complete the first drawing. *Dating each entry in portfolios is critical to their successful use.*

Checklists and *rating scales* are tools that keep a record of knowledge and skill acquisition based on teacher observations of individual children. Checklists are usually prepared by the school district or a school's team of teachers to follow children's learning in a specified area, such as literacy or numeracy development. Rating scales utilize ranking terms to record the level of development in children, such as *never, sometimes, usually,* and *always.* The teacher keeps these records handy when he or she works in the classroom in order to check immediately what she observes. In literacy, the teacher might want to know if children can follow directions, take part in discussions, or repeat rhyming words (Shores, 1997).

Commercially prepared checklists and rating scales are also available, though their goals may differ from those of the school or school district. Wortham's (1995) analysis of checklist use is that they are easy to use, but they can be time consuming and limit the time teachers spend with children. Rating scales are useful for measuring behaviors that might not otherwise be easy to assess, though they tend to be highly subjective. A sample simplified kindergarten mathematics checklist is shown in Figure 6.8.

Anecdotal narratives or *anecdotal records,* as they are often called, are descriptions of children's classroom behaviors written with factual, nonjudgmental language about real events (Shores & Grace, 1998). Collecting anecdotal writings over time as they relate to an individual child assists teachers in their later review of the child and perceived problems the child may possess. Several entries are more valuable than only two or so. Forming judgments about children on only one or two observations denies children due process. A preponderance of evidence is essential to good evaluations of children's progress.

Teachers often use Post-It notes, jotting notes about their observations as a mnemonic device for writing the anecdotal record at the end of the day. Small cassette recorders can also assist in identifying language samples if these are desired. Some teachers develop anecdotal record forms to help them in accurately organizing information they want to share with parents. As mentioned previously, dating each portfolio record is crucial to its use with parents and administrators.

Anecdotal records are included in the Cumulative Folder when the school year ends. Teachers' use of nonjudgmental comments demonstrates sensitivity to the developmental essence of learning, and their focus is on what children are capable of doing. Teachers must eliminate their biases and judgments about children's behavior to protect themselves from legal actions from parents. Figure 6.9 demonstrates appropriate and inappropriate anecdotal comments.

Portfolios are excellent tools to use in planning a parent conference because they are a collection of individual work samples from the classroom. Telling parents

FIGURE 6.8 Mathematics Checklist

Child's Name_____						
Skill	**Yes**	**No**	**Date**	**Date**	**Date**	**Date**
Reads numerals 1 through 10						
Writes numerals 1 through 10						
Counts to 20 by rote						
Counts to 20 rationally						
Uses concrete objects to solve addition problems						
Uses concrete objects to solve subtraction problems						
Chooses the shape that comes next in a three-shape pattern						
Chooses the shape that comes next in a four-shape pattern						
Identify simple shapes: square, circle, rectangle, triangle, and oval						
Measures classroom furniture with nonstandard measure						
Counts to 20 by twos						
Identifies odd and even numerals						

their child needs to work on recognizing letters will be easier if a checklist documenting the child's progress is available. Showing parents samples of children's invented writing is evidence that their literacy is growing. Concrete examples of children's work support the teacher's objective view of the child, forming a foundation for recommendations that are made about his or her progress.

Parent Conferences

Classroom teachers are actively engaged in keeping parents informed about school progress at every grade level, and kindergarten is no exception. Teachers' responsibility for parent conferences include

1. Contacting parents for conferences (or using designated school district parent-teacher conference dates)
2. Planning what will be said to the parents during the conference
3. Collecting work samples and preparing notes for the conference

FIGURE 6.9 Appropriate and Inappropriate Anecdotal Comments

Appropriate Comments	Inappropriate Comments
Jeremy is beginning to take an active role in class discussions.	Jeremy's social and emotional development is so poor, he is incapable of participating in class discussions.
Destiny cried today when another child took her toy away.	Destiny does not know how to be assertive.
Rafael screamed and stomped his feet when he couldn't join the other children in the Block Center three times this week.	Rafael has temper tantrums all the time.
Tommy hit Jennifer when she actually bumped into him during line-up.	Tommy's self-centeredness causes problems for him.
Sanjay has a positive attitude toward school attendance.	Sanjay is a model student who will always perform well.

4. Welcoming parents and helping them feel at ease during the conference period
5. Encouraging a dialogue about the child and fostering a collaborative school-home relationship
6. Providing a specific set of recommendations that parents can use at home to assist with children's growth

One major suggestion for conducting successful parent conferences is to set a positive tone, limiting negative comments about children's performance to one or two major concerns. Whatever concern is mentioned, possible solutions should also be shared with the parent (Shores & Grace, 1998). No parent should ever depart from a conference feeling defeated. The teacher-parent relationship (and the trust parents feel about schools) is developed gradually through professional interactions that convey the teacher's concern for the children in her or his care. (For more information about parent conferences, see Chapter 11.)

Report Cards

In kindergarten, most communication with parents takes place within the framework of a parent conference. These are usually required twice a year, during the fall and near the end of the school year. Some school districts use a combination of conferences and report cards to keep parents apprised of children's achievement. If readiness tests are administered, an end-of-year conference with parents or guardians is essential.

When kindergarten report cards are used, they focus on several areas of development, not just intellectual development (see Figure 6.10). Classroom behavior is analyzed, and evaluations of social and emotional development are often described.

State by State

Kindergarten Mathematics Standards

Tennessee's kindergarten mathematics standards, shown here, are an example of state academic standards. For clarification about each standard as it relates to 5-year-olds, go to the Tennessee Department of Education website (www.state. tn.us/education).

KINDERGARTEN

Number and Operations

Content Standard 1.0 The student will develop number and operation sense needed to represent numbers and number relationships verbally, symbolically, and graphically and to compute fluently and make reasonable estimates in problem solving.

K.1.1 Understand numbers, ways of representing numbers, relationships among numbers, and number systems.

K.1.2 Understand meanings of operations and how they relate to one another.

K.1.3 Solve problems, compute fluently, and make reasonable estimates.

Algebra

Content Standard 2.0 The student will understand and generalize patterns as they represent and analyze quantitative relationships and change in a variety of contexts and problems using graphs, tables, and equations.

K.2.1 Sort and classify objects by size, number, and other properties.

K.2.2 Represent and analyze patterns and functions.

K.2.3 Use concrete, pictorial, and verbal representations to develop an understanding of the language and symbols of mathematics.

K.2.4 Illustrate general properties of operations.
       [no accomplishments for this learning expectation at the Kindergarten level].

K.2.5 Analyze change in various contexts.
       [no accomplishments for this learning expectation at the Kindergarten level].

Geometry

Content Standard 3.0
The student will develop an understanding of geometric concepts and relationships as the basis for geometric modeling and reasoning to solve problems involving one-, two-, and three-dimensional figures.

K.3.1 Analyze characteristics and properties of geometric shapes.

K.3.2 Specify locations and describe spatial relationships.

K.3.3 Recognize and apply flips, slides, and turns.
       [no accomplishments for this learning expectation at the Kindergarten level].

continued

Measurement

Content Standard 4.0

K.4.1 Demonstrate understanding of units of measure and measurable attributes of objects.
K.4.2 Apply appropriate techniques and tools to determine measurements.

Data Analysis and Probability

Content Standard 5.0

The student will understand and apply basic statistical and probability concepts as they organize and analyze data and make predictions and conjectures.

K.5.1 Develop, select, and use appropriate methods to collect, organize, display, and analyze data.
K.5.2 Apply the basic concepts of probability.

Information shared on the report card relates to the emergent literacy skills observed in children shared earlier in the chapter. See Figure 6.10 for a sample report card.

Involving Parents or Guardians in Classroom Activity

One strategy for promoting trust between parents and schools is to invite parents into the classroom as volunteers. Field trip supervision was described previously in this chapter as one technique for involving parents, but other options are possible. Sometimes parents are volunteers who participate on a regular basis. One kindergarten teacher did not feel qualified to teach music in her classroom, so she invited a child's mother to teach music to her children on a weekly basis. Other tasks parents can absorb are:

- Supervising specific center activity (such as the Computer or Art Center)
- Individually assisting children who need special instruction
- Preparing for a classroom celebration
- Assisting with project development
- Regularly reading books to children
- Teaching children special games
- Monitoring children during lunch or library time
- Participating in family learning nights designed to instruct parents in strategies to use in the home to extend learning

Sometimes, schools plan for special mother-child or father-child breakfasts or lunches. Parents and guardians will bring cupcakes or cakes in for children's birthdays. Certainly, parents are involved with Parent-Teacher Organizations if they choose, and holiday celebrations prompt this level of involvement. Other family

FIGURE 6.10 Sample Report Card

Bay St. Louis-Waveland School District					

North Bay Elementary
740 Dunbar Ave.
Bay St. Louis, MS 39520
(228) 467-4757

Progress Report (K-3)

1999-2000

Waveland Elementary
1101 St. Joseph St.
Waveland, MS 39576
(228) 467-6630

STUDENT: _____

TEACHER: _____   Grade: _____

E - Excellent progress   S - Satisfactory progress   N - Needs Improvement

Reading	Reporting Period	1	2	3
Progress				

Comments 1: _____

Comments 2: _____

Comments 3: _____

Language Arts	Reporting Period	1	2	3
Progress				

Comments 1: _____

Comments 2: _____

Comments 3: _____

Math	Reporting Period	1	2	3
Progress				

Comments 1: _____

Comments 2: _____

Comments 3: _____

Learner Characteristics	Reporting Period	1	2	3
Accepts learning challenges				
Follows directions				
Asks questions				
Focuses on learning tasks				
Participates in class discussions				
Able to work with others				
Able to work alone to complete tasks				
Self-starter, initiates learning activities				
Demonstrates self control				
Respects others and their ideas				
In classroom				
Out of classroom				
Completes home practice				

Dear Parents:
If you would like to schedule a conference, please call the school office for a date and time. Thank you!

First Reporting Period   (1)
Please sign below and return the report to your child's teacher.

_____   _____
Parent Signature   Date

Second Reporting Period   (2)
Please sign below and return the report to your child's teacher.

_____   _____
Parent Signature   Date

Third Reporting Period   (3)
Please sign below and return the report to your child's teacher.

_____   _____
Parent Signature   Date

Student promotion or retention is based on the student's portfolio, profile, and progress report.

members can also be involved in classroom experiences. Grandparent Days are popular during the month of September. (See Chapter 11 for other information about parental involvement.)

⭐ ISSUES FACING KINDERGARTEN TEACHERS

Kindergarten teachers understand many of the issues facing them as professionals. Occasionally they are called on for solutions to the following problems.

Research on Teacher Nurture

Newman and Dickinson's review of early literacy research (2001) shows a strong connection between teacher nurturing and student achievement. Collaboration among schools, families, and social services is a critical factor in children's development, well-being, and growth. An old adage, "Children care to learn when teachers learn to care," is a poignant reminder of the influence teachers of young children wield. Other findings that Newman and Dickinson report are:

- High-quality instruction in classrooms correlates with the professional development of educators.
- Professionals must acknowledge that children learn in a variety of ways and plan accordingly.
- Achievement gaps exist between children from middle-income families and children from low-income families.
- Teachers must be sensitive to the developing identities of children.

Push-Down Curriculum

naeyc

Early educators have long been overwhelmed by the tendency of schools to push academic achievement expectations down the grade-level hierarchy. The public believes that if teachers start early enough, children can learn more knowledge more quickly. This thinking is a result of mounting concerns that children in the United States are not competing adequately internationally and began during the space-race era of the 1960s and 1970s. This phenomenon, referred to as the *elementary error* (Bredekamp & Rosegrant, 1992), was discussed in Chapter 1.

Elkind (2001) reminds educators that early childhood is a time when guided, hands-on learning is critical, that introducing the world of symbols too early in life is dangerous, and that learning is a complex process and should not be hurried. The work of David Weikart and Larry Schweinhart (1999) also suggests that developmentally appropriate curriculum yields positive long-term results.

naeyc

The National Association for the Education of Young Children defines guidelines for developing appropriate curriculum practices. They include teachers' commitment to (1) creating a community of learners, (2) teaching to enhance development and learning, (3) constructing appropriate curriculum, (4) assessing children's learning and development, and (5) establishing reciprocal relationships with families (Bredekamp & Copple, 1997).

Recognizing Children with Disabilities

Teachers in early education are aware that children need services that cannot be provided in normal classroom experiences. For the most part, young children enter school for the first time as kindergartners; and teachers of 5-year-olds face this issue specifically. The Council for Exceptional Children's Division for Early Childhood (DEC) (Sandall, McLean, & Smith, 2000) views parents as partners in the assessment process, emphasizing the concept that practices with young children must be appropriate. Other concerns of the DEC are the authenticity and usefulness of assessment procedures, whether they are individualized to children, and the sensitivity of professionals who work with families. Teachers have a number of school personnel and resources to assist them in determining what services children need. (For more information about children with special needs, see Chapter 4.)

Teacher Reflection

All teachers, no matter what grade they teach, reflect on their teaching abilities. Reflections take place daily and weekly, sometimes immediately after teaching a lesson or interacting with an individual child. Teachers reflect on their practice at the end of the school year. The purpose of this reflection is to aid them in improving their classroom practices with children. Reflection motivates teachers to call in parents for conferences about their children, talk about classroom problems with the school counselor or a school administrator, or pursue workshops or graduate study in order to become a more effective teacher.

SUMMARY

On the surface, teaching kindergarten children appears to be easy. The schedule has long blocks of time for children to play in centers, and curriculum standards and assessment procedures are not prescribed as specifically as they are for teachers in the elementary grades. Generally, 5-year-olds have even tempers, and they make the transition into school with poise and confidence. Their curiosity and eagerness to learn contribute to the success they will feel in school if it is planned with their needs in mind.

However easy kindergarten appears, teaching kindergarten requires a commitment to nurturing the potential in children. Teachers of 5-year-olds must recognize that conceptual development is time consuming, be keen observers of children's activity, be ready to take advantage of teachable moments as they occur, and be prepared to establish positive school-home relationships. Good kindergarten teachers can form positive foundations for children's lifelong learning.

DISCUSSION QUESTIONS

1. Interview a kindergarten teacher about assessment practices. Share your findings with your classmates in a class discussion.
2. Recall your experiences with report card time during elementary school. Share with your classmates what was positive and what was less positive about these experiences. What is your attitude about grading young children?

SUGGESTED CHAPTER ACTIVITIES

1. Observe in a kindergarten classroom organized by a teacher with many years of experience. Notice all the visual markers and signals designed to assist children with classroom routine and management. Which ones of these organizers will you use in your classroom?
2. Review Frederick Froebel's philosophy (described in Chapter 1) about working in kindergarten. How does his early practice compare to modern-day kindergarten programs?
3. Develop a file of fingerplays and songs appropriate for use in kindergarten classrooms.

Chapter Seven

Teaching in a First-Grade Classroom

CHAPTER OVERVIEW

★ Have you thought about your first teaching experience? What will you need to know to be successful?

★ What are the roles that teachers accept when they are hired by a school district?

★ How do you plan for the first day of school?

★ Does the school district nurture its first-year teachers so they will have a feeling of competence?

★ What reading skills do children need to achieve during the first year?

★ How do teachers prepare for the year's end?

FIND OUT THE ANSWERS TO THESE QUESTIONS BY READING THIS CHAPTER.

Six-year-old children are inquisitive, congenial, and fun-loving children who enjoy learning. Teachers who work with 6-year-olds often see a great deal of academic growth during the year they are together, as youngsters begin to become more independent in their abilities to read, write, and understand mathematical concepts. A broad range of study topics interests first graders, and teachers discover that they are usually fairly easy to motivate as learners. If first graders have had appropriate experiences with others before entering first grade, they exhibit social and emotional maturity, indicating their readiness to understand others' viewpoints and to adjust more readily to the rigors of group instruction and to working independently.

Physically, 6-year-olds weigh approximately 50 to 60 pounds, and children usually gain about 6 or 7 pounds during the first-grade year. They have 24 teeth (varying based on the appearance of their six-year molars, and their front baby teeth often become loose during the school year). Becoming "snaggle-toothed" is a prized hallmark of the first-grade year, and teachers occasionally see children pulling out their own teeth during the school day! Certainly, children do wiggle the loose tooth until it comes out on its own.

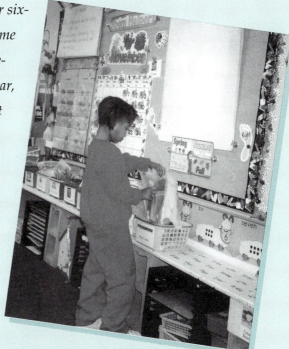

Children are still active during this time period, but they are now capable of sitting still for 30 to 40 minutes at a time, if teachers plan appropriate breaks that will allow children to stretch or wiggle (using fingerplays or songs, for example) during required sedentary school

experiences. They participate eagerly in independent games and activities, and a classroom library is appealing to this age. The transition to first grade will occur easily if children have had positive preschool experiences. Only on occasion will children respond negatively to the required structure that first grade demands.

Children enjoy socializing with their classmates, and typically teachers observe first graders inviting friends and classmates to birthday parties or for overnight visits in their homes. A popular activity is exchanging telephone numbers, and teachers may discover that children will also call them at home if their phone number is available. Outside activities become important, too, especially if the community has Brownie troops, Camp Fire groups, or sports programs designed for boys and girls. T-ball and soccer are popular for youngsters, but gymnastic and dance programs are specifically attractive to 6-year-old girls.

Children have upsets during the year about lost or stolen personal items, deaths of family members, pets, or even news events that attract national attention. Their reactions to emotional disruptions are to be expected, but if they are provided with explanations from caring adults, most children do not become overly alarmed with events that affect them. Children who experience death of a parent or divorce, for example, need referral to school counselors or to other community agency personnel who can assist them with their severe problems. Their families may also need to be included in counseling sessions.

School began at 7:45 in the morning, and now, at 5:00 p.m., Ms. Thomas looked around her newly decorated room and thought to herself, "Well, I'm as ready as I'll ever be. I can't wait to meet my children." Her bulletin boards were in order; materials were easily accessible for conducting the first day of school with poise and confidence. Other teachers had told her that parents often accompanied their children to school on the first day, so she was prepared to get acquainted with them as they arrived by providing a number of independent activities for children to choose as they came into her classroom.

This was Ms. Thomas's first teaching job, and she had spent the past several days attending required school district meetings with the superintendent, her principal, and her teaching team as well as special meetings with other new teachers to orient her to school district policies and health and safety procedures. She had met the custodial staff, the school librarian, the music teacher, the physical education teacher, the cafeteria personnel, and the school nurse, and she had a brand new copy of the school's first-grade curriculum guide on her desk.

Her student teaching experience the previous spring had been successful, and she was hopeful that this first year of teaching would be favorable as well. She was somewhat apprehensive about the first days of school, because she had heard from more experienced teachers that these were important to the overall tone and implementation of the entire school year. She was acquainted with the community, and she had an awareness of the demographics of the children who would be in her classroom. Fortunately, she had only 19 children enrolled in her class, which would make the first days easier; but she also knew that the number could change after Labor Day, a time when late enrollees often arrived at school.

She had just enough time to get home and change clothes and return to the local high school cafeteria for a "Meet the New Teachers" barbecue cosponsored by the Chamber of Commerce and the school district's Board of Trustees. Ms. Thomas recognizes that her position as an educational leader in the city was critical to her tenure at her assigned elementary school.

☆ WHAT FIRST GRADERS ARE EXPECTED TO LEARN

First grade appears to be an extremely important grade in the K–12 hierarchy because of the expectations parents and school districts have for 6-year-olds' achievement levels. From an intellectual standpoint, the demands on first graders are high. If they are not already reading, the teacher's goal is to ensure that children are reading by the end of the school year, with the long-range goal that they will become independent readers by the end of third grade. Basal texts usually have a vocabulary reading list of approximately 150 words, and children should read environmental print with ease.

By the end of first grade, children should be able to do simple addition and subtraction facts, be able to tell time on the hour and half-hour, and have some rudimentary knowledge of money. Many school districts expect first graders to be able to count to 100 by 1s, 2s, 5s, and 10s. They will have a basic understanding of the term *holiday,* and they know their own birth dates. Children should have learned their addresses and phone numbers during their kindergarten year, but in grade 1 they will be able to tell other pertinent information about reaching their parents or guardians in case of an emergency.

Individual states have their own standards, and possession of a specific certification level demonstrates that educators have basic understanding of children's achievement in each grade level. In addition, school district curriculum guides describe the knowledge children should acquire throughout their time in school.

Teachers who work with 6-year-olds emphasize specific skills that may not have been required of them previously. These skills include

- Attentive listening: putting on one's "listening ears" or "zipping one's mouth" so that listening will be easier (for an example of a classroom listening chart, see Figure 7.1)
- Remembering simple classroom rules

Nebraska's Mathematics Standards

Teachers acquaint themselves with state standards before entering classrooms for the first time. Awareness assists their instructional planning to ensure that children learn what they need to learn before third grade end-of-grade tests. This sample of standards shows **Nebraska's** expectations for mathematics by the end of first grade:

NEBRASKA MATHEMATICS STANDARDS, GRADES K–1

1.1 Numeration/Number Sense

1.1.1 By the end of first grade, students will communicate the sequential nature of the number system.

1.1.2 By the end of first grade, students will communicate the mathematical relations of the number system.

1.1.3 By the end of first grade, students will recognize numbers and applications in everyday situations.

1.1.4 By the end of first grade, students will demonstrate the value of numbers (0–20) using concrete objects.

1.2 Computation/Estimation

1.2.1 By the end of first grade, students will demonstrate the concepts of addition and subtraction up to 10.

1.2.2 By the end of first grade, students will determine the reasonableness of proposed solutions to mathematical problems.

1.3 Measurement

1.3.1 By the end of first grade, students will compare two or more items or sets using direct comparisons or nonstandard units of measure for the following attributes: length (shorter/longer), height (taller/shorter), weight (heavier/lighter), temperature (hotter/colder). Nonstandard unit examples are length of a human foot, hand span, new pencil, a toothpick, block, and so on.

1.3.2 By the end of first grade, students will recognize tools of measurement and their appropriate use, such as clocks, calendar, ruler, balance scale, and thermometer.

1.3.3 By the end of first grade, students will tell time to the half-hour using an analog and digital clock.

1.3.4 By the end of first grade, students will identify the different units of measurement used in their environment, such as cents, dollars, pounds, gallons, liters, meters, miles, minutes, and hours.

1.3.5 By the end of first grade, students will demonstrate an understanding of orientation in time for past, present, future, earlier, and later.

1.4 Geometry/Spatial Concepts

1.4.1 By the end of first grade, students will compare relative position and spatial relationships, such as left/right, above/below, over/under, up/down, and near/far.

1.4.2 By the end of first grade, students will identify, describe, and create circles, squares, triangles, and rectangles.

1.5 Data Analysis, Probability, and Statistical Concepts

1.5.1 By the end of first grade, students will count and collect information about objects and events in their environment, such as what is your favorite candy bar, who has a brother, how many pets, and who is going to the library.

1.5.2 By the end of first grade, students will organize and display collected information using objects and pictures.

1.5.3 By the end of first grade, students will make comparisons from displayed data, such as more, less, and fewer.

1.5.4 By the end of first grade, students will describe the steps used in collecting and analyzing information.

1.6 Algebraic Concepts

1.6.1 By the end of first grade, students will identify, describe, extend, and create a variety of patterns, such as objects, sounds, movements, shapes, numbers, and colors.

1.6.2 By the end of first grade, students will sort and classify objects according to one or more attributes, such as size, shape, color, and thickness.

1.6.3 By the end of first grade, students will identify and describe patterns in their environment.

- Participation in group discussions and group instruction
- Asking children to raise their hands to talk during group discussions or in response to questions asked by the teacher
- Following directions for completion of classroom tasks or making transitions from activity to activity within the classroom
- Following routines about participating in groups or choosing and using centers in the classroom
- Taking responsibility for keeping the classroom fairly neat and clean
- Learning how to line up at the door for transitions to other parts of the building

FIGURE 7.1 Listening Chart

Good Listening Rules
Open ears.
Look.
Listen.
What did the speaker say?

- Sharing and caring for classroom materials, understanding the need to save discarded materials for other projects (a classroom recycling center or scrap box assists in this endeavor)
- Delivering messages and report cards to parents or guardians and bringing responses back to school
- Acknowledging that the main purpose of being in school is for learning and accepting the role children must take to be successful at school

⭐ ORGANIZING THE CLASSROOM

Ms. Thomas's room is one of the larger classrooms on her wing, yet preparing the room for all of the centers she would like to have for her class is still a challenge. She has decided to capitalize on a few centers, having one center that will change each time a new social studies theme is studied. The first-grade team believes in having themes that last for prolonged periods of time (four to six weeks, if possible), and Ms. Thomas happily agreed that this plan was appropriate. She was concerned that weekly themes would be required of her, and she felt that week-long topics limited what children could learn about each of the subjects.

The specific centers she selected for her classroom include a Book Corner, an Art Center, a Computer Center, a Writing Center, Games and Puzzles, and a Discovery Center (see Chapter 3 for descriptions of these centers). She grouped the desks and chairs the children would sit in daily in a special formation that allowed for group work. They would also be easily disbanded and regrouped if classroom management strategies require separating specific individuals who are unable to work independently of one another. Her classroom looks like the floor plan shown in Figure 7.2.

The individual features she has added to her classroom are much like those of other first-grade teachers in her school and are designed to give a personal touch to the room. Besides the centers, provisioned with adequate materials to meet the needs of the children, other markers include the following.

- Welcome sign on the door showing her name and the grade she teaches
- Teacher-made calendar with typical monthly icons (small schoolhouses for August, fall leaves for September, pumpkins for October, turkeys for November, etc.) and shape or color cards to help children learn patterning
- American and state flags
- Responsibility pocket chart and name tags so that assigned tasks can rotate throughout the school year (for an example of a responsibility chart, see Figure 7.3)
- Center selection chart with children's name tags available to encourage easy decision-making processes
- Birthday bulletin board showing each child's birthday and provisions for children with summer birthdays (Ms. Thomas checked registration rosters to determine if any family would have religious objections to children's birthdays being displayed and recognized)

FIGURE 7.2 A First-Grade Classroom Layout

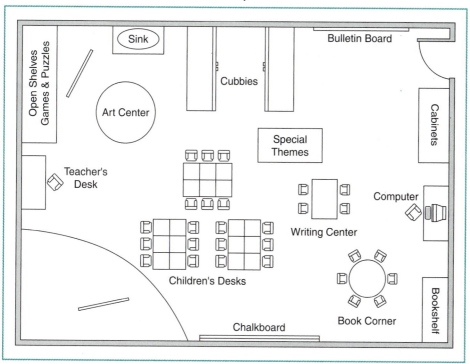

- Attractive signs marking each of the classroom centers
- Names on the children's cubbies and desks
- Chart showing the general rules that guide good behavior in the classroom
- Blank chart available for a first-day brainstorming session to set the rules the children want to guide their classroom activity (this discussion will occur early in the morning of the first day, when Ms. Thomas talks about the democracy she hopes her classroom will achieve)
- Area rug for Circle Time or book reading
- Alphabet chart prominently displayed at the front of the room
- Preplanned system for children being out of the classroom for unscheduled restroom breaks
- Plenty of crayons, markers, pencils, writing paper, construction paper within easy reach of the children (the school district requires that children purchase a list of school supplies in local stores, but Ms. Thomas knows not all children will arrive with them on the first day of school)

FIGURE 7.3 Responsibility Chart

Who Will Help?

Line Leaders
Chalkboard
Plants
Pet
Librarian
Errands

⭐ SCHEDULE OF THE DAY

The teaching team in Ms. Thomas's school works together with their school building principal to establish the schedule for the day. Specific requirements from the state education agency establish the amount of time that is spent on each content area, and the demand for reading instruction is high in first grade. The classrooms in the building have no restroom facilities, and the schedule for restroom breaks is set in conjunction with other classes using the restroom down the hall. Keeping to a tight schedule for going to the cafeteria, library, gym, and other school building facilities is part of the responsibility of every teacher in the school. A typical first-grade schedule would look like this:

7:45	Children enter the classroom
7:50	Teachers collect lunch money or other fees for insurance, school pictures, or special programs
7:55	Morning rituals (pledge to the flag, morning song, and announcements by the school principal)
8:05	Classroom routine (check calendar; count children; review of independent work assigned for the day)
8:15	Social studies
8:40	Handwriting instruction
8:50	Language arts/independent work
9:30	Physical education
9:55	Restroom break
10:05	Attendance is taken and reported
10:05	Language arts/independent work
11:10	Lunch
11:30	Restroom break
11:40	Book reading or storytelling (children rest for a while)
11:55	Mathematics
12:25	Music (twice a week); science (twice a week); library time
12:55	Check independent work
1:05	Recess
1:25	Restroom break
1:35	Integrated thematic study (projects, dramatic play, fine arts activities, additional writing experiences, and individualized instruction, as necessary)
2:15	Review the day's schedule/preliminary planning for the next day
2:30	Songs, fingerplays or poems
2:40	Room cleanup/prepare for dismissal
2:50	Dismissal to school buses (or to private transportation)
3:00	School day is over

☆ THE FIRST DAY OF SCHOOL

The first day of school is exciting yet full of apprehension for parents and their chil-dren. If parents have positive attitudes about children's entrance into the elemen-tary grades, children will arrive in the classroom eagerly awaiting what first grade will bring them. Having an attractive classroom with opportunities for children to make choices is still important in first grade, but longer periods of group time will be allotted to whole-group instruction.

The agenda for the first day of school is that the teacher uses her time establish-ing classroom rules and introducing children to their environment while defining what is expected of them when they are at school. She is aware that children have a need to feel comfortable and at ease, and her patient guidance will ease the fears they may have about their new situation.

Many teachers have a discussion on the first day of school about the classroom being our "home away from home," suggesting that everyone has a part in mak-ing this room a special place to be. This classroom family concept helps in foster-ing prosocial behaviors within children and provides children with information about how to get along with one another while at school. Teachers are aware that the days that follow this first one will be repetitive as they remind children of the classroom rules and their responsibilities in the new environment.

Wise teachers utilize the first day with their class to talk about acceptable mod-els of behavior in school. Their secondary concern is what children are learning, though they also introduce the classroom to children, explaining many of the ex-periences children will have while they are at school. What children learn becomes more important as the year progresses, but how they behave is the main goal of the first day and weeks of school. Caring teachers also search for signs of discomfort and fearfulness in their children, attempting to relieve stress within their students as the day progresses.

The first day of school provides a strong foundation for children's conceptual-ization of the expectations their teacher has of them. The teacher guides, instructs, encourages, and nurtures her young learners while giving children a sense of well-being and anticipation about the year to come. The first day needs to be well planned, and the teacher needs to conduct the business of welcoming children and their parents in a professional and confident manner. Having a realistic view of children's learning and what they will remember from the first day experience will assist in setting the stage for learning for the remainder of the school year.

When Ms. Thomas ends her first day, she discusses with children what they have learned during their day at school. She knows parents or guardians are going to ask the inevitable question: "What did you do at school today?" She wants to avoid having the children respond, "Nothing." Consequently, she spends about 10 min-utes before children leave the classroom for their transportation home reviewing what they have accomplished. Her parting comment is, "Now you can tell your family what you did at school today." Teachers serve as public relations agents, too.

⭐ THE MAJOR EMPHASIS IN FIRST-GRADE CURRICULUM

Teaching reading consumes much of the first-grade curriculum. State and school standards set expectations that first-grade children will move to second grade knowing how to read. Many kindergarten teachers feel pressure to begin early reading, but first-grade teachers know their job is to teach children to read. First-grade teachers know about beginning reading instruction and the theoretical foundation of high-quality reading education.

Opposing Views of Teaching Reading

One approach is *whole-language instruction,* growing out of the research conducted by Ferreiro and Teberosky (1982), Clay (1966) and others (Goodman, 1986; Durkin, 1966; Itzkoff, 1986) during the latter half of the twentieth century. These researchers' work focused on determining how children learn to read and write. They noticed that many children came to school already reading, and Durkin (1966) labeled these early readers as "pencil-and-paper kids."

Pencil-and-paper children came from environments that placed a premium on literacy activities, and their parents often taught them how to read with informal strategies that allowed children to explore and experiment with print in playful ways. When mothers prepared the grocery list, their children would imitate the observed writing behaviors by developing their own grocery lists. When children pretended to be waiters at the dinner table each evening, their parents joined in the play by placing their pretend dinner orders and observed as children wrote the menu on a writing pad. Writing pretend prescriptions, preparing job application forms, or scribbling the names of one's favorite books are activities that emerge from spontaneous play in the home.

The whole-language approach attempts to replicate experiences in the classroom similar to those children have in their homes. Teachers plan classroom activities that allow children to explore and experiment with print. The emphasis is on the five main areas of literacy development—listening, speaking, reading, writing, and thinking. Comparatively, none of the literacy skills is deemed to be greater than any other. Whole-language teachers believe all literacy skills are necessary to reading comprehension.

Activities that might occur in whole-language classrooms are:

- Children participating in informal talk and discussions with their peers
- Children learning how to take turns in group discussions about topics that are being studied in the class
- Teachers taking time to talk to children individually and in small groups
- Teachers writing what children say about topics of study on classroom charts or writing stories that individual children dictate
- Teachers providing writing materials in classroom centers to encourage children to write (notepads in the Home Living Center or in the Restaurant

Center, for example; charts in the Science Center for children to record the growth of a plant)

- Teachers planning time during the day for children to write or draw in individual journals
- Teachers providing time for children to act out their favorite stories
- Teachers reading many books to children
- Teachers organizing instruction to develop class-made books about topics of study
- Teachers encouraging children to write their own books

Teachers recognize that strong listening and speaking abilities are precursors to reading and writing, and they provide an environment that allows children to express themselves verbally. The classroom is no longer a quiet place. The tomblike atmospheres of yesteryear's schools have been transformed into hives of activity that focus on learning by doing. Youngsters are reading and writing about what happens in their classroom or other everyday experiences.

The whole-language approach is attractive to teachers who believe that direct instruction does not meet the needs of all children and can damage some children's disposition to learn. Unfortunately, teachers do not always know how to manage balanced literacy classrooms efficiently. Whole-language classrooms work well if teachers (1) have classroom experience, (2) thoroughly understand the reading/writing process, (3) are able to meet individual needs of children as they arise, and (4) are easily able to articulate how their classroom instruction is teaching children to read and write.

The *back-to-basics movement* is a second approach that emerges periodically when parents and legislators question how effectively children are learning to read. This approach emphasizes phonics instruction and numerous drill and practice sessions to assist children in learning basic reading and writing skills. Often, this approach is implemented despite children's experiential background and interest in reading. Teachers who adopt the back-to-basics approach dogmatically introduce specific skills to children whether or not these skills are relevant to their students and use continued practice activities to reinforce the skills. State education agencies are charged with keeping track of children's progress with end-of-grade tests (usually at the end of third grade).

Chall describes the back-to-basics movement in research she reports in *Learning to Read: The Great Debate* (1983). The emphasis in the back-to-basics movement is on direct instruction of letters of the alphabet, sound/symbol connections, vocabulary development, and word-attack skills. Chall's research review (1967) indicates that direct instruction produces better word recognition skills. The direct instruction method is firmly entrenched in most public school classrooms because of the use of basal readers, which carefully define the skills children are to learn when lessons in the textbooks are presented. An overemphasis on skills causes alarm among reading experts who believe children are denied opportunities they might have had to make sense of print on their own. The back-to-basics movement de-emphasizes the joy, pleasure, and creativity in learning to read and focuses on the nitty-gritty elements of phonics instruction.

What Teachers Are Saying

Reading Instruction

"My past teaching experiences have taught me that I need to use the basal text, phonics instruction, balanced literacy—anything I can find to teach children reading." —*a first-grade teacher*

"When children read something that is relevant to them and they are interested in it, they are engaged in the reading process. Each step is visible, especially as you watch children move from the emergent stage to fluency." —*a first-grade teacher*

"I have a multitude of literacy centers that I rotate in and out each week as the need arises. Each week we have four new literacy centers; the names of these centers change as well. I guess you could say that I have an integrated reading curriculum that includes science, social studies, and some math." —*a first-grade teacher*

Balanced Literacy Approach

naeyc

Within recent years, the International Reading Association and the National Association for the Education of Young Children (1998) merged the opposing approaches to reading and attempted to curtail the divisiveness caused by the polarization of their ideas. The **balanced literacy approach** acknowledges the strengths of each approach and allows teachers to organize lessons utilizing strategies from both camps (Machado, 1999). Progress in the balanced literacy approach begins with children's initial strengths and weaknesses, allowing children to acquire information about literacy at their own pace.

⭐ FIRST GRADE AND READING INSTRUCTION

First-year teachers are occasionally frightened of teaching children how to read. The process seems mystical, and none of us remembers how we learned to read as children. If teachers have collected adequate data about what children know about print, then reading instruction is actually a simple process. Reading instruction is basically connecting children's knowledge about print with the printed page. If they can recognize the word *stop,* as an example, then they should be able to find the word *stop* on a page as many times as it is written. What follows is a description of the usual methods of introducing print to children.

Basal Reader Approach

The *basal reader approach* is a common method for teaching reading to children. The strengths of the basal reader approach are:

1. Use of a controlled vocabulary that is repeated throughout the textbook
2. Planned presentations of new words to children and stories in the text that allow for practice of the new vocabulary
3. Sequential development of skills thought to be essential to children becoming independent readers
4. Teachers' manuals designed to assist even the weakest or ill-prepared teacher in organizing for instruction

First-grade reading textbooks include preprimers (usually two or three) and two readers for the year.

Curricular materials often accompany the basal text for the purpose of enhancing lesson plan presentations by the teachers. Big books, pocket charts and flash cards, and worksheets or workbooks designed to support children's practice of skills as they are introduced are staple items provided by publishers. Other instructional materials such as puppets, posters, and ancillary books for additional practice in reading are examples of items publishers prepare for classrooms as marketing techniques to sell their product to teachers.

Textbook companies have made tremendous strides within the last two decades in improving the literature offered in their textbooks. Publishers are including a variety of genres and deleting racism and sexism in story selection as a result of the criticism by women and minorities during the 1960s and 1970s about the quality of the literature presented to children in classrooms. Photographs and artistic layouts of story presentations are more realistic and nonfiction information is included in greater quantity (Sowers, 2000).

Ms. Thomas's school district uses one of the state-adopted basal texts. Having all the materials provided for her teaching provides more security in tackling the process of teaching reading. She is planning other numerous classroom strategies to supplement what children are learning from the adopted textbook, because of her goal to provide a language-rich classroom that will encourage children to become readers. Implementing the language experience approach (described in the following section) and adapting individualized reading techniques with her children will further develop children's reading abilities.

Language Experience Approach

Another commonly used approach to reading is the *language experience approach*, often referred to as the LEA. Simply designed, this approach gives teachers freedom to experiment with reading instruction and focuses on children's acquiring a wide range of vocabulary based on their interests. The teacher plans an activity that all children will experience in common, such as a discussion about an object that she has brought to class or having a field trip to a community site.

The second step in the approach uses the common experience to collect and write down children's thoughts about the event. Usually this record is developed in a group discussion, but individual descriptions can also be written for the children on pictures they have drawn about the experience. Eventually, a chart emerges that compiles the children's understanding of the class's experience using its vocabulary and perceptions to finalize the writing. The teacher asks the children to read and reread their descriptions.

Follow-up activities include preparing individual copies of the chart for children to include in a book they will eventually take home to share with parents. Often, a class book becomes a record of the LEA, and teachers encourage children to go back and read their efforts at later times. This final step in the LEA process provides reading practice that is essential to children's ability to become independent readers. Occasionally, class projects develop that extend the language learning children are doing. For example, a first-grade class who has visited a local high-school theater production might return to their classroom and organize their own theatrical production complete with scripts, programs, and tickets, providing an outlet for children's reading and writing.

Roach Van Allen presents an in-depth description of the LEA approach in *Language Experiences in Communication* (1976). His work, along with others (Raines & Canady, 1990; Collins & Shaeffer, 1997) gives teachers insight about implementing LEA in classrooms. Their research on LEA is positive, and its usage in classrooms indicates that children have an intense interest in learning to read. Children feel good about their accomplishments, and LEA classrooms demonstrate high levels of self-esteem. A major problem of the language experience approach is the limitation in tracking the vocabulary children are acquiring. Even within one classroom group, children remember and use vocabulary that is relevant to each one of them. In addition, vocabulary may not be repeated and skill development is not sequential in nature.

LEA usage appeals to creative, experienced teachers who find the basal reader approach confining and unimaginative. No assurance exists, however, that children will exit first grade with a basic vocabulary that will match the needs of the second-grade requirements for reading or end-of-year exit tests children take in third grade. Ms. Thomas plans to use an LEA in October when she brings in a pumpkin for jack-o-lantern carving. Her sample lesson plan is on page 259.

Individualized Reading Instruction

Individualized reading instruction is appropriate at any age when children are reading. Its principal goal is to assist young readers in becoming independent in their abilities to read. Children are responsible for selecting what they want to read and keeping records of the materials they have completed. Often, commercial programs such as *Fox in a Box* (Adams & Treadway, 2000) or an informal reading inventory prepared by the teacher are available in the classroom for children to take tests when they are ready to move to another reader. Completion of a record of this type, plus reading to the teacher at a convenient time, formulates the evaluation process, which serves as verification that the child is progressing at a normal rate.

Using an individualized reading approach in the classroom is time consuming, and teachers discover that they need to be highly organized to be successful with this method. They need to know what every child in the classroom is reading and at what level, and they need to be available to hear the child read during the school

Ms. Thomas's LEA Lesson

Lesson Title: Learning about Scarecrows and Pumpkins

Objectives: After this lesson, children will be able to

- Identify the use of a scarecrow
- Identify the color of pumpkins
- Describe how pumpkins grow
- Tell a variety of uses for pumpkins
- Write a language experience story about pumpkins

Focus:

Have a commercial scarecrow and large pumpkin placed on the Circle Time rug. Allow for a few minutes of discussion about the items as children arrive for Circle Time. As children tell what they know about each item, hold up Rau's (1971) book *Shoo, Crow! Shoo!*

Body of the Lesson:

1. Read the book to the children, giving them an opportunity to discuss the pictures.
2. Tell the children that pumpkins are fruits that grow from seeds on vines in gardens. Ask why scarecrows are important to farmers keeping away crows. Remind children that this is autumn (or fall), and tell them that this is the time when pumpkins are harvested.
3. Use a webbing technique to brainstorm uses for pumpkins (pies, breads, soups, roasting the seeds, making jack-o-lanterns, decoration).
4. Tell the children that each will assist in cutting the pumpkin during Center Time, pulling out the seeds, drying them, and roasting the pumpkin seeds for a snack later in the week.

Closure:

Ask children to name a word that starts with the letter *p* as they choose centers.

Follow-Up Activities:

Call various groups to assist with carving the jack-o-lantern throughout Center Time.

Evaluation:

As children come in small groups to carve the pumpkin, ask them questions about where pumpkins grow, their uses, and when they are harvested.
Note: The language experience activity would occur at the end of the week as children recall all of the details of carving the pumpkin into a jack-o-lantern.

Resources:

Commercial scarecrow; large pumpkin; dull knives; aluminum pans for placing pumpkin seeds, drying them, and roasting them; D. Rau, *Shoo, Crow! Shoo!* (1971).

Thanks to Kelly Carlson and Becky Franke, Sam Houston State University seniors, for sharing their lesson plan with us.

week (more than once, if possible). Teachers also need the abilities to identify children who require work on specific skills (syllable analysis or understanding and reading compound words, for example) and prepare small-group instruction for those who have the same problems with reading. The goal of individualized instruction is to provide opportunities for children to become independent readers with goal-setting abilities (Karabenick, 1998).

Key Word Vocabulary

Sylvia Ashton-Warner's groundbreaking work in the 1960s led to her books *Teacher* (1963) and *Spearpoint* (1972), which describe the approach known as *key word vocabulary*. Ashton-Warner worked with Maori children in New Zealand, children whose lifestyles and language-impoverished backgrounds did not match the school's expectations of their readiness for reading instruction. Ashton-Warner wanted to connect with the children on a level that was appropriate for them and, at the same time, support them as they began to understand the need for print in their lives.

The key word vocabulary approach is essentially an individualized approach growing out of the children's personal experiences. Ashton-Warner simply asked children what words they wanted to learn—any word was acceptable. The words they named were written on individual cards and held together with a steel ring. Every day the children came to school, they added a word to their own personal list. At the end of the week, a review of the words with each child indicated which word would remain on the ring and which would be deleted. A periodic review of all the words in the vocabulary would also eliminate specific words that no longer had meaning for the child.

The words the children selected, usually nouns and adjectives, related to children's family lives or to community events, words such as names of family members or holidays being celebrated. Thus, this approach focuses on words with intense emotional relevance—words that communicate fear, anxiety, or stress to a child. Within a few months, words essential to forming sentences emerge, and children begin putting words together to develop and share thoughts about their personal experiences.

One teacher successfully used the key word vocabulary with 4-year-old children, and its merits on a personal level obviously nurture children's interest in reading (Adams & Warner, 2001). The key word vocabulary is not a widely used system for reading instruction, but it has benefits for a supplemental approach in classrooms. Its use is particularly noteworthy for children with limited experiential backgrounds in literacy.

Determining Children's Readiness for Reading

If reading readiness tests have not been administered in kindergarten before children enter the first grade, one of the teacher's first chores is to determine how "ready to read" children are and what needs to be done if they are not ready.

Dimensions of Diversity

Classroom Practices

Teachers of young children can effect change within their children by adopting strategies that will promote broader understanding of other cultures. Here are some recommendations:

- Pronounce children's names accurately, avoiding shortening names when they are difficult to pronounce.
- Display photographs and pictures in the classroom representing the cultural diversity of America.
- Identify and highlight the cultural diversity of your own classroom and community.
- Invite guests to the classroom who represent other cultures.
- Routinely share language, art, music, and food from other cultures, not just when the focus is on a special week or holiday.
- Discuss news events relating to cultural diversity.
- Integrate diversity principles into everyday classroom activity.
- Share your personal heritage with children and help them realize that all people have differences in the manner they live their lives.
- Assist children in valuing the richness that diversity brings to our common heritage.

Most schools will administer a formal reading readiness or achievement instrument, such as the Metropolitan Reading Readiness Test, MRT-6, Level 2 (Nurss & McGauvan, 2000) or Early Screening Inventory (Hills, 1987), but the teacher's classroom observations also serve as a basis for the child's evaluation. Teaching teams may establish a checklist of skills that teachers can use to informally evaluate children through the first two or three weeks of school. Generally, teachers look for the following abilities in children:

1. An understanding that print has meaning
2. Knowledge of alphabet letters and their sounds
3. Ability to recognize their own name and letters that are within them as well as a number of other children's names
4. Basic sight word recognition
5. Ability to read environmental print (stop and exit signs, names of well-known business establishments in the community, speed limit signs, isolated words that possess relevancy for them, and commercial brand names on food and household commodities)
6. Experimentation with print and what it can do
7. Obvious pleasure in having books read to them

FIGURE 7.4 First-Grade Checklist

Child's Name _____	Teacher _____			
Skill	**Date**	**Date**	**Date**	**Date**
Can write own name				
Recognizes capital letters				
Recognizes lowercase letters				
Explains the use of a period				
Explains the use of a comma				
Explains the use of an exclamation mark				
Explains the use of a question mark				
Explains why some letters are capitalized				
Reads most words in basal reader				
Reads print in the school				
Takes readers home regularly				
Checks books out from library				
Reads orally with fluency				
Can retell stories when requested				
Takes pride in reading				

Ms. Thomas is planning a variety of small-group and individualized activities to evaluate children's reading skills during the Integrated Thematic Study time frame scheduled during her day. The checklist defined by the first-grade curriculum is shown in Figure 7.4. Recording children's strengths and weaknesses using individual checklists will assist in planning basal reader instruction and, eventually, in reporting children's progress to their parents.

⭐ INTEGRATED TEACHING AND LEARNING

Ms. Thomas's goal for achieving a successful reading program correlates with her ability to use the basal reader approach, and she dutifully studies the manual each evening in order to be well planned for the next day's instruction. The key word vocabulary approach appeals to her because she knows her children will need assistance in fostering their interest in reading. She plans to use LEA with her social studies themes, and she wants to integrate many language-rich strategies to enhance literacy instruction in her classroom.

Integrated learning, based on child development theory and the interests of children, is supported by *Learning to Read and Write: Developmentally Appropriate Practices for Young Children* (Neuman, Copple, & Bredekamp, 1999). *Integration* implies that planned activities in the classroom accomplish multiple objectives at once. Children who set up a classroom pet shop while studying pets are using organizational skills, as well as intellectual processes in language, mathematics, social studies, and the arts, to complete their project. Children's involvement depends on their interests and the knowledge they bring to the task. The teacher's facilitation of each project provides lifelike experiences focused on consolidating knowledge and skills children have (Katz & Chard, 2000). The integrated thematic study time session scheduled after lunch is an excellent hour for implementing language development techniques, but Ms. Thomas will use some of the following integrated learning strategies at other times of the day as well.

Journals or Logs

Teachers can encourage children to write in *journals* or *logs* on a daily basis on a variety of topics. Some teachers ask children to write as they arrive each morning before formal activities begin. A topic for writing is placed on the chalkboard as children enter the room, and they are asked to write a sentence or two before they are given permission to choose other center activities. Initially, children may not be able to write, but they can draw their perceptions of the topic assigned.

Other teachers use journals to provide an opportunity for children to write about an ongoing social studies project in the classroom or to keep a record of science information they are acquiring. This type of journal writing takes place within the daily scheduled time for social studies or science. As the study progresses, children's writing is kept in folders (or the teacher could collect them) for later assembly as a book on the topic. Taking child-prepared books home is an outstanding tool for helping parents recognize what their children are learning at school.

If children are studying the zoo, for instance, and the study for the day has focused on the elephant, children can write a story about the elephant and draw a picture to save for an individual book about the zoo. Or children may follow through with another art activity prepared by the teacher to correlate with the theme (sculpting salt-dough elephants or using playdough to make elephant replicas).

Keeping journals or logs is commonplace in first-grade classrooms, but Ms. Thomas is aware that the majority of the kindergarten teachers in her school have also used them. Her goal is to build on what the children have already been accomplishing in their previous experience. She knows that their ability to write more successfully will depend on the individual assistance she can give to children during the scheduled writing time. Her task will be to evaluate the writing she observes to determine which children need special instruction about writing techniques. Some may require information about the formation of sentences or even paragraphs, while others will need to know basic rules of punctuation, capitalization, or spelling. Children's dictionaries are available in her Writing Center and Book Corner, and she knows children will use these when they comprehend their importance in the writing process.

Class Books

Making *class books* is an activity that accompanies journal and log writing, and class books support children in consolidating the knowledge they are acquiring during the school year. Basically, class-made books are collections of writing children are completing, and Ms. Thomas is planning to use class books with each social studies theme the first graders are studying during the year. The themes predetermined by the first-grade team include Home, School, Fall, Harvest Time, Winter, Transportation, Farm, Zoo, and Summer Fun. When first grade is over, parents will have nine child-made books that display their child's learning during the first-grade year.

Other books could emerge that show children's ability to write and publish a story in book form. Some schools plan special "authors' days" when parents are invited to school to hear their children read the books they have written, either in the classroom or in a schoolwide presentation in the gym or all-purpose room. Occasionally, schools invite children's book authors to come to the classroom to speak to the children. Children progress in their own development as writers when they know that writing books is a real occupation.

Word Walls

Word walls are another technique designed to make basic vocabulary for writing available in the classroom. The primary reason for developing word walls is children's need to have written words visible when they begin their formal writing. Additionally, they are essential to encouraging informal writing. Teachers use large sheets of butcher paper, poster board, and chalkboards to write down words children suggest for a specific assignment. The collections are left in the room for several days (sometimes for weeks) so that children will find words when they are required to write. Word walls are a support strategy for vocabulary development that relates to the thematic study in the classroom.

In the beginning of the school year, children usually suggest nouns and verbs for the class word wall because of these words' relevancy to children's work. As the year progresses, children add words they need for more substantial writing products. Conjunctions, prepositions, adverbs, and articles appear when children want to write readable sentences that others can comprehend. Soon, children learn words like *the, and, but, for, into, because,* and *maybe* as a result of their exposure to these words on the classroom's word wall.

Thematic Vocabulary Development

Teachers who do not use the word wall concept often use another approach to thematic vocabulary by asking children to brainstorm words they need for writing and reading about a predetermined classroom topic. During a lesson presentation, the teacher requests that children suggest words they want to learn in connection with the selected theme. As children make their choices, she will write the words on a chart or on the chalkboard (or perhaps on an overhead transparency). Displaying the words during the thematic study is helpful while children write about the study for a class book to share with others or individual books that will be taken home.

While studying the topic Rodeo, one group of students brainstormed the following words for their writing assignment:

horse	cowboy	cowgirl
rope	saddle	ride/rider
saddle blanket	arena	barrel racing
wagon	horseshoe	bull
steer	calf scramble	bronco
cattle	race	rodeo clown

The teacher's role in the brainstorming activity is to help children recognize the words they might need during their writing. She suggests words for the list if she discovers an omission that children will need later. The strength of this activity is that words can be added continually throughout the thematic study as they are introduced.

In-Class Library

An *in-class library* (or Book Corner, Ms. Thomas's name for this center) conveys the message to children that books are essential, yet pleasurable, components of living and learning. While she was an undergraduate, Ms. Thomas started a collection of books she wanted for her children by joining one of the children's book clubs her university's early childhood organization had organized and made available to its members. Her parents and friends had given her a number of fine-quality publications to complement her growing library, and she discovered that garage sales were a good source for expensive books that families were ready to discard at inexpensive prices. She found that the school stored outdated basal readers in one of the storerooms in the school, and her team leader told her that these were available for checkout for her in-class library.

The in-class library correlates well with the class Writing Center and Computer Center. Locating the library near both of these entities scaffolds the writing and reading activities in the classroom. As the year progresses, the rotating collection of books relates to the themes children are studying, the seasonal weather and climate of the region, and to community happenings and events. Ms. Thomas has chosen not to allow her personal books in the in-class library to go home with children. As soon as children are reading, she makes available the school's basal readers, the library books checked out from the school's library, and the outdated basal texts she found in the storeroom.

Book Clubs

Book clubs allow families to purchase books at low cost because they are ordered in bulk. Ms. Thomas intends to offer books to parents through a book club, and she asked her team leader about the school's policy for participation in book clubs.

Three well-known book companies and their addresses are:

Scholastic Book Club
555 Broadway
New York, NY
   10012
212.343.6100
www.scholastic.com

Troll Book Club
100 Corporate Drive
Mahwah, NJ
   07430-9986
1.800.541.1097
www.troll.com

Trumpet Book Club
P.O. Box 3730
Jefferson City, MO
   65102-7503
http://trumpetclub.com

Many schools provide the *My Weekly Reader* series for their classrooms because this publication presents current news and information to children in an easy-to-read format. Contact information for *My Weekly Reader* is:

Weekly Reader Corporation
P.O. Box 120023
Stamford, CT 06912-0023
1.800.446.3355
www.weeklyreader.com

Ms. Thomas's school has been ordering *My Weekly Reader* for its primary-age children for many years, and she has requested *Ranger Rick* as a resource for the in-class library. *Ranger Rick* is available by contacting:

National Wildlife Federation
11100 Wildlife Center Drive
Reston, VA 20190-5362
www.nwf.org/wildlife

School Library

The *school library* provides a treasure chest of literature for children's blossoming interest in reading and writing. Most schools have scheduled times for first graders to go to the library, while others invite teachers to make appointments for their classes to visit at prearranged times. Fortunately, Ms. Thomas's librarian wants the school's first-grade groups to come to the library weekly, and their first trip is planned for the second week of school. In the beginning of the school year, the children listen to books and stories the librarian reads, but eventually they begin checking out books to take home to read.

The librarian commits her energies to supporting the teachers in her school, and she talks to each teacher before school starts about the areas of interest they want their children to learn. Not only does she have a wealth of books on a variety of topics, but she orders videos, flannel board sets, recordings, films, computer programs, and puppets, which enhance the literature experience. The children always notice the puppet and doll collection in the library because the librarian displays them prominently for easy access. She uses them in her storytelling sessions, but teachers can check them out occasionally for classroom use. Ms. Thomas makes a note to herself to arrange for the *The Little Engine That Could* train model when the transportation theme is scheduled.

Word Games

Word games appeal to children and challenge them as well. Teachers use these games to help children discover the fun in words. Several appropriate games for first graders follow.

What Word Rhymes? The teacher shares three words, two of which rhyme. Children are to respond by naming the words that rhyme (example: *wall, tall, chair*). When children have experience with this game, they can take turns naming their own words that rhyme. This game assists in the development of phonemic awareness.

What Word Is Missing? The teacher puts a series of sentences on a chart with one word missing. Children read the sentence and tell what word is missing. The first letter of the word and the number of letters in the word can be given as clues to the children.

   Examples:

   Raul p _ _ _ _ with his toy truck.
   Abby and Beth sang a s _ _ _.
   The puppy barked at the k _ _ _ _ _.

One variation of this game is to eliminate the clues and allow children to experiment with a variety of words that actively complete the sentence. Use of this game promotes semantic and contextual awareness.

Configuration Clues. This game is best played with the words that are part of the thematic vocabulary development or are introduced as part of the basal reader instruction. Configurations are similar to puzzles, because letters must fit the predrawn outlines the teacher has drawn on a chart or on the chalkboard. The examples might have a number of answers, but the clue is that the words will be selected from the vocabulary list for the week's theme. Here are some suggestions for the School theme:

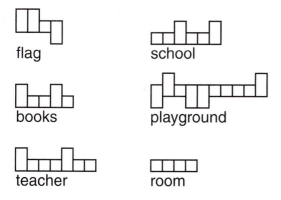

flag

school

books

playground

teacher

room

A game of this type supports children's acquisition of sight words and draws attention to the shapes of letters and words.

What Words Go Together? The teacher develops this game in two ways: One is a verbal experience and the other is a written activity. The goal for the children is to select the word that does not match the others for obvious reasons. The verbal activity is one strategy for helping children become better listeners. The written experience moves children to another level of reading comprehension because they determine the pairs of words based on pictures (teacher-made flashcards or commercial items) or written words. The latter activity occurs after children have achieved the ability to read basic sight words. One sample of this game is naming the following words or showing pictures for children to choose which one goes with the others:

sofa	bed	television set	refrigerator
song	book	puppy	poem

Playing this game enhances vocabulary development.

Word for the Day Word for the Day is a technique Ms. Thomas remembers from her own years in elementary school, when her teachers displayed a special word for the day in the classroom and introduced it to children during early morning ritual time. The special word often related to a school or community event or seasonal and holiday celebrations. Ms. Thomas's objective with this strategy is to challenge independent learners and call attention to words as *words,* a critical factor in children's ability to begin reading known as *metacognition.* The game serves as a foundation for vocabulary development and sight word recognition.

Her specific plan during the first weeks of school is to introduce words that relate to the children's new experience of attending school. The word *school* is the first word she plans to present, with follow-up words being *cafeteria, gym, library, lunch, classroom, playground, principal, custodian,* and *teacher.* Many days the word she selects relates to the thematic study going on in the classroom, but she recognizes that eventually children will begin requesting their own words for the day.

Folder Games

Folder games are familiar to classroom teachers because they are useful at many grade levels for extending the skills children are learning in almost any curriculum area. Math and spelling folder games are common in first-grade classrooms, but Ms. Thomas intends to prepare several to allow practice in reading with syllabication, prefixes, and suffixes to practice structural analysis, and word meanings for vocabulary development. Reading skills correlate with basal reading instruction introduced before the folder game is added to the Book Corner. Examples of two reading folder games are Match the Picture to the Word and Draw a Line Under the Root Word:

Match the Picture to the Word Folder Game

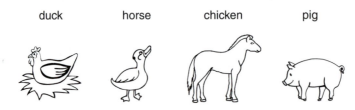

Draw a Line Under the Root Word Folder Game

sings	jumping	walked	talks
marked	looking	picked	running
climbed	meeting	swinging	eaten

Laminating folder games protects the materials and allows multiple usages by children.

⭐ READING INSTRUCTION

Commercially prepared basal readers are the most widely used approach to teaching reading in America's schools. Jalongo (2000) reports that over 90 percent of classrooms use only basals or basal texts in combination with other approaches for reading instruction. The main component of the basal reader approach is the group experience.

Classroom Reading Groups Teachers use a variety of grouping strategies to implement prereading, reading, and postreading activities (Sowers, 2000). One grouping strategy is labeled as *guided reading*. Daily instruction presented to small groups provides for vocabulary development and an overview of the story children will be reading during the prereading phase. Children read silently or orally during the reading phase, and they each have a book to use as individuals take turns reading. Follow-up postreading activities are designed to strengthen skills that are introduced during the prereading and reading phases.

Most often, guided reading groups are formed because of children's abilities. Teachers use their knowledge of children's experiential background, readiness test results, and classroom observations of their interest and motivation to read in order to determine the group placement for each child. Utilizing small-group instruction provides efficient instructional methodology. Individualized reading instruction is time consuming, and teachers have only a set time frame for ensuring that their children are reading by the end of the year.

Occasionally, teachers use *flexible groups,* a strategy that allows them to work with small groups of children who have been identified as having specific instructional needs. During the reading phase, children demonstrate their understanding of reading skills and teachers make time to strengthen the weaknesses they observe. These skills include

Letter recognition: Being able to name individual letters and recite the alphabet

Sound/symbol connection: Being able to identify letters by naming words that begin with the sound and comprehending that vowels have long and short sounds

Phonemic awareness: Understanding that sounds are joined together to form words, words are divided into syllables, and words rhyme and have rhythm

Vocabulary development: Knowing that words have meaning

Semantic clues: Awareness that printed words and their meanings provide hints about what an unknown word might be

Contextual clues: Awareness that the story and pictures in a book provide information about the words on the page

Sight words: Being able to recognize words immediately when seeing them
Decoding: Being able to use what is known about letters to read a new word
Structural analysis: Being able to use what is known about syllables, prefixes, suffixes, and compound words to read an unknown word

The development of these skills is important in helping children to become independent readers. Using flexible groups supports skill acquisition, and their implementation is certainly in the best interests of each child. Teachers recognize that children need to move to other groups on occasion, and flexible grouping assists teachers in determining whether individuals are ready to be placed in another group because of their changing ability levels.

Periodically, teachers organize *special-interest groups,* a fluid and dynamic grouping strategy that attracts children's interest because of an ongoing topic of study or availability of books in the classroom. Special-interest groups develop after children are reading somewhat fluently, and a set of books arouses their curiosity. Teachers use the guided reading process to instruct their learners, keeping in mind that various children read at different comprehension levels.

Large-group instruction in classrooms is an option as well, but children are reading at their own individual levels when large-group instruction occurs. The purpose of large-group instruction is to introduce a skill to children that they all need to know. A game such as Word for the Day is one example of an activity appropriate for large-group instruction. Most of the children will recognize the word if it has relevancy to them, but individualized or small-group instruction is necessary for children to retain it as a sight word. Activities that encourage children to name rhyming words or identify prefixes or compound words are other games that require large-group participation. In all instances, it is recommended that group instruction be short, expectations be reasonable and relevant, skills be applied immediately, and children's understanding be checked (Fields & Spangler, 2000).

Another strategy to assist children's development in reading is the *individual reading conference.* Conferences begin as children become more accomplished with the reading process and do more independent reading in and out of the classroom. Scheduling an individual conference with the teacher supports one-on-one attention from the teacher and gives her insight about the child's progress. The teacher can make notes of strengths and weaknesses, and can keep an accurate record for reporting to parents. Some school districts develop checklists and rating scales designed specifically for assessing children's reading abilities. The reading conference is guaranteed to give the teacher the firsthand observation of reading ability that is required on first-grade report cards.

The time-consuming nature of individual conferences, however, prevents extensive use of this strategy. Teachers have only a set amount of time with children each day, and small- and large-group instruction provides more efficient application of that time. Ms. Thomas is aware of her school's well-developed parental involvement program. She plans to utilize volunteers' time in her classroom for individualized reading sessions. She also intends to encourage parents to listen to their children read at home when they bring home readers, thus extending their reading ability. One-on-one adult attention to children's reading appears to relate to their success as readers (Allington & Walmsley, 1995).

The Basal Reading Lesson

The basal reader text alleviates Ms. Thomas's fears about planning daily reading lesson plans. Her knowledge of reading instruction is current because she completed four courses in reading when she was at the university. The theoretical knowledge she acquired had served her well during student teaching experiences and other preservice field experiences. She happily noticed that the lessons in her teacher's manual advised her about promoting interest in the reading activity, games to play for practicing skills, how to introduce vocabulary, questions to ask during the reading phase, and follow-up activities to extend the reading experience.

Shared Reading

Occasionally, *reading aloud to children* is overlooked in first-grade classrooms because the assumption is that children are already reading and they do not need to have books read to them. How faulty this thinking is! Reading models are necessary, and children continue to discover the pleasure and joy that reading can bring when someone reads to them. Planning a set time each day for books to be shared builds on children's own emerging knowledge about reading. Demonstrating verbal expression and the value of reading fluently is essential to children's oral reading development. Ms. Thomas plans on reminding parents that children continue to find pleasure in nightly book reading or storytelling sessions.

Whatever choices are made about reading instruction, first-grade teachers recognize that differences exist among children in their classrooms. One overlooked factor that affects children's reading ability is their visual acuity. Problems can result if children have difficulty fixating, focusing, or making accurate interpretations about what is observed (Ilg, Ames, Haines, & Gillespie, 1978; Shonkoff & Phillips, 2000). As Neuman, Copple, and Bredekamp (1999) write: "Given exposure to appropriate literacy experiences and good teaching during early childhood, most children learn to read at age six or seven, a few learn at four, some learn at five, and others need intensive individualized support to learn to read at eight or nine" (p. 14).

Reading Recovery

Despite the best efforts of teachers and parents alike, some children struggle with the reading process. To assist the struggling reader, some schools implement a program called *Reading Recovery*. Developed by Marie Clay (1985), Reading Recovery is a method of individualized instruction for children, identified early in the first-grade year, who are not acquiring reading skills as effectively as their peers. The designated Reading Recovery teacher, required to have special training, diagnoses each child's problem and uses daily individualized lesson plans to assist children in overcoming their difficulties. Emphasis is on teaching children (1) searching strategies to allow for more appropriate predictions about unknown words; and (2) self-monitoring and cross-checking strategies to help them evaluate their reading as they participate in the reading event.

Issues and Trends

Reading and Brain Research

Drs. Bennett and Sally Shaywitz indicate that through brain research the following characteristics define successful readers during kindergarten through grade 3:

- Are aware of print
- Recognize letter shapes and their names
- Know spoken words can be broken into smaller sounds
- Know letters represent sounds
- Can blend sounds together
- Process larger letters and units
- Develop automaticity and fluency
- Develop comprehension strategies

The Shaywitzes also recognize risk factors for preschoolers:

- Heredity
- Delay in speech production
- Difficulty learning and recognizing rhyme
- Problems with pronunciation
- Difficulty using the right word in speech
- Difficulty learning letters

Source: www.schwablearning.org.

The typical Reading Recovery lesson occurs in two sessions and includes several components. Sowers (2000) describes the lessons as follows:

(1) at the end of the first lesson, the child reads aloud a book that is preselected by the teacher or child; (2) at the next lesson, the child reads the same book aloud again; (3) during the reading the teacher observes the child's reading carefully and makes notes of difficulties and strategies; (4) the teacher asks questions and encourages the child in developing skills of analyzing the words and texts and in increasing her self-monitoring abilities; (5) a story or message is written by the child to demonstrate the connection between reading and writing; (6) the teacher uses her observations to select a book that is appropriate for the child; and (7) the young reader reads that book aloud. (p. 217)

⭐ HANDWRITING AND SPELLING INSTRUCTION

Formal manuscript handwriting instruction begins in first grade (see Chapter 5 for information about informal manuscript handwriting instruction). Generally, first graders use lined paper for the first time. Daily lessons showing children how to form letters, how to place letters and words on the page, and how to keep consistent spacing and alignment among letters and between words compose the bulk of handwriting instruction children receive. Often, schools adopt their own handwriting style, and teachers can refer to their curriculum guides for a description of the systematic approach to handwriting instruction.

Manuscript handwriting, assumed to be easier for young children to implement, was not introduced into America's schools until 1922 by Marjorie Wise, an English educator, who brought the style from England to Teachers College, Columbia University (Thornton, 1996). Manuscript forms are basically straight lines, slanted lines, circles, and curves (similar to partial circles), sometimes referred to as a block manuscript form or printscript. The Zaner-Bloser Company prepared a popular example of the block manuscript style (see Figure 7.5).

A common alternative that school districts choose is a published handwriting series. The benefits of a district adoption are: (1) the series can be used from first grade throughout the elementary grades; (2) workbooks, which demonstrate letter formation and allow

Formal writing instruction is one component of first-grade classrooms. Children struggle to apply appropriate techniques to produce readable writing.

for practice, often accompany the series; and (3) teachers' manuals are available to help with instructional strategies appropriate for the grade level.

D'Nealian handwriting is another handwriting series used widely with primary-age children (Thurber, 1999). The purpose of D'Nealian is to introduce curves and loops to children at an earlier age, so that the transition to cursive writing will be easier for children to make (see Figure 7.6). Whatever style is selected, two recommendations are that (1) classroom charts and chalkboard writing need to demonstrate the specific style the district has selected, and that (2) teachers in earlier grades should model the preferred manuscript style to children (Machado, 1999).

One of the benefits of a handwriting series is that it offers teachers specialized information about teaching left-handed writers. Manuscript instruction in first grade is rather easy for both right- and left-handed writers because the paper placement is straight up and down. Critical differences appear, though, when cursive writing is introduced. Right-handed writers need the top of the paper slanted slightly to the left, and left-handed children need the top of their paper slanted slightly to the right.

Spelling instruction is similar to handwriting instruction in that schools prescribe a specific approach in their curriculum guides or adopt a published spelling series. Some districts allow teachers to develop their own spelling lists for their children. The flexibility of this third approach is that teachers often know the words children are interested in and which ones relate to ongoing classroom instruction. The word *taxi*, for instance, is not necessarily the word that all children need to

FIGURE 7.5   Zaner-Bloser Manuscript

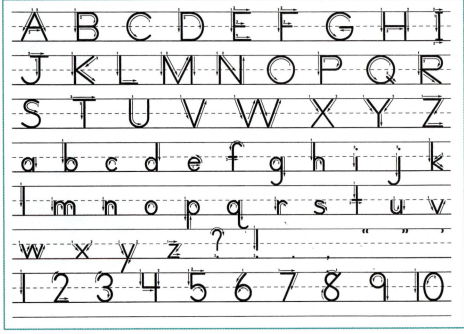

Copyright © Zaner-Bloser, Inc.

FIGURE 7.6   D'Nealian Manuscript

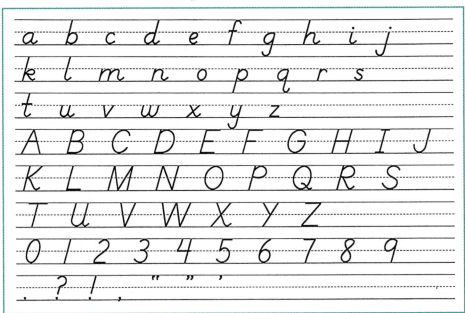

learn to spell. Because the word relates to the Transportation theme planned during the first-grade year, however, it becomes an important word for children to learn.

In first grade, spelling instruction does not usually begin immediately. Children must have some knowledge of print and an understanding of the reading process before they can be successful with spelling activities. In addition, children need opportunities to experiment with letters and words, and what they do for the first few months of first grade should be an extension of the invented spellings they began in kindergarten (see Chapter 6 for information about invented spelling).

Teachers should remember that children become independent spellers over time, often not until after third grade (Brewer, 2001). Instruction in first grade focuses on commonly used words, words that have similar sound-symbol connections, and words that are relevant to children. Teachers often present words possessing familiar phonemic characteristics. Rhyming words are an excellent resource for first spelling lists. Asking first graders to learn to spell *tall, ball, call, fall,* and *mall* requires a change in only the first letter when they are written. Auditory discrimination of first letters in each of these words permits children to accurately spell all of the words in the list.

Teachers commonly use spelling lists to reinforce phonetic information that has been taught to the class. If the silent /e/ concept is a skill children are learning during reading lessons, then a spelling list composed of words such as *lake, make, take, bake,* and *rake* reinforces the original instruction. A study of digraphs would produce a spelling list that uses examples of digraphs (such as /ai/ as in *nail, mail, tail,* and *pail*). Consonant blends (/br/, /bl/, /cl/, /cr/, /gl/, /gr/, /pl/, /pr/, /st/, /tr/, and others) yield excellent spelling lists. Reading series sometimes suggest spelling words to accompany their lesson plans.

Writing Conferences

The writing conference is a strategy supporting reading, handwriting, and spelling instruction. Ms. Thomas plans to use the writing workshop during her scheduled Integrated Thematic Study (see the schedule on page 252). During this period, children will be able to bring their journals or other independent writing for Ms. Thomas to review and recommend changes to strengthen the writing process. The conference is interactive in nature, and Ms. Thomas will remind herself that first graders' writing does not need to be perfect. Guiding children to recognize what they already know about print is the overriding concern during the conference session (Fields & Spangler, 2000). Asking questions such as, "Is a question mark the correct punctuation for this sentence?" or "Have you thought about the word *many* instead of *lots* in this sentence?" shows children another way to look at the writing they are doing.

Ms. Thomas's purpose in using the writing workshop is to give her 6-year-olds reasons to write. Journal writing or logs are a natural approach to the writing workshop activity. Most often, the group will have a writing assignment correlated with the social studies theme. For the Farm theme, children may be required to write a story about *horses* to be placed in an individual folder for later compilation into a book to take home as a record of the thematic study. Children may also be asked to draw pictures to illustrate their stories.

The writing samples children bring may result from products they began during the Language Arts/Independent Work sessions from the morning schedule. Children sign up for individual conferences with her, and eventually she will encourage youngsters to have peer conferences. Children's development in writing suggests, as first graders, that they are arriving at the stage known as *conventional writing* (refer to the stages of writing described in Chapter 6 for a definition of this stage). The writing conference promotes practice with the writing activity, and teachers and parents alike will find pleasure in the growth children make during the year.

☆ CLASSROOM MANAGEMENT IN FIRST GRADE

Six-year-old children are more capable of controlling their own behavior than they were in previous years. The good-natured quality of their personalities also assists the teacher in developing positive management and discipline in her classroom. If she is well organized and has plans for meeting children's intellectual, social, and physical needs, then management becomes all the more easy to achieve. Basically, first graders want to be good. They have a desire to conform to the school's expectations of their behavior.

Characteristics of effective classroom management practices are:

- Planning a variety of interesting, challenging, and productive classroom activities that will keep children busy throughout the day
- Emphasizing children's abilities to maintain self-control
- Acknowledging children when they demonstrate acceptable behaviors in public and private recognition (this recognition can be in the form of verbal praise or nods and smiles)
- Complimenting children for positive behaviors (sharing, taking turns, and being sensitive to one another's needs)
- Reminding children of the rules in preparation for daily instruction or for special events (such as field trips)
- Calling on children for responses when it appears their interest is distracted
- Asking children with self-management issues to sit near the teacher during group instruction
- Utilizing a signaling system to indicate to children when they have become too loud
- Planning efficient transition times from activity to activity (refer to Chapter 6 for further discussion of transitions)
- Reprimanding children privately when infractions occur
- Taking action when some children need firmer controls (removal from a favorite activity or calling parents for conferences about the child's problems)
- Following school policies if children need to be removed from the classroom (Reynolds, 2001)

Some public schools adopt rules that every classroom in the school will use. Usually, these rules are broad in scope and easy to remember (see Figure 7.7). Each teacher in the school uses the guidelines in his or her own way, interpreting what the rules mean for the individual classroom. The benefit of this practice is that the rules can be conveyed to parents through the use of parent handbooks. Therefore, teachers present a concerted effort to adopt practices children can understand and follow, and discipline problems are more easily communicated to parents because of the common language used by all professionals in the school.

FIGURE 7.7 Schoolwide Classroom Rules

> **School Rules**
>
> Respect yourself.
> Respect others.
> Respect school property.

New teachers become aware within the first few months that management is an ongoing process in the classroom. Some days and weeks will be calmer than others. A child who seems to have made strides following class rules will suddenly become surly and belligerent. Another child who has had trouble attending during group time will make a turnaround and become more compliant for a few weeks before regressing into previous troublesome behavior. School lore suggests that phases of the moon and weather changes affect children's behavior.

Management styles reflect teachers' preferences and personalities. Children's going to the pencil sharpener at any time bothers some teachers, because noise from sharpeners distracts others. Teachers who dislike the grinding noise of a pencil sharpener can schedule a set time for children to use the sharpener. One teacher manages a classroom that is cluttered with children's work; another teaches children to take time to clean up after themselves at preappointed times during the school day. Daily classroom activity is an interaction between teachers and children. The critical issue in classroom management is the nature of the adult's relationship to the children in her class. Positive approaches are most successful (Marion, 2003).

⭐ ACCOUNTABILITY ISSUES IN FIRST GRADE

The three principal goals in first-grade classrooms are (1) children learning to read, (2) development of conventional writing, and (3) acquisition of basic math skills. Though most states do require end-of-grade tests beginning with third grade, end-of-grade tests for first graders are not expected. School districts are conscious of the impending third-grade exam, and they often designate budget resources for purchasing or developing an achievement test to give to first and second graders. This practice is their assurance that children are progressing adequately toward third-grade test objects.

Two common tests administered in first grade are the California Achievement Test, referred to as the CAT (Perfection Learning Corporation, 1993), and Gates-MacGinite Silent Reading Test (MacGinite & MacGinite, 2000). Ms. Thomas's school district uses the CAT to channel second-grade instruction to improving weak skill development areas.

Working with Parents

First-grade teachers accept greater responsibility in reporting to parents because the stakes are higher. Prekindergarten teachers are concerned with socialization skills, and kindergarten teachers work toward helping 5-year-olds conceptualize what it means to be in school. First-grade teachers become more directly involved with academic achievement because state standards demand it and the public expects it. Ms. Thomas's school has these four strategies for communicating with parents.

Parent Conferences

Schools support opportunities for teachers and parents to talk to one another. Often, an initial parent conference is scheduled early in the school year, at least by the ninth week. In first grade, the conference may actually be in lieu of sending home the first report card. Other schools plan a second parent-teacher conference at the end of the school year. Schools usually connect with the business community so that "conference days" are advertised and employers are aware that their employees may need to go to school sometime during the time frame. (See Chapter 6 for more information about organizing a parent conference.)

Portfolios

These collections of children's work are defined more thoroughly in Chapter 6, and the description of this strategy there is similar to what first-grade teachers expect for portfolio development. Portfolios demand more of children in first grade, however. Children now have greater control over the material that is placed in the portfolio. They have choices about writing samples and artwork that are included, and they have the freedom to remove an item if they decide it is no longer important.

Teachers continue to place checklists, rating scales, photographs, and other data in the portfolio because these artifacts are tools for communicating during parent-teacher conferences (McGee & Richgels, 2000). They will need to explain to children the reasons they have included their selections, of course. The coordination of efforts between teachers and children with portfolio development is another example of the interactive nature inherent in the teaching-learning process described in Chapter 3.

Parents and teachers conference whenever and wherever they can. Occasionally, conferences are spontaneous, though most are planned and scheduled in advance.

Thursday Take-Homes

Beginning about the second month of school and after the first parent conference or Open House, communication to the home becomes a weekly process with Thursday *take-home* papers. A collection of the week's work (workbook pages from reading or math texts, samples of children's writing, or other materials of note) is stapled together and sent home with each child for parents to review. Teachers include a cover page asking parents to look at their child's work, sign that they have done so, and return the papers on Friday morning. If the material is not returned, teachers telephone the parents to remind them that the take-home collection needs to be returned. Take-homes are an excellent strategy for reporting achievements between scheduled report card dates.

Report Cards

The majority of American school districts begin sending home report cards in first grade, either on a six-week or nine-week basis. They are divided into two basic reporting areas: academic accomplishments and behavioral assessments. Parents want to know if their children are achieving, but they also want to know if they are being "good." If parent-teacher conferences and interval reports to parents (such as Thursday take-home papers) are communicating well, the report card assessments should not surprise parents. They will have been informed already.

☆ CELEBRATING HOLIDAYS

School districts have set policies about the celebration of holidays. Taking instructional time to discuss and read about a special day is appropriate in classrooms if the time is productive. Writing about the holiday and having a well-prepared art or music lesson to accompany the lesson is a good experience for children. School administrators frown on spending an inordinate amount of time on holidays because they interrupt instruction and cause undue stress and chaos within classrooms, especially if they are mishandled. School districts often limit the number of celebrations during the school year, or they organize special fall festivals to replace Halloween celebrations.

Hendrick (2003) recommends that teachers look carefully at the values that are being transmitted during any celebration. Christmas celebrations are difficult to ignore because so much data in the environment tell children that the holiday is near. Teachers may decide to provide equal discussions of Hanukkah and Kwanzaa during the month of December, depending on the demographic representation in their classrooms. The concept of giving is an easy one to develop in classrooms without overemphasis on Santa's deliveries or the gaudiness and greediness of the holiday.

Evidence exists that children comprehend holidays as time spent away from school. In one action research study, a majority of kindergarten children in the teacher's class were unable to tell what a holiday was or describe why it was celebrated (Warner & Adams, 1996). A 1979 Supreme Court ruling in *Florey v. Sioux Falls School District* bans teaching religious ideas inherent in holidays such as Easter and Christmas, though their secular and cultural emphases could be addressed (Taylor, 1996).

Eliminating biases and stereotypes associated with inaccuracies handed down from generation to generation is another consideration. Did George Washington really chop down that cherry tree? Or did the Pilgrims actually dress with large white collars and unique hats? Good teachers always consider the accuracy of any information they are sharing with children.

Ms. Thomas's school permits teachers to celebrate by having parties for the Christmas season and Valentine's Day. Classroom parties are one-hour, end-of-the-day events planned by homeroom mothers and members of the school's Parent-Teacher Association (PTA). The parents plan activities (with teacher input), usually consisting of games and refreshments, and provide all party paraphernalia (paper plates, cups, utensils, party hats, etc.) Ms. Thomas assists by sending home requests for donations to the party (favors or refreshments), and she invites families to attend the function if they are able.

Successful celebrations relate directly to the teacher's ability to maintain children's recognition that they are still members of the classroom and that classroom rules remain intact. Recognizing children's limitations in sustaining self-control, keeping a positive attitude about children's need for social activity, and discovering the team-building nature of parties are essential ingredients to successful celebrations.

☆ OTHER RESPONSIBILITIES FOR FIRST-GRADE TEACHERS

Ms. Thomas's first and foremost responsibility is classroom teaching. Like all teachers who enter the field each year, she is hopeful that she will be the best teacher she can be. Her training prepared her well, and the school district's orientation meetings have helped her comprehend its policies and procedures. An experienced first-grade teacher is her mentor because the district wants to ensure she is doing a good job and feel that she is being effective. The state she teaches in requires attendance at a number of professional development activities throughout the year that provide additional knowledge about her professional position. Preservice teachers learn during their student teaching semester that other responsibilities are expected of them. Among these duties are:

- *Regularly scheduled faculty meetings:* The principal of the school sets the meetings, and teachers are given a calendar for the year showing the dates and time for the meetings. Most schools have only one meeting a month (generally at the end of the school day in the middle of the week), but some principals schedule them more often. The purpose of the faculty meeting is to keep teachers abreast of events and concerns relating to a smooth-running school environment. Occasionally, teachers have additional assignments and meetings if they are serving on district or campuswide curriculum committees. Each year that school districts adopt new textbooks (approximately every five or six years), teachers spend numerous hours after school assisting in the decision-making process. At times, teachers serve on district committees during the summer months to develop new curriculum guides or classroom instructional materials.

- *Bus duty:* If schools hire a sufficient cadre of aides, this duty becomes their responsibility, not the teachers'. Otherwise, teachers rotate their participation with this duty. Ms. Thomas will be responsible for the first-grade afternoon departure every five weeks. Morning arrival is scheduled, too, but children usually enter school at staggered times, and teachers in the entire school have morning duty. Consequently, Ms. Thomas will only need to have morning duty about four times during the school year.

- *Breakfast or lunch duty:* Volunteers in Ms. Thomas's room take the major role in supervising breakfast and lunch in the cafeteria. Each first-grade teacher takes turns being available in the cafeteria to coordinate problem solving that might arise while the first-grade children are eating (such as a child's becoming ill or disruptive). Ms. Thomas's schedule requires that she monitor breakfast about four times during the year and lunch every fifth week. The schedule for bus and breakfast/lunch duty is planned by the principal or assistant principal and given to the teachers during orientation meetings at the beginning of the year.

- *Evening programs:* Ms. Thomas's awareness of special school events was slim because she did not have to participate in these before becoming a full-time teacher. Her memory of her own elementary years gives her a limited understanding of Open House because she recalls going to school with her parents on two or three different occasions. She soon learns that all members of the first-grade team and their classes host the March program. The team leader mentions this at the beginning of the year, charging the teachers to think of ideas they might contribute to the overall success of the program. Evening programs and Open House night (scheduled early in the school year) are public relations activities for parents and families to come to school and meet the professional team in a nonthreatening atmosphere. Members of the school team want the school to be an inviting, comfortable place, and special events (even potluck suppers) accomplish this goal.

- *Working with other professionals in the building and district:* The responsibility of working on committees is mentioned under the section titled *faculty meetings,* and new teachers discover quickly that getting along with the team and other professionals in the building is essential for overall success and satisfaction with their jobs. School operations are easier if teachers understand the roles of administrators, other teachers, special-interest teachers (librarians, music teachers, and technology coordinators), custodians, and cafeteria personnel and show appropriate respect for their positions.

- *Visits to other district campuses:* Ms. Thomas learns that she has the opportunity to visit a number of first-grade classrooms during the fall semester, and she looks forward to becoming acquainted with individual teachers who are familiar with first-grade teaching. The primary school supervisor coordinates the planned visits, which are designed to demonstrate for new teachers how high-quality first-grade classrooms are conducted.

⭐ ENDING THE SCHOOL YEAR

The end of the school year is as busy as the beginning. The last weeks before the final day of school are hectic. Children become more difficult to manage because they look forward to the summer months. Even first graders succumb to the emotional excitement of the last days of school. Teachers, of course, are still attempting to teach, because they value the instructional time they have remaining with their group. The final report cards are due for parents, and last-minute conferences with parents of children who need to be retained or are required to go to summer school consume teachers' energies. Field days, if schools plan them, are scheduled during the final weeks; and events of this nature cause added chaos for children and their teachers.

End-of-year requirements usually include the following:

- Inventorying classroom instructional materials
- Returning textbooks to the school's storage room
- Removing bulletin boards and teaching materials and storing them in classroom closets
- Cleaning off the teacher's desk and storing materials and mementos in drawers or closets
- Finding a good home for the classroom pet(s)
- Removing plants from the classroom for summer survival
- Directing children in collecting their personal belongings before leaving the classroom
- Finalizing reports and grade books and filing them in appropriate places (often in the principal's office)

One monumental task teachers face is recording data about children in cumulative folders. *Cumulative folders* summarize the progress children have made during the school year for future reference. Teachers specify what books children have read (basals as well as independent readers) during the school year and what they know about mathematics, and achievement test scores (if administered). They also write a paragraph or two about children's social and emotional development and their classroom behavior. Information about their height and weight is included.

Cumulative folders describe how children have performed in their grade level. They are passed on through the elementary grades for other teachers to read, and data from each grade is included at the end of the school year. Cumulative records are essential in assuring that children's progress is appropriate. They are mailed to another school in the district or to other communities or states if youngsters relocate.

 **SUMMARY**

Teaching first grade is a challenging responsibility for anyone who is assigned to this level. Six-year-olds are enjoyable because they have achieved a certain level of maturity to discover pleasure by participating in group activities. School districts want their new teachers to have success as teachers, and they provide orientations, mentor teachers, and classroom visits to assist them in their journey through the year.

First-grade teachers spend much of their time teaching children to read, write, and learn addition and subtraction processes. New teachers in the field find that planning lessons and developing classroom materials require consistent dedication, but they also reserve time for parent interactions, faculty meetings, and other duties required of them by their school.

DISCUSSION QUESTIONS

1. Interview a first-grade teacher about her strategies for reading instruction. Which strategies described in this text does she use? What other strategies does she use? Discuss her answers with others in your class.
2. Recall the approach your first-grade teacher used when you learned to read. How did her instruction resemble contemporary approaches? Compare your memories with those of another person in your class.

SUGGESTED CHAPTER ACTIVITIES

1. Locate the consonant blends located in this chapter and prepare a spelling list of words appropriate for first graders. Challenge yourself to develop an extensive list using other blends not mentioned in the textbook.
2. Talk to a left-handed adult. Ask her to describe childhood memories of learning to write while in elementary school. Were they positive?
3. Try manuscript handwriting with your opposite hand for a day.
4. Prepare a classroom chart of one of your favorite poems (appropriate for first-grade children), demonstrating your manuscript handwriting.
5. Prepare a set of folder games designed to teach the reading skills defined in this chapter.

Chapter Eight

Teaching in a Second-Grade Classroom

CHAPTER OVERVIEW

★ How does an inclusion classroom work?

★ How does a teacher meet the needs of children when they are reading on different levels?

★ Are there standards for mathematics instruction and how are they used?

★ How have the standards for social studies changed instruction?

★ How does a teacher plan for instruction when she is teaching in an inclusive classroom?

READ THIS CHAPTER TO FIND THE ANSWERS TO THESE QUESTIONS.

Teachers of 7-year-olds often believe that they have the best of the teaching jobs. Most children beginning second grade are able to read, write, and "do" math. Although not all children will be on grade level in these areas, children are able to do more independently and are able to grasp more complex learning as they study topics in greater detail. Children at this age still seek to please the teacher and enjoy coming to school. They embrace new topics of study with enthusiasm, as many a librarian can testify. In studying insects, for example, many of the children go to the library and check out books on insects. Children continue this pattern throughout the school year. Parents also report that the children share their new knowledge with everyone in the home.

Physically, individual differences in growth remain great at this age, and the teacher needs to be sensitive to this fact. Girls who are very tall and boys who are very short may both experience self-esteem problems unless the teacher takes the time to explain development to the children. It is helpful to use real-world examples of people who were extremely short as children and yet attained normal height as adults. This also opens an opportunity to talk to the children about development in the academic areas. Just as children don't grow at the same rate, neither do they learn to read, write, and "do" math at the same rate. By pointing to examples of well-known people who have exceptional talent or abilities, the teacher can help children to realize that having trouble learning to read in second grade does not mean that they are "dumb" and will forever be behind in reading ability. Albert Einstein is an excellent example of a child who failed to learn to read in first or second grade.

Other physical changes occur in children this age. The cerebral cortex of the brain increases slightly in surface area, and researchers believe the brain functioning may change because of the influence of hormones that are secreted by the adrenal glands beginning around the age of seven or eight. Body growth occurs in spurts and lulls, and fine-motor and gross-motor skills improve, which support athletic skills and participation in sports and organized games (Berk, 1999).

Social skills are continuing to improve during this year. Feelings are still easily hurt when children are excluded from a group. Two or more girls will band together and exclude another girl from playing on any given day. The members of the "in group," however, will change from day to day and different girls will be excluded on different days. Boys continue to enjoy rough-and-tumble play and need careful supervision in order to prevent accidents and injuries.

Mrs. Strabinski teaches in a second-grade classroom at Jeter Street Elementary, a middle-class elementary school in a relatively small city of approximately 100,000 people. Her district believes in full inclusion and has seen to it that all the teachers receive the training they need to be effective. The teachers also receive support from the special services department of the district and from the special education faculty and staff at the school. In Mrs. Strabinski's classroom, 3 of her 21 children have special needs. Jacob has Down syndrome, Hannah has cerebral palsy, and Faneisha has asthma and allergies.

Jacob has been at Jeter Street Elementary since he began school in prekindergarten. His parents retained him in prekindergarten because they felt he needed extra time to learn the social skills that are stressed there. Jacob is now 8 and, though one year older than the other children chronologically, mentally he is functioning on a level equivalent to the beginning of kindergarten, or that of a 5-year-old child.

Hannah is new to Jeter Street Elementary, and she has just moved here from a very large district where she had been in a self-contained special education classroom with children who had severe mental retardation and physical problems. Hannah has cerebral palsy and is not able to speak; she uses a wheelchair at school. Today is Hannah's first day at Jeter Street. After her parents enrolled her this morning, the counselor escorted Hannah and her parents to Mrs. Strabinski's classroom. Mrs. Strabinski welcomed Hannah to the class and introduced her to the children. Since she didn't previously know of Hannah's arrival, Mrs. Strabinski has to quickly make some arrangements for Hannah. For example, Hannah's wheelchair does not fit under the table, and Mrs. Strabinski makes a mental note to address this problem after school today with the special education teacher. Mrs. Strabinski pairs Hannah up with another girl in the classroom and sends them off to the Listening Center so that she can talk for a few minutes with Hannah's parents. Mrs. Strabinski asks the parents for a copy of Hannah's Individualized Education Plan (IEP). Unfortunately, they do not have a copy, so the office will have to request Hannah's

With the proper support, inclusion can work.

records from her old school. She also asks about a communication board, a board or machine with pictures or words that Hannah can touch to communicate with people on a very basic level. Although Hannah had one at her old school, her parents offer, she was not allowed to bring it with her.

After the parents leave and the other children settle back into the morning routine, Mrs. Strabinski sits down with Hannah. She talks to Hannah and tells her that the first thing they must do is to find some way to communicate. She asks Hannah to nod or make a noise to let her know she understands. Hannah nods her head and makes a happy-sounding noise. After further questioning, Mrs. Strabinski goes to the computer and prints a simple sheet that she will glue to a piece of cardboard; this is Hannah's first communication board. On this board she places a smiley face with the word "yes" under it, a frowny face with a "no" under it, and a picture of a toilet and a glass. Hannah is a happy, engaging child with a ready smile. Because of her training, Mrs. Strabinski realizes that the fact that Hannah cannot speak does not mean that she has severe mental retardation. Without an IEP, Mrs. Strabinski does not know what Hannah has been able to do and what her objectives are for this school year.

Over the next few days, Mrs. Strabinski notices that Hannah seems to be intently looking at books during science, reading, and social studies and paying close attention during instruction. She believes that Hannah will be able to learn to read, and she begins teaching Hannah letters, sounds, and words. Hannah catches on so quickly that Mrs. Strabinski begins adding more words and ponders other ways to help Hannah communicate. By the time the IEP arrives and Mrs. Strabinski looks at it, Hannah has already learned 15 sounds and letter names as well as a basic vocabulary of 20 words.

Mrs. Strabinski is shocked by Hannah's IEP. According to her IEP, Hannah is to be working on life and self-help skills, not academic skills. Mrs. Strabinski talks to the educational diagnostician and the parents and arranges for an admission-review-dismissal (ARD) meeting to change her IEP. Mrs. Strabinski believes that Hannah not only can learn all the academic skills necessary for second grade, but she may actually be gifted. Because Hannah could not speak and lacked fine-motor ability, no one realized previously how much intelligence she possessed. Had she been placed in the same type of classroom as in her previous district, Hannah might have remained locked into classes that offered limited academics and the world of reading might never have opened to her. Mrs. Strabinski looks at Hannah and is thankful that her district not only believes in inclusion but supports it in a way that ensures this philosophy is successful.

Although Hannah has little control over her fingers, Mrs. Strabinski decides to use the computer to try to teach Hannah to type using one finger. Hannah learns to type "Hannah" that very same day. Now Hannah can type the letters and sounds when Mrs. Strabinski works with her on the letter names and sounds. Hannah is now able to use inventive spelling and the computer to express her wants and needs.

In addition to Hannah and Jacob, Mrs. Strabinski has Faneisha in her class. Faneisha does not receive special education services but does receive accommodations in the general education classroom under Section 504 (see Chapter 4) because she has asthma and allergies. Faneisha has an inhaler that is kept in the nurse's office at school. (The school does not allow children to keep their inhalers in the classroom.) On bad days, she has to go to the nurse's office every few hours and use her inhaler. Mrs. Strabinski did not realize until this year that constant coughing, not just wheezing, can be a sign of asthma. The medication that Faneisha sometimes has to take for her allergies causes her to be sleepy and have attention problems. Mrs. Strabinski has also become aware that sometimes Faneisha is sleepy in school because of nighttime asthma attacks. Because of the problems Faneisha is having with allergies and asthma, Mrs. Strabinski has been asked by Faneisha's doctor to try to identify asthma and allergy triggers in the school. The doctor has asked her to keep a log of dates, times, and circumstances of asthma and allergy attacks at school.

⭐ INCLUDING CHILDREN WITH SPECIAL NEEDS

naeyc

Inclusion, as a value, supports the right of all children, regardless of their diverse abilities, to participate actively in natural settings within their communities. A natural setting is one in which the child would spend time had he or she not had a disability. Such settings include, but are not limited to, home and family, play groups, child care, nursery schools, Head Start programs, kindergartens, and neighborhood school classrooms. (NAEYC, 1998, p. 1)

In 1993, nearly 5 million children between the ages of 3 and 11 were receiving special education services. Of these children, 69 percent were included in the general education classroom at least 40 percent of the time (Winter, 1997). This number has continued to grow. Some general education teachers have been very successful with inclusion, whereas others have not. Because inclusion is not going to go away, studies are now being conducted to determine why this philosophy has been successful in some instances and why it has failed in others. One such study by Smith and Smith (2000) revealed four factors that made the difference between successful and unsuccessful inclusion.

The first factor was training. Whereas all the participants in the study stated that their undergraduate training did not prepare them for inclusion, some of the participants were able to receive training through the school's in-service efforts. Even this training, however, was viewed as insufficient to provide teachers with the skills and information that they needed. The most effective training consisted of spending time in a successful teacher's classroom and observing that teacher's interactions with students. It was also recommended that administrators also undergo training in order to have a better understanding of the day-to-day requirements of inclusion.

The second factor was class size. The smaller the class size, the more likely a teacher was to view himself or herself as being successful. The number of children with special needs per class was also a consideration. Teachers who viewed themselves as successful had class sizes ranging from 13 to 21 including no more than four children with special needs. Teachers with similar class sizes felt unsuccessful when they had more than four children with special needs. Some classes had as many as eight children with special needs in one classroom. The mix of disabilities was also an important factor in success. Classrooms that had children with ADHD, emotional disturbances, autism, and severe disabilities magnified problems for the teacher. Administrators, therefore, must look at types and intensities of children's disabilities and not just the number in assigning children to inclusion classrooms.

The third factor was support. All the teachers responded that they could not be successful without support, and the quality and quantity of this support was a determining factor in the success or failure of inclusion. Support came from a special education teacher, general education paraprofessionals, special education paraprofessionals, and building administrators. Administrators were seen as providing uneven support. Their support, or lack of support, was viewed in terms of how they handled the teacher's time through the schedules they set and the personnel they hired to support the program.

The fourth factor was time. Time is needed to plan lessons and their accommodations and modifications, to make or procure special materials, and to collaborate with relevant personnel. Teachers were giving up their personal time, lunch time, bathroom time, and home time to plan the lessons and their modifications. One study found it typical for teachers to work the equivalent of one extra day per week at home planning and doing other schoolwork. Administrators may further burden teachers by requiring extra meetings and other responsibilities. Administrators should be facilitators when it comes to finding time for teachers to plan and collaborate. Teachers should not be expected to find the time themselves (Smith & Smith, 2000).

NAEYC supports the development of training programs that prepare families, administrators, and teachers for working in inclusive settings. The organization supports research that contributes to the development, evaluation, and dissemination of full inclusion; it also supports services and systems for improving options for inclusion, thereby contributing to knowledge of state-of-the-art services. These

naeyc

services should be based on the needs and preferences of individual families and children (NAEYC, 1998).

Mrs. Strabinski firmly believes in inclusion. Besides the fact that it is the law, Mrs. Strabinski holds the philosophy that all children should be valued and that including children with special needs helps not only those children, but also the other children in the class. She believes in individualizing instruction for all her children, so it is not really difficult for her to follow an Individualized Education Plan (IEP) for Jacob and Hannah. Indeed, because of the help and support that she receives from the special education teacher, there have been few problems. When making accommodations and modifications for Jacob and Hannah, the special education teacher and Mrs. Strabinski have worked together to determine if they can do the same activities but with modifications. If not, they discuss whether or not they can do the same skill at a simpler level or if they need to do a different skill that is related to the topic being studied. Using this approach for modifications, Mrs. Strabinski has discovered that Hannah can do most of the same activities but that modifications have to be made because of her physical limitations. For Jacob, most of the modifications amount to simpler skills or different skills in a related area.

The special education teacher helps Mrs. Strabinski evaluate the classroom for both Hannah and Jacob. No special accommodations or modifications of the classroom are needed for Jacob, but because Hannah uses a wheelchair, the room has to be arranged so that she can navigate about the room. This means that the aisles have to be wide enough for her wheelchair. Having a desk or table that her wheelchair will fit under is another requirement for her to work using the limited fine-motor skills that she has.

Both Jacob and Hannah need modifications made to the materials in the classroom. Jacob is functioning on a level lower than any of the material currently in the classroom. The special education teacher has material on his level and she has brought it to the classroom. Mrs. Strabinski has also talked to a kindergarten teacher and has borrowed some other materials such as software for the computer. Modifications and accommodations for Hannah involve finding ways to help her be as independent as possible as she interacts with the curricular materials. She is able to move the manipulatives in math as long as they are spread out on her desk and do not require special placement or hooking together.

Other modifications and accommodations are extra time for completion of assignments, shortened assignments, extensive use of the computer for Hannah, and alternative assignments for Jacob. Mrs. Strabinski knows that both Hannah and Jacob will benefit from having a peer tutor or a buddy. She doesn't want to make them feel different, so she announces that all the children will have a study buddy. She chooses the study buddies for each child this first time, being careful to choose children for Jacob and Hannah who are willing and eager to assist them. All the children are excited about having study buddies, and Mrs. Strabinski feels good about the way she has handled this.

Mrs. Strabinski is not left unaided in the classroom. Every week she plans with the special education teacher. Together they decide on content for both Jacob and Hannah and determine when Mrs. Strabinski will need extra assistance in the classroom. The special education teacher works with an instructional aide, so plans are

What Teachers Are Saying

Inclusion

"Although our classrooms are not labeled inclusion, we all teach to a wide range of ability levels, from those who need constant challenge to those in need of one-on-one assistance."—*a first-grade teacher*

"I can modify, but with all the other needs in my room I find it hard to give them [the special children with special needs] the extra time they need."—*a second-grade teacher*

Mrs. Strabinski agrees with this teacher, but experience has helped her find time and different ways to provide the extra needed assistance for these children. She uses peer tutors constantly in her class, and not just for her children with special needs. She also has an arrangement with a fourth-grade teacher who sends students down to act as teacher aides. Mrs. Strabinski also contacted the local AARP and found several retired teachers who welcomed the opportunity to volunteer in her classroom.

"The type of children we are getting in the schools now are much different than those that we had when I first started teaching. It is very challenging to deal with these students who have very unique family situations and special needs. Experience is the best teacher for dealing with special needs students."—*a first-grade teacher*

made for one or the other of them to assist Mrs. Strabinski at certain times. These times may vary from week to week, depending on the activities that are planned.

WHAT SECOND GRADERS ARE EXPECTED TO LEARN

Second grade is a time for children to refine and expand on the skills they learned in first grade. It is a stable year for children. They are used to being in school and are expected to learn just enough new information to keep them challenged and busy. Second graders are able to read more complicated books, receive instruction in writing narratives and how-to papers, work with larger numbers in math and learn to regroup in both addition and subtraction, and move beyond the community in their social studies.

Reading

Children in second grade have many different levels in their reading. Because learning to read is developmental, some children learn to read quite well in first grade whereas others do not learn until they are in second grade (Bredekamp & Copple, 1997). The teacher needs to support each child's ability level.

Teachers use a variety of materials for reading instruction in second grade. They still use big books for shared reading and whole-class instruction for certain concepts. For instance, a teacher who wants to focus attention on the use of exclamation marks might use a big book that presents numerous examples. The teacher can point out the exclamation marks, read the sentences with expression to show why the exclamation mark is used, and have the children practice reading the sentences with strong feeling. Basal readers are also available for reading instruction. Classroom sets of different book titles may come with the basal or may have been purchased by the school specifically for second grade. Some basal series also include small sets of books. These sets have levels that vary from easy to hard for second graders. The school library may also have other reading material such as class sets of books, small sets of books with a cassette tape for a Listening Center, and books on CD-ROM. Mrs. Strabinski discovered a few years ago that the librarian has a generous budget. When Mrs. Strabinski wanted to have multiple copies of several books available to use with small groups, she found the books in a catalog, wrote out all the information necessary for ordering the books, and turned in the list to the librarian with a request, if money was available, for these titles to be purchased through the library. To her delight, all the books she requested were purchased. Since then, she keeps a list of materials and books that she wants to have available in the library and submits it to the librarian. Because few other teachers do this, the librarian will order most of the materials that she requests.

Reading skills that are taught in second grade include the following:

- Elements of a story (characters, setting, plot, solution)
- Prediction
- Sequence
- Author's purpose in writing
- Drawing conclusions
- Classifying
- Word-attack strategies (phonics, context clues)
- Realism and fantasy
- Cause and effect
- Main idea (Afflerbach, Beers, Blachowicz, Boyd, Diffily, Gauntz-Porter, Harris, Leu, McClanahan, Monson, Perez, Sebeste, & Wixson, 2000)

Writing and Language Arts

Second graders are able to write for longer periods of time and may write on a specific topic for several days. They are able to pick up a piece they did not finish and remember what they intended to write. Only disposable basal language books are used. This means that the children actually write in the language book and the pages can be torn out and taken home. The language book combines grammar skill instruction, study skill instruction, and instruction in listening, speaking, and writing. Children are expected to write narratives, how-to papers, poems, letters, and simple reports.

Language and writing skills taught in second grade include:

- Different types of sentences
- Parts of a sentence
- Nouns, verbs, adjectives, adverbs, pronouns
- Plurals
- Alphabetical order
- Dictionary skills
- Library skills
- Capitalization
- The writing process
- Critical thinking
- Listening
- Speaking

Mathematics

Second-grade math basals generally begin with a review of addition. Most basals begin with simple addition problems using picture cues but quickly progress to sums to 10s and then three addends, all without picture cues. Manipulatives are an important part of math instruction in second grade. Children need to use a variety of objects as they make number equations or sentences. Manipulatives also help children as they are exposed to increasingly more complex word problems. Some common manipulatives used in second grade are snap cubes, base ten blocks, small clocks, collections of buttons, shells, paper clips, beads, coins, geoboards, and pattern blocks.

Math skills taught in second grade include:

- Addition up to hundreds with regrouping
- Subtraction up to hundreds with regrouping
- Writing numbers to 999
- Counting to 1,000
- Place value
- Problem-solving skills and strategies
- Meaning of multiplication
- Meaning of division
- Fractions up to sixths
- Estimation
- Measurement of time, weight, capacity, length, calendar, temperature
- Money
- Plane geometry
- Using calculators
- Using computers (Charles, Barnett, Briars, Crown, Johnson, Leinwand, Van de Walle, Allan, Cooley, Elliot, Ling, Ramirez, Renfro, Thompson, & Park, 1999a).

Science

As children become better readers and more logical, concrete thinkers, they are able to understand and explore their world in new ways. In second grade they learn to read pictures, graphs, and charts. They do simple experiments, make observations, record or draw results, compare, and make inferences from the results. The topics studied in science in second grade are more challenging and in-depth as they study about plants, weather, heat, light, simple machines, magnets, and rocks (Baptiste, Jr., Daniel, Hackett, Moyer, Stryker, Vasquez, Flood, & Lapp, 2000). (See Chapter 9 for the National Science Education Standards and the scientific process.)

Social Studies

The focus of social studies broadens in second grade and moves from the study of the community to the study of the country and even to an overview of the earth. Social studies at this level includes history, government, geography, economics, citizenship, culture, and study and thinking skills.

Social studies skills that are taught in second grade include:

- Community, state, country, world
- Geography skills (compass rose, map skills)
- Citizenship
- Geography (oceans, continents, types of land and water)
- Weather
- Natural resources
- History (European explorers and settlers, Native Americans, American Revolution, Civil War, immigration and expansion)
- Economy (working, trade, transportation, goods and services, money)
- Government (Constitution, U.S. government, Washington, D.C.)
- Famous Americans
- Significant landmarks
- Significant holidays
- Cultures (holiday celebrations)
- Study skills (calendars, flowcharts, time lines, main idea, bar graphs)
- Thinking skills (alike and different, sorting, ordering, predictions) (Boyd, Berkin, Gay, Chase, Geiger, Cummins, Kracht, Glenn, Pang, Hahn, Risinger, Hickey, Sanchez & Meszaros, 2003).

⭐ ORGANIZING THE CLASSROOM

The teacher should organize the classroom for second graders in much the same way that it is organized for first grade. There should be numerous centers for the children to use during the day. Although the academic skills are noticeably harder and the amount of paper-and-pencil types of activities has increased, the children still need time to learn through exploration and hands-on activities. The centers that the teacher places in the room are an extremely important part of this development, and they need to have activities for a wide variety of levels and abilities so that all the children can be successful. The number and placement of centers depends on the size and arrangement of the classroom. One teacher, in a very small classroom, used cabinet space and plastic boxes for her centers. These "centers" were self-contained and the children got them out of the cabinet and used the centers at their desks or

Materials placed in plastic tubs make portable centers for children to use independently.

on the floor. Though not ideal, this was certainly more acceptable than assigning various worksheets to keep the children busy who finish their work quickly.

Because children should have ample time during the day for pleasure reading, the reading center and classroom library are essential. At this age children can be taught to function as librarians. The teacher can set up the class library with cards in the backs of the books. A child (the Librarian) can be trained to check out the book, date-stamp the card, and file the card in an index card box behind the appropriate letter tab (in alphabetical order). The child can even be trained to send out overdue notices using preprinted forms that require limited information to be written on them. Librarian is one of the choice jobs in the second grade! Books should include a wide range of levels, from emergent reading to chapter books. The teacher may be supplied with books from the library on a rotating basis but can also build a collection by obtaining free books from the book clubs that commonly solicit orders in elementary schools.

Another popular center in the second-grade classroom is the Engineering Center. If the children are provided with motorized construction sets, such as Erector sets, they can build actual vehicles and machines that move. Although plans are usually included for different projects in these types of sets, some children will invent their own vehicles and machines. This center provides children with the opportunity to problem-solve on a concrete basis as they build and try out different designs in their machines. Small clipboards with paper and pencils should be kept in this center for children to take notes and sketch ideas.

The Writing Center should be equipped with a multitude of colored paper, writing paper, stencils, markers, die-cut shapes and pictures, glue, rubber stamps, and many different colored ink pads and stickers. One way to involve the children in this center is to show the children how to make cards for their family and friends. Multiple copies of blank books in various shapes and sizes also encourage the children to write. When the center is kept supplied with materials, children remain enthusiastic about writing.

The Science Center can contain simple experiments that the teacher has written out and laminated on cardstock for the children to try. In addition to these experiments, there should be magnifying glasses, microscopes, and a variety of items to look at with these tools. Children and parents can participate in providing items for the Science Center. Nature walks around the school can provide leaves, seed pods, feathers, rocks, and sometimes even fossils, depending on the area of the country. Parents might contribute teeth from horses, bones from cows, or other unusual items that the children will find interesting. Clipboards should be a part of this center, too, because they allow the children to record and sketch what they see or learn. If this center can be placed near a window, binoculars and a telescope can be added for the children to use as they explore the world outside the classroom. A bird feeder can be placed outside the window and a clipboard kept nearby for graphing the types of birds that visit the feeder. Children can also sketch birds that come to the feeder and use a bird reference book to try to identify them.

The arrangement of the furniture in the classroom is important. Often second-grade classrooms come equipped with desks for the children. If the children have individual desks, these desks can be pushed together and function as tables. This allows the children to do cooperative learning activities even when classroom size is limited and real tables are not available. The teacher should have at least one large rectangular table or horseshoe table to use for small-group instruction. When it is not being used by the teacher for small-group instruction, this table also offers a place for the children to spread out as they work on special projects.

Children can be assigned, or apply for, class jobs. Teachers who use class jobs with their children find that children respond well and really consider the classroom to be their own. Class jobs depend on the particular needs of each classroom.

Class Jobs

Computer Assistant: turns on the computer and printer, loads programs, and makes sure the computer is turned off at the end of the day.

Science Center Assistant: oversees the Science Center, makes sure that supplies needed are kept available, cleans and straightens the center at the end of the day.

Librarian: checks classroom books in and out, reshelves the books, sends out overdue notices.

Writing Center Assistant: straightens materials, informs teacher when new markers, stamp pads, and other materials are needed.

Attendance Clerk: hands the teacher the list of children absent each day and delivers the attendance sheet to the office or posts it outside the door.

Floor Inspector: notices paper and trash on the floor and requests that the child closest picks it up (this is a good job for a child who has ADHD and needs to move). This job is introduced through role playing. During the role play the "Inspector" points out trash to the teacher and asks the teacher to pick it up. The point is made that even though it is not the teacher's trash, the teacher picks it up because he or she is closest to it.

Second graders also need help in learning organizational skills. These skills are especially important for children with special needs, many of whom are disorganized and always losing things. The teacher can begin by having the children use take-home folders, which can be simple pocket folders. The first day of class the teacher instructs the children to label each pocket. The pocket on the right is labeled "Return to school" and the pocket on the left is labeled "Keep at home." That first day the training begins. There are numerous papers for the children to take home the first few days of school, and the teacher uses this as an opportunity to begin the organization training. As papers are passed out to the children, the teacher has the children open their folders and place the papers in the correct pockets. Training the children to place important papers that need to come back to school helps ensure that field trip permission slips and homework are returned. Using a supply box or closable plastic bag helps keep crayons, pencils, scissors, and glue readily available. The children may also use a pocket folder for a writing folder. One side can be labeled "Work in progress." The other side holds the list of topics the child is interested in, editing mark sheets, and special problem words particular to that child.

FIGURE 8.1 Editing Marks

^	Insert letters or words here
¶	Make a new paragraph
(	Close up; no space
∩	Transpose
≡	Capitalize
℘	Delete

Children are usually required to bring several packs of notebook paper to school. The disorganized child ends up throwing most of his or her paper away because it is loose in the desk and becomes all wrinkled and crushed. If the teacher collects all the paper and puts paper out in central locations in the classroom, the children can be trained to pick up five to ten sheets of paper as needed and to place the paper in a special folder. This activity not only preserves the paper, but it also helps cut down on the mess that children can end up with in their desks. Time should be allotted at the end of every day for the children to straighten their desks and be sure that their take-home folders are organized and ready to be put into their backpacks.

LEARNING STYLES

Children have different styles of learning, or preferred ways of learning and processing information. **Learning styles** are based on this preferred sense that a person uses in learning new information. Many learning styles have been identified and studied over the years. In the field of education, the term *learning style* often refers to whether children are visual, auditory, tactile, or kinesthetic learners. Most school classrooms present instruction geared toward children who are visual or auditory learners, but some children learn best through the tactile or kinesthetic styles. Each style has its strengths and weaknesses. The successful teacher uses the child's preferred style as an entry point into the content and then strengthens the learning by using the other styles to reinforce it (Teaching and Learning Center, 2001).

Visual learners remember what they see or read and need to see information written down. Graphs, flashcards, charts, and diagrams and pictures all aid them in learning new material. Visual learners have difficulty with information that is only presented orally (Teaching and Learning Center, 2001).

Auditory learners remember what they hear, need phonics, and learn by listening. They can become distracted, however, by noise and visual stimuli such as pictures. With these learners the teacher uses explanations, lectures, discussions, audiotapes, songs, and rhymes and has the student read aloud (Teaching and Learning Center, 2001).

Tactile learners learn best through touch and movement. They like to imitate, role-play, build models, and have hands-on lessons. They have trouble remembering what they see and hear. They can remember what they have done, however. Touch and movement are very important to them as they learn (Teaching & Learning Center, 2001).

Kinesthetic learners are closely related to tactile learners and sometimes the two are even grouped together as one learning style. Kinesthetic learners learn best when they are able to move their bodies and use their small or large muscles as they learn. They often may be labeled hyperactive because they wiggle and tap their feet when they sit. They learn as they "perform." They like working with their hands and may be good at art or working with tools (Kinesthetic Learners, 2000). The teacher uses their strengths by encouraging these children to act out a story that was just read or to solve a math problem by using manipulatives.

A teacher planning a lesson should plan it for the whole class. The teacher begins by writing down exactly what all the children need to learn and how this content will be taught. After this step, a teacher who wants to address the learning style of her individual children will ask herself who in her class cannot master this lesson in the manner that it is presented, adding the names of specific children who she feels will have difficulty. Then, using her knowledge of those children, she can add to the original lesson plan various ways to incorporate activities to meet all the learning styles. In math, she may use several different types of manipulatives as she demonstrates a concept, have each child use manipulatives along with her, or have the children dramatize the problem and solution (Ebeling, 2000).

☆ SECOND GRADE AND READING INSTRUCTION

The director of the National Institute of Child Health and Human Development was charged by Congress in 1997 to convene a national panel to assess the effectiveness of various approaches to reading instruction. The director, in consultation with the Secretary of Education, formed a panel of scientists, reading teachers, colleges of education representatives, educational administrators, and parents to study reading instruction and to disseminate the findings and make recommendations about effective reading instruction. The ensuing report was based on the results of experimental studies and formal, evidence-based analyses of current research (National Reading Panel, 2000).

When the National Reading Panel published its findings in 2000, Mrs. Strabinski saw an advertisement in one of her professional journals that the report was available, at no charge, to any interested party. Mrs. Strabinski ordered a copy of the report because she wanted to provide the very best instruction possible to her children. In the report, Mrs. Strabinski read that teaching phonemic awareness (PA) to children caused an improvement not only in PA, but also in reading and spelling. She read that the instruction should be in small groups and should focus on the manipulation of one or two types of phonemes (the smallest unit constituting spoken language) rather than multiple types. This manipulation influenced spelling outcomes more when the children manipulated the phonemes with letters, an activity done with letter tiles (National Reading Panel, 2000). Mrs. Strabinski felt that phonemic awareness instruction would be very beneficial for those of her children who were functioning at an emergent reading level. Now she had to find information that would help her determine how to teach phonemic awareness.

Using the references listed in the National Reading Panel's report, she found a study cited that listed the order of instruction from easy to difficult.

1. Identification of pictures with the same beginning sounds
2. Blending onset (initial consonant or consonant cluster) and rimes (the vowel or vowel and consonants that follow the onset) into words
3. Blending phonemes into words
4. Deleting a phoneme from a word and saying the word that remains
5. Segmenting words into phonemes
6. Blending phonemes into nonwords (Schatschneider, Francis, Foorman, Fletcher, & Mehta, 1999, p. 446)

After further research on the subject, Mrs. Strabinski found many other studies that supported the NRP's finding that phonemic awareness was a strong predictor of future reading ability and poor phonemic awareness was a characteristic of adults who were poor readers (Adams, Foorman, Lundberg, & Beeler, 1998). And so, Mrs. Strabinski began small-group instruction of phonemic awareness. She used letter tiles and pictures with the same and/or different initial consonant sounds for her emergent readers. She tested the other children in her class based on these six levels and formed groups based on the needs of the children. She knew from the NRP report that spending between 5 and 18 hours teaching PA during the school year had a significant impact on the acquisition of phonemic awareness as well as on reading and spelling ability (National Reading Panel, 2000). She knew that she could easily implement PA instruction into her language arts block of time. Using the letter tiles with the emergent readers would be especially beneficial to

Jacob in learning his letter names and sounds and would strengthen any other children who were weak in this area.

In second grade, a teacher may have children functioning on many different reading levels. Some may have learned to read in kindergarten, others in first grade, and others are still on an emergent level. All the children need to have instruction tailored for their specific needs. One way for the teacher to meet this goal is with guided reading. In guided reading the teacher works with a small group of children selected according to their individual needs in reading through a story.

The lesson begins with an introduction to the text that stimulates the children's interest and related background knowledge. The children do a picture walk through the book, discussing the illustrations and concepts related to comprehension of the text (Morrow & Asbury, 2001). Generally, the book is read by all the children simultaneously. The teacher uses this and other books to help the children learn basic concepts about print (see Chapter 7); different word-attack strategies such as phonics, what makes sense, and reading on; and other context clues and reading strategies that aid in comprehension. Children at this level are grouped homogeneously because of the need to focus on concepts about print and reading strategies (The Wright Group, 1995). During the lesson the teacher is constantly observing and assessing the children, and children join or leave a group based on this assessment.

The children keep and read the same book for several days. Unlike round-robin reading, where children get to read only a sentence or two individually, all the children read the book aloud several times. In addition to reading it together during their group, the children are encouraged to read it with each other, to other children, and to their parents or family at home. Mrs. Strabinski was happy to note that the National Reading Panel's report supported oral guided reading as a means of improving children's fluency, word recognition, comprehension, and overall reading achievement. The report found clear improvements in the children's performances, regardless of their ability level, with greater gains made by poor readers (National Reading Panel, 2000).

As the children move to the fluency level, guided reading is still important, but the children can be grouped more heterogeneously. Children can choose books based on their interests. The focus of guided reading for these children is on the development of the concepts about literature. These concepts include the story structure, literary terms, literary devices, and literary strategies. Children work on identifying the beginning, middle, ending, and sequence of events for story structure. Literary terms include character, setting, problem solution, point of view, and genre. Similes, metaphors, alliteration, and onomatopoeia are some of the literary devices that the children come to learn. And the literary strategies of using the table of contents, dictionaries, retelling, and comparing and contrasting will be introduced (The Wright Group, 1995). Minilessons are used during the session to teach a literacy element or language structure. The teacher asks focus questions that help the children predict and confirm, follow the plot line, or understand other elements.

Besides having groups for guided reading, the teacher needs to have flexible groups based on children's interests. The teacher may also use nonfiction books that cover many different topics. Nonfiction books allow children to use thinking processes as they sequence information, differentiate fact and fiction, understand cause and effect, draw conclusions, and generalize from information (The Wright Group, 1995). Nonfiction books may be science, history, archeology, or biography. Having a wide variety of these books available allows the children to develop interests in several areas. Allowing them to choose which books they want to read provides them with the opportunity to be grouped with more advanced children and read more challenging material. Motivation and interest can help spur the children to read material that is at a higher level.

In the second grade, children improve their comprehension and understanding of different types of literary material by practicing and using skills such as predicting, summarizing, main idea, cause and effect, drawing conclusions, sequencing, fact and opinion, comparing and contrasting, and making judgments based on information provided. The National Reading Panel (2000) found seven categories of comprehension instruction that seemed to have a scientific basis for improving comprehension. These types of instruction are:

- Comprehension monitoring, where readers learn how to be aware of their understanding of the material
- Cooperative learning, where students learn reading strategies together
- Use of graphic and semantic organizers (including story maps), where readers make graphic representations of the material to assist comprehension
- Question answering, where readers answer questions posed by the teacher and receive immediate feedback
- Question generation, where readers ask themselves questions about various aspects of the story
- Story structure, where students are taught to use the structure of the story as a means of helping them recall story content in order to answer questions about what they have read
- Summarization, where readers are taught to integrate ideas and generalize from the text information (p. 15)

Children also work on their ability to figure out new vocabulary words through the use of phonic skills, context clues, and structural analysis strategies. Root or base words are studied with prefixes and suffixes as a part of vocabulary development. Stories that the children read become more complex and increase in length as children become more independent in their reading ability.

Keeping up with the most current research by reading the journal *Phi Delta Kappan,* Mrs. Strabinski noted that a critique on the fluency report of the NRP summary reported problems with the research as far as silent reading was concerned. The NRP's summary reported that silent reading was not an effective strategy for increasing fluency. The critique, however, cited the small number of studies reviewed, the fact that there was no statistical difference between the groups who read silently versus the groups who did not have silent reading, and the discounting of many studies that showed strong evidence of a connection between silent reading and literacy growth (Krashen, 2001).

Mrs. Strabinski, though interested in the study by the National Reading Panel, has restricted herself to those parts of the study that she feels have value in her classroom and for her specific group of children. Because of the problems associated with the study on fluency reported in the *Phi Delta Kappan* previously, she began scanning the journal each month for responses and comments about other areas of the report by the National Reading Panel. Mrs. Strabinski is looking for articles that examine the various aspects of the report and provide information that will help her decide which areas of the report can be viewed as valid and reliable. She is wary of making sweeping changes in the education program of children based on any specific report.

One of the first published responses on the National Reading Panel's report was a critique of the report on phonics published in the *Kappan*. The critique was excellent and offered Mrs. Strabinski exactly the information she was seeking. The article focused on the methodology, generalizability of results, reliability, and validity of the NRP's report. A problem immediately brought to the attention of the reader was the small number of studies that were actually used—a mere 38. These studies did not all address the same phonics skills and did not include reading comprehension or application of phonics skills in authentic situations as necessary criteria in determining outcomes. The focus was on word recognition, not comprehension. The student population studied consisted only of kindergarten and first-grade children who were at risk for developing reading problems, low-achieving readers, and older disabled readers. It did not include normally achieving or high-achieving children, or children with limited proficiency in English. The actual number of studies reported by the subgroup studying phonics instruction and low-achieving readers was only eight. The NRP's summary report, however, generalizes its findings to all children (Garan, 2001). Mrs. Strabinski realizes that this cannot be generalized to all children when three very prominent groups were not even included in the study, and so both the **reliability** and **validity** of the summary report must be viewed with caution. Her conviction was further strengthened when she read the critique on the fluency report a few months later.

A major problem with the summary report, according to the article in the *Kappan*, is that it is not an accurate reflection of the reports of the subgroups. The subgroup on phonics instruction reports that there were insufficient data to draw any conclusions about normally developing readers and the effects of phonics instruction. Yet the summary report of the NRP claims that phonics instruction does produce significant benefits for children in kindergarten through sixth grade (Garan, 2001).

Much of the report from the NRP is supported, however, by many studies. In addition to the importance of phonemic awareness instruction, the comprehension section also has merit. When children are in second grade or older, they need to be reading high-quality literature to help them develop a joy of reading. Continued drill and practice on phonic skills is counterproductive. They also need to read expository texts (content knowledge). This helps improve their background knowledge and vocabulary. Research shows that background knowledge is also a strong predictor of reading comprehension. Children should use the new vocabulary in a variety of ways to make those words their own. The words can be used in class discussions, discussions among children, and their journals as they write about what they are learning. Children can also be taught to monitor their own comprehension by asking themselves if they understand what they have just read and by summarizing it to themselves (Learning First Alliance, 1998).

☆ NAEYC's POSITION ON READING AND WRITING

As a member of NAEYC, Mrs. Strabinski decided to check the NAEYC website for information on reading and writing. She found a helpful list of goals for second graders, what teachers can do, and what parents and family members can do to help children learn to read and write. This is the information she found on the website.

naeyc

Second graders can

- Read with greater fluency
- Use strategies more efficiently (rereading, questioning, and so on) when comprehension breaks down
- Use word identification strategies with greater facility to unlock unknown words
- Identify an increasing number of words by sight
- Write about a range of topics to suit different audiences
- Use common letter patterns and critical features to spell words
- Punctuate simple sentences correctly and proofread their own work
- Spend time reading daily and use reading to research topics

What teachers do

- Create a climate that fosters analytic, evaluative, and reflective thinking
- Teach children to write in multiple forms (stories, information, poems)
- Ensure that children read a range of texts for a variety of purposes
- Teach revising, editing, and proofreading skills
- Model enjoyment of reading

What parents and family members can do

- Continue to read to children and encourage them to read to you
- Engage children in activities that require reading and writing
- Become involved in school activities
- Show children your interest in their learning by displaying their written work
- Visit the library regularly
- Support your child's specific hobby or interest with reading materials and references (NAEYC, 1998, pp. 3–4)

Issues and Trends

No Child Left Behind and Reading Instruction

According to this law, reading should be taught using methods that have proven to be scientifically based. This refers to research that is systematic, empirical, involves rigorous data analysis that provides valid data, and has been accepted by a peer-reviewed journal and/or approved by a panel of experts. Furthermore, school districts must ensure that new teachers hired after 2002–2003 are highly qualified. This means that they must be licensed or certified by the state; have at least a bachelor's degree; and pass a state test that demonstrates their knowledge of subject matter and skill in teaching reading, writing, math, and other basics of the elementary school curriculum. A teacher may be fully certified but will not be considered highly qualified until he or she has demonstrated competency in the subject matter. Teachers who have had certification or licensure requirements waived for any reason will not be considered highly qualified (No State Left Behind, 2002).

★ READING INSTRUCTION IN MRS. STRABINSKI'S CLASSROOM

Mrs. Strabinski uses a mixture of materials and strategies for her reading instruction. She has collected big books through the years and uses them with many of the themes that she teaches because the children still like participating in shared reading with big books. She also uses small, leveled books for guided reading groups and small sets of books for interest group reading. All of these materials are supplementary and are supplied by the district. The district also supplies reading books that are either on a lower or higher level than that of the average second grader. This resource gives her additional materials to use in meeting the needs of all her children.

The district has the policy that all teachers in grades kindergarten through third grade must do a running record with each child in their classroom every other week, a task for which all teachers received training. The process is fast, simple, and provides the teacher with information about the child's oral reading ability. The teacher chooses a book on the child's level and, using checkmarks, records on a blank sheet of paper the reading behavior. Each correct word receives a check. Incorrect words are recorded over the word that should have been read. Other marks are used to show omissions, self-corrections, repetitions, insertions, requests for help, and teacher telling the child the word (Jalongo, 2000). The teacher can use this record to analyze mistakes, looking for patterns of mistakes, strengths, and weaknesses. The running record can also be used to determine if the book the child is reading is an independent-level, instructional-level, or frustration-level book for that child.

The word walls in second-grade classrooms become more complex (see Chapter 7). The teacher has a large sheet of paper or poster board for each letter of the alphabet. These are placed in alphabetical order around the classroom and new, high-frequency words and frequently misspelled words are added as the children want to learn how to spell these words. Words from units of study or projects can also be added to the wall. If the large sheets of paper or poster board are laminated, the teacher can erase and add new words throughout the year. This keeps the lists to a manageable size. Additional word walls can be developed as the children learn different skills. Word walls can be constructed to show word families and rhyming words, contractions, homophones, prefixes and suffixes, and plurals using -s, -es, and -ies (Gruber, 1999).

Mrs. Strabinski has given great thought to meeting the needs of both Jacob and Hannah. Jacob is unable to read any of the classroom materials, so she has borrowed material from the kindergarten teacher in her building for him. Jacob is responding with enthusiasm to the simple little books that have two words per page and proudly reads his books to the other children. Mrs. Strabinski does not keep him isolated from the other children, however. He also participates in the big books with all the other children and is a member of the emergent-level guided reading group. Although he is unable to read these books, Jacob is beginning to listen and look at the pictures and is learning other concepts of print.

Hannah has a different set of problems. Because she had previously been in a class with children who had severe cognitive deficits, Hannah has little reading ability. Because Hannah is far behind in her academic areas and able to do a very limited amount of independent work, Mrs. Strabinski has included Hannah in all of the reading groups. After reviewing her university course notes on including children with special needs in the classroom, Mrs. Strabinski developed a low-tech device that allows Hannah to turn the pages of the books by herself: large paper clips on each page of the books. Mrs. Strabinski points to each word in Hannah's book as the children read. She has noticed that Hannah's eyes are now moving to each word. Hannah seems intensely interested in all the books. During the language arts period of the day, when Hannah is not in a reading group or participating in a whole-group shared reading, she is at the computer slowly typing out new words and sentences. Though she will never be able to type in the regular fashion, Hannah gains speed as she learns the positions of the keys. Seeing the progress that Hannah has made in this very short period of time has Mrs. Strabinski again wondering what Hannah's life could have been like had she been included in a general education classroom from the first time she entered school.

Mrs. Strabinski does not use many worksheets in her classroom during reading. Instead, she has the children actively involved with the books they are reading. Depending on the book or story that the children have read, Mrs. Strabinski chooses one of several activities for the children to extend their knowledge. She has some children rewriting their book using different characters or settings. Others re-create the story on a large piece of paper that is used as a "walking story." Their "walking story" is placed under a piece of plastic carpet protector and the children can walk on it as they read each panel. Other children do door panels in which they illustrate a character from the story and have the character saying something about the story. Other children make flip books that include questions and answers based on the story. Murals of the stories, story boards that depict the sequence of the story, and character studies are also completed and displayed in the classroom or outside the classroom for other children to read and share. The children are always excited about sharing their work with other children and visitors.

WRITING INSTRUCTION IN SECOND GRADE

Mrs. Strabinski uses the language basal as a supplemental resource in her classroom for grammar instruction and some dictionary and study skills instruction. It provides her with a scope and sequence for these skills, but she then expands on these skills using the reading material in the classroom. Although the basal includes writing instruction, Mrs. Strabinski uses the writing process with her class in addition to teaching the children the specific writing types required by the state. (For information about the writing process, see Chapter 9.)

One writing area that Mrs. Strabinski focuses on with her children is how to make their stories more interesting to the reader—how to paint pictures in the minds of the readers with words. Mrs. Strabinski uses many examples from the books in her classroom. She not only tells the children that a good introduction to a story makes the reader want to keep reading, she shows them examples from the books in the classroom. She takes a sentence and removes the adjectives and adverbs that the author used and reads the altered sentence to the children. The children talk about the information provided in the sentence, and then Mrs. Strabinski adds the words that were left out and the children discuss the difference these words made in the sentence. Using this format, Mrs. Strabinski introduces adjectives and adverbs to her class and shows how the addition of these words make the writing much more interesting.

Next, she takes a beginning sentence from one of the children's stories that reads, "One day a boy went to a store." She brainstorms with the children all the different types of words they could use to describe this day and writes their suggestions on the board. They talk about weather words, words describing time of day and the month, and any other words the children can come up with that describe the day (Slack, 1993). The children then work in groups and discuss ideas for expanding this sentence using the brainstormed list on the board. The groups then share how they changed the sentence with the rest of the class.

The Class's Brainstormed List

hot	summer	winter	rainy
cold	cool	wet	fall
spring	snowy	autumn	windy
breezy	stormy	cloudy	dark
hazy	freezing	sunny	warm
April	May	December	March
afternoon	morning		

After discussing and sharing their improved sentence with the class, she lets the children develop and improve their own introductions. The children get out their writing folders and rewrite or write an introductory sentence for one of their stories. Mrs. Strabinski uses this same technique to help the children improve their narrative writing. Other minilessons that she teaches include brainstorming location words; sound adjectives; smell adjectives; taste adjectives; touch adjectives; size, color, and shape adjectives; and interesting verbs and adverbs. All of these lessons are done for the purpose of helping children elaborate when they write.

Besides narratives, children in Mrs. Strabinski's district are expected to learn to write how-to papers. Second graders are assessed by the district at the end of the year on these two types of writing. Because writing how-to papers is new to second grade, Mrs. Strabinski uses concrete activities with the children before she even begins to teach the children how to write the paper. She uses art projects, cooking experiences, and simple experiments in class, and then she models for the children the steps involved in writing. After numerous experiences such as these, she will provide a relatively simple activity for the children to do, such as making cheese toast, and have the children practice writing their first how-to paper. She provides prompts on each section of the paper, and there is much discussion in the classroom between the children and the teacher about writing this paper. Mrs. Strabinski continues providing children with these experiences at various times throughout the year, and by the end of second grade her students have become quite good at writing how-to papers and narratives.

How does Mrs. Strabinski modify writing for both Jacob and Hannah? Although Jacob is functioning on a kindergarten level, he is still not able to write his name. Jacob's writing instruction and independent writing time consist of many opportunities for him to practice writing his name and making letters with a variety of materials. He is also encouraged to draw and write, even if it is just pretend writing. Mrs. Strabinski uses letter tiles, magnetic letters, a salt tray for tracing the letters in his name, markers, magic slates, small chalkboards, and paper and pencil as she encourages him to learn how to write his name and begin independent writing. She saved Jacob's very first writing this year. She carefully dated it and put it in his portfolio with a note explaining what Jacob said he had written. This was a paper with circular scribbles on it. She is pleased to note that now he puts a "J" on his paper for his name and that his writing is beginning to look more like letters. Because she is familiar with how children learn to draw and write, she is able to explain to Jacob's parents that he is making progress in writing.

Hannah presents a different set of problems for Mrs. Strabinski. Hannah is unable to hold a pencil and write. Mrs. Strabinski had used the computer to make a communication board for Hannah her first few days in school. She also discovered that Hannah has enough control over her hands to be able to sit at the computer and punch individual keys with the index finger on her right hand. As Hannah's reading has improved, so has her ability to spell and write. She is able to write and communicate by using one of the classroom laptops, so Mrs. Strabinski lets Hannah keep one of the laptops at her desk. Hannah uses the laptop for all her subjects. She can type answers to math problems, write, take her spelling test, and communicate with the other children and Mrs. Strabinski with the laptop. Mrs. Strabinski is thankful that she used some of the technology money last year to purchase a laptop for the classroom.

Recently, as Mrs. Strabinski was talking to Hannah's mother about a new idea she had for Hannah, Hannah's mother broke down and cried as she thanked Mrs. Strabinski for teaching Hannah to read, write, and use the computer. She said her little girl had been locked in a prison and that no one before Mrs. Strabinski had even tried to find the keys to free her. She said that Mrs. Strabinski would always have a special place in her heart because Mrs. Strabinski opened the door and gave Hannah the tools to lead a new, fuller life.

Steps to Help Children Who Are Having Difficulty Writing

Careful observations of children help the teacher decide on interventions for children who are experiencing difficulty writing. Reluctant writers are those children who realize their writing skills are not equal to the other children, have very few words that they know how to write, and are often unable to read what they wrote. The teacher needs to work with these children on a daily basis to help them acquire confidence and a writing vocabulary of high-frequency words that will improve their writing and not make it so laborious. During the daily individual conferences with these children, the teacher has them read what they wrote and immediately reinforces or teaches skills based upon their writing (Depree & Iversen, 1994).

Some children don't even know how to begin and will just sit with a blank sheet of paper in front of them. These children are a little more challenging, and the teacher also needs to work with them individually every day. Often, a teacher who asks such a child what he wants to write about is greeted with silence. The teacher can proceed in one of two directions when this happens. If the teacher knows the child is interested in animals, for example, the teacher can ask the child a question about a specific animal and then model for the child how to write a caption for a picture based on the information the child gives. The child then draws the picture to go with the caption. Or the teacher can use a picture previously drawn by the child and ask the child to tell her about the picture. The teacher can then ask the child what he would like to write about the picture. The teacher stays by the child and assists him until he has written the sentence. If the child has very limited skills, the teacher and child may cowrite the sentence. The teacher may help the child to hear the initial sounds and final sounds in the words and writes the letters that go in between. The teacher may also write the harder words in the sentence. For example, the child has a picture of a dog playing in front of a house and wants to write the sentence "A dog is playing by the house." The teacher helps the child write the sentence "A dog is *playing by* the *house.*" The child has sounded out or knows the words *a, dog, is,* and *the.* The teacher has supplied the other words for the child. When children have difficulty writing, they may become discouraged or distracted if they perceive writing as too hard, especially if they are expected to write every word in the sentence. The teacher's support helps them build their confidence and their speed, and they begin to think of themselves as writers (Depree & Iversen, 1994).

☆ MATH INSTRUCTION IN SECOND GRADE

In 1989, the National Council of Teachers of Mathematics (NCTM) published the *Curriculum and Evaluation Standards for School Mathematics.* **Standards** are statements used to judge quality and value. The Mathematics Standards are statements about what is valued and were written to help judge the quality of a mathematics curriculum (Eisenhower, 2000). These standards were developed in response to the call for reform in teaching mathematics. Before the development of these standards, traditional instruction focused primarily on rote learning and the practice of skills (Fuson, Carroll, & Drueck, 2000). This document has provided the basis for curriculum reform throughout local districts and the country. With increased understanding through research about how children learn mathematical concepts, the needs of society as technology advances and the world becomes more global have added impetus to the change in teaching mathematics (Van de Walle, 1998).

These standards were followed in 1991 by the *Professional Teaching Standards for School Mathematics* and by the *Assessment Standards for School Mathematics* in 1995, and the National Council of Teachers of Mathematics believes that these standards can help ensure that all children receive a high quality mathematics education. These standards have influenced state standards, instructional materials, and classroom practice to varying degrees (National Council of Teachers of Mathematics, 2000).

NCTM's *Principles and Standards* incorporates and builds on the previous standards as it continues to sustain the effort to improve children's school mathematics education. This document offers guidance and vision as it sets forth a comprehensive set of goals for mathematics instruction from prekindergarten through grade 12. Specific curriculum decisions are left to the local school districts. *Principles and Standards* is a resource for teachers and administrators to use in examining and improving their mathematical program. It can be used to guide the development of curriculum, instructional materials, and assessments. It also keeps dialogue ongoing at all levels about how best to teach children mathematics (National Council of Teachers of Mathematics, 2000).

Principles and Standards outlines a comprehensive and ambitious curriculum for all children in mathematics. Ten standards have been proposed. The first five describe content goals in the areas of number and operations, algebra, geometry, measurement, and data analysis and probability. Expectations are identified and discussed for each Content Standard. The next five standards describe the processes of problem solving, reasoning and proof, connections, communication, and representation, and each grade carries a description about what each Process Standard looks like at that grade level. The standards are integrated strands that support the learning of mathematical ideas, not separate topics for study (National Council of Teachers of Mathematics, 2000).

Computers and calculators are now welcomed in the classroom. People no longer fear that letting children use these aids will undermine their education. What calculators and computers have done is to allow less emphasis to be placed on low-level skills and more emphasis to be placed on higher-level thinking skills and problem solving. Guided work using calculators enables children to focus on problem solving and explore numbers and patterns. Teachers can help children in recognizing when it is more efficient to use a calculator and when to do the calculation mentally (National Council of Teachers of Mathematics, 2000).

Problem solving is seen as the primary focus of all math instruction. Children need to be presented with the opportunity to think, reason, formulate problems, and evaluate results. They also need to be able to communicate mathematical ideas to others through talking and writing, to use visual aids such as charts and graphs to explain mathematical ideas, and to interpret and use mathematical language. Reasoning should be a part of the curriculum from kindergarten through school. This means that children are expected to see and extend patterns, use logical reasoning to defend their position, and decide if an answer is correct. Children should be taught math in a way that lets them see the connections between this discipline and other academic areas. They can also see the connections within mathematics— for example, between addition and subtraction, multiplication and division. In this way, math is seen as relevant and meaningful. Children learn mathematics through "doing math," and they construct meaning as they engage in math in a problem-solving environment (Van de Walle, 1998).

These standards have not been welcomed and accepted by everyone, however. As with the great debate over phonics or whole language, there is now debate over use of the NCTM standards versus the traditional approach to teaching mathematics. Traditionalists are skeptical that children will be able to discover, or construct, knowledge without a strong focus on teacher-led instruction. Supporters of the standards accuse the traditionalists of having a simplistic view of constructivism. They point out that children construct this knowledge through experiences with manipulatives and reflections lead the children to understand the abstract. Traditionalists point to all the failed math reforms of the last century, such as the New Math movement in the 1950s and 1960s, and see the standards as a repeat of history. Reformers point to research that shows that most children do not understand the material, even if they are able to work problems and come up with correct answers. In today's world there is an ever-increasing need for math skills as science and technology proliferate.

Although research can be cited to support either position, one concern that has merit is the finding that classroom teachers themselves have a lack of the content knowledge necessary to be effective teachers of mathematics (Loveless, 2001). The debate over the standards will continue to rage. If this conflict mirrors the reading "war," then the best approach for teaching mathematics is one that incorporates both approaches.

Standards-Based Curriculum

In an effort to reform the curriculum taught in the public schools this past decade, the term *standards based* has evolved. Standards in each curriculum area have been written by many national groups and incorporated into some curriculum materials. There is controversy, however, over just what is meant by standards and how the use of standards-based materials differs from traditional methods of teaching. Curriculum reform has been concerned with the inclusion of more than just knowledge and

State by State

Pennsylvania's Academic Standards for Mathematics

The state of **Pennsylvania** has developed academic standards for several subject areas, one of which is mathematics. While the standards are only listed beginning with third grade, it is obvious that earlier grades must do their part if children are to successfully master the standards in grades 3, 5, 8, and 11. The standards are broken down into 11 different categories ranging from numbers, number systems, and number relationships to concepts of calculus. The following are examples from their Academic Standards for Mathematics for grade 3.

2.1 *Numbers, Number Systems, and Number Relationships*
> 2.1.3.A   Count using whole numbers (to 10,000) and by 2s, 3s, 5s, 10s, 25s, and 100s.

2.2 *Computation and Estimation*
> 2.2.3.G   Explain addition and subtraction algorithms with regrouping.

2.3 *Measurement and Estimation*
> 2.3.3.A   Compare measurable characteristics of different objects on the same dimensions (e.g., time, temperature, area, length, weight, capacity, perimeter).

2.6 *Statistics and Data Analysis*
> 2.6.3.D   Form and justify an opinion on whether a given statement is reasonable based on a comparison to data (Pennsylvania Academic Standards for Mathematics).

skills components that predominate in traditional curriculum materials. Reform focuses on the addition of understandings and processes as well as knowledge and skills that constitute competency in a field (Trafton, Reys, & Wasman, 2001).

Trafton, Reys, and Wasman (2001) describe six central characteristics of standards-based mathematical materials. The first characteristic is that they are comprehensive and focus on a core that applies to all students. The core prepares students for the workforce as well as for continued advanced study of mathematics. The second characteristic is coherence. Coherence is promoted through an initial emphasis on core ideas so children see the subject as an integrated whole. These core ideas then provide the anchor for connections and links to related ideas and applications. The third characteristic is the development of ideas in depth. Core ideas are developed at differing levels of depth, depending upon the maturity of the children. These ideas are introduced early in a child's schooling and are revisited throughout the grades with deeper depth and sophistication. The fourth characteristic promotes sense making. Children are able to learn, understand, and use information in new situations that are based on their previous experiences.

The fifth characteristic is engagement of children. This means more than hands-on activities. The focus is rather on intellectual engagement of the children. The work arouses the curiosity of the children, is interesting and within their reach.

Physical engagement is important and stress is placed on the use of manipulatives and active learning. The classroom encourages exploration and risk taking. The sixth and last characteristic is motivation. Traditional curriculum materials do include a few application problems, whereas in standards-based materials applications are often the focus of the work. The children are able to see that knowledge is not the only goal, but that knowledge can be used as a tool for solving problems. Standards-based instruction represents a substantial change in the way instruction occurs in the classroom and requires a different curriculum and a very different classroom environment from much of current practice.

Mrs. Strabinski's district is very concerned that children become problem solvers. Mrs. Strabinski knows that problem solving is not limited to math. Many times during the school day the children are presented with opportunities to develop problem-solving skills. These problems might occur on the playground during recess, in the computer lab as the children try to figure out a problem with the computer, or working with puzzles or the Erector set. The basis of all problem solving, wherever it is found, is to understand and solve the problem. Once the problem is understood, then the child can make plans for solving it. These plans are then implemented and evaluated. Children will frequently use strategies like Guess and Check: The child makes a guess, tries it, and if it fails, tries something else. Helping children understand why a solution didn't work helps them become better problem solvers. Teachers can support the children by asking questions that promote reasoning. Some questions that the teacher might want to ask are the following:

- Are you sure . . . ?
- How do you know . . . ?
- What else can you find that works like this?
- What if . . .
- I wonder why . . . (Copley, 2000, p. 37)

Mrs. Strabinski employs several techniques with her children to enhance their problem-solving ability. She begins by using real-life examples that have meaning for her children and allows them to act out the solution. She does not teach the children to look for key words such as *more than* or *less than*, but she teaches them to think about what is happening and to convert it into a situation where they can use manipulatives (Tucker, Singleton, & Weaver, 2002). This starts at a concrete level. The children are able to "see" the problem, and often the solution becomes evident. They may actually act out the problem as they try to understand it. After many opportunities involving acting, Mrs. Strabinski moves to the use of manipulatives to represent the different parts of the problem. The children can explain the problem to one another using manipulatives in both the explanation of the problem and in figuring out the solution. They can work with partners to discuss and explain a problem, and they can explain it to the teacher when the teacher states that he or she doesn't understand the problem (Tucker, Singleton, & Weaver, 2002). Mrs. Strabinski's next step is to have the children draw a picture or some sort of representation of the problem and the solution. She makes sure to use both examples—when to add and when not to add—in order to teach children to think about the problem before deciding on the appropriate operation. She began using this method last year after attending a workshop on problem solving and has found it to be very effective.

Although these skills are sometimes introduced in first grade, second grade is the level at which children are held accountable for learning how to do addition and subtraction problems with regrouping. Mrs. Strabinski takes the time to explain to her children's parents that regrouping is the same thing they used to call "carrying" or "borrowing." In introducing the concept of regrouping in addition, she makes use of many manipulatives such as snap cubes and base ten blocks. The children are given numerous experiences with place value activities before actually seeing problems written on a worksheet. These activities allow the children to understand the concept before they attempt to do a written problem.

Jacob's IEP states that he will learn to count objects to 10, recognize the numerals from 1 to 10, and write the numerals from 1 to 10. Mrs. Strabinski makes use of the same manipulatives that the other children are using. She makes several learning games that he can play by himself or with others that involve counting and numeral recognition. She uses peer tutors with him to help reinforce his counting. Mrs. Strabinski has Jacob and his peer tutor count out the unit blocks into groups of 10s for the activity she plans to do on place value. Jacob gives each child two groups of 10s (20 blocks). When the children are doing their math problems on paper, Jacob is practicing writing his numbers from 1 to 10. Mrs. Strabinski also has him count different groups of objects and record the number on a Post-It note. She made up a game called "Clear the Desk" that she has taught Jacob and the other students. Number cards from 1 to 10 are dealt out to the players. The teacher or another student draws numbers from another set of cards and calls out the number. The children check their desks for the number called. The child with the number removes it from his desk. The first child to "clear the desk" is the winner (adapted from Lasater, Johnson, Fitzgerald, & Simpson, 1999). She also works with Jacob on counting and his writing of numerals, and uses a computer to reinforce his learning of numbers and counting. Jacob enjoys using the computer and the other children also enjoy participating in the counting games.

Hannah, because of her lack of fine-motor skills and speech, is part of a three-person team. She listens as the children talk and discuss the problems and act them out. Her job in the group is to write the problem showing the numerals and the correct operation, and she uses the computer to do this. Mrs. Strabinski also types, or has an aide type, math problems on Hannah's computer. Instead of writing the answers, Hannah simply types in the answers on her computer and prints out the page. At first, Mrs. Strabinski was modifying the amount of work that Hannah did because she was not familiar with addition. Now Hannah has become quite good at addition and quickly finishes her work.

When children finish their work in class, they can go to the Math Center, which contains many different types of math-related activities. Hannah can't do the puzzles, pattern blocks, geoboards, or some of the other activities, but she can play the board games with the assistance of the other children. She is always looking for someone to play *Sorry*™ with her. She is also able to use the various computer programs, either independently or with another child. Her new IEP states that she will learn to do simple addition and subtraction problems. She has already mastered all the objectives in reading and math that are on the new IEP that was developed shortly after she came to Jeter Street Elementary. Mrs. Strabinski is delighted and has made arrangements with Hannah's parents and the other members of the ARD committee to develop a new IEP for Hannah. This will be her second IEP in less than six months!

Mrs. Strabinski uses a mixture of cooperative grouping, partners, and individual work in her classroom. She is always looking for innovative ways to integrate several subjects into meaningful activities for the children. One activity that she uses every year that the children find especially enjoyable incorporates math, science, and reading. This is her *Three Billy Goats Gruff Project* (Burk, Snider, & Symonds, 1992). Activities cover a two-week period. The children read several versions of the story of *Three Billy Goats Gruff*. They read books written from the troll's point of view. They use a Venn diagram to compare different versions. They graph individual children's choice of favorite versions and compare the results. Mrs. Strabinski has them design a troll they can make from a toilet paper tube, chenelle sticks, google eyes, buttons, ribbon, felt, tissue paper, and any other small items that can be glued onto the tube. Once Mrs. Strabinski has decided on the materials that are available, she sets up a store in the classroom and asks a parent to volunteer as the Store Clerk. The children are each given 25¢ to spend at the store. Before they can go to the store, however, they must design and plan their troll on paper, then figure up the cost of the materials and how much change they will receive back. After doing this, they go to the store, purchase their materials, and make their troll. (See Figure 8.2)

◎◎ **Dimensions of Diversity** ◎◎

Meeting Diverse Needs

Research shows that girls and boys basically start on a par with similar math ability when first beginning school. Somewhere during their schooling, however, many girls lose their confidence in their ability to do math and fewer pursue upper-level math courses in high school. As a result, there are far fewer women than men in math-related careers such as science and technology. How can the early childhood teacher encourage a child's interest in math?

- Have a positive attitude toward math and let the children see all the ways math is used in daily life.
- Structure math activities so children will be successful.
- Give boys and girls equal turns and turns of equal length.
- Provide attention and encouragement to all children.
- Use mixed-sex groupings and encourage the children to help each other; especially encourage the girls to help the boys.
- Talk about women who have careers in math, science, and technology and have books that portray women in these careers.
- Encourage parents to value math ability in their girls as much as in their boys. (Copley, 2000)

Other activities they engage in include writing a history for their troll and describing its family and life before its encounter with the Billy Goats Gruff. They will also design a story map of the river and the two grassy areas on a large piece of paper to meet the dimensions given to them by the teacher. For example, the river must be 6 inches across at the widest part. The story map is used when the children design a bridge to span the river at its widest point.

The day after they make their story maps, the children are divided into small groups. Each group is given three round rocks that represent the three Billy Goats. The children weigh and order their rocks from lightest to heaviest. The rocks may be decorated to resemble the Billy Goats. Using a small amount of modeling clay, toothpicks, and a strip from a manila folder approximately 2 inches by 7 inches, they plan and design a bridge that crosses the river on their story map at its widest part. The bridge must be at least 1 inch in height and capable of supporting Mrs. Strabinski's super Billy Goat (the largest rock of all). The children are to use their heaviest "goat" to test their construction before they are ready to try super Billy Goat.

When the children have designed and built their bridge, Mrs. Strabinski places her Billy Goat on it. If it holds, the children have been successful. Usually the bridge collapses and the children will have to try another method of construction. When the children run out of ideas, Mrs. Strabinski gives them a hint by telling them to think about connecting round pieces of clay with the toothpicks in a crisscross pattern.

FIGURE 8.2 Troll Material List

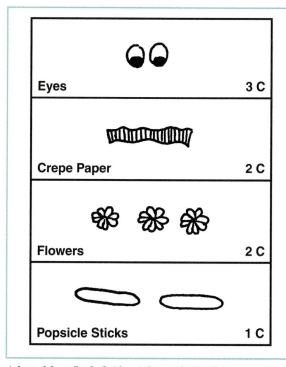
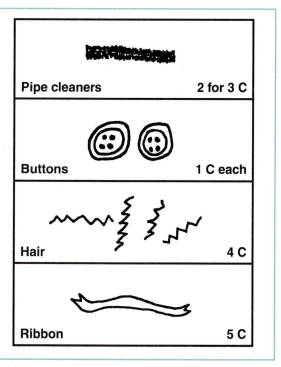

Adapted from Burk, Snider, & Symonds (1992). Form and Artwork by Lauren J. Grein.

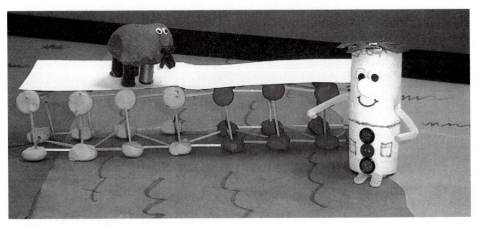

Children can learn to plan, measure, create, and problem-solve while engaging in learning activities. (Artwork by Lauren J. Grein.)

As the children work on the various activities in this unit, they are measuring, weighing, designing, creating, problem solving, collaborating, adding, subtracting, making change, drawing, reading, and writing.

☆ TEACHING SOCIAL STUDIES IN SECOND GRADE

In 1992 social studies was defined by the National Council for the Social Studies (NCSS) as "the integrated study of the social sciences and humanities to promote civic competence" (p. 1). Social studies in the elementary school combines many disciplines such as archeology, economics, geography, history, sociology, religion, the humanities, and natural sciences. The main purpose for studying social studies is to help children become good citizens and be able to function in a democratic society in an increasingly complex world (National Council for the Social Studies, 1996).

The Social Studies Standards are thematically based and organized around ten themes:

    I. Culture
   II. Time, Continuity, and Change
  III. People, Places, and Environments
  IV. Individual Development and Identity
   V. Individuals, Groups, and Institutions
  VI. Power, Authority, and Governance
 VII. Production, Distribution, and Consumption
VIII. Science, Technology, and Society
  IX. Global Connections
   X. Civic Ideals and Practices

The themes are interdisciplinary and interrelated. For example, to understand culture, children need to understand people, places, and environments; civic ideals and practices; and time, continuity, and change (National Council for the Social Studies, 1996). Knowledge is constructed by the children as they engage in the integrated study of the social sciences. The children learn to use certain essential skills for acquiring information and constructing new knowledge. These skills include reading comprehension, study skills, reference and information search skills, technical skills, thinking skills, decision-making skills, personal skills, group interaction skills, and social and political participation skills (Expectations of Excellence, 1994).

The purpose of the standards is threefold: to serve as a framework for social studies design, to guide teachers in designing instruction by providing examples of classroom practice, and to provide performance expectations to guide curriculum decisions. These standards help address the content themes that are essential at each grade level. They also define student performance at early, middle, and high school levels, and they help students become citizens who can address pertinent issues and promote civic ideals and practices (National Council for the Social Studies, 1996).

Examples of the use of the standards from the National Council for the Social Studies' *Expectations of Excellence* (1994) are given for early grades, middle grades, and high school. Theme V's example is for second grade. Theme V deals with Individuals, Groups, and Institutions, and in the example the children brainstorm issues of concern for their community. Then they work in small groups and address one of those issues. They determine if there are any organizations in the community dealing with their issue and they investigate any recent activities conducted by that organization. Each group reports back to the class and the class then chooses three or four organizations in which they are particularly interested. The children develop proposals suggesting ways that they can contribute to these organizations and present their proposals to the organizations. The children keep individual journals of their activities as they become personally involved. Their journals are evaluated for accurateness of information, clarity of writing, and thoroughness.

Many different entities have joined the bandwagon and written standards for different disciplines. Individual states have either written their own standards or modified standards from another organization. Even the U.S. Department of Defense Education Agency (DoDEA) has published standards (U.S. Dept. of Defense Education Agency, 2001). Their standards for social studies also have ten themes, and eight of the themes even carry the same titles as the standards developed by the National Council for the Social Studies (NCSS). Even the themes that carry different titles seem to address the same topics. The DoDEA's theme of Citizenship is described in terms similar to Civic Ideals and Practices from NCSS, and Space and Place of the DoDEA's standards is part of the People, Places, and Environments of the NCSS.

The purpose of social studies instruction is to engage children in experiences that increase their understanding of the different concepts and skills addressed in the social studies curriculum. Actively engaging children increases their motivation, helps them develop skills, and enhances the learning of all students of all ability levels. One unique strategy that incorporates active learning is **spatial dynamics.** Students engaging in spatial dynamics create large-scale models that allow them to participate in learning. The use of spatial dynamics also enhances the learning of children whose preferred learning style is tactile or kinesthetic (Siler, 1998).

Using this approach in a second-grade classroom means that the teacher would study the curriculum and determine which information could be enhanced by this type of presentation. One topic studied in second grade is that of the Native Americans and the arrival of the Europeans. The classroom can be set up to represent Europe and the New World. Children research and add features to this construction, and the teacher uses their construction to talk to them about the coming of the Europeans and the impact of this on the Native Americans. When the teacher is trying to explain about neighborhoods and the community, the classroom can be arranged as a neighborhood with streets and shops. When the teacher is trying to explain about economics and trade and transportation of goods, setting the room up as a distribution center aids in their understanding of these concepts.

Another type of spatial dynamics involves using models. The teacher may save soft drink flats and have the children construct a Native American village on the flat. Depending on the tribe being studied, the children may construct teepees or hogans or lodges. The children can build campfires out of sticks collected on the playground and add other details that tell about life in the village. In studying their state, they can use the flat, trace a large outline of their state, and add geological features to the state by using clay, playdough, or plaster. Salt dough is easy to make and can be allowed to harden and then painted the appropriate color for the mountains or lakes.

Whatever type of spatial dynamics is used, the teacher can use the children's own work to explain, elaborate, and interest the children in the topic under study. Obviously, spatial dynamics requires more time than reading a chapter in the book about the topic, but the level of understanding and the ability of the children to remember the material make it a very attractive and interesting way to teach them, and so it is an excellent use of instructional time (Siler, 1998).

In the early childhood classroom, social studies is often constructed around themes or units and can be integrated across several disciplines as the children study a topic. A unit on the weather might involve science, math, and language arts skills in addition to studying appropriate dress for the weather and types of weather. Use of the Internet allows children access to a wide variety of materials. Eyewitness accounts of major events can be found where the children can listen to words written hundreds of years ago by someone who actually witnessed an event. These words are recorded as a clip on the Internet and read with expression by an actor or announcer. Children believe that they are hearing about an event that just happened when they listen to an eyewitness account of the hardships suffered by the first settlers during the winter months.

There are also virtual field trips available that include visits to the White House, trips to museums, and even tours of the Egyptian pyramids. After viewing virtual field trips, the children can actually participate in making their own virtual field trip. By using a digital camera or camcorder, the children can offer a virtual trip of their school, classroom, or some local site (Risinger, 1999).

Though few modifications and accommodations need to be made for Hannah in the area of social studies, Jacob is another matter. Because Jacob is functioning on a kindergarten level, the major portion of the social studies lessons are inappropriate for him. Mrs. Strabinski has made modifications for him. When the class was studying maps and the compass rose, Jacob was constructing a model of the classroom using the Lego blocks. When the class was studying trade and the cost and transportation of goods, Jacob was learning the names of coins (pennies, nickels, dimes, and quarters) and was practicing sorting the coins into groups. And when the class was studying the effects of the weather on the environment, Jacob was studying about rain, wind, ice, and snow. He learned what to wear when going outside and the vocabulary associated with these weather words.

★ Working with Parents

When children with special needs are included in the general education classroom, parents may have concerns about the quality of the education that their child is receiving and how well their child is fitting into the classroom. Parents will be concerned that their child may be excluded by the other children, or made fun of because of the child's disability. The teacher needs to help assuage the parents' fear. One way to do this is to keep a record of the child's behavior and interactions within the classroom and share these with the parents on a regular basis. The teacher begins by making a brainstormed list of behaviors that describe the interactions within the classroom and with other children. This list contains statements such as "works cooperatively in a group," or "plays with other children during recess." Sharing this type of information, in addition to academic information about the child, gives the parents a truer picture of their child and how their child is doing in the classroom. It also alerts the teacher to social problems that might need to be addressed. For example, the teacher notices that a child is isolated at lunch. No one wants to sit beside him. After the teacher notes this, she then tries to determine the reason that the other children are behaving in this manner. The cause of the problem may be a lack of appropriate social behavior on the part of the child with special needs, who may be reaching over and eating the other children's lunches, or chewing and talking with his mouth open, or doing some other behavior that the other children find offensive. Once the teacher has determined what the problem is, she can begin to intervene and teach the child the appropriate behavior.

Observations are done both in structured situations, such as working in a cooperative group, as well as in unstructured settings, such as free choice center time. Parents are concerned about the emotional well-being of their child as they are about academic gains. Teachers need to plan for and communicate to the parent the child's progress in both areas.

☆ TRANSIENT CHILDREN AND EDUCATION

Transient children are those who move from school to school. The reasons for this constant movement vary from moving because the rent is due to divorce to foster care to following the crops. Although schools are not being held accountable for the test scores of children who have been in their school for less than 120 days, these children are often at risk for delays in growth and development, 35 percent more likely to fail a grade, 77 percent more likely to have behavior problems, more likely

Issues and Trends

Magnet Schools

In the late 1960s, with the legally enforced desegregation of U.S. public schools, school administration began seeking a way to encourage parents to volunteer to have their children bused instead of forced busing for desegregation purposes and thereby reduce racial isolation. McCarver in Tacoma, Washington, in 1968 was the first school of its kind in the nation to attempt to reduce segregation by having parents choose to send their children to the school. The school offered continuous progress for students at their own pace. These first schools were called "alternatives," not magnet schools, and they were organized to guarantee continuous progress in education and offered an alternative to regular public education.

In 1971 a high school in Dallas, Texas, opened that was designed around career strands, attracting students from all racial backgrounds and socioeconomic levels. It even offered classes for adults in the evenings.

The term *magnet* may have come from a school that was opened in Houston, Texas, in 1975 that focused on the visual and performing arts, because it was reported that the school seemed to work like a magnet in attracting children. The term became used in 1975 to describe types of schools that received fiscal assistance from the federal government.

Magnet schools today still reduce racial isolation but are considered a superior choice for a child even in districts that are not ethnically diverse. Children choose these schools based on their interests (Waldrip, 2000).

Magnet schools have not gone uncriticized. It has been charged that districts use magnet schools as a veneer of desegregation that actually leaves the majority of minority students worse off than before. Nonvoluntary teachers in a magnet school may find that they have to alter their teaching style to fit the program. Teachers may also find that the principal takes a stronger, firmer hand in running the school, which can lead to teacher dissatisfaction (Klauke, 1988).

---

to fail to graduate from high school, and frequently to have more personal problems than do other children. Some schools reporting lower test scores also report high rates of mobility of the children. It appears that this constant moving hinders children's educational progress (Bainbridge, 2003).

☆ SUMMARY

Teachers will continue to be expected to teach children with special needs in inclusive settings, and so it becomes important to understand not only the course material, but how to make modifications for these children in the general education classroom. Using cooperative grouping in the classroom allows all children to be included. Children in second grade are at many different levels in reading, and teachers have to provide instruction that is appropriate for each level. Teachers can use mathematics and social studies standards to help ensure that the children will be prepared for life after school. Because these standards offer more hands-on learning, using them helps children to have a better understanding of concepts. When teachers use manipulatives and models during instruction, teaching becomes more effective and children gain a deeper understanding of the material.

⭐ DISCUSSION QUESTIONS

1. Discuss the factors that are important for inclusion to be successful.
2. What are the four learning styles that apply to the field of education, and what are the characteristics of each style?
3. Discuss the controversy over the National Reading Panel's report.
4. What is NAEYC's position on reading and writing?
5. Discuss standards-based curriculum and instruction as it applies to both mathematics and social studies.

⭐ SUGGESTED CHAPTER ACTIVITIES

1. Interview a second-grade teacher in a district near you about his or her school's reading instruction program. Ask about guided oral reading, silent reading, phonemic awareness training, and comprehension skills instruction.
2. Visit an inclusion classroom. Observe the modifications that the teacher makes. Interview the teacher and ask the teacher how he or she feels about inclusion. Ask about the number and type of children with special needs, the support provided by the school and the district, and the time allotted by the school for planning.
3. Use a math lesson from a second-grade book. How would you make modifications for children who are gifted? How would you modify for children with moderate cognitive disabilities? Can they do the same task, or do you need to have a different task?
4. Go online, find the website for the National Council of Teachers of Mathematics, and print a copy of their Number and Operation Standard and Problem Solving Standard for Grades Pre-K–2. Using these standards, plan a math lesson for second grade.
5. Using a second-grade social studies book or topic, plan a spatial dynamic lesson for one of the topics. List what skills will be taught, how the skills will be taught, and what the children will be expected to learn.
6. Make a listing of virtual field trips and their addresses that are available on the Internet.

⭐ WEBSITES

National Council for the Social Studies (www.socialstudies.org)
National Council of Teachers of Mathematics Standards (www.standards. nctm.org/document/chapter4/numb.htm)

Chapter Nine

Teaching in a Third-Grade Classroom

CHAPTER OVERVIEW

★ How is the third grade different from second grade?

★ How are reading and writing taught in third grade?

★ Do standards exist for science?

★ How do you prepare children for state-mandated testing?

★ Math and science are key components of the third grade. What are some of the skills typically taught in each?

THIS CHAPTER WILL ANSWER THESE QUESTIONS.

While 6- through 8-year-olds are usually grouped together under general characteristics, third-grade teachers notice definite differences between children in second and third grades. Eight-year-olds are very independent and can work for longer periods of time by themselves on classroom projects. They begin to enjoy board games and other games with rules. Their writing is smaller, and they use regular notebook paper and have the fine-motor control to learn to write in cursive. Their thought processes have become more logical, and most have progressed into Piaget's concrete operational stage. This is the stage where they understand that changes in appearance do not constitute a change in amount. They are able to "conserve." They understand that pouring a liquid from a tall glass into a short glass does not change the amount of the liquid. Though it may look like there is more liquid in the tall glass, only the appearance has been changed because nothing has been added or taken away.

Socially, 8-year-olds can attend to more cues in a situation, such as facial or body expressions, in interpreting the feelings of another. The emotions of pride and guilt are governed by the child's personal responsibility and a parent or teacher does not have to be present for the child to experience these. Self-esteem becomes more realistic, and children are able to describe themselves in terms of character traits such as being honest, short-tempered, or friendly. They can also understand how someone can experience two different emotions at the same time, such as being happy and sad. They can be happy that they got a present, but sad or disappointed that it wasn't what they wanted (Berk, 1999).

In the classroom, teachers notice that 8-year-olds are able to use memory strategies and have improved attention spans. They use number concepts to master more difficult mathematical skills, and they use reading to learn new knowledge about topics and subjects of interest. Vocabulary rapidly increases, and 8-year-olds have developed the ability to give clear directions (Berk, 1999).

Ms. Chang has taught third grade for 10 years at Carver Elementary. Carver Elementary is located in a rural area with a local population of approximately 19,000. Children are bused into Carver from the surrounding areas, with some children spending up to one and a half hours on the bus each way. The majority of the children come from lower socioeconomic homes. Many live on farms or outside the city limits. The class consists of a mixture of children who are white, black, and Hispanic, with some migrant children. The migrant children's parents follow the crops from season to season and Ms. Chang can expect these children to move to another school later in the school year.

In Ms. Chang's state, all children will take a state-mandated test that assesses the children's math and reading ability. The state rates schools by the children's performance and the results are published in the local newspaper. Principals are under pressure to meet the required percentage-passing rate, and third-grade teachers feel pressure to find ways to help all the children have a successful year—which translates, according to administrators, into passing the test.

☆ WHAT THIRD GRADERS ARE EXPECTED TO LEARN

The foundation for many new academic skills that children will need in the years to come is laid in third grade. All the academic areas suddenly include many more skills and new knowledge to be mastered. The ability to read and write becomes critical for the completion of assignments. Mathematical skills increase in complexity, and children are exposed to new and more advanced content in science. Each of these areas, with the skills and knowledge required, is defined here.

Reading

Whether teachers use basal materials or a more integrated approach to reading, the same basic skills are expected to be taught in third grade. The basal program provides the teacher with lessons for the specific skills to be taught, and most basals now use good literature collected in books that look more like anthologies than the traditional, older versions of basals that included controlled vocabulary. The basal should not be the only type of reading instruction offered, however. Third graders are certainly ready for chapter books and books related to themes or topics being studied in class.

Reading skills typically taught in third grade are:

- Sequencing events in a story
- Drawing conclusions based on information in a story or paragraph
- Identification of cause and effect
- Main idea and supporting details
- Identifying the author's purpose in writing
- Identification of characters in a story and analysis of the characters and their actions
- Listening skills
- Speaking skills, including delivering a speech, telling a story
- Understanding another's point of view
- Identifying parts of a book
- Locating information using graphs, charts, tables, and other reference resources
- Identifying the different types of writing—plays, poems, narratives, folktales, fables, periodicals, fiction, nonfiction
- Identifying the parts of a story—setting, characters, plot, solution
- Making predictions based on information read
- Listening and following directions
- Using context clues as an aid in deciphering unfamiliar words
- Comparing and contrasting different stories, characters (Afflerbach, Beers, Blachowicz, Boyd, Diffily, Gaunty-Porter, Harris, Leu, McClanahan, Monson, Perez, Sebeste, & Wixson, 2000)

Writing and Language Arts

In third grade, writing and language arts skills also are taught more in depth. Writing becomes more refined, and children are expected to compose not only narratives and how-to papers, but also compare-and-contrast papers as well as persuasive pieces. Children are expected to spend more time using the writing process—prewriting, writing, proofreading, and publishing their work. The specific writing and language arts skills taught in third grade are:

- Types of sentences (statements, questions, commands, explanatory)
- Punctuation
- Nouns (singular, plural, possessive, common, proper)
- Subjects and predicates
- Abbreviations
- Compound and complex words
- Verbs (regular, irregular, past, present, future tense)
- Contractions
- Prefixes and suffixes
- Adjectives and articles
- Pronouns
- Adverbs (McCallum, Strong, Thoburn, & Williams, 1990)

Children enjoy sharing what they write.

Spelling

Spelling skills in third grade focus on more complex phonic skills, generally patterns in words. These skills are:

- Blends
- Digraphs
- Long vowels and variant vowel combinations
- Contractions and compound words
- Base words and endings
- Changing final *y* to *i* and adding *-es*
- Synonyms
- Word patterns
- Multiple meanings (Hackney & Lucas, 1998)

Mathematics

Whereas math skills in second grade consisted of mainly expanding and refining skills learned in first grade, with the addition of regrouping skills, the third grade adds new math skills to be mastered, such as multiplication and division. The specific math skills taught in third grade are:

- Place value through 999,999 (read, write, compare, and order whole numbers)
- Money

- Fractions (naming, writing, comparing, estimating)
- Addition and subtraction problems involving whole numbers through 999
- Learn and apply multiplication facts through 10s
- Division
- Geometric patterns
- Solids and shapes
- Measurement (including metric)—capacity, weight, temperature
- Time
- Perimeter
- Area
- Volume
- Problem solving (Charles, Barnett, Briars, Crown, Johnson, Leinwand, Van de Walle, Allan, Cooley, Elliott, Ling, Ramirez, Renfro, & Thompson, 1999).

Science

Many science skills are taught through the various topics that occur in the third-grade curriculum. These general units are life science, physical science, earth science, and the human body. Life science includes the world of plants, the world of animals, life cycles of animals, and environments where animals and plants live. Physical science includes measuring matter, simple machines, and sound and light. Earth science includes the moon, the earth and its resources, and measuring weather. The human body includes the senses and choosing foods wisely. The ability to read maps, charts, graphs, and tables are also part of the curriculum. Other skills addressed through the science curriculum are:

- Investigation through experiments, hypotheses
- Observation
- Collecting and interpreting data
- Classifying
- Predicting
- Controlling variables
- Designing and constructing a model (Charles, Barnett, Briars, Crown, Johnson, Leinwand, Van de Walle, Allan, Cooley, Elliott, Ling, Ramirez, Renfro, & Thompson, 1999).

⭐ ORGANIZING THE CLASSROOM

Most third-grade classrooms are supplied with individual student desks. How the teacher arranges these desks depends upon his or her own philosophy about children and learning. Desks may be arranged in traditional rows or may be pushed together to form a table. The table arrangement allows children to work in cooperative groups more easily but may make it harder for individual children who have an attention problem, or are very social, to focus on the instruction that the teacher provides at the board or overhead. However the desks are arranged, all children need to have a clear view of the board or overhead.

Learning centers remain appropriate for the third-grade classroom. These centers mirror, to a great extent, the ones listed in Chapter 7 for first grade, but they are more complex. The Writing Center may include specific tasks such as writing advertisements and/or descriptions for a favorite toy, writing a letter to a pen pal, or writing a paper or article for publication in the classroom newspaper. Contents and activities in all these centers will be driven by the skills that the children are expected to learn in third grade. Teachers can review the skills listed in their grade-level material (also listed in the section on what children need to know in this chapter) in planning activities for the various learning centers.

The majority of third-grade classrooms contain at least one computer. The teacher can decide if the computer will function as another center or just how it will be used. If it is connected to the Internet, the computer can be used as a research tool as the children learn about different science and social studies topics. The children may also use the computer to publish a piece that they have taken through the writing process.

Other noticeable differences in the third-grade classroom, as compared to the earlier grades, are:

- Cursive alphabet displayed on the wall
- More chapter books in the Reading Center
- Nondisposable textbooks for math
- Regular notebook paper
- Class set of calculators
- Electronic keyboards for learning typing skills to use with the computer
- Posters that address academic skills such as punctuation and multiplication
- Longer periods of time spent on independent work such as reading and writing
- Increased amount of homework

⭐ THIRD GRADE AND READING INSTRUCTION

Teachers tend to teach reading to third-grade children in a whole-group or whole-class mode. The teachers may use the basal, with its preplanned lessons, for reading instruction, or they may decide to use trade books in their reading instruction, or some combination of the two. When trade books are used, they must be analyzed before the reading lesson to determine teaching points and skills that can be taught with the specific book. These teaching points and skills, such as point of view or inference (for example), are often taught to the children in minilessons and then reinforced, as needed, in small groups. Small groups of children can work with the teacher and reread the story as they work on specific reading strategies such as word-attack skills.

Generally, the children engage in some type of independent writing after the reading. It may be as simple as writing in a response log or as complicated as rewriting the story and changing some element of the story, such as the characters or the setting (Combs, 2002). The teacher may employ one of several methods when the children read this way. He or she may ask the children to read silently and then discuss what was read; they may read the selection chorally; they may read portions aloud on an individual basis; or they may share the reading with the teacher.

Using a class set of chapter books, the teacher can also do book studies. During third grade, children will begin making the transition from picture books to chapter books. As they make this transition, it is helpful if the teacher uses whole-class shared reading and moves from reading aloud to reading along. Chapter books help introduce children to high-quality literature and will, hopefully, lead to a life-long love of reading.

At first, the children read along, either orally or silently, as the teacher reads the chapter aloud. The teacher calls attention to specific points in the chapter. These points may deal with new vocabulary, new concepts, or new strategies for comprehension. Children then meet in small groups to discuss the story. Of course, the teacher has already prepared them for this activity by working with the children and teaching them how to discuss the book (Combs, 2002).

In Ms. Chang's class this year, as every year, she has a wide range of abilities and reading levels. She already knows that the basal and other grade-level reading materials are too hard for her students who are still reading on a first-grade level and too easy for her students who are reading on a fourth- or fifth-grade level. Fortunately, the company that supplied the basal readers also has supplied leveled books for children who are above or below grade level. In addition, the school also has purchased reading material on several different levels. This will allow Ms. Chang to meet the needs of all her children.

As Ms. Chang plans her schedule for each day, she includes small guided reading groups (see Chapter 8 for more information on guided reading). All children can participate in the whole-class book studies, but the guided reading groups are composed of students reading on close to the same level. For the readers who are behind, Ms. Chang plans to meet their guided reading group every day. This intensive instruction period helps these children make the progress they need to catch up to the other children. The average children will also receive guided reading, using the story that the class is reading as a whole. Ms. Chang will meet with this group at least three days a week.

Recognizing the needs of the advanced children in her class, Ms. Chang gives them the opportunity to study and read more advanced materials. She plans to meet with this group two days a week. This group is more independent than the other groups and, with training, they can actually meet every day. Three of those days the children meet by themselves to read and discuss the book. The other two days Ms. Chang meets with their group and introduces them to new ideas, concepts, and vocabulary related to the book.

Ms. Chang also uses units in her classroom to integrate reading, writing, math, and science. One of Ms. Chang's favorite units is her unit on chocolate. The children read books such as *Chocolate-Covered Ants* (1990) by Stephen Manes and *Chocolate Fever* (1978) by Robert Kimmel Smith. In *Chocolate Fever*, the main character, Henry Green, loves chocolate so much and eats so much chocolate that he breaks out in spots all over his body. These spots smell like chocolate. Using this book as the starting point for her unit on chocolate, Ms. Chang uses many activities that incorporate science, math, and art skills with language arts. During one activity the children, after observing several different candy bars, are blindfolded and taste small pieces of the candy bars. Using only their senses of smell, touch, and taste, they try to determine what kind of candy they are eating (Instructional Fair, 1988).

During this week the children use the chocolate theme in several areas of the curriculum. As another activity in working with alphabetical order, the teacher has them brainstorm all the brands of candy bars they can think of and then put them in alphabetical order. Using the information they gained from tasting the candy bars, the children create graphs using the candy bars and record their favorite candy bar. Another day they use skills of measuring and following directions when they follow a recipe and make no-bake chocolate cookies in class.

During writing they make a book and decorate it to look like their favorite type of cookie and write a story based on that cookie. Several children make their books look like a chocolate chip cookie. Others write poems in the shape of a chocolate kiss (Teacher Created Materials, 1987). Some of the children are interested in the Hershey Corporation after Ms. Chang tells them that the streetlights in Hershey, Pennsylvania, are shaped like chocolate kisses. They decide to write letters to the Hershey Corporation and inquire about the process of making chocolate. Ms. Chang also uses the chocolate topic as a springboard to social studies. The children learn where and when chocolate was first used. This discussion leads to increased interest in the archeology of South America and the Inca and Aztec civilizations.

Ms. Chang thoroughly enjoyed teaching her chocolate unit, and she felt that the children's learning was enhanced. They have been asking her to do another unit because this one was so much fun. According to one of Ms. Chang's publications from NAEYC, integrating the curriculum is strongly supported in light of current brain research. When topics cross discipline areas, children are more able to understand and apply concepts. This is especially true when topics are related to the children's interests (Bredekamp & Copple, 1997). Ms. Chang is now talking to the children about planning another unit.

naeyc

Ms. Chang has arranged her schedule so that she will be teaching language arts all morning and math, science, and social studies in the afternoon. Ms. Chang had the opportunity to team-teach this year with Mr. Young. Under this arrangement she would have taught her children language arts in the morning; after lunch, her children would be taught math, science, and social studies by Mr. Young while she taught his children language arts. Although several teachers in her school are exchanging children like this, Ms. Chang decides that she prefers to keep her children all day.

There are advantages and disadvantages to both types of teaching. One advantage of team teaching is that each teacher has more time to prepare for each lesson because fewer lessons are taught each day. There is also very little down time during the school day. Each morning and afternoon session is packed with instruction and practice, and the children seem to remain focused and on task. This rigid schedule allows for no flexibility, however. If the children are interested and want to continue with what they are learning, or if they need extra help in grasping a concept, there is no leeway to continue the lesson. They must wait until the next day because the children have to move to the other teacher. When a teacher has the children all day, she can adjust the schedule and allow the children to continue with something that is of great interest, or dip into another subject's time allotment to reteach a skill that the children are having problems learning, rather than having to wait until the next day to address a problem.

Another disadvantage of team teaching is the lack of time to work one on one with children. When the teacher has the children all day, she can make time during the day to work individually with children who need extra help. If Sam is weak in reading but strong in math and always finishes math quickly, the teacher can use part of the math period to work with him in a one-on-one situation on his reading. Because Ms. Chang's class has such a wide spread in abilities, she chooses not to team-teach with Mr. Young in order to have more time to help her students individually and to have more flexibility in her schedule.

Informal Reading Inventories (IRI)

An **informal reading inventory (IRI)** is a type of reading test that is given to children to help discover their independent reading level and to help diagnose reading problems. (See Figure 9.1.) A teacher will be able to draw some conclusions about a child's reading ability after this assessment. Although directions for specific IRIs may vary, they share many commonalities. The inventory usually consists of two parts: graded word lists and graded passages. The graded word lists consist of words from each "grade." With the exception of first grade, where there are three lists (preprimer, primer, and first grade), the other grade levels have just one list. The IRI may also have two different forms, A and B, to allow the teacher to retest a child later using different materials. Often these graded lists have 20 words. The children read these words in isolation, and then the teacher uses this information to select a reading passage that is a level below where the child got all the words from the graded list correct. This allows the child to start out successfully, and the teacher is able to check his or her comprehension at the lower level. The teacher does not start the child off reading the third-grade passage even though the child is in third grade.

As the child reads a graded passage, the teacher will mark words that are mispronounced, substituted, omitted, inserted, repeated, reversed, or not attempted. Comprehension is checked by questions at the end of the selection. The teacher will have the child continue reading graded passages until the instructional level of the child is determined. Generally, this will be the passage that the child is able to read and demonstrate comprehension, and 90 percent of the words will be read correctly with a 75 percent comprehension level. Below this level the material is considered to be in a frustration level. Books that are in the frustration level are too hard for the child. The instructional level is that level where the material is sufficiently challenging, not too difficult or too easy (Wiener & Cohen, 1997).

By analyzing the graded paragraph, the teacher can notice specific problems the child is experiencing. The teacher can pick up on reversals of words such as *was* and *saw* and can determine if certain phonic skills are weak (such as long vowel or

FIGURE 9.1 Sample Third-Grade IRI Paragraph

Narrative

Concept Questions

What does the word "celebration" mean?

_____

_____

_____ (3-2-1-0)

What does it mean for you to miss someone?

_____

_____

_____ (3-2-1-0)

If you are sad, how can someone cheer you up?

_____

_____

_____ (3-2-1-0)

How many candles are on a birthday cake?

_____

_____

_____ (3-2-1-0)

Score: _____ /12 = _____ %

_____ FAM _____ UNFAM

Prediction:

_____

_____

A Special Birthday for Rosa

Today was the day Rosa had eagerly been waiting for, her birthday! She was very happy but she also felt sad. This would be the first birthday that she would <u>celebrate</u> without all her family around her. The company that Rosa's father worked for had given him a wonderful promotion. But this meant that Rosa, her parents, and her little brother,

Jose, had to move to another state. Rosa liked her new home and friends. But, she really wanted to <u>celebrate</u> her birthday with her grandparents, aunts, uncles, and cousins all around her.

They had sent presents but it wouldn't be the same if she couldn't thank them in person. They wouldn't be there to watch her blow out all the candles. And what kind of a birthday would it be without listening to her grandparents' stories about growing up in Italy and Cuba? Also, four people could never sing as loudly or joyfully as her whole family could sing together!

That night, Mama made Rosa's favorite meal. Afterwards, there was a beautiful cake. Mother, Father, and Jose sang "Happy Birthday" while the eight candles <u>glowed.</u> Rosa made a wish, took a deep breath and blew out all the candles. "I know I won't get what I wished for," she said to herself, "but I'm going to wish for it anyway."

Then it was time for the presents. Rosa's father gave her the first present. It was a video-tape. "I think we should play it right now before you open any more presents," her father said. He put the tape into the player. Suddenly, there on the television screen was the rest of Rosa's family smiling and waving and wishing her a happy birthday. One by one, each person on the tape asked Rosa to open the present they had sent. Her father put the tape on pause while Rosa did this. Then they explained why they had chosen that gift especially for Rosa. After all the presents were unwrapped, her family sang some favorite songs and Rosa, her mother, father, and Jose joined in.

Then, Rosa's grandfather spoke to her. "Rosa, this is a new story, one you have never heard before. I am going to tell it to you as a special birthday gift. It is about my first birthday in this country when I was very lonely for my friends and family. It is about how I met your grandmother." When Grandfather was finished, he and Grandmother blew Rosa a kiss and the tape was finished.

continued

FIGURE 9.1 *continued*

Rosa felt wonderful. It was almost like having her family in the room with her. Rosa hugged her parents and her little brother. "I didn't think I would get my wish but I did," she said. That night, when Mama and Papa came to say goodnight to Rosa, they found her in bed, already asleep, with the videotape next to her. It had been the best birthday ever. (487 words)

Number of Total Miscues

(Total Accuracy): _____

Number of Meaning-Change Miscues

(Total Acceptability): _____

Total Accuracy		**Total Acceptability**
0–9 miscues ___	Independent ___	0–9 miscues
10–48 miscues ___	Instructional ___	10–24 miscues
49+ miscues ___	Frustration ___	25+ miscues

Rate: 487 × 60 = 29,220 / _____ seconds = _____ WPM

Retelling Scoring Sheet for A Special Birthday for Rosa

Setting/Background

_____ Today was Rosa's birthday.
_____ She was happy
_____ but she also felt sad.
_____ This would be the first birthday
_____ she would celebrate
_____ without all her family
_____ around her.
_____ Her father had been given a promotion.
_____ Rosa,
_____ her parents,
_____ and her brother had to move
_____ to another state.

Goal

_____ Rosa wanted to celebrate her birthday
_____ with grandparents
_____ aunts
_____ uncles
_____ and cousins around her.

Sample Word Lists

		Identified Automatically	Identified
1.	lunch	c	
2.	celebrate	c	
3.	believe	belief	
4.	claws		c
5.	lion		c
6.	rough	rug	sc
7.	wear	c	
8.	tongue		c
9.	crowded	c	
10.	wool	c	
11.	removed	removed	sc
12.	curious		kircus
13.	sheep		c
14.	electric		c
15.	worried	c	
16.	enemies	enemy	
17.	glowed		c
18.	clothing		c
19.	swim		c
20.	entrance	entray	sc

Total Correct Automatic _6_ /20 = _30_ %
Total Correct Identified _11_ /20 = _55_ %
Total Number Correct _17_ /20 = _85_ %

LEVELS		
Independent	Instructional	Frustration
18–20	14–17	below 14
90–100%	70–85%	below 70%

variant vowel sounds). She can also check the fluency of the reading (how smoothly a child reads, not slow and haltingly), check the child's comprehension by the answers that the child gives about the main idea and supporting details, check on the child's understanding of the meanings of the words in the paragraph, and determine the child's ability to answer questions where inference skills must be used to determine the correct answer.

Ms. Chang's school does not require assessment at the first of the school year. Ms. Chang, however, has decided to do an IRI on each child the first month of school and then at the end of the school year. Not only does this double assessment show the growth that her children make, it is also a good starting point for dialogue with the parents. She knows from past experience that some parents believe that their child is reading at a much higher level than he or she actually is. Using the results from the IRI, Ms. Chang communicates to the parents the actual reading level of their child. Doing this makes sense to Ms. Chang because she has heard rumors of teachers who are being sued because parents claimed that their child made no progress during the year. By doing this testing, Ms. Chang also develops a good understanding of each child's strengths and weaknesses and can provide better instruction based on those strengths and weaknesses.

Using Computers to Teach Literature

By third grade, children begin to have favorite authors. Favorite authors can be the basis for the children to engage in author studies. Many authors have their own websites, and the children can use the Internet to gather information about their favorite author's life. The children may do this in cooperative groups. They may gather all the books by their author from their school library and read and discuss those books. Topics for discussion are themes about which the author writes, the purpose the author has in writing these books, the author's own experiences, and the similarities and differences among the books (Jody & Saccardi, 1998).

Books on CD-ROM are also appropriate for third graders. These books are actually one step up from books on tape in that many of them highlight the words on the screen as they are read aloud to the child. This is another way to strengthen the reading skills of weak readers. The use of these programs should not be limited to weak or struggling readers, however, as most third graders find these books very enjoyable.

⭐ PROFESSIONAL DEVELOPMENT IN READING

Periodically, Ms. Chang's school pays for her to attend training or a workshop that will help strengthen her skills in specific areas. Last year, Ms. Chang attended training on using the writing process in third grade. She was also able to attend a two-day training on working with children of poverty. The first training she has received this year she learned about through reading the professional journals to which her school subscribes.

Ms. Chang has been concerned about the poor reading ability of several of her students. As she was reading the journal *Reading Research and Instruction,* she came across an article that specifically addressed reading fluency. The article stated that speed and effortlessness of children's reading was highly correlated with comprehension and that research supported instructional methods that increase reading fluency by repeated readings, hearing fluent readers, and monitoring a child's progress (Hasbrouck, Ihnot, & Rogers, 2000). Ms. Chang felt that this approach might help some of her weaker readers and so she used the Internet to find the next training site for this method. Fortunately, she found a two-day training that was within 45 minutes of her home. The training was not free, but her school sets aside money each year for this very purpose and so Ms. Chang was able to apply and have the cost covered by her school.

☆ SPELLING INSTRUCTION IN THIRD GRADE

Ms. Chang uses a combination approach to spelling in her classroom. She uses the basal speller provided by the state, but she also uses words from the children's own writing that they are constantly misspelling. The basal has 20 different words for each week of school that the children are expected to learn how to spell. Fifteen of these words are new words and five are review words. The review words are words that the publisher has chosen because they are commonly used by children in their writing. To this list Ms. Chang adds words for each individual child. These are the words that Ms. Chang observes the child consistently misspelling as she works with him or her during writing conferences.

This basal is newly adopted by the district this year. Last year's basal had 15 third-grade words and five challenge words. When spelling textbooks came up for adoption last year, Ms. Chang served on the committee that evaluated the new spelling books. She felt that, given her school's student population, a text that reviewed words on a consistent basis would be more beneficial to her children than textbooks that had only challenge words.

The basal is arranged with a lesson for each day of the week. The words for each week typically highlight a certain skill or pattern among the words. The words this week have the pattern *aw* and *au*. On Monday, Ms. Chang gives the children a practice spelling test. After the practice test, the children check their own test. They circle the parts of the words that they missed and look at those mistakes. Ms. Chang points out to them that they already know most of the word and now need to concentrate on the part of the word that they missed.

Ms. Chang served on her school's Technology Committee last year and was instrumental in getting laptop computers for all the children in third grade. The children now get out their computers and type the spelling words. They will print these words and take them home for the parents to help them learn the words. Each child also adds his or her own additional words to the list.

Each day of the week the spelling book has a different lesson using the spelling words. On Tuesday, the children practice proofreading a selection and finding errors in words that use *au* and *aw*. On Wednesday they learn about the dictionary and how to interpret an entry in the dictionary. On Thursday they work on using context clues and the meanings of the words. And on Friday the children take their spelling test. Obviously, with all the children having different extra words, Ms. Chang had to come up with an efficient way to test the children on these words. She gives all the children the test on the basal words during spelling instruction time. After the group-administered spelling test, the children fold their papers in half with the spelling words folded to the inside and begin their independent writing. As they are writing, Ms. Chang moves from child to child and calls out the individual spelling words to each child. This doesn't take as long as it might seem because Ms. Chang has it so well organized.

Ms. Chang knows that the first question the parents ask their children when they see them on Friday afternoon will be, "How did you do on your spelling test?" Ms. Chang makes it a point to always grade and return the spelling tests before the children leave school on Friday. She has arranged her daily schedule so that spelling comes before her conference period, so she has her conference time to grade the children's tests. The parents of her children are most appreciative of this arrangement. Ms. Chang has found that this system helps parents maintain their interest in their children's spelling and work with their children each week with the spelling words.

Ms. Chang also makes use of a word wall in her classroom. The children used word walls in first and second grade, but Ms. Chang has changed it to reflect the spelling patterns that the children are learning in third grade. For instance, after teaching the children about making plurals by changing the *y* to *i* and adding *-es*, Ms. Chang adds words that follow this pattern to her "Plurals" word wall. She has already added *s* and *es* on the plurals wall and now has three columns. The first column is headed by *–s*, the second by *–es*, and the third by *–ies*. Under each of these are words that follow this pattern (Gruber, 1999).

⭐ WRITING INSTRUCTION IN THIRD GRADE

Ms. Chang uses the writing process with her children. This means that she views writing as a process. The children have a block of time each day that is set aside for writing. Minilessons are given about some aspect of writing, children write independently, and then share their writing (Combs, 2002). Children may begin the school year by brainstorming a list of topics or subjects that interest them. This helps them to come up with ideas for their writing. Once they decide on a topic, they engage in prewriting. During prewriting, the children plan their writing. They may do this through a list, drawings, brainstorming ideas, or use of devices such as the Venn diagram. This prewriting helps children develop the focus of their writing. Once this focus has been developed, the children begin writing. The children are actually composing during this period, and the goal of this period is sustained writing. Ms. Chang allows the children to write without interference during this time. When they have finished writing, the children move into the editing phase.

They look at their work for correctness, both of meaning and of spelling and grammar, and they begin to use proofreading skills during this time. They may also ask other children to read and provide feedback to them as well as having a conference with the teacher about their work (Comb, 2002).

The **writing conference** is the heart of the writing process. During these 5-minute individual conferences, the teacher works with a child to help that child improve his or her writing. The teacher may ask questions about what the child has written, suggest a direction for the writing, help the child to elaborate a story plot, or guide the child to include more descriptive phrases and words that paint mental pictures for the reader. The teacher may ask questions that help the child realize that there is not enough detail for the reader to understand exactly what the writer intends.

Questions That Can Be Asked to Help Children Elaborate

- I don't understand why . . .
- What did the _____ look like when . . . ?
- How did the hero feel?
- Where did this happen?
- What was the time of day, weather, season?
- What happened next?
- What was the problem?
- How did he/she solve the problem?

Ms. Chang also uses this time to work on language arts skills that she notices are missing in the child's writing, such as capitalization of proper nouns. Conferences can occur anytime during the writing process. Children usually sign up for a conference with the teacher, and the teacher confers with several children a day. When she is not conferring separately with children, Ms. Chang moves around the room and visits with children about their writing. These are sometimes referred to as "squat" conferences, because the teacher squats beside the child's desk as she talks to the child.

When a child has progressed to the point that he or she wishes to take a piece to the publication stage, then that piece is rewritten to be free from errors. A published piece is ready to be shared with others and, like any other published work, it should be as near perfect as possible. Not all of the children's writing will end up as published pieces. If children get tired of the subject, they are allowed to file that piece in their writing folder. They may or may not finish that piece later. That decision is left up to the child.

Writing Folders

Each child should have a writing folder. These folders may be as simple as a file folder or as elaborate as a specially decorated expandable folder. Each folder contains the child's writing in progress. In addition, the writing folder may contain items copied by the teacher that will assist the child in writing.

Possible Contents of a Writing Folder

- Brainstormed list of topics that interest the child
- Writing in various stages of progress
- Editing marks sheet that shows symbols such as ^ for inserting words or sentences (see Chapter 8 for example of this sheet)
- Words for descriptive writing such as weather words, feelings words, other adjectives
- A list of the first 100 most common words, in alphabetical order
- List of words that the child frequently misspells
- Sheet of guidelines in question format for the child to check his or her work at the end of the rough draft and the finished piece. Questions such as: Have I proofread my work to myself? Did I begin each sentence with a capital letter?

Although children are usually allowed a choice of topics, they still need to receive instruction in the different types of writing. Many states have requirements for specific types of writing that children are expected to master at certain grade levels. Teachers need to provide developmentally appropriate activities that are the basis for teaching the children how to successfully do these types of writing.

In third grade, after reviewing how-to and narratives, the children are instructed in compare-and-contrast writing. Concrete experiences should be orchestrated with the children's active participation in data collection, starting simply and then moving to the more complex. Simple experiences might involve tasting pretzels and potato sticks and then discussing the similarities and differences. In preparing for the compare-and-contrast writing, children should be exposed to many examples, and the teacher should model the thought processes and steps for writing, then actually write one together with the children, before expecting the children to do this on their own. More complex activities such as the teacher's reading two different versions of the traditional *Three Little Pigs* and the story *The True Story of the Three Little Pigs* (1989) by Jon Scieszka and then comparing and contrasting them would be a possible next step. At the level of third grade, the paper will basically have four paragraphs—an introduction, how they are similar, how they are different, and a conclusion.

A persuasive paper is less easy for the children to grasp. Before children can even begin to write a persuasive paper, they must have experiences that will give them something to persuade someone about. Again, the teacher starts on a simple, concrete level before going to a level where the children are expected to persuade someone to accept an idea. The children may tell the class why they really like a certain candy or cereal. The teacher will want to have the children practice oral persuasion. They might study and write advertisements for candy or cereal or a special toy before attempting to write a persuasive paper.

Research into best practices for both reading and writing indicate that children of teachers who used high-quality literature and engaged their students in exten-

Dimensions of Diversity

Meeting Diverse Needs

When teachers use literature in the classroom for reading instruction, they should be especially sensitive to the type of books selected. When the class reads a whole book, special emphasis is placed on the content and message of that book. Teachers should select materials that will allow all the children in the classroom to see themselves in the characters portrayed in the books. This means that multicultural books will be among those chosen for whole-class study. The main characters should reflect both male and female roles and not be stereotypical of a gender. The family structures portrayed should also include the diversity that exists in today's culture. Not every family is a two-parent family, and the stories chosen should be reflective of family types in today's society (Combs, 2002).

sive reading and writing activities significantly outperform children whose teachers did not teach in this manner. The teachers of the high-performing children also taught skills in the context of meaningful experiences. The teachers of low-performing children taught skills mainly in isolation. This study was actually conducted with third-grade children. Teachers of the high-performing children read with the children in small and large groups, used trade books, organized choral reading of poetry and dramatic response to literature, read aloud to children, and wrote in response to literature. Children read, discussed, and wrote about the books they read: How did the characters feel? What in the story makes you think that? The children also responded in writing to open-ended questions and shared their pieces with the rest of the class (Cantrell, 1999).

Teachers of low-performing children centered their instruction around sets of sight words and commercially prepared programs and basals. The children read long lists of sight words, read from the basal in a "round robin" format, completed phonics worksheets, and used a phonics program in the computer lab to drill on phonic skills in isolation. Students only wrote two or three days a week for a 30-minute period. Writing consisted mainly of finishing story starters and answering questions in content areas (Cantrell, 1999).

This research demonstrates that teachers have a definite effect on the reading and writing ability of their children. The instructional methods used by teachers have a substantial impact on children, and the methods that researchers have been saying are the best, most developmentally appropriate practices indeed are.

PORTFOLIOS USED AS ASSESSMENT

Many schools currently use portfolios as one means of assessing their children. Portfolios that show growth are collections of children's work that document the progress a child made during the school year. These portfolios contain material that is selected by the child and is accompanied by a reflection written by the child as to why he or she has included this piece in the portfolio. Writing pieces are documented from rough draft to the published piece. Even children in kindergarten participate in choosing their best writing and reflecting upon it. Kindergarten teachers usually transcribe the comments made by their children and include these reflections in the children's portfolios.

Material for the portfolio is not restricted to the child's writing but may include audiotapes of the child's reading ability, drawings, pictures of constructions, even videotapes of plays or creative dramatics produced by the children. As with any collection of data in the school, the date of the work is crucial. Without a date on materials, it is not possible to show how the child has grown in skills over time. The date is a way of organizing the material to show the growth that the child has made. The portfolio may also contain information from the teacher in the form of checklists, running records with miscue analysis, anecdotal records, and other informal assessments (Wiener & Cohen, 1997). (See Chapter 8 for more information about running records.)

The portfolio is usually shared with the parents sometime during the school year. Some schools even have portfolio parties, for which children send their parents formal invitations to come view their portfolios. When parents view the portfolio, they are able to see what their child has learned, is learning, and is having problems learning. Parents are also able to talk to their child about the work in the portfolio, pointing out areas of strength and areas that need more work.

Scoring Children's Writing

In Ms. Chang's state, the children are not assessed on their writing by the state until fourth grade. However, Ms. Chang's district still expects her to help prepare the children for the state writing assessment that is done in fourth grade. The district has developed scoring guidelines for third-grade children. Ms. Chang is expected to have the children produce each type of writing (narrative, how-to, persuasive, compare and contrast) and then score the children's writings to see how they are progressing. The district also expects this information to be submitted by every teacher in every elementary school to the coordinator of elementary education in the central administration building. This information is used by the coordinator to predict how well the children will perform on the state test next year in fourth grade. Looking at the scores, the coordinator decides which, if any, schools need staff development and/or special materials to help their third graders improve their writing skills. The district wants the teachers to use a **writing rubric.** The rubric describes for Ms. Chang what an "average" writing paper would look like for each score. Papers are scored on a scale of 1 to 4, with 4 considered commendable, 3 proficient, 2 nearly proficient, and 1 limited achievement.

The different scores, or levels, are defined by the following descriptors. Level One papers are barely comprehensible and have minimal content, incomplete sentences, inadequate or inaccurate use of vocabulary and language structures, and inaccurate spelling, punctuation, and capitalization. Level Two papers are judged to be somewhat complete and mostly comprehensible, with other areas also being

State by State

Writing Assessment in Florida

In **Florida,** children are given a writing folder containing one writing prompt, two lined pages for the written response, a separate sheet for planning and prewriting, and 45 minutes total time for the assessment. The state uses a six-point scale rubric to score their children's writing. The state writing assessment begins in fourth grade.

6 points	writing is focused; sense of wholeness; clear; sentences are complete; and few, if any, errors in mechanics, usage, and punctuation.
5 points	writing is focused; organizational pattern may have some lapses; with rare exceptions, sentences are complete; generally follows the conventions of mechanics, usage, and spelling.
4 points	writing is generally focused but may include extraneous material; some sense of completeness; little variation in sentence structure but most are complete; generally follows the conventions of mechanics, usage, and spelling.
3 points	writing is generally focused on topic but may include extraneous material; organization attempted but may lack a sense of completeness; little, if any, variation in sentence structure; conventions of mechanics and usage are usually demonstrated; commonly used words usually spelled correctly.
2 points	writing is related to the topic but includes extraneous material; little evidence of organization; gross errors in sentence structure; errors in basic conventions of mechanics and usage; commonly used words may be misspelled.
1 point	writing only minimally addresses topic; little organization; gross errors in sentence structure and basic conventions of mechanics and usage; commonly used words may be misspelled (Florida Department of Education, 2002).

rated with the term *somewhat.* Level Three papers, proficient papers, are complete, with adequate use of vocabulary and language structures and mostly accurate spelling, punctuation, and capitalization. Level Four are judged to be superior in all areas (Fairfax County Public Schools, 2002).

A proficient narrative writing piece by a third grader, for example, shows organization skills that include a beginning, middle, and end. The middle is well developed, including description of several events, a problem, and a solution. The characters and setting in the story are elaborate. The majority of the words are spelled with conventional spelling. Correct capitalization and punctuation is used throughout the piece. Vocabulary reflects the level of an average third grader. A paper with these characteristics would be scored as a Level Three paper. The district has sent all the third-grade teachers the scoring rubric along with samples from each of the levels. The teachers score and return the writing samples of their students to the central office.

⭐ LANGUAGE ARTS INSTRUCTION IN THIRD GRADE

The third-grade language arts or language book most likely combines grammar instruction with writing instruction. Teachers who teach writing as a process may use the book primarily to teach the grammar that needs to be taught in third grade, get ideas for minilessons to be taught during writing instruction, and to be an aid in preparing for state assessment tests where the children have to find mistakes in written passages and identify those mistakes as ones in capitalization, punctuation, or spelling. The grammar includes the different parts of speech, tenses of verbs, irregular and helping verbs, mechanics of writing, dictionary (and other reference sources) skills, and use of a thesaurus.

⭐ HANDWRITING INSTRUCTION IN THIRD GRADE

Third grade is the "usual" year that teachers begin instruction in cursive handwriting. Although some schools begin cursive at the end of second grade, Ms. Chang's school has decided to wait until third grade for this instruction. This allows the fine-motor skills of the children to become more developed and also adds to the prestige of being in third grade.

Ms. Chang introduces a letter each day and the children practice making that letter. She models how to make the letter using the board or the overhead projector and then talks the children through the process. She begins with the easier letters first, such as *i* and *t*, before adding letters that are more complex. Unlike her own experience in school, Ms. Chang does not have the children write row after row of the letters they are learning. She does have the children practice several times, trying each time to make the letter better. As they practice, she moves around the room and monitors the children as they form the letters. Ms. Chang has known teachers who did not do this monitoring, and the children suffered as a result. What can happen if the teacher doesn't monitor the children? The children may develop strange ways of making the letter, and even though the letter may look perfect, if it is not made correctly the child will not be able to write complete words with the fluid motion of the cursive style. Ms. Chang has the children circle their best letter. Interestingly enough, many children choose to make rows and rows of letters on their own, especially at first when they are so pleased to be learning how to write in cursive.

⭐ MATH INSTRUCTION IN THIRD GRADE

The math standards discussed in Chapter 8 are used by teachers in all grade levels as they plan and implement mathematics instruction. Math books should be evaluated using the standards and changes made in instruction accordingly.

In third grade, children are expected to be able to add and subtract much larger numbers than before, regrouping more than once. It is also the time that multiplication skills and division skills are taught and mastery is expected. Third graders are expected to have memorized their multiplication facts through 10 by the end of third grade.

Like any math skill, multiplication should be taught to third graders using concrete activities relevant to their lives. The teacher arranges for these experiences for the children. Starting with small numbers, the teacher can set up word problems for the children to aid in understanding. For example, the teacher can tell a story such as this: *One day Joe went to the store on his way to baseball practice and bought six packages of sour gumballs. Each package had two gumballs in it. He wants to share the gumballs with his friends at practice, but he needs to know how many gumballs he has altogether to be sure he has enough for all of them. How many gumballs does he have?* Helping the children work through real-life problems such as this makes the concept of multiplication easier to understand.

Next, the teacher can let the children use counters or chips to solve similar math problems. After this, the teacher will want to move to a step where the children are taught to "draw" the problem and the solution in some fashion. Drawing a representation helps children understand the problem instead of trying to use strategies such as key words (Fuson, Carroll, & Drueck, 2000). When teachers teach key word strategies, they instruct the children to look for words such as *how many more* that indicate the operation that should be used in the solution of the problem. This strategy does not help children understand the problem and how to find the solution, and it does not always work; questions can be worded so that the key words indicate addition when the child really needs to subtract to solve the problem.

Once children have received a good foundation in multiplication, they are ready to learn their facts. Children need to be taught strategies that help them recall the facts. Teaching children to use counting for this stage of their learning is inefficient. Children seldom master the fact 3×4 through activities where they count the elements in three rows of 4. What they must understand is the commutative property of multiplication. Once children understand that 3×4 is the same as 4×3, they can begin to use five different strategies to learn their multiplication facts. Using these strategies helps to support children as they move the facts into long-term memory. The following strategies are presented by Van de Walle (1998) in his book *Elementary and Middle School Mathematics: Teaching Developmentally*.

The first strategy is for children to realize that they already know facts that have 2 as a factor and that these are equivalent to addition doubles. Understanding the commutative property, they will now realize that 2×8 is equivalent to $8 + 8$ and 8×2. Games can be played in which the teacher says a number and the children say the double.

The second strategy is the 5s facts. Children can practice counting by 5s (also needed for telling time and counting money and usually learned in first grade). Once they can count by 5s to at least 45, they can be introduced to problems such as 3×5 by being shown three rows with five dots. Three times five means there are

FIGURE 9.2 The Relationship between 3×5 and 5×3

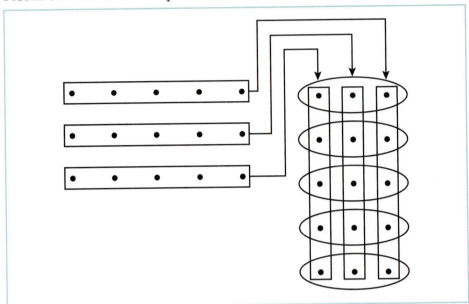

three rows with five dots per row. To show 5×3, the children can turn the rows into columns and circle three across with yarn or a rubber band, producing 5×3 (see Figure 9.2).

The next strategy is to teach the children that 36 of the facts have a factor that is either 0 or 1, that 0 times any number is always 0, and that 1 times any number is always the same as that number. Zero should be presented as sets of nothing.

Facts with a factor of 9 can be easy to learn even though the product will be large. Children can be taught two patterns for mastering 9s. "The tens digit of the product is always one less than the 'other' factor (the one other than nine), and the sum of the two digits in the product is always nine" (Van de Walle, 1998, p. 155). For example, $9 \times 3 = 27$. One number less than 3 is 2 (the 10s digit) and $2 + ? = 9$. Two plus seven equals nine. The answer is 27.

The last strategy deals with the remaining 25 facts that are not learned using the first four strategies. Teachers can have children memorize these remaining facts or can use this last strategy, that is not as easily understood, to help the children learn these facts. The last strategy involves relating these facts to facts already known. The child knows that $5 \times 7 = 35$. To figure out 6×7, the child can add 7 and 35. This strategy will only work if the child is able to do the mental math necessary to add 7 and 35.

As teachers expect children to master their times tables, many may wonder if timed math tests will help them. Timed math tests do not help children master math facts. Children who can perform well under pressure do well. Those who do not perform well under pressure, or work more slowly, may become fearful about their ability to perform math and this will have a negative impact on their learning (Van de Walle, 1998).

Helping children master their multiplication facts is an important part of the third-grade math curriculum. Teachers should help children develop and use efficient strategies in dealing with facts. Repeated counting is not an efficient strategy. Children need to practice using efficient strategies like those already mentioned that will help them as they try to retrieve the facts (Van de Walle, 1998).

Division is also taught in third grade. Again, good teaching begins with concrete experiences and is related to everyday situations. Word problems help children understand division. Using problems that children can relate to helps make division meaningful. The teacher can tell the children that they have 20 chocolate chip cookies and five children get to share them. The teacher can then ask the children: How many cookies will each child get? The problem can be done using counters for the cookies and can actually be counted onto five small paper plates that represent the children. When children have mastered multiplication facts, division becomes easier because they use their multiplication fact knowledge in working division problems.

Teachers need to keep in mind that math concepts are not easy for all children. Children who have logical-mathematical intelligence, as described by Howard Gardner (1983), excel in math. Other children are able to learn math concepts and skills but it will simply take longer, and the teacher cannot assume that something that seems easy will be easy for all children. The vocabulary of mathematics in and of itself causes difficulty. Terms such as *quotients, subtrahends, minuends, products, differences, integers,* and other math-related terms need to be carefully explained to the children (Cornell, 1999).

Though other more traditional areas will be addressed in third grade (time, measurement) Ms. Chang also intends to implement probability experiments into her math curriculum because of an article from *Teaching Children Mathematics* that she read recently. This article addresses the mathematical standard that says that children consider the likelihood or probability of events. She has planned three different probability experiments for the children. They will flip a coin 25 times, recording the results each time; they will spin a spinner and record whether the needle lands on red, green, yellow 25 times; and they will roll a die 30 times and record the results. These experiments will help them begin thinking in terms of likelihood that an event will happen (Edwards & Hensien, 2000).

Like reading, commercial material for math instruction varies greatly from those that focus on direct instruction, to traditional materials, to those that attempt to teach based on the mathematical standards. In a study done by Fuson and colleagues (2000), third graders who used a math program based on the standards outperformed traditional students in the areas of place value, numeration, reasoning, geometry, data, and number-story items. They even outperformed seventh-grade students in the area of reasoning.

Regardless of the type of materials used, teachers should conduct their lessons using manipulatives to demonstrate concepts and allow children to use manipulatives as they seek to build a conceptual understanding of mathematics. Teachers should also check for understanding, look at the mistakes children are making, and try to determine where they are making mistakes. Asking children who are confused to tell you what they don't understand is not helpful. Children can rarely identify what it is they are having problems with or what they don't understand (Cornell, 1999).

⭐ SCIENCE INSTRUCTION IN THIRD GRADE

In 1995, the National Academy of Sciences released the National Science Education Standards. These standards define the skills and knowledge that our children should develop throughout their K–12 education in order to graduate from high school scientifically literate. Science is seen as an active process where children observe and describe, read and seek information, ask questions and make hypotheses, gather information, and suggest explanations. The standards identify and describe eight categories: inquiry, unifying concepts and processes, physical science, life science, earth and space science, science and technology, science in personal and social perspectives, and history and the nature of science (Peters, 1996).

The standards include content that students should know as well as assessment standards for that knowledge. There are also science teaching standards and professional development standards for teachers. The teacher is seen as the critical factor for students' achievement of scientific literacy. The science teaching standards address how to plan, implement, and assess the scientific experiences of the children. Children are expected to construct knowledge and theories based on their experiences as opposed to rote memorization of scientific facts and definitions. All children benefit when science is taught in this manner. Children engage in hands-on activities that stimulate their minds. In addition to hands-on learning, children use scientific processes; engage in scientific debate; and use writing and speaking to communicate what they have observed, understood, learned, or wondered about (Peters, 1996).

The role of the teacher with the children is one of a facilitator who encourages and models the skills of scientific inquiry and openness to new ideas while retaining the skepticism that characterizes science. The teacher also leads discussions among children about scientific ideas (Peters, 1996). In addition to being facilitators, teachers are also responsible for assessing the children. Teachers engage in ongoing assessment of their teaching and children's learning, use multiple methods and gather data about their children systematically, and guide the children in self-assessment. They also use the student data to interact with colleagues, students, parents, and others, reporting and reflecting on student achievement as they strive to improve their teaching (Peters, 1996).

As teachers plan activities to aid children in inquiry, children become more adept at understanding the vocabulary of science and the words will have meaning to them instead of being definitions they can spout from memory using words they don't understand. The outcomes of the inquiry process are developed as children ask questions based on an activity or observation, use scientific skills to design and implement experiments, make and prove or disprove hypotheses as they use the scientific method, communicate the data and the results they achieved, and develop the ability to understand scientific research (Peters, 1996).

According to *Inquiry and the National Science Education Standards* (2000) "inquiry teaching and learning have five essential features that apply across all grade levels" (p. 24). These five features help define and distinguish inquiry-based teaching and learning from the general term *inquiry.*

1. "Learners are engaged by scientifically oriented questions" (p. 24). These questions fall into two different categories: ones that ask why and ones that ask how. Often *why* questions must be changed into *how* questions to lend themselves to the scientific inquiry process. A question about why sunlight affects plants can be investigated by children if changed into a question about how sunlight affects plants.
2. "Learners give priority to evidence, which allows them to develop and evaluate explanations that address scientifically oriented questions" (p. 25). Children use their senses, instruments, and control conditions as they gather data over a period of time. They observe, take measurements, chart data, and gather evidence from the teacher or other sources.
3. "Learners formulate explanations from evidence to address scientifically oriented questions" (p. 26). Explanations are based on reason and supported by the evidence that the children have gathered as they propose new knowledge.
4. "Learners evaluate their explanations in light of alternative explanations, particularly those reflecting scientific understanding" (p. 27). Explanations are reviewed and evaluated based on the evidence. Other possible explanations are generated as children dialogue, then compare and check their results with each other and with the teacher and/or other source material. Explanations are also examined for biases or flaws in reasoning.
5. "Learners communicate and justify their proposed explanations" (p. 27). Sharing results allows children an opportunity to practice effective communication and provides other children with the opportunity to question those results and suggest alternative explanations.

Obviously, the more a child is able to engage in self-direction, the closer that child will be to inquiry-based teaching and learning and the less the amount of direction needed from the teacher or the materials.

Ms. Chang has read a report on the science standards and is looking at the science textbook that she uses with new eyes. She notices that the third-grade book does begin with an explanation for the children of the scientific process and process skills.

The Scientific Process

1. State the problem—this is the question you want answered.
2. Formulate a hypothesis—this is a possible answer and it can be tested.
3. Identify and control the variables—choose one variable to change when you test your hypothesis.
4. Test your hypothesis—do experiments, repeat the experiments to be sure you get the same results.

continued

5. Collect your data and record your results—write, draw, list, measure, or write.
6. Interpret the data—organize it using graphs, charts, diagrams, and look for patterns.
7. State your conclusion—based on the evidence you gathered.
8. Inquire further—use what you learned. (Cooney, DiSpezio, Foots, Matamoros, Nyquist, Ostlund, Chamot, Cummins, Kahn, Sipkovich, & Weinberg, 2000)

The scientific skills listed by the textbook include observing, communicating, classifying, estimating and measuring, inferring, predicting, making operational definitions, making and using models, formulating questions and hypotheses, collecting and interpreting data, identifying and controlling variables, and conducting experiments (Scott Foresman, 2000). Ms. Chang has decided to use the standards to try to implement science into other areas in the curriculum as the school year proceeds instead of depending solely on the science book to provide science instruction for the children.

Shortly after she made this decision, her students became fascinated with a new jet spy plane just declassified by the government. Suddenly, the children were asking many questions about how planes get off the ground and how they are able to fly. Ms. Chang remembers hearing one of the first-grade teachers in her building talk about using projects to investigate topics that her first graders are interested in and how the projects can be used for instruction in many academic areas. After talking to the first-grade teacher, Ms. Chang decides to investigate the topic of airplanes and flight to see if this would be a suitable project for her children. She checks the science book for information on airplanes and flight and finds that these topics are not addressed at all. So Ms. Chang begins a search on the Internet. She discovers many useful sites that will be beneficial to her and the children in the study of flight and airplanes. She becomes excited when she finds actual experiments and demonstrations that the children can engage in that will aid in their understanding of how airplanes are able to fly. Figure 9.3 is a sample of what she found on the Internet.

Ms. Chang's class engaged in the project and investigated how airplanes are able to fly. The children not only used science skills, they also had to apply math skills. They used language arts skills as they read and researched and wrote about airplanes and learned new vocabulary. They then used the knowledge gained to explain and demonstrate to another third-grade class how airplanes fly.

After this project, Ms. Chang was so excited about all the children had learned and the skills they had used across several academic areas that she looked for other ways to integrate math and science into the curriculum. She also found that she could use literature as a springboard for more activities. Looking through her collection of children's books, she found the book *Who Sank the Boat* by Pamela Allen (1982). The story is about some animal friends who go rowing in a boat. When the last animal, the mouse who was lightest of all, got in, the boat sank. Using this idea, she had the children work in groups to design and build boats. Then, using plastic

FIGURE 9.3 Experiments with Air and Lift

Demonstrations

A. Air has weight and exerts pressure.

Place a ruler on a table so that it extends about 8 cm (3 in.) over the edge, and hit the end of the ruler. Reposition the ruler on the table, and cover it with a flat sheet of newsprint. Hit the end of the ruler again, and observe what happens.

B. Faster-moving air exerts less pressure than slower-moving air.

Suspend two table tennis balls from string as shown with about 1 cm (0.5 in.) space between them. Blow a stream of air directly between the table tennis balls, and observe what happens.

C. A difference in air pressure above and below an object causes lift.

Hold a strip of paper with your hand just below your mouth. Blow air across the top of the paper, and observe what happens.

Source: Nova, 2001.

zoo animals and tubs of water, she had the children predict how many animals their boats would hold before it sank. They tested their hypothesis and then discussed how they might increase the number of animals the boat could hold before it sank. This discussion led the children to decide to try to figure out which animals were the lightest and put the lightest animals in the boats first.

Ms. Chang helped the children build a balance scale using a ruler with bathroom cups attached on each end. The children first experimented by placing different plastic animals into the cups. They quickly found that this balance was not sensitive enough for them to determine the relative weights of the animals. Under Ms. Chang's guidance and through posing questions, the children decided to place an animal in one cup and add something small to the other cup until it balanced. They could then count what was added and determine the lightest animals. They looked around the room and tried different items such as the 1s blocks from the base ten set, crayons, paper clips, and rubber bands. They ended up using the rubber bands because they were the lightest. After figuring out the relative lightness of each toy animal, they repeated their experiment with the boat. During their investigation they practiced many science skills and math skills. They also kept a science journal so that they could document their findings.

At the end of this experiment, the children excitedly asked Ms. Chang what they were going to do the next week. Their enthusiasm kept Ms. Chang thinking and coming up with new ideas the rest of the school year. Ms. Chang had made a very important discovery. The children were learning the skills and knowledge that they needed without relying totally on the textbooks. They were also practicing these skills in a meaningful way instead of through worksheets.

⭐ SOCIAL STUDIES INSTRUCTION IN THIRD GRADE

Instruction in social studies in third grade consists of a more in-depth study of the communities in our country, both past and present. Topics might include the early settlements in our land, Native American communities past and present, citizenship and our government, jobs, money, and production of goods (Boyd, Berkin, Gay, Chase, Geiger, Cummins, Kracht, Glenn, Pang, Hahn, Risinger, Hickey, Sanchez, & Meszaros, 2003b). For more detail on implementing the social studies standards from the National Council for the Social Studies, see Chapter 8.

⭐ TEAM MEETINGS

Ms. Chang is serving this year as the team leader for third grade. In this position, the district pays her a small stipend to handle the additional work and responsibility that goes with this position. As team leader, Ms. Chang attends meetings, as needed, with the principal and other team leaders from the different grade levels. She then reports back to her team members what she has learned in the team leader meeting. At the last team meeting, the principal told the attending teachers that the district was forming a Curriculum Writing Committee and a Textbook Committee, and each school needed to send one member from each grade level to serve on these committees. The principal also notified the teachers of changes that would have to be made in their daily schedules because the photographer was coming to school to take the children's pictures.

Team meetings are a part of school life for teachers.

Ms. Chang called a grade level meeting, disseminated this information to her team, and asked for volunteers to serve on these committees. The Curriculum Committee would meet through the summer as teachers wrote curriculum to be used by all third-grade teachers in the district. The curriculum they wrote would be published in a curriculum guide and would be used by third-grade teachers throughout the district for teaching writing. Although the teachers would be expected to work on this project during the summer, they would be paid for their time.

The Textbook Committee would review all the new math books and make a decision about which book to adopt. As part of this committee, the third-grade teacher from each school would receive materials from all the various publishers, review all the materials, present the materials to the team, receive the team's input on which materials they wanted to use, and then meet with the district committee and decide as a district which of the materials to purchase.

As team leader, Ms. Chang also is in charge of doing the extra paperwork that is involved in her grade level. She submits a budget to the principal that reflects the needs of her third-grade team. She may also do the paperwork to arrange any field trips that are planned. And she takes any concerns that the other third-grade teachers have back to the principal and/or other team leaders.

In addition to grade-level meetings, Ms. Chang's school occasionally meets in vertical teams. *Vertical teams* consist of teachers from several different grades. She met with second-grade and fourth-grade teachers the previous week to discuss the areas and topics of the curriculum that overlap and are taught each year. They discussed which topics could possibly be removed or scaled back in one of the grade levels and more heavily emphasized in another. It was found that plants were taught in all three grade levels, so the teachers decided that third grade could remove the plant topic from the curriculum in order to spend more time on the scientific process and more depth on other topics. These meetings also pointed out the need for more time to be spent in third grade on basic understanding of multiplication because that seemed to be a real weakness for the fourth graders.

⭐ SITE-BASED MANAGEMENT

Ms. Chang has also been asked to serve on the school's **site-based management** council. Carver Elementary was one of the first schools in the district to develop effective site-based management (SBM). Ms. Chang is somewhat familiar with SBM but has asked for additional information before she makes a decision on whether or not to be part of the council.

Between 1986 and 1990, more than one-third of all school districts in the nation had implemented some version of SBM. SBM was modeled from industry after it was found that factory workers had increased satisfaction when given the opportunity to share in decision making (Holloway, 2000). SBM emphasizes shared decision making in the school among the principal, teachers, and community members. Eighty percent of the schools have an SBM council, but many are ineffective. To be effective, the people on the council must have genuine authority over the budget, personnel, and curriculum (Holloway, 2000). The principal leads and shares power and responsibility and all information is distributed throughout the school and the community (Site-Based Management, 2002). Four major obstacles to successful SBM have been noted.

1. SBM is considered as an end in itself.
2. Principals work from their own agenda and are perceived as autocratic.
3. The power to make decisions in centered in a single council.
4. Little energy or commitment is given to make it work effectively.
   (Wohlstetter & Mohrman, 1996)

Issues and Trends

No Child Left Behind

The No Child Left Behind Act will result in assessment of all children, in all states, in reading and math in grades 3 through 8. Progress and achievement will be measured every year. The data will be disaggregated according to race, gender, and other criteria (such as disadvantaged) and will be available in annual report cards on school performance and on state performance. These reports will help parents, teachers, administrators, and citizens note the progress of a particular school or state in closing the achievement gap between the various groups of children as well as how well children are achieving overall (No Child Left Behind Fact Sheet, 2002).

☆ STATE STANDARDS AND MANDATED TESTING

In 1990 President George Bush and the country's governors adopted national education goals for educational improvement. States were to establish challenging content and performance standards for all students. The state and federal government policy since then has required schools to have high academic standards, be accountable for student outcomes, include all children in reform initiatives, and have the flexibility necessary to foster instructional change (Goertz, 2001).

Title I provisions of the Improving America's Schools Act of 1994 required states to set high standards in at least reading and mathematics, to assess the student's performance against these standards, to hold schools accountable for the achievement of all the children, and to align their Title I programs with state policies. Forty-nine states have developed these standards at least in reading and mathematics, and 48 of these states have statewide assessment in these areas (Goertz, 2001).

All states have not come up with the same quality of standards, however. Some states have more rigorous standards while others have only broad, general goals that must be interpreted by the local school districts. There is also no agreement among the states about what constitutes low performance. A school that might be considered low performing in one state would be considered acceptable in another state. This inequity becomes a real problem because there are rewards and consequences for high and low performance. High performance may be rewarded with substantial bonuses, whereas low performance may result in threats of school closures, withholding of financial aid, firing of the principal, and/or moving the teachers to other schools. Bonuses are seen as a symbol of accountability by the

Mandated testing can be stressful for children.

public and a reward to be sought after. Being labeled low performing is an embarrassment to teachers and carries the risk that the state will take over the school. Teachers also face the possibility of expanded work hours for the training necessary to raise the performance of the children (Elmore & Fuhrman, 2001).

Since the development of these standards, tests, and accountability policies, some positive and some negative results have been observed. On the positive side there has been more attention given to the state curriculum, more standardization of the curriculum across schools within the state, higher expectations for student performance, and more support for low-performing schools and children. On the negative side there has been the overuse of instructional materials that are formatted like the state tests, neglect of subjects and topics that are not assessed by the state tests, and even the active discouragement of students (at the high-school level) from taking more higher-level courses out of fear that these students will lower the school's scores in these areas (McColskey & McMunn, 2000).

Schools have also engaged in short-term, quick-fix strategies to boost scores. These strategies are less likely to support the reforms that are needed to help prepare children for a successful future. Some of the more worrisome strategies are:

- Purchase of test-preparation workbooks
- Reduced emphasis on projects and subject matter that are not tested
- Attempts to motivate children through contests with cash rewards for best posters or slogans dealing with the test
- Encouraging children to sign contracts saying they will do their best on the test and what they will do to get ready for the test
- Creating bulletin boards that count down to test day
- Regularly giving classroom tests that mirror the state test
- Teaching test-taking strategies to children and sending poor test takers to the counselor for additional help with test strategies
- Having children take practice tests over the four- to six-week period before the actual test
- Buying computer programs developed for the sole purpose of raising test scores through practicing items written in the test format and using them either weekly or sometimes even daily
- Choosing staff development workshops that claim to raise test scores (McColskey & McMunn, 2000).

Other reasons for caution in the use of tests: possible loss of self-esteem by children who receive low scores, lowering of expectations for groups of children, distortion of curriculum, and the perils of the multiple-choice format, which confuses young children to the point where even strong readers may select the wrong answer from the limited choices given. Test scores are used to decide which children will be placed in the gifted and talented program or receive special tutoring, and they may become the basis for grouping children homogeneously into classrooms (Perrone, 1991).

Concern over the use of test scores and testing in general has been raised by several educational organizations. NAEYC's position is that testing is done to improve services and outcomes for children, and any resulting decisions about a child should be based on multiple sources of information, never on a single test score.

naeyc

These other sources would include systematic observations by teachers that are carefully recorded over time, samples of the child's work, and observations and anecdotes from parents and other family members (NAEYC, 1987).

Unfortunately, states are making decisions about curriculum based on test scores that their children achieve on state-mandated tests. Current studies and surveys are revealing some surprising and disturbing trends brought about because of these state tests. The most alarming finding is that the increase in children's scores may not translate into actual learning gains by the children but rather results primarily from students' familiarization with the tests. In North Carolina, a survey found that 80 percent of the teachers reported that children were spending more than 20 percent of their instructional time practicing for the state test. More than 28 percent of the teachers reported that children were spending more than 60 percent of the instructional time practicing for the test. The test preparation has become the instruction, especially in the lower socioeconomic schools and in minority classes.

The effect of this overemphasis is that these children are receiving little instruction in art, science, thinking skills, and other areas not assessed on the state tests. The very groups, minorities and children of poverty, that need the real gains that education can provide to become leaders for tomorrow are the ones receiving the most test practice and the least real academic instruction (McColskey & McMunn, 2000). Spending huge amounts of time practicing for the tests is often not the teachers' choice. Principals, or even school districts as a whole, decide practice policies for the teachers. In some instances, school districts have been known to send out worksheets weekly, one or more for each day of the week, to all the teachers to use with the children.

Even in schools where extensive practice is not mandated by the principal or the district, teachers may still spend large blocks of time on drilling for the test, and favorite units and themes that help integrate the academic subjects and make school more relevant for children will be left out. Indeed, some schools have done exactly this. Instead of making fundamental changes in the way children are taught, emphasis is placed on test-taking skills (Goertz, 2001). This policy is completely contrary to what experts say should be done. Experts say that only a relatively short period of time is needed to prepare children for the format of the test. This finding is collaborated by research that found a one-hour intensive reading readiness tutorial had the same impact on test results as two years of skill-directed instruction (Kohn, 2001).

Unfortunately, many schools begin in September to teach to the test by repeated worksheets that drill children in the skills that will be evaluated on the state test. By the time the children actually take the test in the spring, many are already tired of the repeated practice. Teachers have also been known to add to children's stress by constantly telling them they will not pass the test in the spring unless they pay attention. Though these teachers may have good intentions and are trying to motivate their children, this can cause children to become anxious, have nightmares, hate school, and fear the test. This type of comment can have an especially negative consequence on children in states where children are not allowed to graduate or go to the next grade level until they have passed the state test. Some districts have even chosen textbooks for their children based solely on how closely those textbooks mirror the state assessment tests.

Districts often fail to recognize that the single most important factor affecting the learning of children in any given classroom is the teacher, not the materials used and certainly not the amount of practice for a state test. Ms. Chang and Ms. Riley are cases in point. Both teachers are using the same reading approach and the same reading materials, yet Ms. Chang's children have consistently outscored Ms. Riley's children. The difference is not in the children: Both teachers have approximately the same number of children from the lower socioeconomic group, the same number from the middle class, approximately the same number of boys and girls, and ethnic diversity. The difference is in the quality of the teaching.

Ms. Chang received her test data last year showing her children were having trouble with the concept of inference. Ms. Chang thought about how she could bring this concept down to a more concrete level and came up with activities that would help children really understand what inference means. She began by bringing in objects from around her house that would allow the children to infer something about her family. She brought an old beat-up basketball that her brother used and asked the children to tell her something about her brother. They said, of course, that he must love basketball. She asked them why they said this. They said because the ball was so worn. She brought in her dad's army boots that were size 13. They inferred that he was large. After doing activities like this, she brought in comics from the newspaper. Many comics are only humorous if the reader can infer. Using these comics, Ms. Chang asked the children to tell her something in the first frame of the comic that was a fact. After working on facts, she asked what kinds of things they could infer and why they thought this. Ms. Chang used descriptive sentences, big books, trade books, and role playing for several weeks before she ever introduced the children to inference in a reading selection or on a worksheet. When Ms. Chang's children took the state assessment test, 94 percent of her children passed the questions on inference. In the previous year, approximately 76 percent of Ms. Chang's children had mastered inference on the state test.

Ms. Riley, on the other hand, also noticed that her children had not done as well as she hoped on the inference portion of the state test. Her approach to solving this problem involved having the children do inference worksheets for homework every night, answer inference questions in their textbook, and post and read a list of words that might indicate that the question was an inference question. Though Ms. Riley's percentage passing inference did rise, the children quickly forgot what inference was and the percentage increase was slight in comparison with Ms. Chang's data.

Schools that can resist the temptation to use quick-fix strategies might work to increase student learning, and hence test scores, by making use of four categories of long-term strategies. These strategies are:

- Using the state, national, and district standards to develop clear instructional goals that can be used by the classroom teacher
- Using a "less is more" approach to curriculum by either developing or buying high-quality materials that match the instructional goals
- Supporting collaboration by providing teachers with the time to discuss meaningful and challenging work that they have used successfully with their children so that other teachers can benefit by incorporating these lessons and strategies into their classroom instruction

- Understanding the place of assessment in the school and developing assessment instruments that will go beyond factual recall and will involve children in higher-level thinking skills (McColskey & McMunn, 2000).

Statewide assessment is a fact of life in today's schools. Given that this is so, teachers need to respond to these tests in a proactive manner. Teaching to the test is not in the best interest of the children. Children will become bored with worksheet after worksheet and will not get the enriched educational experiences that will make them the inventors and problem solvers of the next generation. Teachers need to practice good teaching, using recognized effective methods and spending only a few weeks "getting ready for the test." After the test results are back, teachers need to analyze the test data of their children, notice the areas where there are general weaknesses, and think of creative, concrete ways to teach those concepts to their children.

 What Teachers Are Saying

State-Mandated Testing

"I get so stressed in the spring when it is time for our state-mandated tests. It is so sad to me that no one seems to care that a child has progressed from reading on a first-grade level to a beginning third-grade level. All that administrators and the state care about is whether or not the child can pass that state test."

—*a third-grade teacher*

Ms. Chang's response to this teacher is that not all administrators are like this. Should a teacher find himself or herself with an administrator such as this, however, Ms. Chang suggests that the teacher begin sharing with that administrator from the very first of the year about the level of the children and the progress that they are making. This all should be documented by the teacher through teacher-made assessments and tests.

"I had a child in my classroom who could barely read on a first-grade level, but my school refused to test him for special ed until after he took our state reading test. When he took the test, he finished in 10 minutes because he just bubbled any answer. Other children took one to two hours to complete the test. Now, I thought, he will get the help he needs. Guess what—when the results came back, he passed! Then I really had to battle to have him tested." —*a third-grade teacher*

Ms. Chang points out that when teachers in previous grade levels have truly evaluated a child on his or her ability and this is reflected on the report card, unaccountably passing this test will be less of an issue. Ms. Chang points out that not all third-grade teachers are focused only on the state tests.

"I am lucky that my classroom is large enough to have centers. I love using centers to reinforce skills and to give children meaningful activities to do when they finish their work, instead of more worksheets. I have math, science, listening, reading, social studies and art centers." —*a third-grade teacher*

★ Working with Parents

Because Ms. Chang's third graders will have to take the state-mandated test in reading and math in the spring and this is a huge concern to parents, Ms. Chang keeps her parents informed of their child's progress throughout the year. Though Ms. Chang is not a believer in drill-and-practice worksheets for her children, she does believe that her children will pass this test if she employs good instructional methods. She communicates this to her parents so they will not think their children are going to come up short on the state test. Ms. Chang has found that the children only need four to six weeks to learn the format of the test. The rest of the school year she devotes to teaching the children the knowledge and skills that are in the third-grade curriculum.

Ms. Chang does send home examples of skills that will be tested in the spring after she has taught the children and they have practiced these skills. She asks the parents to work with their children and reinforce these skills. This week they have studied missing numbers in math. The children are expected to know what number comes before and after a given number. Ms. Chang has taught the children how to recognize the patterns in numbers and the children have quickly learned this skill. Now she sends home a note to the parents, giving a few examples and asking the parents to practice this skill with their children. In reading they have focused on sequencing events in stories. Ms. Chang has sent home a note to the parents about this skill and used the "Little Red Hen" story as an example. By using a story with a simple story line, she hopes to make it easier for parents to understand what their children were expected to do when asked to state the sequence of events in a story.

Ms. Chang has received positive feedback from her parents using this method. The children feel successful, the parents feel involved, and the additional practice and one-on-one attention that the parents can provide strengthen children's learning.

★ SUMMARY

Third grade is a pivotal year in the education of young children. The knowledge and skills in all subject areas become more complex. Because of state standards and mandated testing, children, teachers, and parents are feeling increasingly stressed. Some schools and teachers have attempted to deal with this stress and raise their test scores by spending increasing amounts of time on drill-and-practice type activities. Teachers and administrators need to resist any pressure that results in a narrowing of the curriculum to areas assessed on these tests. Children need to be actively involved in their learning—to have real, authentic reasons to read, write, and use their math and science skills.

★ DISCUSSION QUESTIONS

1. Discuss reading, writing, and math expectations for third-grade children.
2. Describe the various methods teachers use during reading instruction.
3. Discuss the writing process and the types of writing children are expected to master in third grade.

Issues and Trends

After-School Programs

There is currently an upswing in after-school programs offered to working parents with young, school-age children. The goals of these programs include keeping children safe, assisting with homework, improving academic achievement, and offering these programs at a rate that working families can afford.

The YMCA has such a program in the elementary schools called Prime Time. Prime Time hours may run from 6 a.m. to 6 p.m. Children are supervised at school. Fees vary according to income, and discounts are offered for more than one child. Children receive help with homework, have a snack, play sports and board games, and have playground time (YMCA Prime Time Before & Afterschool Program, 2003).

The Afterschool Alliance is a nonprofit organization that is working to ensure that all children have access to an after-school program by 2010. In October 2000, the Afterschool Alliance launched Lights on Afterschool. This event continues to take place in October of each year. The purpose of the event is to call attention to the importance of after-school programs. The Alliance has 60 national partners, such as 21st Century Community Learning Centers, J.C. Penney Afterschool, Boys and Girls Clubs of America, Junior Achievement and YMCA. In 2001, Arnold Schwarzenegger, the actor, accepted the role of chair of Lights on Afterschool (Lights on Afterschool, 2002).

4. What are the five essential features that apply across all grade levels in inquiry teaching and learning?

⭐ SUGGESTED CHAPTER ACTIVITIES

1. Visit a school in your district and look at its in-adoption reading and math textbooks. Using the information in this chapter, construct a rubric that can be used to evaluate a reading or math textbook.
2. Using the five essential features for inquiry teaching and learning, evaluate a third-grade science textbook and suggest changes that could be made to a particular lesson based on these features.
3. Use the five essential features for inquiry and develop a science lesson for third-grade on a topic not taught in the science book.
4. Obtain several third-grade writing samples. Discuss how the samples might be scored. Talk about strengths and weaknesses of each piece.
5. Visit your state website and find the third-grade standards. Does your state have an assessment test tied to these standards? How easy are these standards to use and understand as a basis for planning instruction?
6. Interview a third-grade teacher and ask how the children's test scores are used. Are scores tied to additional money for the school? Are there penalties for low performance?

Chapter Ten

Using Technology in the Early Childhood Classroom

CHAPTER OVERVIEW

★ Are you familiar with current practices and usage of computers in the classroom?

★ Do you know how to evaluate software and websites for use in the classroom?

★ Are you familiar with the basic vocabulary related to the computer and to the Internet?

★ Do you know how to integrate the computer into a lesson?

★ What are the various ways that a computer can be used in the classroom?

★ What are some of the other types of technology used in the classroom?

READING THIS CHAPTER WILL PROVIDE KNOWLEDGE ABOUT USING TECHNOLOGY IN THE CLASSROOM.

There is a real danger in using technology in the classroom for technology's sake when it may not enhance children's learning, and teachers need to ask themselves in each instance if this is the case. Using laser discs when it would be better to have the children do hands-on activities, depending on computer programs to determine comprehension levels of children instead of doing individual assessments, using computer programs to "teach" skills that will be tested by state tests instead of providing teacher instruction, and using the computer merely as a play center are all common ways teachers use technology, but they are not best practices for young children. Teachers should use technology to enhance children's learning by showing them things they could not otherwise see. Technology can greatly enhance all parts of a teacher's lesson. Using technology at the beginning of a lesson during the focus can capture children's attention and desire to learn more about a subject. Using technology during the presentation of the content material can add another dimension to the learning environment, as video clips and graphics can greatly enrich knowledge and understanding of the topic being studied. Technology can make a subject come seemingly alive for the children as it transports them to places outside of the classroom, and can make learning more meaningful. Seeing pictures of a volcano erupting does not compare to actually viewing an eruption on a video clip that shows the colors and sounds and force of that same eruption.

Teachers can also show children how to incorporate technology into their everyday lives, both at home and school, through use of the Internet, email, and production capabilities of technology.

Our children are facing a world that is constantly changing and becoming more complex in all areas. Businesses are constantly updating methods used in everyday operations and increasing the use of computers and other types of technology. Employers will expect our children to graduate from school with the technology skills necessary for the jobs of the twenty-first century. Parents also want their children to be prepared for either a job or entrance into a college or university when they graduate.

But what exactly is technology? "Broadly speaking, technology is the way people modify (invent, innovate, change, alter, design) their natural environment to suit their own purposes . . . but more generally it refers to the diverse collection of knowledge and processes that people use to extend human abilities and to satisfy human wants and needs (Dugger, 2001, p. 514)." Modern technology ranges from improved communication and wireless networks to advances in engineering and other areas that improve the lives of human beings. As most other industrialized countries incorporate technology education into their K–12 grade schools, the United States stands in stark contrast by the lack of emphasis placed on technology (Dugger, 2001).

With the International Technology Education Association initiative and the release of the *Standards for Technological Literacy: Content for the Study of Technology* (2000), schools in the United States began attempting to implement technology standards. *Standards for Technological Literacy* focuses on the skills and knowledge that students in grades K–12 should be able to do to be considered technologically literate. The National Educational Technology Standards (NETS) for Students is perhaps the most well-known set of standards. Benchmarks are provided for each of the 20 standards at grade levels of K–2, 3–5, 6–8, and 9–12. These standards are based on the belief that the study of technology should be a part of every student's basic educational program. These standards list six broad categories. Within each category are 10 performance indicators that are to be introduced and mastered by the

FIGURE 10.1 "Teacher, look what I made!"

This is my house.

children. Standards have been set for grades prekindergarten to grade 12. These standards are actually divided into four separate sets: pre-kindergarten–2, grades 3–5, grades 6–8, and grades 9–12. The broad categories are basic operations and concepts; social, ethical, and human issues; technology productivity tools; technology communication tools; technology research tools, and technology problem-solving and decision-making tools (International Technology Education Association, 2000).

Profile for Technology-Literate Students: Grades Pre-K to 2:

1. Be able to use input devices (mouse, keyboard) and output devices (printer, monitor) as children successfully operate computers, tape recorders, VCRs, and other technologies.
2. Be able to use a variety of technology and media for directed and independent learning.
3. Be able to communicate using accurate terminology.
4. Be able to use multimedia resources (multimedia encyclopedias, software).
5. Be able to work with others while using technology in the classroom.
6. Use ethical and positive social behavior while using technology.
7. Responsibly use technology systems and software.
8. Create multimedia products.
9. Be able to use technology resources for problem solving and communication of thoughts, ideas, and stories.
10. Be able to use telecommunications to gather information and communicate with others, with support from teachers or others. (National Educational Technology Standards, 2001)

Using the definition of technology previously stated, many various types of technology can be identified in the schools. The primary form that comes to mind is the use of the computer, yet technology also includes, but is not limited to, such things as overhead projectors, tape recorders, calculators, and laser disks.

In the United States and many other countries, computer literacy is now considered a component of the curriculum. Districts have technology budgets and teachers are being required to show in their lesson plans how they are teaching computer skills in their classrooms. Though technology does not consist of only computer-related hardware but includes other items such as overheads, digital cameras, and tape recorders, schools tend to consider technology and computers as synonymous. A 1999 Department of Education survey of 3,560 teachers found that only 20 percent of the teachers in kindergarten through twelfth grade considered themselves to be well prepared to incorporate computers into their classroom. Research has shown that children benefit the most when computers are integrated into the curriculum. Despite workshops and training for teachers, many teachers still are using computers in isolation instead of in the integrated manner that is needed. In elementary schools, computers are most commonly used in drill and practice or playing educational games rather than being used in a productive mode, such as for word processing, drawing, spreadsheet programs, or database programs (Berg, Benz, Lasley, & Raisch, 1998).

⭐ CURRENT PRACTICES IN THE CLASSROOM

Ashmus (2001) has described seven categories of computer use in the school classroom, addressing both the teacher's and child's use of the computer. One use restricted to the teacher is as an administrative tool: to write letters or notes, make tests, send e-mails, keep a grade book, and search on the Internet. For children, it may be used as a presentation tool, for e-mailing, for doing research and publishing, or for remediation.

As technology advances in society, school districts are becoming more concerned that their teachers master the skills associated with these technological advances. Though most districts seek to encourage their teachers to stay current, the Northwest Independent School District near Dallas, Texas, has tied teachers' pay raises to computer proficiency. The teachers in this district have been told that they will receive no pay raises until they prove that they are proficient at computer skills predetermined by the district (Houston Chronicle, 2001). Once the teachers have demonstrated their skills, they will also become eligible for additional technology tools. Some of the skills that the teachers are expected to have mastered include surfing the Web, e-mailing, creating web pages, using scanners, and building a spreadsheet. The teachers have been given five years in which to prove mastery of these skills. Other schools have withheld computers from teachers until they show mastery of the basics of computer operations. Twenty-two states have their own accountability plans that track technology accountability and technology use (Roberts, 2001b). Schools are developing self-assessment instruments for teachers to track and evaluate their technological skills. Levels range from non-use to the ability to design, create, and troubleshoot problems using a variety of technologies. The *National Educational Technology Standards* (2001) also addresses the skills of teachers. The NETS standards are somewhat more stringent. Teachers are expected to design and develop multimedia products, learn to use distance learning, participate in online collaborative projects, and design and develop web pages.

Other schools have chosen to address the lack of skills among their teachers through the use of computer labs. These schools have attempted to provide children with high-quality computer instruction by placing all their computers in one room and hiring a computer instructor. Children typically are scheduled for the computer lab one day a week. This has resulted in a lack of integration of the computer into all areas and has minimized the value of the computer as a useful and practical tool. By using computers in this manner, children fail to view the computer as an integral tool to be used in their everyday classroom learning.

However, this does simplify the assignment of a computer "grade," which is now required on some school report cards. Those districts that choose to have a computer teacher often find that the general education teacher feels that he or she is relieved of the responsibility of seeking ways to integrate the computer into his or her instruction. The situation is further complicated by the fact that most schools are unable to find and hire true computer instructors. Some schools simply hire an instructional aide to load the software before the classes come to the lab and to be

What Teachers are Saying

Their Computer Lab

"The computer lab in our school is so outdated that it is almost worthless."—*a second-grade teacher* (Schools and districts vary greatly in how they spend their technology budget. A teacher has the opportunity to join the technology committee and thereby have some say in how those dollars are spent.)

"We have two computer labs in our school; one is an Internet lab. We use the Internet lab 45 minutes a week. Each child has use of one computer. My children know how to start up, type in an appropriate child site, play, and shut down properly. I facilitate problems that arise." —*a kindergarten teacher*

"We only get to go to the computer lab for 30 minutes every other week."
—*a kindergarten teacher*

"We use our computer lab twice a week for an hour."—*a kindergarten teacher*

"My children get to use our computer lab once a month."—*a second-grade teacher*

an extra pair of hands in assisting the general education teacher. Teachers then use drill-and-practice software and educational games as their only instruction in the computer lab.

Another unfortunate use of the computer lab is occurring as more states are adopting mandated testing for children. More software is being developed that provides children with test practice. This leads to computer labs where children work their way through screen after screen of testing items. Subjected every week to this type of practice, children soon learn to dread going to the computer lab.

Instead of being used for drill and practice or educational games, the computer should be used to develop creative and problem-solving skills and as a tool for research and for product presentation. A truly integrated curriculum uses the interrelationships among the disciplines to learn about a specific topic. Children studying dinosaurs, for example, will use their reading ability to increase their knowledge of dinosaurs; their math ability to determine how large dinosaurs were through measuring activities; their writing ability by keeping a science journal; and their computer skills to do online research about dinosaurs and to prepare and present a report on a particular dinosaur.

COMPUTER LITERACY

Computer literacy is the ability to use computers coupled with an understanding and knowledge about computers. In our world, computer literacy is becoming as important as traditional literacy involving reading and writing. Today more children from middle and upper socioeconomic status homes are beginning school with some computer skills. The problem is that children from poorer families are not afforded the same exposure to computers in their homes and now are in danger of being computer illiterate. Thus, it is crucial that their teachers incorporate computer usage into the curriculum in an integrated manner and not just use the computers for drill and practice and for playing games.

Integrating the computer into the daily activities of the children does not mean simply inserting the computer as another area of study, but incorporating it into the existing curriculum in a meaningful way. Unfortunately, many early childhood teachers lack the understanding of how to do this. This integration comes through planning computer activities. In using technology in a specific lesson, the teacher must decide where in the teaching sequence the most effective placement for a technology component will be. Looking at three major components of the teaching sequence—the focus, the actual teaching, and the closing—the teacher decides which areas to use technology in. Using technology in the focus section allows for a novel experience that stimulates the children's interest. Using technology in the teaching portion allows children to use technology to conduct research and prepare products displaying what they have learned. Using technology in the closing section of the teaching sequence can leave children with enthusiasm about the subject and can lead to their continued study of the subject matter (Aloia, 1998).

Teachers need to become very familiar with the computers and the software in their classrooms. The best way to gain this familiarity is to spend time with the computer exploring at length each software program while thinking about how each program could be incorporated into specific lessons. A survey by Berg and colleagues (1998) of teachers who were considered by their principal to be exemplary technology users in their classroom revealed that 95 percent of these teachers developed their computer skills on their own. Computer skills cannot be learned in a single workshop, which only provides an introduction to a computer skill. To be able to use this training effectively in the classroom, the teacher must use the computer and practice what he or she has learned. Berg also found that exemplary teachers used their computers predominantly for productivity activities, not basic skills or drill and practice.

⭐ COMPUTER USAGE

Often those schools that utilize the computer lab approach provide at least one computer in the classroom. It is the teacher's decision as to how and to what extent this computer will be utilized. Often these computers are used as a separate center or as reinforcement for completing individual seatwork.

Children younger than age 3 learn by exploration with their bodies: their mouths, hands, eyes, ears, and legs (Haugland, 1999b). For these children, computer use is not generally recommended. By age 3, few children will display sustained interest in the computer, preferring instead to play with concrete materials (Anselmo & Zinck, 1987). These children are developing their language and manipulative abilities, and their main avenue of learning is primarily through exploration and discovery (Hill, 1996). Moderate use of the computer by 4-year-olds has been noted (Anselmo & Zinck, 1987). For children ages 3 and 4, the computer should be just another center (Haugland, 1999b). Appropriate software should be loaded each day and children should be allowed to use the computer. Some children may want to just stand behind the computer at first and watch other children use it. This seems to be especially true of children who have had very limited previous exposure to the computer. To help these children become more at ease with the computer, they could be paired with children who are more comfortable and capable computer users. Other children will display competence at the computer. In either case, the teacher should give minimal instructions. The role of the teacher is one of facilitator as children actively explore the computer. The teacher should become involved only if children are experiencing a problem with the software or when the teacher notes that an explanation can lead a child to an increased understanding of the program or computer. Kindergartners enthusiastically embrace the computer and are easily engaged in active software programs. In first grade and subsequent grades, as children become more interested in the world around them and are able to communicate more effectively through reading and writing, the computer can become one of the tools that they use to explore key concepts and obtain information about topics that interest them (Ortega & Ortega, 1995). Computer usage generally increases with the age of the child.

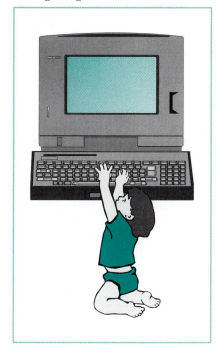

FIGURE 10.2 Children Are Using Computers at Younger and Younger Ages

A prime concern about the use of computers in any early childhood classroom has to be one of developmental appropriateness. If the computer is used in a developmentally appropriate manner, children will be able to interact with the computer and control the computer in a way that they can understand. Because the program or software that is being used determines the amount of control that the child has over the computer, developmentally appropriate software would be software that allows the child to control when to return to the main menu, exit from the program, or move to another screen.

The National Association for the Education of Young Children (NAEYC) adopted a position statement on technology and young children ages 3 through 8 in April of 1996. The entire position statement may be viewed at the NAEYC's website (www.naeyc.org/resources/position_statements/pstech98.htm), but the following points illustrate its position.

naeyc

> Although now there is considerable research that points to the positive effects of technology on children's learning and development (Clements 1994), the research indicates that, in practice, computers supplement and do not replace highly valued early childhood activities and materials, such as art blocks, sand, water, books, exploration with writing materials, and dramatic play. Research indicates that computers can be used in

developmentally appropriate ways beneficial to children and also can be misused, just as any tool can (Shade & Watson 1990). Developmentally appropriate software offers opportunities for collaborative play, learning, and creation. Educators must use professional judgment in evaluating and using this learning tool appropriately, applying the same criteria they would to any other learning tool or experience. They must also weigh the costs of technology with the costs of other learning materials and program resources to arrive at an appropriate balance for their classrooms.

naeyc

NAEYC further states that the teacher must make a professional judgment in determining the use of technology based on its cultural, age, and individual appropriateness. Used appropriately, technology can enhance the cognitive and social skills of children. Technology should be integrated into the curriculum and is only one of several options that are used to enhance children's learning. Equitable access to computers must be promoted for all children and their families. Care must be taken that the technology is free of stereotyping and violence. Teachers and parents should actively advocate appropriate technology applications. Through this collaboration, publishers would be encouraged to develop software that shows nonviolent ways to solve problems. The software should also reflect gender, cultural, and other types of diversity. Teachers need to receive appropriate training and ongoing support to be prepared to make appropriate decisions regarding technology use in their classrooms.

⭐ SOFTWARE FOR THE EARLY CHILDHOOD CLASSROOM

Besides being interesting and motivating, a good computer program will reinforce a child for the correct answer and give instruction for wrong answers. Computer programs can read to children, help children learn the sounds of the alphabet and basic math and science concepts, have the ability to recognize children's voices, and be able to play high-quality music and full-motion video (Buckleitner, 1999). Children generally find these types of programs fun and want to spend time "playing" on the computer.

naeyc

NAEYC's position statement on technology and young children also lists specific recommendations for early childhood professionals as they advocate for more appropriate technology applications. The organization suggests that parents and teachers communicate with software publishers and encourage them to create a balance of programs for boys and girls, create programs that foster collaboration instead of competition, reflect nonviolent ways to solve problems, have features that cater to the needs of children with different abilities, and make previewing easier for parents and teachers (NAEYC, 1996).

As teachers and parents are bombarded with a virtual plethora of software, and as software becomes more available and affordable, it becomes critical for the teacher and parent to have some means of evaluating the software that children will be using.

Software Evaluation

With the advent of computer usage in the early childhood classroom, the task of the teacher in evaluating materials moved from simply evaluating books with a two-dimensional, ink-on-paper format with little changes in the process for the last 300 years to evaluating new material, software, that is multidimensional and interactive. Now the teacher needs to decide how important is it for the child to be in control rather than having the software control what the child is able to see and do, what types and variety of activities are provided and what they are teaching, how the program portrays people and their interactions, and whether different abilities are accommodated as well as evaluating the quality of the program (Buckleitner, 1999). The teacher's theoretical orientation is also important in making decisions about software. There is software based on constructivist thinking in child development, in which children explore and develop their own meaning, and there is software that takes a behaviorist approach to the activities presented in the software program by using reinforcement for correct responses (Buckleitner, 1999).

In the early 1980s, with computers emerging as a novel and exciting addition to the classroom, substantially more research was done on evaluating software than is being done today. In 1996, evaluations of software began to appear online. Some online databases that publish evaluations of software allow anyone to respond to a particular software program. Amazon.com, an Internet bookstore, is one of many that publishes just such a website (Buckleitner, 1999). A teacher can quickly be connected to these evaluation sites by searching the Internet using the terms *software evaluation, reviews of children's software,* or *children's software.* Universities, magazines, and other organizations have websites that often include ratings of software programs used by children.

Evaluation scales are also found in great number on the Internet. There are scales developed by school districts for their teachers to use; scales published by national organizations, universities, and well-qualified professionals; and scales published by individuals who don't list their credentials and leave the viewer with no way to rate the reliability or validity of the scales presented on their sites. These instruments vary from simplistic to very involved, and from hard to understand and score to easy to understand and score. Many scales have been used and specific software evaluated, but only now are researchers beginning to study the relationship between the evaluation score on particular instruments and children's preferences. In a study done by Escobedo and Evans (1997), children were videotaped as they chose from 13 software programs that had been rated as developmentally appropriate using the Haugland and Shade scale. Although results showed that programs that were identified as developmentally appropriate by the instrument showed some positive relationship to children's preferences, some programs rated inappropriate were actually preferred by the children. The study did show that what was most important to the children was the opportunity to interact with the computer. Though children may sometimes prefer software that is developmentally inappropriate just as they may prefer candy to fruit, developmentally appropriate software is a must for the early childhood classroom. Teachers must make decisions based on what is good for the children, what meets the needs of the children, and whether the cost of the software is justified by the benefits to children.

A review of software evaluation scales reveals many consistencies across the various scales, whether or not they purport to show developmental appropriateness. Of 10 evaluation scales picked at random from the many available online, seven emphasized the importance of the child, or learner, as the one in control of the program: being able to exit a game or activity and return to the main menu, being able to save and print. It helps the child be in control when directions to the program are offered verbally as part of the program itself. It also helps the child be more independent when icons are used that symbolize the actual function. For instance, a child who wants to erase something he or she has written can choose the icon showing an eraser. Likewise, a child who wants to write a message can choose the pencil icon. All the evaluation instruments did stress the importance of the learning objectives and the depth and accuracy of the information provided to the children. The instruments ranged in simplicity of form from seven items to four pages in length. The more detailed evaluation instruments included items that scored the age-appropriateness of the software, the quality of graphics, the inclusion of sound, freedom from bias or stereotypes in the presentation, activities for a broad range of abilities, ease of use after an introduction to the program, and absence of errors in content, grammar, spelling, and punctuation.

Publishers may list a wide range of ages for their software. As teachers evaluate the software, they should question if the range listed by the publisher is actually appropriate for all the ages listed. Sometimes the content may be inappropriate even if the skill level is appropriate. It is hard to make software that is appropriate for 12-year-old children also be appropriate in skill level and content for 3- or 4-year-old children. Even programs that focus on a narrow age range still need to have a low entry level for a child to feel successful while still offering more challenging levels for the more advanced children.

Several of the instruments address developmental appropriateness. One system that has been specifically developed for the early childhood classroom is the Haugland Developmental Software Scale (1999a). The Haugland scale is one of the more detailed evaluation instruments. The user of this scale rates the software on key areas such as age appropriateness, process learning, and use of a real-world model. There are two ways that this scale differs from others. The first way is the category of nonviolence. Not only is the software screened to see if it is free of violent characters and actions, it is also assessed for models of positive social values. In addition to no violent characters, the software is assessed for objects that can be used for violence, such as guns and swords, and whether the children are engaged in violent actions within the program. Interestingly enough, nonviolence was not mentioned in any of the other nine evaluation instruments, some of which were actually developed by school districts and universities.

The second way this instrument differs from the others is in the evaluation of absence of bias. Though most of the other instruments list freedom from bias, race, or gender, Haugland's instrument goes much further. The Haugland instrument checks for programs that offer multiple languages; show mixed gender and role equity; and portray people of diverse cultures, ages, abilities, and diverse family styles.

Evaluating software can be a very time-consuming process because it is important for the teacher to explore thoroughly every part of the program. As a part of this exploration, it is important for the teacher to anticipate ways that the child may react to the program and push keys that a child might push. This will show potential problems and limitations of the program. Even after a favorable evaluation of a software program, the teacher needs to watch how the children actually use it. Some programs contain a game for children to play after they engage in the educational portion of the program. By observing the children, the teacher can see if they are circumventing the educational part of the program in order to play the game. This is a common occurrence, and teachers are constantly amazed at the ability of young children to figure out how to do this.

Instructions for a program are a concern with software for the very young and/or special-needs children. Do the instructions require reading? If so, these groups will be immediately limited in the use of the program. If the instructions are verbal, is the voice readily understandable and does the program use words that children will understand?

Being able to escape to the main menu is a very important option. Teachers and children become frustrated when a lesson is started and must be completed or the computer must be restarted in order to stop the lesson and return to the main menu.

More than likely, schools will have a substantial inventory of software they have already purchased. After evaluating the software for developmental appropriateness, a record of the software, its score, and a list of all its features should be made. A brainstormed list of all the areas this software could be used in would be a practical addition to the record. Keeping such a list allows teachers to have at their fingertips the skills and content covered by each software program and helps them in planning appropriate integration activities.

WEBSITES

The advent of the Internet has allowed our children to move beyond the school walls as they interact with children and experts from all over the world. The Internet allows children to take field trips and explore areas and subjects in a way that was never possible before. Museums, organizations, schools, businesses, and individuals have published websites that can be visited and information that can be gleaned for many school activities.

Schools must have access to the Internet to use websites in their instruction. A survey of the state of technology across the United States (31 states out of 50 responding)) conducted by *Technological Horizons in Education Journal (THE),* found that a majority of elementary-level classrooms have at least one computer with Internet access (Roberts, 2001b). The state of Virginia reported 100 percent of their elementary and middle school classrooms had computers with Internet access. Funding is generally obtained through several sources: state departments of education, federal funds, local funds, and gifts and grants.

In the past few years there has been an explosion of new websites, many of which are excellent and others that are providing children with incorrect or misleading information. In using the Internet for research, children need to use the same critical reading skills that they would with any other form of written work. Just because something is written on a website does not mean that it is correct. This poses a danger not only for children, but also for their parents. Parents come to school and approach their child's teacher with information that they have gotten off the Internet and present it to the teacher as fact. Because of this, it is important for teachers themselves to know how to assess and evaluate information from the Internet.

In assessing information from the Internet, several questions should be asked before considering the information trustworthy. First, is the site from a nationally recognized organization? Obviously, information from this type of site can be considered more reliable than a site published by an individual. If the site is not nationally recognized, is it affiliated with a recognized organization? If an individual publishes the site, it must be viewed with caution because many people who publish these sites have an ax to grind or propaganda to transmit. Is the site selling a book or type of treatment? These sites must be considered an advertisement. Their primary goal is to sell their product, and their information may be less than accurate or even distorted. In areas such as science, where knowledge is quickly expanding, websites may not always be updated in a timely manner and the information may be dated or no longer accurate.

Children can be taught to think critically about what they see on the Web. They also need to realize that the Web might not be the best research tool to use when they are seeking information. Often they might be able to find the information they need in a few minutes by picking up a book. The Ithaca College Library lists suggestions for children using the Web.

- Be sure that the Web is the place the child needs to be. Old materials will often not show up on the Web. Not everything is on the Web.
- Question the authority of all sources found on the Web.
- Try to find out who the author of the page is. Check the site's top level domain—.com, .org, .net, .gov, .edu, or geographic code. A tilde (~) usually means that the site was created by someone given space on the Web server and is a personal page created by a person possibly lacking credentials.
- Identify the reason the page exists. Is it trying to sell something, persuade, or inform?
- Look at the material presented. Check the spelling, grammar, the date the page was last updated, and the kinds of sources linked to the page.
- Understand that web pages are different from pages found on the Web. Although books and periodicals are accessible through the Web, web pages generally do not refer to this type of source. Libraries contain online, full-text materials available in databases. It can be harder for a child to determine the quality of an article or journal when it is viewed online. (Henderson, 2000)

When children are ready to use the Internet, teachers must be aware that unless some type of blocking program is installed, they can easily and unintentionally access pornographic or adult sites. Blocking programs will limit, to a certain extent, access to information on the Internet because these methods usually focus on key words. A legitimate search, however, can be stymied by use of a word that is blocked.

FIGURE 10.3 Website Evaluation Rating Scale

Name of Website _____

Site Address   _____

Rate each item on a scale of 1 to 3: 1 = below average, 2 average, and 3 above average.

Site loads quickly	1	2	3
First screen lists site's content	1	2	3
Navigates forward, backward, and easily through site	1	2	3
Instructions simple and clear	1	2	3
Verbal instructions	1	2	3
Child able to use independently after instructions	1	2	3
Icons' purposes clear	1	2	3
Instructions can be bypassed	1	2	3
Can exit site at any time	1	2	3
Appropriate for age/ages listed	1	2	3
Ability levels vary from easy to hard	1	2	3
Learning objectives clear	1	2	3
Learning objectives are reached through discovery	1	2	3
Free from content error	1	2	3
Advertising is limited or inappropriate	1	2	3
No violent characters	1	2	3
No violent actions	1	2	3
Free from stereotypes	1	2	3
Graphics load quickly and are clear	1	2	3
Includes sound	1	2	3
Colorful	1	2	3
Includes animation	1	2	3
Prints	1	2	3
Shows diverse people	1	2	3
Site functions well during high traffic times	1	2	3
Cautions given when prompting for personal information	1	2	3

Total each column   _____   _____   _____

Add all three columns for a total score   _____

Scoring: 70 to 75 = superior
                62 to 69 = good
                54 to 61 = average

Some websites function in a very similar manner to software, and the evaluation instruments are remarkable similar. Figure 10.3 shows one type of evaluation instrument used for websites. Like software evaluation instruments, a multitude of evaluation instruments is available for websites published on the Internet. Instruments should be examined and used based on the information that the teacher is most interested in having for the children. One significant different between software and websites is the inclusion of commercial promotions and ads on the websites. Another difference is that the speed with which the website loads and runs is somewhat determined by the number of "hits," or people attempting to log on to the website at any given time.

Websites for children can be classified into four types: information, communication, interaction, and publication (Haugland, 2000). *Information sites* help children learn more about topics that they find interesting. *Communication sites* allow children to e-mail other children or adults. Children may ask an "expert" questions. Interaction sites function in a similar manner to software programs. Publication sites publish the work of the children (Haugland, 2000).

A first skill children need in order to gain information from the Internet is knowing how to go to a given address. Since all letters, numbers, and symbols must be exact, this sometimes presents a problem for children who are inattentive to details. Once having learned to locate an address, children are ready to begin to learn how to use the search engines to find information about topics of interest. From here children learn how to copy and paste information from websites into a word processing program. Children may also learn to e-mail their teachers and friends.

☆ BASIC INTERNET TERMS FOR TEACHERS

Many teachers use terms related to the Internet but have no real understanding of these terms and could not even explain what these terms mean. As technology use increases, it becomes important for teachers to understand these terms in order to understand discussions with computer technology-support people as well as with children. The following terms should be considered basic knowledge for the early childhood teacher. Most definitions are from *The Computer Desktop Encyclopedia* (Freedman, 1996).

Internet	The Internet is made up of more than 100,000 interconnected networks in over 100 countries, composed of commercial, academic, and government networks. Originally developed for the military, the Internet became widely used for academic and commercial research and users had access to unpublished data and journals on a huge variety of subjects. Today, the Internet has become commercialized into a worldwide information highway, providing information on every subject known to humankind (p. 461).
World Wide Web	An Internet facility that links documents locally and remotely. The Web document is called a web page and links in the page let users jump from page to page (hypertext), whether the pages are stored on the same server or on servers around the world. Pages

	are accessed and read via a web browser such as Netscape Navigator or Internet Explorer (Freedman, 1999, p. 1030).
Web browser	Access to the Internet is achieved through an Internet browser. The browser enables a user to get information from a server (a computer that stores information). The http code allows the browser to retrieve the information requested from the server. Microsoft's Internet Explorer and Netscape Navigator are the most common browsers (Reksten, 2000).
Home page	The first page that appears when a website is accessed. It serves as a table of contents to the rest of the pages on the site or to other websites (Freedman, 1999, p. 406).
Search engines	Software that searches for data based on some criteria (p. 799). Search engines help users find information. Examples of search engines are named Yahoo, Google, and Web Crawler. Searches may be conducted based on subject, title, or author. Results will be displayed by the number of "hits" found, the title of the site, the address, and sometimes a brief description of the site.
Uniform resource locators (URL)	The address that defined the route to a file on the web or any other Internet facility (Freedman, 1999, p. 947). The http code tells the browser that it is looking for a web page and the rest of the address tells the browser the name of the server that holds the web page.

⭐ COMPUTER SKILLS NEEDED BY CHILDREN

Children as young as 3 years old are able to begin learning the skills necessary for independent use of the computer. These skills include how to turn the computer off and on, how to select and load software, how to use the keyboard, how to follow the directions, how to identify the basic parts of the computer (monitor, keyboard, mouse, computer, and printer) and how to print and save their work. Instruction in these skills must take place at the computer. A teacher who is trying to teach a child a multistepped method for loading software, for example, should do an analysis of the task and make note of all the individual steps necessary for loading the software. The teacher should then teach the child using these steps. If a child is unable to complete a skill on his or her own, the teacher should assist the child in completion of the task. The child should be allowed and encouraged to complete as much of the task as possible. This teacher is acting as a support, or scaffold, as the child learns the skill. Keys needed for the operation of software may be marked in some way on the computer. Keys may be color coded by placing self-adhesive dots on the keys. For example, a child who wants to quit or escape a program can push the escape key, the one with the red dot.

As children become more familiar with the computer and are ready for word processing programs, they will learn the skills and terms needed to use these programs.

Possible Word Processing Skills/Lessons

Children will learn how to:

Delete	Use bold and italics
Highlight	Capitalize letters
Change font style	Use underline
Change font size	Center work
Justify left	Cut and paste
Import clip art	Import graphics from the Web
Use spell checker	Use grammar checker
Save to a disk	Load and print from a disk

By third grade, most children should be able to use these skills in their work. One benefit of a computer lab is that these skills can be taught to the entire class at one time. These skills should be taught, however, in the context of an authentic task. For example, when writing a story, children can learn to boldface and center the title and change the font size and style. Because this learning is occurring in an authentic context, children will have more interest in learning. Those skills can be practiced repeatedly with all the following stories that the children write.

Other skills on the computer include home row keyboarding ability. The home row is the row with the keys A, S, D, F that the fingers of the left hand rest on when typing, and J, K, L, keys that the fingers of the right hand rest on when typing. Home row is usually taught at the beginning of third grade. Children also need to know how to log on to the Internet, locate a web page when given the address, and use a search engine to find information. The speed with which computer skills are obtained depends on the child's prior exposure to and interest in the computer. Children who have already been using the computer at home will be familiar with many of the basic vocabulary terms that are needed when learning how to use the computer. Technology standards should be utilized, whether they be local, state, or national, to ensure that no skills are overlooked.

☆ BASIC COMPUTER VOCABULARY FOR CHILDREN

The following are terms that children begin to learn and use as they develop computer skills. Children should not be expected to memorize these definitions; rather, the teacher needs to know and understand these definitions in order to explain the terms to the children. As children use these terms to describe activities they are doing, they become part of the children's vocabulary (Definitions from Freedman, 1996).

boot	To cause the computer to start executing instructions.
CD-ROM	(compact disc read-only memory) A compact disc format used to hold text, graphics, and hi-fi stereo sound.

click	To select an object by pressing the mouse button when the cursor is pointing to the required menu option or icon.
crash	Occurs when the computer is presented with instructions or data it cannot recognize or the program is reaching beyond its protective boundary. If the program is running on a personal computer under a single-task (one program at a time) operating system such as DOS, the computer locks up and has to be rebooted.
cursor	A movable symbol onscreen that is the contact point between the user and the data.
desktop	An on-screen representation of a desktop.
disk	A direct access storage device.
disk drive	A peripheral storage device that holds, spins, reads, and writes magnetic or optical disks.
drag	To move an object onscreen during which its complete movement is visible from starting location to destination.
graphics	The creation and manipulation of picture images in the computer.
hardware	Machinery and equipment such as monitors, keyboards, and printers.
icon	A small, pictorial, on-screen representation of an object (file, program, disk, etc.) used in graphical interfaces.
keyboard	A set of input keys.
load	To copy a program from some source, such as a disk or tape, into memory for execution.
menu	An on-screen list of available functions, or operations, that can be performed currently.
modem	A device that adapts a terminal or computer to a telephone line.
monitor	A display screen used to present output from a computer, camera, VCR, or other video generator.
mouse	A popular pointing device that is used to move the cursor onscreen.
printer	A device that converts computer output into printed images.
program	A collection of instructions that tells the computer what to do.
pull-down menus	A menu that is displayed from the top of the screen downward when its title is selected.
restart	To resume computer operation after a planned or unplanned termination (Freedman, 1996, p. 768).
save	To copy the document, record, or image being worked on onto a storage medium.
scanner	A device that reads a printed page and converts it into a graphics image for the computer (Freedman, 1996, p. 790).
software	Instructions for the computer. Software tells the hardware how to process the data.

sound card	An expansion board that allows a computer to output sounds.
video card	(display adapter) An expansion board that plugs into a desktop computer that converts the images created in the computer to the electronic signals required by the monitor (Freedman, 1996, p. 250).
virus	Software used to infect a computer. After the virus code is written, it is buried within an existing program. Once that program is executed, the virus code is activated and attaches copies of itself to other programs in the system. Infected programs copy the virus to other programs.
window	A scrollable viewing area on screen.

⭐ Working with Parents

Teachers are able to show parents how their children are using technology in school by hosting a Computer Family Night. After deciding on a date and time, the children can type and print personal invitations to their families. As families arrive in the computer lab, a digital camera or video camera is used to take their picture and this picture is put onto a disk. After the disk is loaded into the computer, the parents can add a 30-second message in their native language, scan photos brought from home,

Computer Family Night showcases children's computer skills.

and type information about their family. The families learn to create a slide show and then share it with a family that they do not know. Reviews by the parents from such nights reveal that parents are impressed with what their children are learning and enjoyed participating in the program (Early Literacy Technology Project, 2001).

CARE OF THE COMPUTER

In addition to basic skills on the computer, children should be taught the basic care and cleaning of the computer. Care of the computer can be a task that is shared by the teacher and the children as a normal part of the daily routine.

Children's Role in the Care of the Computer

Just as they are taught the proper way to play with and use paint in the Art Center, children need to be taught how to take care of the computer. Fingers that are sticky from a lunch or snack need to be washed off before using the computer. Cups

Issues and Trends

Parents' View of Software Assistance in Preparing for State-Mandated Tests

A national survey conducted in 2000 by Harris Interactive and sponsored by Sylvan Learning Center and the Association for Supervision and Curriculum Development found an interesting pattern of responses to the question, "Do you believe additional preparation outside of school could help your child perform better on state-mandated assessments?" Those parents who were least familiar with the tests (83 percent) felt the need for outside preparation. An overwhelming 87 percent of these parents believed software would be of more assistance than options offered at school, such as special workshops and help sessions (National Survey Gauges Parent Perceptions of State-Mandated, Standardized Tests, 2000).

What is disturbing about this survey is these parents' seeming belief that software is more beneficial to preparing their children for state tests than is working with a teacher. This belief is not at all supported by current research. Most software programs, to date, are not of great assistance in preparing children. Working with a teacher in a one-on-one situation or in small groups continues to be the best. Working with a teacher allows the teacher to evaluate the child, discuss misconceptions, and talk about why an answer is right or wrong. The child's faulty thinking and reasoning can be corrected by the teacher, which can lead to greater understanding of the concept or skill.

of water, juice, and/or food can be a hazard to the computer and need to be kept well away from the Computer Center. Children can be taught to take a cloth and wipe off the monitor screen. Disks should be kept in a central location, neatly organized in some fashion in a storage box. Disks can be color coded in several ways. They can be color coded by difficulty of the program or by subject. All reading programs could be coded green, for instance. As with any center, the children are taught the proper use and handling of all the components.

The Teacher's Role in the Care of the Computer

Some basic cleaning needs to be done on a regular basis to keep the computer running smoothly. Always remember to unplug the computer before cleaning it with any cleaner. To remove the fingerprints and dirt from the standard screen, use window cleaner sprayed onto a soft rag. Never use paper towels because they can scratch the screen. If the screen has a chemically treated filter to remove glare, use only the special cleaner that came with the filter. Regular window cleaner may dissolve the chemicals on the filter. The keyboard may be cleaned by spraying a window cleaner on a soft rag and wiping down the keyboard. Never spray the cleaner directly on the keyboard because this might cause an electrical short. If the mouse is the older, standard type with a ball on the underside, the ball should periodically be removed and washed with a mild soap. To remove the ball, turn the mouse over and use your thumbnail to turn the door that holds the ball. After washing the ball, dry it and clean the rollers in the mouse with a cotton cloth, removing any grime and dirt, before putting the ball back. For further instructions on the care and cleaning of computers, refer to Shade (1996).

INTEGRATING THE COMPUTER INTO THE CURRICULUM

Integrating the computer or any technology into the curriculum begins with planning. As with any good lesson, the teacher begins planning the unit or theme with a survey of all the material available—books, maps, manipulatives, and the like along with available software and websites. It is helpful to keep a comprehensive list of software and websites with descriptions of their content, adding to the list as new software is purchased and websites are discovered. Teachers should be encouraged to share not only their lists, but also how they are integrating the software and websites. The time spent planning a unit or theme is a crucial component of a successful lesson. Planning allows the teacher to ensure that the unit's learning objectives will be taught and can increase interest in the lesson by utilizing a variety of ways to introduce and teach the objectives.

Teachers can also use the Internet to find lessons that other teachers have written and used successfully that already have technology integrated into the lesson. These lessons may be published by the teachers' school on the school website, by the teachers, or as a part of another website. One example has the teacher introducing an ABC book to children in kindergarten. The teacher tells the children that they will make an ABC book for their classroom. The children brainstorm words that begin with a few of the letters, take pictures with a digital camera, watch the teacher load the pictures into the computer, and use cutting and pasting to import the picture into a word processing document. The teacher can then type, or assist the child in typing, a couple of sentences under the picture. The sentences might read: (child's name) _____ found a (item) _____. (Item) _____ starts with the letter _____ (Woodside, 2001).

Getting Started

When a teacher is adding technology to a unit that already exists, some simple steps will help with the organization and provide important information to other teachers who attempt to use this same lesson. The following plan was developed by a second-grade teacher for a unit on dinosaurs.

I. List All Available Resources for the Theme or Unit

These resources should be listed by the category into which they fall: types of books, manipulatives, software, websites, and music. (Be sure to include descriptions of software and websites.) For example: You are planning a unit on dinosaurs. Here is a partial listing of resources for this theme.

Nonfiction books:	*Dinosaurs: The Real Monsters,* Dougal Dixon
	Dinosaurs: A Closer Look, Dougal Dixon
	A Golden Guide to Fossils, F. H. T. Rhodes, H. S. Zim, & P. R. Shaffer
Fiction books:	*The Berenstain Bears and the Missing Dinosaur Bone* by Stan & Jan Berenstain
	Danny the Dinosaur by Syd Hoff
	Dinosaur Dinner: With a Slice of Alligator Pie by Dennis Lee
Manipulatives:	dinosaur cookie cutters
	plastic dinosaur figures
	assortment of fossils
Software:	*Kid Pix* (Broderbund, 1992)
	CD-ROM Encyclopedia
	Storybook Weaver (MECC, 1992)
	I Can Be a Dinosaur Finder (Educational Insights)
Websites:	American Museum of Natural History (http://amnh.org) includes videos and fossil remains on display
	National Geographic Dinosaur Eggs (www.nationalgeographic.com/dinoeggs) children can hunt and hatch dinosaur eggs
	National Museum of Natural History (www.mnh.si.edu)
Music:	Three Dinosaurs Dreadly (Developmental Learning Materials (DLM); storyline similar to *Three Billy Goats Gruff*
	My Weekly Reader dinosaur songs

II. Make a List of Content Areas, Centers, and Ideas for Instruction

Computer Center

1. Have children research dinosaurs using the software and the websites.
2. Have children write about dinosaurs using *Kid Pix* or *Storybook Weaver*.
3. Visit the National Geographic site and hatch dinosaur eggs.

Math

1. Measure length of triceratops, T-Rex, and stegasaurus.
2. Make dinosaur-shaped cookies.
3. Trace cookie cutters on graph paper and figure which dinosaur shape has the greatest area.
4. Set up a grid in the Sand Table by stringing yarn across the Sand Table and tape labels to the grid (letters for columns and numbers for rows). Bury three chicken bones that have the meat boiled off. Display a poster paper (laminated) grid beside the Sand Table and mark the coordinates where the bones are buried.Have children read the poster board grid and dig for the bones. Children then can rebury the bones in a new location and change the poster board grid to mark the location (Davidson, 1989).

Science

1. Classify dinosaurs.
2. Use plastic dinosaurs and have children write descriptions of the dinosaurs in their science journal.
3. Compare fossils by size and weight. Use reference materials to determine what the fossil is.
4. Which dinosaur could move the fastest? Support your position with research.

Reading

Read fiction and nonfiction books about dinosaurs.

Writing

Have children write a report on a dinosaur of their choice.

Computer Lab

During a regularly scheduled lab time, have children type their dinosaur report on the computer. Bolding, centering, indenting, capitalization, and spell checking are the skills they will be working on in the lab.

Drama

Have the children design and make dinosaur costumes for the musical "Three Dinosaurs Dreadly." DLM includes a tape with the story sung by the characters. Have students perform their "musical" for other classes.

Art

1. Use plaster of paris and the plastic dinosaurs and make footprints of these dinosaurs.
2. Draw and label parts of the dinosaurs.
3. Design, either on paper or using the computer, a make-believe dinosaur that has yet to be discovered.

III. Preview the Software in the School

As new (and old) software is previewed, the teacher can brainstorm all the possible ways that this software might fit into the themes that are taught during the year.

Brainstorm a List of Ways to Integrate the Computer

1. In studying letter writing in class, use the computer to write a letter to a pen pal.
2. In studying adjectives, use the program *Kid Pix* and have children write a descriptive phrase, save it to a disk, and exchange disks. The children will then illustrate the disk that they have exchanged. Put these together in a slide show for the children.
3. Make a wish list for Christmas or birthday.
4. Make a word problem and have another child figure out the answer.
5. When a child discovers how to do something in a program, let him or her be the classroom expert and instruct others.

How many more ways can you add?

IV. Keep Updating Your List

Throughout the year, keep updating your list, including all types of materials and ideas, not just software and websites.

 **STUDENT COMPETENCIES**

As schools attempt to implement computer literacy programs and technology plans, teachers will be required to develop *competencies*, or *expectancies*, about the use of the technology. These competencies are broad statements that apply to all students. The teachers at Walt Disney School (Reksten, 2000) developed the following expectancies for all their students. These expectations are representative of many other schools. Examination of these expectancies in light of the National Educational Technology Standards (NETS, 2001) reveals some similarities but shows expectations at a level significantly below what the NETS feels children need to know.

All students at Walt Disney School will

1. Apply a variety of software applications to the creation of grade-level curriculum projects in language arts, math, science, history/social science, and fine arts.

2. Access and analyze reference information within curriculum in a variety of media formats using CD-ROM and laser disc media and telecommunications with educational research agencies, and be able to access current information on the World Wide Web.
3. Be provided with opportunities to develop the thinking skills of application, synthesis, analysis, and evaluation through the completion of technology-enhanced curriculum projects.
4. Collaborate in heterogeneous groupings to share information and access diverse student talents in the production of technology-enhanced curriculum projects (p. 47).

Schools such as the Walt Disney School will find that they will need to revisit their expectations for children and technology as they attempt to meet the NET Standards. Comparing the two expectations, it is apparent that the NET Standards are more rigorous and embrace all types of technology. The NET Standards expect children to be able to use VCRs, tape recorders, digital cameras, drawing tools, camcorders, and all other technologies. Children are expected to communicate about technology using accurate terminology, be responsible, and demonstrate positive social and ethical behavior in using technology (NETS, 2001).

Children need to be exposed to software that offers them the opportunity to create. Microsoft's *PowerPoint* and Corel's *Presentations* software allow children to incorporate graphics and pictures as well as sound and video clips into presentations. Young children can even create their own web pages. According to the NET Standards, young children are expected to develop the ability to use graphics and sounds in presentations that they develop.

After schools set their competencies for their children, it becomes the responsibility of teachers to implement them. The principal way for children to meet these technology standards is through the process of integrating the computer and other technologies into everyday lessons. These competencies are the goals for all children. The objectives that allow the children to reach these goals are found in each teacher's lesson plans. Teachers' effectiveness at integrating technology into everyday lessons will determine whether these goals will be achieved or not.

⭐ THE TEACHER'S USE OF THE COMPUTER

Teachers are using computers in ever-expanding ways. Computers are being used to calculate grades and generate reports to parents, to assess children in basic skills, to conduct research as units are developed, to communicate with colleagues and the office, and to assist children with special needs. There are software programs specifically designed for teachers that will average grades and generate several different types of reports using those grades. Grades can be entered into the computer and the computer will calculate the grade based on a strict average or a weighted average. A weighted average is one where the teacher determines the "weight" of each type of grade. For example, homework assignments might count only 10 percent of the entire grade, tests might count 50 percent, class participation 10 percent, and daily work 30 percent. Using weighted averages allows the teacher much more flexibility in determining grades than does the standard average, where all grades are equal.

Several assessment programs are available for use with children. The child takes a short test in reading (or math), and the computer scores the child's responses, generates a printed report, and assigns a reading (or math) level to the child. These programs, while providing a teacher with information, should not be used by the teacher as the sole assessment instrument. The information from this one assessment might not even be accurate, depending on the child's interest in the story or attitude that day. The most reliable information about a child's functioning is gathered by the teacher in one-on-one sessions where the teacher listens to the child read and can ask the child questions. These sessions provide the teacher not only with the number of answers that are correct, but also information on the fluency of the reading and insights into problems that the child is experiencing by an analysis of the errors the child makes. Computer programs, however, can provide the teacher with quick checks to see if reading comprehension is improving. In using such a program to assess children, remember that this is just one tool and results may not be accurate if the child does not take the assessment seriously and half-reads questions and/or simply guesses answers.

There are programs on the market to encourage and motivate children to read. Most of the programs work in a similar manner. In one such program, the Accelerated Reader (AR), children read books on their reading level and then take a computerized quiz on the content. The program consists of disks with tests that are loaded onto the computer. Disks generally have tests for books covering several reading levels. Teachers may develop a test for an individual book in their classroom and load it into the program. Several program disks may be loaded on the computer, thereby increasing the number of books available for tests. A list of the books tested on the disk is supplied. To fully use the program, the school must purchase any of the books that are not already available. If teachers want tests for certain favorite books, they have to find the program that lists those books and the school has to purchase the program. Once the program has been purchased, books that will be tested need to be gathered together and marked with their reading level. Children may then select a book, read it, and take a test on the book. Reading levels for the books are listed by the grade level of the book and a decimal that represents the number of months into the school year. So a reading level of 2.4 listed on a book would mean that the book is on a second-grade, fourth-month level. The program has a teacher-override capability that allows the teacher to manipulate the student records. The children are not able to retake a test on a book unless the teacher uses this override feature. The tests are multiple choice and range from 5 to 10 questions per book. Difficulty of the book and number of questions answered correctly award points. Points are saved and can be used to "buy" items at the AR store. The items in the store carry a "price" that is listed in point value. Another method of redeeming points has been the use of parties. For a basic point value, children can purchase pizza and a drink. Added items such as cookies and candy would cost additional points.

While these programs do encourage children to read, there are some very real dangers in the way that schools have actually used these programs. These programs provide reading practice, not reading instruction, but some schools use them as the sole reading program for the children. Because these programs do not provide reading instruction, the children are, in effect, receiving no instruction in reading. Another concern about these programs is that they may also limit children's book selection. Many children either do not want to read a book that is not on their AR list or are being forced to read books that might not interest them because the books are on the list. Because programs containing the tests are expensive, the number of books per level may be greatly limited. Some teachers demand that a child read every book in a level whether the child is interested in the book or not. So what happens? The child is not interested in the book, doesn't read it carefully, and misses the questions on the test. The teacher decides that this child's comprehension is weak and that he or she is not ready to progress to the next reading level.

Although teachers of the future will be expected to use multimedia in presenting and teaching lessons to children, few teachers are trained in how to do this. A program such as *Hyperstudio* or *PowerPoint* allows the teacher to incorporate video clips into classroom presentations. One unique concept is the "Magic Wall." The teacher, using one of the walls in the classroom, creates the Magic Wall. The wall needs to be light colored. Two overhead projectors placed on the floor approximately 10 feet from the wall allow children to see the wall without having to gaze through or over the machines. The teacher selects eight pictures that are important to the topic being studied and fits them to two 8½" × 11" sheets of paper, then has a transparency made. After the transparencies are made, a frame for the pictures is made out of black paper and attached to the transparencies. Attaching colored plastic to the picture (such as those used for theme covers) may also highlight pictures. Each picture is further covered by a piece of construction paper a child lifts in a revelatory process. Any topic or subject can be enhanced using a Magic Wall (Swartz, 2001). If the teacher possesses a projection system for the classroom computer, this can also be incorporated into the lesson and provide the children with imported video clips and slide shows. The children can also project their work for the entire class to see. Old filmstrips can be used and incorporated into the lesson as well as new technology such as laser discs and CD-ROMs (Swartz, 2001).

A teacher's lack of knowledge and skills may make him or her more comfortable using computers in more traditional ways. Overhead slides, crossword puzzles, calendars, letters to parents, homework, lab data sheets, field trip permission slips, signs, and posters are typical products generated by teachers using computers.

There are several basic computer competencies that all teachers should possess, however. Teachers should be able to use a word processor, know how to import graphics into documents, know how to use e-mail, know how to do searches on the Internet, and be able to use a simple spreadsheet. Without these minimum skills, it will be impossible for the teacher to instruct children in the basics of using the computer as a tool.

As more teachers become accustomed to using and exploring the Internet, teachers are finding and using websites that have actual lesson plans for the classroom. Care must be taken and good judgment exercised here because some of these lessons present misinformation or lessons that are harmful to children. One such lesson teaches kindergarten children how to lie in such a way so as not to get caught. With care, the discriminating teacher can find new and interesting ideas and lessons on a great variety of subjects.

Distance learning has been tried in some districts, with mixed results. Originally, distance learning consisted of one-way video and two-way audio interactions. The children could see and hear the teacher, but the teacher could only hear

State by State

Hawaii and Computer Technology

Hawaii is one state that is following a step-by-step technology plan to enable all children to achieve the National Education Goals. This plan is part of Hawaii's *Goals 2000 State Improvement Plan.* The overall framework addresses goals and objectives in the following areas:

Networks	Computers in schools need to be connected to a high-speed network.
Voice	Many schools have antiquated systems that need replacing.
Video	Distance learning programs produced by Hawaii Department of Education (HDOE) do not reach all schools and communities.
Data networks	Approximately 115 of 242 schools have started to cable their campuses for connecting classrooms, offices and libraries.
Neighbor Islands	Some remote schools are in areas where telecommunication network services are unavailable.
Instructional Integration	HDOE surveys indicate needs to be addressed:

- Equalize access in remote areas.
- Increase integration of technology.
- Coordinate technology and telecommunication resources.
- Increase linkages to education resources in the states.
- Integrate technology into local programs.
- Provide service that can guide educators to technology based and other resources that support national standards.
- Develop an up-to-date technology plan.

Progress is being made: 100 percent of the schools, 61 percent of the buildings, 66 percent of the classrooms, and 64 percent of the computers are networked. In addition, 96 percent of the schools now have cable connections (Hawaii Department of Education, 2002).

the children. This made it very difficult to judge how well the lesson was progressing. Some districts tried to offer a second language to their children in kindergarten and lower elementary grades through this method. Some schools canceled after only a few lessons because children were bored and found it too difficult, or too much help was expected from the teacher in the classroom with the children. The teacher in the classroom with the children was of limited help because of lack of familiarity with the language being taught. Current distance learning provides two-way video and audio. Any distance learning, however, needs to provide for interaction, constructivist learning, and more than merely talking heads (Swartz, 2001).

Teachers express concern about using computers, especially in the early childhood classroom. They are afraid that children will become involved in solitary play and miss the interaction necessary for the development of social skills. Actually, computers can facilitate cooperative learning in the early childhood classroom. Interaction between children at the computer can be encouraged by positioning the computer near a favorite center, where many children can easily see it. This stimulates peer interaction, use of language, and cooperative play. The teacher can further encourage social interaction by placing chairs for several of the children, instead of the usual one chair, in front of the monitor (Haugland, 1999b; Anselmo & Zinck, 1987). As with any center, the computer should be located such that the teacher can easily monitor the center.

☆ OTHER TYPES OF TECHNOLOGY USED IN SCHOOLS

Technology and computers are synonymous terms for many teachers, yet technology and computer education are not synonymous. Technology in the early childhood classroom consists of not only computers, but also such items as televisions, VCRs, laser disc players, tape recorders, overhead projectors, calculators, camcorders, musical keyboards, digital cameras, and assistive technology. Children should be allowed suitable use of all the available types of technology that are in the classroom. Teachers usually use televisions, VCRs, and overhead projectors in presenting information, whereas children in early childhood classrooms use calculators, musical keyboards, tape recorders, and assistive technology. Children seldom use camcorders and digital cameras although they can be taught to use them.

Digital Cameras

Children as young as age 3 can be taught to use the digital camera and take pictures. These pictures can then be printed and displayed around the classroom. Language is facilitated as the children look at and talk about their pictures.

Overhead Projectors

Most overhead projectors are used by teachers to model how to do a problem, present information, or even as a form of worksheet. Children are highly motivated when they get to use the overhead. Placing the overhead on a small cart or desk allows the children easy access to it. Children can use the overhead to play teacher in kindergarten and first grade if the teacher provides blank slides and overhead pens for the children to use. Children can also go to the overhead and work and explain problems to the other children, correct spelling and punctuation in a sentence, or even write a story on an overhead slide and share it with the class. With older children, the overhead lends itself to cooperative learning activities. For example, the teacher can divide the class into small groups and have each group of children come up with a word problem. The recorder for the group writes the question on the overhead slide, and the reporter for the group presents the slide to the rest of the class for the class to solve. Of course, before the children present the problem, they have to be able to solve it. This also gives the children the opportunity to teach the other children how to solve the problem.

Tape Recorders

Tape recorders are typically used by teachers in listening centers. However, the tape recorder could also be used by the children in other ways. Children can record books for younger children, record a story or poem as a present for their parents, or record something for the classroom listening library. The teacher can record the science and/or social studies lessons for children who may have a reading disability. The children who need to hear the lesson as they read silently then have it available for use when needed. The teacher can record spelling words for children to take a practice test. The teacher records the word and pauses, allowing the child to write the word. After the pause, the teacher spells the word and the child is able to receive immediate feedback on the correctness of the word he or she wrote. Another pause follows. This allows the child to correct the word if it is wrong.

Laser Disc Readers

Laser discs are usually directed toward the science area. Laser discs are the size of large records. The teacher may quickly find the desired lesson by putting in the number that corresponds to that lesson. Though most lessons provide the children with video clips that enhance their learning, the teacher needs to make sure that the laser disc is enhancing the lesson and not being used just for convenience. For instance, one laser disc lesson for kindergarten explains the difference between living and nonliving. The disc shows a photograph of a rock and says, "This is nonliving." It then shows an insect, and as the insect moves the program says, "This is living." Children would benefit more from going outside and picking up their own rocks, touching them, feeling them, observing them, discussing them, and then observing an ant or other insect. They would have actually experienced living and nonliving rather than simply seeing it on the laser disc. Good teachers also look at the concept to be taught, then the material available to teach that concept, and always choose the method that actively involves children.

Camcorders

With the advent of smaller and smaller camcorders, children are now able to effectively record their own projects and productions. Even if the school has one of the older, heavier types of camcorders, children can still use the camcorder if it is secured to a tripod. As with any equipment, children must be trained in the use of the camcorder. Under the teacher's supervision, children can write a story, design costumes, practice acting it out, and then record it. Hand puppets or characters drawn and attached to craft sticks can also be made and used in productions instead of children taking the parts, which allows the more fantastic stories to be filmed.

Assistive Technology

Assistive technology is the use of technology to assist the child with special needs. It includes "any item, piece of equipment, or product system whether acquired commercially off the shelf, modified, or customized, that is used to in-

---

Dimensions of Diversity

Meeting the Needs of Diverse Learners through Technology

Digital cameras can now be paired with computers to allow "no-touch" computer access. The digital camera is trained on whatever part of the body the child is able to move. The computer is programmed to recognize any small or large movement and triggers a mouse click. This allows children with severe involvement of their muscles to successfully operate the computer independently.

Another computer modification is the "smart" keyboard, a keyboard that talks. This type of communication system makes it possible for children who are unable to talk to use the computer to do their talking for them. The child can type in a message, and the computer speaks the message. The computer also offers shortcuts for messages, and text may be stored for later use.

Issues and Trends

State Compliance and the No Child Left Behind Act

As states seek to comply with the No Child Left Behind Act, computers will play a very important part. The law requires that adequate yearly progress (AYP) be calculated for four subgroups: ethnicity, economically disadvantaged, English-language learners, and disability. States must collect the data and then disaggregate it to track the progress of these subgroups. Some states have gone beyond this mandate and are using a sophisticated data-analysis system that allows them to compare schools within the state that have similar demographics. This system compares a single school to the next nine most like it in the state, based on the demographic information in the system (No State Left Behind, 2002). Some states allow parents, teachers, administrators, and interested parties to access a school's scores though the state education agency's website.

crease, maintain, or improve functional capabilities of individuals with disabilities" (IDEA, 1997). There are two types of assistive technology: low tech and high tech. Low-tech devices are simple, inexpensive, and sometimes even homemade yet allow a child to perform a function independently. Examples of low-tech devices are a paper clip used to help a child with fine-motor problems in turning the pages of a book or a pencil grip that allows a child to grasp a pencil. Other low-tech devices are simple switches that allow toys to be activated, communication boards, joysticks, and taped stories. High-tech devices are more expensive and commercially developed and include not only computers, but also portable Braille notetakers, programmable power wheelchairs, voice-driven word processors, screen magnifiers, speech synthesizers, alternative keyboards, reading machines for children who are blind, and a host of various software programs (Snider & Badgett, 1995).

INTERNATIONAL SOCIETY FOR TECHNOLOGY IN EDUCATION

The International Society for Technology in Education (ISTE) is a nonprofit professional organization dedicated to promoting the appropriate uses of information technology and to support and improve learning, teaching, and administration in K–12 education and teacher education. Members are provided with information, networking opportunities, and guidance as they face the challenges of incorporating new technologies into their schools. ISTE's website contains many links to resources and lesson plans for teachers trying to find ways to implement technology in their classrooms. (International Society for Technology in Education, 2000).

 Summary

Integrating computers and other technology into the classroom becomes increasingly important as our civilization becomes more technical. As part of this integration, it becomes necessary for teachers to develop skills for evaluating software and websites as these proliferate. Technology should be a tool that children use and should encompass not only computer skills but other areas of technology as well. Computer skills especially need to be developed in the early childhood classroom. Teachers need to develop their own technology skills and become confident about using these skills in their classrooms.

Discussion Questions

1. What is the profile of technology-literate students?
2. Discuss how computers are currently being used in the classroom.
3. Describe and explain what other types of technology are found in the classroom.
4. What is assistive technology? Give several examples.

Suggested Chapter Activities

1. Gather names of software programs commonly used in the school and go online and find out if they have been evaluated and the rating they received.
2. Using the evaluation instrument for websites, rate a website that might be used by children.
3. Develop a list of software and website resources for a topic that could be taught in an early childhood class.
4. Visit an early childhood classroom and observe how technology is being used. Write a report on how the teacher could further integrate technology into his or her classroom.

WEBSITES

Dinosaur Exhibit (www.hcc.hawaii.edu/dinos/dinos.1.html)
Division for Early Childhood of the Council for Exceptional Children (www.dec-sped.org)
International Society for Technology in Education (www.iste.org)
NASA Spacelink (www.spacelink.msfc.nasa.gov)
Quest: NASA's K–12 Internet Initiative (www.quest.arc.nasa.gov)
Smithsonian Institution (www.si.edu)
The White House for Kids (www.whitehouse.org/kids/index.asp)

Chapter Eleven

Working with Parents or Guardians

CHAPTER OVERVIEW

★ How many ways can you list for parents to be involved at school?

★ What are some forms of communication with parents or guardians?

★ How does a teacher conduct a parent-teacher conference?

★ What are some home learning activities that can involve parents?

★ Do you know how to effectively communicate with parents or guardians?

★ What are the rights of parents and students?

THESE QUESTIONS AND MORE WILL BE ANSWERED IN THIS CHAPTER.

Most experienced teachers tell beginning teachers that problems with parents are not a significant part of the teaching experience. Most parents care for their children and want to be partners with the teacher. Unfortunately, when a teacher has problems with parents, those problems are usually such that the teacher forgets how easy and helpful 99 percent of the other parents are. So a beginning teacher who hears other teachers moaning about problems with parents should ask about other parents in that teacher's classroom. Any teacher who teaches for a significant period of time is more than likely to have an experience with a parent that is less than pleasant. By far the vast majority of parents, however, are kind and helpful to the teacher.

Most experienced teachers have collections for cards, notes, and letters from parents who have expressed their thanks for the love, care, and education that the teacher has given their child. These cards are constant reminders to teachers about why they became teachers. The following comments are from one teacher's collection.

"We want to thank you for all your help and care you have shown this past year to our precious son. You kept on trying to teach him to read when everyone else had given up."

"You may not remember us, but you had my son in third grade. He is now 23 and we all still feel you are the best teacher he ever had."

"My daughter still remembers her second-grade year in your class. She is now in sixth grade, but you are still her favorite teacher."

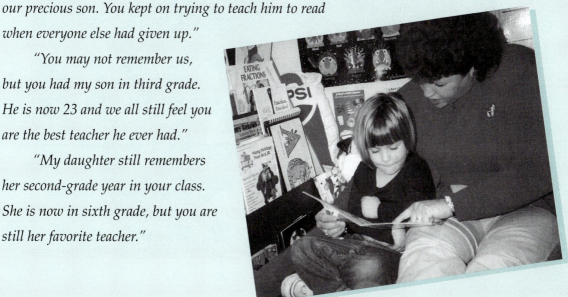

Working with parents or guardians is a very complex issue in today's society. Parents and teachers lead busy lives, and finding time and ways to communicate can become a real problem. There is no doubt that effective communication is extremely important for successful collaboration. Schools continue to seek new ways to communicate with parents and to involve them in their child's education. Parents need to understand the rights they have in the school system, and teachers also need to understand these rights. Working together as partners, parents and teachers can greatly maximize a child's educational experience.

PARENT INVOLVEMENT

In today's fast-paced world, involving parents in school life becomes very challenging. No longer do the majority of children live in a two-parent home where the mother stays at home while only the father works. The most common type of home situation for children is the two-wage-earner home where both mother and father work outside the home (Berk, 1999). Add to this the increasing number of working single-parent homes and it is no wonder that schools are having problems involving parents. In attempting to involve parents, it is important to have the expectation that parents want to be involved and have a vital interest in their children, but

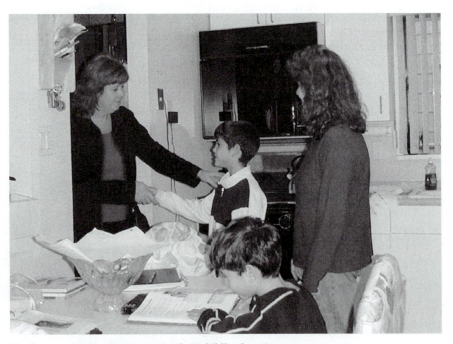

Teachers need to involve parents in their child's education.

that there will be time limitations, especially for single parents. These parents may become involved if they are needed for special projects and have control over time and choice of their projects (Wirth, 1991).

Schools have attempted to involve parents in their children's education by various strategies. In Newton, North Carolina, schools have formed agreements with major employers in the area so that school counselors or teachers may visit parents on the job (Gutloff, 1995). At the other end of the spectrum, some schools take parents to court and sentence them for their children's truancy. Other innovative attempts to involve parents range from making a parent resource room on the school campus to using an old mobile home as a parent resource room on wheels (Gutloff, 1995). Back-to-school nights, parent education groups, school home-activity packets, telephone tutors, and educational videos for loan are some of the more common attempts by schools to involve parents (Berger, 2000).

When parents and teachers work together and share responsibilities for children and the children see this cooperation, children will be motivated to do better in school (Center on Education Governance, 1996). In order to work most effectively with the school, parents need to understand that the school belongs to them and is there to serve the needs of their children. Parents need to learn about the school rules and policies and be aware of discipline and behavior problems that occur in school. Parents can also become active participants by volunteering, joining the local parent-teacher organization, or becoming a community representative. A first step for all parents is to feel comfortable in the school (Center, 1996). Parents may have uncomfortable feelings about being in the school that are carryovers from their own student days. Warm, caring, concerned teachers can build a bridge for the parents that allow them to relate in new ways to being in the school.

There are three basic ways for parents to be involved in their children's schooling. The first is direct parental involvement (Flaxman & Inger, 1992). Parents have been used as volunteers in classrooms, assisting the teacher in preparing materials, setting up activities, and actually working with children. Parents have assisted individual children in practicing academic skills, have read to small groups of children or to the class (Barbour & Barbour, 2001), or have assisted the teacher in class projects. Even parents who have no time to come to the school and volunteer can be involved by working at home making learning games for the teachers to use in centers, typing class newsletters, or coloring and cutting out materials for learning centers and activities.

Parents also serve on advisory committees or site-based decision-making teams in the school. These teams include parents, people from the community, the principal, selected teachers, and school personnel (Berger, 2000). This team, or site council, "works to improve education for children and make educational decisions by using collaborative efforts involving all stakeholders" (Schmaus, 1996, p. 44). The power exerted by these boards will vary greatly depending on whether they have only advisory or have policy-making capacities (Couchenour & Chrisman, 2000).

The second way parents can be involved is through training programs. These programs support parents as their children's first teachers. The training can focus on areas such as self-discipline, helping their child with study habits, communication skills training, and other parenting skills. Programs are generally arranged at times for the convenience of the parents, no fees are charged to attend, and even babysitting is sometimes provided (Flaxman & Inger, 1992).

The third model of parent involvement is one of family resource and support. In the past decade, many schools have begun to offer a great range of programs and activities. These programs and activities are only indirectly related to the children's education, but they provide services to the parents such as job counseling and training, health clinics, home visiting services, substance abuse treatment, resource and referral centers for social services, support and discussion groups, and before- and after-school child care for working parents (Flaxman & Inger, 1992).

☆ INVOLVEMENT OF FATHERS

Involvement of fathers in their children's school is linked to their children's class standing, enjoyment of school, retention, suspension and expulsion, and extracurricular activities. Even after controlling for potentially confounding factors such as household income, parents' education, and the mother's involvement (in two-parent families), the father's involvement has a distinct influence on these outcomes. In two-parent homes, the father's involvement is significantly associated with the children's enjoyment of school, reduced likelihood of retention, and greater likelihood that their

It is important to involve fathers in their children's education.

children will get mostly A's. Single-father families with high father involvement also show a significant association with the children receiving mostly A's and reduced the likelihood of suspension or expulsion (Nord, Brimhall, & West, 1998).

Teachers may facilitate the involvement of fathers by making the effort to talk to them as they drop off their child at school, schedule conferences at a time when the father can come, have a special conference with the noncustodial parent (if the court permits this), plan programs and events in the evenings, and use videos to show their children in the classroom (Berger, 2000).

Absent Fathers

It is unfortunate for our children that many fathers are not a part of their children's lives. Fathers may have made the choice not to be involved with their children, or they may be physically absent because of military service, divorce and remarriage, incarceration, or job-related travel. Other fathers may be physically present but emotionally absent (Frieman & Berkeley, 2002).

Children with absent fathers need to be involved with good male role models. Because most early childhood teachers are female, the teacher must make an effort to find and recruit males to volunteer in the classroom. Teachers may look to retired community members or various service groups in town. Many schools require any person who is actively involved in the classroom to have a criminal background check before being allowed in the classroom. The teacher also needs to spend some time with the volunteers and explain to them why they are so valuable and to train them for the work they will be doing with the children (Frieman & Berkeley, 2002).

Helping Fathers Develop Positive Parenting Skills

Many fathers lack positive parenting skills. As the breadwinner in the home before the divorce or separation, many fathers may have experienced only a limited amount of quality time with their children. Now, either as the **custodial parent** or the parent whose children are visiting him, they will be playing a far more active role in their children's lives. Three areas have been identified as issues fathers face: how to praise their children, how to put their needs first, and how to deal with mistakes (Frieman & Berkeley, 2002).

Fathers generally have not had much practice at being supportive of their children in the ordinary, everyday sense. They may know how to praise outstanding accomplishments but do not realize that their children look to them for approval in many of the small, everyday events in their lives. Teachers can model this for the fathers as they praise the child's daily victories to the fathers, whether by phone, e-mail, or a note home (Frieman & Berkeley, 2002).

As the head of the household before the divorce, the father was socialized to be considered the most important member of the family. Now he must learn to put his children's needs ahead of his own. He may have had a very hard day at the office, but when he comes home now, he cannot hide away in front of the television set and relax for a few hours. If his children are staying with him at this time, he must see to their needs. They need to be fed, possibly need help with their homework, or need a ride to some activity. Although some fathers already put their children first, for many it will be a real change from the way they have lived their lives previously (Frieman & Berkeley, 2002).

Teachers can help fathers do a better job of planning for events by sending newsletters announcing upcoming activities. Fathers can also be acknowledged for their participation in school events through this same newsletter, which may encourage other fathers to attend. Articles can be included that talk about the contributions of fathers to the classroom as well as the importance of the children having good male role models (Frieman & Berkeley, 2002).

Fathers who themselves were raised in a family where the father did not acknowledge mistakes and the father's word was law may have a hard time admitting to their children that they have made a mistake. They will worry that admitting to a mistake will compromise their authority with their children. This is far from the truth. Children have greater respect for fathers who admit to mistakes and correct them.

Teachers can assist fathers by meeting and talking with them independently of their former wives. The teacher can offer information about the child and even possibly make suggestions. Meeting with the father alone makes it less likely that his pride will get in the way when it comes to working with his children (Frieman & Berkeley, 2002).

⭐ PARENT CHALLENGES

Unfortunately, not all parents are equally easy and cooperative when it comes to discussing and handling problems and situations concerning their children. Two very different types of parents that teachers may encounter are reticent parents and difficult parents.

Reticent Parents

Reticent parents are parents who are reluctant to become involved with the school life of their children. Parents themselves have suggested several ways to reach out and involve reticent parents. These include urging the children to encourage and remind their parents about school activities, inviting parents to visit school any time and reassuring them that they will be warmly welcomed, visiting parents in their homes, conveying to parents and children that language differences can be overcome, and sending notes to parents from time to time (Lee, 1995). Determining the reason for a parent's reticence suggests ways to the teacher of encouraging participation by the parent. Reticence should not be viewed as unconcern. Rather, it may have its roots in past experiences, language differences, or simply the necessities of putting food on the table and paying the bills so that parents have no time to take a more active part.

Difficult Parents

Occasionally, teachers have to deal with parents who, for whatever reason, are unreasonable. When it becomes evident that there are major problems between the parents and the teacher, the teacher should hold all conferences in the presence of a third party. This third party should be the principal, assistant principal, or the counselor. In addition, notes should be taken, reviewed by all participants, and distributed after the meeting to all parties. By involving this third party and keeping detailed notes of the meeting, there is less chance for misunderstandings later. Doing this also helps protect the teacher and the school from litigation.

One Teacher's Response to a Difficult Parent

It was only two weeks into the school year and Mrs. King was having trouble with stealing in her first-grade classroom. One of the parents called to tell Mrs. King that her son's milk money had been stolen every day this past week. Mrs. King asked the mother to mark the quarter with a red spot on the side rim and instruct her son to tell Mrs. King when he noticed the quarter was missing. The next day the boy came to Mrs. King and whispered that his quarter was missing. Mrs. King stopped a few minutes early before lunch time and told the class that she wanted to do a lesson on money. The children were instructed to bring their quarters that they had for milk or ice cream and sit at the circle. Mrs. King had all the children with quarters line up and was starting to count the money when Phillip, the child whose quarter was stolen, raised his hand and said that his quarter was gone. Mrs. King asked Phillip if his quarter was marked in any way. Phillip said that his mother had made a red mark on the edge. Mrs. King inspected all the quarters that the children were holding and sure enough, there was Phillip's quarter in Randy's hand. Mrs. King finished the lesson on counting quarters and sent the children to lunch, except for Randy. When she talked to Randy in private, Randy admitted taking the quarter so he could buy ice cream. Mrs. King told Randy that she would have to call his parents and sent Randy to lunch. Mrs. King called and reached Randy's father. Mrs. King explained the situation and assured the father that it was quite common for young children to take things that didn't belong to them, but that it was important for Randy to understand that this was wrong. Randy's dad was very supportive and appreciative of the phone call and assured Mrs. King that he would talk to Randy. Mrs. King felt good about the way this had turned out until she received a call from Randy's mother after school. Randy's mother was very aggressive, verbally abusive, and accused Mrs. King of being a racist and of picking on her son unjustly. Although upset by the mother's treatment, Mrs. King remained calm and reiterated to the mother the fact that this is common among young children. The mother hung up on Mrs. King. For the next four months, the mother sent scathing notes to Mrs. King about any little thing, badmouthed Mrs. King to other parents, and closely watched everything that Mrs. King did. Mrs. King responded by maintaining a professional attitude and responding to hateful notes with polite, courteous notes.

What Teachers Are Saying

Working with Parents

"I would really love teaching, if it weren't for having to deal with parents and administrators."—*a prekindergarten teacher*

"Our colleges and universities need to spend more time preparing new teachers for handling difficult students, parents, and situations."—*a first-grade teacher*

The vast majority of parents do not fall into this category. Experience helps new teachers develop ways to deal with difficult parents. Successful teachers find that listening, acknowledging the reason the parents are upset, showing respect, and remaining calm will settle down most parents.

"I feel very fortunate to have support from my school staff and parents to meet the needs of one of my students this year."—*a third-grade teacher*

One afternoon Mrs. King noticed Randy's mother standing outside the door. Randy was at his PE class and his mother had arrived early to take him to the doctor. Mrs. King went to the door, invited the mother in, and asked her if she would like to help grade some math papers. Mrs. King told her she could grade Randy's first and put on it "Graded by Mom." This mother did exactly that. Because Mrs. King had always maintained a professional manner in dealing with her and because of this invitation, Randy's mother's entire attitude toward Mrs. King changed. She now told everyone that Mrs. King was the best teacher in this elementary school and wanted her other son to have her as his teacher. Mrs. King learned two very important lessons from this experience. First, she learned the importance of always acting like the professional that she is. And second, she learned that Randy's mother had experienced extreme discrimination all through her life and had learned to mistrust people of other races. As Mrs. King learned about how Randy's mother had suffered through the years, she came to understand why she had reacted as she had. Now Mrs. King and Randy's mother are true partners in Randy's education and this partnership is based on mutual respect and trust.

⭐ COMMUNICATION BETWEEN PARENTS AND TEACHERS

Communication between parents and teachers should be ongoing and continuous, not relegated to only those times when problems arise. A phone call or brief note as an introduction and welcome to parents and child before the first day of school will be most appreciated by the parents and helps to establish a foundation for a good relationship. The first day of school is also a great time to make that first connection with parents. A brief note sent home that day can smooth the way for further communications that might not be of such an agreeable nature later. Positive communication is especially important for the teacher to make with the child who has a reputation for being "trouble." After years of only hearing from the teachers when there is a problem, a positive note or phone call establishes the teacher, in the parents' eyes, as different from all previous teachers. This teacher is capable of seeing the good in their child, and so the parents will usually respond to this teacher in a supportive way when he or she does call about a problem.

Prekindergarten and kindergarten teachers will be called upon to relieve the worries and anxieties of the parents as their children begin the school experience. These teachers need to realize that, along with the joy of teaching these little ones, there will be much more parent-teacher dialogue. Parents of children this age are also more likely to call the teacher at home, if they can find a phone number. Some early childhood teachers freely give out their home phone number, whereas others will have an unlisted number. One danger of giving out the home phone number is that some parents will abuse this privilege and call several times a week over insignificant matters. The teacher is then placed in the position of not answering the phone, using an answering machine or caller ID to screen the phone calls, or taking the direct approach of telling the parent that he or she is calling too frequently. Receiving calls only at school poses a different set of problems: Sometimes the teacher doesn't get the message that the parent called, calls can only be returned during the teacher's conference time or after school, few phones are available in the school for teachers to use, and a teacher may be unable to reach the parents that same day. The teacher has to decide which method will be best for him or her.

Teachers need to assure parents that they consider communication to be two-way and encourage parents to let them know when their child is unhappy or struggling with some problem. Children may be bullied without the teacher's knowledge unless the parents call the teacher and report the problem.

Notes, letters, and forms are also effective methods of communicating with parents. Notes may be as simple as a smiley face on a small piece of paper to let the parent know that their child had a good day or may consist of a few lines about a specific incident, concern, need, or accomplishment. The following examples show that very short notes can provide a parent with a great deal of information.

NOVEMBER 5

Shakita knew all her letter sounds!

MARCH 3

Your suggestion is helping! Bobby finished his work today!

Letters can be sent detailing upcoming events such as field trips, classroom needs, special activities, or pending tests. Forms can also be used as a means of keeping parents informed about their child's progress in academics and behavior. (See Figure 11.1.) These forms may be tailored to the grade level and the needs of the children. The purpose of such forms is to keep parents informed so that there will be no surprises at report card time.

Some schools are experimenting with voice mail systems as an alternative means for parents and teachers to communicate. Voice mail is different from answering machines. Voice mail can be sent day or night and accessed from any telephone. Voice mail can be used to inform parents of upcoming events, homework assignments, or other school news (Cameron & Kang, 1997).

Barriers to Communication

Parents and teachers have the same goals for children: to be successful, to be able to perform well academically, and to be happy at school. Despite these common goals, both teachers and parents will at times put up roadblocks to communication. There are various reasons for this behavior. Parents may view teacher comments as criticism of them, their child-rearing practices, or their intelligence. Other parents may remember when they were in school and have negative feelings associated with their experience. Parents may be indifferent to education, too busy, or too caught up in personal worries to have the time or energy left over for their child's educational concerns. Other parents may become caught up in what they perceive as their rights and the rights of their children (Berger, 2000). The teacher hears comments like, "I know my rights!" Understanding why parents are reacting the way they are goes a long way in determining the teacher's method of trying to open communication. If, for instance, the parent has bad feelings from the time when he or she was in school, the teacher can show how things have changed and ease the parent's mind about the treatment the child will receive. In every case, it is important for the teacher to break down these barriers and bring about open communication.

Many times the blame for lack of communication falls on school personnel, not the parents. Teachers may be extremely busy with all the demands placed on them by the school and/or school district as well as having busy personal lives. Teachers may fear reporting to parents that their child is not achieving as expected and so ignore the problem. Teachers may feel threatened by parents who question them about the curriculum or teaching methods or make suggestions about teaching methods and strategies based on parents' past experience or even something they saw on television. A teacher may claim to be the "authority" in the area of teaching, effectively locking parents out of the decision-making process (Berger, 2000). Teachers need to realize that parents know their children and may have valuable insights and suggestions based on this knowledge. Teachers especially need to realize that delaying telling a parent that a child is having problems is not only not helpful, it further delays the child's getting help. A parent has every right to be upset when a teacher tells the parent about a problem that was noticed several months before. Time has been lost in that child's education that can never be regained.

Harmful repercussions of reporting a child's action at school are the one consideration that may prevent a teacher from open, honest communication with a

FIGURE 11.1 Sample Weekly Progress Report

Weekly Progress Report

Name _____ For the ____ six weeks

S = Satisfactory   P = Shows Progress
N = Needs Improvement   U = Unsatisfactory

	1st	2nd	3rd	4th	5th
Reading					
Writing					
Math					
Science					
Social Studies					

All Areas Satisfactory Unless Checked

Is attentive and follows directions					
Works independently/completes tasks					
Completes work on time					
Keeps materials organized					
Works well with others					
Is courteous					
Obeys school/classroom rules					
Appropriate restroom behavior					
Appropriate cafeteria behavior					
Appropriate hall behavior					

Comments: See back

My conference time is _____. The school phone number is _____.

Please initial

1st week _____ 2nd week _____ 3rd week _____ 4th week _____ 5th week _____

parent. Unfortunately, this may happen sometimes, and a parent may severely punish, spank, or even beat a child because of a teacher's phone call about a problem at school. If the child is beaten, this is abuse and must be reported to the proper authorities (see Chapter 12 for more information on child abuse). If the child is beaten or abused, the teacher must carefully consider when, how, and which problems need to be communicated to the parents.

Effective Communication

Teachers can choose to view parents as either partners or subordinates. When teachers treat parents as partners, they empower the parents to help their children. When teachers treat parents as subordinates, parents sense rejection and may participate little, if any, in their child's education (Berger, 2000). Teachers who want to work with parents need effective communication skills. These skills include

1. Giving total attention to the speaker by establishing eye contact and demonstrating through body language that interest is being focused on what the parent is saying.
2. Restating the parent's concerns by attempting to clarify what has been said and trying to discern the parent's meaning and feeling and avoiding responses that are judgmental or critical.
3. Showing respect for the parent by recognizing his or her concerns and opinions.
4. Acknowledging the parents' feelings and recognizing how much you can discuss with parents. The teacher may need to work on establishing a relationship with the parents before being completely open about concerns for their child.
5. Tailoring discussions with language that fits the parents' ability to understand and tailoring the discussions to fit the parents' emotional ability to handle the situation.
6. Being careful of parents who may not be able to handle the child's problems by avoiding provoking or accusing them.
7. Emphasizing that no one is being blamed and that teacher and parent have to work together to help the child.
8. Remembering that arguments leave no one the winner, but being calm, quiet, and enthusiastic about the child's good points before mentioning problems will help control the situation.
9. Protecting the parents' egos by not making them believe they are to blame for their child's difficulties, focusing on plans for helping the child, and giving parents credit for their achievements (Berger, 2000).

CHILDREN OF DIVORCE

When parents become divorced, teachers must make the effort to keep both mother and father informed about their child. Conferences should be held with both parents, if the parents are not hostile to each other. Parents who have unresolved differences have been known to get into a shouting match at a joint conference. In cases such as this, the teacher can meet with each parent separately. If newsletters are going home, each parent should receive one. If the child is involved in a play or some other school activity, the teacher should ensure that both parents are invited.

The teacher should be sensitive to the fact that many children will live with a single parent. Mother's Day activities can be very painful for a child whose mother has abandoned him. Instead of making a card for a mother, the teacher can talk about making a card for someone who loves you and takes care of you. This might be the father, grandparents, or even aunts and uncles.

The parents may alert the teacher that a divorce is impending. This allows the teacher time to prepare for helping the child through this difficult situation. The teacher can also better understand changes in the child's behavior patterns by knowing that there are serious problems in the child's home.

One caution needs to be given in cases when the divorce has been long and bitter and one parent has been denied custodial or even visitation rights. Schools should have a policy that all children are picked up only after going through the office. If a parent arrives and tries to pick up the child, the teacher needs to send that parent to the office first. Children's folders may be marked with some sort of red flag that says that this child cannot be picked up by anyone but the custodial parent. Parents have been known to kidnap their children from school, and teachers need to be part of the protective layer that helps keep children safe.

PARENT-TEACHER CONFERENCES

Many new teachers are intimidated by the parent-teacher conference. Following some simple guidelines can help the new teacher deal with this stress and be successful in dealing with parents. Preparation before the conference is essential. The teacher should be knowledgeable about the child and have written notes on the child's academic strengths and weaknesses. If the child is experiencing problem behavior, the teacher should choose only one problem for this first conference and only mention this problem after making a positive comment. Parents will definitely be on the defensive if a teacher says to them as soon as they walk into the room, "Thank goodness you showed up! I just don't know what to do about Jimmy's behavior." The conference will deteriorate after a comment such as this, and parents will become protective and defensive. Again, focus should be placed on only one problem. The teacher should choose the problem that irritates him or her the most, even though it may not be the child's biggest problem. By solving it first, however, the teacher may overcome a major hurdle in the relationship with the child.

It is important to remember that the vast majority of parents truly care for their children and want what is best for them. Parents who seem oppositional to school personnel may be that way because of the manner in which last year's teacher dealt with them, so the first guideline is to always start with positive information about a child. This is generally an easy task, but there may be a child in the class about whom a new teacher says, "There is nothing positive I can say about this child." In this case, the positive comment may be something simple: a comment on an academic strength, personality trait, or even a personal habit.

Examples of positive comments given by a teacher about difficult children:

"Mary always comes promptly to our classroom in the mornings."

"Jack really enjoys reading."

"Harry is such a good writer."

"Susie is always so clean and neat."

After giving a positive comment or two, the teacher can then begin to review the child's academic strengths and weaknesses. The same principle applies to academic weaknesses that applies to problem behaviors. If a child is extremely weak in all academic areas, a general statement can be made that lets the parent know the child is behind and identifies one or two areas that will be addressed first. It is important for the teacher to tell the parents that they are partners in the educational process. The teacher states that the parents have vital information about the child and a vital part to play in the success of the educational experience. The child will be able to realize the most progress if they work together as a team.

After talking about the problem, the teacher should solicit ideas from the parents about possible solutions. If the problem is behavior, ask the parents if they have ever had similar problems with the child and, if so, what they found to be effective. Also question the parents about the child's interests. A teacher may be able to use the child's interests in a certain topic as a springboard to academic instruction. In case the parents do not have any suggestions, the teacher should be sure to have some. The teacher is the professional, and parents expect him or her to have some suggestions or ideas about possible intervention strategies. Parents will not have much confidence in a teacher who tells the parents that he or she was hoping that the parents would have some ideas because he or she doesn't have a clue about what to try. It is important at this stage for the teacher to write down any proposed suggestions, strategies, or interventions. These notes serve as a reminder for the teacher of what was discussed and what new steps will be implemented for this child. They also help ensure that the teacher does not forget and follows through in a timely fashion.

Finishing the conference on a positive note, being sure to thank the parents for coming, promising to get back with them in a timely manner, and reassuring them that working together will make a difference in their child's educational experience are all actions that build rapport with the parents. As soon as possible, the teacher should implement the strategies discussed during the conference and report back to the parents. If the teacher fails to report to the parents, the parents will assume that the problem has been solved. Communication is the key to working effectively with parents.

Many schools are setting aside entire days for parent-teacher conferences. This may mean that a teacher will have 20 to 25 conferences during one day. When conferences are scheduled back to back, the teacher needs to keep track of the time. Parents, many times, have made special arrangements at work so that they can be there at a specific time. Allowing a conference to go over the allotted time will affect all the conferences scheduled afterward and can cause hard feelings with parents who took off from work in order to be there for their child's conference, only to have to return to work without meeting with the teacher because the teacher didn't stay on schedule. If every conference runs 5 minutes over, it doesn't take long for the entire remaining conferences to become off by a substantial amount of time. Some teachers use a timer to assure that this doesn't happen. If parents are allocated 15 minutes and are 10 minutes late, the teacher should address the fact that the parents are 10 minutes late and state that there are only 5 remaining minutes of their conference time. If there are no major problems to be addressed, this time can be spent in talking in generalities about the child or one specific area. If there are major problems to be addressed, the time might be best used to reschedule the conference.

Any time a teacher holds a conference with a parent, the door to the classroom should be closed. This is especially important on a conference day. Conferences with parents about their child are confidential. If the door is left open, parents may not feel free to confide in the teacher about certain problems for fear of being overheard. Parents waiting in the hall may be tempted to listen in and may gossip about the child. Closing the door provides the confidential atmosphere necessary for serious discussions to take place.

Children as Participants in Parent-Teacher Conferences

In the past few years, some schools have begun including the children in the parent-teacher conference. Children actively participate in collecting work samples, evaluating their schoolwork and behavior, and analyzing their strengths and weaknesses. This is the school's attempt to develop within the child a sense of ownership of his or her education. Teachers report that students are surprisingly honest when evaluating themselves. When parents direct questions to the teachers, the teachers redirect the question to the child. This type of conference requires double the standard amount of time, and children need to be carefully prepared beforehand; they cannot just be "thrown" in. The learning process for children includes instructions on how to evaluate their work and how to determine strengths and weaknesses. Communication and home involvement seem much easier when the student is included in the conference (Denby, 1995). The down side to this type of conference is that the parent may not be able to, or want to, share some pertinent information because the child is present.

The Unscheduled Conference

The unscheduled conference occurs when the parent shows up at the door unexpectedly. This often occurs when a parent has a concern about something specific. The teacher needs to respond by making the time to listen and responding to the concern (Vaughn, Bos, & Schumm, 2000). Even though it may be inconvenient, time should be taken to hear the concerns of the parent and to deal with the problem. Taking time with parents builds the rapport that is necessary for the child's successful learning. If a problem is important enough for parents to come to school, then more than likely it is a problem that affects the education and/or emotional well-being of the child, and the teacher will certainly want to resolve the issue.

Unscheduled conferences can also occur outside school. The teacher may be at the local library or discount center when she is waylaid by a parent wanting to discuss his or her child. The problems that these parents may want to discuss range from the simple to the highly complex. Even though this is not the time the teacher would choose to have a conference, it is important to listen and respond to the parents' concerns. If it is of an extremely confidential nature, the teacher may want to suggest that they meet when they can have some privacy. Many times, however, the parent wants to talk about it now.

☆ NON-ENGLISH-SPEAKING PARENTS OR GUARDIANS

Occasionally, teachers have students whose parents do not speak English. When this is the case, teachers need to have an interpreter at the conference. Sometimes, it may be necessary for the child to fulfill this role, if the language is not a common one. Notes, letters, and report cards will also need to be translated into the native language of the parents.

Issues and Trends

Using Technology to Communicate with Non-English-Speaking Parents

In 1970, Congress passed legislation that mandated schools will communicate with parents in a language they can understand. It wasn't, however, until 1990 that the Office for Civil Rights began to aggressively enforce this. Some districts have spent hundreds of thousands of dollars on contract translators, and other districts have tried to use their bilingual teachers as translators. Neither of these methods has proved satisfactory. Districts do not have huge amounts of money to spend, and using teachers took them out of the classroom and away from teaching the children. Approximately 10 million children live in a home where English is not spoken. As schools sought solutions to this problem, businesses began forming that would professionally translate and publish the standard documents a district uses into the languages that are needed (TransAct, 2003).

Services have also sprung up on the Internet that are available to the schools. When non-English-speaking parents arrive at school, the office staff will ask them which language they speak or to point to their language. The secretary or office personnel can go to the Internet site and pull up the appropriate school papers to welcome them to the school and to allow them to register their child. The documents mirror the English form so that the staff knows what each line contains. Wake County Public School System has a huge diverse population with more than 100 languages spoken in the county and has begun to use this service to meet the needs of the parents (Wake County School System, 2002).

Though steps like this are certainly helping schools communicate with non-English-speaking parents, it does not address the day-to-day needs a teacher might have to communicate with them. There are Internet sites available for someone to type in a message and have it translated, but the quality of the translation is sometimes in doubt and may lead to misunderstandings.

Dimensions of Diversity

Working with Parents from Diverse Cultures

Poorly educated parents, regardless of their cultural background, often fail to see themselves in the role of teachers of reading, writing, and math to their children (Laosa, 1980). Understanding this may help teachers as they attempt to involve these parents in their children's education. When materials and homework are sent home with the children, this often encourages parents to interact in educational ways that they would unlikely do if this material had not been sent home (Cultural Diversity and Early Education, 2001). These parents do not understand how children learn or how to provide learning opportunities to their children in the home. Parents have even been known to deny their young children access to books and writing materials under the mistaken belief that this will harm their child's formal education (Cultural Diversity and Early Education, 2001). These types of beliefs may cause tensions among the school, teachers, and other school personnel. This tension is caused because of the misunderstandings between what the school expects and what the parents expect of the school. Parental practices at home may also be in conflict with what the school sees as appropriate practices (Cultural Diversity and Early Education, 2001).

These problems may be further complicated by language differences between home and school. Parents may fear that, as their children learn English, they will have problems communicating with their children. They worry that their influence over their children will diminish as the children learn an unfamiliar language (Cultural Diversity and Early Education, 2001).

Differences between cultures can also be the cause of misunderstandings. A Mexican-American family might all go to school with their child on the first day as an expression of unity and support for their child. The teacher might view this influx of the family as an indication that the child is spoiled and has been "babied" (Cultural Diversity and Early Education, 2001).

Another problem arises when children from culturally or linguistically diverse backgrounds qualify for and receive special education services. Teachers find that they are seeking ways to involve these parents in making decisions about their children. Parents may resist involvement for a variety of reasons ranging from language differences to mistrust of the U.S. education system. Mistrust may exist where families feel disenfranchised in the community. Schools may also add to the problem by treating recent immigrant parents, for example, a family from Ghana, the same as they treat their African-American families. Obviously, there is little similarity in the backgrounds and experiences of these two families. Parents may react by feeling angry, alienated, and undervalued. Other parents may resist involvement in decisions about their children because they defer to school personnel who are viewed as the experts (Parette & Petch-Hogan, 2000).

continued

Different approaches must be tried with these families if the school wants to involve them. Use of community liaisons or family advisory councils offer these families a different way to present their concerns, issues, or desires. The liaison would be a well-respected member or leader from the community in which the family resides. Schools should use native-speaking individuals to make the initial contact with the parents and provide interpreters for meetings at the school. Finally, schools should attempt to identify who the real decision maker is in a particular family. In some cultures, this might not be the parents, but an extended family member such as the grandmother. All of these are important aspects of involving the families of children with disabilities from diverse backgrounds (Parette & Petch-Hogan, 2000).

Help for schools and individual teachers is now readily available and only a click away with today's technology. Websites, such as the one from Columbia University, provide resources, directories of services, publications, articles, parent guides, and other Internet links to assist schools and teachers in meeting the diverse needs of their children (Equity and Cultural Diversity, 2002).

⭐ PARENTING STYLES

In dealing with parents, it is important to recognize that there are different parenting styles and that a parent's pervading style affects not only the way the child behaves in class, but also determines how a teacher responds to the parent during conferences.

There are four styles of parenting: authoritarian, authoritative, permissive, and uninvolved. Of these styles, the authoritative style of parenting is the best and tends to produce children who are happy, self-confident, self-controlled, independent, friendly, and cooperative. *Authoritative* parents enforce limits and insist on obedience while showing affection for their child, listening to their child's point of view, and encouraging participation in family decision making. *Authoritarian* parents insists that the child obey and adopt a "Do it because I said so" attitude. Their children tend to be unhappy, withdrawn, anxious, and may react with hostility when frustrated. The *permissive* parent avoids making any demands on the child and sets no limits on behavior. These children tend to be dependent, nonachieving, and immature. The *uninvolved* parent provides little support beyond caring for children's physical needs. This may be because the parents are depressed, live in poverty, or have so much stress that they can't be concerned about their children. These children tend to have poor emotional control, low tolerance for frustration, difficulties in school, and delinquency in their teens (Berk, 1999).

Obviously, the style of parenting is an indication to the teacher of the best method of working with the parents. Parents who are uninvolved because of poverty or depression must be given help before they can be able to handle the added pressure of problems with their children. The teacher may be able to influence authoritarian and permissive parents by educating them in good child-rearing practices—not, however, by pointing out that they are not doing a good job of raising their children, but by offering them specific suggestions about specific problems.

⭐ HOME VISITS

Teachers can gain a wealth of information about a child by making a home visit. It is best, in today's world, for a teacher to be accompanied by another person such as another teacher, the school nurse, the school counselor, or an aide. Visits should be scheduled in advance. Parents should be informed about the purpose of the visit. For the prekindergarten or kindergarten child, this could be to make connections with the child and home or might even be part of the school policy. The teacher should arrive on time, and the parents should know how long the teacher is planning to stay. If refreshments are offered, the teacher should be gracious and accept. The teacher should be careful not to judge the physical surroundings and conclude that the home environment is not good for the child. By listening and responding to the parents' questions, much information can be gained and shared by parents and teacher alike. This receptivity is as important as completion of the teacher's agenda (Brewer, 2001).

The visit can be used to discuss special school policies, such as homework, special teaching methods or strategies, special needs of the child, the school's discipline policy, and/or the classroom discipline policy. If the teacher sends home special projects or activities during the year, this is an excellent time to show and explain how these projects will work. A home visit is the perfect opportunity to explain to parents how the classroom works and presents an opportunity to clear up any misconceptions that the parents might have. One teacher used this opportunity to tell the parents how play in the classroom is actually the vehicle through which their child was learning complex skills that would be the basis for skills that would be learned in later years and how this learning was taking place in a very effective manner without the use of worksheets.

Occasions may arise when it becomes imperative for the teacher to make a home visit without being able to notify the parents ahead of time. If the parents have no phone and are unable to read, the teacher may tell the child that a home visit will be made. This message may not make it home to the parents, however, so the teacher should be prepared for taking the parents by surprise. This type of visit should be reserved for serious concerns affecting the child and only after all other means of notifying the parents have failed.

⭐ CHILD INFORMATION SHEET

At the beginning of school, it is especially helpful to send home an information sheet for the parents to fill out. (See Figure 11.2.) These forms provide the

FIGURE 11.2 Sample Student Information Sheet

Student Information Sheet

Name of child _____ Date of birth _____

Mother's name _____

Father's name _____

Lives with both parents: Yes _____   No _____

Step-parent's name _____

Brothers' and sisters' names and ages _____

_____

_____

Other people living in the home _____

_____

Allergies _____

Medications _____

Religious affiliation (optional) _____

Any current problems the teacher should be aware of _____

_____

_____

Any major life changes in the last 2 years (divorce, death) _____

_____

_____

Home phone # _____ Mother's work # _____

Father's work # _____ e-mail _____

Best time to call _____

Other emergency contact person and phone number _____

_____

Talents that parents can share with class (read to class, available for field trips, cooking, talk about occupation, special interests, etc.)   _____

_____

Interests of your child _____

Pets? _____ Favorite book _____

Favorite Activities _____

_____

Thank you for taking the time to fill out this form. We look forward to a great year!

teacher with much personal information about each child in the class. For example, asking the names and ages of all the children *currently living in the home* may provide the teacher with important information. The teacher may find that although the child only has one brother, his mom's sister and her three children are also living in the home at this time. Now the teacher can understand why the child is so tired at school. He is sharing his room, and possibly his bed, with several other children. Some schools have student information sheets that are sent home to everyone. When the school does not request this information, some teachers devise their own.

⭐ HOME LEARNING ACTIVITIES

Teachers are continuously seeking ways to involve the entire family in the educational process. Teachers also want to provide home access to technology to all children in their classroom. In trying to incorporate these two goals, teachers are trying more innovative ideas. One teacher received a grant and purchased a computer that went home with the children, along with a description of three projects to be done: draw a picture; write a story; and answer a survey about who in the home, besides the student, used the computer, and did the family enjoy having the computer? This computer went into mostly lower socioeconomic homes. It was carried to and from school in all kinds of weather, with long commutes on the school bus (up to one and a half hours one way). For two years the computer went out twice a week, every week, and was still in perfect working condition at the end of this period. Parents, children, friends, and relatives all gave the program high marks. Children looked forward with great anticipation to their turn. The computer stayed with the child for three days, and all in the family were encouraged to use it. When it was returned, it was connected to the classroom printer and pictures, letters, or whatever had been done was printed, shared with the class, and sent home with the child. The program was discontinued, however, when the teacher left the district. Programs that can put computers into lower socioeconomic homes could help, in a small way, to close the gap in computer literacy between the poor and middle to upper classes.

Other teachers have purchased tape recorders and recorded books and sent them home with the children in backpacks. A writing suitcase can be put together and equipped with paper, markers, pens, pencils, scissors, colored paper, glue, and other appropriate materials. This suitcase helps, albeit temporarily, to put materials that motivate children to write and draw into the homes of children whose homes are bare of these materials (Rich, 1985).

Home literacy bags can be put together that encourage family participation in the children's early literacy development. These bags may include a book and several activities to do at home based on that book. All the materials necessary for the activities are included in the bag. "The bags put appropriate, good-quality literature directly into the hands of parents, and offer informal, interactive activities for extending children's language and literacy acquisition" (Barbour, 1998/99, p. 72).

☆ STUDENT HANDBOOKS

Many school districts provide parents with a handbook that details the district's discipline management plan, attendance policies, programs, grading, testing, report cards, and all other pertinent information that a parent might want to know about the district, its policies, and its programs. Answers to many of parents' specific questions can be found in these handbooks, which not only provide parents with a wealth of information, but also help teachers new to the district understand policies and procedures. Teachers need to be familiar with the information provided in the handbook for the district in which they are teaching.

☆ PARENTS' AND STUDENTS' RIGHTS

By law, both parents, whether married, separated, or divorced, and a student who is at least 14 years old all have the right to inspect the records on the child that the school holds and passes on each year. *Student records* are those records that are maintained in any way by the public schools (Boston Public School Handbook, 2000). When parents' rights have been legally terminated, they will be denied access to the records for their child, if the school is given a copy of the court order terminating these rights. Although parents are entitled, by state law, to have access to the district's written records concerning their child, this does not include all records that may exist, however. A teacher's personal notes on a student do not have to be made available to the parents. Written records that parents may access include:

1. Grades
2. Attendance records
3. **Psychological records**
4. Test scores
5. Disciplinary records
6. Health and immunization records
7. Counseling records
8. Teacher and counselor evaluations
9. Reports of behavioral patterns (Galena Park ISD Handbook, 2000)

Psychological records are those records that contain the results of IQ testing and achievement tests. Before giving information about students to others, the school must obtain written permission from the parents, with the following exceptions: teachers and school officials with a legitimate need, state or federal officials for use in evaluating and auditing programs, accreditation organizations, researchers, administrators of a district into which the student is transferring, financial aid officials, and officials responding to health emergencies (Berger, 2000).

Under the Family Educational Rights and Privacy Act of 1974, "Parents have the right to inspect all instructional materials, including teachers' manuals, films, tapes, or other supplementary material, that will be used in connection with any survey, analysis, or evaluation" of any program or activity, if that program or activity is funded even partly by the U.S. Department of Education.

Compulsory Attendance

Although parents also have the right to choose where and how their children are educated, all states have compulsory attendance laws that require parents to see that their children regularly attend school. Parents may choose to home-school their children, enroll them in public school, or send them to a private school (Berger, 2000).

Pledge of Allegiance

In 1943, the Supreme Court found in favor of Jehovah's Witnesses parents when it ruled that children do not have to salute the flag and say the pledge of allegiance if it violates their religious beliefs or is a matter of conscience. The children do, however, have to stand quietly and not disrupt the others (West Virginia State Board of Education v. Barnette, 1943).

Discrimination

In 1964, Congress enacted the Civil Rights Act, which prohibits discrimination by any recipients of federal funds. This act states "that no person in the United States shall, on the grounds of race, color, or national origin, be excluded from participation in, be denied the benefits of, or be otherwise subjected to discrimination under any program or activity receiving Federal financial assistance from the Department of Education (Sec. 601)." This law applies to most schools because they receive federal money. Schools are not allowed to separate students based on race. This does not apply to students who are placed in bilingual education based on their limited ability to speak English. This placement is supported by the Elementary and Secondary Act (1965) and the 1974 Supreme Court ruling in *Lau v. Nichols*.

Sex discrimination was addressed in 1972 with Title IX of the Educational Amendments and provides that no person shall be excluded on the basis of sex under any program receiving federal funds. Educational institutions that receive federal funds cannot:

1. Exclude students of one sex from participation in any academic, extra-curricular, research, occupational training or other educational program or activity.
2. Subject any student to separate or different rules of discipline, sanctions or other treatment.
3. Apply different rules of appearance to males and females (for example, requiring males to wear their hair shorter than females).
4. Aid or perpetuate discrimination against any person by providing significant assistance to any agency, organization, or person which discriminates on the basis of sex in providing any aid, benefit, or service to students.

5. Assign pregnant students to separate classes or activities, although schools may require a student to obtain a physician's certificate as to her ability to participate in the normal educational program or activity as long as such a certificate is required of all students for other physical or emotional conditions requiring the attention of a physician.

6. Refuse to excuse any absence because of pregnancy or refuse to allow the student to return to the same grade level that she held when she left school because of pregnancy.

7. Discriminate against any person on the basis of sex in the counseling or guidance of students or the use of different tests or materials for counseling unless such different materials cover the same occupation and interest areas and the use of such different materials is shown to be essential to eliminate sex bias (Berger, 2000).

⭐ HOME SCHOOLING

The main reason that parents choose to home-school their children is that parents perceive this to be best for their children. Such parents feel that their children receive a better education at home than they would receive in public school. The second reason parents give for home schooling is religious beliefs. Some parents use the public school curriculum, and others purchase materials marketed for parents who want to home-school. These materials may be religious in nature if the parents are home-schooling for religious purposes (Toppo, 2001).

Approximately 1.7 percent, or 850,000, of children are being taught at home. These children are more likely to live in a two-parent home, and a higher percentage of these parents have college degrees. In the majority of the families, only one parent works and the average annual income is less than $50,000, with a significant number earning less than $25,000 (Toppo, 2001).

⭐ CHILDREN WITH DISABILITIES

Many federal laws have been passed to protect individuals with disabilities from discrimination. In 1997, PL 105-17, the Individuals with Disabilities Education Act (IDEA), required schools to include students with disabilities to a greater extent in the general education curriculum. (See Chapter 4 on students with special needs for more information.)

⭐ CORPORAL PUNISHMENT

Corporal punishment is still allowed in 23 of the 50 U.S. states. During the 1999–2000 school year, 457,754 students received corporal punishment (National Coalition to Abolish Corporal Punishment in Schools, 2001). Corporal punishment

State by State

Family and Community in the State of Massachusetts

The Massachusetts Department of Education's website has several areas of interest to parents. In Massachusetts, parents are allowed to send their children to schools in communities other than the city or town in which they live, with tuition being paid by the sending district. Under the menu item, Accountability and Targeted Assistance, parents can review the results of the various schools' performance ratings. Those schools that are rated underperforming are further critiqued on progress (or lack of progress) that they are making in attempting to improve. Parents are also able to access information on special communities (special education, gifted and talented, early learning), adult basic education (GED, family literacy), alternative education (various options), and student support (support services, scholarships, tutoring aid) under the menu item, Family and Community (Massachusetts Department of Education, 2002).

in the schools is usually administered in the form of paddling or spanking. In some districts the principal or assistant principal administers the punishment in the presence of a witness, who quite often is the child's teacher. In other districts, teachers are expected to do the actual paddling, again with a witness present. Schools do not have to get prior permission from parents, but even in some schools that regularly paddle students, parents may submit a written request that their child not be paddled. The United States and Canada (and one state in Australia) are the only industrialized countries that still allow corporal punishment (NCACPS, 2000). The courts have consistently upheld the right of the school to administer corporal punishment to children (Ingraham v. Wright, 1977). Even with this assurance, teachers who administer corporal punishment may find themselves in the middle of unpleasant legal procedures. Teachers in states allowing corporal punishment need to advocate for children and seek to change this policy.

⭐ VALUES AND CHARACTER EDUCATION

The current trend in education is toward a renewal of values or character education (Sanchez, 1998). This is seen as necessary as more newspaper headlines detail shootings, stabbings, and other violent crimes that are being committed by children. Many see a need to teach values in the schools because it appears that many of the parents of our children do not. The teaching of values is seen as a possible way to stem the violence that is cropping up in our schools and in our society. Approximately one out of five schools nationwide offers some sort of values or character education (Hart, 1995).

Once the decision is made to attempt to teach values, the problem lies in what values to teach that do not infringe upon the beliefs or rights of any one group in our society. Polls do show that more than 90 percent of the people polled, regardless of faith or no faith, agreed that democracy, patriotism, moral courage, honesty, acceptance of all peoples, and caring for friends and family are values that could be taught in schools (Leo, 1999). Prominent educators believe that values should be at the "core of the school curriculum for the purpose of systematically developing the character of the student" (Sanchez, 1998, p. 1).

Once the values that will be taught have been established, exactly how to teach values to children in early childhood is subject to much debate. Young children are egocentric, and some believe that young children need to be taught codes of behavior and provided with experiences that help them realize that the world does not revolve around them (Suh & Traiger, 1999). Some schools give values education slight status by hanging posters that declare values, and others attempt to implement a comprehensive approach for teaching values.

The area of social studies seems to offer the best fit into the curriculum for values education. In learning how to accept all people, regardless of race or religion, children can listen to or read books that talk about people from other ethnic groups. Sometimes the teacher will want to use nonfiction books about real-life people and the struggles that they have overcome. Other times the teacher can use fiction that presents what a child's or person's life is like or even books that describe how children are mistreated because of the color of their skin, their religion, or a handicap. After reading the book, the teacher will ask the children, "How do you think the boy in this book felt when . . . " "How would you feel if this happened to you?" This kind of questioning encourages children to see others as similar to themselves.

One often-overlooked component of any values education program is that of having the adults, teachers and parents, model appropriate behavior for the children. How the teacher or parent interacts with a child sends a powerful message to that child. If a teacher allows children to be rude and hurt another child's feelings by calling that child a name, then that teacher has given all the children his or her tacit approval to treat people in this manner. Simple statements made by the teacher—such as, "In our school, we play with everyone. We don't exclude someone because she is different."—set the tone for what is and is not acceptable behavior in the classroom.

⭐ HELPING CHILDREN DEAL WITH TERRORISM AND DISASTERS

When national headlines, television stations, and radio stations broadcast extensive coverage of terrorist acts or natural disasters, children come to school with concerns and possibly misinformation. They may feel scared and worried about the future. It is the teacher's job to help these children as they struggle to understand a world that is not safe and secure.

In the wake of the World Trade Center terrorist attack in 2001, help and guidance for teachers began to appear on the Internet addressing these very issues. Psychologists, counselors, doctors, and education specialists have all published helpful advice for teachers and parents. Teachers and parents need to be calm when talking with children. Inviting children to share what they know or understand with others in their classroom helps the children to verbalize their feelings (Greenman, 2001). It is important for the teacher to share at this time, too. The teacher should share his or her feelings in an appropriate manner. This is also a time for the teacher to correct any inaccuracies or misconceptions that the children might be harboring. Allowing children to describe how they feel about what has happened, sharing the stories of the people who were heroes during the incident, and pointing out all the good people who are acting in a caring way all help children deal with the event or disaster. Talking about ways that the children could help and make a difference to the people involved, such as direct, monetary aid or offering food, clothing, bedding, and/or toys to boys and girls who lost all of their possessions, is also helpful. Allowing the children to draw or paint what they are feeling or what they

Teachers are an important source of comfort to young children.

know about the incident gives them an outlet for their feelings. Offering them reassurance that the teacher will keep them safe and reassuring the children that they are safe here at school helps give them feelings of safety (Davis & Keyser, 2001). It is important for the teacher to help children realize that the perpetrators of an act may be of one ethic group or race but that not all the people of this group are to be feared or treated like criminals or hated because of this. In discussing terrorism and hatred, the teacher needs to make children aware that terrorists come in all colors and live in all places. They can be told that terrorists do these terrible things because they don't know how to live and get along with people when they have disagreements (Greenman, 2001). The teacher must offer the children reassurance that he or she will keep them safe, if indeed they are relatively safe (Davis & Keyser, 2001). Even so, children may need extra physical comfort, extra hugs, and smiles.

The classroom should offer the children normalcy through the maintaining of the daily schedule. This normalcy and structure will help the children feel safe. Within the daily schedule, allowing children more time for physical activity will provide an emotional release. The children should be observed and watched for symptoms that suggest anxiety and fear. Young children are not always able to communicate their discomfort with words but may send signals such as reverting back to thumbsucking, bed-wetting, clinging behavior, and problems with eating or sleeping (Ginsberg, 2001). FEMA (2001) has published a Children's Mental Health Checklist to aid parents and teachers in determining the mental status of a child and whether a mental health consultation should be sought. Twenty-five indicators are listed and range from immediate consequences of the disaster or event to characteristics of the child for more than three weeks after the disaster. Headaches, stomachaches, clinging behavior, sleep problems, irritability, and compulsions are a few of the signs children may exhibit. Any suicidal talk or preoccupation with death is a sign for an immediate consultation with a mental health professional (FEMA, 2001).

PARENT PROGRAMS AND INFORMATION SOURCES FOR PARENTS

Many parent education programs have been developed to assist and support parents through training in specific parenting skills. Parents as Teachers and the Even Start Family Literacy Program are two of the programs most familiar to teachers in the public schools. Parent-Teacher Associations (PTA) and Parent-Teacher Organizations (PTO) include parent education as a goal as well as collaboration between the home and school and the dissemination of information for parents. Other organizations such as the National Association for the Education of Young Children provide a website that has a parent section. There are more resources available for parents than ever before, and parents with computers have many of these resources right at their fingertips.

Parents as Teachers

Parents as Teachers is a voluntary family education program designed as a prevention program aimed at forming a close, working relationship between home and school and providing a solid foundation for school success (Educational Programs That Work, 1994). The program begins before birth and continues through age 5. It is founded on the belief that parents are their children's first teachers and that these early years determine school-year success (Parents as Teachers, 2000). Parents are trained as educators using the Parents as Teachers curriculum, which includes sections on guidance of young children, child development, and sensory development. Access to a resource center, parent group meetings, personal home visits, and periodic screening of sensory and educational development are also part of the program (Educational Programs That Work, 1994). During each year of development, parents learn what to expect of their child and how to encourage learning, manage challenging behavior, and promote a strong relationship between parent and child. Activities are offered that encourage intellectual growth, language development, motor skills, and social development (Parents as Teachers, 2000).

Even Start Family Literacy Program

"The Even Start Family Literacy Program was first authorized in 1989 as Part B of Chapter 1 of Title 1 of the Elementary and Secondary Education Act of 1965" (Even Start, 1998, p. 1). This program addresses needs of parents and children from low-income families up to the age of 8. It is an attempt to break the cycle of poverty and illiteracy through parenting education. In 1998, appropriation for this program reached $124 million. Most states administer their own Even Start Programs with this money. The program has three goals: the improvement of parents' literacy skills or basic educational skills, helping parents become partners with the school in educating their children, and assisting children to reach their full potential as learners. Even Start also offers support services such as transportation, nutrition assistance, health care, child care, meals, special care for a disabled family member, referrals for counseling, mental health, battered women, child protective services, employment, and screenings and treatment for substance abuse. Even Start participants are required to participate in all three goal areas. Follow-up research on the program shows gains in children's vocabulary (as measured on the Peabody Picture Vocabulary Test). Children whose parents participated the most recognized the greatest gains. Parenting skills showed significant improvement and the home learning environment improved (Even Start, 1998).

Most projects work with existing early childhood programs such as Head Start. In schools, services are provided in conjunction with required school activities and may take the form of tutoring assistance and homework assistance given in before- and after-school programs, in addition to summer school activities (Even Start, 1998).

Adult services provide help in completing a GED or general instruction in basic reading, writing, and math skills. Parenting education may also be provided in the form of speakers, group discussions, and hands-on activities that increase parents' understanding of normal child development and their role in their children's education (Even Start, 1998).

Parent-Teacher Association (PTA)

The National PTA is the largest child advocacy, nonprofit organization of parents, teachers, students, and other people from the community in the United States. It has almost 6.5 million members and chapters in all 50 states, the District of Columbia, Department of Defense schools overseas, and the U.S. Virgin Islands. Its mission is to support and advocate for children in the schools, community, government, and other organizations that make decisions about children. It also assists parents in developing skills and encourages parent involvement in public schools. The National PTA supports programs in arts education, health and safety, family television viewing, environmental issues, parent involvement, and family issues such as self-esteem, sex, and peer pressure. Their Children First website (www.pta.org) contains information on a wide variety of topics such as helping children with homework and discussions of school violence. The website contains hundreds of free documents for parents. It also provides current news about child-related issues and parenting issues (PTA, 2001).

PTAs have business meetings, conduct fundraisers, and provide for special needs of the school. These needs might include new playground equipment, books for the library, or even an emergency fund for the school nurse. PTA meetings are often held in conjunction with a program performed by the children from the school. This is done in an attempt to involve more parents in the PTA.

When schools are members of the PTA, a certain percentage of local dues will be remitted to the national organization. Dues, or membership fees, are very reasonable. Some schools, however, feel that sending part of their money to a national organization is not in the best interest of their school and have formed separate parent-teacher organizations.

Parent-Teacher Organizations

When schools elect to form an organization not related to the National Parent-Teacher Association, the name PTA cannot be used. Schools often call this organization their PTO. Many of these groups function in the local school in a similar manner to the PTA, but without the resources and goals of a national organization. They collect dues and conduct fundraisers to supply school needs.

National Association for the Education of Young Children (NAEYC)

Organizations such as the NAEYC provide parents with free, high-quality information on many topics. From the NAEYC's homepage, parents can choose the Parents item on the menu and can access *Early Years Are Learning Years* articles. These articles can be accessed by topic or by dates and include such diverse subjects as inclusion, child care, and child development. In addition, parents can find an accredited child care program in their neighborhood, titles of books of special interest to parents, and a list of brochures on various topics of interest to parents (NAEYC, Home Page).

 **SUMMARY**

There are many aspects to working with parents and involving them in their child's education. Family situations add to this problem because families face a shortage of time and, in some cases, resources. Despite these problems, teachers and schools need to seek ways to actively involve parents. Effective communication is the cornerstone for working with parents, and it is helpful for both teachers and parents to know and understand their rights within the school environment.

Organizations exist that help parents develop parenting skills and provide a wealth of information on many topics as well as training in parenting skills. These organizations may also provide services for the entire family and work in conjunction with the school.

⭐ DISCUSSION QUESTIONS

1. What are some challenges that schools face in dealing with parents, and how are these addressed?
2. What are some barriers to communicating with parents?
3. Discuss effective communication in dealing with parents.
4. What rights do parents and students have?
5. Discuss the different types of the programs available to parents.

⭐ SUGGESTED CHAPTER ACTIVITIES

1. Obtain a copy of the student handbook from a district near you. What types of information are presented in the handbook? What is the district's policy about corporal punishment?
2. Attend a PTA meeting and note the business discussed. Was the meeting planned in conjunction with a program involving children? Approximately how many people were in attendance?
3. Gather examples of types of communication sent home to parents. What types of information is being provided?
4. Where does your state fall on the corporal punishment issue? Is it allowed?
5. Do a mock parent-teacher conference in which you, the teacher, have to present some unwelcomed information.
6. Visit a website for parents and report on the types of information available to the parents.

Chapter Twelve

Becoming an Early Childhood Professional

CHAPTER OVERVIEW

★ Do you know the purpose of a code of ethics?

★ What are your ethical responsibilities?

★ Can you identify the signs of child abuse and neglect?

★ What are some of the professional organizations that teachers may join?

★ Can you describe the different types of portfolios?

★ What are the roles and responsibilities of teachers?

★ Do you know the characteristics of effective teachers?

READING THIS CHAPTER WILL PROVIDE THE ANSWERS TO THESE QUESTIONS.

I have had two children go through the public schools. During their time in school, my children have had wonderful teachers for the most part. Unfortunately, they have also had teachers whom I thought were unfit. When my son was in third grade, I went to the principal and demanded that he move him into another class. This third-grade teacher did as little as possible with the children. As a concerned parent, I always looked over my son's papers. He kept bringing home these reading test papers with 18 out of 20 questions wrong. He used an answer key and graded the tests himself. I finally said to him that there was no way he was reading the passages. He said the teacher didn't care if he read the passages or not, she just checked off that he had turned it in! So while some people (the teacher, I am sure) viewed me as a troublemaker, I only took the action of having him switched after this incident and several others like it. Most of the teachers were willing to work with me for the good of my children, and I have a great deal of respect for them. I am more than willing to work with my children's teachers. They have been trained and educated in how to teach my child, but I really have appreciated those teachers who sought my advice and considered themselves partners with me.

Beginning teachers often attempt to model themselves after more experienced, exceptional teachers. This is an important part of learning to be a good teacher. Studies of successful teachers have been helpful in determining certain common characteristics and skills. This chapter provides new or preservice teachers with information that they need as they begin their first year of teaching. It also focuses on characteristics of successful teachers and assists the new or preservice teacher in developing an understanding of ethical responsibilities, self-evaluation, various roles of the teacher, and teacher responsibilities. Information about developing professional portfolios, professional organizations, professional development, and collaboration with others in the school are essential elements for a successful first-year experience.

⭐ CODE OF ETHICS

"Ethics is the study of right and wrong, duty and obligation. It involves critical reflection on morality. [It is] a conscious deliberation regarding moral choice" (Feeney & Freeman, 1999, p. 5). Because a person's individual morality and values influence the thinking that occurs in the decision-making process when one is dealing with ethical issues, teachers must use standards as a guide when they are confronted with ethical decisions. Codes of ethics have been developed by many

Effective teachers facilitate children's learning.

Issues and Trends

New-Teacher Induction Programs

With the high turnover rate of new teachers, baby boomers beginning to retire, and the teacher shortages that some areas of the country are experiencing, districts and states are beginning to implement induction year programs. These programs provide new teachers with models and mentors and support groups to help them through all the different aspects that a first year teacher faces. More than half of the states have some type of induction program, yet more than half of beginning teachers are not participating in anything more than school orientation. When the district throws new teachers into the classroom with a sink-or-swim attitude, the attrition rate is five times higher than among experienced teachers. Financing these programs generally depends on whether or not they are mandated by the state. If they are, states may supplement local support (Promising Practices, 1998).

What are some characteristics of promising programs? New teachers are provided with assistance with everyday problems, and this special attention helps new teachers be reflective about their teaching, make it through their first year more easily, and increase the likelihood that they will come back the following year. Mentors receive compensation for their help and opportunities for professional growth as they work with the new teachers, sometimes in conjunction with colleges and universities. Some induction programs are being offered in conjunction with graduate schools and combine graduate seminars or coursework with the induction program so that new teachers have some graduate credit at the end of their induction year. (Promising Practices, 1998). This can also be helpful for teachers who teach in states that require them to receive a certain number of hours of training a year, or over a period of several years, in order to remain certified in that state.

organizations as a means of guiding teachers in making decisions about professional conduct.

Morality refers to beliefs about right and wrong, duties, and obligations (Feeney & Freeman, 1999). Personal values (i.e., fairness, truth, justice) are shaped by upbringing, culture, religion, and life experiences, especially early childhood experiences. Personal values and personal morality shape the way a teacher responds to situations that occur in the classroom and deals with parents and other people in the school setting. Personal values and morals cannot be solely relied on when making decisions in the workplace because people have differing values and morals. Thus, a code of ethics provides a consistent means for teachers to use, regardless of past experiences or upbringing.

Professional ethics, or a code of ethics, helps guide a teacher in decision making. It provides a standard "of conduct based on core values" (Feeney & Freeman, 1999, p. 9). Besides guiding a teacher's decision, a code of ethics also provides a justification for a difficult decision. A code of ethics is a powerful tool that is too often ignored by teachers. One way to help teachers make significant improvement in the practice of early childhood education is to help them grasp the potential help within the code of ethics (Feeney & Freeman, 1999).

NAEYC's Code of Ethical Conduct

naeyc National Association for the Education of Young Children (NAEYC) standards of ethical behavior are based on six core values that are rooted in the history of early childhood education, with responsibilities stretching over four areas of professional relationships. NAEYC (1997) states that these core values are:

- Appreciating childhood as a unique and valuable stage of the human life cycle
- Basing our work with children on knowledge of child development
- Appreciating and supporting the close ties between the child and the family
- Recognizing that children are best understood and supported in the context of family, culture, community, and society
- Respecting the dignity, worth, and uniqueness of each individual (child, family member, and colleague)
- Helping children and adults achieve their full potential in the context of relationships that are based on trust, respect, and positive regard (p. 1). The four areas of professional relationships covered by these core values are the relationships dealing with "children, families, colleagues, and community and society" (p. 1). Each of the four areas describes ideals and principles when defining practices. "Ideals reflect the aspirations of practitioners. The principles are intended to guide conduct and assist practitioners in resolving ethical dilemmas encountered in the field" (p. 1).

Relationships with Children

It is important for the early childhood teacher to treat each child with respect and to maintain a classroom environment that is safe for the child both physically and emotionally. All children are included to the fullest extent possible, respecting the uniqueness of each child and recognizing his or her potential. All children receive the support services that they need. The teacher also needs to understand child development, recognizing that children develop at different rates and need to be treated accordingly. This understanding forms the basis for appropriate activities that are planned in the classroom.

The guiding principle in relationships with children is to do no harm to them. This means that children must not be discriminated against for any reason. The teacher also involves parents and other staff who have relevant knowledge in making decisions concerning the children. Adaptations to all areas of the learning environment must be made to facilitate that child's learning. Teachers must help ensure the safety of children by reporting suspected child abuse or neglect.

Ethical Responsibilities to Families

Teachers have a responsibility to collaborate with families and develop the relationships necessary for the child's success. Teachers must respect each family and its values, customs, culture, beliefs, and language. Teachers must involve families in significant decisions and inform them of school policies and accidents involving their child while maintaining confidentiality. Family members must have access to the classroom and to their child's records.

Ethical Responsibilities to Colleagues

Teachers should develop relationships with co-workers based on trust, respect, and cooperation. Information and resources should be shared. Care must be exercised when expressing opinions about the conduct of others, and only statements based on firsthand knowledge that is relevant to the children or programs should be expressed. Professional behavior requires a teacher to talk to a colleague first when there is concern about his or her professional behavior and attempt to resolve the matter before talking to the principal.

Responsibilities to Employers

Teachers are expected to provide the highest quality of teaching possible and to do nothing to diminish the reputation of their school or child care facility unless laws are being violated. When teachers do not agree with policies, they should direct their efforts toward change through action within the school or child care facility (NAEYC, 1997).

Teachers who are faced with an ethical dilemma should seek guidance from this code of conduct as they are trying to make a decision. This code of ethics provides teachers with a means of discerning ethical behavior. In the November 1999 issue of *Young Children,* readers were asked to respond to an ethical dilemma. A child's parents did not think that he was being challenged in kindergarten and wanted the child to spend part of the day in the first-grade classroom reading from basals and doing worksheets. The teacher saw her program as developmentally appropriate and the child had been successful in all areas. The question was how the teacher should prepare for the next conference and which parts of the Code of Ethical Conduct applied in this situation. Responses were published in the July 2000 issue. Teachers responding to the question cited the importance of developmentally appropriate practices but failed to mention family involvement in significant decisions as they work toward providing for that child's unique set of needs. Respondents seemed to be defending the program instead of recognizing that this was an opportunity to work collaboratively with parents to enhance the child's learning.

Becky is in your kindergarten classroom. She has autism and sometimes screams when upset. This behavior disturbs the other children in the classroom. Mary's mother has made an appointment with you to discuss Mary and "other problems." You believe that she is going to ask you several questions about Becky and request that Becky be removed from your classroom so that Mary will not be disturbed. Using the Code of Ethics, discuss how you will handle this situation.

☆ CHILD ABUSE AND NEGLECT

naeyc

In addition to keeping the children safe in the classroom, the NAEYC Code of Ethical Conduct addresses the importance of reporting abuse and neglect to the proper authorities. In 1998, 903,000 children in the United States were victims of maltreatment, with an estimated 1,100 children dying from abuse (Child Maltreatment, 1998). With numbers such as these, it is important for the teacher to be able to recognize the signs of child abuse and neglect. The teacher has a legal and moral obligation to report all *suspected* child abuse or neglect. If a teacher fails to report abuse or neglect to the proper authorities, that teacher could be prosecuted. Reporting to the school nurse, counselor, or principal *does not* release the teacher from the responsibility of reporting an incident. Unfortunately, a teacher may work under a principal who does not want the abuse or neglect to be reported. That teacher is still accountable for reporting the incident, even if a principal has told him or her not to do so.

Signs of Abuse and Neglect

The Child Abuse Prevention and Treatment Act (CAPTA) defines abuse and neglect as acts or failure to act that results in, or presents a risk of, "death, serious physical or emotional harm, sexual abuse or exploitation. There are four main types of maltreatment: physical abuse, neglect, sexual abuse, and emotional abuse" (NCCAN, 2000, pp. 1–2). The National Clearinhouse on Child Abuse and Neglect (NCCAN) provides the following definitions for each of these types.

Physical abuse is characterized by the infliction of physical injury as a result of punching, beating, kicking, biting, burning, shaking, or otherwise harming a child. The parent or caregiver may not have intended to hurt the child; rather, the injury may have resulted from overdiscipline or physical punishment.

Child neglect is characterized by failure to provide for the child's basic needs. Neglect can be physical, educational, or emotional. *Physical neglect* includes refusal of or delay in seeking health care; abandonment; expulsion from the home or refusal to allow a runaway to return home; and inadequate supervision. *Educational neglect* includes allowance of chronic truancy, failure to enroll a child of mandatory school age in school, and failure to attend to a special educational need. *Emotional neglect* includes such actions as marked inattention to the child's needs for affection, refusal of or failure to provide needed psychological care, spouse abuse in the child's presence, and permission of drug or alcohol use by the child. The assessment of child neglect requires consideration of cultural values and standards of care as well as recognition that the failure to provide the necessities of life may be related to poverty.

Sexual abuse includes fondling a child's genitals, intercourse, incest, rape, sodomy, exhibitionism, and commercial exploitation through prostitution or the production of pornographic materials. Many experts believe that sexual abuse is the most underreported of child maltreatment because of the secrecy or "conspiracy of silence" that so often characterizes these cases.

Emotional abuse (psychological/verbal/abuse/mental injury) includes acts or omissions by the parents or other caregivers that have caused, or could cause, serious behavioral, cognitive, emotional, or mental disorders. In some cases of emotional abuse, the acts of parents or other caregivers alone, without any harm evident in the child's behavior or condition, are sufficient to warrant child protective services (CPS) intervention. For example, the parents/caregivers may use extreme or bizarre forms of punishment, such as confining a child in a dark closet. Less severe acts, such as habitual scapegoating, belittling, or rejecting treatment, are often difficult to prove, and CPS may not be able to intervene without evidence of harm to the child. (p. 2)

When Children Report Abuse

When a child reports to a teacher that he or she has been beaten, whipped, or otherwise mistreated and then begs the teacher to tell no one, the teacher should never promise not to tell. This is a promise that cannot be kept, even if the child is frightened and says that he or she will get "whipped" for telling. If a child tells the teacher that there are marks all over his or her back, the teacher cannot lift the child's shirt and look for marks. The teacher must ask permission from the child before raising the shirt. If the child says no to this request, then the teacher may not look at the back. Even the school nurse is not able to examine the child's back without gaining permission from the child to do so. It is important to remember that if a child tells the teacher that he or she has been abused, the responsibility for reporting the abuse falls on the teacher. The person who is told or who suspects the abuse is the one, by law, who is required to report that abuse.

Children seldom lie about being abused. However, the teacher does need to be very careful when a child reports abuse or neglect, or even has an injury, to carefully question the child to determine if this is abuse or if the child is calling a spanking being abused. Parents have the right to discipline their children but not to beat them. A few states have taken a hard stand against even spanking children. Not all injuries are abuse. Some children are prone to accidents. There have been rare instances in which parents have been accused of abuse and children have been removed from the home only to find later that the child had a physical ailment that led to broken bones.

⭐ PROFESSIONAL ORGANIZATIONS

Professional organizations for teachers range from special-interest groups to national and international organizations. National organizations usually provide teachers with news about legislation related to education and strive to protect teachers' rights, to improve teaching, and to influence legislators in areas concerning teaching. Many of these organizations disseminate information through a journal or newsletter. These organizations often offer a teacher the opportunity to buy liability insurance that is specific to the teaching environment and relatively inexpensive. There are three major national multidiscipline organizations: the Association of American Educators, the American Federation of Teachers, and the National Education Association.

Association of American Educators (AAE)

The AAE, the newest professional organization, is a nonunion, nonprofit, nonreligious organization that believes schools must integrate character and citizenship into academics and that values that transcend cultures, such as integrity, respect, compassion, cooperation, loyalty, and diligence, must be taught to our children. This organization holds that public education must aim to develop the child's character as well as intellect.

American Federation of Teachers (AFT)

The AFT began in 1916 when a handful of teachers met in Winnetka, Illinois, in one of the teachers' basement. Their intent was to create a strong union committed to their interests as teachers. The AFT is affiliated with the American Federation of Labor and Congress of Industrial Organizations (AFL-CIO) union and has an estimated membership of 500,000. Their journal is called *Changing Education.* The AFT has grown into a union that represents not only workers in education, but also public service and health care workers.

National Education Association (NEA)

The NEA, the oldest and the largest of the teacher organizations, was founded in 1857 and has approximately 2.5 million members. The NEA, as a union, regularly lobbies legislators on educational topics, such as fighting attempts by Congress to privatize public education and the restructuring of education. The NEA provides its members with a weekly e-mail newsletter that includes educational updates from national, state, and local levels. Policy is set though an annual Representative Assembly with elected delegates. The NEA publishes *Today's Education.*

Liability Insurance

One of the main reasons that teachers join a national organization is to obtain liability insurance. It is unfortunate that teachers need to be covered in this manner, but in today's litigious society it is becoming necessary. A favorite threat of older students has become, "My daddy is going to sue you." Anyone can sue a teacher for anything. Teachers are being sued for failure to teach a child to read and for promoting a child who was not on grade level, and these suits can occur several years after the teacher has had the child. Insurance buys peace of mind for teachers. The organizations often offer liability insurance, at an extra cost, to teachers. One policy, for example, offers $1 million of protection per occurrence per member. The insured is covered in cases of injury to a child under a teacher's supervision, failure to educate, violation of a child's civil rights, improper instruction, and accusations of abuse. Also covered are attorney's fees up to $35,000. The insured party, however, is not covered if found guilty of criminal acts.

OTHER PROFESSIONAL ORGANIZATIONS

Other professional organizations include international organizations such as Phi Delta Kappa and specialty organizations for a wide variety of fields, interests, and levels.

Phi Delta Kappa (PDK): An International Organization

Phi Delta Kappa is an international teacher association that promotes high-quality education, particularly public education. Members are teachers and other professionals in education, including college and university professors. PDK also includes administrators and students enrolled in programs leading to teacher certification as well as graduate students. There are 661 local chapters worldwide, and the house journal, *Kappan,* includes articles on current educational topics and concerns. Other services offered are travel seminars, job listings, student services, educational research, and professional development opportunities.

Specialty Organizations

There are numerous specialty organizations for teachers. These organizations are composed of people who have the same teaching field or area of interests or specialization. For instance, early childhood, math, science, reading, or special education teachers may choose to join the following organizations:

National Association for the Education of Young Children
National Council of Teachers of Mathematics
National Science Teachers Association
International Reading Association
Council for Exceptional Children

A professional organization exists for virtually every field, interest, and level. Many of these organizations also have local chapters or affiliates that meet regularly. One compelling reason for an educator to belong to one of these organizations is to have the opportunity to share information with others in the same field. Training is geared toward needs in that specific area, and their journals provide the latest information in the field. This kind of professional connection enriches the educator by providing new and exciting ideas to use in the classroom.

☆ PROFESSIONAL DEVELOPMENT

As in any profession, gaining one's teaching certification does not mean that the person knows everything and is no longer expected to continue learning. *Professional development*, sometimes referred to as *staff development*, is an ongoing process that is intended to improve, enhance, or introduce new skills and competencies. Many states require teachers to continue their education through professional development in order to keep their certification. This development may take the form of graduate hours at a university or workshop hours offered by various groups.

Since 1983 and the publication of *A Nation at Risk* (published by the National Commission on Excellence in Education after studying the quality of U.S. education), professional development has focused on "overcoming deficits in student knowledge or on reshaping the structure and organization of schooling" (Sparks & Hirsh, 2003, p. 1). Before this time, professional development had a "sit-and-get" format: Teachers sat through a workshop and were expected to "get" the information presented. Today, professional development is presented in a how-to model that provides teachers with step-by-step ways to implement new ideas and methods. Development is ongoing, hands-on practice with follow-ups and peer coaching as teachers are immersed in these new methods and activities (Stronge, 1997).

These teachers are participating in professional development training.

A growing body of research shows that teachers are the single most important factor in a child's learning. Good teachers can elicit outstanding responses from children, whereas poor teachers can cause children to make no significant progress in learning. The way to improve education is through professional development for teachers. A study by the National Center for Education Statistics (NCES) in 1998 found that only 56 percent of teachers use instructional strategies aligned to high student performance. The other teachers use methods that were employed when they were students.

Professional development can help teachers refine and advance skills they learned in college. Development that is grade or subject specific can have a dramatic impact on teacher effectiveness as the material presented is tailored to that grade or subject. Eighty-five percent of teachers receiving professional development report that it has improved their teaching by providing them with new information and teaching practices (NCES, 1998).

School-Initiated Professional Development

There are several dangers inherent in school-initiated professional development. "Research shows that one of the most effective forms of professional development takes place when teachers have opportunities to work together and learn from each other" (Sparks & Hirsh, 2003, p. 12). Yet when teachers request time for this type of collaboration, administrators say that it would not be approved by the state as professional development. Many schools use the one-shot and/or schoolwide workshops because all the faculty and staff can be assembled in one place and receive the training at the same time. However, these workshops lack the connectivity that is needed to improve teaching. Other forms of development have taken the form of "feel-good" sessions, ice-breaker activities, consultant-driven presentations, "make-it and take-its" (where teachers actually make an instructional aid), and games and role-playing activities in place of content (Stronge, 1997). When new methods are presented, kindergarten teachers need to receive information on how to implement the method at the kindergarten level. Very little is gained from material presented at a third-grade level, and vice versa. Another danger arises when schools look to fill development days with an inexpensive trainer simply to save money. Schools need to survey the needs of teachers and then seek a trainer based on these needs. Sometimes schools or districts contract with a professional trainer who disseminates incorrect, useless, or even harmful information to teachers and administrators using an untested method as a quick fix for educational problems. To combat this problem, the National Staff Development Council calls for schools to use research-validated practices and require trainers to present evidence that their programs work.

Good professional development exhibits the following characteristics.

- Results driven and job embedded
- Focused on helping teachers become deeply immersed in subject matter and teaching methods
- Curriculum centered and standards based

- Sustained, rigorous, and cumulative
- Directly linked to what teachers do in their classrooms (Sparks & Hirsh, 2003, p. 5)

Early childhood teachers also can seek appropriate professional development through NAEYC. NAEYC offers professional development for early childhood teachers through conferences, seminars, and outreach activities. Journals, brochures, and videotapes are also a source of teacher preparation and training (NAEYC Home Page, 2002).

Professional development needs to be viewed as an integral part of the teaching profession. Its importance also needs to be communicated to the general public, who often view professional development days as play days for teachers. Increasing professional development for teachers is a major key in affecting change in the classroom. Until schools begin to consistently provide high-quality professional development, teachers will continue to struggle for actual change in schools to meet the challenges of today's changing world.

☆ TEACHING PORTFOLIOS

There are three basic types of professional portfolios. The *employment portfolio* is used to present the qualifications of a teacher applying for a position. This is a showcase portfolio that presents the teacher's strengths and best work, exhibits the full range of teaching skills, and works to persuade an employer to hire the teacher. The *evaluation portfolio* is used to present material for evaluation by a principal and

What Teachers Are Saying

Professional Development

"I hate our staff development days. They are the biggest waste of time and money. We need to have grade-level-specific development. What I need in kindergarten is not the same as what teachers need for third grade."—*a kindergarten teacher*

With site-based management, teachers can have input into their school's staff development. This means that teachers need to be proactive and take the time to identify needs for staff development, find qualified people, and sell the idea to the principal and others on the site-based management team.

"The best professional development activity I ever had was when my principal got substitutes for all the kindergarten and first-grade teachers and brought in a person who talked with us about integrating reading, writing, and science. After her lecture, we followed her into one of our first-grade classrooms, and she used the children in that classroom to demonstrate what she had just taught. It was awesome!"—*a first-grade teacher*

is used for professional development. It includes documentation of specific criteria set by the school, district, or state. Some states require this type of portfolio for teacher evaluation. The final type of portfolio, the *professional development portfolio,* is intended to foster professional growth. Its sole purpose is self-evaluation (Green & Smyser, 1996).

★ ORGANIZING A PORTFOLIO

There are several methods for organizing a portfolio, but perhaps the simplest one to remember is the *five I's* (Smyser & Green, 1994; Green & Smyser, 1996). The I's stand for the title of each section: *introduction, influences, instruction, individualization,* and *integration.*

Introduction

The introduction contains the teacher's background information. This may be in the form of a résumé and should include teaching experiences, experiences with children, and professional development as well as autobiographical information.

Information That Could Be Included

- Autobiography
- Résumé
- Teaching credentials
- Statement of philosophy of education
- Current teaching situation with description of school and students

Influences

This section attempts to capture the flavor of the classroom environment that the teacher has created. It includes evidence of room displays and arrangement as well as specific grade-level or subject items that the teacher uses. Statements explaining the value and importance of each item presented accompany the items.

Information That Could Be Included

- Photos of bulletin boards
- Floor plan of classroom
- Listing and brief description of learning centers
- Annotated bibliography of books used
- Teacher-made materials
- Computer software/websites along with a description of how they are used
- Classroom management philosophy
- Discipline plan—school/district/personal
- Classroom schedule
- Classroom groupings (may include photos of cooperative learning)

Instruction

This section reflects actual teaching, the planning and delivery of instruction. Therefore, it is important to include sample lesson plans, units, instructional aids, and descriptions of hands-on experiences. A reflective statement that reveals how these items are used effectively is a very important part of this section.

Information That Could Be Included

- Lesson plans
- Handouts
- Videotape of a lesson
- Student products
- Photos of students working and/or products
- Thematic teaching units
- Learning center activities
- Schedule showing small-group, whole-class, individual instruction

A teacher who lives in a state, such as Texas or Virginia, that evaluates students with a competency-based instrument will want to include in this section a listing of some of those competencies and how they are being taught in the classroom through activities and lessons designed by the teacher. States have employed differing names for these competencies and ways of listing them. In Texas, they are called the Texas Essential Knowledge and Skills, or TEKS; in Virginia, they are called the Standards of Learning. These can be viewed, as well as those for other states, by going to each state education agency's website. (See Chapter 1.) The manner in which the competencies are listed determines how they are addressed in a portfolio.

Virginia lists the Standard of Learning E/W.K.5 (K being a standard for kindergarten) as the following:

- The student will understand how print is organized and read.
- Hold print materials in the correct position.
- Identify the front cover, back cover, and title page of a book.
- Follow words from left to right and top to bottom on a printed page.
- Match voice with print, associating oral phonemes, syllables, words, and phrases with their written forms. (Virginia Education Agency, p. 3)

Because Texas breaks down its competencies into individual items, each one of the points listed in the Virginia standards is a separate objective here.

110.1 K.5B The student is expected to know that print moves left to right across the page and top to bottom. (Texas Education Agency, 1997)

Using the Texas competency, or objective, as an example to be listed in a portfolio, the teacher could address this competency by including a copy of songs that are sung in class on a regular basis. A photo of a student standing before the song chart and using a pointer to point to the words as the other children sing the song could accompany the copy of the songs. This objective could be further enhanced by an explanation that the song being sung has been rewritten using the child's name and that every child is featured during the year by a familiar song rewritten to include that child's name. How motivating to a child to sing a song with his or her name in it!

> Jimmy has a favorite ball, favorite ball, favorite ball.
> Jimmy has a favorite ball; it is a soccer ball. (Sung to the tune of "Mary Had a Little Lamb")

The reflective statement accompanying this objective would explain how the children are chosen, how and when the songs are presented and sung, and how these factors facilitate the mastery of the objective.

Individualization

This section focuses on describing how the teacher is meeting individual needs of students. Student achievement is one measure of teacher effectiveness. This area can be addressed by means of assessment instruments, teacher-made tests, informal reading inventories, learning style modifications, special education accommodations, and cultural diversity. This part of the portfolio shows how the teacher seeks to individualize instruction for each child in the attempt to help each child reach his or her full potential.

Information That Could Be Included

- Evaluation instruments
- Samples of student work
- Samples of teacher-made tests
- Individualized assignments/lessons
- Use of special resources
- Grouping arrangements
- Graphs or charts showing beginning and ending levels of students
- Special methods used in teaching (kinesthetic)
- Individual tutoring of students
- Individual modifications/adaptations made for students

Special emphasis needs to be placed on how the teacher is meeting the needs of the special learners in the classroom, whether these learners are slow learners, children with disabilities, or children who are gifted and talented.

Integration

In this section of the portfolio, the teacher summarizes and brings together all of the information from the other parts of the portfolio into statements that reflect professional goals and objectives as well as thoughts on his or her philosophy of education. A teacher's self-evaluation is presented along with reflections on improvements to make in the future.

Information That Could Be Included:

- Self-evaluation
- Philosophy of education
- Formal teacher evaluations
- Peer evaluations
- Awards and honors
- Letters from parents/students
- Plan of action

In developing a portfolio, the teacher places emphasis more in certain areas than others, depending on the type of portfolio. If the portfolio is to be used as a self-evaluation, for instance, the teacher should be given a rubric to use in the evaluation, and the areas evaluated become the main areas addressed by the portfolio. If the portfolio is used to obtain a teaching position, the teacher should highlight the instruction and integration sections. If the portfolio is used for professional development, obviously the reflective portions and the integration section would be highlighted. It is beneficial for teachers to develop and keep updated some type of portfolio that showcases their skills as professionals.

⭐ SELF-EVALUATION

The goal of self-evaluation for the teacher is to improve teaching skills. "The perceived poor performance of American students on national and international tests has been associated, in part, with unsatisfactory performance by teachers" (Stronge, 1997, p. 217). In response, many districts require teachers to evaluate their teaching. Whether districts require it or not, good teachers engage in self-evaluation because they are professionals and want to strengthen their performance in the classroom. Performance in the classroom is strengthened during self-evaluation because a teacher takes stock of all aspects of the profession and reflects honestly on each, making note of his or her areas of strengths and weakness. Self-evaluation will be a continuous, ongoing process. Just as good teachers are constantly assessing students' learning, they are also constantly assessing their own teaching and making the necessary corrections along the way. When schools or districts mandate that a teacher do a self-evaluation, it is done to satisfy a requirement and the impact that self-evaluation can have on the teacher's teaching skills may be minimal. Contrast this approach with that of the teacher who is constantly engaging in self-evaluation. The teacher who is constantly engaging in self-evaluation is in a continuous process of ever-improving teaching skills and professional growth.

How to Begin Self-Evaluation

The goal of self-evaluation is to improve instruction. All self-evaluation should be focused on what is happening in the classroom. The easiest place for a new teacher to begin is with the lessons that are being taught in the classroom. Stephen L. Yelon

FIGURE 12.1 Ten Powerful Instructional Principles

1. *Meaningfulness*   Does the instruction help students make meaningful connections before, during, and after instruction?
2. *Prerequisites*   Have the subskills, rules, principles, concepts necessary for the understanding of the new material been analyzed and included in the instruction?
3. *Open communication*   Are the objectives of the lesson clear, and has appropriate feedback been provided to the students?
4. *Essential content*   Is the essential content clear and organized and illustrated with examples and demonstrations?
5. *Learning aids*   Are appropriate aids such as graphic organizers, checklists, or models used to help students understand the concept?
6. *Novelty*   Is instruction varied and creative and does it keep the attention of the students?
7. *Modeling*   Is the four-step approach used to demonstrate performance?
   Telling students they will perform what will be demonstrated.
   Telling students what to observe in the demonstration.
   Saying each step and then doing it.
   Asking students to commit the steps to memory before performing them.
8. *Active and appropriate practice*   Do the students receive guided practice, independent practice, varied practice, advanced or remedial practice?
9. *Pleasant conditions and consequences*   Has the teacher anticipated conditions and consequences to prevent undesired behavior and to reward desired behavior?
10. *Consistency*   Are the content and instructional methods related to the objective and the real world? (Yelon, 1996, pp. 271–277)

(1996) has identified ten powerful instructional principles that are employed by effective teachers, teachers who are able to motivate and increase student learning. Using these principles, which are listed in Figure 12.1, a teacher can carefully examine a lesson and assess areas of strength and weakness of any given lesson. Of course, any areas of weakness would be carefully examined and ways to strengthen these areas would be noted by the teacher. If mandated by the district, self-evaluation is done one time during the school year. Self-evaluation once a year, however, does not allow the teacher the opportunity to make constant changes in his or her teaching style, refining each lesson part until all parts become quality parts.

A teacher has just taught a lesson on finding seeds in fruits and vegetables in a kindergarten classroom. During the part of the lesson on the actual search for the seeds, some of the children began throwing and grabbing fruits and vegetables. Using these principles to evaluate the lesson, a teacher can quickly see that principle 9 was not adequately planned and thought through. Now the teacher can re-think the lesson and either determine ways to prevent the undesired behavior from

State by State

Missouri's Career Ladder

The state of **Missouri** has a career ladder program. The goal of this program is to recognize and retain master teachers, provide opportunities for professional growth, improve student achievement, support education goals, and provide a salary supplement. There are three levels, or stages, each with increasing requirements. For example, to achieve Stage I, a teacher must have five years' teaching experience in Missouri public schools; for Stage II seven years' teaching experience; and for Stage III ten years' teaching experience. Documentation is kept that shows that a teacher met the expected performance level on all criteria of the district's Performance-Based Teacher Evaluation System and exceeded expectations 10 percent of the time for Stage II and 15 percent for Stage III. Teachers also must document professional activities and responsibilities that relate to programs and services for children. These must occur outside of contracted time, not during the regular school day. The teacher cannot receive any compensation from any source for these activities (Missouri Department of Elementary and Secondary Education, 2002).

happening again, or ask advice from a master teacher on this matter. Regardless of which option is chosen, the teacher will address this area when she plans the next lesson before the lesson is conducted.

Besides reflecting on each lesson taught, a teacher needs also to examine each learning center and activity that the children are doing and ask the following questions.

What am I trying to teach with this activity/learning center?
Are the activities leading the children to mastery of these objectives?
What could I add that would increase the learning from this activity?
Am I doing this activity for an educational purpose in addition to the fact that the activity is cute and fun?
Is the center (activity) being used in the way I intended?

Self-reflection on these questions is crucial for the teacher. Many times a teacher will plan a learning center only to find that the children are not using the center in the manner intended and therefore the desired skill is not being reinforced. The teacher who is constantly self-evaluating will recognize this fact and make the necessary changes.

ROLES OF A TEACHER

The teacher assumes many roles, both in and out of the classroom. These roles include guidance counselor, nurse, child development specialist, and child **advocate,** in addition to that of teacher and facilitator of learning. Although little training is devoted to the roles of guidance counselor and nurse, the teacher will often be the first person to whom a child turns when in difficulty, whether it is a health problem or an emotional upset. Teachers who are open and friendly with their children will find that those children will turn to them when they are troubled. The beginning teacher needs to talk with the school counselor and nurse to determine procedures for referrals should problems arise. The teacher may be the first to notice that a child is depressed, or is having trouble learning, or seems unable to see the chalkboard. The teacher can then seek the appropriate help for the child.

Child Development Specialist

As a child development specialist, the teacher needs to be familiar with the characteristics of the age of the children he or she is teaching. It is only by becoming familiar with the characteristics of each age that the teacher can plan appropriate lessons and activities. This awareness also helps the teacher know when a child is outside the "normal" development areas and may need special assistance. The early childhood teacher might be the first to notice that a child's language is delayed and can seek help for the child with a therapist. When a child is the first child in a family, parents often do not have the frame of reference for "normal" development and may not realize that their child is exhibiting characteristics of a delay in a given area. The early childhood teacher may be the one who notices the problem and brings it to the attention of the parents. This means that the teacher must be well grounded in child development.

This knowledge of child development also allows the teacher to assure parents that their children are displaying normal behavior for their age. Many parents become concerned when their children reverse a few letters and believe that this is dyslexia. The teacher who is familiar with age-related developmental characteristics can reassure these parents that it is quite common for children of this age to reverse letters and that there is no cause for concern.

Child Advocacy

A teacher needs to assume the role of child advocate. This role transcends the classroom and expands into a child's family, society, and government. "When professionals are advocates, they try to create change in the social environment of children by bringing their expertise, beliefs, and concerns before the general public. Beyond simply informing the public, advocates for children seek to make the public more receptive to children's needs" (Fennimore, 1989, p. 3). The early childhood teacher who is an advocate for children steps beyond the borders of the classroom and becomes involved in the process of influencing society for the betterment of children's lives. Problems observed by the early childhood teacher are often very complex and have no simple answer, but this will not cause the teacher to accept a situation and not seek to change it. Some common areas where teachers become involved deal with discrimination, child abuse and neglect, school violence, television violence, and poverty, as well as issues that directly impact the education of the children, such as developmentally appropriate classrooms. Certainly, in the classroom a teacher advocates for the fair treatment of all children and seeks to eliminate sexism, racism, elitism, handicapism, and ageism (Fennimore, 1989).

Teachers have the opportunity to influence the community as they interact socially with parents, friends, and others. When conversations turn to schools and education, an advocate takes that opportunity to dispel mistaken beliefs and ideas. For example, many people view professional development days as holidays for teachers and see little value in them. When a friend or neighbor mentions this fact, the teacher has the opportunity to share the value and importance of such days. Other opportunities may revolve around attempts to change school policy that is detrimental to children, as teachers write letters to the editors explaining situations in the schools or contact state and national representatives over important issues.

Advocacy has three different forms: personal advocacy, public policy advocacy, and private-sector advocacy. An early childhood teacher can fit in wherever he or she feels comfortable and to the level he or she feels comfortable. Personal advocacy is generally informal and involves sharing personal views with other individuals and groups. The teacher thereby raises awareness of an issue. Public advocacy challenges school boards and local, state, and federal policy makers and agencies in an attempt to influence those entities by calling attention to problems and proposing solutions. Private-sector advocacy educates business leaders about implementing family-friendly work policies and challenges manufacturers of children's toys, games, and videos that contain unnecessary violence (Robinson & Stark, 2002).

There are several advocacy activities in which early childhood teachers can become involved. They can share current research with fellow teachers and parents, join an organization's public policy committee, write a letter to the editor, volunteer to speak at a school board meeting advocating for a certain policy, or talk with employers of working parents and ask for specific family-friendly policies such as time off to attend school conferences (Goffin & Lombardi, 1988).

⭐ RESPONSIBILITIES OF THE TEACHER

The responsibilities of a teacher are multifaceted and broad. The teacher controls the classroom environment, the curriculum, and the assessment and guidance of young children. In addition, he or she must communicate with parents and collaborate with other professionals in the school.

The Environment

The primary responsibility of a teacher is to educate the children and maintain a safe, secure, and relaxed environment for the children. All children should feel welcome in the classroom. There is nothing sadder than seeing a teacher single out a child, pick on that child, and make that child's life at school miserable. Unfortu-

Dimensions of Diversity

The Needs of Interracial Children

If interracial children do not understand that their identity consists of two or more cultures, they may have feelings of guilt and loneliness and feel that they must choose one ethnic identity over the other or one parent over the other. Agencies and schools contribute to the problem when they want children classified according to one race. Teachers can help their children's identity development by reading high-quality children's literature that depicts people who are interracial. Books can help give children an understanding of people and their cultures and provide teachers with opportunities to discuss feelings and emotions that are felt by the characters in different situations. Extensions can also be planned that allow children to explore their heritage. Children can mix paint to match their own skin color and then draw themselves, survey eye or hair colors of classmates and graph the information, bring in photographs of themselves and their parents, or research their ancestry. These are just a few activities that might help a biracial child feel accepted in school (Mazzeo & Jones, 2002).

nately, this happens all too often. A teacher is a professional, and as a professional the teacher is responsible for the education of all the children in his or her class-room. A teacher may have a hard time liking a certain student, but this is no excuse for giving that child any less than the others are receiving.

All children must feel safe and accepted in the classroom. The teacher should model kindness and not accept unkind behavior of the children toward each other. The teacher who does this is rewarded with children who act kind and caring. The teacher who ignores children's behavior and allows them to pick on and torment each other is failing to help the children become accepting of differences, and the children will not feel safe in the classroom. It is plain to an observer which teachers provide a friendly, safe, accepting environment for their children. These teachers have the children who love to come to school and are happy the majority of the time.

The Curriculum

In the public schools teachers have curriculum guides from the publisher available to aid in planning their lessons in addition to guides that have been written by the school district and/or state. These are *guides* and should not be followed word for word, but rather adapted to the needs of the children that are in the classroom. For instance, a teacher one year may have an exceptionally bright first-grade class that already knows the names and sounds of the alphabet. The curriculum guide says the teacher should spend the first four weeks reviewing the letters and sounds. For this class, this is an obvious waste of time. Another year the teacher may have a class in which the majority of the children did not learn the sounds of the letters in kindergarten. This teacher may need to spend more than four weeks reviewing and learning letter sounds. Each year a teacher needs to assess his or her class and teach the children based on their strengths and weaknesses. The curriculum guides are used only as aids in planning instruction.

In today's fast-paced education system that puts many demands on children, teachers need to carefully assess what they are teaching, how they are teaching, and ask themselves if they are using the time they have with the children efficiently. A teacher cannot afford to waste time by having play days on Fridays or showing long videos as rewards for good behavior. It is unfortunate that some teachers tell their children that if they work hard Monday through Thursday, they will be rewarded on Friday with a play day or a full-length movie. One-fifth of an instructional year can be wasted this way and the teacher who does this has done a great disservice to the children.

Assessment of Children

Teachers need to be constantly assessing their children's learning. Teachers should assess their students at the beginning and at the end of the school year as well as continuously throughout the year. Teachers need to share the beginning-of-the-year assessment with the children's parents. Open, honest sharing with parents precludes any problems and misunderstandings that might come from parents who believe their child is further along than the child actually is. Some teachers exhibit fear of parents and are reluctant to share with parents that a child is behind. A teacher who does not inform parents when their child is experiencing difficulty does not allow those parents the opportunity to help or get extra help for their child. Teachers need to view parents as part of the team when it comes to their child's education and be honest and open about the level and functioning of the child.

Assessment is built into the curriculum in the form of skill tests, tests at the end of chapters, and district- and/or state-mandated tests. A teacher who relies on these types of assessment to determine strengths and weaknesses of the children has waited too long. Assessment should be an ongoing process that the teacher engages in throughout the day. After instruction on a new skill, a teacher should be constantly moving about the room and listening and watching the children as they practice this new skill. This way the teacher can immediately spot and reteach those children who are having problems. A teacher who waits and tests the children at the end of the chapter on subtraction, for instance, has allowed those children who did not understand the concept to practice doing it the wrong way for days or weeks. It will be much harder to help these children learn the skill now. Even the teacher who graded the math sheets at the end of the day has lost the opportunity to offer intervention immediately to those children who are weak on the concept. Had this teacher been monitoring the work of the children during their independent practice stage, the children would have received feedback immediately and would not have practiced the skill in an incorrect way.

There is also a danger with too much formal assessment. When a teacher uses a formal assessment instrument, instruction time is lost. How much time depends on the length of the instrument. What tends to happen, though, is that after the formal assessment the teacher is not inclined to teach until he or she has graded the test. So a day of instruction has been lost.

Assessment does not have to be formal, but it does need to be continuous. The teacher should always be watching and listening and making note of who needs extra help as well as which children have understood the concept.

Guidance

Teachers teach their early childhood children more than just the curriculum, they teach the skills necessary to be successful and ways to form and maintain relationships. Teachers do this by helping children solve their own problems instead of always solving the problems for them. Teachers who use the problem-solving approach help children become assertive and not get stuck in the role of victim. This practice also develops the skills necessary to be successful in our society, where skills such as negotiation are essential.

Communicating with Parents

The teacher has the responsibility to effectively communicate with a child's parents or guardians about the progress their child is making. Parents should not be viewed as adversaries, but rather as partners in the child's education. (See Chapter 11 for more information on working with parents.)

Collaborating with Other Professionals

As more services become available to children in the public schools, the ability to successfully collaborate becomes more important. Collaboration involves professionals working together for the benefit of a child. It is based on the principle of sharing. Goals and responsibilities are shared, in their development and their implementation. True collaboration is voluntary, not forced. In the inclusive classroom, collaboration means the general education teacher and the special education teacher work together to ensure that the needs of the special education child are met. Collaboration with a speech therapist means that the general education teacher knows what sounds a child is working on in speech and reinforces the lessons in the everyday activities of the classroom.

Teachers are collaborating with teachers of other grade levels to align the curriculum, plug holes in weak areas, and share strategies and new methods. When teachers share students and one teacher teaches language arts and the other teaches math and science (team teaching), they must be sure to collaborate in planning homework and special activities. When teachers fail to collaborate, children suffer by ending up with unreasonable amounts of homework.

Teachers often find themselves assigned to districtwide committees that involve collaboration in writing curriculum, reviewing textbooks, and helping determine district policies and standards. The ability to collaborate becomes essential as the teachers determine how to best meet the needs of the children.

✩ WORKING IN THE SCHOOL COMMUNITY

Two of the most important people in the school the teacher should cultivate are the custodian and the secretary. These two people are the backbone of the school and have the ability to help a teacher in many ways. Unfortunately, some teachers act in demanding ways toward these employees or treat them as part of the fixtures of the school. The teacher who is friendly to the custodian benefits by the attention that is paid to his or her classroom. If a light goes out, it may be fixed immediately or several days may pass before the light bulb is changed. The custodian's response sometimes depends on how the teacher has treated the custodian. The custodian is a valued member of the school staff and should be treated as such, not in a menial, degrading manner or as a person of no consequence. The teacher who is courteous to the secretary may receive gentle reminders of items that are due in to the principal that the teacher who is demanding, rude, or arrogant does not get. Good manners and friendliness go a long way when dealing with anyone at the school.

The principal is the instructional leader of the school and carries the responsibility for all that happens there. If a teacher is having difficulties with a parent, it is always a good idea to visit with the principal and detail the problems. It helps the principal to be prepared should that parent call to complain. Likewise, the principal should be informed of any activity a class is engaging in outside the classroom. If a teacher wants her class to write and sell books as a fundraiser, for example, the principal needs to be informed and give prior approval for the activity.

Many teachers think the school nurse has an easy job and should take care of any and all of the children's ailments. This is a wrong perception. Good school nurses are extremely busy and see many children each day. Each time a teacher sends a child to the nurse, the nurse has to document in the child's records the visit, the cause of the visit, and the treatment done. Some children try to go to the nurse to get out of the classroom. The savvy teacher evaluates the need before sending the child and confers with the nurse about treatments for recurring ailments. If a child has a scratch with a scab on it, for instance, there is nothing the nurse can do. It is important for the child to learn how to wash and apply a bandage to a small sore, and minor scrapes and scratches can be treated by the child with the teacher's supervision. Of course, a child with any serious injury or head injury should be immediately sent to the nurse or brought to the attention of the office should there be no school nurse.

By watching the children, a teacher can quickly determine which ones are trying to visit the nurse just to get out of class and which ones have a real need for medical care. A teacher who knows that schools cannot give out medication without a doctor's prescription can pass this information on to the child who is asking for an aspirin for a headache. The teacher also needs to communicate to the parents that medicine sent in a child's lunch or backpack cannot be administered by the teacher.

The nurse is also a very important resource for the early childhood teacher. The school nurse can aid in obtaining free vision tests and glasses, dental work, and medical assistance for underprivileged children. Many nurses welcome the opportunity to come into the classroom to conduct lessons related to health topics.

The educational diagnostician is the person in the school who conducts the testing on a child who is suspected of having some type of learning disability. Usually several schools in a district share an educational diagnostician. A child's testing may be done over a period of days. IQ tests are given as well as tests to determine the child's level of academic performance.

Unfortunately, not all schools have a full-time counselor, and even those lucky enough to have one find that the counselor has other duties besides counseling. Counselors often are in charge of the state-mandated testing procedures and reports that must be filed. Some counselors try to conduct small-group sessions on death, divorce, dealing with anger, self-control, and other needs of the children. Information a child shares with the counselor is privileged, so the fact that the counselor does not share what a child reveals should not offend the teacher.

Parent-Teacher Organizations

Most schools will have some type of parent-teacher association (PTA) or parent-teacher organization (PTO). These organizations can be a help to a teacher who has a child with special needs, and they can also help meet the needs of underprivileged children in the classroom. If there is a child who needs clothing, shoes, or school supplies, these organizations generally help. If the organization does not have a fund set aside for the nurse, the teacher might ask for one to be created. The nurse can use this fund to purchase medications for children when their parents fall on hard times and they have no money for medication.

☆ CHARACTERISTICS OF EFFECTIVE TEACHERS

Researchers through the years have identified many behaviors of effective teachers. *Effective behaviors* are those teacher behaviors that are associated with student achievement. Kauchak and Eggen (1998) have identified 10 such behaviors: attitudes, effective use of time, organization, communication, focus, feedback, monitoring, questioning, pacing, review, and closure. Cruickshank, Bainer, and Metcalf (1999) believe that effective teachers understand how to get to know their students, plan for instruction, present material, evaluate information, motivate students, and use effective questioning techniques. Such teachers are knowledgeable about their subject matter and adaptable, or flexible, in their teaching.

Although these authors identify seemingly different behaviors, they actually over-lap in many areas.

Attitudes and Getting to Know Your Children

Teachers who are effective in the classroom have adopted an attitude of high expectations for all their children. They use praise, sincere praise, much more than criticism to motivate their children. Praise becomes insincere when teachers move from child to child saying, "Good job!" Praise that is sincere is given when deserved and is very specific. "You have used such descriptive adjectives in your story that I can see the setting in my mind." Effective teachers believe that they can make a difference in children's lives (Hunt, Touzel, & Wiseman, 1999).

Teachers may obtain information about the children from several sources. The cumulative records are records that are kept by the school on each child from the first day that he or she enrolled at that school. These records include personal information, school attendance, year-end academic grades, standardized test scores, teacher observations, and other miscellaneous information such as health data, psychological reports, and written communications between the parents and the school (Cruickshank, Bainer, & Metcalf, 1999). These records are available for parents on request, so teachers should be careful about what they write here about their students. These records may also help a teacher understand a child. They may show that a child's poor performance occurred after the child lost a parent. The teacher who is aware of this loss can observe the child and make the necessary referrals to help the child cope with the loss. One danger of reading cumulative records, however, can be seen in the case of the teacher who responds to the information with the attitude that this child will be nothing but trouble or who won't expect much from a child based on past performance.

In 1971, Phi Delta Kappa began offering an in-service program for teachers called Teacher Expectations and Student Achievement (TESA). This program is based on research that showed that teachers called less frequently on students they perceived as low achievers than on those they perceived as high achievers, and that teachers gave preferential treatment to children who were high achievers. Low achievers soon learned that they would not be called on as often if they looked puzzled. This perception led to a cycle in which children who were low achievers believed that the teacher viewed them as less able because the teacher did not call on them in class. Such children then concluded that the teacher thought they were not very smart. Children who are called on less often are not active participants in the learning process and are not receiving an equal opportunity to learn (Phi Delta Kappa, 1980). Although this training originated in 1971 and was copyrighted in 1980, it continues to be applicable today. All children should be actively engaged in learning and should be called on in class in an equitable manner.

Information can also be gathered about children by observing them. Observations can be *formal*, planned observations to gain specific information, or *informal*, unplanned, spontaneous observations. Formal observations generally yield more useful information. A teacher notices that a child, Joan, is having difficulty settling down and getting to work every morning. During a formal observation, the teacher makes an observation checklist (Cruickshank, Bainer, & Metcalf, 1999). This checklist may include questions such as:

- Did Joan walk in the door upset?
- What did she do when she first came into the room?
- Whom did she interact with in the room?
- What behaviors were exhibited?
- How long did it take for her to settle down?
- What aided her in settling down?

The answers to these questions reveal whether Joan arrived at class already upset or whether someone upset her after she arrived. It also directs the teacher as to what interventions might be tried with Joan. Issues that should always be addressed in formal observations include at what time the behavior is occurring, with whom the behavior occurs, what happened immediately before the behavior occurred, and what happened immediately after the behavior occurred. This information provides the clues to understanding the behavior exhibited.

Teachers learn about their students' lives by talking to them.

Another way to gain information about children is simply to talk with them and ask them questions. Children are generally happy to share information about themselves with their teacher. Time needs to be spent building trust between the teacher and the child. Questions can be directed toward likes, hobbies, activities, friends, and pets. This information also provides the teacher with ways to motivate the child. A child who doesn't like to read but likes dogs may be motivated to read books about dogs.

A final way to gain information about children is through their parents. Some teachers send home a form the first day of school that asks for personal information such as names and ages of brothers and sisters, favorite activities, health problems, parents' names, and best times to reach the parents. It may also include a section for information about events in the child's life that the teacher should know. (See Chapter 11 for a sample copy.) A parent may reply that there is a new baby in the house and that situation is causing problems, or a grandparent just moved in and took the child's room and now the child is sleeping on the sofa in the living room or on the floor in the parent's room. Calls to parents can also yield a wealth of information that helps a teacher understand a child.

Effective Use of Time

Research has found that the greater the time spent on instruction, the greater the results in student achievement. Time for instruction is either allocated or dictated by the daily schedule. The daily schedule reflects the actual amount of time spent on each subject area, as well as lunch, physical education, music, art, library, computer lab, and recess. Even if an hour is devoted to math, for instance, the actual instructional time is less than this because children gather materials and settle down to work. Time on task is the time that children actually engage in learning activities and varies from child to child depending on the attention that the child displays (Hunt, Touzel, & Wiseman, 1999).

Organization and Planning

Organization in early education has two aspects. The first aspect is the organization of the classroom. This organization includes routines established by the teacher in the areas of management. Does the teacher begin on time, have materials ready, have established routines for collecting papers and moving between centers or activities? The second aspect of organization concerns the lesson. Is the material arranged in a sequential manner, are there graphics to aid in understanding the materials, are there activities that allow hands-on experiences, is the pace of the lesson right where children neither feel rushed nor get bored (Hunt, Touzel, & Wiseman, 1999)?

Planning means that the teacher must decide what to teach and how to teach it, and the children need to be informed of what they are expected to learn. Materials need to be gathered, and the teacher needs to decide how to evaluate the lesson, extend the lesson for the more able students, and remediate the lesson for the less able students. The lesson should be related to the total plan of instructional goals for the year, the term, the unit, and the week (Cruickshank, Bainer, & Metcalf, 1999).

Communication, Presentation, Focus

Hunt, Touzel, and Wiseman (1999) state that "educational research has identified a positive link between language clarity and student achievement. The message for the teacher, obviously, is to be as clear in the use of verbal *communication* as possible" (p. 11). This calls for precise terminology (no vague or ambiguous words), connected discourse (not rambling or disjointed), transition statements that link information together and provide clues to the children as to the important information.

The purpose of a *presentation* is to convey information, facts, ideas, and concepts. Good presentations come about through careful preparation and knowledge of the material. *Focus* means that the children's attention must be engaged. Children should be told what they are expected to learn and do. Enthusiasm and humor help maintain the children's interest, as do audiovisual aids (Cruickshank, Bainer, & Metcalf, 1999).

Feedback and Evaluation

Teachers need to provide children with information on the correctness or accuracy of their work. *Feedback* may be oral or written. Oral feedback obviously is the easiest for teachers to administer, but it needs to be more than one or two words such as "Correct." Effective feedback tells the child not only that he or she is correct or incorrect, but also explains why this is so (Hunt, Touzel, & Wiseman, 1999).

Evaluation is a form of feedback and can take many forms. It may be in the form of a standardized test, a paper-and-pencil test, a teacher-made test, or simply an observation. Evaluation is a measure of how well a teacher can teach, not just what the children have learned (Cruickshank, Bainer, & Metcalf, 1999). All evaluation should be used to direct instruction and make decisions about instruction. Does a lesson need to be presented in a different way because most of the children failed to grasp the concept?

Monitoring and Motivating

Teachers who are good *monitors* are aware of what is going on in their classroom at all times. They see and recognize the children whose attention is lapsing and change their presentation to engage these children (Hunt, Touzel, & Wiseman, 1999). Likewise, these teachers *motivate* by using animated gestures, maintain eye contact with the children, quickly deal with off-task behavior, maintain an appropriate pace to their lesson, add movement to sustain interest, and vary their voice, pitch, and inflection to make their delivery more interesting (Cruickshank, Bainer, & Metcalf, 1999).

Questioning

Questions asked by teachers can call on low-order thinking skills or higher order thinking skills. Questions shape the learning environment for the children and the teacher's skill in asking questions can help enhance the higher level thinking skills (Hunt, Touzel, & Wiseman, 1999). Lower level skills are reflected in simple factual questions. Higher level thinking skills are ones that deal with analysis, synthesis, or evaluation (Cruickshank, Bainer, & Metcalf, 1999). Questions fall into two categories: convergent or divergent. Convergent questions are those that proceed from broad to specific information. Factual questions fall into this category. Divergent questions are those that require thinking to proceed from specific to general. Students must expand on information to generate an answer. These questions require the children to hypothesize, infer, or predict. When studying the effects of the sun on plant life, a divergent question might be to ask the children what would happen if the atmosphere became so polluted that the sunlight no longer reached the ground (Cruickshank, Bainer, & Metcalf, 1999 & Hunt, Touzel, & Wiseman, 1999).

Good teachers allow sufficient thinking time for children after asking a question. Early research showed that teachers typically wait less than 1 second from the time they ask a question until they call on a child. Effective teachers allow 3 to 5 seconds for children to respond. Research showed that this wait time produced more thoughtful and longer responses (Cruickshank, Bainer, & Metcalf, 1999). Five seconds can seem like an extremely long time and the effective teacher must train the other children not to call out answers. Children should be called on, even when they have not volunteered. As mentioned earlier, it is imperative that a teacher call on all the children equally (Cruickshank, Bainer, & Metcalf, 1999).

Pacing

Proper *pacing* of the lesson is very important for the early childhood teacher. A lesson presented at too fast a pace loses the attention of the children as quickly as a lesson paced too slowly. In the case of the too-fast lesson, the children may become frustrated at not being able to keep up. In the too-slow lesson, the children may become distracted and inattentive as they wait for the teacher to continue.

Review and Closure

Review may occur at any point during the lesson. The purpose of review is to help children summarize what has been taught and link that information to information about to be presented. *Closure* is actually the review that comes at the end of the lesson. It provides an opportunity for children to state in their own words what they have learned. By asking the children to explain what they have learned, the teacher is able to assess their depth of understanding, providing the teacher with a beginning place for the next lesson (Hunt, Touzel, & Wiseman, 1999).

Knowledgeability and Adaptability

Effective teachers *know* the material they are presenting and they *know* their children. This combination leads teachers to plan effective, interesting lessons. Therefore, each year's lessons are different, based on the needs and interests of the children. Lesson plans from previous years are not simply copied into lesson plan books, nor are the same things taught in the same ways to each successive year's children. In addition, effective teachers review and prepare for each lesson; they don't try to "wing it."

Effective teachers also need to be *adaptable* and flexible. A good teacher who sees that the lesson is either too easy or too hard for the children will discontinue the lesson, regardless of whether or not a supervisor is in the classroom. In the case of the lesson that is too hard, a teacher who continues to muddle through will end up confusing the children even more. Time needs to be spent on reflection about why the lesson was too hard. Were necessary prior skills missing? If the lesson is too easy and the children have already mastered the objective, it is a waste of precious time to continue, and the children will be bored and may act up. The effective teacher plans for enriching activities for more advanced children, and the entire class can move on to this part of the lesson. In this case, the teacher should acknowledge to the children that he or she is moving on because they already possess this knowledge. Likewise, when children are becoming frustrated and unable to understand a lesson, a teacher should tell them that he or she is stopping the lesson and will rethink how to teach the lesson so that it will be easier for them to understand. It serves no purpose for a teacher to announce to the class that they should have learned this in the previous grade. An effective teacher takes children where they are and begins teaching from that point. If material from the previous year needs to be reviewed or taught, then that will be done. The children are never blamed for not learning the material. "The ability to recognize the need for change and to adapt instruction accordingly is probably the most difficult task for beginning teachers" (Cruickshank, Bainer, & Metcalf, 1999, p. 321).

Beginning teachers need to consider the qualities of effective teachers and seek to develop these skills. As with any profession, the more time, thought, and energy devoted to the development of skills, the quicker and stronger the skills become.

People who become successful early childhood teachers experience the thrill of making a difference in children's lives. Relationships developed with children and their families have been known to last a lifetime. Early childhood teachers have the added responsibility of setting the stage for future learning. The child who feels successful in the early grades will go on to enjoy learning. All early childhood teachers should view their role as one of turning children on to learning and making school a safe, happy, fun place to be.

⭐ SUMMARY

This chapter contains information that beginning teachers will need as they begin their careers in the public schools. The attitude of teachers is extremely important as they wrestle with personal beliefs, codes of conduct, self-evaluation, and the skills necessary to become effective teachers and to work successfully in the school environment. Children's lives are shaped by their teacher's enthusiasm for teaching and their knowledge about the subject matter. Effective teachers also understand how to plan, implement, evaluate, and adapt their lessons to meet the needs of the children in their classes.

⭐ DISCUSSION QUESTIONS

1. Discuss NAEYC's Code of Ethical Conduct.
2. What are the different types of child abuse? What are their signs?
3. Discuss the pros and cons of the different types of portfolios.
4. Use the characteristics of effective teachers to plan a lesson for an early childhood class.

⭐ SUGGESTED CHAPTER ACTIVITIES

1. What is your philosophy of education? After writing a philosophy of education, share and discuss it with a veteran teacher.
2. Plan a lesson that could be included in your portfolio for a specific objective and write a reflection on how this lesson teaches the objective, how it is motivating to children, and where it fits into the instruction of the objective. Is this lesson used to introduce, practice, or reinforce the objective?
3. Using the example given on page 443, the lesson on searching for seeds in fruits and vegetables, explain how a teacher could plan so as to maintain control of the children during the search activity.
4. List some of the current local, state, and national issues that relate to children. How would a child advocate address these issues?
5. Observe in an early childhood classroom, making notes on behavior informally observed. On which behaviors could the teacher conduct a formal observation?
6. Observe reading or math in a first-, second-, or third-grade classroom. Note the amount of time the children spent on getting ready and putting up materials along with other distractions that occurred and resulted in loss of instruction time.
7. Have small groups of students develop and present the various sections of a portfolio.

 **WEBSITES**

NAEYC's Code of Ethical Conduct (www.naeyc.org/resources/position_
   statements/pseth98.htm)
National Clearinghouse on Child Abuse and Neglect Information
   (http://nccanch.acf.hhs.gov/index.cfm)

Developmental Red Flags for Children Ages 3 to 5

Social-Emotional Development

- Does not seem to recognize self as a separate person, or does not refer to self as "I"
- Has great difficulty separating from parent or separates too easily
- Is anxious, tense, restless, compulsive, cannot get dirty or messy, has many fears, engages in excessive self-stimulation
- Seems preoccupied with own inner world; conversations do not make sense
- Shows little or no impulse control; hits or bites as first response; cannot follow a classroom routine
- Expresses emotions inappropriately (laughs when sad, denies feelings); facial expressions do not match emotions
- Cannot focus on activities (short attention span, cannot complete anything, flits from toy to toy)
- Relates only to adults; cannot share adult attention, consistently sets up power struggle, or is physically abusive to adults
- Consistently withdraws from people, prefers to be alone; no depth to relationships; does not seek or accept affection or touching
- Treats people as objects; has no empathy for other children; cannot play on another child's terms
- Is consistently aggressive, frequently hurts others deliberately; shows no remorse or is deceitful in hurting others

Motor Development—Fine Motor, Gross Motor, and Perceptual

- The child who is particularly uncoordinated and who
    - Has lots of accidents
    - Trips, bumps into things
    - Is awkward getting down/up, climbing, jumping, getting around toys and people
    - Stands out from the group in structured motor tasks—walking, climbing stairs, jumping, standing on one foot
    - Avoids more physical games
- The child who relies heavily on watching own or other peoples' movements in order to do them and who
    - May frequently misjudge distances
    - May become particularly uncoordinated or off balance with eyes closed
- The child who, compared to peers, uses much more of her or his body to do the task than the task requires and who
    - Dives into the ball (as though to cover the fact that she or he cannot coordinate a response)
    - Uses tongue, feet, or other body parts excessively to help in coloring, tracing, or performing other high-concentration tasks
    - Produces extremely heavy coloring
    - Leans over the table while concentrating on a fine-motor project
    - When doing wheelbarrows, keeps pulling the knees and feet under the body, or thrusts rump up in the air
- The child with extraneous and involuntary movements, who
    - While painting with one hand, holds the other hand in the air or waves
    - Does chronic toe walking
    - Shows twirling or rocking movements
    - Shakes hands or taps fingers
- The child who compulsively craves being touched or hugged or may
    - Cling to, or lightly brush, the teacher a lot
    - Always sit close to or touch children in a circle
    - Be strongly attracted to sensory experiences such as blankets, soft toys, water, dirt, sand, paste, hands in food

- The child who has a reasonable amount of experience with fine-motor tools but whose skill does not improve proportionately, such as
  - An experienced child who tries but still gets paste, paint, sand, water everywhere
  - A child who is very awkward with, or chronically avoids, small manipulative materials
- The child who has exceptional difficulty with new but simple puzzles, coloring, structured art projects, and drawing a person, and who, for example, may
  - Take much longer to do the task, even when trying hard, and produce a final result that is still not as sophisticated compared to those of peers
  - Show a lot of trial-and-error behavior when trying to do a puzzle
  - Mix up top/bottom, left/right, front/back, on simple projects where a model is to be copied
  - Still does a lot of scribbling

Speech and Language Development

- Articulation. Watch for the child
  - Whose speech is difficult to understand, compared with peers
  - Who mispronounces sounds
  - Whose mouth seems abnormal (excessive under- or overbite; swallowing difficult; poorly lined-up teeth)
  - Who has difficulty putting words and sounds in proper sequence
  - Who cannot be encouraged to produce age-appropriate sound
  - Who has a history of ear infections or middle ear disorders

  Note: Most children develop the following sounds correctly by the ages shown (i.e., don't worry about a 3-year-old who pronounces *t*).
  - 2 years—all vowel sounds
  - 3 years—*p, b, m, w, h*
  - 4 years—*t, d, n, k, h, ng*

- 5 years—*f, j, sh*
- 6 years—*ch, v, r, l*
- 7 years—*s, z,* voiceless or voiced *th*
- Dysfluency (stuttering). Note the child who, compared with others of the same age,
  - Shows excessive amounts of these behaviors:
    - repetitions of sounds, words (*m-m-m-; I-I-I-I*)
    - prolongations of sounds (*mmmmmmmmm-mmmmmmmm*)
    - hesitations or long blocks during speech, usually accompanied by tension or struggle behavior
    - putting in extra words (*um, uh, well*)
  - Shows two or more of these behaviors while speaking:
    - hand clenching
    - eye blinking
    - swaying of body
    - pill rolling with fingers
    - no eye contact
    - body tension or struggle
    - breathing irregularity
    - tremors
    - pitch rise
    - frustration
    - avoidance of talking
  - Is labeled a stutterer by parents
  - Is aware of her or his dysfluencies
- Voice. Note the child whose
  - Rate of speech is extremely fast or slow
  - Voice is breathy or hoarse
  - Voice is very loud or soft
  - Voice is very high or low
  - Voice sounds very nasal
- Language (ability to use and understand words). Note the child who
  - Does not appear to understand when others speak, though hearing is normal
  - Is unable to follow one- or two-step directions
  - Communicates by pointing, gesturing
  - Makes no attempt to communicate with words
  - Uses parrotlike speech (imitates what others say)

Has small vocabulary for age

Has difficulty putting words together in a sentence

Uses words inaccurately

Demonstrates difficulty with three or more of these skills:

>   making a word plural
>
>   changing tenses of verb
>
>   using pronouns
>
>   using negatives
>
>   using possessives
>
>   naming common objects
>
>   telling function of common objects
>
>   using prepositions

Hearing

- Speech and language. Look for the child

  Whose speech is not easily understood by people outside the family

  Whose grammar is less accurate than that of other children of the same age

  Who does not use speech as much as other children of the same age

  Who has an unusual voice (hoarseness, stuffy quality, lack of inflection, or voice that is usually too loud or soft)

- Social behavior (at home and in school). Look for the child who

  Is shy or hesitant in answering questions or joining in conversation

  Misunderstands questions or directions; frequently says "Huh?" or "What?" in response to questions

  Appears to ignore speech; hears "only what he wants to"

  Is unusually attentive to speaker's face or unusually inattentive to speaker, or turns one ear to speaker

  Has difficulty with listening activities such as storytime and following directions

  Has short attention span

  Is distractible and restless; tends to shift quickly from one activity to another

Is generally lethargic or uninterested in most day-to-day activities

Is considered a behavior problem—too active or aggressive, or too quiet and withdrawn

- Medical indications. Look for the child who

  Has frequent or constant upper respiratory tract infections, congestion that appears related to allergies, or a cold for several weeks or months

  Has frequent earaches, ear infections, throat infections, or middle ear problems

  Has had draining ears on one or more occasions

  Is mouth breather and snorer

  Is generally lethargic; has poor color

Vision

- Eyes

  Are watery

  Have discharge

  Lack coordination in directing gaze of both eyes

  Are red

  Are sensitive to light

  Appear to cross or wander, especially when child is tired

- Eyelids

  Have crusts on lids or among lashes

  Are red

  Have recurring sties or swelling

- Behavior and complaints

  Rubs eyes excessively

  Experiences dizziness, headaches, nausea on close work

  Attempts to brush away blur

  Has itchy, burning, scratchy eyes

  Contorts face or body when looking at distant objects, or thrusts head forward; squints or widens eyes

  Blinks eyes excessively; holds book too close or too far; inattentive during visual tasks

  Shuts or covers one eye; tilts head

Checklist for Diversity
in Early Childhood Education and Care

How do we support diversity in early childhood classrooms? Genuine diversity begins with respect for each and every individual and grows with adults' understanding that culture is a powerful part of children's development. In early childhood settings, this means that each and every child and family feels respected and valued.

This checklist includes features of the culturally diverse, developmentally appropriate early childhood classroom. It can help you think through the fundamental issues of diversity in early childhood education and care. Remember that some of these features may be appropriate for very young children but not for primary-grade children, and vice versa. Few programs have all of these features, but all early childhood programs can and should have some of these features and demonstrate that they are working toward the others.

Interactions in the Classroom

❑ Are children encouraged to talk with each other?
❑ Are there times when children can tell imaginative and true stories of their own experiences?
❑ Are children encouraged to listen to everyone's ideas as they work on projects in groups?
❑ Do they have opportunities throughout the day to work and play in pairs and small groups as well as in mixed-age groups and alone?
❑ Does the teacher help children who do not speak English to participate in conversations?
❑ Does the teacher really listen to the children?
❑ Does she respond to children's specific ideas and questions instead of making general comments like "Good idea," or "We'll get to that later"?
❑ Does the teacher pay attention to and use different communication styles?
❑ Does she sit at the children's eye level?

❑ Does the teacher intervene when children hurt each other's feelings?
❑ Does she help children figure out reasons for conflicts and support their problem-solving rather than simply discouraging insults?
❑ Does the teacher observe rather than lead the activity in the room much of the time?

Family Involvement

❑ Does the teacher see family members as resources?
❑ Are family members encouraged to visit classrooms at any time?
❑ Does the teacher solicit family participation?
❑ Does she make arrangements as necessary to accommodate all family members, including persons with disabilities and extended family members?
❑ Does the teacher consider children's home cultures in planning center or school events?
❑ Do working parents receive enough notice of assignments and special activities to allow them to fully participate?
❑ Are announcements, newsletters, etc., spoken and written in families' home languages?
❑ Are activities inexpensive enough for all to participate?
❑ Are activities, materials, and resources in the classroom open ended about the nature of families, instead of suggesting, for instance, that every family has "a mommy and a daddy"?

Community Involvement

❑ Do children have many informal opportunities to meet parents and other community members who work in various capacities? For example, do they meet the father who is a blind executive, or the merchant who is Vietnamese?

❏ Do teachers encourage visitors to talk with individual children and with small groups as well as with whole classes?

❏ Do centers and schools recognize that all people are important, instead of occasionally celebrating a few well-known persons such as Martin Luther King, Jr.? Do they recognize persons in children's own families who contribute to the community?

❏ Does the center or school use senior citizens as resources? What about high school students?

❏ Are children able to take field trips to various nearby locations so that they can learn about their own community?

Physical Environment

❏ Does the classroom seem to be the children's place or the teacher's place?

❏ Are children's creative artworks displayed throughout the room?

❏ Is a bulletin board available to the children as a work space for notes and plans and for works in progress?

❏ Are there "mailboxes" where children can leave private messages for each other and for teachers?

❏ Is there a show-and-tell display area? Are photographs and artifacts of the children's families evident?

❏ Does the teacher continually replace or rearrange materials in classroom centers to support children's changing interests? For example, does the dramatic play center lend itself to a fishing pier as well as the traditional "housekeeping"?

❏ Do materials in the room reflect the cultural diversity of the children and of the world?

❏ Do dolls and other toys reflect different ethnic backgrounds and physical abilities?

❏ Is there a large quantity and wide variety of classic and contemporary picture and story books?

❏ Are high-quality, culturally diverse children's periodicals, such as *Cricket*, *Spider*, and *Ladybug*, available?

❏ Does the teacher demonstrate the world's variety of languages in her classroom?

❏ Do labels in the classroom reflect children's home languages? Are some labels in Braille?

Curriculum

❏ Does the curriculum incorporate each child's personal experiences?

❏ Does the curriculum reflect that different individuals view and interpret the world differently?

❏ Are children able to suggest topics for exploration?

❏ Does the teacher suggest that children pursue interesting ideas through different forms and media? For example, would the teacher suggest that a child experiment with creating a self-portrait in crayon, pencil, and then collage? Would he invite a preschooler to expand a block construction, or a second-grader to write a second draft of a story, adding more details?

❏ Does the teacher recognize and support children's different learning styles?

❏ Does the school honor all children's efforts instead of focusing on academic stars?

❏ Does the teacher pay attention to individual children's interests and provide opportunities for them to pursue those interests?

❏ Does the teacher frequently group children according to their interests, instead of grouping them by ability?

❏ Does the teacher discourage bias? For example, does he support a girl's interest in science or math?

❏ Do children have many opportunities to express themselves and explore ideas through art, music, and plays?

❏ Do children have many opportunities to write notes, letters, lists, diaries, stories, and songs?

❏ Does the teacher treat children's writings seriously by publishing some and sharing it with other classes, families, etc.?

❏ Does the program measure each child's accomplishments in comparison to that child's earlier work through the use of portfolios?

Resources

Derman-Sparks, Louise & A.B.C. Task Force. (1989). *Anti-bias curriculum: Tools for empowering young children.* Washington, DC: National Association for the Education of Young Children.

Grace, C. & Shores, E. F. (1991). *The portfolio and its use; Developmentally appropriate assessment of young children.* Little Rock, AR: Southern Early Childhood Association.

Katz, L. G., Evangelou, D. & Hartman, J. A. (1990). *The case for mixed-age grouping in early education.* Washington, DC: National Association for the Education of Young Children.

McCracken, J. B. (1993). *Valuing diversity: The primary years.* Washington, DC: National Association for the Education of Young Children.

Credits

Authors: Nelle Peck, M.Ed., and Elizabeth F. Shores

Advisors: Carol Brunson Phillips, Ph.D., and Louise Derman-Sparks

Bonus Chapter!

Our bonus chapter, "Teaching in a Fourth-Grade Classroom," follows.
It is intended for use in those states in which early childhood certification
extends to the fourth grade.

Teaching in a Fourth-Grade Classroom

CHAPTER OVERVIEW

★ Have you ever thought about teaching fourth grade?

★ Are content demands greater in fourth grade than they are in previous grades?

★ What is departmentalization? Do all fourth grades use departmentalization as a practice?

★ What is cooperative learning?

★ What opportunities for extracurricular experiences are open for fourth-grade children?

READ THIS CHAPTER TO DISCOVER ANSWERS TO THESE QUESTIONS AND MORE.

Nine-year-olds are energetic, enthusiastic, curious children who possess a zeal for living that resembles younger children's zest, but they are more physically capable of showing their muscle to the world. They push, shove, and maneuver themselves into groups and interact with others confidently and magnanimously. When they choose projects they like, they tackle them with interest and enjoyment. Sometimes their zealousness results in loud disputes and disagreements, but they make up with friends quickly and easily.

Teachers who work with fourth graders find pleasure with their children. These youngsters are mature enough to take responsibility for their schoolwork and, for the most part, respect their teachers and classroom rules. Unlike younger children, they are capable of taking care of their belongings, and they manage their social relationships with ease. They understand the school environment and are able to work with others. They still need hands-on activities to comprehend abstract information, but their abilities to attend to instruction is increasing, especially if they are interested and motivated.

Nine-year-olds are still physically active, and their interest in sports is increasing. Males are most likely to have favorite sports teams, but both genders participate in sports (such as soccer and softball). Their desire to win in competitive events is keen, but the long-term goal in sports involvement appears to be geared more toward social experiences with others their age. If the adults who work with them in sports activities are

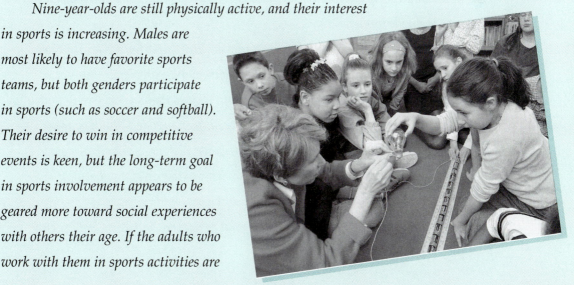

supportive and encouraging, children become confident about themselves as athletes.

Physically, fourth-grade children are in a period of slow growth. Hormonal changes are beginning to occur with some females, and a few children will experience the onset of menses. Males lag behind females physically, but their age allows them to move with dexterity and agility and some possess great strength (which they often like to flaunt to their classmates).

Intellectual growth is a key component of fourth-grade studies. From a curriculum standpoint, experiences in fourth-grade classrooms are generally less child centered and more focused on content. By fourth grade, children should be reading independently. Selection choices are broader, and teachers are able to address reading problems with greater individuality. Reading interests are broad, and gender-specific choices should be available for children. Writing activities require more sophistication, and language arts lessons focus on complex grammar and detailed approaches to enhance writing assignments. Nine-year-olds are capable of conducting research studies individually and in small groups, allowing for complementary study with social studies and science topics. Mathematics requires that fourth graders know the multiplication facts and how to divide proficiently.

Consistent relationships with adults are still important to fourth graders. Their needs for guidance and adult intervention with problems have not disappeared. Young girls face obstacles with cliques that evolve among fourth graders, because of emerging feelings of "being an outsider." Both genders occasionally need individual discussions about good hygiene and strategies for assisting them in becoming more attractive to their friends. The peer group is becoming an integral factor in decisions children make about friendships and personal relationships, and this trend continues as they enter puberty.

Mr. Gedelian's classroom is the most appealing fourth-grade classroom to children in his school, because of his interest in science. Hamsters, gerbils, mice, birds, snakes, and rabbits are in cages along the windows and in the back of the room. Nestled among the cages are plants of all varieties, available as food for the animals and instruction for his students. His school district, in a medium-sized rural community, also owns an Outdoor Center within walking distance to Mr. Gedelian's school, and he has already planned four field trips to the Center in preparation for the zoological and botanical studies he likes to introduce each year.

Four teachers work in the fourth-grade wing of the school, and Mr. Gedelian is team leader by virtue of his tenure in the school system. For several years the team has taught using departmentalized instruction. Each teacher begins the morning with a long block of instruction focusing on reading and language arts (including spelling) with their homeroom group of approximately 22 to 25 children. Physical education is provided to each group in the morning, and the music teacher visits each classroom in the afternoon. After lunch, each group rotates among the four teachers for mathematics, social studies, science, and health education. This system has worked well because each teacher has an opportunity to plan lessons in a favorite area of expertise. The team works together to organize similar plans for reading and language arts instruction.

During the summer, Mr. Gedelian thought about a teaching experience that would provide a capstone experience for the fourth graders who are leaving their

Teaching teams work together to maximize planning and teaching for their respective grade levels.

school and going to middle school in the fall. He plans to present his idea during the first faculty meeting with the hope that the other teachers will agree to the plan. A state park south of the community allows children and chaperones to rent a few cabins for a weeklong stay at the end of the school year. Mr. Gedelian would like the fourth graders to spend a week at the park continuing their classroom study, participating in nature study, preparing their own meals (with parental and teacher assistance), and organizing for sing-alongs, plays, skits, and ghost stories in front of an open campfire in the evening. His vision is for the trip to be a highlight of the children's fourth-grade year. The plan would capitalize on integrated unit study and the teachers could coordinate various activities to extend the learning about the Westward Pioneer Movement, the last unit of the school year. The children could plan a year-long fundraising project to raise funds for the trip. Parental involvement would be essential in helping youngsters organize for the experience. Mr. Gedelian believes that the school district will view this plan as an event worthy of media focus and a genuinely fine public relations activity.

WHAT FOURTH GRADERS ARE EXPECTED TO LEARN

Fourth grade, like second grade, is a year that builds on skills that were taught during the previous year, extending the complexity of those skills and introducing some new ones. The academic areas include new knowledge to be mastered and facts to be learned. Assignments are more in depth and may require extensive writing as children research and prepare more complex reports on various subjects. Mathematical skills continue to increase in complexity, as do science concepts and content. The focus of social studies is generally state specific. Each of these areas, with the skills and knowledge required, is defined here.

Reading

The basal reading series targets skills that improve reading comprehension, vocabulary development, phonics, oral language, listening skills, grammar, and research and study skills. In addition, suggestions are offered for implementing technology, assessment, individual and small-group activities, social studies, music, and art connections (Afflerbach, Beers, Blachowicz, Boyd, Diffily, Gaunty-Porter, Harris, Leu, McClanahan, Monson, Perez, Sebeste, & Wixson, 2000). Again, as stated in previous chapters, the basal should not be the only type of reading instruction offered. Fourth graders may find chapter books and books related to themes or topics studied in class of great interest. New reading skills typically taught in fourth grade include:

- Paraphrasing
- Modified nouns
- Conducting an interview
- Reading strategies such as self-questions
- Summarizing

- Generalizing
- Literary devices (similes and metaphors)
- Atlas/maps
- Expository nonfiction
- Taking notes
- Words with multiple meanings
- Diagrams
- Visualizing
- Steps in a process
- Fact and opinion
- Study strategies
- Advertisements
- Electronic media
- Biographies
- Giving oral reports
- Expressing an opinion
- Idioms
- Making judgments
- Drawing conclusions
- Using the dictionary/glossary (Afflerbach, Beers, Blachowicz, Boyd, Diffily, Gaunty-Porter, Harris, Leu, McClanahan, Monson, Perez, Sebeste, & Wixson, 2000)

Writing and Language Arts

In fourth grade, writing and language arts skills begin to help the children organize and present information, as in writing research reports. Children are expected to use more complex and compound sentences in their writings along with conventional spelling. Children generally use writing more in all subject areas as they read and answer questions, do experiments and record results, and write to communicate and share ideas with their peers. Specific writing and language arts skills taught in fourth grade include:

- Use of commas
- Quotation marks
- Paragraphs
- Using adjectives to improve sentences
- Using transition words
- Using adverbs
- Writing how-to directions
- Prepositional phrases
- Conjunctions
- Appropriate use of pronouns and their referents
- Imagery and sensory words
- Descriptive paragraphs (Afflerbach, Beers, Blachowicz, Boyd, Diffily, Gauntz-Porter, Harris, Leu, McClanahan, Monson, Perez, Sebeste, & Wixson, 2000)

Spelling

Spelling skills in fourth grade, as in third grade, focus on more complex phonic skills and generally focus on patterns in words. These skills are:

- Schwa sound
- Prefixes
- Suffixes
- Alphabetical order
- Comparatives and superlatives
- Irregular plurals
- Contractions
- Vowel patterns
- Silent consonants
- Syllabication (Hackney & Lucas, 1998; Afflerbach, Beers, Blachowicz, Boyd, Diffily, Gaunty-Porter, Harris, Leu, McClanahan, Monson, Perez, Sebeste, & Wixson, 2000)

Mathematics

Fourth-grade mathematics not only builds and expands on previously learned skills, but the types of problem-solving questions that children are expected to be able to solve become more sophisticated. Children learn how to read and write numbers in the trillions as they expand on their knowledge of place value. Multiplication and division become more complex and new concepts and skills are introduced. Specific math skills taught in fourth grade include:

- Polygons
- Parallelograms
- Angles
- Addition of multidigit numbers
- Subtraction of multidigit numbers
- Decimals to thousandths
- Logic problems
- Using a protractor
- Comparing fractions
- Powers of 10
- Estimation
- Converting fractions to decimals
- Converting fractions to percents
- Using a calculator
- Drawing to scale
- Perimeter
- Area
- Three-dimensional shapes
- Volume
- Money

- Fractions (naming, writing, comparing, estimating)
- Addition and subtraction problems involving whole numbers through 999
- Learn and apply multiplication facts through tens
- Division
- Geometric patterns
- Solids and shapes
- Measurement (including metric)—capacity, weight, temperature
- Time
- Perimeter
- Area
- Volume (University of Chicago School Mathematics Project, 1999).

Science

As in third grade, the scientific process, or method, is taught and experiments and/or observations are stressed in each unit. The units mirror those listed in the third grade but include increasingly more difficult concepts, vocabulary, and material. Life science includes classification of living things, animal characteristics, reproduction, and survival. Physical science includes measuring matter, work and energy, electricity, and magnetism. Earth science includes soil, rocks, and changes in landforms, water, and oceans. The human body includes skeleton, muscles, organ system, blood, and the effects of tobacco, drugs, and alcohol. As in third grade, the ability to read maps, charts, graphs, and tables are also part of the curriculum. Other skills that are addressed through the science curriculum that are new to fourth grade are:

- Classifying organisms
- Investigating interaction between living and nonliving things
- Soil
- Constructing graphs and charts
- Interpreting information
- Vertebrates and invertebrates
- Electrical pathways
- Circuits
- Making and transforming electricity
- Motions in the oceans
- Alcohol, drugs, and tobacco
- Mass and density
- Using diagrams
- Using tables
- Reading maps and charts (Cohen, Cooney, Hawthorne, McCormack, Pasachoff, J. M., Pasachoff, N., Rhines, K. L., & Siesnick, 1991).

Social Studies

The progression of social studies generally follows a pattern from kindergarten (self), first grade (family), second grade (neighborhood), third grade (community), to fourth grade (state and/or region of the country) (Wade, 2002). Children learn about their state history, geography, resources and government. Some skills and concepts that are new to fourth grade include:

- Importance of debate
- Social issues
- Attempts to reform social, political, or economic conditions
- Historic events
- Different points of view
- Primary and secondary sources
- Characteristics of an ecosystem
- Relationship among price, supply, and demand
- Cultures
- Using latitude and longitude
- Reading an elevation map
- Reading a population map
- Using atlases
- Writing an outline (Boehm, Hoone, McGowan, McKinney-Browning, & Miramontes, 1997)

☆ THE SCHEDULE AND CLASSROOM LAYOUT

The fourth-grade team spends two days at the beginning of each school year orgaizing the coordination of the departmentalized instruction concept. Their principal provides them with a schedule showing daily restroom breaks for each homeroom, lunch, physical education, and music and weekly library assignments. The homeroom classes rotate after lunch in 40-minute cycles to complete the day by 3:10 when the children who ride buses are dismissed. Some children stay at school for after-hours tutorials, whereas others leave the classroom to participate in a YMCA program in the school because their parents work. A few parents pick up their children after school, and a few others walk home. Often this latter group will remain to assist their teachers in cleaning the classroom, putting up bulletin boards, or running errands for their teachers. Mr. Gedelian is a popular teacher, and he usually has after-hours help from children who enjoy his company and guidance. He is aware of accusations students make about sexual advances, and he ensures that several children are in his classroom when students are present.

All of the fourth-grade classrooms have individual desks with an open shelf to place books and chairs on that can be pushed under the desk. This style does not discriminate against left-handed or large children and allows teachers to push desks together for group work. The desks have a recessed spot for pencils and pens and are large enough to hold all of the textbooks the children are assigned plus whatever supplies they need for class work. Most of the children maintain a fairly neat desk management, but a few need continual reminders about cleaning their messes at the end of the school day.

The classrooms are small, but children have lockers in the hall to place their personal belongings, such as sweaters, coats, scarves, and other seasonal clothing. Umbrellas present unique problems on rainy days because there is not an effective way to dry them before placing them in lockers. Fortunately, the teachers have ample closets to store classroom materials and teachers' guides. In Mr. Gedelian's team, the teachers place their desks at the back of the room to leave space for chalk-board and overhead project instruction in front of the room. Most teachers use their desks for individual conferences or for one-on-one work when children need special help.

State by State

Arkansas Virtual School

The virtual school, funded by a five-year grant from the U.S. Department of Education, has become an option in the state of **Arkansas.** Program design provides children in the state, specifically children in low-performing schools, a public school choice that combines successful teaching methods and curriculum with the tools of tomorrow. Other virtual schools exist in California, Colorado, Idaho, Minnesota, Ohio, and Pennsylvania. The virtual schools partner together, sharing curriculum and teaching methods.

According to the Arkansas Department of Education, parents choose a virtual school for a variety of reasons:

- Academic issues (gifted or struggling students)
- Special needs (physical or learning disabilities)
- Concerns about current learning environment
- Need for flexible schedules (military families, extracurricular activities)
- Desire for high-quality education alternatives

The Arkansas Virtual School uses the high-quality education curriculum by K12 Inc., directed by William J. Bennett. The curriculum is based on time-tested learning methods and traditional academic content. The Arkansas Virtual School is federally funded, so there is no tuition, but available student spaces are limited.

The Arkansas Virtual School offers a comprehensive curriculum for grades K–5 that includes:

- K12 curriculum for the school year in six subjects (Language Arts, Math, Science, History, Art, and Music)
- Computer system with printer and Internet connection, provided at no cost
- All instructional materials, including textbooks, workbooks, planning and progress tools, maps, math and science supplies, CDs, and videos
- Access to a certified teacher for guidance, support, and advice
- Optional educational outings to enhance lessons and build a sense of school community

⭐ FOURTH GRADE AND READING INSTRUCTION

The National Assessment of Education Progress (NAEP), authorized by Congress, is the only federally mandated survey of student achievement in various subjects. The NAEP reports on the educational progress of children in grades 4, 8, and 12. In 2000, the NAEP conducted reading assessment with fourth-grade children. Compared to the assessment from 1992, the average scale score has remained relatively stable. High-performing children have made significant progress since 1992, however, whereas low-performing children are performing significantly lower than in 1992. Sixty-three percent of fourth graders were performing at or above the Basic level, 32 percent at the Proficient level, and 8 percent at the Advanced level (National Center for Education Statistics, 2000).

In addition to these percentages, the center compiled results for various subgroups. In 2000, female fourth graders had higher average scores than males, and more females than males achieved at or above the Proficient level. White and Asian children outperformed black, Hispanic and Native American children. Children in central city schools had lower averages than children in urban fringe/large town and rural/small town schools. Children on free or reduced lunch had lower average scores than children who did not qualify for free or reduced lunch. Of these same children, only 14 percent performed at or above the Proficient level compared to 41 percent of noneligible children (National Center for Education Statistics, 2000).

In fourth grade, materials used for reading become more complex, have more difficult vocabulary, and present a greater conceptual load. Reading begins to focus on using materials "as a vehicle for extending the number of words that can be recognized automatically and perfecting the ability to use phonics knowledge to decode words" (Honig, 2001, p. 83). During fourth grade, as most students become more proficient readers, they are able to read new words with as few as four to fifteen exposures. Some children will be able to read a new word after only two or three exposures, whereas some children with special needs may require as many as 50 to 100 exposures before reading the word automatically (Honig, 2001).

Vocabulary development is a very important factor in reading comprehension. Children must know the meanings of words they read in order to comprehend what they read. The material that children read in grades 3 through 9 contains approximately 90,000 different words. In second grade the average reading vocabulary is between 2,000 and 5,000 words. This difference between second grade and later grades means that children need to learn about 3,000 to 4,000 words per year just to stay on grade level. In order to achieve this level, the California State Board of Education in 1999 recommended that children read between 500,000 and 1,000,000 words per year in the early grades (Honig, 2001).

Honig suggests that there are several ways children learn vocabulary: through reading, listening to books read aloud, and receiving feedback about word meanings. When teachers attempt to teach vocabulary, they should focus on three other components: independent word-learning strategies, specific word instruction, and word consciousness (2001). Independent word-learning strategies include using word parts, such as prefixes and suffixes, to learn word meanings (*un-, dis-, -less,*

-ful), using context clues (examples, direct definitions or explanations, restatements) and using dictionaries and other reference aids. Specific word instruction means explaining new vocabulary words the children will read and explaining their meaning before reading the selection. This strategy is useful with words that are not part of children's everyday vocabulary and/or words that present new concepts to children. Not all new words are taught this way, only those that are important to what is to be read and that will be useful to know in the future. Word consciousness involves activities with words such as homophones, puns, and onomatopoeia (Honig, 2001).

Learning to spell, word families, root words with prefixes and suffixes, syllables, and more comprehensive phonic skills also aid children in reading development. Therefore, the teacher needs to focus instruction on these types of skills as the children read from multiple types of materials such as basal readers, chapter books, science and social studies books, histories, and biographies (Honig, 2001).

As in third grade, small groups of children can work with the teacher and discuss not only the reading content, but also reading strategies that enable the children to decode unfamiliar print. The teacher must be sure to match books that are used for reading instruction to the level of the children. This means that children must be able to recognize between 90 percent to 98 percent of the words for the material to be considered instructional. A child who cannot read at least 90 percent of the words will become frustrated; a child who can read 98–100 percent of the words will not progress because of limited opportunity to practice decoding and learning new vocabulary.

Much fourth-grade reading instruction is done in large groups or even whole-class mode. This means that some of the children are not using appropriate level materials and their progress will be limited. As the school year progresses, comprehension for children who are not on an instructional level will worsen. Whereas these children may show progress from recognizing 66 percent of the words to 69 percent, their comprehension level may only be in the 29th percentile (Juel, 1994). The implication for reading instruction is that every classroom needs a wide range of books on many levels, with multiple copies of each book, and that children must be taught on a level that is instructional for them (Honig, 2001).

Children should be frequently evaluated on their reading. Oral reading tests are the most common means of doing this. These tests may be in the form of a running record or a WCPM (words correct per minute) test. In California, children are expected to read 93 WCPM by mid-fifth grade (California State Board of Education, 1999). These tests are used to ensure that children are reading appropriate instructional material. As children progress, they receive harder material. Children are not placed in groups for the entire school year and do not stay in those same groups for long periods of time but are constantly being regrouped according to their needs.

One strategy that is crucial for fourth-grade teachers is to teach children how to decode unfamiliar multisyllabic words. This instruction helps children to recognize the various syllable types as they attempt to come up with approximate or alternative pronunciations. "The most common patterns are VC/CV (bas-ket), V/CV or VC/V (mo-ment, plan-et), VC/CCV (mon-ster), VC/CCCV (in-stru-ment), and V/V (re-act)" (Honig, 2001, p. 90). The teacher can also help students to look for

familiar word parts, learn prefixes and suffixes, look for familiar vowel and consonant patterns, and divide words into syllables (Honig, 2001).

As Mr. Gedelian plans his lessons for each day, he includes small guided reading
groups (see Chapter 8 for more information on guided reading). All children can
participate in the whole-class book studies, but the guided reading groups will be
composed of students reading on approximately the same level. He will plan these
groups so that the needs of all the children in class are met, from the child who is
still struggling to read to the child who is reading several grades above level.

Although Mr. Gedelian's school district is very concerned with the children's
WCPM scores, Mr. Gedelian is more concerned about their comprehension of the
material they are reading. There are four levels of comprehension (Miller, 2000).
The first level is literal or factual comprehension, the "right there" answers to a
question. In interpretive or inferential comprehension, answers are not found directly in the text, but the reader must be able to draw conclusions, make generalizations, summarize, and predict outcomes in order to answer the question. In
textually implicit or evaluative comprehension, the reader must evaluate what is
written for accuracy, truthfulness, biases, propaganda, and fact and fantasy. In
script tally implicit comprehension, the reader combines his or her prior knowledge with the text to arrive at new knowledge (Miller, 2000).

Mr. Gedelian knows that there are three main strategies for developing comprehension: (1) Having children spend a large amount of time reading, (2) teaching comprehension strategies to children, and (3) having children engage in deep
discussions about what they have read (Honig, 2001). The first strategy he meets
by assigning reading for homework and having a substantial amount of silent reading scheduled into the class day. The comprehension strategies that Mr. Gedelian
teaches include helping the children generate questions about what they will be
reading, clarify confusing text, summarize, make predictions, and understand how
the text is organized based on writing type (Honig, 2001).

Honig reports that deep intellectual discussions about what an author has written are rare in today's classrooms. During discussions, children develop higher-
order thinking skills, oral language, listening skills, and social skills and become
motivated to read. The role of the teacher is to model posing good questions, finding the evidence that supports an opinion, elaborating ideas, understanding the author's message, and making connections to other ideas. As Mr. Gedelian struggles
to implement these discussions, he has had the children prepare by looking for and
noting four things: "anything they do not understand or have a question about,
passages or words they think are especially important, connections between different parts of the text, and parts that elicit strong feelings or that they disagree
with" (Honig, 2001, p. 116). He has decided to begin by using a book from the Junior Great Books program.

Junior Great Books

The Junior Great Books program can be found in all 50 states and in countries
around the world. The program intends to make reading and discussing literature
a lifelong pursuit by combining age-appropriate literature with the shared inquiry

method of discussion. Students develop skills that enable them to read carefully, think critically, listen, speak, and write (Great Books Foundation, 2002). Information about participation in this program is online at www.greatbooks.org/programs/junior/.

Reader's Workshop

Reader's Workshop is a method of teaching reading that is structured on the beliefs that children need time to find books that interest them, are allowed to choose what they want to read, share their books, and respect and support each other and that the classroom is structured in a way that supports learning. Reader's Workshop consists of three parts: minilesson, activity period, and sharing time. The minilesson lasts from 5 to 15 minutes and addresses reading strategies, literary skills, or workshop procedures. The activity period occurs as children read, respond, and confer. At individual conferences the teacher discusses prereading, reading, and postreading strategies; may take a running record of the child's oral reading; discusses vocabulary meanings and pronunciations; and reviews or introduces new reading skills. Another part of this period is an assignment. Assignments vary and may include writing a summary, writing predictions with supporting statements, doing Webs of the main characters, or writing what was hard for the child to understand. During sharing time, children get to take turns sharing their books with a few other children. The other children must listen, retell what was heard, or ask a question and give a compliment to the speaker. Children may share by creating projects that include making dioramas, mobiles, bookmarks, and book covers; gathering author information from the Internet; or designing a poster (Wulf-McGrath, 2000).

Reading in Content Areas

Fourth graders are expected to read and comprehend increasingly more difficult and complex texts. Determining the type of writing and applying certain strategies to a text can increase children's understanding of the text. For example, viewing expository text with thoughts of problem/solution, question/answer, comparisons, and looking for common factors may aid in understanding a passage. Using summary statements, bolded type, headings, and subheadings helps the child identify the importance of some information and the organization of the information. Being able to "read between the lines" and infer allows children to have deeper comprehension of the text. The ability to read and interpret graphs, tables, charts, and diagrams also provides another means of understanding the words that are written (Reading Strategies That Assist Content Area Reading, 2002). Many of these skills have previously been introduced in earlier grades, but they become extremely important as the complexity of the material that the children are reading increases.

Using Nonfiction Books

The use of nonfiction material for reading has steadily increased over the years with many titles available for all ages of children on a wide variety of subjects.

Trends in nonfiction include the use of humor, such as *The Magic School Bus: Inside the Human Body* (by Joanna Cole, 1989); unusual formats (pop-ups, lift-flaps books); simplification of advanced topics; emphasis on graphics and illustrations; more evidence of research by the authors; and focus on one aspect of a topic rather than the entire topic. It is essential that accurate information be presented, stereotypes avoided, both pros and cons presented of debatable topics, and clear distinctions made between facts and theories (Freeman & Person, 1992).

Using retelling of expository text obliges the children to remember very specific facts and vocabulary and requires an understanding of concepts that are presented. Reading expository materials also helps prepare the children for the expository writing expected in fourth grade. Children may use the material they are reading as models when they begin writing (Freeman & Person, 1992).

Nonfiction books may also be used in theme teaching. A thematic unit on houses might include topics such as construction (rafters, vents, and studs, for example) and architecture (blueprints, designs, models). Many opportunities for field trips to construction sites, building supply stores, and city hall for permits allow the teacher to plan relevant experiences for the children. A discussion about careers in construction, combined with visits from skilled craftspeople, can also enhance the unit (Freeman & Person, 1992).

Reading Attitude Research

Research indicates a downward trend in reading attitudes over time. As children mature and more leisure options become available to them, their reading attitudes worsen. Children with reading difficulties generally show a sharp decline. The older the child, the wider the difference in attitudes between good and poor readers (Verhoeven & Snow, 2001).

Girls in general tend to possess more positive reading attitudes than do boys. This is evident from as early as first grade and grows more pronounced among older children. These results are not unique to the American culture (Verhoeven & Snow, 2001). Attitudes were found to improve when teachers used high-quality literature, asked questions to activate prior knowledge, avoided denigrating reading group placement, read aloud to the children, and stressed connections between literature and the everyday lives of the children (Verhoeven & Snow, 2001).

Reading Assessment

In fourth grade, being a good reader becomes even more essential for children. Much of the information that children learn and assignments that are given require a substantial amount of reading. Statistics show that an average of 15–25 percent of children in rural, small town, or suburban areas are disabled in reading. In some urban and inner city areas, this percentage can be as high as 50–100 percent (Miller, 2000). These statistics include all types of children with reading difficulties, from those with special needs to second-language learners to children who have received mediocre reading instruction (Miller, 2000).

Some important guidelines for assessment should be considered by teachers (Miller, 2000). Though some are common sense, teachers still may overlook them.

1. *Assessment should drive instruction.* If assessments are given, they should be the basis for the reading lessons. This means that time is spent teaching to a child's weaknesses, and not teaching what the child already knows. This makes instruction individualized to each child. It also means more planning on the part of the teacher.

2. *Teach the child on the child's instructional level.* Using material that is above a child's instructional level hurts a child's motivational level and does not improve his reading. In order to avoid doing this, the teacher must know what the instructional level of the child is and if the material to be used for reading instruction is appropriate.

3. *Assessment should be continuous.* The teacher continuously monitors the child's reading through observation, running records, individual reading inventories, and miscue analysis. This assessment dictates the direction that the teaching takes.

4. *Assessment should be collaborative and reflective.* If more than one teacher is working with the child on reading (general education teacher and special education teacher), the teachers need to collaborate on their instruction. Children also need to be taught to self-assess their own reading ability. This can be done in conjunction with the child's development of a portfolio.

5. *Assessment should be multidimensional.* Assessment must involve more than just standardized tests.

6. *Assessment should be developmentally and culturally appropriate.* Teachers should keep in mind the fact that young children and children who are culturally or linguistically diverse may not perform well on standardized tests and may actually be better readers than those tests indicate.

7. *Assessment should identify strengths as well as weaknesses.* Pointing out strengths to poor readers, as well as working on weaknesses, helps build the self-esteem and self-confidence of these children.

Improving Vocabulary

There are four basic types of vocabulary that children use: conceptual vocabulary, reading vocabulary, writing vocabulary, and potential or marginal vocabulary. *Conceptual vocabularies* refer to meanings. For children, these vocabularies consist of listening vocabulary (mainly learned in the home) and speaking vocabulary (what words the child uses). *Reading and writing vocabularies* are primarily learned in school, and by the fourth grade the reading vocabulary is usually more extensive than the speaking vocabulary. The *potential or marginal vocabulary* consists of words that a child may be able to determine the meaning of by using context clues and/or word structure. It has been demonstrated that the size of a child's vocabulary correlates positively with success in school (Miller, 2000).

Learning new vocabulary is not a simple task. Learning to read new words is the first task defined by Graves (1987) in learning new words. More tasks are involved before a child moves to the last stage of using the new word as part of his or her speaking and writing vocabulary. These tasks include learning the meaning of new words, learning words that represent the concepts that are already known, learning words that represent unknown, or new, concepts, and classifying the meanings of known words.

Vocabulary is best improved through direct experiences. For example, before visiting a planetarium, the teacher can discuss concepts, terms, models, and exhibits that the children are likely to see. On returning to school, the teacher can review the vocabulary and the children can write about their experience. Many experiences can be planned at a local level that will increase children's vocabulary. The teacher needs to think of all the various opportunities that fit into what is being studied in class in science, social studies, or some other subject. This means that trips taken to the courthouse, to small claims court, factories, and the like will actually benefit vocabulary development (Miller, 2000).

Secondhand experiences can assist in vocabulary development, too, and are more practical than direct experiences. Though it is not possible for the class to visit a tropical rainforest, the children can research the topic and construct a rainforest in the classroom. Other secondhand experiences include using the Internet, videos, software programs, watching experiments or demonstrations, looking at pictures, and examining artifacts (Miller, 2000).

A third way to develop vocabulary, and one of the most effective, is through wide reading of books and articles—by children and by the teacher to children. Studies have "found that the amount of free reading done by a child was the best predictor of vocabulary growth between grades two and five" (Miller, 2000, p. 328).

English-Language Learners (ELL)

More than 6 percent of children in the United States are classified as limited English proficient (Scarcella, 1990), with 66 percent of these children in the elementary grades (National Clearinghouse for Bilingual Education, 1995). Fourth grade finds many children dismissed from bilingual programs and included into the general education classrooms, regardless of their English ability. Although most strategies that are used with children with special needs can be effective with ELL children, a few are more specific to their needs. Instead of asking, "Do you understand?" the teacher should ask a specific question to confirm that the child understands what has been said.

A teacher should also provide both oral and written directions to children. In repeating or rephrasing information, the teacher should change the vocabulary that is used. The children also need to be evaluated with alternative methods without lowering the standards for the class. The teacher should use visual materials, manipulatives, and concrete demonstrations, when possible, to aid in understanding. Speaking slowly and distinctly and not exaggerating words is also helpful for ELL children. The teacher must remember not to constantly correct errors of

Issues and Trends

The Law and Bilingual Education

Children whose first language is other than English are protected by several laws. The Civil Rights Act of 1964 prohibits discrimination in any federally funded activity based on race, color, ethnicity, national origin, religion, or creed. Based on this law, the Supreme Court has upheld the rights of children with limited English proficiency, and additional federal laws have been passed to ensure the availability of funds to provide quality programs for these children. Under the law, parents have the right to be notified of the reason their child was selected for a special program, must be provided with alternatives to the program, and have the option of declining to enroll their child in the program. Parents must be presented this information in a language that they can understand. Approximately 4,580,000 children in this country have limited English proficiency (National Association for Bilingual Education, 2003).

vocabulary, comprehension, accent, or structure, as this will have a negative effect on language acquisition. As with any child, teaching to that child's learning style helps the child learn new vocabulary and concepts (Miller, 2000).

Structuring the reading program to include multicultural literature, predictable books, and wordless picture books has been found to aid children in their language development. Learning centers allow children to learn on their own, and cooperative groups allow children to learn from other children. Allowing the children to read in their primary language and/or giving them a choice of which language to read in has also been found to be effective (Miller, 2000). Some books have one page in English and the same page on the opposite side in another language. Children can also listen to books on tape, and many software programs allow for a child to choose the language.

⭐ SPELLING INSTRUCTION IN FOURTH GRADE

Mr. Gedelian believes that his children should have progressed from trying to sound out words by individual letters as they are writing to the more complicated level of spelling patterns. He believes in holding children accountable for correctly spelling words they have learned in previous grades and those that the children consistently use. He works with each child individually to identify words that fall into either of these categories and adds these words to the child's individual spelling list. Though he doesn't want to stifle the children's creativity, he recognizes that some children have developed bad habits about their spelling and make many common errors. Once the children realize that Mr. Gedelian will not accept careless spelling errors, a remarkable change occurs in the children's overall spelling.

Spelling errors generally can be categorized into four areas: (1) errors made because children mispronounce the word, (2) errors made as children write the letters out of order, (3) errors made because there is more than one way to represent a sound (*trane* for *train*), and (4) errors made because of a lack of knowledge about rules and generalizations (change the *y* to *i* and add *-es*) (Honig, 2001). The type of error determines the strategy that Mr. Gedelian employs. If, for example, a child is writing the letters out of order, he could ask the child to sound out the word as written. This will help the child discover the problem. Talking about pronunciation (and different dialects) assists children who are making type 1 errors, teaching phonics can help with type 3 errors, and teaching general rules of spelling and grammar will help with type 4 errors. Many teachers no longer teach rules of spelling and grammar, but some rules, such as those for forming plurals and suffixes, are very useful for children to learn because they apply to many words. (Honig, 2001).

⭐ WRITING INSTRUCTION IN FOURTH GRADE

There seems to be a correlation between poor readers and poor writers by fourth grade, and this correlation between reading and writing ability seems to increase every year thereafter (Honig, 2001). Therefore, improving reading will help improve a child's writing ability. Like reading, a child's speaking vocabulary will also impact that child's writing ability. Children with limited vocabulary produce less sophisticated writings, using fewer descriptive words and a more simple structure.

Writing instruction in fourth grade focuses on helping children to incorporate more sophisticated language and language structures into the various types of writings they learned in previous grades. Children are expected to use more metaphors and similes, more descriptive words, "big" words, and more complex and compound sentences. The amount of writing produced increases. Children are expected to write stories that contain a problem and solution, with several events included in the story. Children are expected to write for longer periods of time and on many subjects as they research and prepare reports.

Writing Instruction and State Tests

Research indicates that the state curriculum and writing test dictate a teacher's instructional practices. Teachers "are surrounded by a myriad of contextual pressures in the school site. These may include the evaluations of administrators, the physical environment of the classroom, the needs of individual children, the attitudes of parents, the prescriptive curriculum, and their relationships with other teachers. . . . Within the social context of these competing measures, it is reasonable to expect that teachers' personal theories about pedagogy will be influenced in contradictory directions" (Brindley & Schneider, 2002, p. 329).

Clear differences were reported in the research between stated instructional perspectives of teachers and their self-reports of classroom practice. For example, teachers recognized the importance of talking and drawing in the writing process but did not explain ways that these activities are connected during writing. Children use talking to direct their writing as well as orally rehearsing or planning their writing. Although 68 percent of teachers surveyed stated that drawing was necessary for writing, none of the teachers included drawing in their description of the writing behaviors of children (Brindley & Schneider, 2002).

Writing on demand was the predominant form of writing in classrooms. Instructional strategies included the assigning of prompts for the children to practice a particular type of writing. Many teachers equated writing instruction with the assigning of topics. Teachers believed that children would score higher on the state writing test when teachers focused on prescriptive test formats, despite research that shows (and university courses that espouse) the best practices of prewriting preparation, responding to literature, writing workshops, journal writing, and taking a piece of writing through the publication process. Once the state test was over, teachers shifted their focus to creative writing, but this was often in the final months of the school year (Brindley & Schneider, 2002).

⭐ MATH INSTRUCTION IN FOURTH GRADE

Much attention is paid to mathematics in fourth grade across the nation and the world because fourth grade is the first year that our children are compared to other children the same age throughout the country and the world. The Third International Math and Science Study (TIMSS) reported that American fourth-grade children score better than the world average and most U.S. children in fourth grade are mastering basic arithmetic skills. However, by eighth grade U.S. children are below average in their math scores. This decline may result because the top-performing countries introduce more advanced mathematics, such as algebra and geometry, in the fourth grade (Mastering Challenging Mathematics, 1997). Within the United States, the National Assessment of Educational Progress (NAEP) has reported that U.S. children are progressing faster in math than in reading and that in most states the gap between minorities and Caucasian children is not narrowing. In fourth grade, only the states of Georgia and Massachusetts narrowed the gap. Eight states have made progress in narrowing the gap between the top and bottom quarters. The number of children scoring at or above the Proficient level rose in seven states, and the average score increased in 15 states (National Education Goals Panel, 2001).

Studies done in elementary classrooms show that even though good teachers provide instructional opportunities to learn and practice mathematics, 75 percent–90 percent of classroom instruction is organized around the mathematics textbook (Woodward & Elliot, 1990). This takes very little teacher planning because the curriculum is the textbook. The teacher puts the pages to be covered in the lesson plan book, does a few examples with the children after explaining how to do the problems, gives them a practice worksheet to do in class, and sends home another worksheet for homework.

In addition, teachers feel the pressure of state-mandated tests and add more practice to the daily math lesson that is often a worksheet in the format of the state test. Teachers often are concerned that children get "the right answers." However,

Instruction in mathematics requires that children understand math concepts in a concrete manner, even in fourth grade.

when teachers want to teach using a constructivist approach, they develop teaching strategies that support children's thinking.

Three basic principles can help teachers encourage children to think, reflect, and master math. The first principle is to encourage children to think about their answers. Does their answer make sense? Math is viewed as more than following a rule or procedure to produce an answer and then blindly believing that that answer is correct. The second principle is to encourage children to think about thinking. How did they get their answer? Did all the children solve the problem in the same way? Are all the answers the same? If not, which one is correct? The third principle is to encourage representations of thinking. Allow children to work with data, decide how to organize the data to solve the problem, and determine how they could share their solution with others. Teachers who teach in this manner produce children who are not tied to a single way of thinking and answering problems, who understand math, not just "do math" (Wakefield, 2001).

Good teachers make math relevant to the everyday lives of children. When teachers fail to do this, children view math as just something you do in school. In reality, there are many examples that can be pulled from the real world to help children understand math vocabulary and concepts. Area can be viewed as raking a lawn, nominal numbers (those used primarily as labels) are seen in radio station numbers, perimeter can be understood through buying a necklace or fencing a yard, ratio can be thought of in terms of servings per bag of chips, and sets are

more easily understood when teachers talk about how the children themselves belong to several "sets," as friends, family members, or team members (Toher, 2001).

Using concrete examples and projects can also give children a reason to want to
learn math. Projects don't necessarily depend on computational skills and allow
children to feel successful "doing math." Paper clips and Scotch tape can be used
to teach a lesson on geometric shapes. Children can write their own surveys, collect their own data, and make graphs that display the results and interpret those
results. Math can be discussed in other subject areas to aid in understanding the
material. A description in a science book or social studies book about the size of a
whale or tall building has little meaning to children. Taking the children to the playground with yardsticks and chalk, then measuring and drawing an approximation
can greatly aid their understanding in the size of what is being discussed (Bernstein, 1999).

As teachers introduce new concepts and skills to children, they should keep in
mind that children need repeated exposures to activities that will gradually widen
their level of competence. These exposures are not repeat experiences. The first exposure should be on a concrete, personal level. The second exposure should focus
on mental and representational aspects of the concept. The third exposure takes the
child to the abstract and symbolic level with practice that moves toward automa-
tion by building speed and confidence (Teaching Math Basics, 2002).

Teachers need to be constantly aware of the amount of *wait time,* the length of
time a teacher waits for a child to respond to a question. The literature clearly indicates that teachers continue to favor boys over girls in this area. Some teachers
give girls less than 1 second wait time. Teachers need to give sufficient wait time
to all children—boys, girls, and children with special needs (Gore & Roumagoux,
1983). Wait time should be at least 3–5 seconds, more depending on the child and
the circumstances.

The Challenge of Metrics

The TIMSS showed that the only content category in which scores for fourth
graders were below the international average was Measurement, Estimation, and
Number Sense. An examination of the released items from the test shows that six
of the eleven test items involved the metric system. In reviewing fourth-grade curriculum guides, the metric system is mentioned, but not heavily emphasized.
Though some may wonder why children should be taught metrics in the first place,
an examination of several items in the news point out the need. In 1999, the Mars
Climate Orbiter, with a $125 million price tag, was lost because one of the contrac-
tors used the standard units of measurement in this country instead of metric units.
In 1983, a Canadian plane almost crashed because it was fueled in pounds rather
than kilograms, less than half the fuel that was needed. As the United States im-
ports more from other countries and as the world becomes more globally oriented,
it becomes very necessary for our children to learn the metric system (Taylor, 2001).

Teachers can begin remedying this lack of understanding of metrics in several
ways. Noticing metric measures in the real world is a first step, such as the 2-liter

bottle and a 5-K run. Activities in the classroom can also point out the metric system. One such activity is called "golden rules." This activity uses "gold bars" that are traded to show the differences among centimeters, decimeters, and meters (Taylor, 2001). Many more activities can be found on the Internet that will assist teachers in providing activities that will help their children understand the metric system.

Accelerated Math

As the National Council of Teachers of Mathematics (NCTM) campaigns for teachers to help children understand mathematics and not just "do math," some schools or even entire school districts are heading in the opposite direction and are using the Accelerated Math Program as their entire math program. Accelerated Math is a computer program that allows teachers or students to print out individualized worksheets for children to do at their desks. After the worksheets are completed, the children enter the answers (multiple choice) on a scan card and run it through an optical scanner. The results are used by the teacher to plan the next worksheet. Teachers can generate individual worksheets for the entire class at the push of a computer key. Although this program will certainly be easy for the teacher, are children gaining the understanding of mathematics that they will need to live, work, and understand a technologically advanced society? Math is more than successfully completing calculations.

Improving Problem Solving

One of the hardest areas for teachers to address is the area of problem solving. Children generally are taught to solve word problems in a systematic, algorithmic manner. One method that offers an alternative strategy is visualization. Children are taught to visualize the problem and draw an illustration to help in understanding the problem and figuring out the solution. Teachers may begin this process by providing children with picture problems. These picture problems help children understand the problem and offer them examples for the time when they begin to draw their own illustrations. After each problem, discussion follows. Use of illustrations also helps ensure that children are not tricked by the problem. One such problem that tricked children was to determine how many minutes it takes to saw a log all the way through into four pieces. Without the illustration, most children multiply 3 minutes per cut times 4, which does not give the correct answer. Using the method of visualization also seems to generate enthusiasm for problem solving among children (Kelly, 1997).

Meeting the Needs of the Mathematically Gifted

Mathematically gifted children need to be challenged in the general education classroom. They should be provided with authentic tasks that need high-level thinking and reasoning. Teachers typically try to meet these children's needs through enrichment activities. This level will still not challenge some children, so the teacher needs to select activities and tasks that are sufficiently challenging for them. It may be necessary to modify the task to meet individual needs (Diezmann & Wafters, 2000).

An example of a challenging problem for fourth graders is to figure out how many handshakes happened at a party where five people met and shook hands for the first time. If this was easy for a child, the teacher could expand the number of people at the party from a few more up to 100 people. With the problem of 100 people, the child would not be able to solve the problem in the same manner as before but would have to think of another way to solve the problem. The teacher could support the child in his or her efforts to solve this problem by making suggestions as needed (Diezmann & Wafters, 2000).

☆ SCIENCE INSTRUCTION IN FOURTH GRADE

Children in fourth grade are exposed to more complex concepts than in previous grades. They begin to see how scientists classify living organisms. They are expected to conduct experiments and be able to draw conclusions from those experiments. The vocabulary and terms become increasingly more difficult as they explore such concepts as buoyancy, density, aquifers, and permeability, among many other terms. Many teachers teach science using the basal provided by their school and simply follow the lesson plan listed in the book. With a little research, however, teachers can find the resources that will offer more experiments and activities that will help children further their understanding of the concepts being taught. The problem is one of time. With all the demands placed on teachers, time is at a premium.

☆ TEACHING SOCIAL STUDIES IN FOURTH GRADE

Some educators feel that the time has come to change the way social studies is taught in schools, with new topics being developed, engaging questions asked and discussed, and civic action projects included. Children in fourth grade might explore the legitimacy of authority, the foundation of our democracy, the beliefs and values that support democracy, whether our government is equitable for all people, how the community government functions, which other countries are democratic, and how their democracies compare to the United States. Children could also have the opportunity to practice democracy in their school, classroom, and community by participating in a democratic process to solve a school problem, writing letters to the local government about a community issue, and attending and participating in a school board or city council meeting (Wade, 2002).

Organizing an Integrated Study on the State

Mr. Gedelian's school district introduces an extended unit each spring to fourth graders about their state's history, government, resources, and pertinent geographical data. The teachers introduce the name of the state capital, state flower, state song, state motto, and state tree, and each teacher integrates the theme into the usual curriculum areas. Reading and language arts support the theme effectively because many books and poems are available for use. The state has a quarterly journal that highlights aspects of the state's historical sites, tourism, and unique foods. The librarian subscribes to this journal to facilitate the fourth-grade study each year. When the theme is introduced, she sets up a book display and wears a period costume to show children how pioneer women dressed in the 1850s.

As part of the early morning homeroom ritual, the children say the pledge to their state flag each day, and the music teacher introduces the state song and other music indigenous to the region during her regular music period. In mathematics, the teacher requires children to prepare graphs showing the state's population growth by race. The mathematics teacher also encourages children to compare population figures from century to century to show how their community has grown. Children search local and school records to discover information about how their school district has evolved and how it compares to neighboring communities in the county and state. One year the children developed and began a project to bring in canned drink tabs to represent each person in the community, a total of about 27,000 people. The project completion was accomplished with three successive groups of fourth graders.

The health education instructor uses the state study to introduce nutrition information to children. They compare current diets and food intake to those of people who lived in the nineteenth century, and she makes a point of talking to children about the diminished availability of food to pioneers, unless they were able to hunt and fish. She requests children to prepare group reports about various food products distinctive to the state, their storage, processing, and packaging and information about interstate commerce. The children are amazed each year to learn their state's food is disseminated worldwide.

Mr. Gedelian uses the integrated unit to introduce content about the state's landforms to his children. Their community is located near one of the state's major rivers, and he knows many of his children have had fishing and boating experiences on the river. During one summer vacation in the western part of the state, he took photographs of the state's mountain range and used the film to prepare a *PowerPoint* presentation that he gives each year. A secondary study focuses on the state's gold mining and distribution. Mr. Gedelian has a strong interest in rock and soil formation, and his enthusiasm for gold mining is contagious. Generally, his students become excited about fossil formation, and they begin searching their neighborhoods for petrified rocks.

The social studies teacher is a native of the state, and she also presents lessons related to the state study that captivate the children. Because she is a descendant of one of the Native American tribes, her knowledge of Indian customs plus her collection of ancestral clothing are appealing to fourth graders. She collaborates with the music teacher to teach a dance her grandmother taught her, and she introduces Native American words to the class. Near the end of the unit, she and the health education teacher co-teach to assist children in making Indian bread over an outdoor fire.

The social studies include a study of government processes, and the fourth graders receive some preliminary information about their local and state governments. Often the teachers invite their state representative and senator to visit the school, depending on their availability. The children are usually curious about the voting process, and the governmental study provides a venue for planning a school election for Student Council representatives in grades 1 through 3. The fourth graders are responsible for soliciting candidates, setting up a polling booth, and supervising the voting process as it occurs. Once the election is completed, the fourth graders count the votes and announce the winners over the school's intercom system.

Cooperative Learning Grouping

The fourth-grade team utilizes a cooperative learning technique for many of their lessons. Cooperative learning appeals to fourth graders because of their needs for social interactions. Most of the time the teachers assign the groups, but periodically the children choose their peers for specific projects and research. Cooperative learning is based on the concept that "what children can do together today, they can do alone tomorrow" (Vygotsky, 1962). Robert Johnson and David Johnson (1987) of the University of Minnesota Cooperative Learning Center provide in-depth information about organizing and implementing cooperative learning groups and emphasize the importance of establishing accountability within the groups as they work together.

The teacher's task is to assess effort, provide feedback, facilitate work, and ensure individual accountability (clcrc.com, 2004). Common ways to structure individual accountability include:

1. Keeping the size of the group small (smaller groups increase individual accountability)
2. Testing students individually
3. Randomly calling on one student to present his or her group's work to others in the presence of the group
4. Observing groups as they work to determine the contributions of each student
5. Assigning a student in each group to serve as checker (the checker asks other students to explain the reasoning and rationale behind group answers)
6. Having students teach what they learned to someone else, a process called *simultaneous explaining* (clcrc.com, 2004)

Mr. Gedelian likes cooperative learning specifically because of the relationship students develop requiring positive interdependence, interpersonal skills, face-to-face promotive interaction, processing, and reflecting on how well the team is functioning. When he uses cooperative groups, he assigns one person to be the leader (or facilitator), one to be a recorder (or scribe), and a third to be a timekeeper and the monitor (or checker).

Dimensions of Diversity

Teaching Tolerance

Diversity issues still arise in fourth-grade classrooms, just as they do in classrooms of younger children. An excellent resource for teachers to prepare for instruction in diversity is www.tolerance.org/teach. Implemented by the Southern Poverty Law Center in Montgomery, Alabama, the website has teacher (and parent) guides to help children learn tolerance. Classroom activities, lesson plans, teaching tools, and monthly e-letters are available to teachers who subscribe to their distribution list. Magazine articles and current event information are also available. Among the choices available online are topics titled "10 Ways to Fight Hate," "101 Tools for Tolerance," "Tolerance in the News," and "Respond to Hate at School."

Issues and Trends

No Child Left Behind versus Public Policy

Though the intent of the No Child Left Behind Act is just that, the reality of public policy, however, means that some children will be left behind. For example, it is known that many factors affect how well a child will learn. One of the factors that puts a child at risk is poverty. In the United States, the child poverty rate is among the highest in the developed nations. Children who live in poverty usually attend underfunded schools. These schools often lack adequate instructional materials and have limited access to technology; school buildings are inadequate both in space and in repair; and the children are usually taught by teachers on the low end of the teacher pay scale. These teachers also may be less qualified as the schools seek people to fill these spots and sometimes resort to uncertified personnel. Children from poverty situations are placed at risk for cognitive development, not only because of the poor diet they may consume, but because of the poorer-quality child care they may receive. Even with children with special needs, the law requires special accommodations but only provides a fraction of the monetary support that these children need (Thomas & Bainbridge, 2002). Until these very real social issues are addressed and changed, it will be very difficult to leave no child behind, and certainly these children will not be all that they can be until there is real change in their everyday environment, health, and nutrition.

Working with Parents

Parents are as important to fourth graders' education as they are in earlier grades. Some fourth graders want to distance themselves from parental interference into their lives, and this phenomenon continues as children grow older. However, when parents and teachers are partners in children's education, the research shows that the quality of education improves when parents are involved in their children's learning (Allingon & Guice, 2002).

Mr. Gedelian promotes relationships with parents every opportunity he has, even before the start of school. During August before the first day of school, he calls the parents of the children assigned to his homeroom section and tells them three things: (1) how much he is looking forward to working with their child, (2) that they are welcome to visit the classroom at any time, and (3) to contact him when they perceive a problem. Gedelian does not care for parents' calling the principal before contacting him first, and he sends home a note the first day that reminds parents that he wants to know when problems arise.

Open House is a time to meet the parents in person if he has not already. He has been in the district for about 10 years, so many of his parents are ones he has met in previous years. During the hour assigned to teachers during Open House, Mr. Gedelian distributes information to parents about how to improve children's reading/language arts learning. Basically, his message is that children need to be reading many books and writing whenever possible (Allington & Guice, 2002). Other recommendations he makes are:

- Clip newspaper articles to share with children
- Memorize a poem and ask the child to memorize one, too
- Ask children to tell about books they are reading
- Continue to read books to children (even in fourth grade)—they never tire of hearing books read aloud
- Purchase books for children for special occasions (birthdays or on Valentine's Day)
- Visit sites in the community or state that relate to folktales and myths children are learning about in school (Perrone, 1994)

One activity Mr. Gedelian suggests is a parent/child journal that each writes in daily. The journal provides an avenue for children to tell about what is going on in their lives, what type of problems they are facing, and requests for allowance increases or tasks to make money. Parents should respond with answers, of course, but they can use the writing time to tell their children how much they care for them. Parents continually report how invaluable the journal becomes in establishing or reinforcing positive relationships with their children (Perrone, 1994).

The mathematics teacher, in conjunction with districtwide efforts to improve mathematics learning, worked with a group of teachers to prepare a set of take-home modules to encourage parents to become math partners. The district's Education Foundation funded the cost of the modules when the teachers wrote a grant proposal describing their desire to have Math Packets for Home Instruction. The first two modules focused on converting fractions to decimals and percents and measuring surfaces. Each teacher participating in the project prepared five packets, which included suggested activities, worksheets for recording answers, a small calculator, a ruler, and an evaluation form for parents to return when the packet work was completed. Children were able to check out a packet for up to a week's time. The teachers involved were hopeful to receive grant funding again another year to add packets to their stock.

⭐ OPPORTUNITIES FOR FOURTH GRADERS

Fourth graders and extracurricular activities go hand in hand. Schoolwork presents its challenges and opportunities, but extracurricular activities allow youngsters to pursue special interests that are not easily available to them in school. Teachers of older children often find that they are sponsors of special programs for children or they request parent volunteers to help children learn outside the classroom.

After-School Programs

Keeping the nation's children safe and helping them learn after school is a major goal of the 21st Century Community Learning Centers program. Passed in 1999, the program provides funding to communities and schools to support after-school programs for children in the elementary ages. A report by the U.S. Departments of Education and Justice on the effectiveness of after-school programs indicates the public's strong desire to make quality after-school programs available to all children. Americans overwhelmingly favor providing school-based programs (93 percent) (Northwest Regional Educational Laboratory, 1999). The public supports these programs for a number of reasons:

- Over 28 million school-age children have both parents (or their only parent) in the workforce.
- At least 5 million children or more are left alone at home each week.
- Many children lose ground in reading if they are not engaged in organized learning over the summer, especially children from low-income neighborhoods.
- School-age children who are unsupervised during the hours after school are more likely to receive poor grades and drop out of school than those who are involved in supervised activities.
- Statistics show that most juvenile crime takes place between the hours of 2 and 8 p.m.
- Children are at much greater risk of being the victims of crime during the hours after school (Northwest Regional Educational Laboratory, 1999)

Reading Is Fundamental

Founded in 1996 by Margaret Craig McNamara, Reading is Fundamental (RIF) has three goals: (1) to promote family literacy programs, (2) to prepare young children for reading, and (3) to motivate school-age children to read more regularly. RIF, the nation's largest family literacy organization, is a nonprofit group targeting the nation's neediest children from birth to age 11. RIF programs offer communities books for children to explore and keep for themselves, involve parents in children's reading, and develop imaginative activities to inspire children to read.

 Most local RIF programs are supported by service organizations such as Rotary International, Kiwanis, Junior League, and PTAs. Corporate alliances, such as the Coca-Cola Company, Nestlé, New York Life, Metropolitan Life Foundation, and

Prudential provide financial backing to communities and to the national program. For more information about Reading Is Fundamental, go online to www.rif.org.

Student Councils

At Mr. Gedelian's school, the fourth-grade classes with a teacher/adviser (one of his colleagues) sponsor the Student Council. Since 1931, the National Association of Student Councils (NASC) has offered assistance to schools wanting to develop and maintain student council programs. NASC's vision statement is to promote and provide "leadership development opportunities to prepare and empower student leaders to serve their schools and communities" (NASC, 2004). Though programs vary from school to school, in Mr. Gedelian's school, fourth graders are eligible for officer positions and the classes in grades 1 through 4 have representatives who meet on a regularly scheduled basis. Their role is to govern as a team to address issues and problems children perceive and bring to the council and to serve as mediators when disputes arise. They also organize and conduct the election each spring to select representatives and officers for the following year.

Youth Patrols

The Youth Crime Watch of America (YCWA) provides information to schools about organizing Youth Patrols in elementary through high school levels. At the elementary school, patrols serve an important role in before- and after-school bus safety. Having a campus patrol offers children partnerships in accepting responsibilities for keeping the school environment safe and free from crime. If the patrol represents a cross-section of the student body, the unit serves as models for peers' behavior and helps build a sense of community within the school. For information about developing a youth patrol, go online to www.ycwa.org.

School Stores

Some local schools plan and implement in-house school stores as a moneymaking project for the Student Council or the Parent/Teacher Association. The stores are manned by the oldest grade in the school, and often school leaders (such as Student Council officers and members) are responsible for overseeing the store. Mainly, school stores sell supplies children need for class work. Examples are consumable items like pencils, pens, paper, graph paper, crayons, and paste or glue. School stores might also sell paraphernalia related to school spirit, such as bumper stickers, T-shirts, pom-poms, or additional items showing the school colors and mascot. When children are in charge of the school store, they manage the store's operation hours, keep records of sales, inventory stock, and order supplies and goods. The experience is an excellent learning activity.

Choir/Band Instruction

During the spring of each year, band and choir directors often recruit children into middle school music programs by coming to elementary school campuses to share

Fourth-grade children love performing for their families and peers.

information and instruction. Music reading instruction, specifically, may begin during the last six or 12 weeks of the fourth-grade year, in preparation for students' move into further training as they graduate to higher grades. In some instances, when music programs are coordinated for K–12 instruction, the music teacher organizes for music instruction on recorders or flutophones during the last two months of school. These instruments are relatively inexpensive, and most parents are able to purchase them or the school district picks up the cost for low-income families. Children who are interested in choral music have opportunities to participate in community-wide children's choirs or in special elementary choirs.

Mediation Programs

According to the Interfaith Peace Center based in Columbus, Ohio, "mediation is the process in which a third-party neutral assists disputants to solve their own problems" (Interfaith Center for Peace, 2004). The Peace Center has been in existence for 20 years. One of their goals is to train individuals to become mediators, and their work extends to elementary schools. The goal of the process is to work with disputing parties to find solutions that are agreeable to both disputants. Mediation programs have three principles as cornerstones: (1) disputants want to solve the problem, (2) solutions are negotiable, and (3) disputants can mediate as equals.

Children who want to become mediators go through a selection procedure developed by the individual school, either by teachers and/counselors. The children who are interested make application for a training program. Training includes information about directing the mediation phases, developing good communication and listening skills, establishing a positive atmosphere, promoting teamwork, solving problems, remaining calm in stressful situations, remaining impartial, helping without judging, and maintaining confidentiality.

Competitions

Spelling bees, science fairs, speaking and dramatic contests, reading contests, bake-off competitions, and 4H fairs and shows become available as options to elementary children who seek involvement in competitive events. Occasionally, local groups plan competitions for children, whereas others are organized at the state or national levels. One of the best-known contests is the Scripps Howard Spelling Bee Contest that encourages children to compete locally, regionally, and nationally for prize money if they can spell well. Other competitions are essay contests, reading contests, dramatic reading contests, athletic events (such as kick, pass, and punt games), and one-act plays. Children who participate in 4H raise and show animals for prizes and awards. Not all children enjoy competitions, but those who do expend effort to be winners.

What Teachers Are Saying

Teaching Fourth Grade

"Due to pressures on specific grade levels and subjects, many teachers are considering other professions." —*a fourth-grade teacher*

Mr. Gedelian responds: "I cannot imagine any other profession as rewarding as teaching. Yes, we have problems; so does the medical profession and the legal profession. Working in a classroom with children is where I want to be. I know I make an impact on children's lives each and every day. I've been teaching for 15 years now, and each and every year, I hear from former students who remember something I said or did that touched their lives. I don't know what will happen when I have to retire!"

"Teachers have a tremendous impact on a child's life. Everything a teacher says or does influences the thoughts and actions of students in ways that may not be realized."—*a fourth-grade teacher*

"Results can be achieved on high-stakes tests by considering what is taught, when it is taught, how it is taught and by making certain that it is taught." —*a Texas elementary school principal*

"Departmentalization can be an effective strategy for providing quality instruction in fourth grade." —*a fourth-grade teacher*

Newspapers in the Classroom Programs

From minipages for children to games to play with the stock market pages, newspapers in education are widespread across the United States. Some local groups sponsor newspapers in education, or news sources provide low-cost subscriptions to educators. Newspapers are windows to the world, and children learn skills in reading, writing, and mathematics by using them. Most newspapers supply teachers with guides to reinforce instruction in basic skill areas, but activities are included to develop higher-order critical thinking abilities, too. Newspapers are capable of enhancing every curriculum focus, from local news and sports coverage to science to fine arts. Newspapers give teachers creative outlets for teaching children of any age.

Outdoor Learning Center

School district outdoor learning centers are available options for children of all ages to conduct scientific and nature studies as part of their general education. They are most often utilized in areas of the country where forests and wildlife abound. Teachers who plan to use the school district's Outdoor Learning Center must reserve it in advance and organize for transportation to the site. On occasion, the center is useful for class picnics or special end-of-year school celebrations. Mr. Gedelian has used his district's center each year as he begins his unit on plants and animals indigenous to the area.

Fundraising

Most elementary schools organize fundraising efforts at some time or another. Fundraising is in conjunction with a stated goal that a class or grade level has set for itself. Numerous companies distribute catalogs through the mail, at professional conferences, or by direct contact with schools to promote their wares. Among the items that youngsters can sell are candy, calendars, candles, nuts, snacks, popcorn, first aid kits, magazines, scented sachets, stationery, wrapping paper and ribbons, dried flower arrangements, or holiday cards and green wreaths. The possibilities are endless. Purchasing new books for the library or buying a special piece of equipment for the classroom or planning a special field trip for children are among the reasons teachers and children occasionally plan fundraising activities.

Young Inventors Awards Program

The Young Inventors Awards Program began in 1996 to challenge children from grades 2 through 8 to invent a new or modified tool in science or technology. Participants must work independently with guidance from adults or teachers to devise, design, and construct a tool that "makes life easier in some way, entertain or solve an everyday problem" (NSTA, 2004). An entry form, plus an Inventor's Log, diagram of the tool, and a photograph of the child using the tool is required for the national competition. The National Science Teachers Association awards $10,000 savings bonds to two first-place winners, though all entrants receive recognition for their achievements. Among 2002 winning entries by fourth graders were a "No Turn Door Knob Opener," a "Parcel Pal," a "Swing Myself Hammock," and a "Magna Broom."

Destination ImagiNation Program

Destination ImagiNation programs, formerly known as Odyssey of the Mind, is a worldwide program serving approximately 400,000 children. Each year volunteers prepare team challenges designed to stimulate the different senses that humans use for learning. Participating schools apply for an opportunity to use the rules of the organization as a springboard for creative solutions to predetermined problems. School teams are formed of up to seven members who choose one of the challenges to complete and work on for several months before regional competitions. Teams present their solutions to teams of appraisers during competition and, if successful, move on to state and national tournaments. Further information about Destination ImagiNation is available online at www.destinationimagination.org.

Girl/Boy Scouts or Camp Fire Girls/Boys

Most people know about scouting groups for children, because the associations have been in existence for almost a century. Boy Scouts of America was incorporated in 1910, and Girl Scouts began in 1912. Fourth-grade boys are eligible to participate in Cub Scout programs, described as family- and home-centered. Cub Scouts develop ethical decision-making skills and emphasize character development, citizenship training, and personal fitness (Boy Scouts of America, 2004).

Girl Scout troops are open to females ages 5 to 17, and fourth-grade girls can be members of Junior Girl Scouts. More than 233,000 troops exist around the world, allowing girls to discover the fun, friendship, and power of girls being together while working to develop each individual's potential for the improvement of society (Girl Scouts of America, 2004).

Also founded in 1910, Camp Fire USA has as its mission to build caring, confident youth and future leaders. Programs focus on reducing sex-role, racial, and cultural stereotypes and encouraging positive intercultural relationships (Camp Fire USA, 2004).

SUMMARY

Teaching fourth grade is a challenge, but teachers who choose this grade find the experience rewarding and emotionally fulfilling. Fourth-grade children are gaining independence academically and socially. Teachers discover that they do not have to spend as much time taking care of 9-year-olds' physical and emotional needs. Content requirements are high and end-of-year tests are demanding, but fourth graders usually manage the stress of school expectations with poise and confidence. Opportunities are open for great involvement in extracurricular activities, and children generally choose activities that match their interests and emerging social abilities.

DISCUSSION QUESTIONS

1. Describe and explain how fourth-grade language arts differs from previous grade levels.
2. What are some important guidelines for assessment that should be considered by teachers?
3. Discuss three basic principles that teachers can use to help encourage children in mathematics.
4. Name and discuss some opportunities that are available for fourth graders.

SUGGESTED CHAPTER ACTIVITIES

1. Observe in a fourth-grade classroom. Are children significantly different from younger children? If so, what are the differences?
2. Interview a fourth-grade teacher in a district near you and ask what types of assessment are used, how often the children are assessed, and how the results are used.
3. Find a listing of Junior Great Books that are appropriate for fourth grade. Plan a lesson for one of the books.
4. Choose a topic appropriate for fourth grade. Make a Web showing all new vocabulary words that a teacher could use with this theme.
5. Evaluate how a fourth-grade math textbook teaches metrics.
6. Take a word problem from a fourth-grade math book and change it so it challenges a gifted child.
7. What competitive events are available for fourth graders in your state?
8. Write a short report on an extracurricular program that you would be interested in sponsoring as a teacher of fourth-grade children.
9. Investigate resources in your state that assist teachers in preparing a unit on the state's history and government. Prepare a bibliography of available children's books for fourth graders about your state.

☆ Glossary

Adaptive behavior how well a child blends in and behaves as other children the same age.

Advocate a person who tries to create change in the social environment of children.

ARD acronym for admission-review-dismissal. This is the meeting that determines and reviews placement of children with special needs.

Assistive technology any item or equipment that is used or modified to improve the functional capabilities of an individual with a disability.

Balanced literacy approach an approach to teaching reading that uses elements of both the phonics approach and the whole-language approach to meet the individual needs of children learning to read.

Behavior contract a contract that a child develops with a teacher that lists the target behavior to improve and positive and negative consequences for doing or not doing the behavior.

Behaviorist theory a theory that utilizes environmental factors to define how children learn knowledge and skills.

Cognitive-developmental theory a theory that refers to children's growth and experiences to define how children learn knowledge and skills.

Computer literacy ability to understand and use computers.

Concept a basic understanding children have about knowledge they are acquiring.

Concrete operations stage the third Piagetian stage that describes children's learning once they understand reversible actions.

Content Mastery a program the allows children with special needs to receive help with their lessons or assignments on an as-needed basis.

Corporal punishment punishment that is administered in a physical form such as spanking or paddling.

Custodial parent parent who has been granted custody of a child by the court.

Developmental domains areas of development within children that relate to their social, emotional, intellectual, and creative learning and physical growth.

Disequilibrium a state of mind that occurs when children are puzzled about concepts they encounter in their learning.

Dispositions basic attitudes toward specific types of learning children develop.

Equilibrium a state of mind that occurs when children understand concepts they encounter in their learning.

Feelings the changing emotions children experience in daily activities.

Formal operations stage the fourth Piagetian stage that describes adolescents' comprehension of adult concepts.

IEP acronym for *individualized education program*. Children who are identified as qualifying for special education have an education plan written specifically for them that includes goals and objectives specific to their needs.

Informal Reading Inventory an assessment instrument that tests children's reading ability. It is usually composed of a list of words for each grade level in addition to a reading paragraph or very short story.

Knowledge information that children acquire.

Learning style the preferred sense that a person uses to learn new information (visual, auditory, tactile, kinesthetic).

LRE acronym for *least restrictive environment*. For most children with special needs, this means the general education classroom.

Maturationist theory a learning theory that defines children's development as important to their abilities to learn.

Multiple intelligences theory a learning theory developed by Howard Gardner that defines various talents children acquire through heredity and environmental experiences.

Nativist theory a learning theory that defines children's learning as natural because of their human traits.

Preoperational stage the second Piagetian stage that defines children's learning as egocentric and limited because of life's experiences.

Psychological records school records that contain the results of IQ testing and achievement tests administered to a child.

Psychosocial theory a learning theory that recognizes the importance of the effect psychological and emotional experiences have on children's knowledge.

Reliability refers to the consistency of test results.

Scaffolding environmental factors organized by parents and adults that affect children's learning.

Site-based management a management style that lets an individual school make decisions that directly impact it (hiring, firing, budgets).

Sensorimotor stage the first Piagetian stage that defines children's learning as being accomplished through sensory and motor activities.

Skills the types of activities children can perform.

Sociocultural theory a learning theory that suggests that children are affected by their social experiences within the context of their cultural environment.

Spatial dynamics use of large-scale models and active learning to help children understand history and concepts.

Standards statements used to judge quality.

Validity the extent to which a test measures what it is purported to measure.

Writing conference a teacher conference with an individual child to help the child to improve his or her writing.

Writing rubric a guideline used to score a child's writing.

Zone of proximal development a term coined by Vygotsky to describe the learning that children can accomplish with adult assistance.

☆ References

Adams, M., Foorman, B., Lundberg, I., & Beeler, T. (1998). The elusive phoneme. *American Educator,* Spring/Summer, 18–29.

Adams, M. J., & Treadway, J. (2000). *Fox in a box.* New York: McGraw-Hill.

Adams, P., & Warner, L. (2001). Action Research: How to find answers to everyday questions. *Dimensions of Early Childhood, 29*(3), 26–30.

Administration for Children and Families. (2001). *Head Start factsheet* [On-line]. Available: http://www.acf.dhhs.gov/programs/opa/facts/headst.htm

Afflerbach, P., Beers, J., Blachowicz, C., Boyd, C. D., Diffily, D., Gaunty-Porter, D., Harris, V., Leu, D., McClanahan, S., Monson, D., Perez, B., Sebeste, S., & Wixson, K. K. (2000a). *Scott Foresman Reading Grade 2.* New York: Addison-Wesley Educational Publishers, Inc.

Afflerbach, P., Beers, J., Blachowicz, C., Boyd, C. D., Diffily, D., Gaunty-Porter, D., Harris, V., Leu, D., McClanahan, S., Monson, D., Perez, B., Sebeste, S., & Wixson, K. K. (2000b). *Scott Foresman Reading Grade 3.* New York: Addison-Wesley Educational Publishers, Inc.

Afflerbach, P., Beers, J., Blachowicz, C., Boyd, C. D., Diffily, D., Gaunty-Porter, D., Harris, V., Leu, D., McClanahan, S., Monson, D., Perez, B., Sebeste, S., & Wixson, K. K. (2000c). *Scott Foresman Reading Grade 4.* New York: Addison-Wesley Educational Publishers, Inc.

Allen, P. (1982). *Who Sank the Boat?* New York: The Putnam & Grosset Group.

Allen, R. V. (1976). *Language experiences in communication.* Boston: Houghton Mifflin.

Allington, R., & Guice, S. (2002). *Learning to read: What research says parents can do to help their children.* [On-line]. Available: http://cela.albany.edu/publication/article/learnread.htm

Allington, R., & Walmsley, S. (Eds.). (1995). *No quick fix: Rethinking literacy programs in America's elementary schools.* New York: Teachers College Press.

Aloia, G. F. (1998). *Journey into technological integration* [On-line]. Available: http://www.ice.net/~edtech/floridaweb

American Psychiatric Association. (1993). *Diagnostic and statistical manual of mental disorders* (4th ed.). Washington, DC: Author.

Anselmo, S., & Zinck, R. A. (1987). Computers for young children? Perhaps. *Young Children*, March, 22–27.

Armstrong, T. (1993). *Seven kinds of smart: Identifying and developing your many intelligences.* New York: Penguin.

Ashmus, D. (2001). But I don't have a computer lab! Using one computer in the classroom. *Southeast and Islands Regional Technology in Education Consortium* [On-line]. Available: http://www.seirtec.org

Ashton-Warner, S. (1963). *Teacher.* London: Secker and Warburg.

Ashton-Warner, S. (1972). *Spearpoint; Teacher in America.* New York: Knopf.

Association for Childhood Education International. (1992). *Profiles in childhood education 1931–1960.* Wheaton, MD: Author.

Axline, V. (1947). *Play therapy.* New York: Ballantine.

Bainbridge, W. L. (2003). Transient students are education dilemma. The Columbus Dispatch, May 24 [On-line]. Available: http://www.schoolmatch.com/Articles/CDMAY03.htm

Baker, C. (1996). *Foundation of bilingual education and bilingualism* (2nd ed.). Bristol, PA: Multilingual Matters.

Banks, J., & Banks, C., Eds. (1993). *Multicultural education: Issues and perspectives.* Boston: Allyn & Bacon.

Baptiste, H. P., Jr., Daniel, L. H., Hackett, J., Moyer, D., Stryker, P., Vasquez, J., Flood, J., & Lapp, D. (2000). *McGraw-Hill Science Grade 2.* New York: McGraw-Hill School Division.

Barbour, A. (1998/99). Home literacy bags promote family involvement. *Childhood Education*, Winter 1998/99, 71–75.

Barbour, A., & Desjean-Perrotta, B. (2002). *Prop box play, 50 themes to inspire dramatic play.* Beltsville, MD: Gryphon House.

Barbour, C., and Barbour, N. H. (2001). *Families, schools, and communities: Building partnerships for educating children.* Columbus, OH: Merrill.

Barbour, N., & Seefeldt, C. (1993). *Developmental continuity across preschool and primary grades.* Wheaton, MD: Association for Childhood Education International.

Beaty, J. (2002). *Observing development of the young child, third edition.* Upper Saddle River, NJ: Merrill Prentice Hall.

Bennett, C. (1926). *History of manual and industrial education up to 1870.* Peoria, IL: Chas. A. Bennett.

Berg, S., Benz, C. R., Lasley, T. J., & Raisch, C. D. (1998). Exemplary technology use in elementary classrooms. *Journal of Research on Computing in Education, 31*(2), 11–126.

Berger, E. (2000). *Parents as partners in education.* Columbus, OH: Merrill.

Berk, L. (1999). *Infants and children: Prenatal through middle childhood.* Boston, MA: Allyn & Bacon.

Bernstein, R. (1999). How sweet it is. *Instructor,* Vol. 108 (7): 23–27.

Bloom, B. (1964). *Stability and change in human characteristics.* New York: John Wiley.

Bodrova, E., & Leong, D. (1996). *Tools of the mind, The Vygotskian approach to early childhood education.* Englewood Cliffs, NJ: Merrill.

Boehm, A. (2001). *Boehm test of basic concepts.* San Antonio, TX: The Psychological Corporation.

Boehm, R. G., Hoone, C., McGowan, T. M., McKinney-Browning, M. C., & Miramontes, O. G. (1997). *La Historia de Texas* (Spanish Edition). New York: Harcourt Brace & Co.

Boston Public School Handbook. (2000). [On-line]. Available: http://www.boston.k12.Ma.us/info/handbk.htm

Bowman, B., & Beyer, E. (1994). Thoughts on technology and early childhood education. In J. L. Wright & D. D. Shade (Eds.). *Young children: Active learners in a technological age* (pp. 19–30). National Association for the Education of Young Children, Washington, DC.

Bowman, B., Donovan, M., & Burns, M. (Eds.). (2000). *Eager to learn, educating our preschoolers.* Washington, D.C.: National Academy Press.

Bowman, B., Donovan, M., & Burns, M., Eds. (2000). *Eager to learn: Educating our preschoolers.* Washington, D.C.: National Academy Press.

Boy Scouts of America. (2004). [On-line]. Available: http://www.scouting.org

Boyd, C. D., Berkin, C., Gay, G., Chase, L. A., Geiger, R., Cummins, J., Kracht, J. B., Gleen, A. D., Pang, V. O., Hahn, C. L., Risinger, C. F., Hickey, M. G., Sanchez, S. M., & Meszaros, B. (2003a). *Scott Foresman Social Studies: Communities Grade 2.* Glenview, IL: Scott Foresman & Co.

Boyd, C. D., Berkin, C., Gay, G., Chase, L. A., Geiger, R., Cummins, J., Kracht, J. B., Gleen, A. D., Pang, V. O., Hahn, C. L., Risinger, C. F., Hickey, M. G., Sanchez, S. M., & Meszaros, B. (2003b). *Scott Foresman Social Studies: People & Places Grade 3.* Glenview, IL: Scott Foresman & Co.

Bracken, B. (1998). *Bracken basic concept scale, revised.* San Antonio, TX: The Psychological Corporation.

Brain Research and Reading. (2001). [On-line]. Available: http://www.schwablearning.org/brainresearchandreading.htm

Braun, S., & Edwards, E. (1971). *History and theory of early childhood education.* Worthington, OH: Charles A. Jones.

Bredekamp, S., & Copple, C. (Eds.). (1997). *Developmentally appropriate practice in early childhood programs, revised edition.* Washington, DC: National Association for the Education of Young Children.

Bredekamp, S., & Rosegrant, T. (Eds.). (1992). *Reaching potentials: Appropriate curriculum and assessment for young children, Vol. 1.* Washington, DC: National Association for the Education of Young Children.

Breggin, P., & Breggin, G. (1995). The hazards of treating "Attention-Deficit/Hyperactivity Disorder" with methylphenidate (Ritalin). *Journal of College Student Psychotherapy, 10* (2), 55–72.

Brewer, J. (2001). *Introduction to early childhood education, preschool through primary grades.* Boston: Allyn & Bacon.

Brindley, R., & Schneider, J. J. (2002). Writing instruction or destruction: Lessons to be learned from fourth grade teachers' perspectives on teaching writing. *Journal of Teacher Education.* 53 (4): 328–341.

Brisk, M. (1998). *Bilingual education from compensatory to quality schooling.* Mahwah, NJ: Lawrence Erlbaum.

Brody, J. (1999). Diet change may avert need for Ritalin. *New York Times,* Sec.: Health and Fitness. Tues, Nov. 2, p. 8.

Buckleitner, W. (1999). The state of children's software evaluation—yesterday, today and in the 21st century. *Information Technology in Childhood Education.* 211–220.

Building Language Arts Skills. (2002). [On-line]. Available: http://www.teachervision.fen/lesson-plans-6403.html

Burk, D., Snider, A., & Symonds, P. (1992). *Math excursions I: Project-based mathematics for first graders.* Boston, MA: Houghton Mifflin.

Burns, P., & Roe, R. (1985). *Informal reading inventory.* Boston, MA: Houghton Mifflin.

California Department of Education. (2000). *Prekindergarten learning & development guidelines.* Sacramento, CA: Author.

California State Board of Education. (1999). *Reading/ language arts framework for California public schools: Kindergarten through grade twelve.* Sacramento: California Department of Education.

Cameron, C. A., & Kang, L. (1997). Bridging the gap between home and school with voice-mail technology. *Journal of Educational Research, 90*(3), 182–191.

Camp Fire USA. (2004). [On-line]. Available: http:// campfire.org

Campbell, F., & Ramey, C. (1999). *Early learning, later success. The Abecedarian Study.* Chapel Hill, NC: Franklin Porter Graham Child Development Center.

Cantrell, S. C. (1999). The effects of literacy instruction on primary students' reading and writing achievement. *Reading Research and Instruction, 39*(20), 3–20.

Carondolet Historical Society. (1989). *History of des peres school and Susan E. Blow's kindergarten.* St. Louis, MO: Author.

Catron, C., & Allen, J. (1999). *Early childhood curriculum, A creative play model, second edition.* Upper Saddle River, NJ: Merrill.

Center for Literacy. (1995). *Parents and schools: Working together* [On-line]. University of Illinois at Chicago. Available: http://www.ncbe.gw.ued/mispubs.flame/ working.htm

Center on Education Governance. (1996). *Assessment of school based management* [On-line]. Available: http:// www.edwebproject.org/edref/sbm2.html

CHADD. (1999). *School discipline: A position paper prepared by the national children and adults with Attention-Deficit/Hyperactivity disorders* [On-line]. Available: http://222.chadd.org/papers/school_ discipline2htm

Chall, J. (1983). *Learning to read: The great debate.* New York: McGraw-Hill.

Chandler, L., & Dahlquist, C. (2002). *Functional assessment: Strategies to prevent and remediate challenging behavior in school settings.* Upper Saddle River, NJ: Merrill.

Chard, S. (1994a). *The project approach: Developing the basic framework.* New York: Scholastic.

Chard, S. (1994b). *The project approach: Developing curriculum with children.* New York: Scholastic.

Charles, R. I., Barnett, C. S., Briars, D. J., Crown, W. D., Johnson, M. L., Leinwand, S. J., Van de Walle, J., Allan, C. R., Cooley, D. A., Elliot, P. C., Ling, P., Ramirez, A. B., Renfro, F. L., & Thompson, M. (1999a). *Scott Foresman-Addison Wesley Math Grade 2.* Glenview, IL: Scott Foresman-Addison Wesley.

Charles, R. I., Barnett, C. S., Briars, D. J., Crown, W. D., Johnson, M. L., Leinwand, S. J., Van de Walle, J., Allan, C. R., Cooley, D. A., Elliot, P. C., Ling, P., Ramirez, A. B., Renfro, F. L., & Thompson, M. (1999b). *Scott Foresman-Addison Wesley Math Grade 3.* Glenview, IL: Scott Foresman-Addison Wesley.

Chen, J. (1998). *Project Spectrum: Early learning activities.* New York: Teachers College Press.

Child Maltreatment (1998). Reports from the states to the National Child Abuse and Neglect Data System. U.S. Dept. of Health & Welfare. [On-line]. Available: http://www.acf.dhhs.gov/programs/ cb/publications/cm98

Children's Defense Fund. (2000). *The state of America's children, yearbook 2000.* Washington, DC: Author.

Children's Defense Fund. (2001). *Issue basics* [On-line]. Available: http://www.cdfactioncouncil.org/Head %20Start%Basics.htm

Civil Rights Act of 1964. Sec. 601; 78 Stat. 252; U.S. C., 2000d. Cited in the Federal Register, 45(92).

Clark, B. (1992). *Growing up gifted: Developing the potential of children at home and at school* (4th ed.). Upper Saddle River, NJ: Merrill.

Clay, M. (1966). *Emergent reading behavior.* Unpublished doctoral dissertation, University of Auckland, New Zealand.

Clay, M. (1985). *The early detection of reading difficulties.* Portsmouth, NH: Heinemann.

Clay, M. (1993). *An observation survey of early literacy achievement.* Portsmouth, NH: Heinemann.

Clcrc.com. (2004). [On-line]. Available: http://clcrc .org

Cohen, M. R., Cooney, T. M., Hawthorne, C. M., McCormack, A. J., Pasachoff, J. M., Pasachoff, N. Rhines, K. L., & Siesnick, I. L. (1991). *Scott Foresman Science Grade 4.* Glenview, IL: Scott Foresman & Company.

Cole, J. (1989). *The magic school bus: Inside the human body.* New York: Scholastic, Inc.

Collier, V. (1987). Age and rate of acquisition of second language for academic purposes. *TESPL Quarterly, 21,* 617–641.

Collins, N., & Shaeffer, M. (1997). Look, listen, and learn to read. *Young Children, 52*(5), 65–67.

Combs, M. (2002). *Reading and writers in primary grades.* Upper Saddle River, NJ: Merrill.

Cooney, T., DiSpezio, M. A., Foots, B. K., Matamoros, A. L., Nyquist, K. B., Ostlund, K. L., Chamot, A. U., Cummins, J., Kahn, G. P., Sipkovich, V., & Weinberg, S. (2000a). *Scott Foresman Science Grade 2.* Glenview, IL: Addison-Wesley Educational Publishers, Inc.

Cooney, T., DiSpezio, M. A., Foots, B. K., Matamoros, A. L., Nyquist, K. B., Ostlund, K. L., Chamot, A. U., Cummins, J., Kahn, G. P., Sipkovich, V., & Weinberg, S. (2000b). *Scott Foresman Science Grade 3.* Glenview, IL: Addison-Wesley Educational Publishers, Inc.

Copley, J. (1999) *Mathematics in the early years.* Reston, VA: National Council of Teachers of Mathematics.

Copley, J. (2000). *The young child and mathematics.* Washington, D.C.: National Association for the Education of Young Children.

Cornell, C. (1999). I hate math! I couldn't learn it and can't teach it. *Childhood Education, 75*(4), 225–230.

Couchenour. D., & Chrisman, K. (2000). *Families, schools and communities.* Albany, NY: Delmar.

Cruickshank, D. R., Bainer, D. L., & Metcalf, K. K. (1999). *The act of teaching.* Boston, MA: McGraw-Hill.

Culatta, R., & Tompkins, J. (1999). *Fundamentals of special education.* Upper Saddle River, NJ: Prentice-Hall.

Cultural Diversity and Early Education. (2001). [On-line]. Available: http://www.nap.edu/reading room/books/earlyed/contents.html

Darling-Hammond, L. (1997). *The right to learn.* San Francisco, CA: Jossey-Bass.

Davidson, J. I. (1989).*Children & computers together in the early childhood classroom.* Albany, NY: Delmar.

Davis, B. C., & Shade, D. D. (2000). Integrate, don't isolate!—Computers in the early childhood curriculum [On-line]. *Eric Digest.* Available: http://ericece.org/pub/digests/1994/shade94.html

Davis, J. (2001). *Modifying classroom centers to enhance intelligence areas.* Unpublished paper. Huntsville, TX: Sam Houston State University.

Davis, L., & Keyser, J. (2001). *Helping children understand the unthinkable: Strategies for helping kids deal with the attacks on the World Trade Center and the Pentagon* [On-line]. Available: http://www.brighthorizons.com/talktochildren/expertarticles

Denby, J. (1995). Elementary kids in parent-teacher conferences. *Education Digest,* November, 45–47.

Depree, H., & Iversen, S. (1994). *Early literacy in the classroom.* Bothell, WA: The Wright Group.

Dewey, J. (1938/1998). *Experience and education: The 60th anniversary edition.* West Lafayette, IN: Kappa Delta Pi.

Diezmann, C. M., & Wafters, J. J. (2000). Catering for mathematically gifted elementary students: Learning from challenging tasks. *Gifted Child Today Magazine.* Vol. 23 (4): 14–21.

Driscoll, M., & Nagel, N. (1999). *Early childhood education birth–8.* Boston: Allyn & Bacon.

Druin, A., & Solomon, C. (1996). *Designing multimedia environments for children.* New York: John Wiley & Sons.

Dugger, Jr., W. E. (2001). Standards for technological literacy. *Phi Delta Kappan, 82*(7), 513–517.

Durkin, D. (1966). *Children who read early.* New York: Teachers College Press.

Early Childhood Intervention 300.7. [On-line]. Available: http://www.ideapractices.org/law/regulations/searchregs/subpartA/Asec300.7php

Early Literacy Technology Project. (2001). *Computer family night* [On-line]. Available: http://www.mcps.k12.md.us/curriculum/littlekids/cfn_text.htm#activities

Ebeling, D. (2000). Adapting your teaching to any learning style. *Phi Delta Kappan, 82*(3), 247–248.

ECS Special Report. (2002). [On-line]. Available: http://www.ecs.org/clearinghouse/22/88//2288.pdf

Education Commission of the States Special Report. (2002). *No state left behind: The challenges and opportunities of ESEA 2001.* [On-line]. Available: http://www.personal.umich.edu/-dlcohen/ESCNo_State_Left_Behind.pdf

Educational Programs That Work. (1994). The Catalogue of the National Diffusion Network. [On-line]. Available: http://www.ed.gov/pubs/EOTW/index.html

Edwards, C., Gandini, L., & Forman, G., Eds. (1998). *The hundred languages of children, second edition.* Greenwich, CT: Ablex Publishing Company.

Edwards, T. G., & Hensien, S. M. (2000). Using probability experiments to foster discourse. *Teaching Children Mathematics 6*(8), 524–529.

Eisenhower National Clearinghouse for Mathematics and Science Education. (2000). NCTM Standards [On-line]. Available: http://www.enc.org/reform/journals/enc2280/nf_2801.html

Elkind, D. (2001). How to help your children become good readers. [On-line]. Available: http://www.child-reading-tips.com/david-elkind-child-development.htm

Elmore, R. F., & Fuhrman, S. H. (2001). Holding schools accountable: Is it working? *Phi Delta Kappan, 83*(1), 67–72.

Engel, B. (1995). *Considering children's art: Why and how to value their works.* Washington, DC: National Association for the Education of Young Children.

Equity and Cultural Diversity. (2002). [On-line]. Available: http://www.eric-web.tc.columbia.edu/equity

Erikson, E. (1963). *Childhood and society* (2nd ed.). New York: Norton.

Escobedo, T. H., & Evans, S. (1997). A comparison of child-tested early childhood education software with professional ratings. Paper presented at the Annual Meeting of the American education Research Association. Chicago, IL, March 28.

Evans, E. (1971). *Contemporary influences in early childhood education.* New York: Holt, Rinehart and Winston.

Even Start Family Literacy Program. (1998). *The national evaluation of the Even Start Family Literacy Program* [On-line]. Available: http://www.ed.gov/pubs/EvenStart/cj1program.html

Everyday Mathematics—Grade 4. (1999). Chicago, IL: Everyday Learning Corp.

Expectations of excellence: Curriculum standards for social studies. (1994). Bulletin 89. Washington, DC: National Council for the Social Studies.

Fairfax County Public Schools. (2002). [On-Line]. Available: http://www.fcps.k12.va.us

Family Educational Rights and Privacy Act. (1974).

Federal Emergency Management Agency (FEMA). (2001). After the disaster: A children's mental health checklist [On-line]. Available: http://www.fema.gov

Feeney, S., & Freeman, N. K. (1999). *Ethics and the early childhood educator.* Washington, DC: National Association for the Education of Young Children.

Feldman, D. (1994). *Beyond universals in cognitive development, second edition.* Stamford, CT: Ablex Publishing.

Fennimore, B. S. (1989). *Child advocacy for early childhood educators.* New York: Teachers College Press.

Ferreiro, E., & Teberosky, A. (1982). *Literacy before schooling.* Exeter, NH: Heinemann.

Fields, J., & Boesser, C. (2002) *Constructive guidance and discipline.* Upper Saddle River, NJ: Merrill.

Fields, M., & Spangler, K. (2000). *Let's begin reading right* (4th ed.). Upper Saddle River, NJ: Merrill.

Flaxman, E., & Inger, M. (1992). Parents and schooling in the 1990's. *Education Digest,* May, 2–7.

Fleming, D. (1994). *Barnyard Banter.* New York: Holt.

Florida Department of Education. (2002). Curriculum, instruction & assessment [On-line]. Available: http://www.firn.edu/doe/sas/fw/fwaprubr.htm

Frankenburg, W., & Dodds, J. 1992. *Denver II training manual.* Denver, CO: Denver Developmental Materials.

Freedman, A. (1996). *The computer desktop encyclopedia.* Point Pleasant, PA: Computer Language Company.

Freeman, D., & Freeman, Y. (1994). *Between worlds: Access to second language acquisition.* Portsmouth, NH: Heinemann.

Freeman, E. B., and Person, D. G. (1992). *Using nonfiction trade books in the elementary classroom from ants to zeppelins.* Urbana, IL: National Council of English Teachers.

Frieman, B., & Berkeley, T. (2002). Encouraging fathers to participate in the school experiences of young children: The teacher's role. *Early Childhood Education Journal, 29*(3), 209–213.

Friend, M., & Bursuck, W. (1999). *Including students with special needs* (2nd ed.). Boston: Allyn & Bacon.

Froebel, F. (1912). *The education of man.* Trans. Hailmann. New York: Appleton.

Frost, J., Wortham, S., & Reifel, S. (2001). *Play and child development.* Upper Saddle River, NJ: Merrill Prentice Hall.

Fuson, K. C., Carroll, W. M., & Drueck, J. V. (2000). Achievement results for second and third graders using the standards-based curriculum *Everyday Mathematics. Journal for Research in Mathematics Education, 31*(3), 277–295.

Galena Park ISD Handbook. (2000). Houston, TX: Author.

Garan, E. (2001). Beyond the smoke and mirrors. A critique of the National Reading Report on phonics. *Phi Delta Kappan, 82*(7), 500–506.

Gardner, H. (1983). *Frames of mind.* New York: Basic Books.

Gentry, J. R., Harris, K. R., Graham, S., & Zutell, J. (1998a) *Zaner-Bloser, Spell It—Write! Grade 3.* Columbus, OH: Zaner-Bloser, Inc.

Gentry, J. R., Harris, K. R., Graham, S., & Zutell, J. (1998a) *Zaner-Bloser, Spell It—Write! Grade 4.* Columbus, OH: Zaner-Bloser, Inc.

Gersten, R., & Baker, S. (2000). What we know about effective instructional practices for English-language learners. *Exceptional Children, 66*(4), 454–470.

Gesell Institute of Human Development. [On-line]. Available: http://www.gesellinstitute.org

Gestwicki, C. (1999). *Developmentally appropriate practice, Curriculum and development in early education* (2nd ed.). New York: Delmar.

Ginsberg, M. R. (2001). *Helping children cope with disaster* [On-line]. Available: http://www.bright horizons.com/talktochildren/expertarticles/NAEYC article.htm.

Girl Scouts of America. (2004). [On-line]. Available: http://www.girlscouts.org

girlsandboystown. (2001). [On-line]. Available: http://www.girlsandboystown.org/home.htm

Goals 2000. [On-line]. Available: http://www.ed .gov/legislation/GOALS2000/TheAct/index.html

Goertz, M. E. (2001). Redefining government roles in an era of standards-based reform. *Phi Delta Kappan, 83*(1), 62–66.

Goffin, S., & Lombardi, J. (1988). *Speaking out: early childhood advocacy.* Washington, DC: NAEYC.

Goleman, D. (1995). *Emotional intelligence.* New York: Bantam.

Goodman, Y. (1986). *Emergent literacy: Writing and reading.* Norwood, NJ: Ablex.

Gordon, A., & Browne, K. (2003). *Beginnings & beyond* (6th ed.). Albany, NY: Delmar.

Gordon, A., & Klass, D. (1979). *They need to know: How to teach children about death.* Englewood Cliffs, NJ: Macmillan.

Gore, D. S., & Roumagoux, D. V. (1983). Wait-time as a variable in sex related differences during fourth grade mathematics instruction. *Journal of Educational Research.* Vol. 76 (5): 273–275.

Grandin, T. (1999). *Teaching tips for children and adults with autism* [On-line]. Available: http://www .autism.org/temple/tips.html

Graves, M. (1987). Roles of instruction in vocabulary development. In M. G. McKeown & M. E. Curtis (Eds.) *The nature of vocabulary acquisition* (pp. 165–184). Hillsdale, NJ: Lawrence Erlbaum.

Great Books Foundation. (2002). *Junior great books.* [On-line]. Available: http://www.greatbooks.org/ programs/junior/index.shtml

Green, J. E., & Smyser, S. O. (1996). *The teacher portfolio.* Lancaster, PA: Technomic.

Greene, J., Biederman, J., Faraone, S., Wilens, T., Mick, E., & Blier, H. (1999). Further validation of social impairment as a predictor of substance use disorders. Findings from a sample of siblings of boys with and without ADHD. *Journal of Clinical Child Psychology, 28*(3), 349–354.

Greenman, J. (2001). Answering young children's questions [On-line]. Available: http://www.bright horizons.com/talktochildren/expertarticles/ answering_young_children.htm

Gruber, B. (1999). Boost learning with word walls. *Teaching K–8.* Sept. [On-line]. Available: http:// www.TeachingK-8.com

Gutloff, K. (1995). Do parents make you nervous? *NEA Today, 14*(4), 4–5.

H. R. 1350: Summary of Major Changes. (2003). [On-line]. Available: http://www.IdaAmerica.org/ HR1350SummaryFinalBill5–7-03.htm

Hackney, C. S., & Lucas, V. H. (1998). *Zaner-Bloser spell it—write it! Grade 2.* Columbus, OH: Zaner-Bloser, Inc.

Hackney, C. S., & Lucas, V. H. (1998). *Zaner-Bloser spell it—write it! Grade 4.* Columbus, OH: Zaner-Bloser, Inc.

Hackney, C., & Lucas, V. (1993). *Zaner-Bloser Handwriting, a way to self expression.* Columbus, OH: Zaner Bloser.

Hallahan, D., & Kauffman, J. (1976). *Introduction to learning disabilities.* Englewood Cliffs, NJ: Prentice Hall, Inc.

Hart, J. (1995, February 16). Reading and righting: hunting lost values. *The Boston Globe,* pp. 1, 28.

Hasbrouck, J., Ihnot, C., & Rogers, G. (2000). "Read Naturally": A strategy to increase oral reading fluency. *Reading Research and Instruction, 38*(2).

Haugland, S. (1999a). *The developmental scale for software.* Cape Girardeau, MO: K. I. D. S. & Computers.

Haugland, S. W. (1999b). What role should technology play in young children's learning? *Young Children, 54*(6), 26–31.

Haugland, S. W. (2000). Early childhood classrooms in the 21st century: Using computers to maximize learning. *Young Children, 55*(1): 12–18.

Haugland, S. W. (2000). Software Evaluation [On-line]. Available: http://childrenandcomputers.com

Haugland, S. W., & Gerzog, G. (1998). *The developmental software scale for web sites.* Cape Girardeau, MO: K. I. D. S. & Computers.

Haugland, S., & Wright, J. L. (1997). *Young children and technology: A world of discovery.* Boston: Allyn & Bacon.

Hawaii Department of Education. (2002). Hawaii technology planning and goals 2002. [On-line]. Available: http://www.k12.hi.us/~challeng/Goals _2000/Sect_1.html

Head Start Multicultural Task Force. (2001). *Multicultural principles for Head Start programs* [On-line]. U.S. Department of Health and Human Services. Available: http://www.bmcc.org/Headstart/Cultural/

Helm, J., Beneke, S., & Steinheimer, K. (1998). *Windows on learning: Documenting children's work.* New York: Teachers College Press.

Henderson, J. R. (2000). ICYousee: t is for thinking [On-line]. Ithaca College Library. Available: http://www.ithaca.edu/library/training/hott.html

Hendrick, J. (2003). *Total learning: Developmental curriculum for young children.* Boston: Allyn & Bacon.

Hendrick, J., (Ed.). (1997). *First steps toward teaching the Reggio way.* Upper Saddle River, NJ: Merrill.

Henniger, M. (2002). *Teaching young children: An introduction, third edition.* Upper Saddle River, NJ: Prentice Hall.

Herr, J., & Libby, Y. (1994). *Early childhood writing centers.* New York: International Thomson Publishing.

Hewes, D., Ed. (1976). *NAEYC's first half century 1926–1976.* Washington, D.C.: National Association for the Education of Young Children.

Hill, A. M. (1996). Technology in the elementary school. *The Technology Teacher, 55*(6), 19–23.

Hill, P. (1892, 1992). *Kindergarten: A reprint from the American educator encyclopedia, 100th anniversary.* Olney, MD: Association for Childhood Education International.

Hills, T. (1987). *Early screening inventory.* Urbana: IL: ERIC Clearinghouse on Elementary and Early Childhood Education.

Hohmann, M. (1995). *Educating young children.* Ypsilanti, MI: High/Scope Press.

Hohmann, M., Banet, B., & Weikart, D. (1979). *Young children in action: A manual for preschool educators.* Ypsilanti, MI: High/Scope Press.

Holloway, J. (2000). The promise and pitfalls of site-based management. [On-line] *Educational Leadership, 57*(7). Available: http://www.asch.org/readingroom/edlead/0004/holloway.html

Honig, B. (2001). *Teaching our children to read.* (2nd Ed.) Thousand Oaks, CA: Corwin Press, Inc.

Houghton Mifflin Explora Texas. (1997). Boston: Houghton Mifflin Company.

Houston Chronicle. (2001, September 9). *Teacher pay tied to skill on computer,* p. 40A.

Huffman, L., Mehlinger, S., & Kerivan, A. (2000). *Off to a good start.* [On-line]. Available: http://www .nimh.nih.gov/childhp/goodstart.cfm

Hunt, G. H., Touzel, T. J., & Wiseman, D. G. (1999). *Effective teaching: Preparation and implementation.* Springfield, IL: Charles C Thomas.

Hunt, J. (1961). *Intelligence and experience.* New York: Ronald Press.

Hymes, J. (1955). *Behavior and misbehavior.* Englewood Cliffs, NJ: Prentice Hall.

Hymes, J. (1968). *Teaching the child under six.* Columbus, OH: Charles E. Merrill.

IDEA. (1997). [On-line]. Available: http://www.ed .gov/offices/OSERS/policy/IDEAupdates.html

Ilg, F., Ames, L. B., Haines, J., & Gillespie, C. (1978). *School readiness* (rev. ed.). New York: Harper & Row.

Ilg, F., Ames, L., Haines, J., & Gillespie, C. (1987). School readiness. New York: Harper & Row.

Individuals with disabilities education act (IDEA). (2001). Washington, DC: U.S. Government Printing Office.

Ingraham v. Wright. (1977), 430 U.S. 651.

Inquiry and the National Science Education Standards. (2000). Washington, D.C.: National Academy Press.

Instructional Fair, Inc. (1988). Chocolate fever. *Reading to Your Class IF8533* (p. 34).

Interfaith Center for Peace. (2004). [On-line]. Available: http://peace-center.org/mediation.html

International Society for Technology in Education. (2000). Homepage. [On-line] Available: http://www.ISTE.org

International Technology Education Association. (2000). *Standards for technological literacy: Content for the study of technology.* Author: Reston, VA.

Itard, J. 1932. *Wild boy of Averyon.* New York: The Century Company.

Itzkoff, S. (1986). *How we learn to read.* New York: Paideia.

Jalongo, M. (2000). *Early childhood language arts* (2nd ed.). Boston: Allyn & Bacon.

Jalongo, M., & Isenberg, J. (2000). *Exploring your role: A practitioner's introduction to early childhood education.* Upper Saddle River, NJ: Prentice Hall.

Jensen, P., Kettle, L., Roper, M., Sloan, M., Dulcan, M., Hoven, C., Bird, H., Bauermeister, J., & Payne, J. (1999). Are stimulants overprescribed? Treatment of ADHD in four U.S. Communities. *Journal of American Academy of Child Adolescence Psychiatry, 38*(7), 797–804.

Jody, M., & Saccardi, M. (1998). *Using computers to teach literature.* Urbana, IL: National Council of Teachers of English.

Johnson, R. T., Johnson, D. W., & Holubec, E. J. (1987). *Structuring cooperative learning: Lesson plan for teachers/editors.* Edina, MN: Interaction Book Co.

Jones, C. (1991). *Primary grade assessment: What it means and what it does.* Austin, TX: Texas Association for the Education of Young Children.

Juel, C. (1994). *Learning to read and write in one elementary school.* New York: Springer-Verlag.

Karabenick, S., Ed. (1998). *Strategic help seeking: Implications for learning and teaching.* Mahwah, NJ: L. Erlbaum Associates.

Katz, L., & Chard, S. (2000). *Engaging children's minds: The project approach.* Norwood, NJ: Ablex.

Katz, L., & Helm, J. (2001). *Young investigators: The project approach in the early years.* Williston, VT: Teachers College Press.

Katz, L., & McClelland, D. (1997). *Fostering children's social competence: The teacher's role.* Washington, DC: National Association for the Education of Young Children.

Katz, L., Evangelou, D., & Hartman, J. (1990). *The case for mixed-age grouping in early education.* Washington, DC: National Association for the Education of Young Children.

Kauchak, D., & Eggen, P. (Eds.). (1998). *Learning and teaching: Research-based methods* Boston: MA: Allyn & Bacon.

Kelly, J. (1997). Improving problem solving through drawings. *Teaching Children Mathematics.* Vol 6 (1): 48–51.

Kerman, S., & Martin, M. (1980). *Teacher expectations and student achievement.* Bloomington, IL: Phi Beta Kappa.

Kindergarten teacher reading academies. (1999). Austin, TX: Texas Education Agency.

Kinesthetic Learners. (2000). *Characteristics of kinesthetic learners* [On-line]. Available: http://yk.psu.edu/learncenter/acskills/kinesthetic.html

King, E., Chipman, M., & Cruz-Janzen, M. (1994). *Educating young children in a diverse society.* Boston: Allyn & Bacon.

Klauke, A. (1988). Magnet schools (ERIC Digest Series No. EA 26). [On-line]. Available: http://www.ericfacility.net/ericdigests/ed293225.html

Kohn, A. (1993). *Punished by rewards.* Boston: Houghton Mifflin.

Kohn, A. (2001). Fighting the tests: a practical guide to rescuing our schools. *Phi Delta Kappan, 82*(2), 349–357.

Kotulak, R. (1997). *Inside the brain.* Kansas City: Andrews McMeel.

Krashen, S. (2001). Critique of the National Reading Panel report on fluency. *Phi Delta Kappan, 83*(2), 349–357.

Laing, S. (2001). *Annual report 2000–01 of the state superintendent of public instruction.* [On-line]. Available: http://www.usoe.k12.ut.us/siteindex.htm

Laosa, L. M. (1980). Maternal teaching strategies in Chicano and Anglo-American families: the influence of culture and education on maternal behavior. *Child Development, 51,* 759–765.

Lasater, M., Johnson, M., Fitzgerald, M., & Simpson, C. (1999). *Paraeducators: Lifelines in the classroom, module four.* LR Consulting.

Learning First Alliance. (1998). Every child reading. *Learning First Alliance Action Plan.* [On-line]. Available: http://www.learningfirst.org

Lee, F. (1995). Strategies for involving reticent parents. *Young Children, 50,* 4–7.

Leo, J. (1999, November 15). C is for character. *U.S. News & World Report,* p. 20.

Leslie, L., & Caldwell, J. *Qualitative reading inventory— 3.* New York: Longman.

Levine, L., & McCloskey, M. (2002). *ABCs of EFL with young learners* [On-line]. Available: http://www.mindspring.com/_mimcc/ABCs%20of%20EFL%20with%20YOUNG%20LEARNERS.htm

Lights on Afterschool. (2002). About Lights on Afterschool [On-line]. Available: http://www.afterschoolalliance.org/lights_2002/faq.cfm

Loveless, T. (2001). *The great curriculum debate: How should we teach reading and math?* Washington, DC: Brookings Institution Press.

Lowenfeld, V., & Brittain, W. (1947/1967). *Creative and mental growth.* New York: Macmillan.

Lucas, T., Henze, R., and Donato, R. (1990). Promoting the success of Latino language-minority students: An exploratory study of six high schools. *Harvard Educational Review.*

MacDonald, S. (1996). *The portfolio and its use.* Little Rock, AR: Southern Early Childhood Association.

MacGinite, W., & MacGinite, R. (2000). *Gates-Macginite silent reading test* (4th ed.). Itasca, IL: Riverside.

Machado, J. (1999). *Early childhood experiences in language arts.* Albany, NY: Delmar.

Manes, S. (1990). *Chocolate-covered ants.* New York: Scholastic.

Marion, M. (2003). *Guidance of young children* (6th ed.). Columbus, OH: Merrill.

Marotz, L., Cross, M., & Rush, J. (2001). *Health, safety, and nutrition for the young child* (5th ed.). Albany, NY: Delmar Thomson Learning.

Martin, B. (1987). *Here are my hands.* New York: Henry Holt.

Massachusetts Department of Education. (2002). School choice [On-line]. Available: http://finance1 .doe.mass.edu/schoice/1_schoice.html

Mastering challenging mathematics by the end of eighth grade. (1997). Washington, DC: Department of Education.

Mastropieri, M. A., Scruggs, T. E., & Shiah, R-L. (1997). Can computers teach problem-solving strategies to students with mild mental retardation? *Remedial and Special Education, 18*(3), 157–165.

Mazzeo, D. A., & Jones, M. R. (2002). Children's literature that encourages the identity development of interracial children. *Dimensions of Early Childhood, 30*(3), 13–19.

McAfee, O., & Leong, D. (2002). *Assessing and guiding young children's development and learning* (3rd ed.). Boston: Allyn & Bacon.

McCallum, A., Strong, W., Thoburn, T., & Williams, P. (1990). *Language arts today.* New York, N. Y: Macmillan.

McColskey, W., & McMunn, N. (2000). Strategies for dealing with high-stakes state tests. *Phi Delta Kappan, 82*(2), 115–120.

McCracken, J. (1993). *Valuing diversity: The primary years.* Washington, DC: National Association for the Education of Young Children.

McDonald, D. (1979). *Music in our lives: The early years.* Washington, DC: National Association for the Education of Young Children.

McGee, L., & Richgels, D. (2000). *Literacy's beginnings: Supporting young readers and writers, third edition.* Needham, MA: Allyn & Bacon.

McGraw-Hill Science. (2000). Fourth grade edition. Farmington, NY: McGraw-Hill School Division.

Miller, W. (2000). *Strategies for developing emergent literacy.* Boston: McGraw-Hill.

Missouri Department of Elementary and Secondary Education. (2002). Career ladder frequently asked questions [On-line]. Available: http://www.dese .state.mo.us/divteachqual/careerladder/FAQs.htm

Mitchell, A., Stoney, L., & Dichter, H. (2001). *Financing child care in the United States: An expanded catalog of current strategies.* Kansas City, MO: Ewing Marion Kauffman Foundation.

Montessori, M. (1914). *Dr. Montessori's own handbook.* New York: Schocken Books.

Morrison, G. (2001). *Early childhood education today* (8th ed.). Columbus, OH: Merrill.

Morrow, L., & Asbury, E. (2001). *Literacy activities for early childhood classrooms.* Boston: Allyn & Bacon.

Murphy, D., & Goffin, S. (Eds.). (1992). *Understanding the possibilities: A curriculum guide for project construct.* Jefferson City, MO: Missouri Department of Elementary and Secondary Education.

Music Educators National Conference. (1994). *National standards for arts education.* Reston, VA: Author.

Nagy, M. (1948). The child's view of death. *Journal of Genetic Psychology, 73,* 3–27.

National Association for Bilingual Education. (2003). Legislation and policy. [On-line] Available: http:// www.nabe.org

National Association for the Education of Young Children. *NAEYC's First Half Century 1926–1976.* (1976). *Young Children, 50*(6), 462–476.

National Association for the Education of Young Children. (1987). *Standardized testing of young children 3 through 8 years of age.* Washington, DC: Author.

National Association for the Education of Young Children. (1997). Standards of ethical behavior. [On-line]. Available: http://www.naeyc.org

National Association for the Education of Young Children. (2002). *Position statement on linguistic and cul-*

tural diversity. [On-line]. Available: http://www .naeyc.org

National Association for the Education of Young Children. (1993). Position on inclusion. [On-line]. Available: http://www.naeyc.org/resources/position _statements/psdin98.htm

National Association for the Education of Young Children. (1996). Position on technology and young children. [On-line]. Available: http://www.naeyc. org/resources/position_statements/psdin98.htm

National Association for the Education of Young Children Home Page. (2002). [On-line]. Available: http://www .naeyc.org

National Association for the Education of Young Children and the International Reading Association. (1998). NAEYC/IRA position statement: Learning to read and write: Developmentally appropriate practices for young children. [On-line]. Available: http://www.naeyc.org/resources/position -statementspsdin98.htm

National Association for the Education of Young Children and the International Reading Association. (1998). NAEYC/IRA position statement: Learning to read and write: Developmentally appropriate practices for young children. *Young Children 53*(4): 30–46.

National Association for the Education of Young Children & National Association of Early Childhood Specialists in State Departments of Education. (2003). *Early childhood curriculum: Assessment and program evaluation.* Washington, DC: Author. [On-line]. Available: http://www.naeyc.org/resources/ positionstatements/pdf

National Association of State Boards of Education. (1991). *Caring communities: Supporting young children and families.* Alexandria, VA: Author.

National Association of State Directors of Special Education. (2002). *Implementing the No Child Left Behind Act: What It Means for IDEA.* [On-line]. Available: http://www.nasdse.org/downloadnclb .htm

National Association of Student Councils. (2004). *Meet nasc.* [On-line]. Available: http://www.nasc .us/meetnasc

National Center for Education Statistics. (1998). Instructional Strategies. [On-line] Available: http:// nces.ed.gov

National Center for Education Statistics. (2000). The nation's report card: Fourth-grade reading 2000.

[On-line]. Available: http://nces.ed.gov/nations reportcard/pubs/main2000/2001499.asp

National Center for Education Statistics. (2002). *Did you know?* [On-line]. Available: http://nces.ed.gov

National Center for Research on Cultural Diversity and Second Language Learning. (1995). *Fostering second language development in young children* (ERIC Digest #386950). Washington, DC: ERIC Clearinghouse on Language and Linguistics.

National Clearinghouse for Bilingual Education. (1995). *Ask NCBE.* January 20.

National Clearinghouse on Child Abuse and Neglect. Statistical information (2000, March). [On-line]. Available: http://www.calib.com/nccanch

National Coalition to Abolish Corporal Punishment in Schools. (2001). U.S. Statistics on Corporal Punishment by State & Race. [On-line]. Available: http://www.stophitting.com/NCACPS

National Council for the Social Studies. (1996). *Standards and position statements.* [On-line]. Available: http://www.socialstudies.org/standards/l.4html

National Council of Teachers of Mathematics. (2000). *Principles and standards for school mathematics* [On-line]. Available: http://standards.nctm.org/ document

National Education Association. 2002. [On-line]. Available: http://www.nea.org/

National Education Goals Panel. (2001). [On-line]. Available: http://www.negp.gov

National Educational Technology Standards. (2001). [On-line]. Available: http://cnets.iste.org

National Head Start Association. [On-line]. Available: http://www.nhsa.org

National Program for Playground Safety. (2001). *American's playground: Report card.* [On-line]. Available: http://www.uni.edu/playground/report/blank_ report.html

National Reading Panel. (2000). *The report of the National Reading Panel.* (NIH Pub. No. 00–4754.) Jessup, MD: National Institute for Literacy.

National Science Teachers Association. (2004). [On-line]. Available: http://www.nsta.org/programs/ craftsman

National Study of School Evaluation. (2001). *Principles of teaching effectiveness, early childhood programs.* Schaumburg, IL: National Study of School Evaluation.

National Survey Gauges Parent Perceptions of State-Mandated, Standardized Tests. (2000). [On-line].

Available: http://www.ascd.org/cms/index.cfm? TheViewID=1287

National Task Force on School Readiness. (1991). *Caring communities Supporting young children and families.* Alexandria, VA: National Association of State Boards of Education.

Nebraska Department of Education. (1999). *Mathematics standards.* Lincoln, NE: Author.

Neugebauer, B. (1992). *Cultural Diversity.* [On-line]. Available: http://www.esu3.org/ectc/media/bibs/diversity.pdf

Neuman, M., & Bennett, J. (2001, November). Starting strong: Policy implications for early childhood education and care in the U.S. *Phi Delta Kappan, 83*(1), 246–254.

Neuman, S. B., Copple, C., & Bredekamp, S. (1999). *Learning to read and write, Developmentally appropriate practices for young children.* Washington, DC: National Association for the Education of Young Children.

New York State Department of Education. (2000). *The BALANCED VIEW: Early childhood education, Part 1: What research tells us.* Author.

New York State Department of Education. (2002). *Changes in allowable testing accommodations on elementary and intermediate level tests* [On-line]. Available: http://www.vesid.nysed.gov/specialed/publications/policy/changeaccom.htm

Newman, S., & Dickinson, D. (2001). *Handbook of early literacy research.* New York: Guilford Press.

Nilson, B. (2001). *Week by week, Plans for observing and recording young children* (2nd ed.). Albany, NY: Delmar/Thomson Learning.

Nimmo, E., & Nimmo, J. (1994). *Emergent curriculum.* Washington, D.C.: National Association for the Education of Young Children.

No Child Left Behind Act Fact Sheet. (2002). U.S. Dept. of Education [On-line]. Available: http://www.ed.gov/offices/OESE/esea/factsheet.html

No State Left Behind: The challenges and opportunities of ESEA 2001. (2002). Denver, CO: Education Commission of the States.

Nord, C., Brimhall, D., & West, J. (1998). Dad's involvement in their kids' schools. *Education Digest,* March, 29–31.

North Carolina Department of Public Instruction. (1999). *Demonstrating grade level work critical to student promotion.* Raleigh, NC: Author.

Northwest Regional Educational Laboratory. (1999). *After-school programs: Good for kids, Good for communities.* [On-line]. Available: http://www.nwrel.org/request/jan99

Nova. (2001). [On-line]. Available: http://www.pbs.org/wgbh/nova/teachers/Activities/2412_barrier.html

Nurss, J. (2000). *Metropolitan readiness tests (MRT-6), level 2.* San Antonio, TX: The Psychological Corporation.

Nurss, J., & McGaurran, M. (1987). *Early readiness inventory.* San Antonio, TX: Psychological Corporation.

Nurss, J., & McGauvan, M. (2000). *Metropolitan reading readiness tests, MRT-6, Level 2.* San Antonio, TX: The Psychological Corporation.

Office of Special Education Programs. (1999). Children with ADD/ADHD—topic brief [On-line]. Available: http://www.ed.gov/offices/OSERS/Policy/IDEA/brief6.html

Olson, L. (2002). Inadequate yearly gains are predicted. [On-line]. *Education Week,* April, 3. Available: http://www.edweek.com/ew/newstory.cfm?slug=29ayp.h21

Orem, R. (Ed.). (1974). *Montessori, Her method and the movement.* New York: Putnam.

Orlick, T. (1978). *The cooperative sorts and games book.* New York: Pantheon Books.

Ortega, C., & Ortega, R. (1995). Integrated elementary technology education. *The Technology Teacher, 54*(5), 11–16.

Pancheri, C., & Prater, M. (1999). What teachers and parents should know about Ritalin. *Teaching Exceptional Children,* March/April, 20–26.

Parents as Teachers. (2000). *About Parents as Teachers* [On-line]. Available: http://www.patnc.org

Parent-Teacher Association. (2001). [On-line] Available: http://www.pta.org

Parette, H., & Petch-Hogan, B. (2000). Approaching families: Facilitating culturally/linguistically diverse family involvement. *Teaching Exceptional Children, 33*(2), 4–10.

Parten, M. (1932). Social participation among preschool children. *Journal of Abnormal and Social Psychology, 27,* 243–262.

Peck, J., McCaig, G., & Sapp, M. (1988). *Kindergarten policies: What is best for children?* Washington, DC: National Association for the Education of Young Children.

Peck, N., & Shores, E. (1994). *A checklist for diversity in early childhood education and care.* Little Rock, AR: Southern Early Childhood Education.

Pennsylvania Department of Education. (2002). *Academic standards for mathematics.* [On-line]. Available: http://www.pde.state.us

Perfection Learning Corporation. (1993). *California achievement test.* Logan, UT: Author.

Perrone, V. (1991). *ACEI position paper on standardized testing* [On-line]. Available: http://www.udel.edu/bateman/acei/onstandard.thm#children

Perrone, V. (1994). *101 educational conversations with your 4th grader.* Broomhall, PA: Chelsea House Publishers.

Perrone, V. (1991). *Some hard questions about standardized testing.* Olney, MD: Association for Childhood Education International.

Peters, J. M. (1996). *A sampler of national science education standards.* Upper Saddle River, NJ: Merrill.

Phi Delta Kappa. (1980). *Teacher expectations and student achievement.* Bloomington, IN: Phi Delta Kappa.

Phipps, P. (1997). *Multiple intelligences in the early childhood classroom.* Columbus, OH: SRA McGraw-Hill.

Piaget, J. (1962). *Play, dreams and imitation in childhood.* New York: Norton.

Piaget, J. (1977). *The development of thought: Equilibration of cognitive structures.* New York: Viking.

Pierangelo, R., & Giuliani, G. (1998). *Special educators' complete guide to 109 diagnostic tests.* West Nyack, NY: Center for Applied Research in Education.

Promising Practices: New Ways to Improve Teacher Quality. (1998). The induction of new teachers [On-line]. Available: http://www.ed/gov/pubs/PromPractice/chapter5.html

Public Law 94–142. (1992). The individuals with disabilities education act [On-line]. Available: http://www.thearc.org/faqs/p194142.html

Public Schools of North Carolina. (2001). [On-line]. Available: http://www.dpi.state.nc.us

Quam, S. (1995). *First kindergarten in the United States* (3rd ed.). Watertown, WI: Watertown Historical Society.

Raines, S., & Canady, R. (1990). *The whole language kindergarten.* New York: Teachers College Press.

Rau, D. (1971). *Shoo, Crow! Shoo!* Minneapolis: Compass Point Books.

Reading strategies that assist content area reading. (2002). [On-line]. Available: http://www/sarasota.k12.fl.us/sarasota/interdiscrdg.htm

Reksten, L. E. (2000). *Using technology to increase student learning.* Thousand Oaks, CA: Corwin Press.

Reynolds, E. (2001). *Guiding young children, third edition.* Mountain View, CA: Mayfield Publishing Company.

Rich, S. (1985). The writing suitcase. *Young Children,* July, 42–44.

Richards, D. (1997). Child find and problem section 504 identification issues. Austin, TX: Richards Lindsay & Martin, L. L. P.

Risinger, C. (1999). Teaching social studies with the Internet [On-line]. *ERIC Digest.* Available: http://www.ed.gov/databases/ERIC_Digests/ed435582.html

Roberts, J. (2001a). THE Journal's state of the states survey. *Technological Horizons in Education Journal, 28*(10), 40–51.

Roberts, J. (2001b). Standards for technological literacy. *Phi Delta Kappan, 82*(7), 513–517.

Roberts, R. (1965). *Vocational and practical arts education.* New York: Harper & Row.

Robinson, A., & Stark, D. (2002). *Advocates in action: Making a difference for young children.* Washington, DC: National Association for the Education of Young Children.

Rogers, A. (1998, December 7). The brain: Thinking differently. *Newsweek.*

Rothenberg, D. (1995, May). Full-day kindergarten programs. *Eric Digest* (EDO-PS-95–4).

Rousseau, J. (1762/1947). *Emile.* London: Everyman Paperback Classics.

Ryan, L. (1990). Picture-based augmentative communication systems for autistic students. Paper presented at the Mid-South Conference on Communicative Disorders, Memphis, TN.

Sanchez, T. R. (1998). Using stories about heroes to teach values. *Eric Digest* (ED_NO: ED424190).

Sandall, S., McLean, M., & Smith, B., Eds. (2000). *DEC Recommended practices in early intervention/early childhood special education.* Denver, CO: Council for Exceptional Children.

Sanders, S. (2002). *Active for life, Developmentally appropriate movement programs for young children.* Washington, DC: National Association for the Education of Young Children.

Scarcella, R. (1990). *Teaching language minority students in the regular classroom.* Englewood Cliffs, NJ: Prentice Hall.

Schatschneider, C., Francis, D., Foorman, B., Fletcher, J., & Mehta, P. (1999). The dimensionality of phonological awareness: An application of item response Theory. *Journal of Educational Psychology, 91,* 439–449.

Schattman, R., & Benay, J. (1992). Inclusiveness transforms special education for the 1900s. *Education Digest, 5,* 23–26.

Schiller, P. (1999). *Start smart!* Beltsville, MD: Gryphon House.

Schmaus, L. (1996). Parents share in school decision-making. *Education Digest,* April, 44–47.

Schmit, J., Alper, S., Raschke, D., & Ryndak, D. (2000). Effects of using a photographic cueing package during routine school transitions with a child who has autism. *Mental Retardation, 38*(2), 131–137.

Scieszka, J. (1989). *The true story of the three little pigs.* New York: Viking Kestrel.

Scott Foresman Reading—Grade 4. (2000). Glenview, IL.: Addison-Wesley Educational Publishers Inc.

Seefeldt, C. & Barbour, N. (1998). *Early childhood education: An introduction* (4th ed.). Columbus, OH: Merrill.

Shade, D. D. (1996). Care and cleaning of your computer. *Early Childhood Education Journal, 23*(3), 165–168.

Shonkoff, J., & Phillips, D. (Eds.). (2000). *From neurons to neighborhoods: The science of early childhood development.* Washington, DC: National Academy Press.

Shores, E., & Grace, C. (1998). *The portfolio book.* Beltsville, MD: Gryphon House, Inc.

Shores, E. (1997). *Developmentally appropriate assessment (the DLM early childhood professional library 1).* New York: Delmar Publishers.

Silber, K. (1965). Pestalozzi: The man and his work (2nd ed.). London: Routledge and Kegan Paul.

Siler, C. R. 1998. Spatial dynamics: An alternative teaching tool in the social studies. *ERIC Digest.* [On-line]. Available: http://www.ed.gov/databases/ERIC_Digests/ed415179.html

Site-based management: Boon or boondoggle? (2002). Walden University. [On-line]. Available: http://www.education-world.com/a_admin176.shtml

Skinner, B. (1968). *The technology of teaching.* New York: Appleton.

Slaby, R., Roedell, W., Arezzo, D., & Hendrix, K. (1995). *Early violence prevention, Tools for teachers of young children.* Washington, DC: National Association for the Education of Young Children.

Slack, C. (1993). *Foundations for writing.* San Antonio, TX: ECS Learning Systems.

Smilansky, S., & Shefatya, L. (1990). *Facilitating play: A medium for promoting cognitive, socioemotional and academic development in young children.* Gaithersburg, MD: Psychological and Educational Publications.

Smith, M., & Smith, K. (2000). "I believe in inclusion, but . . .": Regular education early childhood teachers' perceptions of successful inclusion. *Journal of Research in Childhood Education, 14*(2), 161–180.

Smith, R. K. (1978). *Chocolate fever.* Old Greenwich, CT: Bantam Doubleday Dell.

Smith, T., Polloway, E., Patton J., & Dowdy, C. (2001). *Teaching students with special needs in inclusive settings.* Boston, MA: Allyn & Bacon.

Smyser, S. O., & Green, J. E. (1994). Teaching portfolios: Application for teacher education. *Ohio-Michigan Journal of Teacher Education, 8*(1), 47–54.

Snider, S. L., & Badgett, T. L. (1995). "I have this computer, what do I do now? Using technology to enhance every child's learning. *Early Childhood Education Journal, 23*(2), 101–105.

Snyder, A. (1972). *Dauntless women in childhood education, 1856–1931.* Washington, DC: Association for the Education of Young Children.

Sobel, J. (1983). *Everybody wins: Non-competitive games for young children.* New York: Walker and Company.

Southern Regional Education Board. (1992). *Readiness for school: The early childhood challenge.* Atlanta, GA: Author.

Sowers, J. (2000). *Language arts in early education.* Albany, NY: Delmar.

Sparks, D., & Hirsh, S. (2003). *A national plan for improving professional development* [On-line]. Available: http://www.nsdc.org/library/NSDOland.html

Spencer, T., Biederman, J., Wilens, T., Harding, M., O'Donnell, D., & Griffin, S. (1996). Pharmacotherapy of attention-deficit hyperactivity disorder across the life cycle. *Journal of American Academy Child Adolescent Psychiatry, 35*(4), 409–432.

Spinelli, C. G. (2002). *Classroom assessment for students with special needs in inclusive settings.* Upper Saddle River, NJ: Pearson Education.

Standing, R. (1957). *Maria Montessori: Her life and work.* New York: New American Library.

Sternberg, R. (2003). *Triarchic theory of intelligence.* [On-line]. Available: http://www.wilderdom.com/personality/L2=2SternbergTriarchiTheory.html

Stork, S. (2000). *Movement education and lesson plan development workbook.* Indianapolis, IN: USA Gymnastics.

Stronge, J. H. (1997). *Evaluating teaching: A guide to current thinking and best practice.* Thousand Oaks, CA: Corwin Press.

Suh, B. K., & Traiger, J. (1999). Teaching values through elementary social studies and literature curricula. *Education, 119*(4), p. 723.

Swartz, J. A. (2001). *The teacher as Aladdin.* Dubuque, Iowa: Kendall/Hunt.

Sylwester, R. (1995). *A celebration of neurons: An educator's guide to the human brain.* Alexandria, VA: Association for Supervision and Curriculum Development.

Taylor, B. (1996). *Education and the law: A dictionary.* Santa Barbara, CA: ABC-CLIO.

Taylor, P. M. (2001). Do your students measure up metrically? *Teaching Children Mathematics.* Vol. 7 (5), 282–288.

Teacher Created Materials. (1987). A poem about chocolate. #355 *Literature and Critical Thinking Book 1* p. 37. Westminister, CA: Teacher Created Materials.

Teachers take revolutionary approach to traditional math challenge. (1999). *T H E Journal.* Vol. 27 (3) 110–113.

Teaching and Learning Center. (2001). Owensboro Community College. [On-line]. Available: http://www.tex.state.tx.us/rules/tac/ch110_128ahtml

Teaching math basics. (2002). [On-line]. Available: http://ivc.uidaho.edu/ed326/background/basics.html

Teaching Tolerance Project. (1997) *Starting small: Teaching tolerance in preschool and the early grades.* Montgomery, AL: Southern Poverty Law Center.

Texas Education Agency. (1997). *Texas Essential Knowledge and Skills.* Austin, TX: Author.

Texas Education Agency. (1997). *Texas prekindergarten curriculum guidelines.* Austin, TX: Author.

Texas Education Agency. Texas Essential Knowledge and Skills (2002) [On-line]. Available: http://www.tex.state.tx.us/rules/tac/ch110_128ahtml

The hundred languages of children. (1987). Reggio Emilia, Italy: Department of Education.

Thoburn, T., Williams, P., Strong, W., & McCallum, A. (1996). *Macmillan Language Arts Today.* New York: Macmillan Publishing Co.

Thomas, D., & Bainbridge, W. L. (2002). No child left behind: Facts and fallacies. *Phi Delta Kappan, 83*(10), 781–782.

Thornton, T. P. (1996). Handwriting in America. New Haven, CT: Yale University Press.

Thurber, D. (1999). *D'Nealian handwriting,* Boston: Pearson Education.

Toher, G. R. (2001). Making sense of math. *Contemporary Education.* School of Education, Indiana State University. Vol. 72 (1): 5–7.

Toppo, G. (2001, August 2). Study: 850,000 children home-schooled. Associated Press. [On-line]. Available: http://www.ap.org/index.html

Trafton, R., Reys, B., & Wasman, D. (2001). Standards-based mathematics curriculum materials: A phrase in search of a definition. *Phi Delta Kappan, 83*(3), 259–264.

TransAct Communications, Inc. (2003). Why TransAct? [On-line]. Available: http://www.transact.com/default.cfm?level=1,2,23

Trawick-Smith, J. (1997). *Early childhood development: A multicultural perspective.* Upper Saddle River, NJ: Merrill.

Tripp, G., & Alsop, B. (1999). Sensitivity to reward frequency in boys with attention Deficit hyperactivity disorder. *Journal of Clinical Child Psychology, 28*(3), 366–375.

Tucker, B., Singleton, A., & Weaver, T. (2002). *Teaching mathematics to all children.* Upper Saddle River, NJ: Merrill.

U.S. Bureau of the Census. (1993). *The Hispanic population in the United States.* Washington, DC: U.S. Government Printing Office.

U.S. Bureau of the Census. (2000). [On-line]. Available: http://www.census.gov/population/cen2000/briefs.html

U.S. Department of Defense Education Agency. (2001). Social Studies Standards. [On-line]. Available: http://www.odedodea.edu/curriculum/g2social.html

U.S. Department of Education and U.S. Department of Justice. (2000). *Working for children and families: Safe and smart after-school programs.* [On-line]. Available: http://www.edpubs/org/webtore/Content/ItemDetails.asp?stritem

U.S. Department of Education. (1993). National excellence: A case for developing American talent. Washington, DC: U.S. Government Printing Office.

U.S. Department of Education. (1998a). Student placement in elementary and secondary schools and section 504 and title II of the Americans with disabilities act [On-line]. Available: http://www.ed.gov/OCR/docs/placpub.html

U.S. Department of Education. (1998b). 20th annual report to Congress on the implementation of the Individuals with Disabilities Education Act. Washington, DC: U.S. Government Printing Office.

U.S. Department of Education. (1998c). *What happens in the classroom.* Washington, DC: U.S. Government Printing Office.

U.S. Department of Education. (1999). *The condition of education, 1998.* Washington, DC: U.S. Government Printing Office.

U.S. Department of Education. (2000). Condition of America's public school facilities. Washington, DC: National Council for Education Statistics.

U.S. Department of Health and Human Services. (2000). *Child maltreatment 1998: Reports from the states to the National Child Abuse and Neglect Data System.* Washington, DC: U.S. Government Printing Office.

U.S. Office for Civil Rights. (1999). [On-line]. Available: http://hhs.gov/ocr/index.html

University of Chicago Mathematics Project. (1999). *Everyday mathematics.* Chicago, IL: Everyday Learning Corp.

Using NAEYC's Code of Conduct to Negotiate Professional Problems. (2000). *Young Children, 55*(4), 86–87.

Utah State Department of Education. (1998). *Handbook and specific directions for administration of the prekindergarten assessment* [On-line]. Available: http://www.usoe.k12.ut.us

Van de Walle, J. A. (1998). *Elementary and Middle School Mathematics: Teaching Developmentally* (3rd ed.). New York: Longman.

Vaughn, S., Bos, C., & Schumm, J. (2000). *Teaching exceptional, diverse, and at-risk students in the general education classroom.* Boston: Allyn & Bacon.

Verhoeven, L., and Snow, C. (2001). *Literacy and motivation: Reading engagement in individuals and groups.* Mahwah, NJ: Lawrence Erlbaum Associates, Inc.

Viorst, J. (1972). *Alexander and the terrible, horrible, no good, very bad day.* New York: Aladdin Books.

Virginia Education Agency. Standards of Learning. 2002 [On-line]. Available: http://www.knowledge.state.va.us/main/sal/solview.cfm?curriculum_abb=E%2F&category_abb=k

Vygotsky, L. (1962). *Thought and language.* Cambridge, MA: MIT Press.

Vygotsky, L. (1967, Summer). Play and its role in the mental development of children. *Soviet Psychology, 5*(3), pp. 6–18.

Waddell, D. (1988). Attention Deficit Hyperactivity Disorder (ADHD) teacher handout. Birdvillele ISD, Ft. Worth, TX: National Association of School Psychologists.

Wade, R. (2002). Beyond expanding horizons: New curriculum directions for elementary social studies. *The Elementary School Journal.* 103 (2): 115–126.

Wadsworth, O. (1985). *Over in the meadow.* New York: Puffin Books.

Wake County Public School System. (2002). New Internet service will help WCPSS improve communication with non-English speaking parents [On-line]. Available: http://www.wcpss.net/news/transact

Wakefield, A. P. (2001). Teaching young children to think about math. *Principal.* 80 (5): 26–29.

Waldrip, D. (2000). A brief history and philosophy of magnet schools [On-line]. Available: http://www.magnet.edu/history.html

Walker, B., Hafenstein, N., & Crow-Enslow, L. (1999). Meeting the needs of gifted learners in the early childhood classroom. *Young Children, 54*(1), 32–36.

Warner, L., & Adams, P. (1996, Winter). Teachers as action researchers in the classroom. *Dimensions of Early Childhood, 24*(1), 22–25.

Warner, L., & Lynch, S. (2001, Summer). Cultivating good classroom behavior. *Children and Families, 15*(3), 56–59.

Warner, L., & Sower, J. (2001). National Survey of Early Childhood Classroom Teachers. Huntsville, TX: Sam Houston State University.

Warner, Laverne. (1999). Self-esteem: A byproduct of quality classroom music. *Childhood Education,* 76 (1), 19–23.

Washington, V., & Andrews, J. D. (Eds.). (1999). *Children of 2010.* Washington, DC: National Association for the Education of Young Children.

Weikart, D. (1971). *Early childhood special education for intellectually subnormal and/or culturally different children.* Ypsilanti, MI: High/Scope Education Research Foundation.

Weikart, D. (1989). *Quality preschool programs: A long social investment.* New York: Ford Foundation.

Weikart, D., & Schweinhart, L., Eds. (1999). *What should young children learn? Teacher and parent views in 15 countries.* Ypsilanti, MI: High/Scope Press.

West Virginia State Board of Education v. Barnette, 319 U.S. 624 (1943).

West, J., Denton, K., & Germino-Hausken, E. (2000). *The condition of education.* [On-line]. Available: http://www.nces.gov/programs/coe

Wiener, R. B., & Cohen, J. H. (1997). *Literacy portfolios: Using assessment to guide instruction.* Upper Saddle River, NJ: Merrill.

Winner, E., & Hetland, L. (2001, Winter). The arts and academic improvement: What the evidence shows, executive summary. *National Art Education Association, 10*(1), 1–4.

Winter, S. (1997). "SMART" planning for inclusion. *Childhood Education, 73,* 212–218.

Wirth, E. (1991). Working parents work for schools. *Education Digest,* November, 21–22.

Wohlstetter, P., & Mohrman, S. (1996). Assessment of school based management. U.S. Dept. of Education [On-line]. Available: http://ed.gov/pubs/SER/SchBasedMgt/title.html

Woodside. (2001). Making a classroom ABC book. [On-line]. Available: http://www.mcps.k12.md.us/curriculum/littlekids/archivelesson_abc_book.htm

Woodward, A., & Elliot, D. L. (1990). Textbook use and teacher professionalism. In Elliot & Woodward (Eds.), *Textbooks and schooling in the United States* (89th Yearbook of the National Society for the Study of Education, Part 1, pp. 178–193). Chicago: National Society for the Study of Education.

Wortham, S. (1995). *Measurement and evaluation in early childhood education, second edition.* Englewood Cliffs, NJ: Merrill.

Wright Group. (1995). *Guided Reading: A Practical Approach for Teachers.* Bothell, WA: The Wright Group Publishing, Inc.

Wright Group. (1995). *Guided reading: A practical approach for teachers.* Bothell, WA: Author.

Wright, J. L., & Shade, D. D. (Eds.) (1994). *Young children: Active learners in a technological age.* Washington, DC: National Association for the Education of Young Children.

Wulf-McGrath, R. (2000). Making the difference with reading instruction: Reader's workshop. *Classroom Leadership Online,* Vol. 4 (1). [On-line]. Available: http://www.ascd.oprg/readingroom/classlead/0009/2sep00.html

Yell, M. (1995). Least restrictive environment, inclusion, and students with disabilities: A legal analysis. *Journal of Special Education, 28*(4), 349–404.

Yelon, S. L. (1996). *Powerful principles of instruction.* White Plains, NY: Longman Publishers USA.

YMCA Prime Time Before & Afterschool Program. (2003). [On-line]. Available: http://www.theplanningcouncil.org/tpcdatabase/iw0mde8z.htm

Zernike, K., & Petersen, M. (2001, August 21). Officials try slowing behavioral drug use. *New York Times,* National Desk sec.

Zill, N., & West, J. (1997). *The elementary school performance and adjustment of children who enter kindergarten late or repeat kindergarten: Findings from national surveys.* Washington, DC: U.S. Department of Education, Office of Educational Research and Improvement.

Zill, N., Collins, M., West, J., & Hausken, G. (1995, December). School readiness and children's developmental status. *ERIC Digest* (EDO-PS-95–15.)

☆ Author Index

⭐ Subject Index

Photo Credits

DATE DUE